MIDWEST STUDIES IN PHILOSOPHY

EDITED BY PETER A. FRENCH, THEODORE E. UEHLING, JR.,
HOWARD K. WETTSTEIN
ASSOCIATE EDITOR ROBERT FELEPPA

Virtually all papers in MIDWEST STUDIES IN PHILOSOPHY are invited and previously unpublished. The editors will, however, consider unsolicited manuscripts that are received by January of the year preceding the appearance of a volume. All manuscripts must be pertinent to the topic area of the volume for which they are submitted. Address manuscripts to The Editors, MIDWEST STUDIES IN PHILOSOPHY, University of Minnesota, Morris; Morris, MN 56267.

The articles in MIDWEST STUDIES IN PHILOSOPHY are indexed in THE PHILOSOPHER'S INDEX.

Forthcoming Volumes:

Volume VI   February 1981 The Foundations of Analytic Philosophy
Volume VII   February 1982 Social and Political Philosophy

Previously Published Volumes:

Volume I   February 1976 Studies in the History of Philosophy . . . . . out of print
Volume II   February 1977 Studies in the Philosophy of Language . . . in print, Rev. Ed., Contemporary Perspectives in the Philosophy of Language
Volume III   February 1978 Studies in Ethical Theory. . . . . in print
Volume IV   February 1979 Studies in Metaphysics . . . . in print

Midwest Studies
in
Philosophy
Volume
V
Studies in Epistemology

Editors
PETER A. FRENCH
THEODORE E. UEHLING, JR.
HOWARD K. WETTSTEIN

Associate Editor
ROBERT FELEPPA

University of Minnesota Press • Minneapolis

121
SZ9
143432
Mar.1988

Library of Congress Cataloging in Publication Data

Main entry under title:

Studies in epistemology.

(Midwest studies in philosophy; v. 5)
1. Knowledge, Theory of—Addresses, essays, lectures.
I. French, Peter A.   II. Uehling, Theodore Edward.
III. Wettstein, Howard K.   IV. Series.
BD161.S717   121   79-26706
ISBN 0-8166-0944-6
ISBN 0-8166-0947-0 pbk.

This volume is dedicated to
the memory of
JAMES W. CORNMAN

Midwest Studies in Philosophy
Volume V
Studies in Epistemology

Midwest Studies in Philosophy
Volume V

The Raft and the Pyramid: Coherence versus Foundations in the Theory of Knowledge

ERNEST SOSA

Contemporary epistemology must choose between the solid security of the ancient foundationalist pyramid and the risky adventure of the new coherentist raft. Our main objective will be to understand, as deeply as we can, the nature of the controversy and the reasons for and against each of the two options. But first of all we take note of two underlying assumptions.

1. *Two assumptions*

(A1) Not everything believed is known, but nothing can be known without being at least believed (or accepted, presumed, taken for granted, or the like) in some broad sense. What additional requirements must a belief fill in order to be knowledge? There are surely at least the following two: (a) it must be true, and (b) it must be justified (or warranted, reasonable, correct, or the like).

(A2) Let us assume, moreover, with respect to the second condition A1(b): first, that it involves a normative or evaluative property; and, second, that the relevant sort of justification is that which pertains to knowledge: epistemic (or theoretical) justification. Someone seriously ill may have two sorts of justification for believing he will recover: the practical justification that derives from the contribution such belief will make to his recovery and the theoretical justification provided by the lab results, the doctor's diagnosis and prognosis, and so on. Only the latter is relevant to the question whether he knows.

2. *Knowledge and criteria (or canons, methods, or the like)*

a. There are two key questions of the theory of knowledge:

(i) What do we know?

(ii) How do we know?

3

The answer to the first would be a list of bits of knowledge or at least of types of knowledge: of the self, of the external world, of other minds, and so on. An answer to the second would give us criteria (or canons, methods, principles, or the like) that would explain how we know whatever it is that we do know.

b. In developing a theory of knowledge, we can begin either with a(i) or with a(ii). Particularism would have us begin with an answer to a(i) and only then take up a(ii) on the basis of that answer. Quite to the contrary, methodism would reverse that order. The particularist thus tends to be antiskeptical on principle. But the methodist is as such equally receptive to skepticism and to the contrary. Hume, for example, was no less a methodist than Descartes. Each accepted, in effect, that only the obvious and what is proved deductively on its basis can possibly be known.

c. What, then, is the obvious? For Descartes it is what we know by intuition, what is clear and distinct, what is indubitable and credible with no fear of error. Thus for Descartes basic knowledge is always an infallible belief in an indubitable truth. All other knowledge must stand on that basis through deductive proof. Starting from such criteria (canons, methods, etc.), Descartes concluded that knowledge extended about as far as his contemporaries believed.[1] Starting from similar criteria, however, Hume concluded that both science and common sense made claims far beyond their rightful limits.

d. Philosophical posterity has rejected Descartes's theory for one main reason: that it admits too easily as obvious what is nothing of the sort. Descartes's reasoning is beautifully simple: God exists; no omnipotent perfectly good being would descend to deceit; but if our common sense beliefs were radically false, that would represent deceit on His part. Therefore, our common sense beliefs must be true or at least cannot be radically false. But in order to buttress this line of reasoning and fill in details, Descartes appeals to various principles that appear something less than indubitable.

e. For his part, Hume rejects all but a miniscule portion of our supposed common sense knowledge. He establishes first that there is no way to prove such supposed knowledge on the basis of what is obvious at any given moment through reason or experience. And he concludes, in keeping with this methodism, that in point of fact there really is no such knowledge.

3. *Two metaphors: the raft and the pyramid*

Both metaphors concern the body or system of knowledge in a given mind. But the mind is of course a more complex marvel than is sometimes supposed. Here I do not allude to the depths plumbed by Freud, nor even to Chomsky's. Nor need we recall the labyrinths inhabited by statesmen and diplomats, nor the rich patterns of some novels or theories. We need look no further than the most common, everyday beliefs. Take, for instance, the belief that driving tonight will be dangerous. Brief reflection should reveal that any of us with that belief will join to it several other closely related beliefs on which the given belief depends for its existence or (at least) its justification. Among such beliefs we could presumably find some or all of the following: that the road will be icy or snowy; that driving on ice or snow is dangerous; that it will rain or snow tonight; that the temperature will be below freezing; appropriate beliefs about the forecast and its reliability; and so on.

How must such beliefs be interrelated in order to help justify my belief about the danger of driving tonight? Here foundationalism and coherentism disagree, each offering its own metaphor. Let us have a closer look at this dispute, starting with foundationalism.

Both Descartes and Hume attribute to human knowledge an architectonic structure. There is a nonsymmetric relation of physical support such that any two floors of a building are tied by that relation: one of the two supports (or at least helps support) the other. And there is, moreover, a part with a special status: the foundation, which is supported by none of the floors while supporting them all.

With respect to a body of knowledge K (in someone's possession), foundationalism implies that K can be divided into parts K_1, K_2, . . ., such that there is some nonsymmetric relation R (analogous to the relation of physical support) which orders those parts in such a way that there is one—call it F—that bears R to every other part while none of them bears R in turn to F.

According to foundationalism, each piece of knowledge lies on a pyramid such as the following:

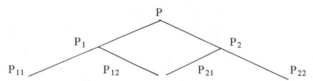

The nodes of such a pyramid (for a proposition P relative to a subject S and a time t) must obey the following requirements:

    a. The set of all nodes that succeed (directly) any given node must serve jointly as a base that properly supports that node (for S at t).

    b. Each node must be a proposition that S is justified in believing at t.

    c. If a node is not self-evident (for S at t), it must have successors (that serve jointly as a base that properly supports that node).

    d. Each branch of an epistemic pyramid must terminate.

For the foundationalist Descartes, for instance, each terminating node must be an indubitable proposition that S believes at t with no possibility of error. As for the nonterminal nodes, each of them represents inferential knowledge, derived by deduction from more basic beliefs.

Such radical foundationalism suffers from a fatal weakness that is twofold:

    (a) there are not so many perfectly obvious truths as Descartes thought; and

    (b) once we restrict ourselves to what is truly obvious in any given context, very little of one's supposed common sense knowledge can be proved on that basis.

If we adhere to such radical foundationalism, therefore, we are just wrong in thinking we know so much.

Note that in citing such a "fatal weakness" of radical foundationalism, we favor particularism as against the methodism of Descartes and Hume. For we reject the methods or criteria of Descartes and Hume when we realize that they plunge us in a deep skepticism. If such criteria are incompatible with our enjoyment of the rich body of knowledge that we commonly take for granted, then as good particularists we hold on to the knowledge and reject the criteria.

If we reject radical foundationalism, however, what are we to put in its place? Here epistemology faces a dilemma that different epistemologists resolve differently. Some reject radical foundationalism but retain some more moderate form of foundationalism. Others react more vigorously, however, by rejecting all forms of foundationalism in favor of a radically different coherentism. Coherentism is associated with idealism — of both the German and the British variety — and has recently acquired new vigor and interest.

The coherentists reject the metaphor of the pyramid in favor of one that they owe to the positivist Neurath, according to whom our body of knowledge is a raft that floats free of any anchor or tie. Repairs must be made afloat, and though no part is untouchable, we must stand on some in order to replace or repair others. Not every part can go at once.

According to the new metaphor, what justifies a belief is not that it be an infallible belief with an indubitable object, nor that it have been proved deductively on such a basis, but that it cohere with a comprehensive system of beliefs.

4. A coherentist critique of foundationalism

What reasons do coherentists offer for their total rejection of foundationalism? The argument that follows below summarizes much of what is alleged aganist foundationalism. But first we must distinguish between subjective states that incorporate a propositional attitude and those that do not. A propositional attitude is a mental state of someone with a proposition for its object: beliefs, hopes, and fears provide examples. By way of contrast, a headache does not incorporate any such attitude. One can of course be conscious of a headache, but the headache itself does not constitute or incorporate any attitude with a proposition for its object. With this distinction in the background, here is the antifoundationalist argument, which has two lemmas — a(iv) and b(iii) — and a principal conclusion.

a. (i) If a mental state incorporates a propositional attitude, then it does not give us direct contact with reality, e.g., with pure experience, unfiltered by concepts or beliefs.

(ii) If a mental state does not give us direct contact with reality, then it provides no guarantee against error.

(iii) If a mental state provides no guarantee against error, then it cannot serve as a foundation for knowledge.

(iv) Therefore, if a mental state incorporates a propositional attitude, then it cannot serve as a foundation for knowledge.

b. (i) If a mental state does not incorporate a propositional attitude, then it is an enigma how such a state can provide support for any hypothesis, raising its credibility selectively by contrast with its alternatives. (If the mental state has no conceptual or propositional content, then what logical relation can it possibly bear to any hypothesis? Belief in a hypothesis would be a propositional attitude with the hypothesis itself as object. How can one depend logically for such a belief on an experience with no propositional content?)

    (ii) If a mental state has no propositional content and cannot provide logical support for any hypothesis, then it cannot serve as a foundation for knowledge.

    (iii) Therefore, if a mental state does not incorporate a propositional attitude, then it cannot serve as a foundation for knowledge.

  c.   Every mental state either does or does not incorporate a propositional attitude.

  d.   Therefore, no mental state can serve as a foundation for knowledge. (From a(iv), b(iii), and c.)

According to the coherentist critic, foundationalism is run through by this dilemma. Let us take a closer look.[2]

    In the first place, what reason is there to think, in accordance with premise b(i), that only propositional attitudes can give support to their own kind? Consider practices—e.g., broad policies or customs. Could not some person or group be justified in a practice because of its consequences: that is, could not the consequences of a practice make it a good practice? But among the consequences of a practice may surely be found, for example, a more just distribution of goods and less suffering than there would be under its alternatives. And neither the more just distribution nor the lower degree of suffering is a propositional attitude. This provides an example in which propositional attitudes (the intentions that sustain the practice) are justified by consequences that are not propositional attitudes. That being so, is it not conceivable that the justification of belief that matters for knowledge be analogous to the objective justification by consequences that we find in ethics?

    Is it not possible, for instance, that a belief that there is something red before one be justified in part because it has its origin in one's visual experience of red when one looks at an apple in daylight? If we accept such examples, they show us a source of justification that serves as such without incorporating a propositional attitude.

    As for premise a(iii), it is already under suspicion from our earlier exploration of premise b(i). A mental state M can be nonpropositional and hence not a candidate for so much as truth, much less infallibility, while it serves, in spite of that, as a foundation of knowledge. Leaving that aside, let us suppose that the relevant mental state is indeed propositional. Must it then be infallible in order to serve as a foundation of justification and knowledge? That is so far from being obvious that it seems more likely false when compared with an analogue in ethics. With respect to beliefs, we may distinguish between their being true and their being justified. Analogously, with respect to actions, we may distinguish between their being optimal (best of all alternatives, all things considered) and their being (subjectively) justified. In practical deliberation on alternatives for action, is it inconceivable that the most *eligible* alternative *not* be objectively the best, all things considered? Can there not be another alternative—perhaps a most repugnant one worth little if any consideration—that in point of fact would have a much better total set of consequences and would thus be better, all things considered? Take the physician attending to Frau Hitler at the birth of little Adolf. Is it not possible that if he had acted less morally, that would have proved better in the fullness of time? And if that is so in ethics, may not its likeness hold good in epistemology? Might there not be justified (reasonable, warranted) beliefs that are not even true, much less infallible? That seems to me not just a conceivable possibility, but indeed a familiar fact of everyday life, where observational beliefs too often prove illusory but no less reasonable for being false.

If the foregoing is on the right track, then the antifoundationalist is far astray. What has led him there?

As a diagnosis of the antifoundationalist argument before us, and more particularly of its second lemma, I would suggest that it rests on an Intellectualist Model of Justification.

According to such a model, the justification of belief (and psychological states generally) is parasitical on certain logical relations among propositions. For example, my belief (i) that the streets are wet, is justified by my pair of beliefs (ii) that it is raining, and (iii) that if it is raining, the streets are wet. Thus we have a structure such as this:

B(Q) is justified by the fact that B(Q) is grounded on (B(P), B(P⊃Q)).

And according to an Intellectualist Model, this is parasitical on the fact that

P and (P⊃Q) together logically imply Q.

Concerning this attack on foundationalism I will argue (a) that it is useless to the coherentist, since if the antifoundationalist dilemma impales the foundationalist, a form of it can be turned against the coherentist to the same effect; (b) that the dilemma would be lethal not only to foundationalism and coherentism but also to the very possibility of substantive epistemology; and (c) that a form of it would have the same effect on normative ethics.

(a) According to coherentism, what justifies a belief is its membership in a coherent and comprehensive set of beliefs. But whereas being grounded on B(P) and (B(P⊃Q) is a property of a belief B(Q) that yields immediately the logical implication of Q and P and (P⊃Q) as the logical source of that property's justificatory power, the property of being a member of a coherent set is not one that immediately yields any such implication.

It may be argued, nevertheless, (i) that the property of being a member of a coherent set would supervene in any actual instance on the property of being a member of a particular set *a* that is in fact coherent, and (ii) that this would enable us to preserve our Intellectualist Model, since (iii) the justification of the member belief B(Q) by its membership in *a* would then be parasitical on the logical relations among the beliefs in *a* which constitute the coherence of that set of beliefs, and (iv) the justification of B(Q) by the fact that it is part of a coherent set would then be *indirectly* parasitical on logical relations among propositions after all.

But if such an indirect form of parasitism is allowed, then the experience of pain may perhaps be said to justify belief in its existence parasitically on the fact that P logically implies P! The Intellectualist Model seems either so trivial as to be dull, or else sharp enough to cut equally against both foundationalism and coherentism.

(b) If (i) only propositional attitudes can justify such propositional attitudes as belief, and if (ii) to do so they must in turn be justified by yet other propositional attitudes, it seems clear that (iii) there is no hope of constructing a complete epistemology, one which would give us, in theory, an account of what the justification of any justified belief would supervene on. For (i) and (ii) would rule out the possibility of a finite regress of justification.

(c) If only propositional attitudes can justify propositional attitudes, and if to do so they must in turn be justified by yet other propositional attitudes, it seems clear that there is no hope of constructing a complete normative ethics, one which would give us, in theory, an account of what the justification of any possible justified action would supervene upon. For the justification of an action presumably depends on the intentions it embeds and the justification of these, and here we are already within the net of propositional attitudes from which, for the Intellectualist, there is no escape.

It seems fair to conclude that our coherentist takes his antifoundationalist zeal too far. His antifoundationalist argument helps expose some valuable insights but falls short of its malicious intent. The foundationalist emerges showing no serious damage. Indeed, he now demands equal time for a positive brief in defense of his position.

5. *The regress argument*

a. The regress argument in epistemology concludes that we must countenance beliefs that are justified in the absence of justification by other beliefs. But it reaches that conclusion only by rejecting the possibility in principle of an infinite regress of justification. It thus opts for foundational beliefs justified in some noninferential way by ruling out a chain or pyramid of justification that has justifiers, and justifiers of justifiers, and so on *without end*. One may well find this too short a route to foundationalism, however, and demand more compelling reasons for thus rejecting an infinite regress as vicious. We shall find indeed that it is not easy to meet this demand.

b. We have seen how even the most ordinary of everyday beliefs is the tip of an iceberg. A closer look below the surface reveals a complex structure that ramifies with no end in sight. Take again my belief that driving will be dangerour tonight, at the tip of an iceberg, (I), that looks like this:

(I)

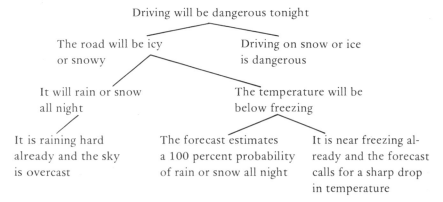

Driving will be dangerous tonight

The road will be icy or snowy

Driving on snow or ice is dangerous

It will rain or snow all night

The temperature will be below freezing

It is raining hard already and the sky is overcast

The forecast estimates a 100 percent probability of rain or snow all night

It is near freezing already and the forecast calls for a sharp drop in temperature

The immediate cause of my belief that driving will be hazardous tonight is the sound of raindrops on the windowpane. All but one or two members of the underlying iceberg are as far as they can be from my thoughts at the time. In what sense, then, do they form an iceberg whose tip breaks the calm surface of my consciousness?

Here I will assume that the members of (I) are beliefs of the subject, even if unconscious or subconscious, that causally buttress and thus justify his prediction about the driving conditions.

Can the iceberg extend without end? If may appear obvious that it cannot do so, and one may jump to the conclusion that any piece of knowledge must be ultimately founded on beliefs that are *not* (inferentially) justified or warranted by other beleifs. This is a doctrine of *epistemic foundationalism.*

Let us focus not so much on the *giving* of justification as on the *having* of it. *Can* there be a belief that is justified in part by other beliefs, some of which are in turn justified by yet other beliefs, and so on without end? Can there be an endless regress of justification?

c. There are several familiar objections to such a regress:

(i) *Objection*: "It is incompatible with human limitations. No human subject could harbor the required infinity of beliefs." *Reply*: It is mere presumption to fathom with such assurance the depths of the mind, and especially its unconscious and dispositional depths. Besides, our object here is the nature of epistemic justification in itself and not only that of such justification as is accessible to humans. Our question is not whether humans could harbor an infinite iceberg of justification. Our question is rather whether *any* mind, no matter how deep, could do so. Or is it ruled out *in principle* by the very nature of justification?

(ii) *Objection*: "An infinite regress is indeed ruled out in principle, for if justification were thus infinite how could it possible end? *Reply*: (i)

If the end mentioned is *temporal*, then why must there be such an end? In the first place, the subject may be eternal. Even if he is not eternal, moreover, why must belief acquisition and justification occur seriatim? What precludes an infinite body of beliefs acquired at a single stroke? Human limitations may rule this out for humans, but we have yet to be shown that it is precluded in principle, by the very nature of justification. (ii) If the end mentioned is justificatory, on the other hand, then to ask how justification could possibly end is just to beg the question.

(iii) *Objection*: "Let us make two assumptions: first, that S's belief of q justifies his belief of p only if it works together with a justified belief on his part that q provides good evidence for p; and, second, that if S is to be justified in believing p on the basis of his belief of q and is to be justified in believing q on the basis of his belief of r, then S must be justified in believing that r provides good evidence for p via q. These assumptions imply that an actual regress of justification requires belief in an infinite proposition. Since no one (or at least no human) can believe an infinite proposition, no one (no human) can be a subject of such an actual regress."[3]

Reply: Neither of the two assumptions is beyond question, but even granting them both, it may still be doubted that the conclusion follows. It is true that each finitely complex belief of the form "r provides good evidence for p via $q_1, \ldots, q_n$" will *omit* how some members of the full infinite regress are epistemically tied to belief of p. But that seems irrelevant given the fact that for each member r of the regress, such that r is tied epistemically to belief of p, there *is* a finite belief of the required sort ("r provides good evidence for p via $q_1, \ldots, q_n$") that ties the two together. Consequently, there is no apparent reason to suppose—even granted the two assumptions—that an infinite regress will require a single belief in an infinite proposition, and not just an infinity of beliefs in increasingly complex finite propositions.

(iv) *Objection*: "But if it is allowed that justification extend infinitely, then it is too easy to justify any belief at all or too many beliefs altogether. Take, for instance, the belief that there are perfect numbers greater than 100. And suppose a mind powerful enough to believe every member of the following sequence:

(σ1) There is at least one perfect number > 100
          There are at least two perfect numbers > 100
              "   three   "   "

If such a believer has no other belief about perfect numbers save the belief that a perfect number is a whole number equal to the sum of its whole factors, then surely he is *not* justified in believing that there are perfect numbers greater than 100. He is quite unjustified in believing any of the members of sequence (σ1), in spite of the fact that a challenge to any can be met easily by appeal to its successor. Thus it cannot be allowed after all that justification extend infinitely, and an infinite regress is ruled out."

Reply: We must distinguish between regresses of justification that are actual and those that are merely potential. The difference is *not* simply that an actual regress is composed of actual beliefs. For even if all members of the regress are actual beliefs, the regress may still be *merely potential* in the following sense: while it is true that *if* any member *were* justified then its predecessors *would* be, still none is in fact justified. Anyone with our series of beliefs about perfect numbers in the absence of any further relevant information on such numbers would presumably be the subject of such a merely potential justificatory regress.

(v) *Objection*: "But defenders of infinite justificatory regresses cannot distinguish thus between actual regresses and those that are merely potential. There is no real distinction to be drawn between the two. For if any regress ever justifies the belief at its head, then every regress must always do so. But obviously not every regress does so (as we have seen by examples), and hence no regress can do so."[4]

Reply: One can in fact distinguish between actual justificatory regresses and merely potential ones, and one can do so both abstractly and by examples.

What an actual regress has that a merely potential regress lacks is the property of containing only justified beliefs as members. What they both share is the property of containing no member without successors that would jointly justify it.

Recall our regress about perfect numbers greater than 100: i.e., there is at least one; there are at least two; there are at least three; and so on. Each member has a successor that would justify it, but no member is justified (in the absence of further information external to the regress). That is therefore a merely potential infinite regress. As for an actual regress, I see no compelling reason why someone (if not a human, then some more powerful mind) could not hold an infinite series of actually justified beliefs as follows:

(σ2) There is at least one even number
There are at least two even numbers
   "   three   "

It may be that no one could be the subject of such a series of justified beliefs unless he had a proof that there is a denumerable infinity of even numbers. But even if that should be so, it would not take away the fact of the infinite regress of potential justifiers, each of which is actually justified, and hence it would not take away the fact of the actual endless regress of justification.

The objection under discussion is confused, moreover, on the nature of the issue before us. Our question is *not* whether there can be an infinite potential regress, each member of which would be justified by its successors, such that the belief at its head is justified in virtue of its position there, at the head of such a regress. The existence and even the possibility of a single such regress with a belief at its head that was *not* justified in virtue of its position there would of course settle that question in the negative. Our question is, rather, whether there can be an actual infinite regress of justification, and the fact that a belief at the head of a potential regress might still fail to be justified despite its position does *not* settle this question. For even if there can be a merely potential regress with an unjustified belief at its head, that leaves open the possibility of an infinite regress, each member of which is justified by its immediate successors working jointly, where every member of the regress is in addition actually justified.

6. *The relation of justification and foundationalist strategy*

The foregoing discussion is predicated on a simple conception of justification such that a set of beliefs β conditionally justifies (*would* justify) a belief X iff, necessarily, if all members of β are justified then X is also justified (if it exists). The fact that on such a conception of justification actual endless regresses—such as (σ2)—seem quite possible blocks a straightforward regress argument in favor of foundations. For it shows that an actual infinite regress cannot be dismissed out of hand.

Perhaps the foundationalist could introduce some relation of justification—presumably more complex and yet to be explicated—with respect to which it could be argued more plausibly that an actual endless regress is out of the question.

There is, however, a more straightforward strategy open to the foundationalist. For he *need not* object to the possibility of an endless regress of justification. His essential creed is the more positive belief that every justified belief must be at the head of a terminating regress. Fortunately, to affirm the universal necessity of a terminating regress is *not* to deny the bare possibility of a nonterminating regress. For a single belief can trail at once regresses of both sorts: one terminating and one not. Thus the proof of the denumerably infinite cardinality of the set of evens may provide for a powerful enough intellect a *terminating* regress for each member of the *endless* series of justified beliefs:

(σ2) There is at least one even number
    There are at least two even numbers
           "   three   "

At the same time, it is obvious that each member of (σ2) lies at the head of an actual endless regress of justification, on the assumption that each member is conditionally justified by its successor, which is in turn actually justified.

"Thank you so much," the foundationalist may sneer, "but I really do not need that kind of help. Nor do I need to be reminded of my essential creed, which I know as well as anyone. Indeed my rejection of endless regresses of justification is only a means of supporting my view that every justified belief must rest ultimately on foundations, on a terminating regress. You reject that strategy much too casually, in my view, but I will not object here. So we put that strategy aside. And now, my helpful friend, just what do we put in its place."

Fair enough. How then could one show the need for foundations if an endless regress is not ruled out?

7. Two levels of foundationalism

a. We need to distinguish, first, between two forms of foundationalism: one *formal*, the other *substantive*. A type of *formal foundationalism* with respect to a normative or evaluative property ϕ is the view that the conditions (actual and possible) within which ϕ would apply can be specified in general, perhaps recursively. *Substantive foundationalism* is only a particular way of doing so, and coherentism is another.

Simpleminded hedonism is the view that:

(i) every instance of pleasure is good,

(ii) everything that causes something good is itself good, and

(iii) everything that is good is so in virtue of (i) or (ii) above.

Simpleminded hedonism is a type of formal foundationalism with respect to the good.

Classical foundationalism in epistemology is the view that:

(i) every infallible, indubitable belief is justified,

(ii) every belief deductively inferred from justified beliefs is itself justified, and

(iii) every belief that is justified is so in virtue of (i) or (ii) above.

Classical foundationalism is a type of formal foundationalism with respect to epistemic justification.

Both of the foregoing theories — simpleminded hedonism in ethics, and classical foundationalism in epistemology — are of course flawed. But they both remain examples of formal foundationalist theories.

b. One way of arguing in favor of formal foundationalism in epistemology is to formulate a convincing formal foundationalist theory of justification. But classical foundationalism in epistemology no longer has for many the attraction that it had for Descartes, nor has any other form of epistemic foundationalism won general acceptance. Indeed epistemic foundationalism has been generally abandoned and its advocates have been put on the defensive by the writings of Wittgenstein, Quine, Sellars, Rescher, Aune, Harman, Lehrer, and others. It is lamentable that in our headlong rush away from foundationalism we have lost sight of the different types of foundationalism (formal vs. substantive) and of the different grades of each type. Too many of us now see it as a blur to be decried and avoided. Thus our present attempt to bring it all into better focus.

c. If we cannot argue from a generally accepted foundationalist theory, what reason is there to accept formal foundationalism? There is no reason to think that the conditions (actual and possible) within which an object is spherical are generally specifiable in nongeometric terms. Why should we think that the conditions (actual and possible) within which a belief is epistemically justified are generally specifiable in nonepistemic terms?

So far as I can see, the main reason for accepting formal foundationalism in the absence of an actual, convincing formal foundationalist theory is the very plausible idea that epistemic justification is subject to the supervenience that characterizes normative and evaluative properties generally. Thus, if a car is a good car, then any physical replica of that car must be just as good. If it is a good car in virtue of such properties as being economical, little prone to break down, etc., then surely any exact replica would share all such properties and would thus be equally good. Similarly, if a belief is epistemically justified, it is presumably so in virtue of its character and its basis in perception, memory, or inference (if any). Thus any belief exactly like it in its character and its basis must be equally well justified. Epistemic justification is supervenient. The justification of a belief supervenes on such properties of it as its content and its basis (if any) in perception, memory, or inference. Such a doctrine of supervenience may itself be considered, with considerable justice, a grade of foundationalism. For it entails that every instance of justified belief is founded on a number of its nonepistemic properties, such as its having a certain basis in perception, memory, and inference, or the like.

But there are higher grades of foundationalism as well. There is, for instance, the doctrine that the conditions (actual and possible) within which a belief would be epistemically justified *can be specified* in general, perhaps recursively (and by reference to such notions as perception, memory, and inference).

A higher grade yet of formal foundationalism requires not only that the conditions for justified belief be specifiable, in general, but that they be specifiable by a simple, comprehensive theory.

d. Simpleminded hedonism is a formal foundationalist theory of the highest grade. If it is true, then in every possible world goodness supervenes on pleasure and causation in a way that is recursively specifiable by means of a very simple theory.

Classical foundationalism in epistemology is also a formal foundationalist theory of the highest grade. If it is true, then in every possible world epistemic justification supervenes on infallibility cum indubitability and deductive inference in a way that is recursively specifiable by means of a very simple theory.

Surprisingly enough, coherentism may also turn out to be formal foundationalism of the highest grade, provided only that the concept of coherence is itself both simple enough and free of any normative or evaluative admixture.

Given these provisos, coherentism explains how epistemic justification supervenes on the nonepistemic in a theory of remarkable simplicity: a belief is justified iff it has a place within a system of beliefs that is coherent and comprehensive.

It is a goal of ethics to explain how the ethical rightness of an action supervenes on what is not ethically evaluative or normative. Similarly, it is a goal of epistemology to explain how the epistemic justification of a belief supervenes on what is not epistemically evaluative or normative. If coherentism aims at this goal, that imposes restrictions on the notion of coherence, which must now be conceived innocent of epistemically evaluative or normative admixture. Its substance must therefore consist of such concepts as explanation, probability, and logical implication—with these conceived, in turn, innocent of normative or evaluative content.

e. We have found a surprising kinship between coherentism and substantive foundationalism, both of which turn out to be varieties of a deeper foundationalism. This deeper foundationalism is applicable to any normative or evaluative property ϕ, and it comes in three grades. The *first* or lowest is simply the supervenience of ϕ: the idea that whenever something has ϕ its having it is founded on certain others of its properties which fall into certain restricted sorts. The *second* is the explicable supervenience of ϕ: the idea that there are formulable principles that explain in quite general terms the conditions (actual and possible) within which ϕ applies. The *third* and highest is the easily explicable supervenience of ϕ: the idea that there is a *simple* theory that explains the conditions within which ϕ applies. We have found the coherentist and the substantive foundationalist sharing a primary goal: the development of a formal foundationalist theory of the highest grade. For they both want a simple theory that explains precisely how epistemic justification supervenes, in general, on the nonepistemic. This insight gives us an unusual viewpoint on some recent attacks against foundationalism. Let us now consider as an example a certain simple form of argument distilled from the recent antifoundationalist literature.[5]

8. *Doxastic ascent arguments*

Several attacks on foundationalism turn on a sort of "doxastic ascent" argument that calls for closer scrutiny.[6] Here are two examples:

A. A belief B is foundationally justified for S in virtue of having property F only if S is justified in believing (1) that most at least of his beliefs with property F are true, and (2) that B has property F. But this means that belief B is not foundational after all, and indeed that the very notion of (empirical) foundational belief is incoherent.

   It is sometimes held, for example, that perceptual or observational beliefs are often justified through their origin in the exercise of one or more of our five senses in standard conditions of perception. The advocate of doxastic ascent would raise a vigorous protest, however, for in his view the mere fact of such sensory prompting is impotent to justify the belief prompted. Such prompting must be coupled with the further belief that one's senses work well in the circumstances, or the like. For we are dealing here with *knowledge*, which requires not blind faith but *reasoned* trust. But now surely the further belief about the reliability of one's senses itself cannot rest on blind faith but requires its own backing of reasons, and we are off on the regress.

B.   A belief B of proposition P is foundationally justified for S only if S is justified in believing that there are no factors present that would cause him to make mistakes on the matter of the proposition P. But, again, this means that belief B is not foundational after all and indeed that the notion of (empirical) foundational belief is incoherent.

From the vantage point of formal foundationalism, neither of these arguments seems persuasive. In the first place, as we have seen, what makes a belief foundational (formally) is its having a property that is nonepistemic (not evaluative in the epistemic or cognitive mode), and does not involve inference from other beliefs, but guarantees, via a necessary principle, that the belief in question is justified. A belief B is made foundational by having some such nonepistemic property that yields its justification. Take my belief that I am in pain in a context where it is caused by my being in pain. The property that my belief then has, of being a self-attribution of pain caused by one's own pain is, let us suppose, a nonepistemic property that yields the justification of any belief that has it. So my belief that I am in pain is in that context foundationally justified. Along with my belief that I am in pain, however, there come other beliefs that are equally well justified, such as my belief that someone is in pain. Thus I am foundationally justified in believing that I am in pain only if I am justified in believing that someone is in pain. Those who object to foundationalism as in A or B above are hence mistaken in thinking that their premises would refute foundationalism. The fact is that they would not touch it. For a belief is no less foundationally justified for having its justification yoked to that of another closely related belief.

The advocate of arguments like A and B must apparently strengthen his premises. He must apparently claim that the beliefs whose justification is entailed by the foundationally justified status of belief B must in some sense function as a *necessary source* of the justification of B. And this would of course preclude giving B foundationally justified status. For if the *being justified* of those beliefs is an *essential* part of the source of the justification of B, then it is ruled out that there be a wholly *nonepistemic* source of B's justification.

That brings us to a second point about A and B, for it should now be clear that these cannot be selectively aimed at foundationalism. In particular, they seem neither more nor less valid objections to coherentism than to foundationalism, or so I will now argue about each of them in turn.

A'.   A belief X is justified for S in virtue of membership in a coherent set only if S is justified in believing (1) that most at least of his beliefs with the property of thus cohering are true, and (2) that X has that property.

Any coherentist who accepts A seems bound to accept A'. For what could be possibly appeal to as a relevant difference? But A′ is a quicksand of endless depth. (How is he justified in believing A′(1)? Partly through justified belief that *it* coheres? And what would justify *this*? And so on . . .).

B′.   A belief X is justified for S only if S is justified in believing that there are no factors present that would cause him to make mistakes on the subject matter of that belief.

Again, any coherentist who accepts B seems bound to accept B′. But this is just another road to the quicksand. (For S is justified in believing that there are no such factors only if . . . and so on.)

Why are such regresses vicious? The key is again, to my mind, the doctrine of supervenience. Such regresses are vicious because they would be logically incompatible with the supervenience of epistemic justification on such nonepistemic facts as the totality of a subject's beliefs, his cognitive and experiential history, and as many other nonepistemic facts as may seem at all relevant. The idea is that there is a set of such nonepistemic facts surrounding a justified belief such that no belief could possibly have been surrounded by those very facts without being justified. Advocates of A or B run afoul of such supervenience, since they are surely committed to the more general views derivable from either of A or B by deleting 'foundationally' from its first sentence. In each case the more general view would then preclude the possibility of supervenience, since it would entail that the source of justification *always* includes an *epistemic* component.

9. Coherentism and substantive foundationalism

a. The notions of coherentism and substantive foundationalism remain unexplicated. We have relied so far on our intuitive grasp of them. In this section we shall consider reasons for the view that substantive foundationalism is superior to coherentism. To assess these reasons, we need some more explicit account of the difference between the two.

By coherentism we shall mean any view according to which the ultimate sources of justification for any belief lie in relations among that belief and other beliefs of the subject: explanatory relations, perhaps, or relations of probability or logic.

According to substantive foundationalism, as it is to be understood here, there are ultimate sources of justification other than relations among beliefs. Traditionally these additional sources have pertained to the special content of the belief or its special relations to the subjective experience of the believer.

b. The view that justification is a matter of relations among beliefs is open to an objection from alternative coherent systems or detachment from reality, depending on one's perspective. From the latter perspective the body of beliefs is held constant and the surrounding world is allowed to vary, whereas from the former perspective it is the surrounding world that is held constant while the body of beliefs is allowed to vary. In either case, according to the coherentist, there could be no effect on the justification for any belief.

Let us sharpen the question before us as follows. Is there reason to think that there is a least one system B', alternative to our actual system of beliefs B, such that B' contains a belief X with the following properties:

(i) in our present nonbelief circumstances we would not be justified in having belief X even if we accepted along with that belief (as our total system of beliefs) the entire belief system B' in which it is embedded (no matter how acceptance of B' were brought about); and

(ii) that is so despite the fact that belief X coheres within B' at least as fully as does some actual justified belief of ours within our actual belief system B (where the justification of that actual justified belief is alleged by the coherentist to derive solely from its coherence within our actual body of beliefs B).

The coherentist is vulnerable to counterexamples of this sort right at the surface of his body of beliefs, where we find beliefs with minimal coherence, whose detachment and replacement with contrary beliefs would have little effect on the coherence of the body. Thus take my belief that I have a headache when I do have a splitting headache, and let us suppose that this *does* cohere within my present body of beliefs. (Thus I have no reason to doubt my present introspective beliefs, and so on. And if my belief does *not* cohere, so much the worse for coherentism, since my belief is surely justified.) Here then we have a perfectly justified or warranted belief. And yet such a belief may well have relevant relations of explanation, logic, or probability with at most a small set of other beliefs of mine at the time: say, that I am not free of headache, that I am in pain, that someone is in pain, and the like. If so, then an equally coherent alternative is not far to seek. Let everything remain constant, *including* the splitting headache, except for the following: replace the belief that I have a headache with the belief that I do *not* have a headache, the belief that I am in pain with the belief that I am *not* in pain, the belief that someone is in pain with the belief that someone is *not* in pain, and so on. I contend that my resulting hypothetical system of beliefs would cohere as fully as does my actual system of beliefs, and yet my hypothetical belief that I do *not* have a headache would not therefore be justified. What makes this difference concerning justification between my actual belief that I have a headache and the hypothetical belief that I am free of headache, each as coherent as the other within its own system, if not the actual splitting headache? But the headache is *not* itself a belief nor a relation among beliefs and is thus in no way constitutive of the internal coherence of my body of beliefs.

Some might be tempted to respond by alleging that one's belief about whether or not one has a headache is always *infallible*. But since we could devise similar examples for the various sensory modalities and propositional attitudes, the response given for the case of headache would have to be generalized. In effect, it would have to cover "peripheral" beliefs generally—beliefs at the periphery of one's body of beliefs, minimally coherent with the rest. These peripheral beliefs would all be said to be infallible. That is, again, a possible response, but it leads to a capitulation by the coherentist to the radical foundationalist on a crucial issue that has traditionally divided them: the infallibility of beliefs about one's own subjective states.

What is more, not all peripheral beliefs are about one's own subjective states. The direct realist is probably right that some beliefs about our surroundings are uninferred and yet justified. Consider my present belief that the table before me is oblong. This presumably coheres with such other beliefs of mine as that the table has the same shape as the piece of paper before me, which is oblong, and a different shape than the window frame here, which is square, and so on. So far as I can see, however, there is no insurmountable obstacle to replacing that whole set of coherent beliefs with an equally coherent set as follows: that the table before me is square, that the table has the same shape as the square window frame, and a different shape than the piece of paper, which is oblong, and so on. The important points are (a) that this replacement may be made without changing the rest of one's body of beliefs or any aspect of the world beyond, including one's present visual experience of something oblong, not square, as one looks at the table before one; and (b) that is so, in part, because of the fact (c) that the subject need not have any beliefs about his present sensory experience.

Some might be tempted to respond by alleging that one's present experience is *self-intimating*, i.e., always necessarily taken note of and reflected in one's beliefs. Thus if anyone has visual experience of something oblong, then he believes that he has such experience. But this would involve a further important concession by the coherentist to the radical foundationalist, who would have been granted two of his most cherished doctrines: the infallibility of introspective belief and the self-intimation of experience.

10. *The foundationalist's dilemma*

The antifoundationalist zeal of recent years has left several forms of foundationalism standing. These all share the conviction that a belief can be justified not only by its coherence within a comprehensive system but also by an appropriate combination of observational content and origin in the use of the senses in standard conditions. What follows presents a dilemma for any foundationalism based on any such idea.

a. We may surely suppose that beings with observational mechanisms radically unlike ours might also have knowledge of their environment. (That seems possible even if the radical difference in observational mechanisms precludes overlap in substantive concepts and beliefs.)

b. Let us suppose that there is such a being, for whom experience of type ϕ (of which we have no notion) has a role with respect to his beliefs of type ϕ analogous to the role that our visual experience has with respect to our visual beliefs. Thus we might have a schema such as the following:

Human	*Extraterrestial being*
Visual experience	ϕ experience
Experience of something red	Experience of something F
Belief that there is something red before one	Belief that there is something F before one

c. It is often recognized that our visual experience intervenes in two ways with respect to our visual beliefs: as cause and as justification. But these are not wholly independent. Presumably, the justification of the belief that something here is red derives at least in part from the fact that it originates in a visual experience of something red that takes place in normal circumstances.

d. Analogously, the extraterrestial belief that something here has the property of being F might be justified partly by the fact that it originates in a ϕ experience of something F that takes place in normal circumstances.

e. A simple question presents the foundationalist's dilemma: regarding the epistemic principle that underlies our justification for believing that something here is red on the basis of our visual experience of something red, is it proposed as a fundamental principle or as a derived generalization? Let us compare the famous Principle of Utility of value theory, according to which it is best for that to happen which, of all the possible alternatives in the circumstances, would bring with it into the world the greatest balance of pleasure over pain, joy over sorrow, happiness over unhappiness, content over discontent, or the like. Upon this fundamental principle one may then base various generalizations, rules of thumb, and maxims of public health, nutrition, legislation, etiquette, hygiene, and so on. But these are all then derived generalizations which rest for their validity on the fundamental principle. Similarly, one may also ask, with respect to the generalizations advanced by our foundationalist, whether these are proposed as fundamental principles or as derived maxims or the like. This sets him face to face with a dilemma, each of whose alternatives is problematic. If his proposals are meant to have the status of secondary or derived maxims, for instance, then it would be quite unphilosophical to stop there. Let us turn, therefore, to the other alternative.

f. On reflection it seems rather unlikely that epistemic principles for the justification of observational beliefs by their origin in sensory experience could have a status more fundamental than that of derived generalizations. For by granting such principles fundamental status we would open the door to a multitude of equally basic principles with no unifying factor. There would be some for vision, some for hearing, etc., without even mentioning the corresponding extraterrestial principles.

g. It may appear that there is after all an idea, however, that unifies our multitude of principles. For they all involve sensory experience and sensible characteristics. But what is a sensible characteristic? Aristotle's answer appeals to examples: colors, shapes, sounds, and so on. Such a notion might enable us to unify perceptual epistemic principles under some more fundamental principle such as the following:

> If σ is a sensible characteristic, then the belief that there is something with σ before one is (prima facie) justified if it is based on a visual experience of something with σ in conditions that are normal with respect to σ.

h. There are at least two difficulties with such a suggestion, however, and neither one can be brushed aside easily. First, it is not clear that we can have a viable notion of sensible characteristic on the basis of examples so diverse as colors, shapes, tones, odors, and so on. Second, the authority of such a principle apparently derives from contingent circumstances concerning the reliability of beliefs prompted by sensory experiences of certain sorts. According to the foundationalist, our visual beliefs are justified by their origin in our visual experience or the like. Would such beliefs be equally well justified in a world where beliefs with such an origin were nearly always false?

i. In addition, finally, even if we had a viable notion of such characteristics, it is not obvious that fundamental knowledge of reality would have to derive causally or otherwise from sensory experience of such characteristics. How could one impose reasonable limits on extraterrestial mechanisms for noninferential acquisition of beliefs? Is it not possible that such mechanisms need not always function through sensory experience of any sort? Would such beings necessarily be denied any knowledge of their surroundings and indeed of any contingent spatio-temporal fact? Let us suppose them to possess a complex system of true beliefs concerning their surroundings, the structures below the surface of things, exact details of history and geography, all constituted by concepts none of which corresponds to any of our sensible characteristics. What then? Is it not possible that their basic beliefs should all concern fields of force, waves, mathematical structures, and numerical assignments to variables in several dimensions? This is no doubt an exotic notion, but even so it still seems conceivable. And if it is in fact possible, what then shall we say of the noninferential beliefs of such beings? Would we have to concede the existence of special epistemic principles that can validate their noninferential beliefs? Would it not be preferable to formulate more abstract principles that can cover both human and extraterrestial foundations? If such more abstract principles are in fact accessible, then the less general principles that define the human foundations and those that define the extraterrestial foundations are both derived principles whose validity depends on that of the more abstract principles. In this the human and extraterrestial epistemic principles would resemble rules of good nutrition for an infant and an adult. The infant's rules would of course be quite unlike those valid for the adult. But both would still be based on a more fundamental principle that postulates the ends of well-being and good health. What more fundamental principles might support both human and extraterrestial knowledge in the way that those concerning good health and well-being support rules of nutrition for both the infant and the adult?

11. *Reliabilism: an ethics of moral virtues and an epistemology of intellectual virtues*

In what sense is the doctor attending Frau Hitler justified in performing an action that brings with it far less value than one of its accessible alternatives? According to one promising idea, the key is to be found in the rules that he embodies through stable dispositions. His action is the result of certain stable virtues, and there are no equally virtuous alternate *dispositions* that, given his cognitive limitations, he might have embodied with equal or better total consequences, and that would have led him to infanticide in the circumstances. The important move for our purpose is the stratification of justification. Primary justification attaches to virtues and other dispositions, to stable dispositions to act, through their greater contribution of value when compared with alternatives. Secondary justification attaches to particular acts in virtue of their source in virtues or other such justified dispositions.

The same strategy may also prove fruitful in epistemology. Here primary justification would apply to *intellectual* virtues, to stable dispositions for belief acquisition, through their greater contribution toward getting us to the truth. Secondary justification would then attach to particular beliefs in virtue of their source in intellectual virtues or other such justified dispositions.[7]

That raises parallel questions for ethics and epistemology. We need to consider more carefully the concept of a virtue and the distinction between moral and intellectual virtues. In epistemology, there is reason to think that the most useful and illuminating notion of intellectual virtue will prove broader than our tradition would suggest and must give due weight not only to the subject and his intrinsic nature but also to his environment and to his epistemic community. This is a large topic, however, to which I hope some of us will turn with more space, and insight, than I can now command.[8]

SUMMARY

1. *Two assumptions:* (A1) that for a belief to constitute knowledge it must be (a) true and (b) justified; and (A2) that the justification relevant to whether or not one knows is a sort of epistemic or theoretical justification to be distinguished from its practical counterpart.

2. *Knowledge and criteria.* Particularism is distinguished from methodism: the first gives priority to particular examples of knowledge over general methods of criteria, whereas the second reverses that order. The methodism of Descartes leads him to an elaborate dogmatism whereas that of Hume leads him to a very simple skepticism. The particularist is, of course, antiskeptical on principle.

3. *Two metaphors: the raft and the pyramid.* For the foundationalist every piece of knowledge stands at the apex of a pyramid that rests on stable and secure foundations whose stability and security does not derive from the upper stories

or sections. For the coherentist a body of knowledge is a free-floating raft every plank of which helps directly or indirectly to keep all the others in place, and no plank of which would retain its status with no help from the others.

4. *A coherentist critique of foundationalism.* No mental state can provide a foundation for empirical knowledge. For if such a state is propositional, then it is fallible and hence no secure foundation. But if it is *not* propositional, then how can it possibly serve as a foundation for belief? How can one infer or justify anything on the basis of a state that, having no propositional content, must be logically dumb? An analogy with ethics suggests a reason to reject this dilemma. Other reasons are also advanced and discussed.

5. *The regress argument.* In defending his position, the foundationalist often attempts to rule out the very possibility of an infinite regress of justification (which leads him to the necessity for a foundation). Some of his arguments to that end are examined.

6. *The relation of justification and foundationalist strategy.* An alternative foundationalist strategy is exposed, one that does not require ruling out the possibility of an infinite regress of justification.

7. *Two levels of foundationalism.* Substantive foundationalism is distinguished from formal foundationalism, three grades of which are exposed: first, the supervenience of epistemic justification; second, its explicable supervenience; and, third, its supervenience explicable by means of a simple theory. There turns out to be a surprising kinship between coherentism and substantive foundationalism, both of which aim at a formal foundationalism of the highest grade, at a theory of the greatest simplicity that explains how epistemic justification supervenes on nonepistemic factors.

8. *Doxastic ascent arguments.* The distinction between formal and substantive foundationalism provides an unusual viewpoint on some recent attacks against foundationalism. We consider doxastic ascent arguments as an example.

9. *Coherentism and substantive foundationalism.* It is argued that substantive foundationalism is superior since coherentism is unable to account adequately for the epistemic status of beliefs at the "periphery" of a body of beliefs.

10. *The foundationalist's dilemma.* All foundationalism based on sense experience is subject to a fatal dilemma.

11. *Reliabilism.* An alternative to foundationalism of sense experience is sketched.

Notes

1. But Descartes's methodism was at most partial. James Van Cleve has supplied the materials for a convincing argument that the way out of the Cartesian circle is through a particularism of basic knowledge. (See James Van Cleve, "Foundationalism, Epistemic Principles, and the Cartesian Circle," *The Philosophical Review* 88 (1979):55–91.) But this is, of course, compatible with methodism on inferred knowledge. Whether Descartes subscribed to such methodism is hard (perhaps impossible) to determine, since in the end he makes room for all the kinds of knowledge required by particularism. But his language when he introduces the method of hyperbolic doubt, and the order in which he proceeds, suggest that he did subscribe to such methodism.

2. Cf. Laurence Bonjour "The Coherence Theory of Truth," *Philosophical Studies* 30 (1976): 281–312; and, especially, Michael Williams, *Groundless Belief* (New Haven, 1977); and L. Bonjour, "Can Empirical Knowledge Have a Foundation?" *American Philosophical Quarterly* 15 (1978):1–15.

3. Cf. Richard Foley, "Inferential Justification and the Infinite Regress," *American Philosophical Quarterly* 15 (1978):311–16.

4. Cf. John Post, "Infinite Regress Arguments," *Philosophical Studies* 34 (1980).

5. The argument of this whole section is developed in greater detail in my paper "The Foundations of Foundationalism" *Nous* (1980).

6. For some examples of the influence of doxastic ascent arguments, see Wilfrid Sellars's writing in epistemology: e.g., "Empiricism and the Philosophy of Mind" in *Science, Perception, and Reality*, especially section VIII, and particularly p. 168. Also I. T. Oakley, "An Argument for Skepticism Concerning Justified Beliefs," *American Philosophical Quarterly* 13 (1976):221–28; and Bonjour, "Can Empirical Knowledge Have a Foundation?"

7. This puts in a more traditional perspective the contemporary effort to develop a "causal theory of knowing." From our viewpoint, this effort is better understood not as an attempt to *define* propositional knowledge but as an attempt to formulate fundamental principles of justification.

Cf. the work of D. Armstrong, *Belief, Truth and Knowledge* (London, 1973); and that of F. Dretske, A. Goldman, and M. Swain, whose relevant already published work is included in *Essays on Knowledge and Justification*, ed. G. Pappas and M. Swain (Ithaca and London, 1978). But the theory is still under development by Goldman and by Swain, who have reached general conclusions about it similar to those suggested here, though not necessarily—so far as I know—for the same reasons or in the same overall context.

8. I am indebted above all to Roderick Chisholm: for his writings and for innumerable discussions. The main ideas in the present paper were first presented in a seminar of 1976–77 at the University of Texas. I am grateful to Anthony Anderson, David and Jean Blumenfeld, Laurence Bonjour, and Martin Perlmutter, who made that seminar a valuable stimulus. Subsequent criticism by my colleague James Van Cleve has also been valuable and stimulating.

The Internalist Conception of Justification

ALVIN GOLDMAN

One possible aim of epistemology is to advise cognizers on the proper choice of beliefs or other doxastic attitudes. This aim has often been part of scientific methodology: to tell scientists when they should accept a given hypothesis, or give it a certain degree of credence. This *regulative* function is naturally linked to the notion of epistemic justification. It may well be suggested that a cognizer is justified in believing something just in case the rules of proper epistemic procedure prescribe that belief. Principles that make such doxastic prescriptions might thereby "double" as principles of justification.

In the first part of this paper I contrast the regulative conception of justification with another, equally tenable, conception. Then, after noting a fundamental worry about the applicability of the regulative conception, I proceed to lay it out in more detail. The regulative justificational status of a doxastic attitude for person S at time *t* depends upon (a) the right set of doxastic instructions and (b) the states S is in at (or just before) *t*.

The regulative conception per se is neutral about the right doxastic instructions. But the question naturally arises: What *makes* this or that set of instructions the *right* instructions? The rest of the paper is devoted to this question. Two approaches are identified: *externalism* and *internalism*. Internalism takes its inspiration from a perspective that has dominated epistemology since the time of Descartes. I try to show that this perspective yields no definite or adequate answer to the question posed here; it provides no adequate conception of the rightness of doxastic instructions. This leaves externalism as the only available option, and I defend its plausibility.

Parts of this paper are positive and constructive. But the bulk of the paper is negative. It tries to undermine a classical epistemological perspective by showing that it cannot answer the question: What are the right doxastic instructions? I do not myself try to answer this question. But I do end the paper on a positive note, with a sketch of a framework within which that question may be answered.

I

In "Doing The Best One Can,"[1] Holly S. Goldman distinguishes two possible functions of a moral principle. First, it can serve as an instrument for making theoretical evaluations of actions. Second, it can serve as a device that an agent can employ to guide his/her activitives. A moral principle may not be equally useful for these two purposes. For example, the standard act-utilitarian principle—an act is right if and only if it would produce at least as much net happiness as any available alternative—is perfectly suitable (which is not to say correct) as an instrument for theoretical evaluation. It specifies conditions that determine the rightness or wrongness of an action. But this principle is not entirely suitable as an action-guiding principle. At the time of action an agent may not know which act would produce the most happiness; he may not even *believe* of any particular act that it would produce the most happiness. Thus it is unclear how to use the act-utilitarian principle to guide his conduct. In an unpublished paper,[2] Goldman suggests that we need distinct principles for decision-making purposes. One possible decision-making principle that might be associated with act-utilitarianism is to choose the act with the highest subjective probability of producing the most happiness. A different decision principle that might be paired with act-utilitarianism is to choose the act that, given your subjective probabilities, has the greatest "expected" happiness. (These two principles are not equivalent. An act with a slightly higher subjective probability than any other of producing the most happiness but a non-negligible chance of producing disaster would be enjoined by the first of these principles but not necessarily by the second.) Whichever decision principle should be associated with act-utilitarianism, the general point is that there are distinct *types* of principles: one for "theoretical evaluation" and one for practical guidance of action.

The concept of epistemic justification calls for an analogous distinction between kinds of theories or principles. On the one hand, a principle of justification might specify the features of beliefs (or other doxastic attitudes) that confer epistemic status. These features may or may not be usable by a cognizer to make a doxastic choice. On the other hand, a principle of justification might be designed specifically to guide a cognizer in regulating or choosing his doxastic attitudes. Here the criteria of justification must be ones to which a cognizer can appeal in the process of making a doxastic decision. That the theoretical and regulative functions of justification principles can be distinct emerges clearly from an account of justified belief I have proposed in another paper.[3] Refinements aside, this account—which I call "Historical Reliabilism"—says that a belief is justified just in case its causal ancestry consists of reliable belief-forming processes, i.e., processes that generally lead to truth. As a theoretical specification of epistemic status, such an account is entirely suitable. But this theory or principle cannot be used by a cognizer to make a doxastic decision; nor is it so.intended. First, at the time of belief a cognizer may not know, or be in a position to find out about, the causal ancestry of his belief; and a cognizer may not know, or be able to tell, whether the processes that composed this ancestry are generally reliable. Thus there is no guarantee that a cognizer can apply the Historical Reliabilist theory to his own case. Second, Historical Reliabilism simply is not a *rule* or *prescription* for choosing beliefs or other doxastic attitudes. It considers an *already formed* belief of a cognizer and says what features are necessary and sufficient for that belief to count as justified. It does not take a cognizer who is trying to decide which doxastic attitude to adopt vis-à-vis a given proposition and tell him what to do (doxastically speaking).

Epistemologists have been interested in theories of justification for at least two reasons. First, many have thought that a necessary condition of *knowing* a proposition is having a justified belief in that proposition. So a full analysis of knowledge requires an indication of the conditions in which belief is justified. Second, many epistemologists have been interested in "doxastic decision principles," i.e., rules for the formation of belief or other doxastic attitudes, e.g., subjective probabilities. Descartes's clearness-and-distinctness test was intended as a criterion to be used in deciding what to believe. And contemporary Bayesianism instructs cognizers to have credence functions, i.e., sets of subjective probabilities, that satisfy the axioms of the probability calculus. Many epistemologists, I believe, have conflated these two interests. They have assumed that a regulative notion of justification is the same notion of justification as the one that appears in the analysis of propositional knowledge. I think this assumption is mistaken. The best candidate for inclusion in the analysis of knowing is the Historical Reliabilist conception of justifiedness, and that notion is not a regulative one. For the purposes of the present paper, however, this issue is incidental. Here I wish to explore the idea of justification in its regulative role, whether or not it has any bearing on the concept of propositional knowledge.

I have introduced the regulative conception of epistemology by means of an analogy with ethics. It is questionable, however, whether the analogy is perfect. Ethics is largely concerned with individual actions, and actions are certainly subject to voluntary control and hence proper objects of self-guidance or regulation. But it is problematic whether doxastic states or attitudes are subject to (direct) voluntary control, and therefore problematic whether there is any point in formulating doxastic decision principles. I suspect that formation, retention, and revision of doxastic states are *not* subject to voluntary control, except perhaps in a restricted domain. Doxastic voluntarism is a dubious doctrine, however cherished it may have been by Descartes and other epistemologists. For the sake of discussion, though, let us proceed on the assumption (at least for a while) that doxastic voluntarism is true, that a cognizer can decide or choose whether to believe a given proposition at a given moment. We can then construe a principle of justification as one that instructs cognizers to adopt or retain certain beliefs (or other doxastic attitudes) in various circumstances. A principle of justification would be analogous to a moral principle that is designed to serve a regulative, or decision-making, function.

Let us be more precise about the relationship between the *justifiedness* of a belief and *doxastic decision principles* (for short, "DDPs"). We may represent a DDP as a function whose *inputs* are certain conditions of a cognizer—e.g., his beliefs, perceptual field, and ostensible memories—and whose *outputs* are prescriptions to adopt (or retain) this or that doxastic attitude—e.g., believing p, suspending judgment with respect to p, or having a particular subjective probability vis-à-vis p. Unless otherwise indicated, I shall here mean by "DDP" a *total* DDP, i.e., a single complete set of principles prescribing all doxastic attitudes a cognizer should have at a single time. Such a total DDP would presumably make use of a variety of different inputs, including those that pertain to perception, memory, induction, and the like.

The justificational status of believing a given proposition, say p, for cognizer S at time t presumably depends in part on the conditions S is in at, or just before, t, e.g., what evidence S possesses. But whether S is justified in believing p at t—whether S "ought," epistemically speaking, to believe p at t—also depends on the correct DDP. Assume that a unique DDP is correct, or right. Then S is justified in believing p at t if and only if the right DDP, when applied to the relevant conditions that characterize S at t, yields as output the prescription "believe p." More generally *S is justified in having doxastic attitude D vis-à-vis p at t if and only if the right DDP, when applied to the relevant input conditions that characterize S at t, yields as output the prescription ⌈adopt attitude D vis-à-vis p.⌉* This general relationship constitutes the basic framework of the regulative view of justification which will be presupposed in the rest of our discussion.[4]

Given this approach to justificational status, several questions obviously become paramount. First, what are admissible sorts of input conditions for a DDP? Which states of a cognizer are relevant to the justificational status of a doxastic attitude? Second, are we right in assuming that there is a uniquely correct DDP? Third, if this assumption is correct, what *makes* a certain DDP right, or correct?

II

Let us begin with the question concerning admissible inputs. In illustrating input conditions, I mentioned various cognitive states of a person, e.g., his beliefs and ostensible memories. It is worth asking, however, why the relevant input conditions should be cognitive states, or, for that matter, why they should be *states* of the person at all. Why could input conditions not be states of the world, or the external environment? On purely formal grounds, the following seems to qualify as a DDP: "For any proposition p, if p is true, then believe p (at any time t)." The input conditions for this DDP are not states of the cognizer; rather, they are the truth-values of the various propositions, or the "states of the world" that make these propositions true or false. But why not allow a DDP with input conditions of this kind? Admittedly, this is an intuitively inappropriate DDP. But what exactly makes it inappropriate?

The answer is straightforward. If a DDP is to be actually *usable* for making deliberate decisions, the conditions that serve as inputs must be *accessible* or *available* to the decision-maker at the time of decision. The agent must be *able to tell*, with respect to any possible input condition, whether that condition holds at the time in question. Now if the truth-value of any random proposition is a possible input condition, a cognizer would have to be able to tell, with respect to any such proposition, whether or not it is true. This requirement is not satisfied. Hence, the general class of truths and falsehoods cannot serve as the appropriate domain (i.e., input conditions) for a DDP.

We now see why a person's current cognitive states are a plausible class of input conditions. It is plausible to hold that for such states a person *can tell*, at any moment, exactly which of them he is in at that moment. So these input conditions would satisfy the requirement of being "accessible" or "available" to the decision-maker. But what exactly do we mean in saying that a person "*can tell*" with respect to a given condition whether or not that condition obtains? Here is a reasonable answer: "For any person S and time t, if S asks himself at t whether condition C obtains at the time in question, then S will believe that condition C obtains then if and only if it does obtain then."[5]

Notice that *past* cognitive states do not satisfy this constraint. It is not true, in general, that if I ask myself at time t whether or not I was in a certain cognitive state G at an earlier time t_0, then I will believe that I was in G at t_0 if and only if I was. I may forget or misremember my past cognitive states. For this reason, cognitive *ancestry* is not among the conditions that can serve as a DDP input. Thus a "historical" theory is excluded as a *regulative* theory of justification.

It is worth exploring some other consequences of our constraint on input conditions. Epistemologists commonly include logical relationships in their epistemic rules. For example, a rule might say: "If you are justified in believing Q, and Q *logically implies* P, then believe P." One input for this rule is the obtaining of a logical implication. But according to our constraint this is not an admissible input. It is not in general true that a person *can tell*, for any propositions Q and P, whether or not Q logically implies P. It appears, then, that many favorite examples of epistemic rules may not be legitimate (portions of) DDPs.

The rule in the previous paragraph poses another question about admissible input conditions. Is the justificational status of a doxastic attitude a legitimate input condition? Is *being-justified-in-believing* Q, as opposed to merely *believing* Q, an admissible input? If we admit (regulative) justificational status as an input condition, we have a threat of circularity in our theory. The aim of specifying a class of inputs and a correct DDP is to provide a theory of justification. If (the notion of) justificational status itself appears in the input conditions, our account would seem to be circular.

The charge of circularity should not be leveled too hastily. If a recursive account of justification were given, it would be unobjectionable to have a *recursive clause* by which the justificational status of believing Q could help determine the justificational status of believing P.[6] However, such a recursive account would also need *base clauses*, and to avoid circularity these base clauses would have to specify non-justificational conditions—substantive or "factual" conditions—for justificational status. So the justificational status of believing P would ultimately be traceable to these substantive conditions, which may be viewed as the relevant inputs. Thus it is appropriate to add the following restriction to our constraint on inputs: inputs must be purely factual, non-epistemic conditions.

This is all I shall say about admissible inputs for a DDP. Let us now turn to the question of what makes something the right DDP, and whether, indeed, a uniquely correct DDP can be demanded.

III

The choice of a DDP clearly depends on the *goals* of cognition, or doxastic-attitude-formation. A very plausible set of goals are the oft-cited aims of *believing the truth*—as much truth as possible—and *avoiding error*. (Some alternative goals will be examined later.) These twin desiderata, however, tend to compete with one another. A "conservative" DDP prescribes more suspension of judgment than does a "venturesome" DDP. Greater conservatism would tend to produce less false belief, which is good, but also less true belief, which is bad. Which of two such DDPs is preferable, on the whole, is a function of how the totality of true belief is weighted as compared with the amount of error. One view would be that a single false belief outweighs a tremendous amount of truth. Another view would be that there is as much positive value in a single (modest) truth as there is negative value in a single (modest) error. For my purposes, this knotty issue can be sidestepped. The issues I wish to raise in this paper are independent of the weighting problem. So let us proceed on the assumption that *some* combination of true belief and error avoidance is what we seek in a DDP.[7]

Given the aim of true belief and error avoidance, the right DDP is apparently one that would produce optimal results in terms of true belief and error avoidance. It is the DDP that would have such optimal results in the long run for the sum-total of cognizers. Or, assuming that what is best for one (human) cognizer is best for others, the right DDP is the one that would produce optimal results for any cognizer taken singly. It is the DDP that God in his omniscience would recommend.

Unfortunately, the foregoing characterization of the right DDP ignores a crucial aspect of traditional epistemology. The foregoing conception rests on an "*externalist*" perspective: the perspective of a Godlike observer who, knowing all truths and falsehoods, can select the DDP that optimally conduces to true belief and error avoidance. Traditional epistemology has not adopted this externalist perspective. It has been predominantly *internalist*, or egocentric. On the latter perspective, epistemology's job is to construct a doxastic principle or procedure *from the inside*, from our own individual vantage point. To adopt a Kantian idiom, a DDP must not be "heteronomous," or dictated "from without." It must be "autonomous," a law we can give to ourselves and which we have *grounds* for giving to ourselves. The *objective* optimality of a DDP, on this view, does not make it right. A DDP counts as right only if it is "certifiable" *from within*.

To illustrate the point, suppose a DDP were proposed that consisted in a very, very long list of propositions to be believed: propositions about individual events and states of affairs, laws of nature, and so on. Belief in these propositions is prescribed *unconditionally*, independent of the cognitive states of the agent. In short, the input conditions for this DDP are the null set. Further suppose that all the prescribed propositions in this long list are *true*. Does that make this DDP a strong candidate for the right DDP? Not at all, according to internalism. This is a DDP that a Godlike observer might give us, not the sort we can legitimately give to ourselves. More cautiously, if we *are* in a position to give that DDP to ourselves, it must be because we have used some other, more fundamental, DDP to ascertain the relevant set of truths. It is that more fundamental DDP which ought to be proposed as the genuinely correct DDP.

The foregoing example, it must be conceded, has oddities that are irrelevant to the point at issue. The DDP in question is counterintuitive because it contains no *general* instructions, no precepts for generating new beliefs from old, no provisions for learning from experience. All these features would naturally be expected in a good DDP. For this reason, let us illustrate the internalist idea with another, more familiar, example: the problem of induction.

Assume for the sake of argument that there is a unique inductive rule that would actually be optimal for predictive puposes. (Specification of an inductive rule will probably require, to meet Goodmanian concerns, either an enumeration of projectible predicates or a set of rules of projection. Assume these are built into the rule in question.) The mere fact of optimality, however, would not be regarded by internalism as a solution to the problem of induction. According to internalism, an inductive rule is right only if we can *justify* the claim that it is optimal, i.e., only if we can *show* that it will lead to truth, or will probably lead to truth, or that it (alone) meets some weaker (e.g., Reichenbachian) test of optimality. *De facto* optimality does not satisfy the internalist. A rule that just *happens* to be optimal is not right unless we *know*, or are *justified* in believing, that it is optimal.

Thus far I have given a rather vague characterization of the internalist conception of justifiedness. In the remainder of the paper I want to explore this conception critically. I shall argue that the internalist conception is either fundamentally confused or unfulfillable. Either (A) there is no definite and acceptable set of conditions that articulate the vague idea of the internalist, or (B) although such a definite set of conditions can be specified, there is nothing—no DDP, or rule of justification—that meets these conditions. In short, what appears to be a comprehensible and attractive conception of justification melts away when examined carefully. Finally, I shall argue that externalism provides a perfectly satisfactory conception of justifiedness.

IV

The crucial question for internalism is: What is the right DDP? We shall not try to pinpoint the particular DDP that is right according to internalism (nor the one that is right according to externalism). Rather, we shall try to see whether there is a definite and acceptable set of conditions that determine what internalism would *count* as the right DDP. We can indicate the sort of condition being sought by formulating the condition appropriate to *externalism*, viz. (1):

(1) DDP X is right if and only if: X is *actually* optimal.

By 'optimal' I mean, of course, optimal in producing true belief and error avoidance. As indicated earlier, the exact weighting of true belief and error avoidance is here neglected.

For reasons given above, (1) does not satisfy the internalist. What, then, *would* do so? Judging by our earlier characterization of internalism, the condition that seems to capture the internalist's conception is this:

(2) DDP X is right if and only if: we are *justified* in believing that X is optimal.

There is a fatal problem with (2), however. It uses the notion of justification! As indicated previously, the aim of a theory of justification is to assign justificational status in *non-justificational* terms. In particular, the aim of a regulative theory of justification is to provide instructions concerning doxastic attitudes that do not presuppose the prior existence, or establishment, of any such prescriptions. If the (regulative) notion of justifiedness is allowed in the condition(s) for the rightness of a DDP, this requirement will clearly be violated. For the rightness of a DDP is one of the two basic components of the theory of justifiedness. In short, proposal (2) is blatantly circular, and inadmissible on purely "formal" grounds.

It will do no better to say, in place of (2), that a DDP must be "certifiable" as optimal, or that we must have "grounds" for believing it to be optimal. Terms like 'certifiable' and 'grounds' are themselves epistemic terms, roughly synonymous with 'justified'. All such terms are equally inadmissible for the purposes at hand. Unfortunately, the initial sketch of the internalist conception utilized these very terms. This suggests that (2) correctly expresses the intuitive idea behind internalism, unacceptable as that idea turns out to be. But there may be other, unobjectionable ways of fleshing out internalism. Let us explore some further possibilities.

In place of (2) we might try (3):

(3) DDP X is right if and only if: we *believe* that X is optimal.

Clearly, (3) avoids the formal problem facing (2). But is it at all plausible? I think not. Suppose we believe some particular DDP X to be optimal for (intuitively speaking) very bad reasons, or for no reasons at all. We may believe it to be optimal out of wishful thinking, sheer confusion, or mere hunch and guesswork. We may believe it to be optimal simply because it pops into our heads, or comes to us in a dream. Is internalism committed to saying, in such circumstances, that X is really right? That doxastic attitudes *ought* (epistemically speaking) to be formed in accordance with X? Surely not. Internalism presumably does not want the rightness of a DDP to be determined by sheer eccentricity, frivolous reasons, or happenstance.

These considerations are just the sorts of considerations that motivate proposal (2). But we cannot go back to (2). Is there anything similar to (2) that does not violate the formal restriction on which (2) itself founders? It may seem promising to recall that a non-regulative theory of justified belief is available: Historical Reliabilism. It may be suggested that no circularity would be involved if we used the non-regulative notion of justifiedness in our theory of the regulative notion. More important, since Historical Reliabilism is a theory formulated in non-epistemic terms, why not use the substance of this theory without employing the term 'justification' (or any of its cognates)? This would yield the following:

(4) DDP X is right if and only if: (A) we believe that X is optimal, and
                                   (B) this belief was caused by reliable cognitive processes.

Unfortunately, (4) founders on another restriction, a restriction peculiar to internalism. The basic idea of internalism is that there should be guaranteed epistemic access to the correctness of a DDP.[8] No condition of DDP-rightness is acceptable unless we have epistemic access to the DDP that in fact satisfies the condition, i.e., unless we can tell which DDP satisfies it. The internalist's objection to externalism's condition of rightness, i.e., actual optimality, is precisely that cognizers may have no way of telling which DDP satisfies it. Internalism's *own* condition of rightness must, therefore, be such that any cognizer *can tell* which DDP satisfies it. But this restriction is not met by (4). In general, we are not in a position to tell how some belief of ours was caused; nor is it guaranteed that we can tell which of our cognitive processes are reliable and which are not.

In addition to the foregoing objections (which are conclusive enough), there are other problems with (2), (3), and (4). A problem common to all three is the use of the term 'we'. To whom does this pronoun purport to refer? To *everyone*? This implies, in the case of (3) and (4), that a DDP is right (according to internalism) only if *everyone* believes it to be optimal. But surely such universal consensus is hard to come by and unreasonable to require.

How is this difficulty to be met in any future proposal? Should 'we' be taken to refer to a *majority* of people? To a *plurality* in favor of a single DDP as compared with any other DDP? Neither of these suggestions is attractive. A more promising solution is to *relativize* DDP-rightness to a cognizer (and a time). This would yield the following analogues of (3) and (4):

(3*) DDP X is right for S at t if and only if: S believes at t that X is optimal.

(4*) DDP X is right for S at t if and only if: (A) S believes at t that X is optimal, and
(B) this belief was caused by reliable cognitive processes.

The relativization solution is a serious step that should not be taken lightly. But let us defer an examination of that issue for a moment.[9] There is still another problem that would face (3*) and (4*) as they stand, a problem related to the one that relativization was intended to solve. Relativization was intended to meet the objection that the same DDP may not be believed *by everyone* to be optimal. But we must also note that some people may not believe of *any* DDP that it is optimal. Indeed, since the notion of a DDP is an abstruse notion, unlikely to be familiar to anyone but a philosopher, it is highly probable that *most* people will not believe of any DDP that it is optimal. It will follow from (3*) and (4*) that no DDP at all will be right for the vast majority of people. This would seem to imply that no doxastic instructions govern these individuals, so that there are no doxastic attitudes that they are justified (or unjustified) in choosing. Certainly this cannot be intended by internalism. Thus what internalism needs is a condition of rightness that does not require *actual belief* by a cognizer in the optimality of some DDP.

To meet this requirement the internalist might say that DDP X is right for person S at time t just in case S *would* believe X to be optimal, given S's antecedent mental states. But would . . . *if what*? If S formed this belief in accordance with the right DDP? Obviously the internalist cannot say that, for it would be a flagrant circularity. What might be said, however, is that S would believe X to be optimal if S used X itself. In other words, X is right for S at t just in case X is "*self-prescribing*" for S at t. This may be written as (5):

> (5) DDP X is right for S at t if and only if: if X is applied to S's (relevant) inputs at t, X prescribes belief in ⌜X is optimal⌝.

One problem with (5) is that it may fail to meet the internalist's restriction that a cognizer should be able to tell which DDP meets the condition. If a DDP is very complex, it may be difficult to tell what it prescribes, in particular, whether or not it prescribes belief in its own optimality. A second problem is even more critical. Two or more incompatible DDPs can each satisfy (5) for the same person and time. Let Y be a DDP that, among other things, prescribes use of the "scientific method" (assuming there is a unique such method). Let Z be a DDP that, among other things, prescribes belief in accordance with ostensible revelations (rather than the scientific method). Then it may well happen that, given S's inputs at t, Y prescribes belief in ⌜Y is optimal⌝ and Z prescribes belief in ⌜Z is optimal⌝. According to (5), *both* Y and Z are right for S at t. But since they are incompatible, they will generate some incompatible doxastic prescriptions. Which of these competing prescriptions should be followed? Which should be used to assess the justificational status of S's doxastic attitudes? (5) cannot answer these questions and is therefore unacceptable.

V

Let us return now to the issue of relativization. It follows, of course, from the strategy of relativization that a DDP which is right for one cognizer may not be right for another. Is such "*epistemological relativism*" acceptable to internalism? It is clear, I think, that internalists have not generally intended any such relativism. They have usually assumed that some uniform set of doxastic principles should govern all human cognizers. Foundationalists think that foundationalism (insofar as it generates doxastic prescriptions) is right for everyone. Coherentists think that coherentism is right for everyone. Bayesians think that Bayesianism is right for everyone. So we will need some special and strong argumentation to sustain the idea that internalism should incorporate relativism.

One possible line of argumentation would attempt to draw an analogy with the distinction in ethics between *objective* and *subjective* rightness.[10] An act is said to be objectively right just in case it actually satisfies the conditions for moral rightness. An act is said to be subjectively right just in case, roughly speaking, the agent's beliefs or evidence concerning the circumstances or consequences of the act suggest that it is objectively right. Subjective rightness involves relativization to the beliefs or evidence of the agent at the time of action. Now it might be suggested that the moral status of objective rightness is analogous to the *ex*ternalist conception of DDP rightness and that the *in*ternalist conception of DDP rightness is analogous to the moral status of subjective rightness. Since the moral notion involves relativization, it is proper for the epistemic notion to involve relativization as well.

Apart from the issue of relativization, the idea of subjective rightness in ethics may hold promise of assistance in our present predicament. After all, the notion of subjective rightness in ethics is usually thought to be tolerably clear. Why not borrow its analysis for the purpose of stating conditions of DDP rightness?

Regrettably, matters are not so simple. There seem to be two basic strategies for analyzing subjective rightness in ethics: (A) Action A is subjectively right if and only if the agent *believes* of A that it is objectively right; or (B) Action A is subjectively right if and only if the agent is *justified* in believing of A that it is objectively right. We may call these the *"doxastic"* and *"epistemic"* approaches, respectively. Neither of these approaches works well when applied to our present topic. When transferred to our topic, the doxastic approach yields (3) or (3*), which proved quite unsatisfactory. (Some of the same criticisms might apply to the *moral* notion as well.) Furthermore, the epistemic approach would yield our proposal (2) (or a relativized version of (2)), which is wholly inadmissible. The moral theorist is entitled to use an epistemic notion to explicate *his* concept of subjective rightness, but *we* are not entitled to use an epistemic notion, for our *explicandum* is itself epistemic.

The ethicist's notion of subjective rightness, then, proves to have less utility for our purposes than we might hope. Still, it may help support the idea of relativization. What we need, however, is not just the analogy from ethics but a particular example that motivates this idea in the epistemic sphere. Here is an example designed to serve this purpose.

Consider two men who belong to different cultures in different historical periods. The first belongs to a prescientific or early scientific community, in which precise methods of experimentation and statistical techniques have never been dreamed of. The second belongs to a scientifically advanced culture and has personally been trained in methodological and statistical techniques. Imagine that each of these men happens to entertain the same scientific hypothesis, H, and that each has the same observational evidence that bears on H. According to the DDP believed by the first man to be optimal, H should be believed. According to the DDP believed by the second man to be optimal, H should not be believed. Now suppose each man adopts the doxastic attitude vis-à-vis H prescribed by his favored DDP. Is each not *justified* in adopting this doxastic attitude? In particular, the member of the prescientific culture isn't justified — at least "subjectively justified" — in adopting his doxastic attitude? After all, the sophisticated techniques of advanced science are, by hypothesis not yet invented. He can hardly be faulted for proceeding as best he can, by his own lights. Is not the DDP he uses at least "right for him?"

Although this example is plausible, it is not wholly convincing. A defender of epistemological objectivism might reply as follows. "It is admittedly *excusable* or *pardonable* for the member of the prescientific community to accept his own DDP — call it W — and for him to form the doxastic attitude prescribed by W. But to say that this is *excusable* is not to say that the resultant doxastic attitude is *justified*. A doxastic attitude is justified only if it is enjoined by proper procedure, and the description of the case presupposes that DDP W is not proper procedure, i.e., is not the right DDP. To be sure, it may be difficult for this cognizer, in his historico-cultural setting, to identify the right DDP. This is why we would not *blame* him for his doxastic act. Still, there is no need to consider him *justified* in believing H. Nor is there need to say that W is in *some* sense a 'right' DDP. The only right DDP is the objectively right DDP. Even internalism should insist on an objectively right DDP, whether or not it is equivalent to the 'optimal' DDP."[11]

I am inclined to endorse this response of the objectivist and conclude that the example in question should not impel the internalist to be a relativist. On the other hand, even if the internalist wants to be a relativist, we have not yet identified conditions that express an adequate version of internalism, either of a relativistic or a non-relativistic variety. Thus we have yet to make cogent sense of the vague intuitions that motivate internalism. Thus far internalism is a mere will-o'-the wisp.

VI

At this juncture the internalist may object that I have ignored the most obvious and straightforward way of specifying his conception. At least since the time of Descartes there has been a reasonably well-defined idea of the *"internal standpoint"* in epistemology. This is the idea of a certain epistemological *starting point*, a position from which all doxastic decisons are to be made. To make doxastic decisions, however, one needs a DDP, and so it is natural to say that the DDP must also be chosen from the same "internal" starting point. This was Descartes's own practice, for his criterion of clearness-and-distinctness was proposed and argued for from this very vantage point.[12] We have, then, a natural way of formulating the internalist's condition for the rightness of a DDP:

(6) DDP X is right if and only if: X is the proper DDP to choose if one chooses a DDP from the internal standpoint.

So formulated, internalism certainly contrasts with externalism, for there is no guarantee that the DDP properly chosen from the internal standpoint would be identical with the optimal DDP.

Is (6) a clear and definite condition for DDP-rightness? That depends on how clear and definite we can make the idea of the internal standpoint and the criteria of "proper choice." I shall argue that, however clear and definite we can make this idea and these criteria, there is no unique DDP that can be generated.[13] In short, even if (6) is a condition that satisfactorily expresses the spirit of internalism, it does not select or determine a preferred DDP. In this sense the internalist conception of a right DDP is *"unfulfillable."*

A merely apparent difficulty for choosing a DDP from the internal standpoint is the threat of a vicious regress. The choice of a DDP requires a criterion of choice, and it might be supposed that this criterion must itself be a DDP: a meta-DDP. But how is *that* DDP to be chosen? By means of a meta-meta-DDP? And so on ad infinitum? This worry rests on a confusion. A DDP is not a proposition but a *policy* or set of conditional *prescriptions*. (*That such-and-such a DDP is optimal* is a proposition; but the DDP is not a proposition.) Since a DDP is not a proposition, the adoption of a DDP is not the adoption of a *doxastic* attitude. Since no *doxastic* attitude is being chosen, no DDP is required. To be sure, some criterion of choice is needed, which does, as we shall see, pose problems. But the criterion in question may be a familiar decision criterion, such as maximizing expected value, not a DDP. Thus no infinite regress is launched.

A somewhat analogous problem, though, is the central problem that confronts the attempt to choose a DDP from the internal standpoint. Although the choice of a unique DDP does not require a prior (meta-) DDP, it *does* require antecedent doxastic attitudes on which to base a choice. To assess the probable consequences of this or that policy of forming physical-world beliefs, for example, one needs some doxastic attitudes toward propositions that describe typical events in the physical world and relationships between the physical world and one's mental states. But such doxastic attitudes are absent in the internal standpoint.

To clarify this point, let us be more precise about the nature of the internal standpoint. As indicated, this standpoint is supposed to be an epistemological starting point. At such a point one should be epistemologically neutral or uncommitted. More specifically, *doxastic* neutrality is required. The whole point of choosing a DDP, after all, is to license selected doxastic attitudes. Until a DDP has been properly chosen, no doxastic attitudes can be licensed, at least no doxastic attitudes toward epistemologically problematic propositions. So the internal standpoint must disallow the use of, or appeal to, prior doxastic attitudes we may happen to have. As in Rawls's "original position," the internal standpoint is a perspective in which principles must be chosen from behind a "veil of ignorance."

I said that no appeal may be made to doxastic attitudes toward epistemologically "problematic" propositions. Which propositions are problematic? Virtually all contingent propositions have generally been regarded as problematic, and doxastic attitudes toward these should certainly be barred from the internal standpoint. A possible exception is first-person-current-mental-state propositions, which are often regarded as unproblematic although they are contingent. We may allow beliefs in these propositions to be used in the internal standpoint, just for the sake of argument.[14] It is unlikely that this will substantially assist the internalist's project anyway.

The foregoing characterization of the internal standpoint is obviously modeled on Descartes's procedure. Yet Descartes himself is not sufficiently thoroughgoing. He advocates the policy of *suspending judgment* on problematic propositions at the epistemological starting point. But suspension of judgment is itself a kind of doxastic attitude. What justifies Descartes in adopting *that* attitude toward the propositions in question? He operates on the assumption that when evidence is inconclusive you should suspend judgment. But this in itself is a partial DDP, and, like any DDP, should first be argued for. Before the selection of a DDP we cannot say that the proper attitude to adopt is suspension of judgment. This is not doxastic neutrality.

It must be admitted, though, that suspension of judgment may be the best approximation to doxastic neutrality, or doxastic nullity. If you have a proposition in mind at all, how else can you avoid commitment? So let us permit the use of suspension of judgment in the internal standpoint. However, suspension of judgment must not be equated with a subjective probability of .5. *Such* a doxastic attitude certainly would be prejudicial.

Let us now see how the absence of usable doxastic attitudes in the internal standpoint makes it impossible to choose a unique DDP. The most popular criterion of choice in decision theory is *maximizing expected value*. Suppose that this criterion is used in trying to make the choice. In the present case maximizing expected value means selecting the DDP that has the greatest expected value as measured by true belief and error avoidance. For each DDP the "expected" verific consequences of adopting it would be computed and then the DDP with the greatest expected value would be chosen. The rub, however, is that the notion of "expected" value is partly a function of *subjective probabilities*. The "expected" value of adopting a given DDP is a function of one's estimate of that DDP's leading to truth and away from error. But we have already seen that no such subjective probabilities vis-à-vis contingent subject matter—at least physicalistic subject matter—can be appealed to in the internal standpoint. Hence the criterion of maximizing expected value cannot be used in the internal standpoint to select a unique DDP.

A concrete example may help. Suppose you are trying to decide whether to choose a DDP that incorporates the rule: "Whenever you experience a certain sequence of sensations, believe the proposition: 'There is a doorknob before me.'" To make this decision you need an assessment of the consequences of including this rule. Will adoption of it tend to produce true beliefs or errors? What proportion of each? Unless you have a (doxastic) estimate of these outcomes, you cannot assess the expected value of this rule. But any such estimate is a doxastic attitude toward a *contingent* proposition and is therefore barred from the internal standpoint. This is so even if phenomenalism is true. Even if phenomenalism is true, any given sequence of sensations is compatible not only with there being a doorknob before you but also with, for example, your hallucinating the feeling of touching a door knob. Since the sequence of sensations is compatible with both states of affairs, an estimate of the verific consequences of adopting the rule in question will depend upon an estimate of the frequency with which you will really encounter doorknobs as opposed to merely hallucinate such encounters. But no such estimates are permitted in the internal standpoint.

My argument for the impossibility of choosing a DDP from the internal standpoint has thus far rested on a particular decision criterion: maximizing expected value. But decision theory has a larger inventory of decision rules, and some of these might dictate a choice without the indicated doxastic attitudes. Consider the criterion of maximin, for example. This criterion tells a decision-maker to choose an option (here, a DDP) whose worst possible outcome is at least as good as the worst possible outcome of any other option (DDP). Trivially, the worst outcome for a DDP that enjoins any beliefs at all is the outcome where all enjoined beliefs turn out false. So the worst outcome of a DDP that never enjoins belief at all—the skeptic's, or agnostic's, DDP—is clearly the best of the worst outcomes. Thus it might appear that maximin *would* generate the choice of a unique DDP from the internal standpoint, namely, the skeptic's DDP.

But why use the maximin criterion when choosing a DDP from the internal standpoint? Why not select, say, the maximax criterion instead? Maximax tells you to choose an option (here, a DDP) whose best possible outcome is at least as good as the best possible outcome of any other option (DDP). Obviously, maximax would generate a very different choice of DDP than maximin would, if it generates any unique choice at all.[15] Maximax would mandate a DDP that prescribes belief most liberally (indeed, profligately), since the best possible outcome of such a DDP—viz., all the enjoined beliefs being true—will be unsurpassed.

Perhaps *some* situations could dictate a preference for maximin over maximax and other situations the reverse preference. But the internal standpoint permits no preference whatever. *Ex hypothesi*, the internal standpoint contains no doxastic attitudes toward (problematic) contingent propositions, so there is no basis for either optimism or pessimism in one's choices. Without a basis for selecting a unique criterion of choice, no unique DDP can be generated from the internal standpoint.

Have I been too restrictive in excluding doxastic attitudes toward virtually all contingent propositions from the internal standpoint? Could we not so specify the internal standpoint as to admit more doxastic attitudes, even beliefs? Well, we certainly *could*, as many epistemologists have done by admitting "premisses" about the uniformity of nature, or the initial credibility or reliability of memory. But on what ground may we impute such doxastic attitudes to the internal standpoint? How are we to choose the particular doxastic attitudes? Presumably the selection should not be made randomly or arbitrarily. Should we choose beliefs that are widespread among human cognizers? This would be a poor rationale, since widespread beliefs may have no claim to epistemological priority. Should we impute beliefs that strike us as epistemically sound? That sort of strategy would seem to rely on *prior* epistemic standards, some prior commitment to a DDP. But the entire rationale for inventing the internal standpoint is precisely to *choose* a DDP (for the first time!). Basing such a choice on some antecedent DDP is indeed self-defeating and invites the prospect of a vicious regress.

Some readers may not be fully convinced by my attack on the feasibility of generating a unique DDP from the internal standpoint. They might feel that recent epistemologists in the foundationalist tradition have succeeded in producing doxastic principles of the sort I have in mind (if not an entire DDP), e.g., such epistemologists as Roderick Chisholm or John Pollock.[16] Are these epistemologists not good examples of internalists, and do they not succeed in displaying the favorable prospects for internalism?

Although Chisholm and Pollock may indeed be foundationalists, I do not think they are thoroughgoing internalists *in the sense of this notion that I have specified*. Whatever the merits of their work, they do not succeed in supporting our version of internalism.

Chisholm's epistemic principles may be viewed as partial DDPs. These rules assign epistemic status to propositions, and this assignment of epistemic status is roughly equivalent to prescribing, permitting, or prohibiting belief. To say in Chisholm's terminology that a proposition is "evident" for a person is to say, roughly, that he ought to believe it. The crucial question is how Chisholm's principles are supposed to be derived. For example, Chisholm endorses the principle, "If you believe that you *perceive* something to have property F, where F is a sensible characteristic, then you ought to believe the proposition that there *is* something which has property F (before you)."[17] Chisholm would presumably be unwilling to endorse either (i) "If you believe that you *telepathize* a person to be thinking thought T, then you ought to believe the proposition that someone (else) *is* thinking thought T," or (ii) "If you believe that you '*clairvoy*' that x will happen, then you ought to believe the proposition that x *will* happen." Why is the principle concerning ostensible perception, but not the principles concerning ostensible telepathy or clairvoyance, to be endorsed? Chisholm proceeds by assuming that "we have at our disposal certain instances that the rules should countenance or permit and other instances that the rules should reject or forbid."[18] In other words, we rely on our commonsensical intuitions or judgments concerning what we know, or what the proper epistemic standards are.[19] This suggests that Chisholm's choice of epistemic principles rests on *prior* epistemic standards, which contravenes the idea of internalism. To put the point slightly differently, Chisholm seems to be engaged merely in codifying or systematizing antecedent doxastic practice, at least reflective doxastic practice. But it cannot be assumed that this practice, or the epistemic standards it expresses, derives from the internal standpoint. There is no guarantee, or even a hint of a guarantee, that our intuitive epistemic judgments could have been properly chosen from the internal standpoint. Hence nothing in Chisholm's discussion alleviates the difficulties for internalism.

Essentially the same point holds for Pollock. Pollock says that the "basic epistemological task" is to "*spell out*" the justification conditions for statements in different areas of knowledge.[20] This apparently means that epistemology should elucidate the set of justification conditions (roughly, the DDP) that we antecedently or commonsensically accept. True, Pollock maintains that the *meanings* of our ordinary physical-object statements, statements about the past, etc., consist in criteria of justification. But even if this is right, it just implies that we have chosen to use words in a way that commits us to certain justification principles (a DDP). There is no assurance, however, or even the glimmer of a suggestion, that such principles have been chosen, or could have been chosen, from the internal standpoint. So Pollock, like Chisholm, offers no comfort to internalism as *I* have delineated it.

VII

The epistemological difficulties of the Cartesian or egocentric position are familiar, and the previous section only reformulates these difficulties within a certain structure or framework. (I believe, however, that this framework makes the problems clearer than they have sometimes been made.) In particular, it is a familiar fact that it is difficult for the internal standpoint to license belief in *contingent* propositions. Still, the domain of logic might seem to be a different kettle of fish. After all, it is (allegedly) an a priori domain. Should the internal standpoint not be able to license doxastic attitudes toward propositions of logic? Should it not be able to generate *certain* doxastic principles (partial DDPs), viz., principles that derive from logic?

The relative tractability of these subjects is an illusion. First let us consider how to generate doxastic principles from logic. An initially attractive principle is this: "For any propositions Q and P, if Q logically implies P, and you believe Q, then believe P." There are two objections to this principle. First, as Gilbert Harman points out,[21] it may be best to abandon belief in Q under these circumstances rather than adopt a belief in P. Second, this principle violates our admissibility constraint on inputs (as we pointed out in section II). People cannot in general tell infallibly whether a putative logical implication really is one or not; hence this condition cannot serve as an antecedent of a doxastic principle.

The principle might be amended to read: "If you *believe* that Q logically implies P, and you believe Q, then believe P." This meets the admissibility constraint, but it does not meet Harman's objection. In fact, Harman's point is doubly troublesome here, since it is also problematic whether you should retain your belief in the putative logical implication; perhaps *that* belief should be abandoned.

A possible further amendment is this: "If you *justifiably* believe that Q logically implies P, and you *justifiably* believe Q, then believe P." This amendment might accommodate Harman's worry, but the resulting principle can serve only as a recursive principle and it focuses our attention on the need for *base clauses* concerning logical relationships (e.g., propositions of the form "Q logically implies P"). In light of our earlier restrictions (see section II), these base clauses must specify *nonepistemic* conditions in which one should believe logical truths.

Bayesians and confirmation theorists of various persuasions have often said that every tautology or logical truth should be assigned a subjective probability of 1.0. In our framework this amounts to the principle "For any proposition p, if p is a logical truth, then believe p (or be completely certain of p)." But this violates our "can tell" constraint on inputs. Ignoring that constraint for the moment, it should be clear that this principle is misguided. In terms of our regulative conception, it says that a person is automatically *justified* in believing (indeed, being certain of) any proposition that is a logical truth. Such a principle has no appeal. It conflates the modal or logical status of a proposition with its epistemic status. Bear in mind that the logical status of a proposition is a matter, like any other, in which mistakes and confusions are possible.[22] A person who is untrained or poorly trained in logic is even more likely to make mistakes, or to fail to "grasp" or "intuit" a logical relationship when one is present. Thus there is no plausibility in saying, of any person whatever, that whenever he entertains a proposition that is a logical truth, he is justified in believing it (indeed, in being completely certain of it).

Thus far the difficulties we have canvassed concerning matters of logic are as much a problem for externalism as for internalism. But our discussion highlights two peculiar difficulties for internalism. First, we have seen that propositions of logic are epistemologically problematic. Beliefs in such propositions, therefore, cannot be allowed in the internal standpoint; they cannot be used to choose a DDP. This exacerbates the difficulty of choosing a DDP from the internal standpoint, for it is hard to *figure out* what doxastic policies to adopt if one cannot employ (beliefs in) truths of logic in one's figuring. Second, our discussion reminds us of the fact that an appropriate doxastic strategy vis-à-vis propositions of logic partly depends on our powers of reasoning and intuition. Well-chosen doxastic instructions should reflect the scope and accuracy of our imaginal and computational faculties. The exact nature of these powers and faculties, however, is a contingent matter, so there cannot be doxastic attitudes concerning them in the internal standpoint. This adds still another reason why no choice of doxastic principles for the domain of logic can be generated from the internal standpoint.

VIII

Internalists may object that I have not been entirely fair to them. Acknowledging the force of the difficulties I have raised, they may hasten to say that these difficulties stem largely from the assumption that true-belief-cum-error-avoidance is the proper goal of cognition. If a different goal is posited, it may be easier to choose a DDP from the internal standpoint.

Is there a plausible alternative goal? One classical candidate is *coherence* among doxastic attitudes. Coherence is a notoriously ambiguous concept, though. One version interprets it as *consistency*: a set of beliefs is coherent if and only if the propositions believed are logically consistent. A set of subjective probabilities is coherent if and only if they conform to the probability calculus. It has often been pointed out, however, that mere consistency (in either form) is an implausibly modest goal. It is too easy (relatively speaking) to obtain a merely consistent set of beliefs. Furthermore, it is unclear on this view why scientists and scholars regard the accumulation of additional evidence, and performance of new tests and experiments, as worthwhile intellectual enterprises. If mere consistency is our aim, new evidence and experiments are irrelevant. We can retain consistent beliefs with as sparse an evidence-base as you please. Evidently, we gather more evidence because more evidence (we assume) will contribute to greater truth-acquisition and/or error-avoidance.

Other forms of coherence have been advanced, *explanatory* coherence being the leading example. The notion of explanatory coherence, though, is far from clear.[23] Furthermore, it is hard to see why it should be regarded as the goal of cognition unless best explanatory hypotheses are likely to be *true*. So it is truth once again that surfaces as the fundamental cognitive desideratum.

Other candidate goals may be mentioned briefly. Peirce regarded the aim of inquiry as the "fixation" of belief, by which he meant the formation of belief in such a fashion that subsequent change is avoided. But why should mere fixity of opinion be sought? Besides, it is too easy a goal to meet, at least if doxastic voluntarism is true. One kind of DDP that meets this goal is a DDP that instructs cognizers to retain beliefs they have held in the past. Unfortunately, there are many different total DDPs that would contain this instruction. There is no way to choose from these DDPs, since they all meet the specified goal. This shows that the goal is too weak.

Another candidate desideratum out of the pragmatist tradition is the goal of "relieving agnosticism." Isaac Levi's treatment renders this equivalent to the goal of maximizing belief "content."[24] But Levi couples this with the goal of error-avoidance, and this again introduces an element that internalism finds difficult to handle. It is clear, moreover, that content-maximization by itself is an implausible *exclusive* desideratum. A DDP could promote this goal by prescribing belief in every proposition, including contradictory propositions, which is radically counter-intuitive. Nor is it plausible to couple content-maximization with mere inconsistency-avoidance. There are indefinitely many consistent-but-detailed sets of possible beliefs. Which of these should be chosen? There would be no criterion of selection from these sets on the basis of this twofold goal.

I conclude that truth-acquisition and error-avoidance is the best candidate for the goal of cognition (or doxastic-attitude formation). Postulation of this goal does indeed pose problems for internalism, but that reflects ill on internalism, not on the goal.[25]

IX

We have surveyed numerous attempts to articulate the vague idea that underlies internalism. Most of these attempts proved unsatisfactory. When we finally formulated a condition that did not seem palpably inadequate, i.e., (6), we found good reason to believe that no unique DDP[26] could be generated from this condition. There seems, then, to be no way of fulfilling internalism's conception of the right DDP. Should we conclude that internalism is a mirage, a conception that beckons to us with no real prospect of satisfaction? Many epistemologists would shrink from this conclusion, since it would leave nothing but externalism to satisfy our need for a theory of justification. But I shall argue that we should be thoroughly content with externalism, that it offers everything one can reasonably expect (if not everything one has always wanted) in a theory of justification.

One objection to externalism is its failure to *guarantee* epistemic access to the optimal DDP, the DDP that externalism says is right. But this fact should not be confused with the claim that the optimal DDP is necessarily *in*accessible. Nothing in the conception of an optimal DDP precludes the possibility of successful identification of the optimal DDP. Furthermore, since two distinct total DDPs can share a large proportion of instructions, the uniquely optimal DDP may be approximated to a greater or lesser extent by numerous sub-optimal DDPs. We may get "close" to the optimal DDP, even if we do not get every detail exactly right. And if we regulate our doxastic attitudes in accordance with a slightly sub-optimal DDP, we may still "do" almost everything correctly, i.e., justifiably; for the great majority of our doxastic attitudes may conform with the right (= optimal) DDP as well as with our approximation to it.

Still, at any given time, we may not be in possession of the right DDP. Can this be reconciled with people's common practice of rendering epistemic appraisals? Certainly it can. People's appraisals of doxastic attitudes as justified or unjustified reflect only their *beliefs* about justifiedness, not the *facts* of justifiedness. When Smith judges Jones's belief to be justified (in the regulative sense), this indicates that Smith *believes* that Jones's belief accords with the right DDP. It does not mean that Jones's belief *does* accord with the right DDP, nor even that Smith is *justified* in believing that it so accords (though doubtless Smith *thinks* that he is justified).

However, many people have great confidence in their epistemic appraisals. Can this be reconciled with the externalist conception, which makes the right DDP difficult to identify? Part of the answer is that ordinary people have no inkling of the theoretical problems and difficulties and may therefore have *misplaced* confidence in their appraisals. With increased sophistication, some of this confidence may fade. The same is true of moral judgments. The mere fact that ordinary people often have great confidence in their moral judgments hardly shows that the correct moral standard (assuming there is one) is easily accessible. The common man's confidence in his moral appraisals may be misplaced.

But do not philosophers, logicians, and statisticians often have great confidence in their epistemic appraisals, which are not so readily dismissible as misplaced? Yes, but many of these appraisals are *negative*, and it is much easier to *fault* a piece of reasoning, or a conclusion, than it is to sustain one. If you can see that a certain pattern of thought will lead systematically to error, you can plausibly conclude that some other pattern of thought is better, and hence that the conclusion in question is not licensed by the optimal DDP. You can do all this without pretending to know exactly what the optimal DDP *is*.

Finally, even *positive* epistemic appraisals do not imply putative knowledge of the *total* optimal DDP. Saying that a certain doxastic attitude accords with the optimal DDP does not suggest that you can specify that DDP, any more than saying that a certain act conforms with (fails to violate) the criminal code implies that you can specify the details of that code in its entirety.

What is most perturbing about externalism, however, may be something entirely different. Suppose that the actually optimal DDP can be found only with difficulty and effort. *What are we supposed to do in the meantime?* How should we form our doxastic attitudes? How should we search for the optimal DDP? Which (meta-) DDP should we use in the search procedure?

The first point to note is that internalism faces the very same problems. Whatever the internalistically right DDP is supposed to be, we could not rely on its falling to us from heaven. We should probably have to work to get it. The same questions, then, arise: how should we form our doxastic attitudes in the meantime? and which DDP should we use in searching for the internalistically right DDP? These worries do not create a special presumption against externalism, since they are of equal significance for internalism.

Furthermore, there is an important reason why these questions and worries probably have no application, either to externalism or to internalism. This point rests on the probable falsity of doxastic voluntarism, at least the radical version of this doctrine which says that doxastic attitudes can *only* be chosen, that they cannot be formed by non-deliberative processes. On the contrary, there are native, or constitutional, doxastic processes that generate beliefs independently of our will and independently of the deliberate selection of a DDP. Perceptual processes automatically produce representations that, unless inhibited by other cognitions, serve as beliefs. Similarly, we are all ground-level inductivists. Expectation based on past experience is part of our animal heritage. Thus we do have means of forming doxastic attitudes before choosing doxastic *principles*. Native doxastic *habits* render the selection of doxastic *principles* not strictly necessary. When we do come to choose doxastic principles, this choice may be based on beliefs formed by antecedent doxastic habits. No meta-DDP is required.

Indeed, a stronger argument can be made. Not only is it *possible* for the choice of a doxastic principle to be based on doxastic habit; it is *necessary*. If every choice of a DDP rests on doxastic attitudes that result from a prior DDP choice, there would be an infinite regress of DDP choices. Such an infinite regress is impossible (at least physically impossible). So if there are any DDP choices at all, they must rest, ultimately, on doxastic habits.

This conclusion jibes with the most plausible reconstruction of how doxastic principle choices come to be made. At the start a creature forms beliefs from automatic, preprogrammed doxastic processes; these beliefs are largely about its own immediate environment. At a later stage of development, at least in a sophisticated creature, beliefs are formed about its own belief-forming processes. The creature comes to believe that certain of its belief-forming processes often lead to error and that others are more reliable. This kind of belief can arise as follows. The creature predicts a certain event, i.e., believes it will occur. The creature then observes its non-occurrence, i.e., believes it has failed to occur. If the creature remembers the earlier belief, it can conclude that the earlier belief was false, hence that the process which generated it is (somewhat) unreliable. These beliefs presuppose, of course, that the creature has a conception of truth and falsity. This need not be a philosophical *theory* of truth but merely a rudimentary conception thereof. (Such a conception would seem to go hand-in-hand with a conception of belief, since believing a proposition is believing it to be true.) Once the creature distinguishes between more and less reliable belief-forming processes, it has taken the first step toward doxastic appraisal. It can then introduce a (non-regulative) notion of *justifiedness*; beliefs are justified if and only if they are produced by (relatively) reliable belief-forming processes. The creature can also begin doxastic self-criticism, in which it proposes *regulative* principles to itself.[27] On the assumption that doxastic states are at least partly subject to deliberate decision, the creature can formulate and endorse DDPs that might avert errors or biases in its native processes.

What is noteworthy in this reconstruction is that the notion of justifiedness, especially the regulative notion, is a late arrival. It does not appear until the creature already has beliefs and a conception of truth. This reverses the scenario that internalism tends to foster. Internalism encourages the idea that the choice of a DDP should antecede all belief, that we must first select a *criterion* of truth—a principle for deciding which propositions are true—before we form any beliefs. But if my description of how things actually go is correct, this order is reversed. Beliefs come before the selection of a DDP. Upon reflection, it is hard to see how things *could* go otherwise, given the kind of creature we are.

If the foregoing discussion is right, the answers to our earlier questions are straightforward. We do have a means of forming doxastic attitudes prior to our (initial) choice of a DDP: we have our native, preprogrammed doxastic processes.

Similarly, there is a straightforward answer to what we should do in trying to identify the optimal DDP. At first we should (and must) use our constitutional doxastic habits. Once these habits generate the choice of a DDP, that DDP should be used (together with the habits which it does not wholly displace) to form any new views about the optimal DDP.

Actually it is an open question whether *any* doxastic processes can be deliberately influenced. If all doxastic processes are, in Hume's terminology, "permanent and irresistible," then the entire conception of a DDP has no application whatever. A middle ground is possible, though. *Some* doxastic processes may operate independently of the will and may not be modifiable by voluntary means: *other* doxastic processes may be subject to reflective and voluntary direction. In this case—which is the most convenient one for present purposes—there would be points of application for DDPs, but there would also be automatic processes that operate prior to the appearance of reflective choice in the doxastic domain.

Notice that even if the *doxastic* domain does not admit of voluntary intervention, there is still scope for deliberate self-guidance in the intellectual sphere. There are doubtless other events or states—distinct from doxastic states themselves—that can be voluntarily controlled and have indirect influence on doxastic attitudes. The search for evidence (e.g., deployment of the sensory apparatus in purposefully selected directions) and the search for, or attention to, hypotheses on deliberately chosen topics are examples of voluntary processes that have a major impact on our beliefs. So even the falsity of *doxastic* voluntarism would not undermine the regulative orientation of epistemology.[28] However, we might have to substitute the idea of a CDP—a *cognitive* decision principle—for that of a DDP—a *doxastic* decision principle.

The perspective advanced in our recent discussion has salient points of contact with epistemological "*contextualism*," e.g., the version of this approach adopted by W. V. Quine. Quine emphasizes that there is no point of cosmic exile.[29] We have to start, epistemologically speaking, from the beliefs we have at a given time. Similarly, Karl Popper emphasizes that rational inquiry can consist only in criticism of antecedently held belief. We do and must start from an uncritically held body of opinion, or mental structure.[30] The same view is expressed by C. S. Peirce: ". . . there is but one state of mind from which you can 'set out,' namely, the very state of mind in which you actually find yourself at the time you do 'set out'—a state in which you are laden with an immense mass of cognition already formed, of which you cannot divest yourself if you would . . .".[31]

My contextualism, however, is only a view at the *meta-theoretical* level. It only answers the question: How should we go about choosing a criterion of justifiedness, i.e., a DDP? My answer to *this* question is entirely neutral with respect to the specific criterion of justifiedness that should ultimately be chosen, i.e., the optimal DDP. That DDP could turn out to be some sort of "*foundationalist*" DDP. Its belief-prescriptions might reflect the idea that there is a special class of propositions that should be believed quite independently of other beliefs and from which all other beliefs should be inferred. I do not mean to *endorse* this sort of foundationalism.

I cite it only to illustrate the point that, whereas Quine, for example, is a thorough-going opponent of foundationalism, my own *two-leveled* theory allows more room for epistemological flexibility. On the meta-level—"How can we try to identify the right DDP?"—I take a contextualist position. But on the basic level—"Which DDP is the right DDP?"—any answer is viable (in principle).[32]

The reader may feel that this very flexibility is a weakness of my discussion. If I have not specified the right DDP, or even the general form of the right DDP (foundationalist, coherentist, etc.), what has been accomplished? Two important things, I believe, have been accomplished. First, we have elucidated the general idea of a regulative conception of justifiedness and shown how justificational status, so conceived, depends upon (a) the cognizer's current states and (b) the right DDP. Second, we have articulated the only tenable conception of DDP-rightness (externalism) and disposed of an illusory rival conception (internalism) that traditional epistemology suggests. We have thereby provided two fundamental building blocks of any fully detailed regulative epistemology, at least any regulative epistemology that seeks to guide *doxastic* choices.[33]

Notes

1. In A. I. Goldman and J. Kim, eds., *Values and Morals* (Dordrecht, 1978). See p. 194.

2. "Moral Decision Principles."

3. "What is Justified Belief?," in George S. Pappas, ed., *Justification and Knowledge* (Dordrecht, 1979).

4. One general problem with this approach is the assumption of a uniquely correct DDP. Suppose instead that two or more DDPs are *"tied"* for best and that some of these make conflicting prescriptions. In particular, suppose one DDP tells S to believe proposition p and another tells S to disbelieve it. Which doxastic attitude vis-à-vis p is S justified in adopting? The solution is to say that a cognizer is justified in having doxastic attitude D vis-à-vis p at *t* if and only if there is *at least one best* DDP that prescribes D vis-à-vis p at *t*. This is tantamount to saying that a cognizer is justified in adopting D vis-à-vis p just in case he is *permitted* to have D vis-à-vis p and that he is permitted to have D vis-à-vis p if at least one best DDP prescribes it. This is indeed quite plausible. In fact, apart from the problem of multiply correct DDPs, there is much to be said for linking justifiedness with a *permission* to adopt the indicated doxastic attitude rather than a *prescription* to do so. Even a single DDP may contain permissions as well as prescriptions and prohibitions, and it is plausible to say that a doxastic attitude is justified if it is permitted.

For purposes of simplicity, however, I am going to bypass these issues. First, I shall link justifiedness to what is prescribed rather than to what is permitted. Second, I shall generally assume that there is a uniquely right DDP. More precisely, I shall ignore the problem of "ties." In later discussion when I *do* admit the possibility of there not being a uniquely correct DDP, I shall have in mind not the possibility of ties but the possibility of correctness being relativized to different cognizers.

5. Is this explication of "can tell" too strong? Admittedly, it may be controversial whether even current mental states meet the requirement as formulated. In all likelihood, such states as *stored* beliefs, especially the *totality* of one's stored beliefs, do not satisfy this constraint. But we can live with such consequences. The regulative conception need not try to decide precisely which states (if any) satisfy its constraint on inputs. This would only have to be decided by anyone seeking to *use*, or *apply*, the regulative conception. For simplicity I am just assuming that a variety of current cognitive states do satisfy the constraint.

Still, we can entertain the prospect of weakening the explication in the text. But something like it seems needed. A principle cannot be a genuine decision-principle unless a person can actually be guided by it, i.e., act in conformity with it. He must be able to bring it about that he executes an output-prescription when and only when the corresponding input-condition is fulfilled. To do this, it seems, he must have the power to tell, or detect, when each input condition (antecedent of a principle) is or is not fulfilled.

6. More precisely, we are not interested in a recursive "account" of justification but in a recursive DDP, i.e., a recursive set of doxastic principles. The consequent of a doxastic principle will not be something of the form "you are justified in believing Q," but rather something like "believe Q." Hence, perhaps a better schema for an inductive (or recursive) member of a recursive set of principles would be this: "If, given your present inputs, this DDP instructs you to believe Q, and Q bears such-and-such a relation to P, then believe P."

7. The indicated goal may bias the choice of a DDP in favor of "belief"-principles as opposed to "subjective-probability"-principles. To avoid this bias we could elaborate the goal by giving positive value to assignments of subjective probabilities greater than .5 to truths and negative value to assignments of subjective probabilities greater than .5 to falsehoods. In the remainder of our discussion, however, I shall ignore this complication.

8. It is part of the regulative conception in general—hence common to both externalism and internalism—that a cognizer must be able to tell which *input* conditions obtain. But here we are discussing *DDP-rightness*, not input conditions. The regulative conception *per se* imposes no requirement of epistemic access to the right DDP. It merely says that a doxastic attitude is justified if it is prescribed by the DDP that is *in fact* right, whether or not the cognizer knows it is right. Internalism goes further by seeking to make it a condition of a DDP *being right* that a cognizer can know or tell that it is right (or optimal).

9. If relativization is permitted, we need a slight amendment in the basic relationship between justifiedness and DDP-rightness. That relationship would then be formulated as follows: S is justified in having doxastic attitude D vis-à-vis p at *t* if and only if the right DDP (*or the DDP that is right for S at t*), when applied to the relevant input conditions that characterize S at *t*, yields as output the prescription ⌈adopt attitude D vis-à-vis p⌉.

10. For a distinction between objective and subjective justification in epistemology, see John L. Pollock, "A Plethora of Epistemological Theories," in Pappas, ed., *Justification and Knowledge*. It is arguable that Keith Lehrer's view in *Knowledge* (London, 1974) is a form of subjectivism or relativism. On the other hand, it might be construed as a kind of non-relativistic coherentism.

11. A more difficult case is proposed by Holly Goldman, Suppose that a cognizer uses the right DDP—call it R—to decide which DDP is right, and R prescribes belief in the *false* proposition that DDP W is right. Then this cognizer is *justified* in believing that W is right. (Suppose also that W prescribes belief in its being right.) Now suppose he considers whether to believe proposition p, and W prescribes belief in p. On the other hand, R prohibits belief in p. Is the cognizer justified in believing p? According to the basic structure of the regulative approach (see section I), he is not so justified, since the right DDP does not prescribe belief in p. On the other hand, there is a strong temptation to say that he *is* justified in believing p. After all, he is justified in believing that he is justified in believing p, and it is an attractive principle that if one is justified in believing that one is justified in believing p (JJp), then one is justified in believing p (Jp). However, we are not forced to accept this principle, and an epistemological objectivist is well advised not to accept it.

12. However, it is not clear that all traditional epistemologists have tried to *select* a DDP from the internal standpoint. Many have simply presupposed some (inadequately specified) DDP and explored the question whether this DDP, when applied to the internal standpoint, prescribes our commonsensical beliefs, e.g., belief in the external world. Thus, what I am here calling "internalism" may not correctly describe most historical epistemology. Nonetheless, if epistemology accepts the doxastic regulative enterprise, the selection of a DDP is absolutely central, and criteria for the rightness of a DDP are equally crucial. Once this problem is posed, it seems consonant with the epistemological tradition to suggest that DDP-rightness be judged from the internal standpoint.

13. Indeed, there is not even a *small group* of DDPs that can be picked out as best.

14. It might be thought that the regulative conception itself automatically confers special status on first-person-current-mental-state propositions, for the regulative conception (RC) presupposes that cognizers can infallibly form beliefs about their own current mental states. We should avoid misunderstanding, however. The RC just lays down a *constraint* on input conditions (the antecedents of DDPs), i.e., that they must meet the "can tell" requirement. The RC does not say which *specific* conditions meet this requirement, if any. *I* claimed that, plausibly, a person's cognitive states—at least many such states—meet this requirement. But the RC per se makes no commitment on this point. In any case, even if it is *true* that such-and-such mental states meet this requirement, it does not follow that beliefs in propositions describing these states should be allowed in the internal standpoint. These propositions may still be epistemologically problematic.

15. It is doubtful that maximax would select a unique DDP. There are infinitely many incompatible DDPs that prescribe equally profligate belief-formation. The best outcomes of each of these will be equally good.

16. See Roderick M. Chisholm, *Theory of Knowledge* (Englewood Cliffs, N.J., first edition, 1966, second edition, 1977) and John L. Pollock, *Knowledge and Justification* (Princeton, 1974).

17. The formulation here includes some rewording of my own.

18. Chisholm, *Theory of Knowledge*, first edition, p. 24.

19. See *ibid.*, second edition, p. 16.

20. *Op. cit.*, p. 21.

21. Gilbert Harman, *Thought* (Princeton, 1973), p. 157.

22. This is stressed by Hume, among others. See *A Treatise of Human Nature*, book I, part IV, section I.

23. See Lehrer, *Knowledge*, chap. 7.

24. Isaac Levi, *Gambling with Truth* (New York, 1967).

25. Still another possible goal is the satisfaction of needs or desires. But it is not easier for internalism to generate a DDP for this goal than for the goal of true-belief-cum-error-avoidance. Indeed, need or desire satisfaction will depend heavily upon truth-acquisition and error-avoidance.

26. Or even any small set of best DDPs.

27. I do not mean to imply here that the non-regulative conception of justifiedness must temporally precede the regulative conception.

28. This point is also made in "Epistemics: The Regulative Theory of Cognition," *The Journal of Philosophy*, 75, no. 10 (October 1978):509–23.

29. W. V. Quine, *Word and Object* (Cambridge, Mass., 1960), p. 275.

30. Karl Popper, *Objective Knowledge* (Oxford, 1972), pp. 71–72.

31. Justus Buchler, ed., *Philosophical Writings of Peirce* (New York, 1955), p. 256.

32. One might think that the regulative conception (RC) is biased in favor of foundationalism. Is it not committed to the idea that we have infallible access to our own cognitive states? And is this idea not peculiar to foundationalism? Two comments are in order. First, as indicated in notes 5 and 14 above, the RC does not say *which* states of a person, if any, have this special status. It merely lays down a *constraint* on inputs. Second, it is not true that infallible access to cognitive states is a thesis peculiar to foundationalism. Coherentism is committed to the same sort of thesis. In particular, it is committed to the assumption that we can tell what our own current *beliefs* are. Unless we can tell what (all) our current beliefs are, we cannot tell whether they satisfy the requirement of coherence (whatever exactly this requirement is), nor can we adjust our beliefs to meet that requirement.

33. Some of the ideas in this paper germinated during research that was sponsored by the John Simon Guggenheim Foundation and the Center for Advanced Study in the Behavioral Sciences. For many helpful suggestions and criticisms I am indebted to Holly Goldman, Louis Loeb, and Terence Horgan.

Externalist Theories of Empirical Knowledge

LAURENCE BONJOUR

Of the many problems that would have to be solved by a satisfactory theory of empirical knowledge, perhaps the most central is a general structural problem which I shall call *the epistemic regress problem*: the problem of how to avoid an infinite and presumably vicious regress of justification in one's account of the justification of empirical beliefs. *Foundationalist* theories of empirical knowledge, as we shall see further below, attempt to avoid the regress by locating a class of empirical beliefs whose justification does not depend on that of other empirical beliefs. *Externalist* theories, the topic of the present paper, represent one species of foundationalism.

I

I begin with a brief look at the epistemic regress problem. The source of the problem is the requirement that beliefs that are to constitute knowledge must be *epistemically justified*. Such a requirement is of course an essential part of the "traditional" conception of knowledge as justified true belief, but it also figures in at least most of the revisions of that conception which have been inspired by the Gettier problem. Indeed, if this requirement is understood in a sufficiently generic way, as meaning roughly that the acceptance of the belief must be epistemically rational, that it must not be epistemically irresponsible, then it becomes hard to see how any adequate conception of knowledge can fail to include it.

How then are empirical beliefs epistemically justified? Certainly the most obvious way to *show* that such a belief is justified is by producing a justificatory argument in which the belief to be justified is shown to follow inferentially from some other (perhaps conjunctive) belief, which is thus offered as a reason for accepting it. Beliefs whose justification would, if made explicit, take this form may be said to be *inferentially justified*. (Of course, such a justificatory argument would usually be explicitly rehearsed only in the face of some specific problem or challenge. Notice also that an inferentially justified belief need not have been *arrived at* through inference, though it often will have been.)

The important point about inferential justification, however, is that if the justificandum belief is to be genuinely justified by the proffered argument, then the belief that provides the premise of the argument must itself be justified in some fashion. This premise belief might of course itself be inferentially justified, but this would only raise a new issue of justification with respect to the premise(s) of this new justificatory argument, and so on, so that empirical knowledge is threatened by an infinite and seemingly vicious regress of epistemic justification, with a thoroughgoing skepticism as the eventual outcome. So long as each new step of justification is inferential, it appears that justification can never be completed, indeed can never really even get started, and hence that there is no justification and no knowledge. Thus the epistemic regress problem.

What is the eventual outcome of this regress? There are a variety of possibilities, but the majority of philosophers who have considered the problem have believed that the only outcome that does not lead more or less directly to skepticism is *foundationalism*: the view that the regress terminates by reaching empirical beliefs (a) that are genuinely justified, but (b) whose justification is not inferentially dependent on that of any further empirical belief(s), so that no further issue of empirical justification is thereby raised. These non-inferentially justified beliefs, or *basic beliefs* as I shall call them, are claimed to provide the foundation upon which the edifice of empirical knowledge rests. And the central argument for foundationalism is simply that all other possible outcomes of the regress lead inexorably to skepticism.[1]

This argument has undeniable force. Nonetheless, the central concept of foundationalism, the concept of a basic belief, is itself by no means unproblematic. The fundamental question that must be answered by any acceptable version of foundationalism is: *how are basic beliefs possible?* How, that is, is it possible for there to be an empirical belief that is epistemically justified in a way completely independent of any believed premises that might provide reasons for accepting it? As Chisholm suggests, a basic belief seems to be in effect an epistemologically unmoved (or perhaps self-moved) mover. But such a status is surely no less paradoxical in epistemology than it is in theology.

This intuitive difficulty with the idea of a basic empirical belief may be elaborated by considering briefly the fundamental concept of epistemic justification. There are two points to be made. First, the idea of justification is generic, admitting in principle of many different species. Thus, for example, the acceptance of an empirical belief might be morally justified, or pragmatically justified, or justified in some still different sense. But a belief's being justified in one of these other senses will not satisfy the justification condition for knowledge. What knowledge requires is *epistemic* justification. And the distinguishing characteristic of this particular species of justification is, I submit, its internal relationship to the cognitive goal of *truth*. A cognitive act is epistemically justified, on this conception, only if and to the extent that is aimed at this goal—which means at a minimum that one accepts only beliefs that there is adequate reason to think are true.

Second, the concept of epistemic justification is fundamentally a normative concept. It has to do with what one has a duty or obligation to do, from an epistemic or intellectual standpoint. As Chisholm suggests, one's purely intellectual duty is to accept beliefs that are true, or likely to be true, and reject beliefs that are false, or likely to be false. To accept beliefs on some other basis is to violate one's epistemic duty—to be, one might say, *epistemically irresponsible*—even though such acceptance might be desirable or even mandatory from some other, non-epistemic standpoint.

Thus if basic beliefs are to provide a suitable foundation for empirical knowledge, if inference from them is to be the sole basis for the justification of other empirical beliefs, then that feature, whatever it may be, in virtue of which an empirical belief qualifies as basic, must also constitute an adequate reason for thinking that the belief is true. And now if we assume, plausibly enough, that the person for whom a belief is basic must *himself* possess the justification for that belief if *his* acceptance of it is to be epistemically rational or responsible, and thus apparently that he must believe *with justification* both (a) that the belief has the feature in question and (b) that beliefs having that feature are likely to be true, then we get the result that this belief is not basic after all, since its justification depends on that of these other beliefs. If this result is correct, then foundationalism is untenable as a solution to the regress problem.[2]

What strategies are available to the foundationalist for avoiding this objection? One possibility would be to grant that the believer must be in possession of the reason for thinking that his basic belief is true but hold that the believer's cognitive grasp of that reason does not involve further *beliefs*, which would then require justification, but instead cognitive states of a different and more rudimentary kind: *intuitions* or *immediate apprehensions*, which are somehow capable of conferring justification upon beliefs without themselves requiring justification. Some such view as this seems implicit in most traditional versions of foundationalism.[3]

My concern in the present paper, however, is with an alternative foundationalist strategy, one of comparatively recent innovation. One way, perhaps somewhat tendentious, to put this alternative approach is to say that according to it, though there must in a sense be a reason why a basic belief is likely to be true, the person for whom such a belief is basic need not have any cognitive grasp of this reason. On this view, the epistemic justification or reasonableness of a basic belief depends on the obtaining of an appropriate relation, generally causal or nomological in character, between the believer and the world. This relation, which is differently characterized by different versions of the view, is such as to make it either nomologically certain or else highly probable that the belief is true. It would thus provide, *for anyone who knew about it*, an undeniably excellent reason for accepting such a belief. But according to proponents of the view under discussion, the person for whom the belief is basic need not (and in general will not) have any cognitive grasp of any kind of this reason or of the relation that is the basis for it in order for this basic belief to be justified; all these matters may be entirely *external* to the person's subjective conception of the situation. Thus the justification of a basic belief need not involve any further beliefs (or other cognitive states) so that no further regress of justification is generated. D. M. Armstrong calls this an "externalist" solution to the regress problem, and I shall adopt this label.

My purpose in this paper is to examine such externalist views. I am not concerned with problems of detail in formulating a view of this kind, though some of these will be mentioned in passing, but rather with the overall acceptability of an externalist solution to the regress problem and thus of an externalist version of foundationalism. I shall attempt to argue that externalism is not acceptable. But there is a methodological problem with respect to such an argument which must be faced at the outset, since it determines the basic approach of the paper.

When viewed from the general standpoint of the western epistemological tradition, externalism represents a very radical departure. It seems safe to say that until very recent times, no serious philosopher of knowledge would have dreamed of suggesting that a person's beliefs might be epistemically justified simply in virtue of facts or relations that were external to his subjective conception. Descartes, for example, would surely have been quite unimpressed by the suggestion that his problematic beliefs about the external world were justified if only they were in fact reliably related to the world—whether or not he had any reason for thinking this to be so. Clearly his conception, and that of generations of philosophers who followed, was that such a relation could play a justificatory role only if the believer possessed adequate reason for thinking that it obtained. Thus the suggestion embodied in externalism would have been regarded by most epistemologists as simply irrelevant to the main epistemological issue, so much so that the philosopher who suggested it would have been taken either to be hopelessly confused or to be simply changing the subject (as I note below, this may be what some externalists in fact intend to be doing). The problem, however, is that this very radicalism has the effect of insulating the externalist from any very direct refutation: any attempt at such a refutation is almost certain to appeal to premises that a thoroughgoing externalist would not accept. My solution to this threatened impasse will be to proceed on an intuitive level as far as possible. By considering a series of examples, I shall attempt to exhibit as clearly as possible the fundamental intuition about epistemic rationality that externalism seems to violate. Although this intuition may not constitute a conclusive objection to the view, it is enough, I believe, to shift the burden of proof decisively to the externalist. In the final section of the paper, I shall consider briefly whether he can discharge this burden.

II

Our first task will be the formulation of a clear and relatively adequate version of externalism. The recent epistemological literature contains a reasonably large number of externalist and quasi-externalist views. Some of these, however, are not clearly relevant to our present concerns, either because they are aimed primarily at the Gettier problem, so that their implications for a foundationalist solution of the regress problem are not made clear, or because they *seem*, on the surface at least, to involve a repudiation of the very conception of epistemic justification or reasonableness as a requirement for knowledge. Views of the latter sort seem to me to be very difficult to take seriously; but if they are seriously intended, they would have the consequence that the regress problem, at least in the form discussed here, would simply not arise, so that there would be no need for any solution, foundationalist or otherwise. My immediate concern here is with versions of externalism that claim to *solve* the regress problem and thus that also claim that the acceptance of beliefs satisfying the externalist conditions is epistemically justified or rational or warranted. Only such an externalist position genuinely constitutes a version of foundationalism, and hence the more radical views, if any such are in fact seriously intended, may safely be left aside for the time being.

The most completely developed externalist view of the sort we are interested in is that of Armstrong, as presented in his book, *Belief, Truth and Knowledge*.[4] Armstrong is explicitly concerned with the regress problem, though he formulates it in terms of knowledge rather than justification. And it seems reasonably clear that he wants to say that beliefs satisfying his externalist criterion are epistemically justified or rational, though he is not as explicit as one might like on this point.[5] In what follows, I shall in any case assume such an interpretation of Armstrong and formulate his position accordingly.

Another version of externalism, which fairly closely resembles Armstrong's except for being limited to knowledge derived from visual perception, is offered by Dretske in *Seeing and Knowing*.[6] Goldman, in several papers, also suggests views of an externalist sort,[7] and the view that Alston calls "Simple Foundationalism" and claims to be the most defensible version of foundationalism seems to be essentially externalist in character.[8] The most extreme version of externalism would be one that held that the external condition required for justification is simply the *truth* of the belief in question. Such a view could not be held in general, of course, without obliterating the distinction between knowledge and mere true belief, thereby turning every lucky guess into knowledge. But it might be held with respect to some more limited class of beliefs. Such a view is mentioned by Alston as one possible account of privileged access,[9] and seems, surprisingly enough, to be advocated by Chisholm (though it is very hard to be sure that this is what Chisholm really means).[10]

Here I shall concentrate mainly on Armstrong's view. Like all externalists, Armstrong makes the acceptability of a basic belief depend on an external relation between the believer and his belief, on the one hand, and the world, on the other, specifically a law-like connection: "there must be a *law-like connection* between the state of affairs Bap [i.e., a's believing that p] and the state of affairs which makes 'p' true, such that, given Bap, it must be the case that p." [166] This is what Armstrong calls the "thermometer-model" of non-inferential knowledge: just as the readings of a reliable thermometer lawfully reflect the temperature, so one's basic beliefs lawfully reflect the states of affairs that make them true. A person whose beliefs satisfy this condition is in effect a reliable cognitive instrument; and it is, according to Armstrong, precisely in virtue of this reliability that these basic beliefs are justified.

Of course, not all thermometers are reliable, and even a reliable one may be accurate only under certain conditions. Similarly, it is not a requirement for the justification of a basic belief on Armstrong's view that all beliefs of that general kind or even all beliefs of that kind held by that particular believer be reliable. Thus the law linking the having of the belief with the state of affairs that makes it true will have to mention properties, including relational properties, of the believer beyond his merely having that belief. Incorporating this modification yields the following schematic formulation of the conditions under which a non-inferential belief is justified and therefore basic: a non-inferential belief is justified if and only if there is some property H of the believer, such that it is a law of nature that whenever a person satisfies H and has that belief, then the belief is true. [197][11] Here H may be as complicated as one likes and may include facts about the believer's mental processes, sensory apparatus, environment, and so on. But presumably, though Armstrong does not mention this point, H is not to include anything that would entail the truth of the belief; such a logical connection would not count as a law of nature.

Armstrong adds several qualifications to this account, aimed at warding off various objections, of which I shall mention only two. First, the nomological connection between the belief and the state of affairs that makes it true is to be restricted to "that of *completely reliable sign* to thing signified." [182] What this is intended to exclude is the case where the belief itself *causes* the state of affairs that makes it true. In such a case, it seems intuitively that the belief is not a case of knowledge even though it satisfies the condition of complete reliability formulated above. Second, the property H of the believer which is involved in the law of nature must not be "too specific"; there must be a "real possibility" of a recurrence of the situation described by the law. What Armstrong is worried about here is the possibility of a "veridical hallucination," i.e., a case in which a hallucinatory belief happens to be correct. In such a case, if the state of affairs that makes the belief true happens to be part of the cause of the hallucination and if the believer and his environment are described in enough detail, it might turn out to be nomologically necessary that such a state of affairs obtain, simply because all alternative possible causes for the hallucinatory belief have been ruled out by the specificity of the description. Again, such a case intuitively should not count as a case of knowledge, but it would satisfy Armstrong's criterion in the absence of this additional stipulation. (Obviously this requirement of non-specificity or repeatability is extremely vague and seems in fact to be no more than an *ad hoc* solution to this problem; but I shall not pursue this issue here.)

There are various problems of detail, similar to those just discussed, which could be raised about Armstrong's view, but these have little relevance to the main theme of the present paper. Here I am concerned with the more fundamental issue of whether Armstrong's view, or any other externalist view of this general sort, is acceptable as a solution to the regress problem and the basis for a foundationalist account of empirical knowledge. When considered from this perspective, Armstrong's view seems at the very least to be in need of considerable refinement in the face of fairly obvious counterexamples. Thus our first task will be to develop some of these counterexamples and suggest modifications in the view accordingly. This discussion will also lead, however, to a fundamental intuitive objection to all forms of externalism.

III

Although it is formulated in more general terms, the main concern of an externalist view like Armstrong's is obviously those non-inferential beliefs which arise from ordinary sources like sense-perception and introspection. For it is, of course, these beliefs which will on any plausible foundationalist view provide the actual foundations of empirical knowledge. Nevertheless, cases involving sense-perception and introspection are not very suitable for an intuitive assessment of externalism, since one central issue between externalism and other foundationalist and non-foundationalist views is precisely whether in such cases a further basis for justification beyond the externalist one is typically present. Thus it will be useful to begin by considering the application of externalism to other possible cases of non-inferential knowledge, cases of a less familiar sort where it will be easier to stipulate in a way that will be effective on an intuitive level that only the externalist sort of justification is present. Specifically, in this section and the next, our focus will be on possible cases of clairvoyant knowledge. Clairvoyance, the alleged psychic power of perceiving or intuiting the existence and character of distant states of affairs without the aid of any sensory input, remains the subject of considerable scientific controversy. Although many would like to dismiss out of hand the very idea of such a cognitive power, there remains a certain amount of evidence in favor of its existence which it is difficult to entirely discount. But in any case, the actual existence of clairvoyance does not matter at all for present purposes, so long as it is conceded to represent a coherent possibility. For externalism, as a general philosophical account of the foundations of empirical knowledge, must of course apply to all possible modes of non-inferential empirical knowledge, and not just to those that in fact happen to be realized.

The intuitive difficulty with externalism that the following discussion is intended to delineate and develop is this: on the externalist view, a person may be ever so irrational and irresponsible in accepting a belief, when judged in light of his own subjective conception of the situation, and may still turn out to be epistemically justified, i.e., may still turn out to satisfy Armstrong's general criterion of reliability. This belief may in fact be reliable, even though the person has no reason for thinking that it is reliable—or even though he has good reason to think that it is not reliable. But such a person seems nonetheless to be thoroughly irresponsible from an epistemic standpoint in accepting such a belief, and hence not justified, contrary to externalism. The following cases may help bring out this problem more clearly.

Consider first the following case:

Case I. Samantha believes herself to have the power of clairvoyance, though she has no reasons for or against this belief. One day she comes to believe, for no apparent reason, that the President is in New York City. She maintains this belief, appealing to her alleged clairvoyant power, even though she is at the same time aware of a massive amount of apparently cogent evidence, consisting of news reports, press releases, allegedly live television pictures, etc., indicating that the President is at that time in Washington, D.C. Now the President is in fact in New York City, the evidence to the contrary being part of a massive official hoax mounted in the face of an assassination threat. Moreover, Samantha does in fact have completely reliable clairvoyant power, under the conditions that were then satisfied, and her belief about the President did result from the operation of that power.

In this case, it is clear that Armstrong's criterion of reliability is satisfied. There will be some complicated description of Samantha, including the conditions then operative, from which it will follow, by the law describing her clairvoyant power, that her belief is true.[12] But it seems intuitively clear nevertheless that this is not a case of justified belief or of knowledge: Samantha is being thoroughly irrational and irresponsible in disregarding cogent evidence that the President is not in New York City on the basis of a clairvoyant power which she has no reason at all to think that she possesses; and this irrationality is not somehow canceled by the fact that she happens to be right. Thus, I submit, Samantha's irrationality and irresponsibility prevent her belief from being epistemically justified.

This case and others like it suggest the need for a further condition to supplement Armstrong's original one: not only must it be true that there is a law-like connection between a person's belief and the state of affairs that makes it true, such that given the belief, the state of affairs cannot fail to obtain, but it must also be true that the person in question does not possess cogent reasons for thinking that the belief in question is false. For, as this case seems to show, the possession of such reasons renders the acceptance of the belief irrational in a way that cannot be overridden by a purely externalist justification.

Nor is this the end of the difficulty for Armstrong. Suppose that the clairvoyant believer, instead of having evidence against the particular belief in question, has evidence against his possession of such a cognitive power, as in the following case:

> Case II. Casper believes himself to have the power of clairvoyance, though he has no reasons for this belief. He maintains his belief despite the fact that on the numerous occasions on which he has attempted to confirm one of his allegedly clairvoyant beliefs, it has always turned out apparently to be false. One day Casper comes to believe, for no apparent reason, that the President is in New York City, and he maintains this belief, appealing to his alleged clairvoyant power. Now in fact the President is in New York City; and Casper does, under the conditions that were then satisfied, have completely reliable clairvoyant power, from which this belief in fact resulted. The apparent falsity of his other clairvoyant beliefs was due in some cases to his being in the wrong conditions for the operation of his power and in other cases to deception and misinformation.

Is Casper justified in believing that the President is in New York City, so that he then knows that this is the case? According to Armstrong's account, even with the modification just suggested, we must apparently say that the belief is justified and hence a case of knowledge: the reliability condition is satisfied, and Casper possesses no reason for thinking that the President is not in New York City. But this result still seems mistaken. Casper is being quite irrational and irresponsible from an epistemic standpoint in disregarding evidence that his beliefs of this sort are not reliable and should not be trusted. And for this reason, the belief in question is not justified.

In the foregoing case, Casper possessed good reasons for thinking that he did not possess the sort of cognitive ability that he believed himself to possess. But the result would be the same, I believe, if someone instead possessed good reasons for thinking that *in general* there could be no such cognitive ability, as in the following case:

> Case III. Maud believes herself to have the power of clairvoyance, though she has no reasons for this belief. She maintains her belief despite being inundated by her embarrassed friends and relatives with massive quantities of apparently cogent scientific evidence that no such power is possible. One day Maud comes to believe, for no apparent reason, that the President is in New York City, and she maintains this belief, despite the lack of any independent evidence, appealing to her alleged clairvoyant power. Now in fact the President is in New York City, and Maud does, under the conditions then satisfied, have completely reliable clairvoyant power. Moreover, her belief about the President did result from the operation of that power.

Again, Armstrong's criterion of reliability seems to be satisfied. But it also seems to me that Maud, like Casper, is not justified in her belief about the President and does not have knowledge. Maud has excellent reasons for thinking that no cognitive power such as she believes herself to possess is possible, and it is irrational and irresponsible of her to maintain her belief in that power in the face of that evidence and to continue to accept and maintain beliefs on this dubious basis.

Cases like these two suggest the need for a further modification of Armstrong's account: in addition to the law-like connection between belief and truth and the absence of any reasons against the particular belief in question, it must also be the case that the believer in question has no cogent reasons, either relative to his own case or in general, for thinking that such a law-like connection does *not* exist, i.e., that beliefs of that kind are not reliable.

IV

So far the modifications suggested for Armstrong's criterion are consistent with the basic thrust of externalism as a response to the regress problem. What emerges is in fact a significantly more plausible externalist position. But these cases and the modifications made in response to them also suggest an important moral which leads to a basic intuitive objection to externalism: external or objective reliability is not enough to offset subjective irrationality. If the acceptance of a belief is seriously unreasonable or unwarranted from the believer's own standpoint, then the mere fact that unbeknownst to the believer its existence in those circumstances lawfully guarantees its truth will not suffice to render the belief epistemically justified and thereby an instance of knowledge. So far we have been concerned only with situations in which the believer's subjective irrationality took the form of ignoring positive grounds in his possession for questioning either that specific belief or beliefs arrived at in that way. But now we must ask whether even in a case where these positive reasons for a charge of irrationality are not present, the acceptance of a belief where only an externalist justification is available cannot still be said to be subjectively irrational in a sense that rules out its being epistemically justified.

We may begin by considering one further case of clairvoyance, in which Armstrong's criterion with all the suggested modifications is satisfied:

> Case IV. Norman, under certain conditions that usually obtain, is a completely reliable clairvoyant with respect to certain kinds of subject matter. He possesses no evidence or reasons of any kind for or against the general possibility of such a cognitive power, or for or against the thesis that he possesses it. One day Norman comes to believe that the President is in New York City, though he has no evidence either for or against this belief. In fact the belief is true and results from his clairvoyant power, under circumstances in which it is completely reliable.

Is Norman epistemically justified in believing that the President is in New York City, so that his belief is an instance of knowledge? According to the modified externalist position, we must apparently say that he is. But is this the right result? Are there not still sufficient grounds for a charge of subjective irrationality to prevent Norman's being epistemically justified?

One thing that might seem relevant to this issue, which I have deliberately omitted from the specification of the case, is whether Norman *believes* himself to have clairvoyant power, even though he has no justification for such a belief. Let us consider both possibilities. Suppose, first, that Norman does have such a belief and that it contributes to his acceptance of his original belief about the President's whereabouts in the sense that were Norman to become convinced that he did not have this power, he would also cease to accept the belief about the President.[13] But is it not obviously irrational, from an epistemic standpoint, for Norman to hold such a belief when he has no reasons at all for thinking that it is true or even for thinking that such a power is possible? This belief about his clairvoyance fails after all to possess even an externalist justification. And if we say that the belief about his clairvoyance is epistemically irrational and unjustified, must we not say the same thing about the belief about the President which *ex hypothesi* depends upon it?[14]

A possible response to this challenge would be to add one further condition to our modified externalist position, *viz.*, that the believer not even *believe* that the law-like connection in question obtains, since such a belief will not in general be justified (or at least that his continued acceptance of the particular belief that is at issue not depend on his acceptance of such a general belief). In our present case, this would mean that Norman must not believe that he has the power of clairvoyance (or at least that his acceptance of the belief about the President's whereabouts not depend on his having such a general belief). But if this specification is added to the case, it now becomes more than a little puzzling to understand what Norman thinks is going on. From his standpoint, there is apparently no way in which he *could* know the President's whereabouts. Why then does he continue to maintain the belief that the President is in New York City? Why is not the mere fact that there is no way, as far as he knows or believes, for him to have obtained this information a sufficient reason for classifying this belief as an unfounded hunch and ceasing to accept it? And if Norman does not do this, is he not thereby being epistemically irrational and irresponsible?

For these reasons, I submit, Norman's acceptance of the belief about the President's whereabouts is epistemically irrational and irresponsible, and thereby unjustified, whether or not he believes himself to have clairvoyant power, so long as he has no justification for such a belief. Part of one's epistemic duty is to reflect critically upon one's beliefs, and such critical reflection precludes believing things to which one has, to one's knowledge, no reliable means of epistemic access.[15]

We are now face-to-face with the fundamental—and seemingly obvious—intuitive problem with externalism: *why* should the mere fact that such an external relation obtains mean that Norman's belief is epistemically justified, when the relation in question is entirely outside his ken? As remarked earlier, it is clear that one who knew that Armstrong's criterion was satisfied would be in a position to construct a simple and quite cogent justifying argument for the belief in question: if Norman has property H (being a completely reliable clairvoyant under the existing conditions and arriving at the belief on that basis), then he holds the belief in question only if it is true; Norman does have property H and does hold the belief in question; therefore, the belief is true. But Norman himself is by stipulation not in a position to employ this argument, and it is unclear why the mere fact that it is, so to speak, potentially available in the situation should justify *his* acceptance of the belief. Precisely what generates the regress problem in the first place, after all, is the requirement that for a belief to be justified for a particular person, not only is it necessary that there be true premises somehow available in the situation which could in principle provide a basis for a justification, but also that the believer in question know or at least justifiably believe some such set of premises and thus be in a position to employ the corresponding argument. The externalist position seems to amount merely to waiving this general requirement in a certain class of cases, and the question is why this should be acceptable in these cases when it is not acceptable generally. (If it were acceptable generally, then it seems likely that *any* true belief would be justified, unless some severe requirement is imposed as to how immediately available such premises must be. But any such requirement seems utterly arbitrary, once the natural one of actual access by the believer is abandoned.) Thus externalism looks like a purely *ad hoc* solution to the epistemic regress problem.

One reason why externalism may seem initially plausible is that if the external relation in question genuinely obtains, then Norman will in fact not go wrong in accepting the belief, and it is, *in a sense*, not an accident that this is so. But how is this supposed to justify Norman's belief? From his subjective perspective, it *is* an accident that the belief is true. Of course, it would not be an accident from the standpoint of our hypothetical external observer who knows all the relevant facts and laws. Such an observer, having constructed the justifying argument sketched above, would be thereby in a position to justify *his own* acceptance of the belief. Thus

Norman, as Armstrong's thermometer image suggests, could serve as a useful epistemic instrument for such an observer, a kind of cognitive thermometer; and it is to this
fact, as we have seen, that Armstrong appeals in arguing that a belief like Norman's can
be correctly said to be reasonable or justifiable. [183] But none of this seems in fact to
justify Norman's *own* acceptance of the belief, for Norman, unlike the hypothetical
external observer, has no reason at all for thinking that the belief is true. And the suggestion here is that the rationality or justifiability of Norman's belief should be judged
from Norman's own perspective, rather than from one that is unavailable to him.[16]

This basic objection to externalism seems to me to be intuitively compelling.
But it is sufficiently close to being simply a statement of what the externalist wants
to deny to make it helpful to buttress it a bit by appealing to some related intuitions.

First, we may consider an analogy with moral philosophy. The same conflict
between perspectives which we have seen to arise in the process of epistemic assessment can also arise with regard to the moral assessment of a person's action: the
agent's subjective conception of what he is doing may differ dramatically from that
which would in principle be available to an external observer who had access to facts
about the situation that are beyond the agent's ken. And now we can imagine an approximate moral analogue of externalism which would hold that the moral justifiability of an agent's action was, in certain cases at least, properly to be determined
from the external perspective, entirely irrespective of the agent's own conception of
the situation.

Consider first the moral analogue of Armstrong's original, unmodified version
of externalism. If we assume, purely for the sake of simplicity, a utilitarian moral
theory, such a view would say that an action might on occasion be morally justified
simply in virtue of the fact that in the situation then obtaining, it would as a matter
of objective fact lead to the best overall consequences—even if the agent planned and
anticipated that it would lead to a very different, perhaps extremely undesirable,
consequences. But such a view seems plainly mistaken. There is no doubt a point to
the objective, external assessment: we can say correctly that it turns out to be objectively a good thing that the agent performed the action. But this is not at all inconsistent with saying that his action was morally unjustified and reprehensible, given
his subjective conception of the likely consequences.

Thus our envisaged moral externalism must at least be modified in a way that
parallels the modifications earlier suggested for epistemological externalism. Without attempting to make the analogy exact, it will suffice for our present purposes to
add to the original requirement for moral justification, viz., that the action will in
fact lead to the best overall consequences, the further condition that the agent not
believe or intend that it lead to undesirable consequences. Since it is also, of course,
not required by moral externalism that the agent believe that the action will lead to
good consequences, the sort of case we are now considering is one in which an agent
acts in a way that will in fact produce the best overall consequences, but has *no belief at all* about the likely consequences of his action. Although such an agent is no
doubt preferable to one who acts in the belief that his action will lead to undesirable
consequences, surely he is not morally justified in what he does. On the contrary,

he is being highly irresponsible, from a moral standpoint, in performing the action in the absence of any evaluation of what will result from it. His moral duty, from our assumed utilitarian standpoint, is to do what will lead to the best consequences, but this duty is not satisfied by the fact that he produces this result willy-nilly, without any idea that he is doing so.[17] And similarly, the fact that a given sort of belief is objectively reliable, and thus that accepting it is in fact conducive to arriving at the truth, need not prevent our judging that the epistemic agent who accepts it without any inkling that this is the case violates his epistemic duty and is epistemically irresponsible and unjustified in doing so.

Second, we may appeal to the connection between knowledge and rational action. Suppose that Norman, in addition to the clairvoyant belief described earlier, also believes that the Attorney-General is in Chicago. This latter belief, however, is not a clairvoyant belief but is based upon ordinary empirical evidence in Norman's possession, evidence strong enough to give the belief some fairly high degree of reasonableness, but *not* strong enough to satisfy the requirement for knowledge.[18] Suppose further that Norman finds himself in a situation where he is forced to bet a very large amount, perhaps even his life or the life of someone else, on the whereabouts of either the President or the Attorney-General. Given his epistemic situation as described, which bet is it more reasonable for him to make? It seems relatively clear that it is more reasonable for him to bet the Attorney-General is in Chicago than to bet that the President is in New York City. But then we have the paradoxical result that from the externalist standpoint it is more rational to act on a merely reasonable belief than to act on one that is adequately justifed to qualify as knowledge (and which in fact *is* knowledge). It is very hard to see how this could be so. If greater epistemic reasonableness does not carry with it greater reasonableness of action, then it becomes most difficult to see why it should be sought in the first place. (Of course, the externalist could simply bite the bullet and insist that it is in fact more reasonable for Norman to bet on the President's whereabouts than the Attorney-General's, but such a view seems very implausible.)

I have been attempting in this section to articulate the fundamental intuition about epistemic rationality, and rationality generally, that externalism seems to violate. This intuition the externalist would of course reject, and thus my discussion does not constitute a refutation of the externalist position on its own ground. Nevertheless it seems to me to have sufficient intuitive force at least to place the burden of proof squarely on the externalist. In the final section of the paper, I shall consider briefly some of the responses that seem to be available to him.

V

One possible defense for the externalist in the face of the foregoing intuitive objection would be to narrow his position by restricting it to those commonsensical varieties of non-inferential knowledge which are his primary concern, viz., sense-perception and introspection, thereby rendering the cases set forth above strictly irrelevant. Such a move seems, however, utterly *ad hoc*. Admittedly it is more difficult to construct intuitively compelling counterexamples involving sense-perception and introspection, mainly because our intuitions that beliefs of those kinds are in fact warranted in *some* way or other are very strong. But this does nothing to establish that the externalist account of their warrant is the correct one. Thus unless the externalist can give some positive account of why the same conclusion that seems to hold for non-standard cases like clairvoyance does not also hold for sense-perception and introspection, this narrowing of his position seems to do him no good.

If the externalist cannot escape the force of the objection in this way, can he perhaps balance it with positive arguments in favor of his position? Many attempts to argue for externalism are in effect arguments by elimination and depend on the claim that alternative accounts of empirical knowledge are unacceptable, either because they cannot solve the regress problem or for some other reason. Most such arguments, depending as they do on a detailed consideration of the alternatives, are beyond the scope of the present paper. But one such argument depends only on very general features of the competing positions and thus can usefully be considered here.

The basic factual premise of this argument is that in very many cases that are commonsensically instances of justified belief and of knowledge, there seem to be no justifying factors explicitly present beyond those appealed to by the externalist. An ordinary person in such a case may have no idea at all of the character of his immediate experience, of the coherence of his system of beliefs, etc., and yet may still have knowledge. Alternative theories, so the argument goes, may describe correctly cases of knowledge involving a knower who is extremely reflective and sophisticated, but they are obviously too demanding and too grandiose when applied to these more ordinary cases. In these cases, *only* the externalist condition is satisfied, and this shows that no more than that is necessary for justification and for knowledge, though more might still be epistemically desirable.

Although the precise extent to which it holds could be disputed, in the main this factual premise must be simply conceded. Any non-externalist account of empirical knowledge that has any plausibility will impose standards for justification which very many beliefs that seem commonsensically to be cases of knowledge fail to meet in any full and explicit fashion. And thus on such a view, such beliefs will not *strictly speaking* be instances of adequate justification and of knowledge. But it does not follow that externalism must be correct. This would follow only with the addition of the premise that the judgments of common sense in this area are sacrosanct, that any departure from them is enough to demonstrate that a theory of knowledge is inadequate. But such a premise seems entirely too strong. There seems in fact to be no basis for more than a reasonably strong presumption in favor of the correctness of common sense, but one which is still quite defeasible. And what it would take to defeat this presumption depends in part on how great a departure from common sense is being advocated. Thus, although it would take very strong grounds to justify a very strong form of skepticism, not nearly so much would be required to make acceptable the view that what common sense regards as cases of justification and of knowledge are in fact only rough approximations to an epistemic ideal which *strictly speaking* they do not satisfy.

Of course, a really adequate reply to the externalist would have to spell out in some detail the precise way in which such beliefs really do approximately satisfy some acceptable alternative standard, a task which obviously cannot be attempted here. But even without such elaboration, it seems reasonable to conclude that this argument in favor of externalism fails to carry very much weight as it stands and would require serious buttressing in order to give it any chance of offsetting the intuitive objection to externalism: either the advocacy and defense of a quite strong presumption in favor of common sense, or a detailed showing that alternative theories cannot in fact grant to the cases favored by common sense even the status of approximations to justification and to knowledge.

The other pro-externalist argument I want to consider does not depend in any important way on consideration of alternative positions. This argument is hinted at by Armstrong [185–88], among others, but I know of no place where it is developed very explicitly. Its basic claim is that only an externalist theory can handle a certain version of the lottery paradox.

The lottery paradox is standardly formulated as a problem confronting accounts of inductive logic that contain a rule of acceptance or detachment, but we shall be concerned here with a somewhat modified version. This version arises when we ask how much or what degree of epistemic justification is required for a belief to qualify as knowledge, given that the other necessary conditions for knowledge are satisfied. Given the intimate connection, discussed earlier, between epistemic justification and likelihood of truth, it seems initially reasonable to take likelihood or probability of truth as a measure of the degree of epistemic justification, and thus to interpret the foregoing question as asking how likely or probable it must be, relative to the justification of one's belief, that the belief be true, in order for that belief to satisfy the justification requirement for knowledge. Most historical theories of knowledge tended to answer that knowledge requires *certainty* of truth, relative to one's justification. But more recent epistemological views have tended to reject this answer, for familiar reasons, and to hold instead that knowledge requires only a reasonably high likelihood of truth. And now, if this high likelihood of truth is interpreted in the obvious way as meaning that, relative to one's justification, the numerical probability that one's belief is true must equal or exceed some fixed value, the lottery paradox at once rears its head.

Suppose, for example, that we decide that a belief is adequately justified to satisfy the requirement for knowledge if the probability of its truth, relative to its justification, is 0.99 or greater. Imagine now that a lottery is to be held, about which we know the following facts: exactly 100 tickets have been sold, the drawing will indeed be held, it will be a fair drawing, and there will be only one winning ticket. Consider now each of the 100 propositions of the form:

Ticket number n will lose

where n is replaced by the number of one of the tickets. Since there are 100 tickets and only one winner, the probability of each such proposition is 0.99; and hence if we believe each of them, our individual beliefs will be adequately justified to satisfy the requirement for knowledge. And then, given only the seemingly reasonable assumptions, first, that if one has adequate justification for believing each of a set of propositions, one also has adequate justification for believing the conjunction of the members of the set, and, second, that if one has adequate justification for believing a proposition, one also has adequate justification for believing any further proposition entailed by the first proposition, it follows that we are adequately justified in believing that no ticket will win, contradicting our other information.

Clearly this is a mistaken result, but how is it to be avoided? In the first place, it will plainly do no good to simply increase the level of numerical probability required for adequate justification. For no matter how high it is raised, short of certainty, it will obviously be possible to duplicate the paradoxical result by simply choosing a large enough lottery. Nor do the standard responses to the lottery paradox, whatever their merits may be in dealing with other versions of the paradox, seem to be of much help here. Most of them are ruled out simply by insisting that we do know that empirical propositions are true, not merely that they are probable, and that such knowledge is not in general relative to particular contexts of inquiry. This leaves only the possibility of avoiding the paradoxical result by rejecting the two assumptions stated in the preceding paragraph. But this would be extremely implausible—involving in effect a denial that one may always justifiably deduce conclusions from one's putative knowledge—and in any case would still leave the intuitively unacceptable result that one could on this basis come to know separately the 99 true propositions about various tickets losing (though not of course the false one). In fact, it seems intuitively clear that I do not *know* any of these propositions to be true: if I own one of the tickets, I do not know that it will lose, even if in fact it will, and would not know no matter how large the total number of tickets might be.

At this stage, it may seem that the only way to avoid the paradox is to return to the traditional idea that any degree of probability or likelihood of truth less than certainty is insufficient for knowledge, that only certainty, relative to one's justification, will suffice. The standard objection to such a view is that it seems to lead at once to the skeptical conclusion that we have little or no empirical knowledge. For it seems quite clear that there are no empirical beliefs, with the possible and extremely problematic exception of beliefs about one's own mental states, for which we have justification adequate to exclude all possibility of error. Such a solution seems as bad as the original problem.

It is at this point that externalism may seem to offer a way out. For an externalist position allows one to hold that the justification of an empirical belief must make it certain that the belief is true, while still escaping the clutches of skepticism. This is so precisely because the externalist justification need not be within the cognitive grasp of the believer or indeed of anyone. It need only be true that there is *some* description of the believer, however complex and practically unknowable it may be, which, together with *some* true law of nature, ensures the truth of the belief. Thus, e.g., my perceptual belief that there is a cup on my desk is not certain, on any view, relative to the evidence or justification that is in my possession; I might be hallucinating or there might be an evil demon who is deceiving me. But it seems reasonable to suppose that if the belief is indeed true, then there is *some* external description of me and my situation and *some* true law of nature, relative to which the truth of the belief is guaranteed, and if so it would satisfy the requirement for knowledge.

In some ways, this is a neat and appealing solution to the paradox. Nonetheless, it seems doubtful that it is ultimately satisfactory. In the first place, there is surely something intuitively fishy about solving the problem by appealing to an in-principle guarantee of truth which will almost certainly in practice be available to no one. A second problem, which cannot be elaborated here, is that insisting on this sort of solution seems likely to create insuperable difficulties for knowledge of general and theoretical propositions. But in any case, the externalist solution seems to yield intuitively incorrect results in certain kinds of cases. A look at one of these may also suggest the beginnings of a more satisfactory solution.

Consider then the following case:

Case V. Agatha, seated at her desk, believes herself to be perceiving a cup on the desk. She also knows, however, that she is one of a group of 100 people who have been selected for a philosophical experiment by a Cartesian evil demon. The conditions have been so arranged that all 100 will at this particular time seem to themselves to be perceiving a cup upon their respective desks, with no significant differences in the subjective character of their respective experiences. But in fact, though 99 of the people will be perceiving a cup in the normal way, the last one will be caused by the demon to have a complete hallucination (including perceptual conditions, etc.) of a non-existent cup. Agatha knows all this, but she does not have any further information as to whether she is the one who is hallucinating, though as it happens she is not.

Is Agatha epistemically justified in her belief that there is a cup on the desk and does she know this to be so? According to the externalist view, we must say that she is justified and does know. For there is, we may assume, an external description of Agatha and her situation relative to which it is nomologically certain that her belief is true. (Indeed, according to Armstrong's original, unmodified view, she would be justified and would know even if she also knew instead that 99 of the 100 persons were being deceived by the demon, so long as she was in fact the odd one who was perceiving normally.) But this result is, I submit, intuitively mistaken. If Agatha knows that she is perceiving a cup, then she also knows that she is not the one who is being deceived. But she does not know this, for reasons that parallel those operative in the lottery case.

Is there then no way out of the paradox? The foregoing case and others like it seem to me to suggest the following approach to at least the present version of the paradox, though I can offer only an exceedingly brief sketch here. Intuitively, what the lottery case and the case of Agatha have in common is the presence of a large number of relevantly similar, alternative possibilities, all individually very unlikely, but such that the person in question *knows* that at least one of them will in fact be realized. In such a case, since there is no relevant way of distinguishing among these possibilities, the person cannot believe with adequate justification and *a fortiori* cannot know that any particular possibility will not be realized, even though the probability that it will not be realized may be made as high as one likes by simply increasing the total number of possibilities. Such cases do show that high probability is not by itself enough to satisfy the justification condition for knowledge. They do not show, however, that certainty is required instead. For what rules out knowledge in such a case is not merely the fact that the probability of truth is less than certainty but also the fact that the person *knows* that at least one of these highly probable propositions is false. It is a necessary condition for justification and for knowledge that this not be so. But there are many cases in which a person's justification for a belief fails to make it certain that the belief is true, but in which the person also does not know that some possible situation in which the belief would be false is one of a set of relevantly similar, alternative possibilities, at least one of which will definitely be realized. And in such a case, the lottery paradox provides no reason to think that the person does not know.[19]

An example may help to make this point clear. Consider again my apparent perception of the cup on my desk. I think that I do in fact know that there is a cup there. But the justification that is in my possession surely does not make it certain that my belief is true. Thus, for example, it seems to be possible, relative to my subjective justification, that I am being deceived by an evil demon, who is causing me to have a hallucinatory experience of the cup, together with accompanying conditions of perception. But it does not follow from this that I do not know that there is a cup on the desk, because it does not follow and I do not know that there is some class of relevantly similar cases in at least one of which a person is in fact deceived by such a demon. Although it is only probable and not certain that there is no demon, it is still possible for all I *know* that never in the history of the universe, past, present, or future, is there a case in which someone in a relevantly similar perceptual situation is actually deceived by such a demon. And, as far as I can see, the same thing is true of all the other ways in which it is possible that my belief might be mistaken. If this is so, then the lottery paradox provides no obstacle to my knowledge in this case.[20]

This response to the lottery paradox seems to me to be on the right track. It must be conceded, however, that it is in considerable need of further development and may turn out to have problems of its own. But that is a subject for another paper.[21]

There is one other sort of response, mentioned briefly above, which the externalist might make to the sorts of criticisms developed in this paper. I want to remark on it briefly, though a full-scale discussion is impossible here. In the end it may be possible to make intuitive sense of externalism only by construing the externalist as simply abandoning the traditional idea of epistemic justification or rationality and along with it anything resembling the traditional conception of knowledge. I have already mentioned that this may be precisely what the proponents of externalism intend to be doing, though most of them are anything but clear on this point.[22]

Against an externalist position that seriously adopts such a gambit, the criticisms developed in the present paper are of course entirely ineffective. If the externalist does not want even to claim that beliefs satisfying his conditions are epistemically justified or reasonable, then it is obviously no objection that they seem in some cases to be quite unjustified and unreasonable. But, as already noted, such a view, though it may possess some other sort of appeal, constitutes a solution to the epistemic regress problem or to any problem arising out of the traditional conception of knowledge only in the radical and relatively uninteresting sense that to reject that conception entirely is also, of course, to reject any problems arising out of it. Such "solutions" would seem to be available for any philosophical problem at all, but it is hard to see why they should be taken seriously.

Notes

1. For a fuller discussion of the regress argument, including a discussion of other possible outcomes of the regress, see my paper "Can Empirical Knowledge Have a Foundation?" *American Philosophical Quarterly* 15 (1978):1–13. That paper also contains a brief anticipation of the present discussion of externalism.

2. It could, of course, still be claimed that the belief in question was *empirically* basic, so long as both the needed justifying premises were justifiable on an *a priori* basis. But this would mean that it was an *a priori* truth that a particular empirical belief was likely to be true. In the present paper, I shall simply assume, without further discussion, that this seemingly unlikely state of affairs does not in fact obtain.

3. For criticism of this view, see the paper cited in note 1.

4. D. M. Armstrong, *Belief, Truth and Knowledge* (London, Press, 1973). Bracketed references in the text will be to the pages of this book.

5. The clearest passages are at p. 183, where Armstrong says that a belief satisfying his externalist condition, though not "based on reasons," nevertheless "might be said to be reasonable (justifiable), because it is a sign, a completely reliable sign, that the situation believed to exist does in fact exist"; and at p. 189, where he suggests that the satisfaction of a slightly weaker condition, though it does not yield knowledge, may still yield rational belief. There is no reason to think that any species of rationality or reasonableness other than the epistemic is at issue in either of these passages. But though these passages seem to me to adequately support my interpretation of Armstrong, the strongest support may well derive simply from the fact that he at no point *disavows* a claim of epistemic rationality. (See also the parenthetical remark in the middle of p. 77.)

6. Fred I. Dretske, *Seeing and Knowing* (London, 1969), chap. III. Dretske also differs from Armstrong in requiring in effect that the would-be knower also believe that the externalist condition is satisfied, but not of course that this belief be justified.

7. Goldman does this most clearly in "Discrimination and Perceptual Knowledge," *Journal of Philosophy* 73 (1976):771–91; and in "What is Justified Belief?" forthcoming. See also "A Causal Theory of Knowing," *Journal of Philosophy* 64 (1967):355–72, though this last paper is more concerned with the Gettier problem than with a general account of the standards of epistemic justification.

8. William P. Alston, "Two Types of Foundationalism," *Journal of Philosophy* 73 (1976): 165–85; see especially p. 168.

9. Alston, "Varieties of Privileged Access," in Roderick Chisholm and Robert Swartz, *Empirical Knowledge* (Englewood Cliffs, N.J., 1973), pp. 396–99. Alston's term for this species of privileged access is "truth-sufficiency."

10. See Chisholm, *Theory of Knowledge*, 2nd ed. (Englewood Cliffs, N.J., 1977), p. 22, where Chisholm offers the following definition of the concept of a state of affairs being *self-presenting*:

> *h* is *self-presenting* for *S* at *t* = Df *h* occurs at *t*; and necessarily, if *h* occurs at *t* then *h* is evident [i.e., justified] for *S* at *t*.

Despite the overtones of the term "self-presentation," nothing in this passage seems to require that believer have any sort of immediate awareness of the state in question; all that is required is that it actually occur, i.e., that his belief be true. On the other hand, Chisholm also, in the section immediately preceding this definition, quotes with approval a passage from Leibniz which appeals to the idea of "direct awareness" and of the absence of mediation "between the understanding and its objects," thus suggesting the non-externalist variety of foundationalism (pp.20–21).

11. Armstrong actually formulates the criterion as a criterion of knowledge, rather than merely of justification; the satisfaction of the belief condition is built into the criterion and this, with the satisfaction of the indicated justification condition, entails that the truth condition is satisfied.

12. This assumes that clairvoyant beliefs are caused in some distinctive way, so that an appropriately complete description of Samantha will rule out the possibility that the belief is a mere hunch and will connect appropriately with the law governing her clairvoyance.

13. This further supposition does not prevent the belief about the President's whereabouts from being non-inferential, since it is not in any useful sense Norman's reason for accepting that specific belief.

14. This is the basic objection to Dretske's version of externalism, mentioned above. Dretske's condition requires that one have an analogously unjustified (though true) belief about the reliability of one's perceptual belief.

15. The only apparent answer here would be to claim that the reasonable presumption is in favor of one's having such reliable means of access, unless there is good reason to the contrary. But it is hard to see why such a presumption should be thought reasonable.

16. Mark Pastin, in a critical study of Armstrong, has suggested that ascriptions of knowledge depend on the epistemic situation of the ascriber rather than on that of the ascribee at this point, so that I am correct in ascribing knowledge to Norman so long as *I* know that his belief is reliable (and hence also that the other conditions of knowledge are satisfied), even if Norman does not. But I can see no very convincing rationale for this claim. See Pastin, "Knowledge and Reliability: A Study of D. M. Armstrong's *Belief, Truth and Knowledge*," *Metaphilosophy* 9 (1978):150–62. Notice further that if the epistemic regress problem is in general to be dealt with along externalist lines, then my knowledge that Norman's belief is reliable would depend on the epistemic situation of a further external observer, who ascribes knowledge to me. And similarly for the knowledge of that observer, etc., *ad infinitum*. I do not know whether this regress of external observers is vicious, but it seems clearly to deprive the appeal to such an observer of any value as a practical criterion.

17. Of course there are cases in which one must act, even though one has no adequate knowledge of the likely consequences; and one might attempt to defend epistemic externalism by arguing that in epistemic contexts the analogous situation *always* obtains. But there are several problems with such a response. First, to simply assume that this is always so seems to be question-begging, and the externalist can argue for this claim only by refuting all alternatives to his position. Second, notice that in ethical contexts this situation usually, perhaps always, obtains only when not acting will lead definitely to bad consequences, not just to the failure to obtain good ones; and there seems to be no parallel to this in the epistemic case. Third, and most important, the justification for one's action in such a case would depend not on the external fact, if it is a fact, that the action leads to good consequences, but simply on the fact that one could do no better, given the unfortunate state of one's knowledge; thus this position would not be genuinely a version of moral externalism, and analogously for the epistemic case.

18. I am assuming here, following Chisholm, that knowledge requires a degree of justification stronger than that required to make a belief merely reasonable.

19. I do not, alas, have any real account to offer here of the notion of *relevant similarity*. Roughly, the idea is that two possibilities are relevantly similar if there is no known difference between them that has a bearing on the likelihood that they will be realized. But this will not quite do. For consider a lottery case in which there are two tickets bearing each even number and only one for each odd number. Intuitively, it seems to me, this difference does not prevent all the tickets, odd and even, from being relevantly similar, despite the fact that it is twice as likely that an even ticket will be drawn.

20. But if this account is correct, I may still fail to know in many other cases in which common sense would say fairly strongly that I do. E.g., do I know that my house has not burned down since I left it this morning? Ordinarily we are inclined to say that we do know such things. But if it is true, as it might well be, that I also know that of the class of houses relevantly similar to mine, at least one will burn down at some point, then I do not, on the present account, *know* that my house has not burned down, however improbable such a catastrophe may be. (On the other hand, knowledge would not be ruled out by the present principle simply because I knew that certain specific similar houses, *other than mine*, have in the past burned down or even that they will in the future burn down. For I know, *ex hypothesi*, that my house is not one of those. The force of the principle depends on my knowing that at least one possibility *which might for all I know be the one I am interested in* will be realized, not just on descriptively similar possibilities being realized.)

21. This response to the lottery paradox derives in part from discussions with C. Anthony Anderson.

22. The clearest example of such a position is in Goldman's paper "Discrimination and Perceptual Knowledge," cited above, where he rejects what he calls "Cartesian-style justification" as a requirement for perceptual knowledge, in favor of an externalist account. He goes on to remark, however, that one could use the term "justification" in such a way that satisfaction of his externalist conditions "counts as justification," though a kind of justification "entirely different from the sort of justification demanded by Cartesianism" (p. 790). What is unclear is whether this is supposed to be a purely verbal possibility, which would then be of little interest, or whether it is supposed to connect with something like the concept of epistemic rationality explicated in section I. Thus it is uncertain whether Goldman means to repudiate the whole idea of epistemic rationality, or only some more limited view such as the doctrine of the given (reference to which provides his only explanation of what he means by "Cartesianism" in epistemology).

Defeated Knowledge, Reliability, and Justification

ROBERT AUDI

Philosophers generally agree that knowledge is not merely justified true belief. But they do not agree on what kind of account of knowledge can best distinguish it from mere justified true belief. A major question dividing them is whether the distinction should be made on the basis of the kind of justification S has for believing p, or on the basis of apparently non-normative concepts such as that of the reliability of the belief, construed in terms of the likelihood that beliefs of the kind in question will be true. I shall call the first sort of approach to the analysis of knowledge *justificationist* and the second sort of approach *naturalistic*.[1] Epistemologists using both approaches have recently been occupied with problems posed by certain examples of what is sometimes called "defeated knowledge."[2] This might be characterized as justified true belief that would be knowledge if it were not undermined by one or another kind of untoward circumstance. A good account of the nature of knowledge must of course do more than rule out defeating circumstances. But this task appears to be one of the most difficult problems confronting epistemology, and many instances of defeated knowledge are challenging test cases for an account of knowledge.

This paper will begin by exploring some recent theories that deal with defeated knowledge. I shall then propose an alternative account of some representative examples of defeated knowledge. No attempt will be made to develop an analysis of knowledge in general; the account proposed is meant only to enhance our understanding, from a justificationist point of view, of defeated knowledge, and to help us determine whether reliability accounts of defeated knowledge, which seem to be the most plausible kind of naturalistic account, are superior to justificationist accounts of defeated knowledge. As I am conceiving a reliability account, it is one that explains the defeat of would-be knowledge that p by showing that S's belief that p is in some way inadequately reliable. By contrast, justificationist accounts explain defeated knowledge in terms of the kind of justification S has for believing p. Only a few current positions can be considered here, and some kinds of defeated knowledge will not be discussed. But the reliability and justificationist views to be studied are, I hope, sufficiently representative to warrant the conclusions I shall draw.

1. RELIABILITY THEORIES

Among the very best reliability theories yet developed is Alvin Goldman's account of non-inferential perceptual knowledge. Our problem can be readily seen through an example from his important paper, "Discrimination and Perceptual Knowledge":

> Suppose we are told that, unknown to Henry, the district he has just entered is full of papier-mâché facsimiles of barns. These facsimiles look from the road exactly like barns, but are really just façades, without back walls or interiors. . . . Having just entered the district, Henry has not encountered any facsimiles; the object he sees is a genuine barn. But if the object on that site were a facsimile, Henry would mistake it for a barn. Given this new information, we would be strongly inclined to withdraw the claim [which we would allow in a normal rural setting] that Henry *knows* the object is a barn.[3]

Henry has a justified true belief that is not knowledge; but it is hard to explain why it is not. Goldman himself points out that his previous account of empirical knowledge, a causal analysis, cannot explain this: "Henry's belief that the object is a barn is caused by the presence of the barn; indeed, the process is a perceptual one"[4] of just the kind that occurs when we *do* acquire perceptual knowledge by observation.

Facts that are simply about the perceiver may also defeat would-be knowledge. Suppose that unbeknownst to S, he has been *hallucinating* barns while driving along. Imagine that he feels normal, that the hallucinatory "barns" "look" to him like real ones, and that he has no reason to suspect anything is wrong. He may then come to a real barn, see it, and justifiably believe that it is a barn. Yet he does not *know* that it is. The reasons are similar to the reasons why Henry does not know. For instance, just as Henry would have taken a facsimile to be a barn had there been one before him, S would have believed there was a barn before him if he had hallucinated one instead of seeing one.

How is an analysis of knowledge to rule out such defeaters? Let us first consider Goldman's treatment of the problem. What he proposes as an explanation of why Henry's would-be knowledge is defeated is roughly this: S has non-inferential perceptual knowledge, of a, that it is F, only if there is no relevant perceptually equivalent state of affairs (such as would obtain if Henry viewed a barn facsimile) in which S *falsely* believes, of the perceptual counterpart of a (e.g., the facsimile), that it is F.[5] This explains why Henry lacks knowledge, because the fact that there are barn facsimiles all around Henry and he *would* believe, of any one of them, that it is a barn makes the state of affairs, Henry's viewing a facsimile from the same angle in the same light, etc., a *relevant* perceptual equivalent. It defeats his would-be knowledge because he cannot perceptually discriminate (under the same conditions of observation) a facsimile from the barn he actually sees. Goldman does not try to specify what makes an alternative relevant, apparently in part because no prima facie satisfactory account of the notion occurs to him.

One may wonder how Goldman would deal with the hallucination possibility I have raised. It seems clear that because S's barn hallucinations are occurring frequently as he drives along and in each case he mistakenly believes he sees a barn, their occurrence is also relevant to his belief that a is a barn, and defeats his would-be knowledge that it is. However, there is presumably no object, a hallucinatory barn, such that S might believe falsely, of it, that it is a barn. Hence the barn hallucinations do not provide perceptually equivalent states of affairs in Goldman's sense. What Goldman suggests is that there must be "neither a relevant perceptual equivalent of the indicated sort (using our present definition of perceptual equivalence) *nor* a relevant alternative situation in which an equivalent percept occurs and prompts a *de dicto* belief that something has F, but where there is nothing that *perceptually* causes this percept and nothing *of which* F is believed to hold."[6] This explains why S's belief that a is a barn is unreliable. For even though there is nothing in the circumstances which he would mistakenly take to be a barn, there are relevant circumstances in which, given the same sensory evidence, he would mistakenly take it that there is one before him.

Before considering some justificationist proposals that also deal with the case, let us examine another important naturalistic position, namely, Armstrong's. His account is more general than Goldman's and seems to have an advantage in having fewer problematic expressions (such as 'relevant alternative').

Armstrong's reliability account of non-inferential knowledge would deal with Goldman's barn case through Armstrong's requirement that if S non-inferentially knows that a is F, then S has a property H, where "there is a law-like connection in nature" such that for any x and any y, if x has H and believes y has F, y does have F.[7] It might seem that this requirement would not rule out Henry's knowing that a is a barn. For it may appear that Henry has such a property and would thus have to be said to know that a is a barn.[8] He might have a "nomic" property (e.g., being affected in a certain way by light rays from a certain sort of object) such that if *anyone* who has that property believes the object in question to be a barn, then it is one. However, Armstrong would probably reply that there is no difference between the way one is visually affected by a barn and the way one is visually affected from the same distance and angle by a mere barn wall artifically supported from behind, since the same sorts of light rays reach one in the same way. Hence there is unlikely to be a suitable H.

This is a plausible response. It also suggests something important about Armstrong's theory: even when S does (visually) know that there is a barn before him, Armstrong should take S's knowledge to be indirect, i.e., to be based on some other knowledge or belief of S's, such as the belief that there is a woody-looking barnlike surface before him. However, it appears that Armstrong would take S's knowledge that a is a woody-looking surface to be direct.[9] This raises no obstacle to dealing with the case of Henry; but one can still imagine defeating conditions for justified true belief of this sort, and it is doubtful that Armstrong's account can rule out all

of them. Take the hallucination example, and suppose S's would-be direct knowledge is the justified true belief that there is a woody-looking surface before him
shaped like a barn wall. Surely his belief could be "perceptually caused" in the normal way by the barn surface S sees, i.e., caused in the way ordinary objects like tables
and chairs cause us to believe they are before us when we perceive them in normal
light. Moreover, there might be a suitable H in virtue of which his belief is *reliable*.
Yet the belief is not knowledge.

To be sure, Armstrong puts important restrictions on H. The one relevant here
is that H be "such that there is a real possibility of the situation covered by the law-
like connection recurring."[10] But surely there is a real possibility of many situations
in which a person has the relevant property, e.g. being visually affected in a certain
way by light rays of a certain character. One might now object that we still do not
have a sufficiently specific H, since light rays from a woody-looking surface would
affect one no differently than light rays from, e.g., a machine that produces optical
illusions or from something that appears qualitatively very similar to a woody-looking
surface yet is not a physical surface at all, or at least not an ordinary one (perhaps a
laser photograph could fit this description). But if this is so, it would not be congenial to Armstrong. For he would then probably have to say that by sight one cannot directly know even that there is a physical surface before one. (For this strong a
belief would not be reliable on the basis of the relevant H.) He would probably not
wish to say this, and in any case the hallucination possibility we are imagining would
defeat this would-be knowledge as well. Perhaps there are minor revisions that would
enable Armstrong's account to deal with these problems, but I cannot explore that
possibility here. I am more concerned with the view as representative of a plausible
reliability theory than with its correctness. The same holds for my concern with justificationist theories, which are the subject of the next section.

2. JUSTIFICATIONIST THEORIES

We have seen how some plausible naturalistic views bear on certain cases of defeated
knowledge. Let us consider how some justificationist accounts of knowledge might
treat the same examples.

It will be instructive to begin with an attractively simple theory suggested by
John Barker: a justified true belief that p constitutes knowledge "if and only if what
isn't known won't hurt, i.e., if and only if there is some way that any other true proposition besides p could come to be known without destruction of the original justification for believing p."[11] This condition does not seem to be met in any case we
have examined. For instance, apparently S cannot come to know that there are facsimiles around him which he cannot tell from real barns, without destroying his *original* justification for believing the object he sees is a barn. This justification might be,
e.g., that a looks to S like a barn or that a *barn* "perceptually causes" S to believe
that he sees a barn. Whatever the justification, it will have to be buttressed with new
information if S is to remain justified in his original belief. Similarly, in our hallucination case, if S is to know that a is a barn, after he discovers he has been hallucinating

barns, S's belief that a is a barn will have to be based at least in part on something new, say a justified belief that he is not now hallucinating a barn.

Barker's necessary condition claim is plausible, perhaps even so obviously true as to be uncontroversial. For if S knows that p, one way in which he could come to know any potentially defeating propositions is in the context of also coming to know how he knows that p. Surely he could come to know how he does, in a manner that enables him to explain away any would-be defeaters.

On the other hand, consider justified true belief that is not defeated knowledge but simply not justified in the right sort of way to qualify as knowledge. Some cases of this kind seem to undermine Barker's sufficient condition claim. Suppose, e.g., that S has a justified true belief that he will lose in a lottery in which he has one out of the 1,000 tickets. Is there not some way he could come to know any other true proposition without destroying his original justification for believing he will lose? It would seem so. Granted, if he comes to know a true causal account of why his ticket will not be selected, then he no longer *needs* his original justification in terms of the probability that he will win in a fair lottery of the relevant sort. But surely this justification is not destroyed by his discovery of the different (and superior) one. Barker's proposal does, however, seem to give us a useful partial characterization of defeated knowledge. For no defeated knowledge seems to satisfy his condition, and defeated knowledge is often clearly such that S's justification would be undermined by discovering certain things of which he is ignorant.

We can learn much from considering how an elaborate recent theory by Marshall Swain could deal with our examples. For Swain, Henry would not know that a is a barn because there is a "significant alternative," C^*, to the actual causal chain, $X \rightarrow Y$, that links the state of affairs, a's being a barn, to Henry's belief that a is one. Swain gives only a sufficient condition for C^*'s being a significant alternative, namely, that

(a) it is objectively likely that C^* should have occurred rather than $X \rightarrow Y$; and

(b) if C^* had occurred instead of $X \rightarrow Y$, then there would have been an event or state of affairs U in C^* such that S would not have been justified in believing that b [e.g., that a is a barn] if S were justified in believing that U occurred.[12]

The idea, as applied to Henry, is this. It is objectively likely that a facsimile should have caused his percepts. If it had, there would have been a state of affairs, e.g. the facsimile's causing Henry to seem to see a barn before him, such that if he were justified in believing that this occurred, he would not be justified in believing that a is a barn. Regarding our hallucination case, S's hallucinating would also be a significant alternative to his seeing a barn. It is objectively likely; and had it occurred, there would have been a state of affairs, e.g. the hallucination's causing him to seem to see a barn, that satisfies (b).

Consider another kind of example, one in which S has a justified true perceptual belief that fails to be knowledge because of some oddity in the causal chain from the relevant state of affairs to the belief. Thus,

Suppose Milton is in a museum looking at a glass box that contains a vase. Entirely unknown to him, the surface of the box is actually a cleverly constructed television screen. For someone looking at the glass box, the visual appearances are precisely what they would be if the surface of the box were clear glass and the vase were being directly observed. Moreover, suppose that the vase whose image is being televised is the vase that is actually in the box. Milton comes to believe that the vase is in the box on the basis of reasons R, and his believing for these reasons is justified. But he does not know that the vase is in there.[13]

Swain deals with this by requiring that a belief constituting knowledge cannot depend on a defective causal chain:

Where S justifiably believes that h on the basis of R, causal chain, $X \to Y$ is defective with respect to this justified belief *if* (a) there is some event or state of affairs U in $X \to Y$ such that S would be justified in believing that U did not occur, and (b) it is essential to S's justifiably believing that h on the basis of R that S would be justified in believing that U did not occur.[14]

Applying this to Milton, we are to assume that the case is very uncommon and that in part for this reason Milton satisfies (a). Presumably (b) holds of him too.

Goldman deals with a similar case—in which S sees a candle before him through a complex system of mirrors whose existence he does not even suspect—by appealing to the notion of a relevant alternative: S does not know that there is a candle before him, since there is a relevant alternative in which, through similar mirrors, he would falsely believe this.[15] Swain, too, can deal with the case. Just as Goldman construes as a relevant alternative S's being appeared to in the same way though the proposition in question is false, Swain can take such states of affairs as significant alternatives even if they are not objectively likely.

3. AN ALTERNATIVE ACCOUNT
OF DEFEATED PERCEPTUAL KNOWLEDGE

In this section, I want to propose a justificationist account of defeated perceptual knowledge. The account is much less broad than Swain's, which applies to non-perceptual as well as to perceptual beliefs; and although it is broader than Goldman's in applying to indirect perceptual beliefs, I do not offer a sufficient condition for any kind of perceptual knowledge, as he does for non-inferential perceptual knowledge. My concern is restricted to defeated knowledge, and there may be kinds of defeated perceptual knowledge not ruled out by the principles I propose.

A major difference between my account and Swain's is that mine makes essential use of the distinction between direct and indirect knowledge and beliefs, whereas for him both are instances of what he calls believing on the basis of a reason. One way of expressing this distinction is to say that S's knowledge or belief that p is direct if and only if it is not *based on* any other knowledge or belief of S's, i.e., roughly, no other belief of his constitutes (or expresses) a reason of his for which he believes p.[16] If S's knowledge that p is based on his knowledge that q, which is his reason for p, then he knows p *indirectly*. Such knowledge has been called inferential; but though all inferential knowledge is indirect, I shall not take S's indirectly knowing that p to entail S's having inferred p from anything else, at least not if inferring is taken, as it usually is, to imply a process of drawing a conclusion from a set of propositions one is in some sense entertaining. Some knowledge and beliefs which it is natural to call perceptual are indirect, and I want to begin by considering a case of defeated knowledge constituted by an indirect belief.

Indirect Perceptual Beliefs

Imagine that S enters an office building and walks down a long corridor toward the person he is going to see. As he passes an open door, he hears the familiar sounds of a typewriter. They strike him as having the muffled quality of sounds produced by the IBM Selectric, and he takes it that a Selectric is being used inside. Let us assume that he is correct in this and that his experience with Selectrics and other typewriters is such that he is also justified in his belief that a Selectric is being used in the room he is passing. Now imagine that all the other offices S will pass on the corridor are experimenting with a new Japanese product which few people, even in the typewriter business, have heard about: the Sonilectric. It works much like the Selectric and sounds so much like it that had S passed one of the other doors he would have believed the Selectric was being used in the room in question. The case is like Henry's in that S's would-be knowledge is defeated by the proximity of relevant circumstances in which he would form a false belief. But it may differ from that of Henry; for here, supposing that we have a perceptual belief, we clearly do not have a direct one, since S's belief that a Selectric is being used is based on his belief that the sounds in question are Selectric sounds.

How should we deal with the case? Since Goldman would presumably not regard S's belief as non-inferential, his account would not apply to it (though, as I shall later suggest, it is easy to see how the account might be extended to deal with the example). For Swain, the defeat of S's knowledge can be explained by pointing out that in the circumstances there is a significant alternative to the actual causal chain from the Selectric to S's belief that a Selectric is being used. For it seems objectively likely that S should have heard a Sonilectric instead, and if he did he would have believed that a Selectric was being used.

I want to suggest a different way of explaining why S's knowledge is defeated here. I shall first propose an epistemic principle that seems to hold for indirect knowledge in general and then proceed to apply it to our example:

> P: If, at t, S's belief that p is essentially based on his belief that q, then, at t, S knows that p, only if, at t, (i) q is true; (ii) S justifiably believes q; (iii) there is a warranting relation, R, that S justifiably takes q to have to p; and (iv) q does, in the circumstance S is in at t, warrant p.[17]

I am using 'warranting relation' broadly and construing (iii) as satisfiable by both *de dicto* and *de re* beliefs. Clause (iii) thus encompasses S's believing that if q then p, believing that q entails p, believing that q is good evidence for p, believing that q indicates p, taking (or believing, if taking is not a kind of believing) q to justify (warrant, show, etc.) p, and so on. Since some of these beliefs can be held by a person who has no epistemic concepts, S can satisfy (iii) without having them. Regarding S's belief that p being based on his belief that q, this relation may hold even if he does not realize it, nor ever entertain q, nor ever entertain the proposition that he takes q to support p, nor ever infer (in any conscious way, at least) p from q. Moreover, even if S's belief that p is also based on his believing some proposition other than q, I shall say it is *essentially* based on his belief that q, only if, other things remaining equal, S would not believe p if he did not believe q. With these qualifications, P seems quite plausible.

Let us now consider some applications of P. First, in our typewriter example it seems plain that S does not satisfy clause (iv): *in* the circumstances, that the sounds he hears have the muffled quality of sounds produced by the Selectric does not warrant (for S) the proposition that a Selectric is being used. For all around him are non-Selectrics producing sounds with the muffled quality he believes he hears. Consider also the example in which S sees a candle through a complicated system of mirrors. On the (perhaps dubious) assumption that S's belief that there is a candle before him is indirect, P implies that it will constitute knowledge only if this proposition is warranted by some other proposition S believes, presumably one roughly to the effect that there is before him a flame-like area at the top of a waxy-looking cylinder. Now in the circumstances this proposition does not warrant the proposition that there is a candle before him. There may be several ways to explain why not. One is that under the circumstances the former is not a *reliable* indication of the latter. Another is that if S realized that the circumstances in question obtained, he would not be *justified* in believing the latter on the basis of the former. I shall return to this contrast.

One may now wonder whether the case of Henry can also be dealt with by using P. This question is difficult to answer. For one thing, it requires determining whether, in the sort of circumstances imagined, Henry's belief, through sight, that a is a barn, is *indirect*, i.e., based on at least one other belief of his. If the belief is direct, then P does not apply to it. The question whether or not such beliefs are direct is important not only for determining the scope of P and similar principles but also for assessing coherentist theories of knowledge. For on the plausible (though by no means self-evident) supposition that if a direct belief constitutes knowledge, it constitutes *direct* knowledge, coherentists will have to construe all empirical knowledge, at least, as constituted by indirect belief. (For as usually understood, coherentists deny that there is any direct empirical knowledge, and sometimes that there is any direct *a priori* knowledge.) It is thus of considerable interest whether perceptual beliefs like Henry's are, despite appearances, indirect. If so, P might be able to explain why Henry does not have knowledge and indeed why many other apparently direct justified true perceptual beliefs fail to constitute knowledge. If not, coherentists would have to undertake the difficult task of showing at least how indirect empirical knowledge may be constituted by direct belief.[18]

Once we take seriously the question whether Henry's belief is indirect, we are confronted with another difficult question. Since it is through sight that he believes that a is a barn, we need to ask whether he *directly sees* that this is so. As I am using this term here, S directly sees that a is F, if and only if he sees that a is F, and does not see this on the basis of seeing that something else is the case. At least typically, if S sees that a is F, on the basis of seeing that p, then his belief that a is F is based on his belief that p; but I shall leave it open whether the former *entails* the latter.

We are now in a position to take up the question whether Henry's belief that a is a barn is indirect. No doubt knowledge through (or at least in part through) sight, that a is a barn, could be indirect. For instance, if Henry is at a considerable distance from a and must struggle to discern its features, in the light of which he concludes that a is a barn, his knowledge that it is will be based on other knowledge of his. But Goldman seems to have in mind a case in which one sees all the typical features and straightaway believes the object to be a barn. Let us explore how one might in this sort of case argue that the belief is nonetheless indirect. I shall consider several of the reasons that suggest this.

First, let us ask whether, in the situation we are imagining, where there are no facsimiles or other defeaters, S would directly see that a is a barn. Might it not be the case that what S directly sees to be the case is simply that there is a roughly rectangular, woody-looking surface before him? This would explain why what he *sees* to be the case seems to be the same even if there is only a (very faithful) facsimile before him; and it would *suggest* that S's belief that there is a barn before him is based on his belief that there is such a surface there.

Another consideration emerges if we imagine S looking attentively at (say) a barn in normal light, at first believing it to be a barn and then strongly suspecting, on the basis of the false testimony of a friend beside him, that it is a facsimile. Suppose that there are no facsimiles and, for the sake of argument, that S does at first directly see that the structure is a barn. How are we to explain his no longer seeing that it is when he is still looking at it under the same perceptual conditions? S's sensory state, as well as the objects and surfaces he sees, are the same. Perhaps what explains why he does not see that it is a barn after the testimony is that his suspicion prevents him from *taking* what he sees to be the side of a barn. On this view, there is no change in what he directly sees to be the case; the change is in what he believes ("sees") on the basis of what he directly sees to be the case. Thus, suppose that another observer, with the same sensory acuity and repertoire of concepts, looks unsuspectingly at the same barn. One might then plausibly argue as follows. What each directly sees to be the case is the same as what the other directly sees to be so. The first does not directly see that a is a barn (nor see that this is so at all, since he does not believe it); hence the second does not directly see this either.

A third consideration arises if we imagine that someone who knows about a barn facsimile nearby tells S about it and asks him how he knows a is a barn. If S's confidence is not easily shaken and he replies without seeking evidence beyond what he has, he might say, "Clearly, that [pointing toward the barn] is the surface of a barn," or "It looks just like a barn seen from this angle—that wall can't possibly be papier-mâché," or "It has exactly the shape and texture of a barn seen from here." Must we suppose that S has *adopted* these beliefs only in response to the questioning and then based his belief that *a* is a barn on them? Perhaps he is making *explicit* the basis on which he took *a* to be a barn. By contrast, imagine asking an ordinary person (in daylight) how he knows that *a* (which he sees) is a red (or a woody-looking) surface. Unless he is philosophically sophisticated, he is unlikely to have any grounds to cite, at least none which constitute his reason(s) for believing that the thing in question is a red surface. For he presumably takes himself simply to see that it is. He may realize, at this point anyway, that he could be hallucinating. But if so, it would not follow that his belief that the surface in question is red was based on his having believed he was not hallucinating. The latter belief is adopted *after* S begins to wonder about his justification for believing he sees something red, whereas it seems arguable that, even before being asked how he knows there is a barn before him, S believes there is a woody-looking surface before him. It is not that such perceptual beliefs as that there is a red surface before one could not be indirect. But ordinarily they do not seem so, whereas beliefs to the effect that something is a barn (car, dog, person) can be plausibly argued to be.

These considerations lend some plausibility to the view that in the kinds of cases we are examining, one's knowledge, through sight, that *a* is a barn, is indirect. But they are quite inconclusive. Granting a difference between what is required to know that there is a woody-looking surface before one and what is required to know that there is a barn before one, nothing said above shows that in order to know the latter one must believe (or know) that there is a woody-looking surface before one (or have other grounds or believe or know any item of evidence). Moreover, though it is plausible to suppose that what S directly sees to be the case is the same whether he sees that *a* is a barn or mistakenly takes a facsimile to be a barn, it is also arguable that since seeing that *a* is *F* entails knowing that it is, and S does not know the facsimile is a barn, *this* difference explains why S directly sees that *a* is a barn, yet does not directly see the same thing to be so when he views a facsimile and mistakenly believes it to be a barn. Similarly, since seeing that *a* is *F* apparently entails believing that it is, we can explain why S ceases to see that *a* is a barn when he comes to suspect it is a facsimile, by maintaining that he is now refusing to believe what he seems to (and previously did) see directly—namely, that *a* is a barn. We need not explain this by saying that what he seems to see directly he in fact saw only on the basis of something else he saw to be so. To be sure, these replies are not themselves conclusive. But they are sufficiently cogent to make it unreasonable to assume that P can account for cases like that of Henry (who, if his belief that *a* is a barn is indirect, would fail to satisfy clause (iv) of P). In any event, there certainly are cases of defeated knowledge constituted by direct beliefs, and the principle I shall propose to deal with these can also explain why, assuming that Henry's belief that *a* is a barn is direct, he does not know that *a* is a barn.

Direct Perceptual Beliefs

Let us consider a case of defeated knowledge constituted by direct belief. Suppose S has only the modest justified true belief that over there is a woody-looking surface, but does not *know* this because he has, without even suspecting it, been hallucinating such surfaces and would have had the same belief had he at the time hallucinated the kind of surface he now sees. Presumably, S's belief here is *direct*, so P does not apply. We thus need a different way of explaining why the belief is not knowledge.

One direction a justificationist can take here is that of a coherence theory of justification, on which there is no direct knowledge or directly justified belief. Harman,[19] e.g., could use P or something like it after all. However, a justificationist, like a naturalist, need not be a coherentist, any more than he need be a foundationalist. How should a justificationist who is not a coherentist construe the case? A Cartesian strategy would be to deny that even S's belief that *a* is a barn surface is direct, and to argue that it is based on, say, a belief that there appears to S to be a barn surface there. Then P again applies: given the hallucinations, S is mistaken (or not justified) in taking the proposition that there appears to him to be a barn surface there, to warrant the proposition that there is one there.

This strategy is not without plausibility, and it brings out that P is neutral between theories of perception that deny we have direct knowledge of the physical world and direct realist views that affirm this. But wherever one might locate direct belief in perceptual experience, there remains the problem of how to explain its defeat—unless, of course, we hold that certain beliefs, such as appearance-beliefs, are *necessarily* knowledge and hence indefeasible. I prefer not to be forced to take that view,[20] and in any case it would be desirable to show that a justificationist need not hold it nor choose between coherentism and retreating inward for direct knowledge.

We may make some headway if we think of perceptual knowledge as a function of success in several interrelated dimensions. If we can locate defeaters in terms of these, we may get a better understanding of defeated direct perceptual beliefs. One important dimension seems to be S's *perceptual capacity* relative to the belief and the circumstances. Are his eyes or ears, e.g., good enough to enable him to know what he believes on the basis of their input? Second, there is *perceptual normality*. If S's senses malfunction, e.g. in such a way that there are gaps in his hearing, then he may be unable to know that Beethoven's "Apassionata" is being played, even though he would ordinarily recognize it and hears very clearly the parts he does hear. Third, *perceptual circumstances* are crucial. The presence of mirrors, e.g., can produce false visual beliefs, and background noise can produce false beliefs about what someone has said to one. Fourth, since perceptual knowledge requires responding to input from the senses, there is the dimension of *cognitive responses to one's senses*. S's perceptual beliefs must be in some sense appropriate to his perceptual state. When, for instance, he has a clear impression of both color and shape before him, he must not believe that there is merely a color before him. There may well be further dimensions of perceptual knowledge to be emphasized, and one could make important distinctions within these four categories. But if we take the above as a point of departure, at least the following conditions for direct perceptual knowledge are suggested:

> (a) S's senses must (as Goldman's case of Henry shows) be sufficiently acute, relative to the proposition in question and the circumstances in which he believes it, to distinguish the relevant sort of object or property from things he

might confuse it with in the circumstances. S must not, e.g., claim to discern precisely the shape of a distant object if he is so far away that its edges look highly blurred. Similarly, given Henry's circumstances, his vision is insufficiently acute to record differences in appearance between a barn and a facsimile.

(b) The sense(s) through which S believes p must be normal. For instance, if S has a loud (illusory) ringing in his ears at the pitch of A 440, he may be quite unable to certify the corresponding note on a piano as in tune even if he has "absolute pitch." Similarly, his senses must not be playing tricks on him, as with certain optical illusions or the hallucinations described above. (In the case of a hallucinatory perceptual belief, I shall speak of the sense(s) *appropriate* to the belief rather than a belief *through* a sense. For although the sense of sight [say] is appropriate [or relevant] to a belief arising from a visual hallucination, S does not, or at any rate need not, "see" the thing in question through sight.)

(c) S's perceptual circumstances must be appropriate for the belief in question. For instance, where the belief is to the effect that a is (say) red, the lighting must not make it appear to have a color it does not have; and where the belief concerns the shape of something, S's orientation to it must not be inappropriate for judging its shape.

(d) S's cognitive responses to his sense impressions must be normal, so that he is not, e.g., failing to believe a is red when his seeing it is producing the usual sensations of red, nor confusing two things—say, horses and cows—when he knows them perfectly well and is having the normal perceptual sensations of them. (It would be difficult to ascertain that the states of affairs described here have occurred, but doing so nevertheless seems quite possible.)

I am not in the least suggesting that S must believe (a) through (d) in order to have direct perceptual knowledge. My suggestion is only that he must be such that he either is not unjustified in believing (a) through (d), or would not be unjustified in believing them, if he did believe them. More positively, I am inclined to think that (a) through (d) are a *presumption* of our ascribing perceptual knowledge to S. In calling them a presumption I mean, not that we ascribe perceptual knowledge to S in a given case only if we believe he satisfies them in that case, but (in part) that if we consider any of them *false* in a given case, then we deny that S knows p.[21]

The counterpart conceptual claim, which seems equally plausible, is that a direct, justified true perceptual belief of S's represents knowledge only if this presumption is true of it. The plausibility of this claim can be seen by imagining someone *denying* that, e.g., S's vision being abnormal is a reason to question his claim (from a distance) to have visual knowledge that a is a barn. Similarly, imagine someone's denying that S's being unjustified in trusting his vision, is a reason to question this claim. Such denials would be prima facie ground for thinking that the person did not share our concept of perceptual knowledge. To be sure, S's vision may be subnormal, yet still perfectly adequate to give him knowledge, at the distance in question, that a is a barn. Similarly, S's being color-blind may not bear on his ability to acquire visual knowledge that a car is passing. Moreover, auditory hallucinations that give S false beliefs may not affect any of his visual beliefs. Nor need colored light or even an opaque (but snug) wrapping affect one's judgment of shape. Some abnormalities are not relevant to the question whether, in the circumstances, S's belief that p represents knowledge. The notions we need are (at least) those expressed in (a) through (d): the notion of the acuity of S's senses, relative to the proposition in question and to the circumstances in which S believes it; and the notions of S's senses, his cognitive responses to his sense impressions, and his perceptual circumstances being relevantly normal with respect to a perceptual belief. I shall have to leave these notions of relevant normality rather vague; but explicating some such notions seems a problem for any theory of perceptual knowledge, and nothing I say should turn on their vagueness.

As in other cases, we can imagine both justificationist and reliability accounts of relevance. For instance, a reliability theorist might argue that S's senses, or S's perceptual circumstances, are not relevantly normal if they render the belief in question unreliable. And a justificationist might argue that they are not relevantly normal if they are such that if S believed that the circumstances obtained, or that his senses had the abnormality in question, then he would no longer be justified in believing that p. I shall return to this problem. But let us first consider how, using the presumption I have formulated, a justificationist account of defeated knowledge might deal with some of the cases we have discussed.

The epistemic principle corresponding to the presumption I am exploring might be formulated along the following lines:

> Q: S's direct perceptual belief that p constitutes, at t, direct perceptual knowledge that p, only if, at t, and with respect to the direct perceptual belief that p, (i) the sense (or combination of senses) through which S believes (or appropriate to S's believing) that p is sufficiently acute to enable S to distinguish the object or property in question from things S might confuse it with in the circumstances; (ii) this sense or combination of senses is not relevantly abnormal; (iii) S's perceptual circumstances are appropriate; (iv) S's responses to his sense impressions are not relevantly abnormal; and (v) S does not unjustifiably believe, or would not be unjustified if, in the perceptual situation he is in at t, he did believe, any of (i), (ii), (iii), and (iv).[22]

In our example, S is hallucinating barn surfaces without knowing it, in such a way that, since clause (ii) is not satisfied, the presumption Q expresses is false. Q thus provides a prima facie explanation of why S's direct justified true belief that a is a woody-looking surface is defeated.

Let us now consider a case in which clauses (i) through (iv) are satisfied, but S is unjustified in believing them, so that clause (v) is not satisfied. Suppose S's senses return to normal, though no one yet knows this; and imagine that S has not realized he has been hallucinating, but *should* have realized it because credible witnesses have told him so. Let us assume that he argues against their testimony plausibly, but inconclusively. We might suppose that he has good reasons to believe his senses are normal, yet is not justified in believing this because his reasons are still not good enough to warrant his rejecting the testimony. He might nevertheless be justified in believing that *a* is a barn, at least where the testimony of his senses to this effect is vivid and steady. For given his firm belief, based on good reasons, that his senses are (relevantly) normal, one can hardly fault him for accepting their vivid steady testimony. It seems, however, that his justified true belief that *a* is a barn is not *knowledge*. The reason is apparently that he is *unjustified* in believing the (true) presumption that his senses are normal.

This sort of example is important for justificationists. If there were no such cases, the presumption they appeal to in dealing with defeated direct knowledge might be held to require no use of the notion of justification. That would not imply that all defeated knowledge could be accounted for on non-justificationist lines, but it would weaken their case for the view that defeated knowledge is best understood on a justificationist theory.

We should also consider how Q might apply to cases like that of Henry if the relevant belief is construed as direct. Suppose that Henry's belief that *a* is a barn is not based on any other belief of his. Notice first that the presence of barn facsimiles is a feature of Henry's circumstances. Similarly, if we imagine him observing a candle through a system of mirrors, as described above, their presence would also be what I am calling a circumstance. Now with respect to the circumstances involving the facsimiles, his senses will not be sufficiently acute. He would confuse facsimiles with barns at the distance in question. Thus, by clause (i) of Q, Henry's belief does not constitute knowledge. Regarding the example involving the mirrors, his perceptual circumstances are not appropriate to the belief in question. Judging location through a complicated system of mirrors of the sort imagined is somewhat like judging color in red light. Here, then, Henry would not satisfy (iii) of Q.

These conditions, like (ii) and (iv), are related to, and to some extent unified by, the idea of justification at least in the following way: if Henry *believed* that his circumstances were as they are in relation to the beliefs in question, he would not be justified in holding them. More generally, it is at least often the case that what undermines S's would-be knowledge without undermining his justification *would* undermine his justification if he believed it. And this makes it natural to say, though it does not require us to say, that much defeated knowledge is defeated because S's *justification* is in some way insecure or defective.

4. RELIABILITY AND JUSTIFICATIONIST THEORIES COMPARED

We have seen how some representative naturalistic and some representative justificationist principles can deal with certain cases of defeated knowledge. I now want to consider some of the relative merits of these approaches to defeated knowledge, focusing mainly on Goldman's position and the justificationist proposal employing principles P and Q.

One thing the positions have in common is neutrality with respect to skepticism. Neither approach favors skepticism or rules it out. Skeptics might accept Goldman's view and then take S's (apparent) knowledge that a is a barn to be defeated by even the mere possibility of a barn facsimile which S cannot visually distinguish from a real barn. They might also accept P and then construe the mere possibility of such facsimiles as showing that S is mistaken (or unjustified) in taking the proposition that over there is a barnlike surface, to warrant the proposition that the object over there is a barn, so that he fails to satisfy (iv) of P. Moreover, though neither of the approaches favors skepticism, both make it easy to see how skepticism can be plausible.

What is the reason for these and other similarities between the approaches? Could it be in part that our intuitions about what alternatives are relevant to indirect justified true perceptual beliefs are based on our intuitions about what alternatives would either (a) undermine S's *justification* for taking some proposition to warrant the proposition about the object (e.g., that it is a Selectric), or (b) falsify the proposition that the former does warrant the latter? Similarly, regarding direct justified true perceptual beliefs, are our intuitions about what alternatives are relevant to whether the belief is knowledge based on our intuitions about the satisfaction of Q or something like it? Since 'relevant alternatives' is an undefined term of art, these questions are problematic. But given the possible justificationist explanations of defeated knowledge we have considered, some burden of showing that the answers are negative, or at least that the terms can be explicated without tacit reliance on justificationist notions, seems to rest on those who hold that the notion of a relevant alternative can be naturalistically analyzed.

Let us suppose, however, that an adequate non-justificationist account of relevant alternatives can be given. Would this be a better account than any justificationist account? This is a large question. I shall simply ask whether there are cases of defeated knowledge which a highly plausible naturalistic account like Goldman's does not explain in as theoretically satisfactory a way as some justificationist accounts. There may be such cases. Consider one of Goldman's own examples involving identical twins:

> Suppose Sam's "schemata" of Judy and Trudy have hitherto been indistinct, so Judy-caused percepts sometimes elicit Judy-beliefs and sometimes Trudy-beliefs, and similarly for Trudy-caused percepts. Today Sam falls down and hits his head. As a consequence a new feature is "added" to his Judy-schema, a mole-associated feature. From now on he will believe someone to be Judy only if he has the sort of percept that would be caused by a Judy-like person with a mole over the left eye. Sam is unaware that this change has taken place and will remain unaware of it, since he isn't conscious of the cues he uses. Until today, neither Judy nor Trudy has had a left-eyebrow mole; but today Judy happens to develop such a mole.[23]

To rule out Sam's knowing the twin with the mole to be Judy, Goldman adds to his account of non-inferential perceptual knowledge the condition that "S's propensity to form an F-belief as a result of percept P has an appropriate genesis."[24]

Goldman does not offer an account of an appropriate genesis. Perhaps a plausible naturalistic account can be given, but apparently none has been developed to date. Let me suggest, however, that some justificationist conceptions of knowledge enable us to account for the case reasonably well. Consider several variants of it.

Suppose first that Sam knows at the time of the accident that he has been unable to tell Judy from Trudy. Then, even after the accident he is not justified in believing, of Judy with the mole, that she is Judy (assuming he has not forgotten his previous inability to tell them apart). This shows that even very high reliability does not entail justification.

Suppose, on the other hand, that Sam has seen only Judy and has not the slightest inkling that Trudy exists. Then, when he sees Judy, he presumably is justified in believing her to be Judy. Again there are two cases. First, there is the sort of case Goldman seems to be imagining: Sam directly believes her to be Judy; and although this is in part because the relevant percept has the mole feature, no inference occurs. Alternatively, Sam may indirectly believe her to be Judy on the basis of taking her to have the mole feature. The latter case could well occur if Sam has come to believe, just after the accident, that he will have to identify Judy at a masquerade party where her face will be heavily made up. Because of the accident, he believes that she has a mole, and when he sees her he takes her to be Judy, believing this, not directly, but on the basis of seeing (and believing) her to have the mole.

In the case involving direct justified belief, we have defeated knowledge. Yet Sam's belief is perfectly reliable; and he has the relevant discriminative powers. Why is it not knowledge? Q would explain this as follows. First, surely Sam's cognitive responses to his senses are abnormal, with respect to a direct perceptual belief that a is F, when an essential part of what causes the belief is the sort of feature of the a-percept which the mole-feature represents. For one thing, it has not been acquired through any perceptual experience, on Sam's part, of a. Nor has the property in question been otherwise appropriately associated with a, e.g. through someone's telling Sam that a has the feature. Intuitively, the idea is that a new feature of one's a-percept does not normally become a necessary or sufficient condition for one's perceptually believing a to be F unless one has *associated* the feature with F or with at least one other a-feature in virtue of which one takes a to be F. This certainly seems to hold when we can say that S knows a to be F *by* the feature in question. One could account for this idea by saying that only by some such association would one's belief that a is F, if based on this feature, be *reliable*, or by saying that only by some such association could one be justified, by virtue of this feature, in taking a to be F.

Our construal involving indirect belief does not embody defeated knowledge, since Sam is not justified in believing, of the woman with the mole, that she is Judy. On the other hand, P can explain why in this case he would not know that she is Judy, even if this belief were not only justified but also reliable and backed by adequate discriminative capacities. For Sam is not justified in believing that only a Judy-like person with a mole is Judy; nor is he justified even in taking the mole to be evidence that its bearer is Judy.

Let us see whether Swain's justificationist account of knowledge can also deal with the mole example, construed in any of the ways I have sketched. There are at least two ways Swain might proceed. First, the causal chain from the mole state of affairs to Sam's belief, of Judy, that she is Judy, might be defective in Swain's sense. For perhaps Sam would be (a) justified in believing, say, that the state of affairs, an accidentally acquired neural property's causing him to be such that he will perceptually take a Judy-like person to be Judy only if she has a mole, did not occur, and (b) justified in believing, of Judy, that she is Judy, only if he would be justified in believing that this state of affairs did *not* occur. It is not clear to me whether Sam satisfies these conditions. For one thing, is it essential to Sam's justification for believing the woman with the mole to be Judy that he would be justified in believing that no such intermediary occurred? And under what conditions would he have to be justified in believing this? Under conditions as they are at the time, if he believed this I suppose he would be justified.

Imagine, however, that someone has told Sam of the strange accident and given him reasons to believe it occurred which he should accept but stubbornly rejects. Now Sam would not be justified in believing that the relevant state of affairs did not occur. He would then apparently not satisfy the condition of Swain's which might otherwise rule out Sam's knowing. Swain would need, I think, to appeal to another of his conditions. Perhaps the state of affairs, Trudy-with-a-mole, would qualify as a significant alternative to the one actually obtaining. To be sure, this state of affairs does not seem objectively likely. However, Swain says, of the objective likelihood of an alternative, only that it is "not *clear* that the objective likelihood of an alternative is necessary for its significance."[25] Since Trudy-with-a-mole apparently might be a significant alternative even if its objective likelihood is small, and since Swain's account can deal with the example just sketched only by construing this state of affairs as a significant alternative, it would seem that Swain should not take objective likelihood to be necessary for significance, even though this leaves his account less definite. Thus interpreted, the account can deal with this and similar examples.

The last few paragraphs have described how a hard case might be treated using (a) Goldman's reliability account of non-inferential perceptual knowledge, (b) principles P and Q, and (c) some of Swain's principles. With this case the latter two sets of principles seem to provide more understanding of why the subject lacks knowledge. I now want to take up a further question that is suggested by this apparent finding: Can the (partial) account of defeated knowledge provided by P and Q give us a reasonable way of characterizing a relevant alternative with respect to perceptual beliefs? Could it be that whenever we find a relevant alternative in such cases, S fails to satisfy P or Q, and that whenever S fails to satisfy P or Q with respect to a justified true perceptual belief, we have defeated knowledge? If this hypothesis is true, P and Q may be taken to give some account of the notion of a relevant alternative for perceptual beliefs. I am not sure that they do, and if they do they are admittedly not much less vague than that notion as introduced by Goldman; but the above hypothesis is to some degree confirmed by the fairly wide range of examples we have considered.

Similarly, P and Q appear capable of enhancing our understanding of what Swain calls a significant alternative. For one thing, they help us see what *sorts* of things make alternatives significant. Roughly, significant alternatives are states of affairs such that (a) they might have occurred instead of certain states of affairs that did occur in the actual causal chain terminating with S's belief that p, and (b) S would not be justified in believing that p if he were justified in believing one (or more) of the former states of affairs to have occurred. If principle Q is correct, then among the former (the defeating states) are states of affairs involving deficiencies in perceptual capacity relative to the belief that p; perceptual abnormalities; untoward perceptual circumstances; and abnormal responses to one's sense impressions. It would be easy to exaggerate the degree to which our understanding of these notions is independent of examples like those we have been working with; but this seems true of all the plausible theories currently in the literature, and if so then even a tentative categorization like the one embodied in Q is worth taking seriously.

It may be objected, however, that P and Q readily lend themselves to a reliability interpretation, so that if they do give an account of relevant alternatives it need not be justificationist. Consider P first. It might be argued, with respect to the justificationist clauses, that in place of (ii) one could put 'S's belief that q is reliable', that one could eliminate (iii), and that in place of (iv) one could put 'in the circumstances S is in at t, q is a reliable indication of p'. Regarding Q, it might be held that for 'S unjustifiably believes, or would be unjustified in believing' one could substitute 'S has an unreliable belief, or would have an unreliable belief'. Would P and Q lose any of their explanatory power if we made these substitutions? To argue that each of the substitutions would produce a significant loss would require a long discussion. I shall make just one point about each principle.

First, it seems doubtful that the notion of warranting in P can be naturalistically analyzed. We might, at least in certain cases, give a naturalistic *explanation* of why a belief is warranted, but that is a different matter. One might try to produce a naturalistic analysis by explicating 'q is a reliable indication of p' as equivalent to 'q strictly implies or inductively supports p'. But not just any degree or kind of inductive support will do. The support must be *adequate*; and it is not clear that such adequacy can be explicated independently of justificationist notions. One reason for saying this emerges if we ask how reliable a belief has to be to count as knowledge. Consider Henry. Suppose he can, in the relevant kind of situation, distinguish barns from facsimiles 95 percent of the time. Have we any way of saying whether this is good enough for knowledge without simply relying on our intuitions about knowledge or justification? Could it be that our intuitions about adequate reliability are guided by, or even dependent on, our sense of (1) whether in the circumstances Henry's discriminative powers are such that for him the proposition that over there is a woody-looking barnlike surface *warrants* the proposition that *that* (the thing that has the surface) is a barn, or (2) whether, if he realized there were facsimiles that he could not visually distinguish from barns at the relevant distance, he would, in the circumstances, be *justified* in taking the former proposition to warrant the latter? One might avoid this move by requiring, as Dretske does, that knowledge be based on "conclusive reasons."[26] For then only completely reliable beliefs would qualify. But it is surely not clear that knowledge does require conclusive reasons.[27]

Similar considerations apply to the proposed reliability construal of Q. When we ask what constitutes, e.g., an unreliable belief that one's senses are relevantly normal, it looks as if we do not have a plausible way of answering except through our intuitions about knowledge or justification. Indeed, the crucial question seems to be whether, in the circumstances, S's senses are reliable enough so that, if he knew their acuity relative to the belief that p, he would still be justified in believing that p. Thus, where S is normal but knows he has been hallucinating barns, it is only when his belief that his senses are back to normal is justified, or reliable *enough* to be justified, that he can again know an object before him to be a barn. His belief need not be completely reliable, in the sense that in the circumstances his being mistaken would be a physical impossibility; and surely, for him to know that there is a barn before him, his senses need not be so acute that, taking his acuity together with the circumstances he is in, it is physically impossible that this belief be mistaken. But it appears that the right sort of reliability may be in some way a function of S's justification for one or another belief or proposition.

One might at this point object that our intuitions about when q warrants (or justifies) p, or about when S is justified in taking q to warrant (or justify) p, are no *less* dependent on our intuitions about whether S knows that p than are our intuitions about whether S's belief that p is adequately reliable to constitute knowledge that p. But I do not think that is so. Surely one thing shown by many cases of defeated knowledge is that it *can* be quite clear that S is justified, even "fully" ("completely") justified, in the ordinary sense of this phrase, in believing that p, or in believing both that q and that q warrants p, when it is also clear that S does not know that p. Perhaps, then, justificationist accounts of defeated knowledge have greater conceptual independence of the notion of knowledge than those reliability accounts —the most plausible, I think—which do not require conclusive reasons. I cannot claim to have shown this, but given the present tendency (as I see it) to prefer reliability theories, it would be enough to have shown that the view is plausible.

Nothing I have said implies that a naturalistic or, in particular, a reliability account of knowledge cannot succeed. My negative purpose has been simply to show that, contrary to the impression many epistemologists seem to have, it is by no means clear that such accounts are superior to justificationist accounts, at least as regards explaining defeated knowledge. This conclusion would gain support if it should turn out that a reliability account—and perhaps most other plausible naturalistic accounts—of defeated knowledge can succeed only by taking knowledge to require conclusive reasons. For in that case, the positions in question face all the problems confronting the conclusive reasons thesis.

My positive aim has been to argue that principles P and Q (or something close to them) provide a useful account of some important cases of defeated knowledge. They are also meant to support my negative aim and to complement Swain's principles. To be sure, both P and Q need further clarification and further study; but that assessment seems to apply to a significant degree to all the currently available plausible accounts of defeated knowledge.

There are kinds of defeated knowledge we have not considered. Nor have we considered justificationist or naturalistic accounts of knowledge in general. But with respect to some important cases of defeated knowledge, we have seen that some justificationist accounts apparently can succeed reasonably well. And I have suggested that our intuitions about what alternatives are relevant might be based on our intuitions about whether certain beliefs are justified or on whether certain justificationist principles are satisfied. Although my arguments by no means show that no naturalistic account of relevance can be given, they do indicate the need for an explication of the notion along naturalistic lines. This is a significant point. It tends to offset what naturalists can gain by pointing out that their vocabulary is already required by the sciences, whereas justificationists need at least one normative notion. It remains to be seen which approach can give a better overall account of knowledge. But if my main points are correct, it appears that at least in dealing with some special problems of defeated knowledge, a justificationist position embodying something like principles P and Q can provide at least as good an account as the currently leading naturalistic theories.[28]

Notes

1. If the apparent distinction between normative and non-normative concepts cannot be sustained, then the contrast between naturalistic and justificationist approaches must be drawn differently. I believe this could be done, but I cannot go into the matter here.

2. See, e.g., Marshall Swain, "Reasons, Causes, and Knowledge," *Journal of Philosophy* 75, no. 5 (1978):229-49; Alvin I. Goldman, "Discrimination and Perceptual Knowledge," *Journal of Philosophy* 73, no. 20 (1976):771-91; Gilbert Harman, *Thought* (Princeton, 1973); John Barker, "What You Don't Know Won't Hurt You?" *American Philosophical Quarterly* 13, no. 4 (1976): 303-8; and Peter Klein, "Knowledge, Causality, and Defeasibility," *Journal of Philosophy* 73, no. 20 (1976):792-812.

3. Goldman, "Discrimination and Perceptual Knowledge," p. 776. Some of the ideas in this paper of Goldman's are discussed or developed in his more recent "What Is Justified Belief?" forthcoming in George S. Pappas, ed., *Justification and Knowledge* (Dordrecht and Boston, 1979). In what follows I try to take some account of Goldman's later paper, particularly in constructing naturalistic interpretations of some justificationist terms. But to discuss that paper seriously would take considerable space and is not required by my purposes here.

4. *Ibid.*, p. 773.

5. *Ibid.*, esp. pp. 785-86. Intuitively, a state of affairs, e.g. S's perceiving *b*, is perceptually equivalent to the state of affairs, S's perceiving *a*, provided S cannot perceptually distinguish between the two. Goldman actually offers conditions necessary *and* sufficient for S's having noninferential knowledge, of *a*, that it is *F*; but only the condition cited in the text need concern us here. Goldman also formulates his conditions for *de re* belief, whereas, for the most part, I shall speak of Henry's (*de dicto*) belief that *a* is a barn. This distinction is important, but for our purposes the more convenient *de dicto* locutions are adequate.

6. *Ibid.*, p. 789.

7. D. M. Armstrong, *Belief, Truth, and Knowledge* (Cambridge, 1973), p. 182.

8. Goldman seems to think that Armstrong's account, at least in its earlier form in *A Materialist Theory of the Mind* (London, 1968), pp. 189-93, cannot deal with such cases. But Goldman's reason for saying this is apparently different from the one suggested here; see "Discrimination and Perceptual Knowledge," esp. p. 779.

9. Armstrong, *Belief, Truth, and Knowledge*, pp. 163-65. Armstrong suggests, e.g., that when we have ordinary perceptual knowledge of a dog, "the presence of a *whole* dog is inferred from more elementary information" (p. 165).

10. *Ibid.*, pp. 171-74.

11. Barker, "What You Don't Know Won't Hurt You?" p. 303.

12. Swain, "Reasons, Causes, and Knowledge," p. 240.

13. *Ibid.*, p. 233.

14. *Ibid.*, p. 238.

15. Goldman, "Discrimination and Perceptual Knowledge," pp. 787-88. (The example is from a paper of Swain's.)

16. It is very difficult to explicate the notion of one belief's being based on another, and few philosophers have offered detailed accounts of the notion. One plausible account is Armstrong's; see *Belief, Truth, and Knowledge*, esp. chap. 14. The notion is also discussed extensively by George S. Pappas in "Basing Relations" (unpublished) and at some length in my "Psychological Foundationalism," *The Monist* 61, no. 4 (1978). For the purposes of this paper, the brief characterization in the text will serve.

17. A more complicated principle is required to deal with cases in which S's belief that p is based on one or more of his other beliefs, where none of this set is a necessary condition for his believing p. At least conditions (i) and (iii), moreover, are controversial. Condition (i) might be held to be too strong because q could be a conjunction with one false conjunct whose *other* conjuncts warrant p sufficiently to enable S to know it despite the error. Condition (iii) would be denied by most reliability theorists, on the ground that if (iv) holds (iii) need not. If the first objection is correct, P can, I believe, accommodate it with minor revision. If the second objection is correct, a more significant change in P would be needed. I am not at all sure that the second objection can be met, but in any case little in this paper turns on clause (iii).

18. Lehrer, at least, has tried to do something that appears to give some support to this, in connection with his example of the gypsy lawyer. See Keith Lehrer, *Knowledge* (Oxford, 1974), pp. 122-26. In my "Psychological Foundationalism," cited in note 16, I have tried to indicate some difficulties raised by this move.

19. See Harman, *Thought*, esp. chaps. 9-11.

20. In "The Limits of Self-Knowledge," *Canadian Journal of Philosophy* 4, no. 2 (1975): 253-67, I have argued that the view is mistaken.

21. Cp. Barker's similar notion of a presupposition of S's; "What You Don't Know Won't Hurt You?" p. 305.

22. Q requires several comments. If perceptual knowledge of objects is in some (or all) cases direct, Q would still apply to it. Q does not require that any particular kind of perceptual knowledge be direct or indirect. With minor revisions, it would apparently hold for indirect knowledge also. Regarding (v), I shall take it to be satisfiable by appropriate *de re* beliefs, e.g. by S's believing his senses *to be* normal. The reference in (ii) to a combination of senses is meant to accommodate cases in which, e.g., S acquires perceptual knowledge, from a distance, that a is a horse, only by virtue of jointly seeing the appropriate shape and hearing the appropriate hoof sounds. Concerning (ii), the notion of a perceptual circumstance is somewhat vague; but no point in this paper will turn on its vagueness.

23. Goldman, "Discrimination and Perceptual Knowledge," p. 789.

24. *Ibid.*, p. 789.

25. See Swain, "Reasons, Causes, and Knowledge," p. 240.

26. See Fred Dretske, "Conclusive Reasons," *Australasian Journal of Philosophy* 49 (1971): 1-22.

27. Some of these difficulties are brought out by George S. Pappas and Marshall Swain in "Some Conclusive Reasons against 'Conclusive Reasons'," *Australasian Journal of Philosophy* 51 (1973):72-76.

28. An earlier version of this paper was given at the University of Minnesota, Morris, and I profited from discussing it with the faculty and students there. I have also benefited from discussion with Alvin Goldman at the time he presented "Discrimination and Perceptual Knowledge" at the University of Nebraska, and that paper did much to generate my interest in doing this one. For helpful comments on earlier versions of this paper, I am also grateful to William Alston, Panayot Butchvarov, George Pappas, Mark Pastin, Thomas Vinci, and Howard Wettstein.

The Multi-Perspectival Theory of Knowledge

MARK PASTIN

Epistemology aims to understand the concept of knowledge. To understand what knowledge is it is necessary to understand what justified belief is. This is not because justified belief is necessary for knowledge in *every* case; I consider cases of knowledge without justified belief later. But in most cases of knowledge, justified belief is necessary for knowledge. The concept or concepts of justification focus the interest of epistemologists. The other components of knowledge, which include at least true belief, are investigated in general metaphysics and in philosophy of mind. Further, our only approach to truth in our beliefs is through justified believing. These considerations underscore the peculiarity of some recent developments in epistemology. Reflection on Gettier examples, examples of social factors influencing knowledge, and examples of discriminative capacities influencing knowledge have led some epistemologists to turn away from concepts of justification and toward concepts of reliability, discrimination among relevant alternatives, and optimal explanation. Often concepts of justification are completely bypassed, with knowledge being explained in terms of these new concepts. But even if these new concepts are taken to explicate a sort of "nouveau-justification," and knowledge is then explained in terms of this nouveau-justification, there is a significant reorientation in understanding of the sort of justification that is relevant to knowledge. I shall argue that these approaches are unsatisfactory, that they fail to explain the cases they are intended to explain, and that a good explanation of these cases is possible without appeal to justification-surrogate or nouveau-justification concepts. I shall offer an account of knowledge, the multi-perspectival account, in which most any traditional concept of justification can be employed, but which relates justification to knowledge in a more illuminating way than a typical justified, true belief approach does. The proposed relation between justification and knowledge enables the multi-perspectival account to explain cases of the above sorts as well as other problem cases.

The strategy is as follows: First, I survey examples of the kinds motivating appeal to justification-surrogate and nouveau-justification concepts. These examples must be addressed by any adequate account of knowledge. I then raise a basic problem for attempts to account for these examples in terms of justification-surrogate and nouveau-justification concepts. I offer an account of knowledge, or, more accurately, of knowledge *attributions*. The account aims to explain the problem cases within a general framework for understanding knowledge assessment. While the multi-perspectival account of knowledge is not a justified, true belief account, it neither appeals to justification-surrogate or nouveau-justification concepts nor, on the reading I favor, adds a fourth condition for knowledge. Finally, the multi-perspectival account of knowledge is assessed. In one sense, the multi-perspectival account yields a no-knowledge view. Knowledge attributions turn out to be indexical and "soft," as well as multi-perspectival. What is said in attributing knowledge depends on contextual factors—on who attributes the knowledge when. There is no fact of the matter as to whether or not a person knows something simpliciter. And knowledge attribution requires—in usual cases—consideration of the "evidential perspectives" of several persons. Rather than continuing to frighten you with bizarre features of my account, I shall let it speak for itself after a look at some examples and other approaches.

1. REVIEW OF DATA

I consider three types of examples that are often cited as grounds for abandoning a justificationist approach to explaining knowledge in favor of reliability, discrimination among relevant alternatives, or optimal explanation approaches.

Gettier cases are the most familiar. A standard case goes as follows: A person S truly believes *that Jones owns a Ford* (F) or *that Brown is in Barcelona* (B). S has evidence justifying F and S believes F. S infers F-or-B from F and thereby justifiably believes F-or-B. F is false, but B, for which S has no evidence, is true. It follows that S has justified, true belief in F-or-B. But S does not know F-or-B. To meet such problems some epistemologists add a fourth condition to a justified, true belief account of knowledge. These attempts suffer from seeming ad-hoc-ness and are open to counterexamples—thus the attractiveness of nonstandard approaches to explaining knowledge.

Examples of the second type to be considered can be called "social cases." These examples involve defeat of a knowledge attribution by evidence that the purported knower does not have. Gilbert Harman has brought these cases to the attention of epistemologists.[1] One such case: S reads in a reliable newspaper *that a dictator has been assassinated* (A). The story is true and was written by a reporter who witnessed the assassination. S justifiably and truly believes A. In addition to the reporter who wrote the story read by S, a number of other reporters witnessed the assassination. These reporters agree among themselves that it would be in the public interest to deny that the assassination occurred, and they issue denials that there has been an assassination. S is in the company of a number of people who are aware of these unrefuted denials, and they either believe that there has been no assassination or do not know what to think. If S were to pay attention to these people, or learn about the denials in some other way, he too would not believe A. But S does not learn of the denials. S's justified, true belief does not constitute knowledge. How can S know, whereas the other people do not, when the only difference between S and the others is that S lacks evidence the others have? Since S has justified, true belief in A but does not know A, it would seem that something beyond or other than justification is needed for S to know A.

Finally, there are discrimination cases of the sort described by Alvin Goldman.[2] Suppose that it visually appears to S *that there is a barn alongside the road* (B). S is an ordinary reliable perceiver, and there is in fact a barn alongside the road where S seems to see a barn. S justifiably and truly believes B. Unknown to S, there are also a number of very realistic barn facsimiles alongside this road, and S would visually take any one of these facsimiles to be a real barn. But if S cannot visually distinguish the real barn from the facsimiles, then, despite justified, true belief in B, S does not know B. Given that S lacks nothing by way of justification for B, it seems that his lack of knowledge cannot be explained in terms of justification.

2. JUSTIFICATION SURROGATES AND NOUVEAU JUSTIFICATION

I now offer a cartoon-stroke impression of accounts of knowledge in terms of justification-surrogate and nouveau-justification concepts. I show how these accounts attempt to explain the above cases and raise a problem for the explanation offered by these accounts. I consider accounts of knowledge in terms of reliability, ability to discriminate among relevant alternatives, and inference to the best total explanation.

First, consider the reliability account, a version of which has been ably defended by D. M. Armstrong.[3] On this account, person S knows proposition P only if S's belief in P is a reliable indication within a certain range of circumstances that P is the case. S's belief in P must be formed in such a way that it is nomically necessary within a certain range of circumstances that if S believes P then P is true. It is too much to require that S's belief reliably indicate that P is true whatever the circumstances, since *any* belief-forming process is unreliable with respect to a given proposition in *some* circumstances.

The defender of the reliability approach will argue that S's belief is unreliable in each of the problem cases. In the Gettier case S's belief does not reliably indicate the truth of F-or-B since S would believe as he does if B were false. The truth of B is not effective in forming S's belief in F-or-B. S is arguably unreliable in the social case since S would believe A even if those unrefuted denials of A accessible to S were true. S would believe the newspaper report of A even if it were incorrect and the sources that deny A were correct. In the discrimination case S is clearly unreliable since he would believe as he does if he were in the presence of a barn facsimile instead of a real barn.

Next, consider the discrimination account, versions of which have been proposed by Alvin Goldman and Gail Stine.[4] On this account, S knows P only if S can distinguish cases in which P is true from relevant alternative cases in which P is false. There is an obvious parallel between the discrimination account and the reliability account—roughly, S's belief in P is reliable in set of circumstances C just in case S is able to discriminate those circumstances in C where P is true from those where P is false. Thus one expects explanation of problem cases to be about the same on these two accounts. The discrimination account maintains that S does not know in the Gettier case because S cannot discriminate the actual case in which F-or-B is true from otherwise similar, relevant alternative cases in which both B and F-or-B are false. S fails to know in the social case because he cannot distinguish the present case in which the newspaper report of S is true and the accessible denials are false from relevant alternative cases in which the newspaper report is false and the denials are true. In the barn case—obvious grist for the discrimination account mill—S does not know because he cannot distinguish barns from nearby barn facsimiles.

Finally, consider the best explanation account, versions of which have been well defended by Gilbert Harman, and recently by Michael Williams.[5] On this approach, S knows P only if P is part of a true, maximal, and optimally explanatory view which is (properly) based on what S believes. This is more a caricature than a sketch of the best explanation account. Features of particular versions of this account, e.g., how an explanatory view is *properly based* on S's beliefs, essential to explanation of problem cases are ignored. Explanation of problem cases is not entirely uniform as on earlier accounts. In the Gettier case the best explanation account maintains that S does not know F-or-B because no true, total view that includes B, or F-or-B, can be based on what S believes. In the social case S fails to know A because a true, maximal, optimally explanatory view would include propositions about what other sources say about A, and these propositions cannot be based on what S believes. In the discrimination case S does not know B since a true, maximal, optimally explanatory view would include propositions about barn facsimiles that cannot be based on S's beliefs.

I have been somewhat unmindful of details in characterizing accounts of knowledge in terms of justification-surrogate and nouveau-justification concepts, and in explaining how these accounts address problem cases. I think the serious problem for these accounts does not lie in detail of formulation or in how the accounts address problem cases. If the accounts are on the right track, if they appeal to the concepts appropriate for explaining knowledge, then a correct formulation in detail of an account of knowledge will follow. And I would be surprised if these accounts were not *formally* able to deal with the problem cases. This is partly because of the problem I find in these accounts.

The problem is that each account appeals to one wholly unexplicated concept, which enables the accounts to deal with the problem cases, and that this key concept cannot in turn be explicated without appeal to a concept of justification that is neither a surrogate- or nouveau-justification concept. On the reliability account, S knows P only if S's belief in P reliably indicates that P is true *in a certain range of circumstances*. Which circumstances? The circumstances must be enough like actual circumstances that the process that results in S's believing P is relevant to the truth of P in the circumstances. But the circumstances should include some enough unlike actual circumstances to offer a test of the process resulting in S's belief. As far as I can tell, the range of circumstances seems to be those circumstances consistent with S's being justified in believing P. If reliable, true belief is to constitute knowledge, the range of circumstances must be restricted to those in which S's justification in believing P is knowledge-producing. It is not surprising that the reliability account distinguishes the problem cases from clear cases of knowing.

On the discrimination account, S knows P only if S can distinguish cases in which P is true from *relevant alternative cases* in which P is false. Which cases are relevant alternative cases? Barn facsimiles are relevant to S's perceiving that this is a barn, but an evil agronomic demon is not relevant. I think that the relevant alternative cases are those compatible with S's being justified in his perceptual belief (perhaps holding S's sensory experiences and other beliefs constant so far as possible). If true belief coupled with the ability to discriminate among relevant alternatives is to yield knowledge, relevant alternative cases must be restricted to those in which S's justification for his perceptual belief is knowledge-producing justification. Again, it is no surprise that the discrimination account segregates the problem cases from uncontroversial cases of knowledge.

Finally, on the best explanation account, S knows P only if P is part of a true, maximal, best explanatory view (properly) based on what S believes. What is it for P to be part of a *best explanatory view (properly) based on what S believes*? The issue of what constitutes a best or better explanation is complex and important. This can be said—P is part of a *best* explanatory view only if P and the rest of the claims constituting the view are justified, perhaps to the maximal degree. Further, if inclusion in a true, maximal, optimal explanatory view, together with true belief, is to suffice for knowledge, it seems essential to require that P and the other claims in the view have knowledge-producing justification. This makes accounting for the problem cases easy but uninformative.

In summary, the problem with justification-surrogate and nouveau-justification accounts of knowledge is that they appeal to a "standard" concept of justification, and at just the point where a "standard" concept of justification fails in an account of knowledge. (I explain what I mean by a 'standard concept of justification' shortly.) It is clear that the accounts do appeal to an unexplicated concept of justification and that this concept is not obviously explicable as a surrogate-justification or nouveau-justification concept. Perhaps, the conclusion that appeal to this concept is in the form of knowledge-producing justification is less clear. But, if we are not to draw this conclusion, the proponents of the accounts must offer *some* measure of appropriate circumstances, relevant alternatives, or goodness of explanation. Substituting an unexplicated justification concept for a standard concept of justification, or for a standard concept of justification and the proviso that justification be knowledge-producing, is not an advance. It is a backward step if we need *both* a standard justification concept and the new "dummy" concept. The point of the account which I shall propose is that a standard justification concept alone suffices to explain knowledge and to sort problem cases from genuine cases of knowing.

The essential feature of a *standard* justification concept is that it is *perspectival*. Whether or not a proposition is justified for a person at a time, in accordance with a standard justification concept, is determined by features of the person's perspective at that time—by the person's perceptual and memory input and by what the person believes on the basis of that input. I do not intend to restrict standard justification concepts to concepts employed in some narrow range of epistemologies. No specific characterizations of perceptual input, memory input, or correct basing or reasoning are presupposed.[6] Some versions of reliability, discrimination, and best explanation knowledge accounts refer to features of a person's perspective in assessing reliability, ability to discriminate, or level of explanation. But a motivating presupposition of these accounts is that perspectival justification, the world *as presented to a person*, is not sufficient to explain knowledge.

Historically, an important problem for epistemology and metaphysics has been to discover connections between what is perspectivally justified for a person and what is the case or probably the case in the world. It clearly is logically possible for a proposition to be perspectivally justified for a person but neither true nor "objectively likely" to be true, in any respectable sense of 'objectively likely'. The problem of bridging perspectival justification and objective reality, though surely of great interest, is not our problem here.[7] A solution to that problem would not account for the relations between perspectival justification, the facts of our problem cases, and an account of knowledge. (Even if we distinguish a concept of "objective" justification that entails truth or probable truth, that by itself does not tell us how the perspectival justification on which our beliefs must be grounded, and criticized, relates to either this "objective" justification or the world.)

3. THE MULTI-PERSPECTIVAL ACCOUNT OF KNOWLEDGE

The approaches we have considered take the moral of the problem cases to be that something other than or in addition to perspectival (or standard) justification is needed to distinguish cases of true belief that are knowledge from those that are not. The problem is that epistemologists, generally, and in thinking about these problem cases, focus exclusively on what is justified *for a purported knower*. I shall propose a *necessary* condition for true knowledge attribution, the *multi-perspectivality of knowledge condition* (MP:C), which requires consideration of several persons' perspectival justification in most knowledge attributions. Particularly, MP:C requires that the perspectives of both the purported knower, to whom knowledge is attributed, and the knowledge attributor (or, in some cases, attributors) be considered. MP:C by itself suffices to account for the problem cases. But I go on to propose a multi-perspectival *account* of knowledge (MP:A) that states both necessary and sufficient conditions for true knowledge attribution. Finally, I consider an interpretation of MP:A that yields an account of the *content* of knowledge attributions, as well as of their truth conditions. In a concluding section MP:C, MP:A, and the account of the content of knowledge attributions are assessed.

The basic idea of MP:C is that of a person being able to put another person in a position to justifiably believe a proposition. I shall speak of a person (or, for later reference, another type of individual) S *at a given time t being able to inform* person

S' *at* time t' *about* a proposition P. Usually a person is able to inform someone about something by sharing his evidence on the topic with the person. When that evidence is added to the background evidence of the person, it puts the person in a position to justifiably believe the proposition in question. But a person, or individual of another type, can inform someone about a proposition merely by being a good indicator of truth in the domain of the proposition. We arrive at a good example of non-evidential informing by taking some liberties with the description of a little boy in D. H. Lawrence's story "The Rocking-Horse Winner."[8] The little boy can, while vigorously riding his rocking-horse, pick the winning horse in races at a local track. The little boy does not pick on the basis of any evidence he has—we may suppose that he does not even know that what he is doing is picking horses to win races. The little boy acquires no evidence about the outcome of his picks. Nonetheless, if we take note of the little boy's ability to invariably call the races correctly, he can put us in a position to justifiably believe that Socrates will win the seventh race. Oracles too are often described in such a way that, although they do not pronounce on the basis of evidence, they can put others in a position to justifiably believe. Thermometers, other similar instruments, and computers inform us although it can only be metaphorically claimed that the instrument or computer has evidence.

It is difficult to precisely characterize the notion of a person (or other type of individual) S at a certain time t being able to inform person S' at time t' about a proposition P. The following characterization is adequate for statement of MP:C although a refinement is needed to elevate MP:C to a full knowledge account.

> S *at* t *can inform* S' *at* t' *about* P: there is a property ϕ such that (1) S has ϕ at t, and (2) if S' should justifiably believe at t' that S has ϕ at t S' would also justifiably believe P at t'.

The consequence of clause (2) must be expanded to read: S' would also justifiably believe P at t' even if S' were not otherwise justified in believing P at t'. Having ϕ may *suffice* for S to put S' in a position to justifiably believe P even if S' already has independent evidence justifying belief in P.

This characterization would profit from clarification at several points. First, if we allow a person to have certain "funny" properties, the person will be able to inform another person about anything. If for any given true proposition P, S may have the property of existing-in-circumstances-in-which-P-is-the-case, then S can inform anyone about the truth of P. Second, if we allow S' to believe that S has ϕ under a "funny" description of S, then S will be able to inform S' about anything. If S' may justifiably believe that S has ϕ by believing that the person is who F (F uniquely applies to S) and exists while P is true (for any true P) has ϕ, then S will be able to inform S' about any true proposition P. Finally, it is unclear what it is for a certain justified belief to suffice for a person to have another justified belief. Although clarification of these points is necessary, I shall be satisfied if all that stands in the way of accepting the proposals to be made is further consideration of these points. There is no reason to think that an account of what constitutes a "funny" property or description will appeal to any concept of justification or knowledge-producing justification. A refinement of the notion of informing offered below solves some problems relating to "funny" properties. Consideration of the notion of sufficient justification is of general importance to epistemology, but particular accounts of this notion make no difference to my proposals or to an explanation of knowledge in terms of perspectival justification.[9]

I turn now to statement of the multi-perspectivality of knowledge condition, which is the heart of my proposals. It is important to note that MP:C is a *necessary* condition for the *truth* of knowledge attributions, for the truth of an attribution by person A at time t_1 of knowledge of P to S at t_2.

> (MP:C)   A's *attribution at t_1 of knowledge of* P *to* S *at t_2 is true* only if S at t_2 is able to inform A at t_1 about P.

That is: If A at t_1 truly attributes knowledge of P to S at t_2, then S at t_2 can put A in a position to justifiably believe P at t_1. MP:C is offered as a necessary condition for true knowledge attribution, and, as such, could be added to a justified, true belief account of knowledge. But a more interesting account of knowledge is obtained by taking satisfaction of MP:C together with true belief to *suffice* for true knowledge attribution.

First, let us see how MP:C addresses the problem cases. In the Gettier case the only property S has by virtue of which he could inform *us* about F-or-B is the property of having such and such evidence for F. Given the way the case is stipulated, and the fact we know that it is so stipulated, we are, despite S's evidence for F, justified in believing that F is false. Given our background evidence in this case, S cannot inform *us* about F-or-B. So according to MP:C we cannot truly attribute knowledge of F-or-B to S.

In the social case the property of S by virtue of which he *might* inform us about A is his having read the newspaper report and having certain evidence concerning the reliability of the newspaper and the reporter. But, given the description of this case, in particular, the fact that the newspaper report has been denied, without refutation, by reliable sources, this property of S cannot put us in a position to justifiably believe A. Of course, within the full description of this case, the evidence which overrides S's evidence for A is in turn overriden, but not on the basis of any property of S. S cannot inform us about A so that, according to MP:C, we cannot truly attribute knowledge of A to S.[10]

In the discrimination case the only property of S by virtue of which S might inform us about B is his having certain sensory experience and supplementary evidence concerning the reliability of this sort of experience vis à vis barn-like objects. But we cannot have a justified belief in B on this evidence, given our evidence concerning nearby barn-facsimiles which present themselves to S exactly as barns do. S cannot inform us about B so that we cannot truly attribute knowledge of B to S.

I think that MP:C gives non-ad-hoc explanations of the problem cases and that it will explain further problem cases. There is another type of case that justificationist epistemologists often ignore or discount. These are cases of knowledge without justified belief. In the conceptually possible but non-actual cases of the rocking-horse predictor and the oracle, we are inclined to attribute knowledge in the absence of justified belief. Knowledge attributions to animals, computers, and instruments such as thermometers, which have justified beliefs only in an extended sense, require explanation or at least explaining away. Even if we do not truly and literally attribute knowledge in these cases, the inclination to attribute knowledge should be explained. And we may doubt that there is actually evidence sufficient for justified belief in some cases in which knowledge is truly and literally attributed on the basis of the knower's memory. There is a tendency to scratch around for something that might serve as memory evidence in these cases, but this scratching reveals the conviction that there *must* be justification rather than the relevant justifying evidence.

If satisfaction of MP:C—together with true belief—is promoted from being a necessary condition for true knowledge attribution to being sufficient the resulting account (MP:A) of true knowledge attribution explains cases of knowledge without justified belief.

(MP:A)   A's *attribution at* t_1 *of knowledge of* P *to* S *at* t_2 *is true* if and only if (1) S believes P at t_2, (2) P is true, and (3) S at t_2 is able to inform A at t_1 about P.

Our inclination to say that the little boy knows who will win a certain race is vindicated—at least if the little boy believes his predictions—because the little boy has a property, that of being reliable with respect to local races, which qualifies him to inform us about the race winners. Something similar would be true of oracles were there any. When the recollections or "memory traces" needed to justify a person in believing something are gone, we can still truly attribute knowledge to the person provided that he is the sort of person likely, given what he once justifiably believed, to be correct about the sort of proposition in question. Conceptual stretching is involved in knowledge attributions to computers, thermometers, and animals. But the stretching is to satisfy the belief condition, not MP:C.

A qualification needs to be entered if satisfaction of MP:C, together with true belief, is taken to be sufficient for true knowledge attribution. There are many kinds of properties that a person might have in virtue of which we, given extensive background knowledge and the justified belief that the person has the property, could come to be justified in believing something. Suppose that S believes that the temperature is exactly $110°$. S has no worthy evidence for this belief and has shown no reliability concerning temperature estimates. Nonetheless, a physiologist S$'$ might be justified in believing that the temperature is exactly $110°$ on the basis of careful observation of the physical condition of S. S$'$ is not thereby in a position to truly attribute knowledge that the temperature is exactly $110°$ to S. The *way* in which an individual can inform is relevant to whether or not knowledge can be truly attributed to him. In particular, it is essential that the individual's belief in P have a role in his ability to inform an attributor about P. With this in mind, we characterize a narrower notion of informing, *cognitive* informing.

S *at* t *can cognitively inform* S$'$ *at* t$'$ *about* P: there is a property ϕ such that (1) S has ϕ and believes P at t, and (2) these two facts about S at t, jointly but not separately, would if justifiably believed by S′ at t′ suffice for S′ to justifiably believe P at t′.

This characterization ensures that the property of a person that qualifies him/her to cognitively inform someone about P be related to what the informer believes. We arrive at an improved statement of MP:A by requiring that a person to whom knowledge is truly attributed be able to *cognitively* inform the knowledge attributor.

> (MP:A/   A's *attribution at* t_1 *of knowledge of* P *to* S *at* t_2 *is true*
> Cognitive-Knowing) if and only if (1) S believes P at t_2, (2) P is true, and (3)
> S at t_2 is able to *cognitively* inform A at t_1 about P.

MP:A/Cognitive-Knowing still allows two distinct kinds of bases for truly attributing knowledge to a person: Knowledge may be truly attributed to a person on the basis of the knower having a belief that via its justification puts the attributor in a position to justifiably believe *or* on the basis of the knower having a belief that, independently of its justification, puts the attributor in a position to justifiably believe. If one finds true knowledge attribution by the latter route, as in the cases of the rocking-horse predictor and the oracle, unacceptable, the requirements for informing and true knowledge attribution can be further restricted:

> S *at* t *can evidentially inform* S′ *at* t′ *about* P: there is a property ϕ such that (1) S justifiably believes P and has ϕ at t, and (2) the fact that S has ϕ at t, conjoined with the fact that S justifiably believes P at t, but not by itself, would if justifiably believed by S′ at t′ suffice for S′ to justifiably believe P at t′.

The notion of evidential informing *allows* S to qualify as an evidential informer *solely* on the basis of evidence that S has, and independently of any reliability-inducing property (since ϕ need play no role in S's ability to inform). This possibility should not be ruled out, and indeed is paradigmatic for some epistemologists, as a proper basis for true knowledge attribution.

> (MP:A/   A's *attribution at* t_1 *of knowledge of* P *to* S *at* t_2 *is true*
> Evidential-Knowing) if and only if (1) S believes P at t_2, (2) P is true, and (3)
> S at t_2 is able to evidentially inform A at t_1 about P.

If we adopt MP:A/Evidential-Knowing, then MP:C plays the role of a fourth condition for true knowledge attribution requiring not only that P be justified for the person to whom knowledge is attributed but also that this knower be able to inform the knowledge attributor in virtue of being so justified.

Introducing the notions of cognitive and evidential informing eliminates some of the "funny" properties that allowed trivial satisfaction of the conditions for simple informing. Cognitive informing requires that the fact of the informer's believing be relevant to his ability to inform, and evidential informing requires that justified believing be similarly relevant. And these requirements are not met in the cases considered involving "funny" properties.[11]

All three versions of MP:A state necessary and sufficient conditions for true knowledge attribution. They do not say what the *content* of knowledge attributions is, what is being claimed in attributing knowledge of P to S at t. The simplest account of the content of knowledge attributions consistent with MP:A is that in attributing knowledge of P to S at t one claims that oneself, the time of attribution, S, P, and t satisfy the conditions of MP:A. Given the reference to a knowledge attributor in MP:A, it is useful to have an indexing device to indicate who is attributing knowledge (verbally or in belief) and when. Thus 'S knows P at $t_{2(A, t_1)}$' expresses a verbal or mental attribution by A at t_1 of knowledge of P to S at t_2. Our account of the content of knowledge attributions, MP:A/Content, is then stated as follows:

> (MP:A/Content)   S *knows* P *at* $t_{2(A, t_1)}$ is the assertion (or belief) by A at t_1 that (1) S believes P at t_2, (2) P is true, and (3) S at t_2 informs me [A] at t_1 about P. (Bracketed 'A' is *our* reference to A, whereas A picks himself out as 'me' or its linguistic/conceptual equivalent.)

Much needs to be said to make MP:A/Content intelligible, let alone acceptable. First, clause (3) of MP:A/Content employs a notion of actual informing as opposed to ability to inform. The notion of actual informing is easily derived from the notion of ability to inform: S at t informs S' at t' about P if there is a property ϕ such that (1) S has ϕ at t, and (2) S' justifiably believes at t' that S has ϕ at t, and this suffices for S' to justifiably believe P at t'. Notions of cognitive and evidential actual informing can be characterized in a parallel way. Second, according to MP:A/Content A's attribution of knowledge to S involves self-reference by A. The nature of self-reference is problematic, and there is always a chance that the problems will spill over into any account involving self-reference. Finally, we must consider how, given MP:A/Content, embedded (B knows that C knows that P) and iterated (B knows that he knows that P) knowledge attributions are to be explained. Extending MP:A/Content in one obvious way, and suppressing time indices, 'B knows that C knows that $P_{(A)}$' comes to '(1) B believes that C knows that $P_{(B)}$, (2) C knows that $P_{(B)}$, and (3) B informs A that C knows that $P_{(B)}$.' One may question whether the appropriate person index in (2) is always 'B' or whether it might sometimes or always be 'A' or 'A,B'. The issue of appropriate indexing here and in cases of iterated knowledge attributions (e.g., 'A' versus 'I' as indices) are complex. Finally, there is a version of MP:A/Content corresponding to each of the three versions of MP:A. These need to be spelled out. It is obvious that full development of an account of the *content* of knowledge attributions along the lines of MP:A/Content is a task for a separate essay.

4. ASSESSMENT

On all of MP:C, MP:A, and MP:A/Content, knowledge attributions are *indexical*. The truth of what is claimed in attributing knowledge depends on who the attributor is and when the attribution occurs. On MP:A/Content, the content of knowledge attributions is also indexical.[12] What is claimed in attributing knowledge is that the purported knower stands in a certain relation to me, or us, or whoever the attributor or attributors are, and to the evidence available to the attributor or attributors. On all the multi-perspectival conditions and accounts, knowledge attributions are *"soft."* There is no single fact of the matter as to whether or not S knows that P. The way to think about whether or not S knows that P is in terms of what informing, cognitive informing, and evidential informing properties S has in relation to other persons. Once these properties are specified, and it is determined whether S truly believes P, there is no other information about S relevant to whether or not S knows P. Finally, while MP:C, MP:A, and MP:A/Content clearly offer a non-standard account of knowledge-attributions, they employ only a standard, perspectival justification concept. Justification enters the picture in two ways. The justified beliefs of the knowledge *attributor* must always be considered in determining what the attributor can be informed of. And the justified beliefs of the person to whom knowledge is attributed must be considered in all cases in which the person is able to inform on the basis of what he justifiably believes. The multi-perspectival conditions and accounts, despite taking a non-traditional approach in relating justification to knowledge, vindicate the focus of epistemologists on concepts of justification and conditions under which beliefs are justified.

Beyond testing multi-perspectival conditions and accounts against the problem cases, it is hard to tell how to best assess a multi-perspectival view. Some epistemologists to whom I have tried to explain these conditions and accounts simply find them "offensive to their intuitions" or, in Berkelean terms, "manifestly repugnent." I think that these reactions are based on a simplistic view of linguistic and conceptual structures which supports the conviction that facts about knowledge must be non-perspectivally "objective" in the way that facts about bricks are. But is it really surprising that we have linguistic and conceptual tools for assessing the evidence and evidence-producing features of others in relation to ourselves and our own evidence?

I shall consider three particularly potent objections to a multi-perspectival view of knowledge. The first objection is that there seems to be as much arbitrariness in the appeal of MP:C or MP:A to background evidence in dealing with problem cases as there is in accounts of knowledge employing surrogate-justification or nouveau-justification concepts. Why is the evidence of the reporters who deny A relevant in the social case? Why do the barn-facsimiles, but not the possibility of an evil agronomic demon, make it impossible for S to inform us about B in the discrimination case? Can we say anything better than that the relevant evidence is that which is knowledge-producing or knowledge-defeating? I think so. I think the answer is that the relevant evidence is exactly that which affects what the knowledge attributor is *justified* in believing. In the social case, the denials of A by the reporters preclude justified belief by the knowledge attributor solely on the basis of what S has read. In the discrimination case, evidence about barn-facsimiles precludes justified belief by the knowledge attributor whereas the possibility of an evil demon does not. These answers admittedly involve an appeal to "intuition," to how we are reflectively inclined to apply concepts. But the intuitions concern only what one is justified in believing. They are *not* "intuitions" about whether justification, which is conceded to be present in problem cases, is appropriate for knowledge, and it is "intuitions" of this latter kind that undermine explanation by surrogate-justification and nouveau-justification accounts. I add tentatively that there is a sense in which appeal to background evidence in evaluation of a knowledge attribution has "widest scope." In considering whether a certain knowledge attribution is true, we must consider what *we* can be informed of. Even when we initially consider a knowledge attribution by someone else, the attribution becomes *our own*, as well as that of the other attributor, by way of our consideration of the knowledge attribution.

The second objection concerns self-attributions of knowledge and Gettier cases.[13] Suppose that S of the Gettier case says of himself "I know F-or-B." Is what S says true? To evaluate S's knowledge attribution is for *us* to consider whether S knows F-or-B, in accordance with the claim of widest scope for relevant evidence. Therefore, we must consider what S can inform us of. But then our earlier comments about this case, to the effect that S cannot inform us about F-or-B because S's evidence concerns only the discredited F, entails that the answer to the above question is "No." This is the correct answer, despite the fact that S can inform *himself* about F-or-B.

The third objection concerns knowledge attributions that are "lucky guesses."[14] Suppose that D has so little evidence concerning nuclear energy, and so little ability to comprehend evidence about nuclear energy, that no matter what S, a nuclear engineer, tells D, D will not be justified in believing propositions about nuclear energy. Let N be a proposition about nuclear energy that S truly, and with strong, unproblematic justification, believes. Although D does not even know that S is a nuclear engineer, D wildly guesses that S knows N. Does D truly attribute knowledge of N to S? One might think that with enough care a property of S can be identified in virtue of which S can inform D about N. But this ignores an assumption of this case, that D simply is too dumb to be a repository for the background information requisite to justified belief in N. I think that we, privy to the description of the case, are first inclined to hold that S knows N and that we then take it to follow that D's attribution of knowledge of N to S is true. We are right about S but wrong about D. I think that we make this mistake because our interest ordinarily is in what *we* are justified in believing given *all* the evidence available. And, if the claim of widest scope for evidence relevant to knowledge attribution is correct, and we are thus implicitly indices for any knowledge attribution we evaluate, it is even less surprising that we assess even D's attribution of knowledge in this case in terms of our own evidence.

The multi-perspectival view of knowledge presented here (MP:C, MP:A, MP:A/ Cognitive-Knowing, MP:A/Evidential-Knowing, and especially the content-interpretation MP:A/Content) requires further elucidation and defense. There are important problems concerning the nature and scope of indices, the role of self-reference, and embedded and iterated knowledge attributions. Still, I hope that this tentative presentation of a multi-perspectival view helps to establish the role of a standard justification concept in explaining knowledge attribution, in even the most puzzling cases, and to demonstrate that the problems of perception, induction, memory, and other minds do not dissolve when concepts of reliability, discrimination, and best explanation are invoked. The moral of the multi-perspectival view is that epistemic virtue is found not in one's own perspectives but in what one contributes to the perspectives of others. Here I fear that I have given you too little occasion for true knowledge attribution.

Notes

1. Gilbert Harman, "Knowledge, Inference, and Explanation," *American Philosophical Quarterly* 5 (1968):164–73, and *Thought* (Princeton, 1973), especially chap. 9.

2. Alvin I. Goldman, "Discrimination and Perceptual Knowledge," *The Journal of Philosophy* 73 (1976):771–91.

3. D. M. Armstrong, *Belief, Truth and Knowledge* (London, 1973). See also my "Knowledge and Reliability: A Study of *Belief, Truth and Knowledge*," *Metaphilosophy* 9 (1978):150–62.

4. See Goldman, "Discrimination and Perceptual Knowledge," and Gail Stine, "Skepticism, Relevant Alternatives, and Deductive Closure," *Philosophical Studies* 29 (1976):249–61. Fred Dretske defends an interesting view that shares components with both reliability and discrimination accounts in "Epistemic Operators," *The Journal of Philosophy* 67 (1970):1007–23 and "Contrastive Statements," *Philosophical Review* 81 (1972):411–37.

5. See Harman, *Thought*, and Michael Williams, *Groundless Belief* (Oxford, 1977).

6. I offer an account of perspectival justification in "A Decision Procedure for Epistemology?" *Philosophical Studies* 35 (1979): 257-268, but I am not relying on that account here. In "A Decision Procedure" I explore the advantages and problems of perspectival justification concepts having different degrees of neutrality among epistemologies.

7. I explore these issues in "Problematic Realism: The Need for Epistemology," *Justification and Knowledge*, ed. George Pappas (D. Reidel, 1974): 151-168.

8. Roderick Firth called my attention to this case in arguing that justified belief is not always necessary for knowledge.

9. I propose accounts of justifying (or warranting) and of sufficient justifying (or warranting) in "Counterfactuals in Epistemology," *Synthese* 34 (1977):479–95 and "Warranting Reconsidered," *Synthese* 37 (1978):459–64.

10. Consideration of this case suggests that MP:C entails that knowledge cannot be truly attributed in certain "extendability" cases. Suppose that S justifiably believes the true proposition N, that there are exactly nine planets. S's evidence for N is E, which is the sort of non-specific information most of us have about the number of planets. We are aware of new evidence B about a bump in Pluto's orbit. B&E supports the claim that there are ten planets and thus supports not-N. If this is the complete story, MP:C correctly prescribes that we cannot truly attribute knowledge of N to S on the basis of S's justified belief in E. Suppose we are also aware of further evidence O which shows that the "bump" is due to an observation error. E&B&O supports N. The application of MP:C in the social case suggests that we still cannot truly attribute knowledge of N to S given that his evidence is just E. E does not suffice to justify N for us. Perhaps, but not obviously. One can argue a disanalogy between this case and the social case. In the social case, the evidence that overrides the initially defeating evidence does so only by independently appealing to A. It makes S's evidence good only by making it redundant. In the "extendability" case, S's evidence is made good by showing independently of N that the apparently defeating evidence is itself defective. I believe it is possible to make this subtle difference between the cases, and application of MP:C to them, hold up. If so, it probably explains our greater inclination to attribute knowledge in this sort of "extendability" case than in social cases.

11. The introduction of these narrower types of informing does not eliminate all "funny" properties. (An even narrower type of evidential informing which leaves the property ϕ out entirely does eliminate all "funny" properties.) For instance, cognitive informing does not rule out the "funny" property of being-such-that-if-S-believes-P-then-P-is-true. The example is courtesy of Richard Creath and Gregory Fitch. Problems concerning "funny" properties and descriptions correspond to problems concerning "funny" warranting relations raised by Fred Feldman in "On the Analysis of Warranting," *Synthese* 34 (1977):497–512. Feldman's paper is a critique of my "Counterfactuals in Epistemology." My responses in "Warranting Reconsidered" should go some way toward dealing with "funny" properties and descriptions. "Funny" descriptions may also be ruled out by requiring that S′ pick out S with a name or the conceptual equivalent of a name.

12. This indexical aspect of knowledge attributions first occurred to me in discussions with Hector Castañeda and in thinking about some of J. L. Austin's comments on promising.

Michael White suggests that certain performative verbs have this sort of indexical character in "A Suggestion Regarding the Semantical Analysis of Performatives," *Dialectica* 30 (1976): 117–34. White's extension of a Stalnaker-style two dimensional semantical analysis to performative verbs may also yield a semantical analysis of knowledge attributions in accordance with MP:A/Content.

13. Romane Clark held my nose to this objection.

14. George Pappas raised this objection in correspondence.

The Standard Definition

OLIVER A. JOHNSON

I f one were to have asked a philosopher to define 'knowledge' twenty years ago, the response would probably have been short, unhesitating, and precise: Knowledge is justified true belief. Not so, however, today. Beginning in 1963, with Edmund Gettier's well-known article "Is Justified True Belief Knowledge?"[1] this *standard definition* has been subjected to attack on a variety of counts, so that it has fallen into considerable disrepute among epistemologists. In this paper I shall attempt to rehabilitate its tarnished reputation by offering and defending a somewhat chastened version of the standard definition.

I have several reasons for undertaking such a task. I think that this definition does capture, within limits that are not so broad as to be defeating, what most serious people mean by the word 'knowledge' when they are speaking seriously. Further, I think that epistemologists have succumbed to attacks on the standard definition prematurely, for the definition is by no means defenseless against criticism. More specifically, it seems to me that many would-be defenders of the definition have conceded the issue by default; rather than pointing out that the most telling criticisms made against it result from ambiguities about its meaning that are capable of satisfactory clarification, they have simply abandoned it altogether. Because I believe this last point to be of great importance, I shall devote most of my essay to it. I shall, that is, be concerned more with the clarification than with the defense of the standard definition. The form of the definition that will emerge from my analysis and which I shall, in the end, defend will thus depart substantially from many of its recent interpretations, to the extent perhaps of proving unpalatable to at least some traditional epistemologists.

To clear the ground for our analysis of the standard definition, perhaps the best way to begin is to inquire into the reasons that have led philosophers, first, to adopt such a definition and, second, to be in the process of abandoning it. It is relatively easy to state these reasons in general terms; to explain them in detail is a much more difficult task. In support of the general acceptance of the definition I think it can be said that philosophers who have adopted it would maintain that the notion of justified true belief does accurately reflect what ordinary users of English mean when they use the term 'knowledge'. In maintaining this they would appear, at least on the surface, to be right. Although the average person may not be explicitly aware of just what he intends to convey when using the noun 'knowledge'—or, perhaps more frequently, the verb 'know'—most people would, after reflection, probably agree that the standard definition does capture their intent. If this proves to be correct, the definition gains substantial support. The strength of this point is given backhanded acknowledgment by those who have challenged the definition. Taking Gettier as our example, it is clear from his paper that his dissatisfaction with the definition rests in large part on his contention that, when we probe beneath surface appearances, we find that the definition does not really capture what people intend when they use the word 'know' seriously. To support his thesis, Gettier offers two illustrations of situations in which someone believes something, his belief is true, and he is justified in believing what he does, yet no thoughtful user of English would admit that he possesses knowledge about what he believes. If Gettier's assessment is correct, I think we must agree with him that the standard definition is seriously compromised.

Clearly we are faced with a problem here, for it cannot be the case that philosophers have been right in believing that the notion of justified true belief explicates what people mean when they use the term 'knowledge', if Gettier is also right in his conclusion that it fails to explicate what they mean. I think that, to resolve this problem, we must delve quite deeply—more deeply, in fact, than most traditional epistemologists and Gettier have done—into the intricacies of the notion of justified true belief itself. Although this notion may appear initially to be free from ambiguity, closer scrutiny will, I think, reveal two alternative interpretations of it. Furthermore, an understanding of the way in which these interpretations differ from each other can provide a resolution to the controversies that have been generated by recent critics of the definition. Before I turn to these alternative interpretations, however, I should like to add a few remarks in further support of the standard definition.

If it be true, as philosophers have generally believed, that people usually do use the term 'knowledge' as equivalent in its meaning to justified true belief, it is reasonable to assume that they do not do so arbitrarily but have reasons for the way they talk. The point that I am raising about the use of the term here, it need hardly be said, is not a verbal one; I am not concerned about the *word* 'knowledge' itself. On the contrary, if I were writing in French, I could make the same point about the word *'savoir'* or, if in German, about the word *'wissen'*. When I say that people have reasons for using the term in the way they do, what I am trying to convey is this: The notion of justified true belief is important, so important that in English, as in other languages, we have developed a standard term to refer to it. The importance of the notion has a practical basis, associated ultimately with the struggle for existence. Man is distinguished by his capacity to think, which is enormous in comparison to that of other animals. Without this ability, I think it is fair to say, he would almost surely have long since gone the way of the dinosaurs. By employing our reasoning capacities in such a way that not only has ensured our survival but, beyond that, has helped us gain the benefits of civilized life that we have gradually achieved through endless millennia, we have had not only to think but to think effectively. The practical human problem can be put in the following way. Because of our mental capacities we can (unlike other animals) have beliefs. We can believe, for example, that irrigation helps the crops grow, that by sailing to the west one can arrive in the east, that the careful keeping of records helps us predict the future, and so on. But we can also believe divergent things, for example, that performing dances makes crops grow, that if one sails to the west one will fall off the rim of the world, or that by observing the stars we can predict the future. Now, through long experience, man has come to recognize that his beliefs are not neutral in value; on the contrary, some beliefs are better than others. The superior beliefs are those that are most effective in promoting the goal of survival and the higher goal of civilized life. Of the criteria that determine the practical value of our beliefs, perhaps the single most important criterion is truth. If not in every individual situation, in the long run a belief that is true is better than one that is false. True beliefs are better, ultimately, because they provide us more aid in attaining the goals for which we strive.

So much, then, for the practical importance of our having beliefs that are true and hence of our having added to our vocabulary a word to express the conception of true belief. But one further point must be made. If we agree that it is valuable to have true beliefs about things, we must still realize that, from a practical standpoint, something more is needed to permit us to exploit this value effectively. We must be able to recognize which of our beliefs are, in fact, true. If we were not able to do so, we would lack the guidance we need in order to determine which of our beliefs we should act on and which not. As a result, our beliefs would be of little practical help to us in the evolutionary process. Hence the necessity of justifying the truth of our beliefs. The process of justification is the only means we have at our disposal that can enable us to determine which of the many things we might believe are true and hence worthy of our belief and commitment to action, and which not. Thus the notion of belief whose truth is justified is of central importance not only to human existence but to the good life as well. It is not necessary to our purposes here to go into the etymological details describing how the word 'knowledge' has come, in the English language, to stand for this more complex notion of justified true belief; suffice it to say that it has. The crucial point is the importance of the more complex notion for which this word stands. Hence it warrants a word in our working vocabulary.

These brief remarks, though quite general, lend emphasis to the view that, whatever its deficiencies may prove to be, the standard definition is neither trivial nor frivolous; rather, it has its roots in a basic characteristic of the human condition. Should we be led to make modifications in that definition, therefore, we must recognize that we run the risk of ending with a concept whose meaning has lost its relevant connection with the human concerns that have generated our traditional notion of knowledge. With this caution in mind, let us now turn to the criticisms that have recently been leveled against the standard definition.

The definition has been attacked in a variety of ways. Exception has, for example, been taken to the view that knowledge is a species of beliefs or that for a belief to qualify as something we know, it must be true. However, beginning with Gettier, the criticisms that have, I think, proved most telling have concentrated on the notion of justification and the role it plays in the definition. I shall, therefore, focus my attention on it. To set the stage for our discussion, let us then agree that knowledge is a subclass of belief. A belief, to qualify as something we know, must satisfy two conditions: (1) It must be true and (2) it must be justified. I shall call these conditions, respectively, the *truth* condition and the *justification* condition of knowledge. For the reasons I have just given, I shall concentrate my remarks in what follows on the justification condition.

The first question that needs to be resolved concerns the meaning of the justification condition. When we say of a certain belief that it is a *justified* true belief, exactly what do we mean to convey by the word 'justified'? The central ambiguity in the standard definition surfaces at this point, for those who accept that definition have answered the question I have just raised in two different ways. On the one hand, some have understood the notion of justification in terms of the epistemic status of the believer. According to their interpretation, if Smith not only believes but knows that *p*, we can say of Smith's belief that *p* (1) that it is true and (2) that Smith is *justified in believing* it. This is the understanding of the justification condition assumed by Gettier in the formulation of the standard definition that he attacks in his paper "Is Justified True Belief Knowledge?"[2] He attributes the interpretation (in somewhat different formulations) to Plato, Chisholm, and Ayer.[3] On the other hand, some defenders of the standard definition have viewed the justification condition in quite another way. According to their understanding of it, if Smith not only believes but knows that *p*, we can say of his belief that *p* (1) that it is true and (2) that he *can justify it to be true*. On this interpretation, satisfaction of the justification condition is not guaranteed by the epistemic status of the believer. Rather, an additional requirement is imposed on him. He must be able to accomplish a very specific task; namely, to justify the truth of what he believes.

The difference between these two interpretations of the justification condition may not be immediately apparent; nevertheless it has, as we shall see later, important consequences. To distinguish the two more sharply from each other, we can note the following logical relationships between them: The second interpretation entails the first; if Smith can justify it to be true that *p*, it follows that he is justified in believing that *p*. However, the entailment does not work in the opposite direction. As Gettier demonstrates in his Case I,[4] even though Smith, on the basis of the evidence he has, is clearly *justified in believing* the proposition "The man who will get the job has ten coins in his pocket," he cannot *justify this to be true* because he deduces it from a proposition, which he believes on the basis of misleading evidence, which is itself false.

These two interpretations of the justification condition can, however, be distinguished from each other in a quite different way, one that will prove of considerable importance to the argument of my paper. The distinction lies in the relationship each one must assume to exist between the justification condition and the truth condition of the standard definition. On the first interpretation, this relationship is contingent. It neither follows from the fact that a belief is true that anyone is justified in believing it nor from the fact that someone is justified in believing something that what he believes is true. The second point is the crucial one; namely, that a belief's satisfaction of the justification condition does not entail its satisfaction of the truth condition. As a result we can say, without contradiction, that Smith is justified in believing that p but $\sim p$. On the second interpretation, although satisfaction of the truth condition does not entail satisfaction of the justification condition (one may believe something that is true yet not be able to justify its truth), satisfaction of the justification condition *does* entail satisfaction of the truth condition (one cannot justify the truth of a false belief). Thus we can say that if Smith can justify that his belief that p is true, his belief must be true, for the proposition "Smith can justify that p, but $\sim p$" states a contradiction. Since much of the discussion that follows will turn on this difference between the two interpretations of the justification condition, it may be convenient to give each of them a name. So I shall call them, respectively, the *contingent* interpretation and the *logical* interpretation of that condition.

Not only can the justification condition be interpreted in these two ways, but one of the interpretations is clearly preferable to the other. To see which of the two it is, we must examine both. I shall begin with the contingent interpretation. That it is beset with difficulties hardly needs remark. One of these has been illustrated by Gettier. Since his argument is short, I shall reproduce it here.

> Suppose that Smith and Jones have applied for a certain job. And suppose that Smith has strong evidence for the following conjunctive proposition:
>
> (d) Jones is the man who will get the job, and Jones has ten coins in his pocket.
>
> Smith's evidence for (d) might be that the president of the company assured him that Jones would in the end be selected, and that he, Smith, had counted the coins in Jones's pocket ten minutes ago. Proposition (d) entails:
>
> (e) The man who will get the job has ten coins in his pocket. Let us suppose that Smith sees the entailment from (d) to (e), and accepts (e) on the grounds of (d), for which he has strong evidence. In this case, Smith is clearly justified in believing that (e) is true.
>
> But imagine, further, that unknown to Smith, he himself, not Jones, will get the job. And, also, unknown to Smith, he himself has ten coins in his pocket. Proposition (e) is then true, though proposition (d), from which Smith inferred (e), is false. In our example, then, all of the following are true: (*i*) (e) is true, (*ii*) Smith believes that (e) is true, and (*iii*) Smith is justified in believing that (e) is true. But it is equally clear that Smith does not *know* that (e) is true. . . .[5]

As Gettier concludes in the passage that follows this quotation, his contention that Smith does not know that (e) is true, even though he believes it to be true and is justified in so believing, rests on his view that we should all agree with him that Smith's belief, even though it satisfies the conditions of the standard definition, is not a case of knowledge. Smith does not know that (e), because his belief that (e) is based on misleading evidence. As a result it so seriously violates our understanding of the concept of knowledge that we would refuse to use this term to describe it. I think it is generally agreed that Gettier succeeds in making his case. If so, we have good reason for rejecting the contingent interpretation of the justification condition, since it has led to the consequence that Gettier illustrates and attacks.

The contingent interpretation, moreover, is vulnerable to another objection, of a quite different kind. To appreciate this criticism it is necessary to make a few preliminary remarks on the subject of definition. Any definition, to be judged acceptable, must satisfy certain conditions. It must, for example, be non-circular. Among the conditions of a satisfactory definition is what I shall call the *applicability* criterion. If we have an object and must decide whether to describe it by a certain term, we must be able to apply the definition of that term to the object, in order to determine whether it satisfies the definition and so falls under the term. Perhaps an illustration will help here; I offer an example of a bad definition. In the folklore of World War II, when mechanical devices (guns, tanks, planes) broke down, the practice developed of attributing the failure to the activity of "Gremlins," who were said to be creatures who went about causing trouble in machines but who disappeared whenever anyone turned his gaze in their direction. Assuming that anyone ever tried seriously to attribute a mechanical failure to Gremlin activity, he would be faced with an obvious insuperable difficulty. He could never succeed in showing that the breakdown was a result of Gremlin activity, because such activity was defined in a way that made it impossible to apply the definition to any concrete case.

If the justification condition is given a contingent interpretation, the definition of knowledge that results falls into the same difficulty as that of Gremlin activity. It becomes impossible to apply it to any belief in order to decide whether that belief satisfies its conditions, hence qualifies to be called knowledge. Suppose Smith believes that p, then claims that he not only believes this but knows it. Can we test his knowledge claim? Specifically, can we determine whether his belief satisfies the conditions that define knowledge? We can begin by asking him what justifies him in believing that p. Suppose he lists his reasons and we judge them to be adequate. He is, we conclude, justified in believing that p; i.e., his belief satisfies the justification condition of knowledge. So far, so good. But Smith cannot know that p unless p is true; truth also is a necessary condition of knowledge. So we must judge p against the truth condition. How should we set about doing this? We cannot say that p satisfies the truth condition because it satisfies the justification condition; for these two conditions are, according to the contingent interpretation of the justification condition, only contingently related to each other. One may, according to this interpretation, be justified in believing a certain proposition even though that proposition is false. And this may be the case with p. If it is, Smith cannot make good his claim to know that p because he has not shown that p satisfies the truth condition of knowledge.

The only apparent way to solve this problem is to adopt the position that one can determine the question whether a belief satisfies the truth condition of knowledge by some means that is independent of one's determination that it satisfies the justification condition. Some epistemologists, at least, claim that this can be done. The question is, How? Since, by hypothesis, the justification condition has been satisfied, no appeal could be made to any reasons that would support the truth of the belief in question. The only alternative left to the believer would be to claim that he recognizes the truth of his belief directly; it is, as philosophers once said, self-evidently true. I shall call this view *intuitionism*, using the term in a broad sense, to refer to any alleged direct recognition of the truth or falsity of a belief, whether this be accomplished by empirical inspection, intellectual cognition, feeling, or in some other way.

The appeal to intuition, as a way of establishing the truth of our beliefs, is, unfortunately, subject to overwhelming objections. In the first place, the notion of self-evident truth cannot be maintained; beliefs simply do not come with the labels 'True' or 'False' affixed to them. Furthermore, when we examine the activity of intuition, as it is used in this context as a way of guaranteeing truth, we run into logical difficulties. Intuition is some kind of activity performed by the believer, whether it be an act of sense perception, or of mental cognition, or something else. Generalizing, we can say that it is a psychological activity. There is no difficulty in our agreeing that such activities do occur; the question at issue is whether their occurrence can establish the truth of any proposition.[6] It can, only if the following proposition states a contradiction: A intuits that $p \cdot \sim p$. But obviously this proposition is self-consistent. To see this, let us flesh it out a bit. When we do, we get something like this: "Smith engages in a kind of psychological activity, which he calls 'intuition' and which consists in his believing (very strongly) that the proposition 'Jones will get the job' is true and that the proposition 'Jones will get the job' is false." The consistency between the two parts of this proposition is apparent; the fact that Smith engages in some kind of psychological activity exercises no logical constraint on a third person's decision about whether or not to offer a job to Jones. Furthermore, the same logical difficulty remains whatever the content of what anyone alleges that he intuits to be true may be.

But here an intuitionist might object, arguing that one *cannot* intuit a proposition to be true unless it is true, hence that the fact of intuition establishes the fact of truth. My response would be twofold. In the first place, the claim is question-begging. If intuition is an activity of the believer, the conclusion I have already reached stands; the fact that an individual is in a certain psychological state, no matter what the word that is used to describe this state, is insufficient to guarantee the truth of a proposition he believes. To claim that it can provide a guarantee, on the grounds that no such act can occur unless the proposition believed is true, is to change the meaning of "intuition." It is no longer simply a description of a psychological activity but has become much more than this. And the "more" that it has become—namely, the direct recognition of the truth of a proposition—begs the question at issue because it assumes that the propositions so "intuited" are true without offering any reasons to support this assumption. If, indeed, propositions came labeled with their truth values, such an assumption would be justified, but unfortunately, as I have already remarked, they do not. In the second place, philosophers (and others) have claimed, on the basis of an appeal to direct intuition, that a wide variety of different propositions are true. Sometimes the propositions claimed to be true are logically inconsistent with each other.[7] But of two propositions inconsistent with each other, one must be false. A method, claimed to be a guarantor of truth, that yields false propositions as true can hardly claim our allegiance.

To recapitulate the argument of the last few pages, we can sum up as follows: If its justification condition is given a contingent interpretation, the standard definition of knowledge is rendered useless. We cannot apply it to any belief in order to answer the question: Does this belief constitute knowledge or doesn't it? Although a decision can be reached regarding the belief's satisfaction of the justification condition, the definition offers no method by which any decision can be reached regarding its satisfaction of the truth condition. The person who, on the basis of this interpretation, claims not only to believe something but to know it as well is thus caught in the same predicament as the World War II mechanic who claimed that the malfunctioning of some motor was a result of Gremlin activity.

Let us now turn to the logical interpretation of the justification condition, beginning our examination by raising the same two objections against it that I have just found to be decisive against the contingent interpretation. Turning first to Gettier's argument, would we, if we applied the logical interpretation, be led to call beliefs like that of Smith in Case I examples of knowledge? To repeat, the situation, as Gettier describes it, is this: Smith believes that the man who will get the job for which he has applied has ten coins in his pocket. His reasons for believing this are that (a) the president of the company has assured him that Jones will be hired and (b) he has just counted the coins in Jones's pocket and found ten. From these premises he infers his conclusion. Although Smith's conclusion is true, it is not Jones but Smith himself who will get the job. Although he is not aware of it, he too has ten coins in his pocket and the president changes his mind and decides to hire him rather than Jones. As I said earlier, I think Gettier is right in concluding that Smith does not *know* that the person who will get the job has ten coins in his pocket. This leads us to the critical question: What would we say about the knowledge-status of Smith's belief if we give the justification condition a logical (rather than a contingent) interpretation? According to the logical interpretation, Smith's belief will qualify as knowledge only if he can justify it to be true. As Gettier's Case I stands, Smith would proceed to do this by the following argument:

(1) The man who will get the job is Jones.

(2) Jones has ten coins in his pocket.

(3) The man who will get the job has ten coins in his pocket.

Although Smith's argument is formally valid, this is not in itself enough to establish the truth of its conclusion. Something more is required, namely, that both its premises be true. But premise (1) is false. Hence Smith has failed to justify the truth of his (true) belief, stated in (3). His belief, as a result, cannot qualify as knowledge, according to the logical interpretation of the justification condition. So that interpretation escapes the criticism embodied in Gettier's Case I.

The question could, of course, still be raised: Granted that the logical interpretation does not fall prey to Gettier's Case I, might it not succumb to some other ingenious counterexample of a similar kind? Although it is difficult to answer such a hypothetical question in the absence of a specific counterexample, I think we can at least say the following: The point of Case I lies in the fact that Smith believes what is true by accident; in normal (i.e., non-rigged) situations, his belief that the man who would get the job has ten coins in his pocket would be false. It is simply the fortuitous, and to him unknown, concatenation of events that makes his belief true. But this kind of situation could not occur if the justification condition is given a logical interpretation, because Smith would know that the man who would get the job had ten coins in his pocket only if he was able to justify this to be true, something he could not accomplish if one of the premises on which he based his conclusion —namely, that he (Smith) had ten coins in his pocket—remained a fact of which he himself was unaware.[8]

Next let us see how the logical interpretation fares against my own criticism of the contingent interpretation. According to that criticism the contingent interpretation makes it impossible for us to apply the definition of knowledge to a belief and thus render a judgment on its knowledge-status. Although we can apply the justification condition, we find ourselves with no way of applying the truth condition. To see if the same difficulty besets the logical interpretation, let us assume (as we did before) that Smith believes that p and that his belief is justified (i.e., satisfies the justification condition). We must now try to determine if it satisfies the truth condition also. Is there any way we can go about doing this? As soon as we ask the question we realize it is redundant; it has already been answered. Since, according to the logical interpretation, a belief's satisfaction of the truth condition is a necessary condition of its satisfaction of the justification condition—one cannot justify the truth of a belief unless that belief is true—it follows *a fortiori* that if Smith's belief satisfies the justification condition it satisfies the truth condition as well. The difficulty we found in the definition of knowledge, on a contingent interpretation of the justification condition, is removed if that condition is given a logical interpretation.

If the only grounds for making a choice between the two interpretations of the justification condition were their respective abilities to meet the criticisms raised by Gettier and myself, it is clear that we should opt for the logical interpretation. Before making this decision, however, we need to investigate that interpretation further, for it has certain consequences that may give us pause. The most serious of these lies in the level of the demands it makes on a belief to qualify that belief as something we know. The requirement it lays down is so stringent that it disqualifies most of the things we believe from counting as knowledge. Indeed, the criticism might be made, it rules out *all* our beliefs and hence leads to skepticism. I shall examine both these objections, beginning first with the more radical one. To do so, it will be necessary to make a few preliminary, explanatory remarks about the meaning of the justification condition, on the logical interpretation.

According to the logical interpretation of the justification condition, when one says that Smith knows that p (i.e., that, for Smith, p is a justified true belief), one implies that Smith can justify p to be true. One is, thus, attributing an ability to Smith. But exactly what is the nature of this ability? Under what conditions should we agree that Smith *can* justify the truth of p? I do not think we can be absolutely precise in our answer to these questions. The meaning of the word 'can', as it functions in this interpretation, can be stipulated only within broad parameters. On the one hand, we should not want to limit our knowledge to beliefs whose truth we can justify immediately and spontaneously, without reflection; on the other, we should not want to broaden it to include all beliefs whose truth we are potentially able to justify. We might say that Smith knows all those things whose truth he *has justified*. In most cases this would appear to be sufficient; however, it would not be satisfactory in situations in which Smith has forgotten how he has justified the beliefs. Then we should probably say that although Smith *knew* these things, he no longer *knows* them. Perhaps we could say that Smith knows that p if he (a) has justified p to be true and (b) remembers that and how he has done this and, therefore, can repeat his justification on demand. Under these conditions it would certainly be correct to conclude, according to the logical interpretation, that Smith knows that p. But the weight of the requirement obviously rests on (b), which imputes to Smith the ability to justify the truth of p. And, as I have just said, I doubt that the meaning of 'can' in the phrase 'can justify' is capable of being precisely stipulated. Perhaps the best we can say is that Smith can justify any p to be true if he can justify its truth in the amount of time that it would normally take people to justify truths of the p-type.

With this preliminary concerning meaning out of the way we can now turn to the two related criticisms of the logical interpretation that I listed a moment ago, beginning with the charge that it leads to skepticism. If, to know something, the argument runs, one must be able to justify it to be true, we are forced to conclude that no one can know anything. However good the reasons people may have for believing certain things, these reasons can never be good enough to justify the truth of what they believe; their beliefs, in spite of the reasons supporting them, still may in fact be false.

As a first attempt to respond to this objection, we might ask why the critic argues that our beliefs may be false, in spite of the reasons we offer in their support. After all, according to the logical interpretation, good (i.e., justifying) reasons consist solely in those reasons that entail the truth of the proposition for which they are offered as reasons. Could not the skeptical critic respond by accepting this and then going on to contend that no such entailing reasons can possibly be given in support of a proposition, thus implying that his original contention that no one can justify any proposition to be true is true? But if this be so, it follows that he can never make his case against the logical interpretation. If no one can justify any proposition to be true, then he cannot justify it to be true that no one can justify any proposition to be true. What his objection to the logical interpretation attempts to do is to rule out *a priori* the possibility of knowledge. But it fails in this attempt, because the assumption underlying the objection makes it impossible for the objection to succeed.

Nevertheless, the critic might still make a point, but a less radical one: "I concede that I cannot *justify* the truth of my skeptical thesis about knowledge; nevertheless, it *may* be true and, if it is, no one can know anything, according to the logical interpretation of the justification condition." To respond to this charge it would seem necessary to show that the proposition "No one can justify anything to be true," although it may be true, is in fact false. We could do this if we were able to justify the truth of some proposition. And this we can readily do. Let us take for an example the proposition "Some propositions are true." If this proposition were false, its denial "∼ (Some propositions are true)" would be true. But the proposition "∼ (Some propositions are true)" entails the proposition "Some propositions are true"; for if it were false, the last proposition would be true and if it were true, the last proposition would still be true, because it itself (i.e., "∼ (Some propositions are true") would be a case of a proposition that is true. Since the denial of the proposition "Some propositions are true" entails the truth of this proposition, we can conclude that it is true *necessarily*.

Let us now turn back to the proposition "No one can justify anything to be true," which our skeptical critic has claimed to be possibly true. It might seem that the argument we have just offered bolsters his case for, if it is necessarily true that some propositions are true, one could conclude that it is possible that the skeptic's proposition is included among them. But let us look further. The proposition "Some propositions are true" is a conclusion we reached by means of an argument. We supported our claim that it is necessarily true by demonstrating its truth. In demonstrating its truth, we justified it to be true. By justifying the truth of this proposition, we justified the truth of the proposition "Someone can justify something to be true," for this latter proposition must be true if we have a case, as we have, of someone's having justified something to be true. Since it is true that someone can justify something to be true, the skeptic's claim "No one can justify anything to be true" must be false. Because it is false, we can disregard it. It follows that if we adopt the logical interpretation of the justification condition, we *know* that we can justify some things to be true for at least the reason that the proposition "We can justify some things to be true" satisfies the sufficient conditions to qualify as knowledge: (1) It is true and (2) we can justify it to be true (because we have just demonstrated it to be so and can repeat our demonstration on demand). We can, as a result, dismiss the objection that adoption of the logical interpretation leads to skepticism.

I turn now to a more serious objection. On the logical interpretation, a belief cannot satisfy the justification condition of knowledge unless it satisfies the truth condition; it is impossible to justify the truth of a false belief. We have, earlier in the paper, already made two points about any definition of knowledge: (1) It must be possible to apply the conditions the definition lays down to our beliefs in order to determine whether these do or do not constitute things we know and (2) we cannot apply the truth condition directly (beliefs do not come labeled either 'True' or

'False'). As a result of (2), the only basis we have, on which we can reach the judgment that a given belief is true, are the reasons we offer in its support. We can say generally of any set of reasons offered in support of a belief that they justify its truth or that they fall short of this goal. If they fall short, then, given the reasons, the belief may be true but it may also be false. But, if a belief may be false in spite of the reasons we have given in its support, we cannot legitimately claim of it that it is something we know because we have not determined that it satisfies the truth condition of knowledge. To be in a position to claim of any belief that it does satisfy the truth condition, therefore, we must be able to say that, given the reasons we have provided in its support, it is true. We can do this, however, only if, given these reasons, the belief cannot be false. It follows, thus, that to be able to certify any belief as satisfying the truth condition of knowledge, we must offer reasons in its support that *entail* it to be true.

This consequence of the logical interpretation gives rise to some serious problems. In the first place it greatly restricts the range of our knowledge. Although we can legitimately claim to know some things because we can justify certain of our beliefs as true (i.e., the reasons we can give in their support entail their truth), our ability to do so extends only to a small proportion of the things we believe. Little of what we believe, therefore, do we really know. Because of the restrictions it puts on what we can know, our definition of knowledge may seem deficient. It fails to accomplish what a satisfactory definition of a term should do; namely, give a meaning to that term which is (at least reasonably) close to the meaning that most people who use the term in their ordinary discourse give to it. As people ordinarily use the term 'knowledge', it is appropriate to talk of someone's knowing something in a far wider range of situations than our definition would ever allow.

What I have just said is, I think, factually correct. We do use the term 'knowledge' much more loosely than my definition would permit. So we must ask: Should we abandon the definition because of the disparity between it and ordinary usage or are the reasons we have given in its support sufficient to counterbalance this deficiency? In the remainder of my paper I shall argue that the factors favoring the definition outweigh its shortcomings, therefore that it should be retained.

To begin, any appeal to the way in which the term 'knowledge' is ordinarily used is fraught with difficulty. So much depends on who is using the term and in what circumstances it is being used. Consider, for example, the difference in criteria that would be demanded if the question were asked, "Do you know if Smith is having an affair with his secretary?" and the situation were (a) two of Smith's neighbors gossiping over a back fence or (b) a lawyer in a divorce proceedings questioning a witness. Ordinary usage of terms like 'knowledge' is very elastic and a case can be made that situations do occur in life (outside of philosophical discussion) in which the criteria applied to this term do approximate in rigor to those laid down by our definition.

But another point about ordinary usage must be added. Insofar as it tends to be more generous in the permitted use of the term, it embraces an interpretation of the two conditions of knowledge that results in an incoherency in the concept. On the one hand, it relaxes the justification condition. Instead of holding that we must justify what we believe to be true before we can legitimately claim to know it, it would (in most circumstances) grant the status of knowledge to those beliefs for which we can offer "good reasons." And, as we have just indicated, the "good reasons" of ordinary usage generally cover a much broader range than the logically coercive reasons demanded of the justification condition on our interpretation of the standard definition. On the other hand, however, the ordinary conception of knowledge makes truth one of its necessary conditions. No one, in conducting the everyday affairs of life or in conversing on any topic whatsoever would find an audience willing to accept the following remark: "I know that so-and-so (I have, after all, good reasons for believing it) but, in fact, so-and-so isn't true." As we have already seen, the demand made by the truth condition can be satisfied only by construing the justification condition in such a way that a belief that satisfies it, in doing so, satisfies the truth condition as well. Since this is not true of the "good reasons" construal of the justification condition, ordinary usage leaves us with an incoherent conception of knowledge. Although, as I said at the very outset, an important criterion of the success of any definition we may offer of knowledge is its consonance with the way in which the word is ordinarily used, this cannot be the only criterion. When ordinary usage is confused and inconsistent, philosophers have an obligation to try to offer clarification and consistency for only by doing so can we advance toward our ultimate objective, to which all other considerations must yield—an understanding of the nature of things.

The "good reasons" construal of the justification condition, typical of ordinary usage, gives rise to an additional problem. On the grounds that good reasons can be given in their support, it lumps together as knowledge beliefs that differ markedly from each other in their epistemic status. For example, most people would probably accept Smith's belief that Jones had ten coins in his pocket as something Smith knew, on the grounds that Smith had counted the coins. They would probably also accept my belief that some propositions are true as something I know, on the grounds that I can demonstrate the truth of this belief. Nevertheless, these two beliefs differ from each other in a significant way. Whereas my belief not only satisfies the truth condition of knowledge, required by ordinary usage, but can also be *shown* to satisfy this condition, Smith's belief may or may not satisfy it and can, in any case, not be shown to satisfy it. Therefore to label the two beliefs by the same name is to obscure a vital difference between them.

This problem can, fortunately, be resolved, since it is a matter of terminology. We might, for example, continue to use the term 'knowledge' in the way that most of us now usually do, to refer to beliefs that, although they may not be true and cannot be shown to be true, can nevertheless be supported by "good reasons." This would allow us to gather under the umbrella of knowledge a vast number of beliefs of common sense, theories of empirical science, and, perhaps, much else besides. We could then separate, as a distinct category, beliefs whose truth we can justify, designating them by some other term; 'superknowledge' is a suggestion. I see no overwhelming objections to this suggestion—although the word 'superknowledge' is perhaps unduly reminiscent of the label on a can of olives. The crucial point is that we maintain the distinction between beliefs whose truth we cannot justify and those whose truth we can, for these are different from each other in an important way.

Nevertheless, let me in conclusion offer an alternative terminological practice, one that has the advantage of not asking us to introduce a new, inflated term into our vocabulary but puts to use words we now possess and commonly employ. Let us reserve the term 'knowledge' for beliefs whose truth we can justify; and for those whose truth we cannot justify but for which we can offer reasons that we believe in some sense to be "good," let us continue to use a term already in both our philosophical and our common vocabularies—'reasonable belief'. Thus, although many of our commonsensical beliefs, as well as the theories of empirical science, etc., cannot be counted strictly as things we know, they can count as things we reasonably believe. According to St. Paul, the just shall live by faith; if I am right, most of the rest of us live (at least most of the time, I hope) by reasonable belief.

Notes

1. E. Gettier, "Is Justified True Belief Knowledge?" *Analysis* 23 (1963):121–23.

2. In *ibid.*, p. 121, Gettier formulates the standard definition as follows:

"S knows that P *IFF*   (i) P is true,

(ii) S believes that P, and

(iii) S is justified in believing that P."

3. Gettier refers to *Theaetetus* 201 and *Meno* 98 in support of his view that Plato would accept such an interpretation of the justification condition; I think there might be some disagreement about his reading of the dialogues on this point. Chisholm's definition, to which Gettier refers, appears in his *Perceiving* (Ithaca, 1957), where he writes: "The following, then, will be our definition of 'know' . . . 'S knows that L is true' means: (i) S accepts L; (ii) S has adequate evidence for L; and (iii) L is true" (p. 16). And Ayer writes, in *The Problem of Knowledge* (Baltimore, 1956), as follows: "I conclude then that the necessary and sufficient conditions for knowing that something is the case are first that what one is said to know be true, secondly that one be sure of it, and thirdly that one should have the right to be sure" (p. 35). For an even more explicit statement of this conception of knowledge, see C. I. Lewis, *An Analysis of Knowledge and Valuation* (La Salle, 1946). Lewis writes: "Knowledge is belief which not only is true but also is justified in its believing attitude" (p. 9).

4. See Gettier, "Is Justified True Belief Knowledge?" p. 122.

5. *Ibid.* This is his "Case I."

6. I use this term here, and later, as a surrogate for 'belief'. For purposes of my argument, the two are interchangeable.

7. Numerous examples could be cited, including several from the philosophical literature.

8. It might be noted, in passing, that the logical interpretation is equally invulnerable to the second of Gettier's two counterexamples, which he calls Case II (see *ibid.*, pp. 122–23).

Lost Justification

GEORGE S. PAPPAS

Often the justification or evidence that a person has for a certain belief at a specific time is evidence he no longer possesses at a later time. In this paper I describe what I think is a fairly typical case of this sort. I then consider what epistemological moral, if any, it is most appropriate to draw from the example presented.

Suppose that a person, S, learns some new things at a certain time. For instance, imagine that S learns that his third grade teacher's name is Mrs. Hatton and that he learns this at the time he is in the third grade. He thus comes to know some specific proposition, P (= the proposition expressed by the sentence "The name of my third grade teacher is Mrs. Hatton."), at a specific time, in this case, let us say, in early Fall 1950. We may suppose that this is wholly new knowledge for S, and we may further suppose that S gains this knowledge on the basis of some evidence available to him at the time. That is, we assume that in 1950, S came to know that P and that he did so on the basis of some evidence he then had. His evidence, for example, might have been that he read the following sentence on the chalkboard: "This is the third grade; the teacher's name is Mrs. Hatton; the room number is 201; . . . etc." His evidence may also have included the fact that he was told by a reliable friend that indeed his teacher for the third grade was to be Mrs. Hatton.

Now consider S many years later, say in 1979. He still knows that P at this later time, since he has remembered his teacher's name, continuously, throughout the interval. This is not to say that he has occurrently remembered during all of those years. His memory with respect to this fact is at best occasionally occurrent during that time. Still, he remembered that P across the twenty-nine years, and he has retained that knowledge without ever having lost it by forgetting. Yet, imagine that S no longer has any of the evidence on the basis of which he originally came to know that P. This is because he has totally forgotten the sentences on the chalkboard and likewise forgotten the testimony of his friend. Indeed, he has so forgotten these matters that, even if he is reminded of these facts by his mother or some other person, he has absolutely no recollection. He replies to her, "Well, if you say so, I guess that's how I learned her name, but I don't remember at all. All I know is that my third grade teacher's name was Mrs. Hatton."

To round out the example, we need to add just one more feature. That is, we also suppose that during the interval, 1950 to 1979, S has not acquired any *new* evidence apropos the fact that P. He has completely lost his original evidence, such as it was, and has gained no new evidence relative to P ever since he first came to know it. He still knows that P, even now, in 1979.

Situations in which a person comes to know some proposition on the basis of some evidence, but where he loses his original evidence while retaining the knowledge, are quite common. Indeed, a great deal of anyone's knowledge at any time is of precisely this sort. Only slightly less common are cases such as I have described wherein the person loses his original evidence but also gains no new evidence concerning the proposition he first came to know. To see the first point, consider a familiar example. Millions of sometime students of American history have learned that Lincoln was President during the Civil War. Further, most if not all of these people learned this fact on the basis of some evidence, typically evidence having to do with reading that Lincoln was President during the war. Yet many of the same people have both lost their original evidence and gained new evidence since their initial learning. They have lost the original evidence in the sense that they have completely forgotten the fact that they read (or heard or whatever) that Lincoln was President during the Civil War. Typically, they have also gained new evidence bearing on the matter: e.g., they will have seen movies, heard lectures, spoken with friends, read other material about the Civil War, and so on. They thus have plenty of evidence for the proposition that Lincoln was President during the Civil War, but they altogether lack their original evidence. Still, given appropriate retention, each knows that Lincoln was President during the Civil War, and each has known this all along.

Many of the same history students, however, never acquired any new evidence concerning Lincoln and the Civil War since their initial learning. They have not lost their knowledge, however, since they have remembered that Lincoln was President at that time. Notice that the two groups of people are similar in an important respect beyond the fact that members of each group learned that Lincoln was President during the Civil War; for each group, the explanation of why their respective members now know that Lincoln was President during the Civil War is that those members have remembered what they initially learned. Acquisition of new evidence is superfluous for members of the first group, and it is nonexistent for members of the second sort of group. Ongoing and current memory is sufficient to account for the fact that such persons have their knowledge of Lincoln, just as ongoing and current memory suffices for S to know that his teacher's name was Mrs. Hatton.

Let us be clear about what is meant by the term 'lost evidence'. In saying that S has completely forgotten his original evidence, and so has *lost* it, I mean to imply that his original evidence does not function *now* to justify his belief that his teacher's name was Mrs. Hatton. Of course, the fact that S once had that evidence is in one way relevant to his now knowing that P, since it was that evidence on the basis of which he first came to know that P. *That* sort of relevance is not lost in any sense.

Situations like those described above, I have said, are very common and familiar. But what shall we say about S and his continuing knowledge of the name of his third grade teacher? For, if S knows now, in 1979, that the name of his third grade teacher is Mrs. Hatton, then S is now, in 1979, justified in believing that the name of his third grade teacher is Mrs. Hatton.[1] But in what does his current justification consist, given that he altogether lacks his original knowledge-producing evidence and that he has acquired no fresh evidence concerning the matter in the meantime?

Two quick answers to these questions concern the description of the example. Thus one might hold that we have erred in supposing that S still knows that P now, in 1979. He *lacks* that knowledge, now, one might argue, *precisely because* he has lost his original evidence as described earlier. Hence the case of S and his "knowledge" of his teacher's name produces no problem, since S does not have that knowledge. Since he lost the evidence, he lost the knowledge. The other quick answer concerns the sense in which S's evidence is lost. It might be conceded that S has completely forgotten his original evidence, and in *that* sense the evidence is lost. Still, one might say, it is that very original evidence which functions, now, to justify his belief that P.

The problem with the first quick answer is that it ignores the fact that S has never forgotten that P, even though he has forgotten his original evidence. Not having forgotten that P across twenty-nine years is sufficient for his now knowing that P. Rejection of this latter claim, I think, would bring with it a rejection of much of what is ordinarily counted as knowledge. The second quick answer faces a different problem. Since S has completely forgotten his original evidence, *oe* (= original evidence), he is not now justified in believing *oe*, and it is problematic whether *oe* is even justified for him.[2] But a person is justified in believing a proposition on the basis of some evidence only if he is justified in believing the evidence he then has. However, since S has completely forgotten *oe*, *oe* does not seem justified for him and, more important, he is not justified in believing *oe*. Thus he does not now know that P on the basis of *oe*; hence, it is not *oe*, his original evidence, which currently functions to justify his belief that his third grade teacher's name was Mrs. Hatton.[3]

Should we say, then, that S's current memory makes up his present justification for belief that P? Perhaps. But what would the content of his memory be? Content candidates include remembering that *oe*, remembering that P, and remembering some other evidence acquired since the initial learning of P. However, we have discounted the role of newly acquired evidence, and *ex hypothesi*, S does not remember that *oe*. Does S know that P, then, on the basis of his current memory that P? That is, does the fact that S presently remembers that P function to justify his belief that P?

It is slightly tempting to say that remembering that P functions as S's evidence in this case. But the correct answer seems instead to be that S's remembering that P and his knowing that P are the same. For, in the sort of context described above, knowing that P just *is* remembering that P. Hence his remembering that P is not the evidence on the basis of which S now knows that P.[4] We need to look elsewhere for S's justification.

Some philosophers have maintained that a person's ostensible memory is epistemologically important.[5] And, taking a hint from such philosophers, we might want to say that S's ostensible memory (his seeming to remember) provides him with the evidence that justifies his current belief that P. Here again, though, we face a content problem: we need to specify what it is that S is said to ostensibly remember. He does not ostensibly remember that *oe*, nor does he seem to remember any new evidence, at least not veridically. Non-veridically seeming to remember is of no help; seeming to remember that Q where Q is false, and where his belief that Q is his sole evidence for the claim that P, does not serve to justify belief that P in the context where S knows that P. We are left with S's seeming to remember that P. But to see that it is not his evidence for belief that P we need only consider that seeming to remember is an occurrence of some sort, an occurrent mental act or event. However, there is no reason to insist that, in the above example, S occurrently seems to remember that P. Even so, S still (perhaps non-occurrently) knows that P. Of course, S *might* seem to remember that P, now, in 1979. The point to emphasize, though, is that he would know that P, now, even if he did not now seem to remember that P. Thus, seeming to remember that P now is not the evidence on the basis of which S now knows that P.[6]

There are still several further matters we have not yet considered. For instance, perhaps S has acquired some *negative* evidence bearing on P, even though he has not gained any positive evidence. Again, doubtless S has considerable background knowledge of disparate sorts, and surely some of it relates to P. Moreover, if S is to actually know that P in 1979, he must be a reliable cognizer; that is, he must not be drugged, drunk, or otherwise impaired with respect to judgments concerning his third grade teacher's name and concerning countless other matters. Then we could say that the evidence that now justifies S in believing that P, or at least contributes to that justification, is his negative evidence relative to P; or that it is his background knowledge; or we could say that it is his knowledge that the conditions then obtaining, with respect to himself primarily, are quite normal. Or one might argue that the union of two or more of these items makes up S's current evidence for his belief that P.

By 'negative evidence' in this context we mean evidence that has the effect of driving down the antecedent probability of P. Thus S might discover one of his own old school report cards in his attic and find that the card says "promoted to the fourth grade" and that it carries the signature of Mrs. Andrews. Such a discovery would constitute negative evidence vis-à-vis P; it would serve to decrease S's justification for his belief that P. Alternatively, S might have what we can call 'competitive evidence' bearing on the claim that P. That is, he might have some evidence that tends to rule out alternatives to P, including the alternative, not-P. Thus S may have positive evidence that the name of his third grade teacher was *not* Mrs. Whitely (since he knows that that was the name of his second grade teacher), and this evidence is competitively relevant to P: it supports ruling out some alternative proposition, say that Q (expressed by "The name of my third grade teacher is Mrs. Whitely."). We can surely agree that S *might* have such negative or competitive evidence, and if so, it would help to support his belief that P. However, there is no necessity to this; S *need* not have such evidence at all, and this fact would not affect his knowledge that P in 1979. It may be true that often a person would have negative or competitive evidence in situations like that described earlier. But equally often a person would lack such evidence, and that lack would not alter the fact that he has retained some piece of knowledge, such as, in our case, knowledge that P. Similar remarks are in order regarding background knowledge relevant to P. While S might have such knowledge sometimes, he need not have it in order to have knowledge that P. Continuing memory that P is sufficient for knowledge. There is nothing problematic in assuming that, in the example described, S lacks suitable background knowledge; we are free to assume that S does not have such knowledge even if in many other situations a person would have appropriate background knowledge. Of course, it is not being claimed that S might lack *all* other knowledge; i.e., it is not being claimed that S knows just one thing, namely that P. A much more restricted claim is being endorsed, namely, that S lacks background knowledge bearing on P. But this fact does not imply that S lacks knowledge that P.

We can agree that S knows, in 1979, that P only if he is a reliable, normal cognizer, one who is not drunk, drugged, deranged, or otherwise incapacitated. In this way, the example described earlier mimics cases of perceptual knowledge. Thus a person gains knowledge, perceptually, that there is a shiny carpet on the floor, in typical cases, only if observation conditions are normal—or at least normal for purposes of carpet and color observation. Such does not always obtain; a person might gain perceptual knowledge of the shininess of the carpet even in situations where some observation conditions are not normal. But it seems plausible to allow that normal observation conditions obtain in the typical cases (the usual cases) of perceptual knowledge acquisition.

Is there any reason, though, for thinking that the fact that he is then a normal, reliable cognizer makes up S's evidence that P is the case? To see why the answer here should be *no*, consider the example of a conceptually impoverished individual, Jones, who altogether lacks the concepts of being drunk, being drugged, being deranged, and the like. The propositions that he is not drunk, not drugged, not incapacitated with respect to certain types of affairs—such propositions would not be justified for Jones. Hence such propositions would not serve as the evidence on the basis of which he then knows some other proposition, say, that there is a shiny carpet on the floor. Nonetheless, this sort of conceptual impoverishment does not prohibit Jones from gaining perceptual knowledge of the shiny carpet. This sort of perceptual knowledge might be itself based on evidence, and perhaps it is generally that way with such propositions as many philosophers have held. But Jones's evidence would not include any of those propositions with respect to which he is conceptually impoverished; it would not include, that is, propositions concerning the normalcy of observation conditions.

This example shows that a person's knowledge may be dependent on normalcy of observation conditions without being *evidentially dependent* on such conditions. And this is the sort of result we can utilize in the case of S and the proposition that his third grade teacher's name is Mrs. Hatton. That is, we can agree that there is some sense in which S's knowledge that P is dependent on a certain form of normalcy obtaining—*he* would not know that P if *he* were not normal in specific ways—without being forced to concede that his knowledge is evidentially dependent on the fact that such normalcy obtains. Thus we are free to assume that S, is not justified in his belief that P on the basis of evidence that consists of propositions concerning the normalcy of specific conditions pertaining to himself.

It might be objected, however, that the immediate preceding remarks help sacrifice any claim that the case of S is common or typical. It may be granted that S *need* not have negative, competitive, or background evidence bearing on P; and similarly concede that S *need* not have knowledge or justified beliefs concerning normalcy of certain conditions. Still, one might argue, a person *would* usually have such evidence and knowledge or justified beliefs. Thus, one could say, the most that has been offered is a logically and empirically consistent example, but still one that is highly atypical.

One reply to this objection is to agree that there are many situations that significantly differ from the one presented here. In a great many situations, a person would indeed have the sort of evidence or knowledge discussed above. However, there are enough situations remaining which are similar in all relevant respects to S and his current knowledge that P, to warrant our saying of the latter that it is a fairly typical situation. That contention is not undermined by the (conceded) fact that many situations are relevantly different from the one discussed here.

Also relevant here is the distinction introduced earlier between being justified in believing P and P's being justified for a person. The latter notion, I have said, does not imply belief that P, whereas the former does. Now doubtless in many situations like that discussed above, negative and competitive evidence, background evidence, and propositions concerning the normalcy of some conditions *would be justified* for the person in question. And, I suspect, it is *this* fact which tempts us into supposing that in nearly all such situations the person will have some evidence for the believed proposition at issue. But this, I suggest, is a mistake. For a person S has evidence, *e*, on the basis of which he knows that P only if S is justified in believing that *e*, and so, only if he believes that *e*. And there are many situations in which a person would fail to have the beliefs required in order to have appropriate negative, competitive, or background evidence, or evidence concerning the normalcy of conditions.[7]

Thus far we have found that none of the natural candidates for the sort of evidence we might attribute to S have been required. And, since I know of no other evidence candidates in this context, it seems safe to tentatively conclude that S *does not have any evidence* on the basis of which he is justified in believing that P. Yet it seems quite plausible to maintain, as was done in setting out the example, that S still does know that P now, in 1979. Moreover, given the reasonable assumption that knowledge implies justification, it is also plausible to maintain that S is justified in believing that P, now, in 1979. But if S knows that P now and if he has no evidence at all for P now, we should conclude that S's knowledge that P, now, is *immediate* or, as I would put it, *non-inferential*. Similarly with justification and for the same reason: lacking all evidence for the belief that P, S's justification for the belief that P is immediate, or non-inferential. Non-inferential, immediate, knowledge is just the knowledge that one has and that one would have even if one were not to have it on the basis of evidence. And non-inferential, immediate justification is just the justification that one has for a proposition and that one would have even if one were not to have any evidence that makes up or helps make up one's justification for believing that proposition.[8]

Maintaining that S knows that P non-inferentially or immediately is apt to be regarded as very counterintuitive, principally on two grounds. First, P is a proposition about the past, and such knowledge, if had at all, is usually reckoned as inferential. Moreover, as I have noted, the situation of S and his teacher's name is *typical*; it is *common* for a person to lose his original evidence for a proposition in much the way S has and to gain no evidence bearing on that proposition later on, while still continuing to know that proposition as long as appropriate memory and some semblance of normalcy is retained. Given the usualness of cases of this sort, it would follow that *much* of any person's knowledge at any time is immediate, or non-inferential, and *this* is surely counterintuitive. On the contrary, it is usually held that there is precious little immediate or non-inferential knowledge, if there is indeed any at all. Indeed, it would seem that even more counterintuitive results will follow: if S knows that P non-inferentially (immediately) and if the sort of situation he is in is quite common, then much of one's knowledge of the past will turn out to be non-inferential (immediate). For many philosophers, these results will suffice to constitute a *reductio* of the foregoing argument concerning S and his teacher's name.

But I tend to think that S's situation vis-à-vis the proposition that P is quite usual and unproblematic; that it is implausible to think that his current knowledge that P is based on any of the proposed pieces of evidence considered above; that S's situation is quite common and familiar; and that knowledge implies justification. And so I tend to allow that the above-mentioned results are counterintuitive, but to insist that they are correct, for all that.[9, 10]

Notes

1. I here accept the thesis that knowledge implies justification. But it has been questioned by some, including C. Radford, "Knowledge—By Examples," *Analysis* 27 (1966):1–11.

2. S's being justified in believing that P, and P's being justified for S, are distinct epistemic facts. The former implies that S does in fact believe that P, whereas the latter does not. P is justified for a person S just in case, were S to believe that P, then his belief that P would be justified.

3. In his "Retained Knowledge," *Mind* 83 (1974):355–71, Alan Holland seems to take a different line on this point since, he argues, in order for a person to have the same knowledge now that he possessed much earlier, he must now have the *same grounds* that he had earlier. But it is unclear whether Holland and I disagree on this matter, since his notion of grounds is not quite the same as my notion of evidence. Evidence, I assume, is propositional; but Holland's notion of grounds is not propositional since on his account, one's grounds are causally related to one's current belief. Nothing that I claim in this paper, so far as I can see, rules out a causal relation holding between S's current belief that P and the event of his coming to have his original evidence.

4. It is thus implied that in the context described, remembering that P is (identical to) knowing that P. But this claim does not itself imply that all remembering-that is knowing-that; still less does it imply that remembering-that propositions entail knowing-that propositions.

5. See, for instance, C. I. Lewis, *Analysis of Knowledge and Valuation* (La Salle, Ill., 1946), chap. 11.

6. One might say that remembering that P implies seeming to remember that P. Hence S would now seem to remember that P, and he always would have done so—as long as he had re-

membered that P, at any rate. Thus, one might argue, rejection of ostensible memory as S's current justifying evidence, as done here, is much too hasty. The problem with this objection, I believe, comes in its first step. For, I would claim, there is no plausible interpretation of 'seems to remember' such that remembering implies seeming to remember.

Note, however, that even if S were to seem to remember that P now, it would not follow that the claim that he seems to remember that P is his evidence for belief that P.

7. One might, of course, deny the assumption made here and allow that some or all of the evidence on the basis of which S knows that P consists of propositions that are (merely) justified for him. (See, e.g., K. Lehrer, *Knowledge* [New York, 1974], pp. 21–23.) However, I doubt if this tack would defeat the overall point made here. For, I would, claim, there are also a great many situations in which one's evidence is lost, as described, and where appropriate negative, competitive, and other evidence is not even justified for the person.

8. See, for instance, J. Cornman, "Materialism and Some Myths About Some Givens," *The Monist* 56 (1972):222, and M. Pastin, "Modest Foundationalism and Self-Warrant," in G. Pappas and M. Swain, eds., *Essays on Knowledge and Justification* (Ithaca, N.Y., 1978), for such accounts of non-inferential knowledge and non-inferential justification or warrant. See, too, W. P. Alston, "Self Warrant: A Neglected Form of Privileged Access," *American Philosophical Quarterly* 13 (1976):257–72. For an alternative characterization, see D. Armstrong, *Belief, Truth and Knowledge* (New York, 1973), part III.

9. An alternative conclusion has been suggested by Marty Perlmutter. He proposes that the lost justification case shows that the customary distinction between immediate and indirect knowledge does not actually apply to ongoing knowledge, but rather to *coming to know*. I find this idea very plausible, in part. But I think a somewhat more plausible view would be one in which we allow that the immediate/indirect distinction applies to knowledge and that a related distinction applies for immediate and indirect coming to know.

10. An earlier version of this paper was presented at the Western Division APA meetings in Denver, April 1979. The remarks of the commentator, Marty Perlmutter, were quite helpful. I have also benefitted from comments and criticisms from Robert Audi, Ray Elugardo, Peter Klein, Bill Lycan, Ausonio Marras, Phil Quinn, and Marshall Swain.

Level-Confusions in Epistemology

WILLIAM P. ALSTON

Uncovering confusions in each other's work is a favorite, almost, one sometimes suspects, the sole, occupation of contemporary American philosophers. I am surely not the only member of this class who has to resist temptations to spend a disproportionate amount of time on such activities. After all, it is so much easier than presenting and defending substantive theses. And it is a lot of fun. Like the rest of fallen humanity, I resist temptation only part of the time, and this is, I fear, the other part. In this paper I will be engaged in uncovering what I take to be some fundamental and pervasive confusions in contemporary epistemology. However, in this instance I have more solid reasons than usual for spending time in confusion spotting. I do think that epistemology is one area in which the practitioners, even (or perhaps especially) the most significant ones, have fallen into certain confusions that have profoundly influenced their systematic constructions. Hence by revealing those confusions one can make an important contribution to the development of epistemology with relatively little effort. At least that is my claim for what I am doing in this paper. You can form your own judgement as to whether it is correct.

The confusions to which I will be calling your attention all involve sloughing over the distinction between epistemic levels, proceeding as if what is true of a proposition, belief, or epistemic state of affairs on one level is *ipso facto* true of a correlated proposition, belief, or epistemic state of affairs on another. The levels I have in mind are those built up by the introduction and iteration of epistemic or pistic operators: 'know that', 'believe that', 'is justified in believing that', and so on. Thus if we begin with any proposition, p, we can build a structure of epistemic levels by using various epistemic operators.

I. p
   S believes that p
   S believes that S believes that p

   . . . . . .

135

II. *p*
      S is justified in believing that *p*
      S is justified in believing that S is justified in believing that *p*

    . . . . . .

III. *p*
      S knows that *p*
      S knows that S knows that *p*

    . . . . . .

We can also have "mixed" items. *S knows that p* can give rise to the higher-level *S believes that S knows that p* or the equally higher-level *S is justified in believing that S knows that p.* My purposes in this paper do not require me to develop precise criteria for determining the relative levels of any two such items. The confusions we will be disclosing are all between items that are obviously on different levels.

<h1 style="text-align:center">I</h1>

My first example concerns the concept of immediate (direct) justification. The contrast between mediate (indirect) and immediate (direct) justification can be most simply and most fundamentally stated as follows.

(1) To say that a belief is mediately justified is to say that what justifies it includes some other justified beliefs of the same subject.[1]

(2) To say that a belief is immediately justified is to say that what justifies it does not include some other justified beliefs of the same subject.

This generic characterization of immediate justification is purely negative. Anyone who holds that some beliefs are immediately justified will have some conception of what can justify beliefs in such a way that no other justified beliefs of the same subject are involved in the justification.

Now the confusion about immediate justification I will be exploring consists just in this: it is confusedly supposed that for S's belief that *p* to be immediately justified it is required that the higher-level belief that *S is justified in believing that p*, or that *S knows that p*, itself be immediately justified; or, even more confusedly, that this is what the immediate justification of S's belief that *p* consists in. Full-blown examples of this confusion can be found in Roderick Chisholm and in Panayot Butchvarov.[2] I will restrict my attention to Chisholm.

Chisholm's version of immediate justification is what we may call truth-justification, justification of a belief by its truth or by the fact that makes it true. To follow Chisholm's presentation of this, a short terminological digression will be required. Chisholm distinguishes several grades of epistemic justification, one of the higher of which is 'evident'. (The exact definition of 'evident' and its distinction from other grades need not concern us here.) The term 'evident' is applied to propositions; if a propostion, *p*, is evident for a subject, S, then S is justified (to a high degree) in believing that p. Chisholm tends to use the term 'justified' in a non-discriminating way to range over all grades of justification.

In the recently published second edition of his *Theory of Knowledge*[3] Chisholm defines his basic notion of immediate justification for empirical beliefs as follows.

> D2.1 h is *self-presenting* for S at t = Df. h is true at t; and necessarily, if h is true at t, then h is evident for S at t. (p. 22)[4]

This conforms to the generic notion of immediate justification I presented above. But Chisholm also presents his version of immediate justification in a quite different way. He introduces his conception of the directly evident by considering the ways in which one might answer the "Socratic" questions "What justification do you have for thinking you know this thing to be true?" or "What justification do you have for counting this thing as something that is evident?" (p. 17)

> In many instances the answers to our questions will take the following form: "What justifies me in thinking that I know that a is F is the fact it is evident to me that b is G" . . . This type of answer to our Socratic questions shifts the burden of justification from one claim to another. For we may now ask, "What justifies me in counting it as evident that b is G?" or "What justifies me in thinking I know that b is G?" . . . We might try to continue *ad indefinitum,* justifying each new claim that we elicit by still another claim. Or we might be tempted to complete a vicious circle . . . But if we are rational beings, we will do neither of these things. For we will find that our Socratic questions lead us to a proper stopping place . . . Let us say provisionally that we have found a proper stopping place when the answer to our question may take the following form:
>
> > What justifies me in thinking I know that a is F is simply the fact that a is F.
>
> Whenever this type of answer is appropriate, we have encountered the *directly evident.* (pp. 18-20)

In this passage and others we get a different picture of what makes a proposition directly evident. According to the definition D2.1, what makes a true proposition, p, directly evident for S, is that its truth makes *it* evident for S; whereas according to the passage just quoted what makes p directly evident is that its truth makes evident (justifies)[5] S's higher level belief that S knows that p (or that it is evident to S that p). The two passages give different answers to the question: what does the truth of p have to justify in order that p be *directly* evident?

There is fairly strong textual evidence that Chisholm simply does not see that the two accounts are different, or, at least, that the realization of their difference is not effectively operative in his mind when he is presenting his position. Not only do we find each account reflected in numerous passages. We even find Chisholm juxtaposing them in the same discussion.

Thinking and believing provide us with paradigm cases of the directly evident.

Consider a reasonable man who . . . believes that Albuquerque is in New Mexico, and suppose him to reflect on the philosophical question, "What is my justification for thinking that I know . . . that I believe that Albuquerque is in New Mexico? . . . The man could reply in this way: "My justification for thinking I know . . . that I believe that Albuquerque is in New Mexico, is simply the fact . . . that I do believe that it is in New Mexico." And this reply fits our formula for the directly evident:

> What justifies me in thinking I know that *a* is F is simply the fact that *a* is F.

Our man has stated his justification for a proposition merely by reiterating that proposition. (p. 21)

Obviously it is the higher-level conception of direct evidence that is being employed throughout most of this passage. But the very last sentence constitutes a reversion to the lower-level conception. If the proposition for which the man is stating his justification was the higher-level proposition *I know that I believe that Albuquerque is in New Mexico*, then he did *not* state his justification by reiterating the proposition. For what he enunciated in stating his justification was not that proposition, but its lower-level correlate, *I believe that Albuquerque is in New Mexico*. Thus he stated his justification for *p* by reiterating *p* only if the *p* in question were that lower-level proposition.

Of course it may be that Chisholm is not *confusing* the two levels but is presenting the matter in such a way as to reflect his *conviction* that, for self-presenting propositions, the truth of *p* generates justification on both levels. Indeed, in a later part of the book Chisholm does espouse, and argue for, a level-bridging principle that might seem to have this consequence.

> . . . if a proposition is evident and if one considers the proposition, then it is evident that the proposition is evident. (p. 114)

This principle does ensure a transfer of evidence from a proposition, *p*, to the higher-level proposition that *it is evident that p*, given that S considers the matter. But it by no means follows from this that the source of evidence is the same on the two levels; hence it does not follow that where the truth of *p* suffices to make *p* evident, *it* will also suffice to make *it is evident that p* evident. The principle quoted above is quite compatible with its being the case that where *it is evident that p* (for some self-presenting proposition, *p*) becomes evident to S upon considering the matter, what makes the higher-level proposition evident is not the mere truth of *p*, but something that is uncovered in the process of consideration. And Chisholm evinces no awareness that the thesis that the truth of *p* generates evidence on the higher level as well as the lower, is one that needs to be scrutinized and defended, whether on the basis of the above principle or otherwise.

In any event, the important philosophical question is not what is or is not going on in Chisholm's mind, but whether the thesis that the source of evidence is the same on the two levels, has important consequences that are likely to pass unnoticed if one simply assumes the thesis without explicitly realizing that one is doing so. I will now point out some of those consequences.

First, if one saddles one's account of immediate justification with the claim that the same kind of justification extends to one or more correlated higher-level propositions, the plausibility of one's account will be reduced. This is certainly the case with Chisholm. Whatever ultimate judgment is to be brought in the matter, it is not totally implausible to suppose that one is justified in beliefs about what one is currently feeling, sensing, or thinking just by the fact that one *is* so feeling, sensing, or thinking. But is it equally plausible that I am justified in supposing that *it is evident to me that I feel tired* just by the fact that I feel tired? Can I be justified in supposing that a certain proposition has a certain epistemic status for me, *just by feeling tired.* One's initial doubts in this matter are increased by considering Chisholm's definition of 'evident'.

> D1.5 *h* is evident for S = Df (i) *h* is beyond reasonable doubt for S and (ii) for every *i*, if accepting *i* is more reasonable for S than accepting *h*, then *i* is certain for S. (p. 12)

And the definition of 'certain' runs:

> D1.4 *h* is certain for S = Df *h* is beyond reasonable doubt for S, and there is no *i* such that accepting *i* is more reasonable for S than accepting *h*. (p. 10)

Leaving aside what it takes to be justified in supposing the acceptance of one proposition to be more reasonable than the acceptance of another, and leaving aside what it takes to be justified in supposing that a certain proposition is beyond reasonable doubt, let us concentrate on the rest of what is involved in a proposition's being evident, viz., a certain comparative epistemic status vis-à-vis all other propositions. More specifically, this comparative status consists in its being the case that no other propositions enjoy a more favorable epistemic status for S except those that enjoy the highest possible epistemic status. Now, is it credible that I should be justified in a belief that is, in part, about the epistemic status of a given proposition vis-à-vis the entire class of propositions, *just by virtue of feeling tired?* At the very least, the claim to higher-level truth-justification raises questions that are quite different from the claim to lower-level truth-justification. Chisholm has saddled his theory with a considerable liability by adding on the higher-level claim.[6]

Moreover, Chisholm need not have taken on this additional liability in order for direct evidence to play its intended role in his system. The course of Chisholm's exposition, and the structure of his theory, makes it clear that the main function of directly evident propositions in his system is to stop the regress of justification and serve as foundations of knowledge. I have argued elsewhere that the demands of the regress argument are amply satisfied by first-level immediate justification and that a foundationalist epistemology based on propositions that enjoy only first-level immediate justification will be in at least as strong a position as any other foundationalism.[7] It is true that Chisholm's methodology requires what we might call "high accessibility" to one's own epistemic states. This position is reflected in the quote from p. 114 given above and in other pronouncements in that same section of the book, such as Chisholm's version of the KK thesis.

(K4) If S considers the proposition that he knows that *p,* and if he does know that *p,* then he knows that he knows that *p.* (p. 116)

However, it remains to be shown that high accessibility requires that what justifies the higher-level proposition that *it is evident to S that p,* or that *S knows that p,* be the *same* as what justifies *p* itself. Chisholm has not so argued, and I am dubious about the prospects.

An equally serious consequence of a confusion of levels (or of an uncritical assumption that correlated propositions on two levels enjoy the same justification) is that the range of candidates for immediate justification is sharply restricted. It is a striking fact that most epistemologists who work with something like our distinction between mediate and immediate justification are markedly penurious in the modes of immediate justification they consider. Chisholm is typical in this regard. He simply notes that when a proposition is rendered evident by its own truth it is thereby *directly* evident, and he fails to consider whether there are other possibilities. Other epistemologists are equally narrowly preoccupied with immediate awareness or with self-evidence as sources of immediate justification.[8] One particularly unfortunate consequence of this parochialism is an obliviousness to the possibility that a belief might be immediately justified by having originated in a certain way, e.g., justified by having been produced by a reliable belief-producing mechanism.[9] Whatever the reason for Chisholm's ignoring immediate awareness, or Lewis's ignoring truth-justification, it seems quite plausible to suppose that the level-confusion we have been discussing is responsible for the widespread neglect of immediate justification by origin. For if one takes it that S is immediately justified in believing that *p* only if S is immediately justified in believing that *S is justified in believing that p,* then one will restrict the range of immediate justifiers to those one supposes will be capable of justifying the higher-level, as well as the lower-level, proposition. As we have seen in discussing Chisholm, it is by no means obvious that the modes of immediate justification favored by level-confusers do meet this requirement; perhaps a judicious assessment would reveal that none do. Nevertheless, it seems much *more* obvious that the fact that a belief was produced by a reliable psychological mechanism is *not* sufficient to justify a belief *about* the epistemic status of that belief; for we are often in the dark concerning the reliability, or other features, of what produces our beliefs. Hence in failing to distinguish between justification on the two levels, one will be led to ignore the possible epistemic relevance of the actual mode of belief-production.

Indeed, even where the possibility is considered, level-confusions may play a decisive role in its evaluation. Consider the following passage from Keith Lehrer's book, *Knowledge.*[10]

Thus, if something looks red to a person, he cannot justifiably conclude that it is red from the formula that red things look red in standard conditions to normal observers, he would also need to know that the conditions are standard and that he is normal. Independent information is, therefore, required for the justification of this perceptual belief. . . . More generally, to justify such a belief requires the information that the conditions that surround a man and the state he is in are such that when something looks red in conditions of this sort to a person in his state, then it is red.

. . . Since a man may hallucinate, he cannot justifiably conclude he sees something as opposed to merely hallucinating unless he has information enabling him to distinguish hallucination from the real thing. (pp. 103-4)

Let us agree that a person to whom x looks red cannot be justified in a perceptual belief that x is red unless "the conditions that surround" him and "the state he is in are such that when something looks red in conditions of this sort to a person in his state, then it is red." But why should we also require that the person *have that information, know* (justifiably believe) that this is so. Why is it not enough that it *be* so? As we read on, it becomes transparently clear that Lehrer is falling into a level-confusion.

. . . the need for independent information arose from the need to determine whether the circumstances in which a person finds himself are those in which a man may justifiably conclude that he is seeing a typewriter or seeing something red.

. . . when a great deal . . . hinges on the matter of whether the person saw a bear-print or something else, . . . then we start to ask serious questions. We seek to determine if the person has information enabling him to decide whether he is seeing things of the sort he says he sees. (p. 105)

Well of course if *that* is what we are (he is) after, we (he) need "independent information." If he is trying to determine whether he is (really) seeing a bear-print (which involves determining whether his perceptual belief that there was a bear-print in a certain place was justified), or trying to determine whether the circumstances of his perception were such as to justify his perceptual belief, then *of course* he needs evidence of the sort mentioned. But that is just to say that he needs such evidence in order to be justified in the higher-level epistemic belief that his original perceptual belief was justified (and to be justified in the beliefs that support that epistemic belief). Lehrer can get from this incontrovertible truth to his central claim that such information is required for the perceptual belief to be justified, only by confusing the two problems — the justification of the perceptual belief and the justification of the higher-level belief that the perceptual belief is justified.

If one restricts oneself to sources of immediate justification that, one supposes, survive a transition to higher levels, the kinds of beliefs one takes to be susceptible of immediate justification will be likewise restricted. Historically, this has meant a restriction (for *a posteriori* knowledge) to beliefs concerning the believer's current states of consciousness. The insuperable difficulties encountered in the attempt to build the whole of *a posteriori* knowledge on such a slim basis have been more than amply documented. Our discussion reveals the role level-confusion has played in generating the supposition that no more extended foundation is available.

Indeed, if one does not distinguish between justification on different levels, one may be, confusedly, led to reject the whole concept of immediate justification. Consider the following argument from Bruce Aune's book, *Knowledge, Mind, and Nature*.[11]

> I would venture to say that any spontaneous claim, observational or intro-spective, carries almost no presumption of truth, when considered entirely by itself. If we accept such a claim as true, it is only because of our confidence that a complex body of background assumptions − concerning observers, standing conditions, the kind of object in question − and, often, a complex mass of further observations all point to the conclusion that it is true.
>
> Given these prosaic considerations, it is not necessary to cite experimental evidence illustrating the delusions easily brought about by, for example, hypnosis to see that no spontaneous claim is acceptable wholly on its own merits. On the contrary, common experience is entirely adequate to show that clear-headed men never accept a claim merely because it is made, without regard to the peculiarities of the agent and of the conditions under which it is produced. For such men, the acceptability of every claim is always deter-mined by inference. If we are prepared to take these standards of acceptabil-ity seriously, we must accordingly admit that the traditional search for in-trinsically acceptable empirical premises is completely misguided. (pp. 42-43)

Here Aune is arguing that beliefs are justified only by inference (from other propositions known, or justifiably believed), which is equivalent to the denial that there are any immediately justified beliefs. But a close reading will reveal that the considerations he advances seem to yield that conclusion only if one is confusing levels. The solid points that Aune makes in support of that claim are the following.

> If we accept such a claim [observational or introspective] as true, it is only because of our confidence that a complex of background assumptions . . . all point to the conclusion that it is true.

> . . . clear-headed men never accept a claim merely because it is made, with-out regard to the peculiarities of the agent and of the conditions under which it is produced. For such men, the acceptability of every claim is always deter-mined by inference.

Now in making these points Aune is not really considering what would justify the *issuer* of an introspective or observational claim, but what it would take to justify "us" in accepting his claim; he is considering the matter from a third-person per-spective. And it is clear that I cannot be immediately justified in accepting *your* introspective or observational claim. If I am so justified, it is because I am justified in supposing that you issued a claim of that sort, that you are in a normal condition and know the language, and so on. But that is only because I, in contrast to you, am justified in believing that *p* (where what you claimed is that *p*) only if I am justified in supposing that *you are justified in believing that p*. My access to *p* is through your access. It is just because my justification in believing *p* presupposes my being justified in believing that you are justified, that my justification has to be indirect. Thus what Aune's argument supports is the necessity for inferential backing for any higher-level belief to the effect that some person is justified in believing that *p*. Only a failure to distinguish levels leads him to suppose that he has shown that *no* belief can be immediately justified.

II

Next let us consider the bearing of level-confusions on the requirements for *mediate* justification, or in less technical terminology, on what it takes for S to have an adequate reason, grounds, or evidence for supposing that *p*. If the justification is mediate, there must be some other proposition, *q*, that is related to *p* and to S's belief that *p* in certain ways. Exactly what ways are necessary? The following requirements are accepted by virtually all who have considered the matter.

(1) *q* is related to *p* in a way that is "appropriate"[12] for purposes of justification.

(2) S believes that *q*.

(3) S is justified in believing that *q*.[13]

Most of the discussion of mediate justification has centered around (1). How must propositions, e.g., about sensory appearances, be related to, e.g., propositions about physical objects in the environment of the perceiver, to serve as adequate grounds for the latter? Must there be an entailment? Will some sort of inductive evidence relationship do? Or is there some special "evidence-conferring" relationship involved?

Again, there is widespread agreement that there must be some "psychological" connection between S's belief that *q* and S's belief that *p*. They cannot just lie "side by side" in his mind: *q* must be "his reason," or at least one of his reasons for believing that *p*. This is often taken to imply that the belief that *p* have been produced by the belief that *q*, or that the former be causally *sustained* by the latter. Sometimes this is further specified to require that S have *inferred p* from *q*, or now be disposed to do so. But whether or not inference is required, there is general agreement that some restrictions must be put on the mode of generation. So let us put as the fourth condition:

(4) S's belief that *p* was produced by, or is causally sustained by, S's belief that *q*, in the right way.

Now we come to further alleged conditions that, I want to suggest, depend for their plausibility on level-confusions. For one thing, various writers[14] hold that if S's belief that *q* is to constitute an adequate basis for S's belief that *p*, not only must *q* be appropriately related to *p*, but S must *know*, or at least justifiably believe, that this is so.

(5) S is justified in believing that q is appropriately related to p.

It seems to me that this is too sophisticated as a general requirement for mediate justification, especially if we take mediate justification to be required for mediate knowledge. Surely creatures like dogs and preverbal children can have mediate knowledge. My dog knows that I am preparing to take him for a walk, and he knows that because he sees me getting out his chain. But such creatures have no concepts of deductive, inductive, or other relations between propositions, and hence are quite incapable of believing, much less justifiably believing, that such relations obtain. Even where S has the relevant concepts, he may not be *justified* in supposing that appropriate relations obtain. He may just unthinkingly assume (truly) that, e.g., his local newspaper is a reliable source of local news. Does this prevent him from learning (coming to know) about local happenings from reading his newspaper (from his knowledge that these happenings are reported in the newspaper)?

Those who introduce condition (5) fail to give anything like a full-dress defense of it. Its proponents seem to take it as having sufficient intrinsic plausibility to make an explicit defense unnecessary. My diagnosis is that this plausibility largely stems from level-confusion. It does seem that I cannot be justified in the higher-level belief that *my belief that q mediately justifies me in believing that p* unless I am justified in supposing that q is appropriately related to p. For unless I am justified in supposing that, how could I be justified in supposing that the appropriate justification relation holds between the beliefs? And so if one does not distinguish between being justified in believing that p and being justified in *supposing that one is mediately justified in believing that p,* then one will naturally suppose that what is required for the latter is also required for the former.

Another widespread requirement is:

(6) S is able, or disposed, to cite q as what justifies his belief that p.

Here, e.g., is C. I. Lewis, disavowing the necessity for a conscious inference from q to p, and replacing that requirement with a combination of (4) and (6).

> . . . whether the ground of judgment is or is not explicitly in mind, is hardly the pertinent consideration, because it could not plausibly be taken to mark the important distinction between attitudes of B having positive cognitive value and those which lack it. Rather the pertinent distinction is between cases in which if the judgment be challenged by ourselves or others, we should be able to assign a basis of it which, whether explicitly thought of in drawing the judgment or not, is so related to it that we could truly say "If it were not for that, I should not have so judged."[15]

Again (6) would seem to be much too sophisticated a requirement, especially if justification is required for knowledge. There are knowing creatures who lack the sophistication, or even the linguistic skills, to respond to challenges by specifying the basis of their beliefs. They include creatures that do not have the use of language as well as language users who do not (yet) have any concept of epistemic justification. Even those sophisticated enough to engage in this kind of palaver may be unable, in particular cases, to identify the real and sufficient bases of their belief. Why, then, has this requirement seemed right to many? Here too level-confusion may play an important role. Requirement (6) seems more plausible as a requirement for being justified in accepting the higher-level proposition that *S is justified in believing that p.* One might well think that I cannot be justified in a claim to justification unless I can point out what does the justifying. But here we cannot pin all the blame on level-confusion. For, in truth, (6) is questionable as a requirement for higher-level justification as well. Why must I be able to *specify, cite,* or *formulate* what it is that justifies me in believing that *p,* in order to *be* justified in supposing that I *am* so justified? This is a special form of the old question of whether I can be justified in accepting a relatively unspecific or general proposition without being able to specify the particular fact(s) that makes it true. It has many forms: can I not be justified in supposing that there are a lot of dots on that surface without being able to say how many? Can I not be justified in believing that there is someone in the room without being able to say who is in the room? Of course it remains to be seen exactly how one could be justified in supposing, unspecifically, that he is (somehow) justified in believing that *p* without being able to say precisely what justifies him. But surely this possibility should not be dismissed without a hearing.

In the light of the point just made, perhaps the main villain in this piece is another widespread confusion in epistemology — one we are not really exploring in this paper — the confusion between 'justification' in the sense of *being* justified and 'justification' in the sense of "showing that one is justified." If one fails to keep that distinction in mind, one is liable to suppose that in order to *be* justified in believing that *p* one must be *able* at least to "justify" one's belief that *p* in the sense of showing that one is justified, i.e., exhibiting what it is that justifies one. And that would explain the plausibility of (6).

III

Finally let us consider the role of level-confusion in certain forms of skeptical argument. First, look at what may conveniently be called "Cartesian skepticism" because of its similarity to what we find in Descartes's *Meditations.*[16] The kind of argument I wish to discuss is directed at some particular knowledge claim and is designed to show that the claimer, S, does not know what he is claiming to know. Let us consider a case in which a person is looking out the window and claims to know that a car is parked in front of his house. (He supposes himself to see a car parked there.) The argument will then proceed as follows.

1. If S's present visual experience is being directly produced by an omnipotent spirit, then S does not know (perceptually) that there is a car parked in front of his house.[17]

2. S does not know that his present visual experience is not being directly produced by an omnipotent spirit.

3. Therefore, S does not know (perceptually) that there is a car parked in front of his house.

Questions could be raised about both premises, but I will not go into that. Instead, I will contend that even if both premises were unexceptionable, the conclusion would not follow. Why should we suppose that S's inability to rule out the hypothesis of an abnormal production of his visual experience implies that his visual experience gives him no knowledge of the physical environment? Any answer to this question will have to derive from our rationale for (1). Let us take that rationale to depend on some kind of (at least partly) causal theory of perceptual knowledge. My visual experiences can give me knowledge of a certain physical object only if that object played a role in the chain of causes leading up to that experience. If those experiences would have been produced exactly as they were (given the particular circumstances in which they occurred) even if that object were not there, then those experiences cannot mediate any knowledge of that object. If this be accepted, then (1) is justified. If S's visual experiences were produced directly by an omnipotent spirit, then they would have been produced in precisely this form even if a car had not been parked in front of his house. Hence, in that case, he would not know in this way, would not have visual knowledge, that there is a car parked in front of his house. But how does the conclusion follow from all that (plus (2)). Granted that an *actual* abnormal production inhibits perceptual knowledge, why suppose that the mere fact that S does not know the production was not abnormal rules out S's knowing about the car? If the object I am eating is made of cardboard, it will not nourish me. But suppose I do not know it is not made of cardboard; it by no means follows just from this lack of knowledge that the object will not nourish me. Its nutrient power, or the reverse, depends on what it *is*, not on what I do or do not *know* about it. Why should we suppose the present case is any different?

Here is a slightly different way of putting the matter. I do not know whether what I am eating is made of cardboard. But that fact leaves wide open the possibility that it is not made of cardboard and that it in fact contains nutrients. Similarly, the fact that I do not know whether my present visual experiences are being directly produced by an ingenious neuro-physiologist leaves wide open the possibility that in fact they are being produced in the usual way by a chain of causes stemming from a car parked in front of my house. And if that possibility is realized, I do have perceptual knowledge that a car is parked in front of my house. Since premise (2) does not rule out the possibility in question, it (with premise (1)) does not establish that I do not know that a car is parked in front of my house.

But then why is this argument so tempting? Again, a level-confusion may be largely responsible. Given a certain assumption, we can derive a higher-level correlate of (3) from our two premises, a correlate that replaces *there is a car parked in front of S's house* with *S knows (perceptually) that there is a car parked in front of S's house.*

3A. Therefore S does not know that he knows (perceptually) that there is a car parked in front of his house.

The assumption in question, a rather controversial one, is that one cannot know that p unless one knows, with respect to each of the necessary conditions of p, that it obtains. Now according to premise (1), one necessary condition of S's knowing (perceptually) that there is a car parked in front of his house is that his perceptual experience is not produced abnormally. But according to (2), S does not know that this necessary condition obtains. Hence (3A): he does not know that he knows (perceptually) that there is a car parked in front of his house. But, granted that (3A) follows from (1) and (2), why suppose that (3) follows? One possible explanation of this supposition is a *conviction* that one cannot know that p without knowing that one knows that p; if that were so, then to show that one does not know that one knows that p is *ipso facto* to show that one does not know that p. However, not many philosophers hold so strong a level-bridging view. Hence I think that the attractiveness of the original argument is largely due to a level-*confusion*. If one fails to distinguish clearly between p and S *knows that* p, one will likewise not distinguish between what it takes to know the one and what it takes to know the other.[18]

Finally, let us consider another kind of skeptical argument, in which level-confusion also plays an important part. This is what we may call "criterion skepticism"; the classical form is in Sextus Empiricus, *Outlines of Pyrrhonism*, bk. II, chap. 4.

> In order to decide the dispute which has arisen about the criterion (of truth), we must possess an accepted criterion by which we shall be able to judge the dispute; and in order to possess an accepted criterion, the dispute about the criterion must first be decided. And when the argument thus reduces itself to a form of circular reasoning the discovery of the criterion becomes impracticable, since we do not allow them to adopt a criterion by assumption, while if they offer to judge the criterion by a criterion we force them to a regress *ad infinitum*. And furthermore, since demonstration requires an approved demonstration, they are forced into circular reasoning.

I should like to work with my own version of an argument suggested by these remarks of Sextus.

> In order for me to be justified in believing that p, my belief that p must satisfy the conditions laid down by some valid epistemic principle (for epistemic justification). But then I am justified in the original belief only if I am justified in supposing that there is a valid epistemic principle that does apply in that way to my present belief. And in order to be justified in that further belief there must be a valid epistemic principle that is satisfied in *that* case. And in order to be justified in supposing that . . . This series either doubles back on itself, in which case the justification is circular, or it stretches back infinitely. Thus it would appear that claims to justification give rise either to circularity or to an infinite regress.

The level-confusion is more readily apparent here than in Cartesian skepticism. This argument has no tendency to show that my being justified in believing that p

depends on conditions that give rise to an infinite regress. On the argument's own showing, what my *being* justified in believing that *p* depends on is the existence of a valid epistemic principle that applies to my belief that *p*. So long as there *is* such a principle, that belief *is* justified whether I know anything about the principle or not and whether or not I am justified in supposing that there is such a principle. What this latter justification is required for is not my being justified in believing that *p*, but rather my being justified in the higher-level belief that *I am justified in believing that p*. I can be justified in that higher-level belief only if I am justified in supposing there to be a principle of the right sort. But it is only by a level-confusion that one could suppose this latter justification to be required for my being justified in the original lower-level belief. The regress never gets started.

This would seem to leave open the possibility that being justified in a higher-level belief, such as the belief that *I am justified in believing that p*, does give rise to an infinite regress or circularity. But that would be a mistake of the same kind. To be justified in that higher-level belief, there has to be a (higher-level) epistemic principle of justification that applies in the right way to the belief in question. But again, all that is required is the *existence* of such a principle. For the justification of that (first-order) higher-level belief, it is not necessary that I be justified in supposing that there is such a principle; only that there be such. Again, what this last justification is needed for is the justification of the still higher-level belief that *I am justified in believing that I am justified in believing that p*. At each stage I can *be* justified in holding a certain belief provided there *is* a valid epistemic principle that satisfies certain conditions. My knowing or being justified in believing that there is such a principle is required only for the justification of a belief that is of a still higher level vis-à-vis the belief with which we started.

IV

In conclusion, let me suggest a more positive moral from this string of polemics. It should be clear that the level-confusions we have been examining naturally lead to ignoring the possibility of what we might call unsophisticated, unreflective first-level knowledge or justification, cases in which one knows that *p*, or is justified in believing that *p*, but, whether because of conceptual underdevelopment or otherwise, fails to attain the more sophisticated, higher-level knowledge (or justified belief) that one has that lower-level knowledge or justification. Of course it may not be immediately obvious that there is unreflective knowledge or justification; the question needs careful consideration. But the point is that so long as we are victims of level-confusion we cannot even consider the possibility of a purely first-level cognition. The new look in epistemology introduced by the "reliability" theories of such thinkers as Dretske, Armstrong, and Goldman is largely built on the claim that first-level knowledge is independent of higher-level knowledge. We will be able to take this "new look" even experimentally, only to the extent that we can free ourselves from the blinders imposed by level-confusion.

Notes

1. We are leaving open the question of what else is required for mediate justification over and above the possession of certain other justified beliefs.

2. Panayot Butchvarov, *The Concept of Knowledge* (Evanston, Ill., 1970), pt. I, section 6.

3. Roderick Chisholm, *Theory of Knowledge*, 2nd ed. (Englewood Cliffs, N.J., 1977).

4. One other terminological guide to the quotations that follow. In the first edition of *Theory of Knowledge* (1966), Chisholm used the term 'directly evident' for the concept expressed above by the term 'self-presenting'. In the second edition the former term is officially reserved for a wider concept, but much of the material that was retained from the first edition still used 'directly evident' in the way 'self-presenting' was defined above. I will use the term 'directly evident' for the concept just defined.

5. What are we to make of the fact that in D2.1 Chisholm speaks of *p* being made *evident* by the fact that *p*, whereas in the passage just quoted he speaks of the higher-level proposition being *justified* by the fact that *p*? Does this indicate that Chisholm is less sure about the degree of justification conferred by the fact that *p* on the higher-level proposition than on the degree of justification it confers on the proposition that *p*? Or does he think that the propositions on both levels are made *evident* by the fact that *p*? For present purposes it is not necessary to settle this question. The point with which we are concerned is simply the relation between claims to some justificatory role of the fact that *p* on the two levels.

6. Similar points can be made for other conceptions of immediate justification. If we hold with Russell, C. I. Lewis, and many others, that beliefs about one's current sensory data are justified by the fact that one is "directly aware" of those states, this has a certain initial plausibility, one that is not shared by the correlated higher-level claim that one is justified in believing that one is justified in holding such beliefs by virtue of being directly aware of sensory data.

7. William P. Alston, "Two Types of Foundationalism", *Journal of Philosophy* 73 (1976): 165-85.

8. For two of the rare attempts to critically compare different putative direct justifiers, see my essay "Self-Warrant: A Neglected Form of Privileged Access," *American Philosophical Quarterly* 13 (1976): 257-72; Butchvarov, *The Concept of Knowledge*, Chap. 1, sec. 6.

9. For some presentations of this possibility see Alvin I. Goldman, "Discrimination and Perceptual Knowledge," *Journal of Philosophy* 73 (1976): 771-91; and my "The Justification of Perceptual Beliefs," unpublished.

10. Keith Lehrer, *Knowledge* (Oxford, 1974).

11. Bruce Aune, *Knowledge, Mind, and Nature* (New York, 1967).

12. If one should try to give a general criterion for "appropriateness," it might be something like this: *q* is related to *p* "appropriately" *iff* the truth of *q* will thereby either guarantee the truth of *p*, or at least make the truth of *p* likely. In other words, the relationship is, or tends to be, truth-preserving.

13. The rationale for (2) and (3) are fairly obvious. How can the fact that *q* is "appropriately" related to *p* do anything to justify *me* in believing that *p* unless I "have" this adequate ground, unless I am in a position to appropriate the epistemic benefits contained therein. And I cannot do this unless it is at least something I believe. And unless I am *justified* in believing it, how can justification (for me) be transferred along the appropriate propositional relation. Some would go further and require that I *know* that *q*. The temporal relations between the beliefs are widely ignored.

14. D. M. Armstrong, *Belief, Truth, and Knowledge* (Cambridge, 1973), p. 151. Brian Skyrms, "The Explication of 'X knows that *p*'" *Journal of Philosophy* 64 (June 22, 1967): 374.

15. C. I. Lewis, *An Analysis of Knowledge and Valuation* (LaSalle, Ill., 1946), p. 328.

16. This argument is not supposed to be an exact replica of anything in the *Meditations*.

17. For a more up-to-date version the omnipotent spirit could be replaced by an ingenious neuro-physiologist.

18. Of course, if (1) were of the form 'If q, then not-p', rather than of the form 'If q, then S doesn't know that p', it would be a different ball game. (Where p is, in our case, *There is a car parked in front of S's house*, and q is *S's present visual experience is being directly produced by an omnipotent spirit.*) For in that case the falsity of q is one of the necessary conditons of the truth of p, and so (2) tells us that S does not know that this necessary condition holds. And so the same reasoning that led us to take the original argument to show that S does not know that S knows that p, would lead us to take this argument to show that S does not know that p. Sometimes Cartsian skepticism is presented in this stronger form and sometimes in the weaker form. Thus when q is *I am dreaming* and p is *I am seated in front of the fire awake*, we have the stronger form, for q does imply not-p. But in our original example, q did not imply not-p. My present visual experience's being produced by an omnipotent spirit is quite compatible with there being a car parked in front of my house at the moment. In this paper I am concerned only with the weaker form. It is worthy of note that the stronger form is more vulnerable to the Moore-Malcolm charge of begging the question. For if q does imply not-p, then the question of whether I know that not-q is directly dependent on whether I know that p. For if I do know that p, which is the point of contention, then, given certain principles of epistemic logic, I *ipso facto* know that not-q.

Knowing Less by Knowing More

CARL GINET

I

It is a well known property of non-deductive inference that you can weaken such an inference by adding to its premises. For example, the conclusion

    (1) Hobart defeated Cornell in their basketball game yesterday,

is supported much more strongly by the premise

    (2) The announcer on the eleven o'clock newscast last night said, "Hobart nipped Cornell 79 to 78 this evening,"

than it is by that premise conjoined with

    (3) The announcer on the eight o'clock newscast this morning said, "Last night Cornell squeaked by Hobart 79 to 78."

This property of non-deductive inference appears to lead to a somewhat surprising conclusion about knowledge. Because of it, it seems, one can pass from knowing a certain fact to not knowing it merely by acquiring more information relevant to whether or not that fact obtains. Suppose that (1) is true. And suppose that, listening to the eleven o'clock newscast last night, I came to know that (2) is true. It certainly seems right to say that upon coming to know that (2) is true I came to know that (1) is true — provided, of course, that I believed that (1) is true on the basis of my knowledge of (2) and of the general background that makes (2) good evidence for (1) and I knew of no evidence against (1). One of the common ways in which we come to know the outcomes of sporting events is by hearing them reported on the radio. But suppose further that I listened to the eight o'clock newscast this morning and came to know that (3) is true. And suppose that at that point and for some time thereafter I knew nothing other than (2) and (3) that was specifically relevant to whether or not (1) is true. Then, certainly, during that period I did *not* know that (1) is true. The same general background that makes (2) by itself strong evidence for (1) makes (3) by itself strong evidence against (1) and so makes the conjunction of (2) and (3), by itself, of no evidentiary value either way with respect to (1). During that period I had no justification at all for believing (1) to be true and therefore certainly did not know it to be true. So: like many others who learned it from last night's newscast, I knew that Hobart defeated Cornell; but, unlike those fortunate ones who missed this morning's newscast, I ceased to know this; and this loss of knowledge was brought about simply by my gaining the knowledge that this morning's newscast said otherwise.

This seems to me, at any rate, the right way to describe such a case. But some may balk at this description. While not wishing to deny that one can cease to know what one once knew, they may resist the idea that one can do this simply by learning more. Knowledge, they may be inclined to say, ought to be more secure than that: though not proof against forgetting, it ought to be proof against further knowledge. Philosophers so inclined may even seek ways to show that it is impossible to know less by knowing more.

One way this might be argued would be by denying that knowledge — the genuine article — can be obtained by non-deductive inference. Just because justification of belief by such inference is vulnerable to defeat by new information (or new justified beliefs), it might be said, such inference cannot provide the sort of justification required for *knowledge*. Unfortunately, this line requires one to deny that a great deal of what passes for knowledge really is so. It requires one to suppose that knowledge is very much harder to come by, and very much more rarely attained, than we ordinarily think it is. Thus it trades a minor touch of insecurity in knowledge for a major loss of means to its attainment. This does not look like a sensible bargain.

II

Those who are disinclined to admit the possibility of knowing less by knowing more may, therefore, be inclined (at least at first) to welcome an intriguing argument stated in the literature a few years ago by Gilbert Harman.[1] This argument does not tamper with the ordinary initial conditions for knowledge. It leaves them as our everyday intuitions would have them. Instead it attempts to provide any one who can once correctly claim to know a thing with a justification for continuing to claim to know it no matter what new information she may acquire.

Harman states the argument in the following way (I have inserted letters to label the various propositions in the argument):

If (a) I know that h is true, (b) I know that evidence against h is evidence against something that is true; so (c) I know that such evidence is misleading. But (d) I should disregard evidence that is misleading. So, once (a) I know that h is true, (e) I am in a position to disregard any future evidence that seems to tell against h.

This statement of the argument has a minor defect that, for my purposes, it is safe and convenient to ignore. Strictly speaking, the first premise is not necessarily true: (b) does not follow from (a). If I know that h is true, then I know that evidence against h is evidence against a truth, *provided* also that my knowledge of h leads me, through my knowledge of the obvious logical connection, to believe confidently that any evidence against h is evidence against a truth. (It is obvious that h entails that evidence against h is evidence against a truth.)

There are, however, some flaws in Harman's formulation that I think we should remedy before going on to evaluate the argument.

First, the subordinate inference from (b) to (c) looks unnecessary. To say that evidence against a truth is misleading is just to say that it is evidence against a *truth*.

Second, it is not as clear as it should be what is meant by the last clause of the conclusion, namely, (e) I am in a position to *disregard* any future evidence that seems to tell against h. This must, I think, be taken to mean that any fact I might in the future come to know I will then be entitled to treat as *no* evidence for me against h, as not weakening the case I have for believing confidently that h is true (however much it might *seem* that I should treat the new information as weakening my case for h).

Third, what premise (d) tells us looks unnecessarily paradoxical. The point is not that I should take what I *recognize to be* evidence against h and, because it is misleading, treat it as no evidence against h. Rather, the point is that if I know that my counting some fact as evidence against h — as weakening my case for h — *would be* to count it as evidence against a truth, then I am entitled *not* to count it as evidence against h. By the same token, the formulation of clause (b) is needlessly paradoxical: it is not that I know that what I *take* to be evidence against h is evidence against a truth but that I know that if I *were* to count something as evidence against h I *would be* counting it as evidence against a truth.

Fourth, the argument must assume that I do not in the future *forget* my knowledge of the truth of h. For this possibility provides an obvious way in which the conclusion of the argument could be false that has not been explicitly ruled out in the premises.

These observations so far suggest the following reformulation of the argument:

For any propositions h and f: if (a) I know that h is true, then (b) I know that, if in the future I come to know that f is true and to count f as evidence against h, I will be counting f as evidence against a truth. But (d) if I know that f is true and that if I count f as evidence against h I will be counting f as evidence against a truth, then I am entitled not to count f as evidence against h; so, if (a) I know that h is true, and I do not forget this knowledge, then (e) if in the future I come to know that f is true then at that time I am entitled not to count f as evidence against h.

This revision of the argument reveals a significant gap in it. The argument, in effect, affirms that (e) follows from (a) by means of (b) and the conditional (d).

But note that (b) is not the same proposition as the antecedent of (d). (b) says: I know that if I come to know that f is true, then, if I then count f as evidence against b, I will be counting f as evidence against a truth. The antecedent of (d) says: I know that f is true and that if I count f as evidence against b, then I count f as evidence against a truth. If (e) is really to follow, these two propositions must be linked by the further assumption that if I know what (b) says I know (and I do not in the future forget this knowledge), then if in the future I came to know that f is true then at that time I know what the antecedent of (d) says I know.

If we add this assumption as a premise, we obtain the following valid formulation of the argument:

For any propositions b and f:

(4) if (a) I know that b is true, then (b) I know that, if in the future I come to know f to be true, my then counting f as evidence against b would be to count f as evidence against a truth;

(5) if (b) I know that if in the future I come to know f to be true then my counting f as evidence against b would be to count f as evidence against a truth, and I do not forget this knowledge, then if in the future I come to know that f is true then at that time I know that my counting f as evidence against b would be to count f as evidence against a truth;

(6) if (d) I know that f is true and that my counting f as evidence against b would be to count f as evidence against a truth, then I am entitled not to count f as evidence against b;

(7) therefore, if (a) I know that b is true, and I do not forget this knowledge, then (e) if in the future I come to know that f is true, then at that time I am entitled not to count f as evidence against b.

If this argument is sound, then what we said about the case of my hearing on the radio conflicting reports of the outcome of a basketball game is wrong. If (1) is substituted for b and (3) for f, the argument tells us that, once I knew that (1) is true (by inference from (2)), then, assuming that I did not forget this knowledge, when I came to know (3) I was entitled to regard the fact that (3) as no evidence at all against the truth of (1). This is enough to convince me that the argument cannot be sound, but, of course, it would not be enough for anyone who dislikes the idea that one can lose knowledge by gaining it and who dislikes it enough to doubt the correctness of what we said about the case of the conflicting newscasts.

There is, however, a stronger reason for suspecting that something must be wrong with the argument. The argument does not depend on anything peculiar to the meaning of 'know'. It works just as well if 'know' is replaced throughout with 'justifiedly believe'. This means that if the argument were sound it would demonstrate that either non-deductive inference does *not* possess the well-known property mentioned at the beginning of this paper (namely, that adding information to the premises can weaken the argument, i.e., weaken the justification that justified belief in the premises provides for belief in the conclusion) or else non-deductive inference is incapable of justifying even belief (much less a claim to know). Thus the argument proves more than even those who like the conclusion might wish to accept.

I think it likely that most philosophers will, upon reflection, agree that the argument must go wrong somewhere. Where? It is valid, in our latest formulation. Which, then, of the three premises is (are) false?

Harman offers a brief diagnosis of the problem:

> The argument . . . overlooks the way actually having evidence can make a difference. Since I now know that [h is true], I now know that any evidence that appears to indicate something else is misleading. That does not warrant me in simply disregarding any further evidence, since getting that further evidence can change what I know. In particular, after I get such further evidence I may no longer know that it is misleading. For having the new evidence can make it true that I no longer know that [h is true] ; if I no longer know that, I no longer know that the new evidence is misleading.[2]

The second sentence here is not entirely unambiguous. The clause 'I now know that any evidence that appears to indicate something else is misleading' could be taken to refer to evidence that I now already possess. But I think that Harman means that, since I now know that h is true, I now know that if I were in the future to take some newly learned fact to be evidence against h I would in so doing be misled. Thus I think he means to accept the first premise of the argument as I have reformulated it, i.e., (4). And I think that this premise should be accepted. When, after hearing the late evening news, I knew that Hobart had defeated Cornell, I also knew that if in the future I were to take some newly learned fact to be evidence against this proposition, I would be taking it to be evidence against a truth. Right after the eleven o'clock newscast I could have said that I know that Hobart defeated Cornell and, therefore, I know — what I see to be an obvious logical consequence — that if tomorrow I hear some newscaster say something to the contrary and take that to be evidence to the contrary, then I will be counting that as evidence against what is in fact a truth.

What Harman goes on to say, after the second sentence of the passage quoted above, does not seem to quarrel with the third premise of the argument as I have reformulated it, i.e., (6). I think that this too is as it should be, provided we understand "count f as evidence against h" in the right way. In the context of this argument this phrase should be taken to mean "count f as weakening the overall case I have for believing h to beneath the strength required for knowing h." (If this latter phrase is substituted for the former throughout the argument, my claim a few paragraphs back that the argument works just as well if 'know' is replaced throughout with 'justifiedly believe' still holds.) On this reading of this key phrase the truth of (6) is plain. I cannot, at the same time, both know that h is true and be required to count my knowledge of f as making my overall case for believing h weaker than what is required for knowing h.

What Harman does question in the passage quoted above, if I understand him right, is the second premise of my reformulation, i.e., (5). (This is the premise that was not explicit in Harman's formulation of the argument quoted earlier.) Here again, I think he is right. This is where the argument leaves the track. What Harman says amounts to this: the basis on which I now know h and the proposition f may be such that my coming to know f would make me cease to know h. This is true and important, but I think it needs spelling out how, in light of this, (5) is false and, perhaps more important, how (5), though false, can seem true.

(5) says that if first I know a certain conditional proposition and, not forgetting this knowledge, I later come to know its antecedent (assuming that when I come to know f I will know that I know it), then I will (if I have my logical wits about me) thereby come to know its consequent. Stated thus abstractly, this looks very plausible. We are taken in because we find such a progression through *modus ponens* quite natural and familiar: it is a common pattern for the acquisition of knowledge. What we overlook is that this progression need not always be possible. There can be conditional propositions whose content is such that, although one may know (justifiedly believe) the conditional in a situation where its antecedent is true, the way in which one knows this (one's justification for believing this) may depend on one's *not* knowing (believing) that the antecedent is true.

Consider, for example, these conditionals:

(8) If he has spoken falsely, I will always be deceived. (For I can never doubt him.)

(9) If there was such a meeting, then I'll be forever innocent of the fact.

It is transparent that I could not know (justifiedly believe) either of these conditionals (in any way at all) except by failing to know (believe) its antecedent. For the content of antecedent and consequent are so related that my knowing (believing) the antecedent means that I do not know (justifiedly believe) the consequent. (Indeed, in these cases, my knowing the antecedent is incompatible with the truth of the consequent.)

Now take (5), substitute (1) for h and (3) for f, suppose the result to be asserted shortly after I have come to know (1) on the basis of (2), and consider the conditional that the antecedent of (5) then says I know, namely:

(10) If I come to know that the announcer on the eight o'clock newscast tomorrow morning says that Cornell squeaked by Hobart 79 to 78, then my counting that announcement as evidence that Hobart did not defeat Cornell will be to count it as evidence against a truth.

(10) is much like (8) and (9). The contents of the antecedent and consequent of (10) are related to each other, and to the basis on which I know (10) in the example, in such a way that I could not know (10) on that basis except by failing to know its antecedent. Had I not come to know (2) until I had already come to know (3) and therewith (knowing that I know it) the antecedent of (10), I could not have known (1) or its logical consequence (10) merely on the basis of knowing (2). Thus the content of (10) and the way in which it is known in this situation

are such that I cannot go on to add to the situation knowledge of the antecedent of (10) without thereby losing knowledge of (10). Thus (10) is here incapacitated for use in the familiar progression through *modus ponens*. As with (8) and (9), knowledge of the conditional cannot consort with knowledge of its antecedent. Therefore, contrary to what we assume when we find (5) plausible, one cannot simply add knowledge of the antecedent to one's already acquired knowledge of the conditional to yield knowledge of the consequent. Premise (5) is involved in somewhat the same absurdity as *A* is in the following dialogue: *A:* "If he spoke falsely, I will always be deceived." *B:* "He did speak falsely." *A:* "Then I will always be deceived." (The absurdity is not exactly the same. The reason my knowing the conditional depends on my not knowing the antecedent in the case of (8), though not in the case of (10), is that the *truth* of the conditional is incompatible with my knowing the antecedent.)

Conditionals the knowledge of which depends on failure to know their antecedents are sufficiently uncommon that one is not likely to have become familiar with the fact that a conditional can have this property that thwarts progression through *modus ponens*. That may be why one may find (5) and this whole argument tempting, or at least find oneself at a loss to identify the snag in it. But once identified, the snag is indisputable and does ruin the argument. It is safe to conclude that in this argument there is no sound basis at all for doubting the possibility of decreasing one's knowledge by means of increasing it.

If I can lose a piece of knowledge just by gaining another, then it follows, of course, that when I have the knowledge I can fail to know that I will not in the future thus lose it. More than this, I can *fail to have justification for claiming to know* that I will not thus lose it. Consider our example. At the time when I know (1) on the basis of (2) and know (by a simple deduction from (1)) that if I come to know (3) and count it as evidence against (1) I will be counting it as evidence against a truth, I need not be in a position to be sure that I will not in the future come to know (3) — even if I know that if I do come to know (3) then I will no longer know (1). Indeed, in the ordinary sort of case, it would seem to be going too far for me to claim to *know* that tomorrow morning's newscast will not contradict what I have just learned from tonight's newscast. From the three premises,

(i) I know (1) on the basis of (2),

(ii) if in the future I come to know (3) and count it as evidence against (1) then I will be counting it as evidence against a truth,

(iii) if in the future I come to know (3), then I will no longer know (1),

all of which we may suppose I now know, there is no legitimate inference to the conclusion that I will not in the future come to know (3). It does not follow deductively and it is hard to see any acceptable inferential principles that would sanction it as a non-deductive inference, in every world in which knowing less by knowing more is possible. So we have another mildly surprising result: I can know something in such a way that at the same time I must admit that I do not know that I will not later be forced by a certain specific development to give up my claim to know it.

III

The possibility of knowing less by knowing more could also be described as the possibility of knowledge that depends on *ignorance* of conflicting evidence. In defending the possibility of such knowledge I do not wish to be misunderstood as defending a different and stronger claim that might be confused with it, namely the claim that whenever a person's ignorance of conflicting evidence protects her *justification for claiming* to know a fact — that is, the person is entitled to claim to know it, but only because she is ignorant of the conflicting evidence — then that person does *know* that fact, no matter what the nature of the conflicting evidence. This claim is now widely recognized to be false.

Its falsity can be seen by making some alterations on the example we have been using. Suppose that (1) is true and that, having heard the eleven o'clock news, I came to know (2) and, on that basis, justifiedly assumed that I knew (1). But suppose that the announcer on the eleven o'clock news slipped up in reading the sheet before her, inadvertently reversing the names 'Cornell' and 'Hobart'. Suppose further that this sheet was typed by a cohort taking a telephoned report and that this cohort slipped up in typing the accurate report he heard, inadvertently reversing the names of the two schools. The announcer announces the truth, but only quite fortuitously, as the result of two coincidental errors canceling each other. In light of this we should, I think, refuse to say that I *knew* this truth on the basis of hearing that announcement.

The contrary evidence of which I am ignorant in this case is the fact that the announcer misread the sheet before her. Not only would this undermine my case for claiming knowledge were I to learn of it, but in just being there, unknown to me, it renders my claim to knowledge false. This is in contrast to the contrary evidence in the earlier example, where my ignorance of it did protect my assumption that I knew the outcome of the game. In both examples my ignorance shielded my *justification* for claiming to know, but only in the first did it also guard the *truth* of the claim (and so create the possibility of losing one piece of knowledge just by gaining another).

What in general is it that divides such cases, in which justification for claiming to know depends on not knowing about contrary evidence, into these two species? What feature of the relation between the already acquired justification and the unknown contrary evidence makes it one sort of case rather than the other? If we had an interesting general answer to this question, we would also have one to the question of what condition must be added to justified true belief in order to get a set of conditions sufficient for knowledge: this condition is just the non-existence of the sort (whatever it is) of unknown conflicting evidence that renders a justified knowledge claim false. The one question comes down to the other. It is a question that has received very extensive discussion in the last decade and a half.[3] This discussion has not produced any interesting general answer that is compelling and widely agreed upon. The reason for this, I believe, is that the question has no interesting general answer.

One relevant suggestion, illustrated by the example given above, is this: Given a particular justification for a knowledge claim, contrary evidence that would render that claim false always differs from contrary evidence that would not do so because the subject's justification for believing the proposition in question would be weakened much more by her learning of the first sort of contrary evidence than it would be by her learning of the second sort. This suggestion is a general answer to the question, all right, and it may well be correct, but it is not very interesting. It is not the revealing sort of answer that we would like to have. It is too meager in content. If this is all that can be said, then the general difference we are interested in is just a matter of the degree of something for which there is no principled way of determining the cutoff point. Whereas we would like it to be determined by some property of the contrary evidence, or its relation to the already possessed justification, that is always clearly present or clearly absent and it reveals some interesting epistemic principle, some interesting fact about the concept of knowledge. All that our unexciting point reveals about the concept of knowledge is that it is vague in yet another dimension.

Plausible candidates for more satisfying general answers are by now familiar. They are things like: the contrary evidence (that falsifies the knowledge claim) must entail that the subject's justification includes a false belief or requires inference through a false lemma; the contrary evidence must entail that the beliefs involved in the subject's justification lack an appropriate sort of causal connection with the fact the subject is justified in claiming to know. I think, however, that the fact we have to face is that, although interesting conditions like these may work for special kinds of knowledge (for example, knowledge by inference or memory knowledge or restricted kinds of perceptual knowledge), none of them applies in every kind of case. If anything works all across the board, it is just the fairly obvious point mentioned above. (Although this is not the interesting general answer that we would have liked to have, the fact that nothing more interesting holds, if it is a fact, is interesting.)

There is some support for this conclusion in the fact that in all the discussion of the question (of which I am aware) no interesting general answer has been proposed for which there is not a counterexample. But what clinches it is that one can construct examples in which nothing more interesting than the obvious point is available to serve as a general basis for the distinction. Consider the following situation.[4] You are visiting a foreign city and come across a public market in which you see many stands piled up with fruits and vegetables. You walk up to one of the fruit stands and look over its enormous display of pears. Your eye lights on a particular pear and you think that it looks unusually delicious. You contemplate buying and eating it. You never question whether what you are looking at is a pear. Now, if this were a normal sort of fruit stand, you would *know* that what you are looking at is a pear. Let us suppose, however, that, although it is a pear and you are, of course, justified in your unquestioning confidence that it is, this fruit stand is out of the ordinary because 99 percent of the things surrounding that pear that look every bit as much like pears as it does are not pears but carefully painted wax imitations, which it amuses this fruit vendor to put in place of the real pears that have been sold. Thus it is extremely lucky that what you are looking at is a pear and not a piece of wax, too lucky for your true belief that it is a pear — justified as it is merely by how the thing looks — to count as knowledge.

But now suppose that the circumstances had been somewhat different. Suppose that only 1 percent of the pear-looking things surrounding the one that has caught your eye were wax imitations and that 99 percent were real pears. In that case, surely, it would *not* be too fortunate that you happen to be looking at one of the real pears in the display for it to be said that you know that what you see is a pear.

Where, between 1 and 99 percent, does one draw the line, on one side of which you know and on the other you do not? No doubt everyone will want to draw it vaguely. There are likely to be differences of opinion about where even a vague boundary should be put. (I am inclined to say that the boundary has been crossed when as many as half of the surrounding pear-looking things are imitations.) The important point, however, is that the only relevant property separating the clear cases on one side from those on the other is the *size* of the ratio of imitation to genuine pears. There is no other interesting property the presence or absence of which explains why you know when the ratio is very small but fail to know when it is very large. There is only the degree of something. The only thing one can say is that the cases where you do not know that you see a pear differ from those where you do because in the first sort of case the contrary evidence of which you are ignorant (the fact that *n* percent of the pear-looking things in the display are imitations) would, if you became cognizant of it, damage your case for believing that you see a pear *too much* more than it would in the second sort of case (where the proportion of imitations is much smaller). It makes it *too* lucky that the basis you happen to have for assuming that you see a pear is a basis for a truth rather than a falsehood. The example offers no other way in which to make the distinction. It follows that this colorless sort of point is the strongest that can always be appealed to in order to distinguish unknown contrary evidence that falsifies a justified knowledge claim from such evidence that does not do thus but merely places one in a position to know less by knowing more.[5]

Notes

1. Gilbert Harman, *Thought* (Princeton, 1973) p. 148. Harman credits Saul Kripke with suggesting the argument to him. I first encountered the argument in a talk that Kripke gave at Cornell in the Spring of 1975.

2. *Ibid.,* pp. 148-49.

3. Since the publication of Edmund Gettier's paper, "Is Justified True Belief Knowledge?" *Analysis* 23 (1963): 121-23.

4. I offered a similar example to make a similar point in *Knowledge, Perception, and Memory* (Dordrecht, 1975), pp. 74-75.

5. It is not certain that even this unexciting sort of point always applies. It may be possible for there to be a pair of cases in which the subjects have justifications for claiming to know the same truth, there exists the same sort of evidence against this truth which would damage

their justifications *equally* badly, were they to learn of it, yet only one of them *knows* the truth in question. Richard Boyd has suggested to me (in discussion) that we might get such a pair of cases by including the supposition that in one case, but not the other, the subject was aware of the possibility of the sort of contrary evidence that in fact existed (while justified in thinking that this possibility could be ignored). I am uncertain, however, that this sort of difference between the cases can, in the fact of the posited similarities, be a good reason for concluding to the further difference that the subject's claim to know is falsified by the existence of the contrary evidence in that case but not in the other. Being aware of the possibility must mean here something more than being aware that it is a *logical* possibility. It must mean something like knowing that one does not know that the possibility is not a fact. But, as I have pointed out above (p. 157), one can *know* something while having to admit that one does *not* know that evidence will not be turned up that will force one to give up one's claim to know it. But then, there may be relevantly different sorts of bases for knowing that one does not know . . . Or there may, for all I know, be some other sort of difference that would do the trick.

I would like to thank John Bennett, Richard Boyd, Harold Hodes, Terence Irwin, Sydney Shoemaker, and William Wilcox for helpful comments on a slightly earlier version of this paper.

Reasoning and Evidence
One Does Not Possess[1]

GILBERT HARMAN

PART 1. THE BASIC ARGUMENT

By reasoning or inference I do not mean a proof or argument in a logician's sense. I mean, rather, a process by which one changes one's overall view, adding some things, subtracting others. As a heuristic aid in studying reasoning in this sense, I shall tentatively assume that our intuitions about knowledge are fairly accurate and I shall also tentatively assume the following two principles:

(P1)   Reasoning that could in certain circumstances give someone knowledge is justified reasoning.

(P2)   Reasoning that depends essentially on the acceptance of a false proposition does not give someone knowledge.

I shall then consider various "Gettier examples," each of which is a *pair* of possible situations in which (a) a person believes something h that happens to be true, (b) in both situations the person is equally justified in believing h, but (c) in one situation that belief constitutes knowledge whereas in the other it does not.[2] Although such examples have often been discussed in connection with attempts to offer analyses of the concept of knowledge, my purpose is different. I aim to use such examples to learn something about reasoning. In this paper I shall show how reflections on Gettier examples, given (P1) and (P2), can suggest principles of reasoning which can then be seen to be independently plausible and for which an independent rationale can be found.

1. Evidence One Does Not Possess

I have argued elsewhere that intuitions about knowledge in certain Gettier examples indicate (1) that there cannot be a purely probabilistic rule of inference and (2) that there is a requirement of explanatory coherence on our beliefs; and I have claimed that the rationale for this is (1) that we could not operate in purely probabilistic terms because that would involve an exponential explosion in the memory capacity needed to handle each new proposition on which we had a view and (2) that our beliefs are subject to a requirement of explanatory coherence because of our need to use our beliefs in achieving our goals.[3]

These results come from considering Gettier examples in which lack of knowledge can easily be attributed to the falsity of an explanatory claim that is essential to certain reasoning. There are other Gettier examples, which are not clearly of the same sort, involving misleading evidence one does not possess. To construct such an example, we take a case (case one) in which someone knows something and then modify it by imagining (case two) that there exists misleading evidence against the proposition in question, evidence of which the person in the example is unaware and such that, if the person were aware of that evidence, he or she would no longer be justified in believing the proposition in question. Concerning many examples of this sort, we are reluctant to say that in case two the person knows the proposition in question to be true, even though all his or her essential explanatory suppositions seem true.

There seem to be two ways in which such misleading evidence can undermine a person's knowledge.[4] The evidence can either be evidence that it would be possible for the person to obtain himself or herself or evidence possessed by others in a relevant social group to which the person in question belongs.

Here is an example of the first kind. In case one, Mary comes to know that Norman is in Italy when she calls his office and is told he is spending the summer in Rome. In case two, Norman seeks to give Mary the impression that he is in San Francisco by writing her a letter saying so, a letter he mails to San Francisco where a friend then mails it on to Mary. This letter is in the pile of unopened mail on Mary's desk before her when she calls Norman's office and is told he is spending the summer in Rome. In this case (case two), Mary does not come to know that Norman is in Italy, although all her explanatory suppositions are correct.[5] Norman's office reports what he told them as the result of his intention then to spend the summer in Rome, an intention he has carried out.

It is important in this case that Mary could obtain the misleading evidence. If the evidence is unobtainable, because Norman forgot to mail the letter after he wrote it, or because the letter was burned up in a mail fire in San Francisco, or because the letter was delivered to the wrong building where it will remain unopened, then it does not keep Mary from knowing that Norman is in Italy.

It is also important that the obtainable evidence not be merely *part* of the evidence Mary would obtain if she were to obtain evidence including that part. All the evidence Mary would obtain must be counted. If Norman's friend in California adds a note explaining the hoax before he mails Norman's letter on to Mary, Norman's letter in her unopened mail in front of her no longer keeps her from knowing that he is in Italy, since that is only part of the relevant evidence Mary would obtain if she were to open the letter.[6]

Here is an example of the second kind. Jane comes to know in case one that Dr. Kirby has been assassinated when she reads about it in the paper. But she does not come to know this in case two if widespread publicity of which she is unaware has been given to credible denials of the story by officials (who hope to defuse an explosive political situation), so that most people do not know what to believe. Nevertheless, Jane's explanatory suppositions in case two are all true. She reads what was written by an eyewitness reporting what he observed.

In this sort of case, the misleading evidence does not have to be obtainable by Jane, who might be locked away in solitary confinement with no one to talk to and no information about the outside world except for this particular issue of the newspaper which a guard has left behind by accident. She still fails to come to know that Dr. Kirby has been assassinated. On the other hand, it is important in this sort of case that the misleading evidence be possessed by others in some relevant social group. Suppose that the official denials are reported only to inmates of a certain prison (in order to prevent a riot there) but not outside. If Jane is a prisoner there, the local awareness of the denials keeps her from knowing that Dr. Kirby has been assassinated. But if Jane is an ordinary citizen not connected in any way with the prison, the fact that the prisoners have heard denials of the story does not keep her from knowing that Dr. Kirby has been assassinated.[7]

2. Principle Q

Given principle (P2), these and similar examples[8] suggest that reasoning always involves essentially the implicit acceptance of the proposition that there exists no unpossessed evidence of a certain sort against the conclusion of that reasoning. We might express this suggestion in the form of the following tentative principle about reasoning.[9]

> (Q) It is essential to one's reasoning for a given conclusion that one accept the proposition that there is no evidence one does not possess, possession of which would make acceptance of the conclusion unjustified, and which, either
> (a) one can obtain oneself, or
> (b) is possessed by others in a relevant social group to which one belongs.

Comment: (Q) says that it is essential to one's reasoning that one accept the proposition that there is no sufficiently strong unpossessed evidence of a certain sort against one's conclusion. I shall be suggesting that there is a sense in which one *explicitly* accepts one's conclusion and needs only *implicitly* to accept the proposition about no counterevidence of the relevant sort. It will turn out, I think, that implicit acceptance of a proposition can be justified in certain cases in which explicit acceptance would not be. (Q) should therefore not be interpreted as saying that one is justified in reaching a given conclusion only if one is justified in explicitly accepting the proposition that there is no counterevidence of the relevant sort, nor does (Q) imply that one knows one's conclusion to be true only if one *knows* there is no such unpossessed counterevidence. But this is to anticipate later discussion.

Because of clauses (a) and (b) in (Q), we can distinguish two principles here, call them (Qa) and (Qb). Let us consider these one at a time.

3. The Rationale for (Qa)

(Qa) tells one not to accept a conclusion unless one is justified in accepting the proposition that there is no obtainable undermining evidence against that conclusion. This sounds very much like a well-known principle of scientific method. In seeking to confirm a universal generalization, for example, it is more important to see whether the generalization holds in a variety of situations than to examine many instances all of the same sort.[10] This is a special case of a more general point, stressed by Karl Popper,[11] that, to "corroborate" a scientific hypothesis, it is not enough to look for positive evidence in favor of the hypothesis; one must also search diligently for evidence against the hypothesis. A hypothesis is corroborated only to the extent that it survives our best attempts to refute it. Popper himself goes on to argue that one should not ever really accept or believe any scientific hypotheses and that one cannot ever know anything in science; but we can appreciate Popper's methodological point and see its relevance, even to more ordinary nonscientific hypotheses, without accepting his skepticism about scientific knowledge and certainly without extending that skepticism into the ordinary nonscientific realm. Indeed I have to reject general skepticism about knowledge since I am assuming (as part of my strategy) that we know roughly what we ordinarily think and say we know. And Popper's methodological emphasis on the search for negative evidence would seem to tie in nicely with (Qa), which says one is not to accept a hypothesis until one is justified in accepting the proposition that there is no obtainable evidence that would undermine it.

Now Popper's principle is sometimes thought to follow from considerations of epistemic or subjective probability. Suppose we can do a test whose outcome will be either e or not-e. Suppose our hypothesis h implies the outcome will be e and is incompatible with the outcome's being not-e. Then, according to Bayes's theorem, the conditional probability of h, given that the test results in e, equals the antecedent probability of h divided by the antecedent probability of e.

$$p(h, e) = \frac{p(h)}{p(e)}$$

So, the more likely our test is to refute h by yielding not-e, the higher the conditional probability of h, given that the test results in e. This is one way to try to make sense of the idea that a hypothesis is corroborated only to the extent that it survives our best attempts to refute it.[12]

But such considerations of epistemic or subjective probability cannot by themselves account for (Qa), which is a principle about when one is justified in accepting a conclusion and not just a principle about the probability of a conclusion.

Principle (Qa) would be false given a purely probabilistic rule of inference saying that one may accept a conclusion if and only if the conclusion has a sufficiently high probability, e.g., at least .90. A conclusion can be acceptable by this criterion even though one cannot accept the proposition that there is no obtainable evidence possession of which would make one's original conclusion unacceptable. Indeed, it may be more likely than not that there is such obtainable evidence.

For example, suppose one knows with certainty that a box contains ten coins, nine fair coins, and one that has a proability of .60 of coming up heads when tossed. One also knows that a coin has been randomly selected from the box and tossed, although one cannot see whether it has come up heads or tails. Then the probability that the selected coin is fair is .90, given what one knows, so the purely probabilistic rule would warrant acceptance of the conclusion that the selected coin is fair. Now, if one should walk across the room to see how the coin has landed and were to discover that the coin has come up heads, one would obtain undermining evidence, since the probability that the coin is fair, given that evidence, would drop to .88 and the purely probabilistic rule would no longer permit acceptance of the conclusion that the coin is fair. But the purely probabilistic rule certainly does not allow one to accept the proposition that there is no such undermining evidence to one's original conclusion. In fact, the probability that there is this particular obtainable undermining evidence is .51; the existence of such evidence is therefore more likely than not. So (Qa) is clearly incompatible with this sort of purely probabilistic rule of inference.

This brings out a serious defect in such a simple purely probabilistic rule of inference. There is something wrong with a rule that allows one to accept a conclusion at a given moment while at the same time realizing that one will probably have to abandon that conclusion a moment later, e.g., when one looks to see how the coin has landed. One's conclusions should be more stable than that.

Of course, in this case, having concluded that the coin is fair, one might simply refuse to look at it to see how it has come up. More generally, once having accepted a conclusion, one might refuse to consider any further evidence that might undermine that conclusion. Although this would make one's conclusions more stable, it is clearly a highly dogmatic and irrational strategy.[13] What we want are stable conclusions without dogmatism.

A more complex rule avoids this problem.

(Z) One may accept a conclusion h if and only if two conditions are satisfied:
   (1) the probability of h is sufficiently high, e.g., at least .9, and
   (2) the probability is also at least .9 that there is no obtainable evidence such that the conditional probability of h, given that evidence, is less than .9.

This rule is, of course, subject to the various problems alluded to above for the simpler purely probabilistic rule — the needed probabilities are not generally available and Gettier examples involving explanatory assumptions cannot be accounted for in terms of (P1) and (P2), given the rule (Z). (Z) is compatible with (Qa), but it provides no purely probabilistic rationale for (Qa) since no purely probabilistic rationale is offered for part (2) of (Z). The rationale for this must be the same as the rationale for (Qa) itself and must derive from our interest in stable conclusions without dogmatism. Let us consider this more carefully.

Accepting a conclusion *h* involves two things: first, one comes to be prepared to take *h* for granted in further theoretical and practical reasoning, and, second, one ends inquiry into the truth of *h*.[14]

To be justified in accepting the conclusion *h*, one must therefore be justified in doing both these things. In particular, one must be justified in supposing there is *no point* to further undogmatic inquiry. One must be justified in supposing that further undogmatic inquiry would not uncover evidence that would affect one's conclusion, that there is no obtainable sufficiently negative evidence. In accepting one's conclusion, one implicitly accepts the proposition that there is no such evidence. So, to be justified in accepting that conclusion, one must be justified in implicitly accepting that proposition. This is just our principle (Qa).

Actually this is oversimplified. (Qa) applies if one fully accepts something, if one accepts something as known. But one can also accept something tentatively, as a working hypothesis, and such tentative acceptance is not subject to (Qa). Furthermore, to accept *h* tentatively, as a working hypothesis, is really to accept *h*. It is not just to accept another proposition about *h*, for example, the proposition that *h* is probable. Nor is it just to *assume* that *h* is true for the sake of argument, as when one assumes that *h* is true in order to derive a contradiction from that assumption, thus showing that *h* is false, or when one shows that a certain conclusion follows from the assumption that *h* is true and also from the assumption that *h* is false. But, even though tentative acceptance is real acceptance, to accept *h* tentatively is not to end inquiry into *h;* it is rather to pursue that inquiry in a certain way. One accepts *h* as a working hypothesis for the present in order to see where one gets. One realizes that one may very well run into difficulty or just not get anywhere. In that case, one should abandon *h* and perhaps try something else. On the other hand, if things work out well, such tentative acceptance may turn into full acceptance of *h* as known. At that point, one's justification for accepting *h* as known will not be at all the same as one's earlier justification for tentatively accepting *h* but will include facts about the way in which the tentative acceptance has worked out. Now one can be justified in accepting *h* merely as a working hypothesis for the present without being justified in the strong supposition that there is no obtainable sufficiently negative evidence against *h* at all; it is enough to suppose, perhaps, that there is no easily obtainable counterevidence. So (Qa) does not apply to tentative acceptance. (This is compatible with our appeal to (P1) and (P2), however, since tentative acceptance of something as a working hypothesis cannot give one knowledge unless it becomes full acceptance of the thing in question as known.[15])

John Dewey has been interpreted as arguing that normally only tentative acceptance in this sense is ever justified, simply because one can rarely satisfy (Qa), this leading to the conclusion that we rarely know anything.[16] More recently, Peter Unger argued in a very similar way that we never know anything at all.[17] And, as already mentioned, Popper appeals to similar considerations in arguing that we never have scientific knowledge. But in practice, people suppose they know many things, even truths of science. My strategy is to suppose that they are for the most part right and, in particular, that they are for the most part justified in accepting such things as known and therefore for the most part justified in implicitly accepting the proposition that there is no obtainable sufficiently negative evidence to a conclusion accepted as known.

This is not to agree with Norman Malcolm[18] and more recently Peter Unger[19] who say that accepting a conclusion as known involves a dogmatic commitment to *disregard* any future negative evidence. Acceptance of something as known involves rather only an implicit belief that there is no such negative evidence. One might later learn something that makes it no longer rational to suppose that there is no such evidence. In that case, one should stop accepting the proposition in question as known and, in doing so, one will not be violating any prior commitment. The fact that accepting something as known ends inquiry does not imply that such acceptance involves dogmatism; it implies, rather, a principle of epistemic conservatism: one is justified in continuing to believe what one believes in the absence of any special reason to doubt a particular thing.

To believe something, to accept it as known, is then not to accept it dogmatically. But this is not to say that such a belief is merely tentative. Accepting something as known ends inquiry into its truth; tentatively accepting something as a working hypothesis does not end inquiry. Once something is accepted as known, one is justified in continuing to accept it in the absence of any special reason to doubt it. When something is tentatively accepted, on the other hand, the mere absence of special reasons to doubt it is not enough to justify its continued acceptance; it is also necessary that the tentative acceptance should prove sufficiently fruitful so that there are positive reasons for such continued acceptance.

(Qa) is a principle about conclusions that are accepted as known, saying that a conclusion of that sort is justified only if one is also justified in accepting the proposition that there is no obtainable undermining evidence. As we have seen, this follows from two points: (a) accepting a conclusion as known ends inquiry into the truth of that conclusion and (b) inquiry should not be dogmatic. Now there is a very good rationale for us to accept certain propositions as opposed to, say, always assigning propositions various subjective probabilities. This is a simple matter of practicality. There is a practical limit to the information we can retain. An attempt to operate without beliefs, relying only on probabilities, requires a memory capacity that is an exponentially exploding function of the number of unrelated atomic propositions involved. This exponential explosion is avoided if one records information primarily by means of beliefs one has adopted.[20]

But why not always accept things only tentatively, as Popper recommends, and never end inquiry? That would also be impractical; there is a limit to the number of investigations one can carry on at any given time. Also, always to accept things only tentatively would bring an unwelcome instability to what one accepts, since the continued acceptance of something tentatively accepted as a working hypothesis depends not only on not having special reasons to doubt that thing but also on the continued fruitfulness of accepting it. It cannot be expected that most things one accepts will be constantly fruitful in ongoing inquiry. So most things now accepted will eventually have to be rejected, given such a policy. But that will cause trouble later, since much information not currently useful would come in handy at some later now unforeseen time.

Why must untentative acceptance that ends inquiry be subject to (Qa)? Why not allow such acceptance even when one suspects there might well be obtainable undermining evidence? One reason has already been mentioned, namely, that allowing this sort of acceptance requires either a dogmatic commitment to ignore further evidence or an unwelcome and impractical instability in what one accepts, allowing one to end inquiry while all the time realizing that one will probably have to reopen it in a moment.[21] Why should such dogmatism be avoided? Because otherwise wishful thinking can bias one's beliefs in a serious way.

4. The Rationale for (Qb)

So much then for (Qa). Let us now briefly consider (Qb), which tells one not to accept a conclusion unless one can also accept the proposition that no undermining evidence against that conclusion is possessed by others in a relevant social group to which one belongs. This, I suggest, reflects the social aspect of inquiry. Inquiry is often a group affair. If one is to be in a position to end the inquiry of a group, one must be justified in supposing that one is in a position to do so. One must be justified in taking oneself to be in a position to know, to be in a position in which others can rely on one's conclusion. J. L. Austin put the point like this: "When I say 'I know', *I give others my word: I give others my authority for saying* that 'S is P'."[22] In accepting the conclusion that 'S is P' as known, one implicitly concludes that one can give others one's authority for saying that 'S is P'. So if one is to be justified in accepting 'S is P' as known, then one must be justified in implicitly concluding that one can give others one's authority for saying that 'S is P'. One is justified in that only if one is justified in the implicit supposition that the others do not have undermining evidence against 'S is P'.

This is not to abandon the conception of inference as a change in one person's overall view. Inference is in the first instance a personal private psychological process. Nor is this to deny that one sometimes reaches purely personal conclusions that do not satisfy (Qb), just as one sometimes reaches tentative conclusions that do not satisfy (Qa). There are, as indicated above, reasons for not restricting ourselves to tentative conclusions. But, given the personal private character of reasoning, one might well wonder what reasons there could be for not restricting ourselves to purely personal conclusions. Why should we ever reach conclusions that are subject to principle (Qb)?

The answer is that a great deal of our knowledge of the world depends on authority. We and our children would not get very far without what is learned from family, friends, teachers, books, newspapers, radio, and television. Even the mastery of language depends on accepting various things on authority.[23] In ordinary life, people have to accept many things not just for themselves but for others as well. But someone is justified in accepting a conclusion as something on which others can rely only if (Qb) is satisfied.

So, we have been able to find a rationale for both parts of principle (Q), for both (Qa) and (Qb). Recall that (Q) was suggested by an examination of judgments about particular cases of knowledge in the light of principles (P1) and (P2). Having uncovered (Q) in this way, we went on to see whether we could discover a rationale for such a principle. We found such a rationale by considering what is involved in accepting something as known and by asking why we should ever accept something as known rather than as a merely tentative and/or as a merely personal conclusion.

PART 2. MORE ABOUT (Q)

1. Indirect Undermining Evidence

With respect to a given conclusion, let us count as *potentially undermining evidence* any evidence one does not possess, possession of which would make acceptance of that conclusion unjustified. And let us count as *actually undermining evidence* to that conclusion any potentially undermining evidence that either (a) one can obtain oneself or (b) is possessed by others in a relevant social group to which one belongs. Then (Q) says that one is justified in accepting a given conclusion only if one is also justified in accepting the proposition that there is no actually undermining evidence to that conclusion.

Actually undermining evidence in this sense need not be directly evidence against the truth of a conclusion. It might be only evidence against the truth of the claim that there is no actually undermining evidence to that conclusion. The point can be seen by considering certain Gettier examples. In case one, Paula comes to know on the basis of her investigation that Quilty is the murderer. Case two is like case one except that there is in Paula's unopened mail before her a letter from her partner Ruth saying, falsely as it turns out, that she (Ruth) has uncovered surprising new relevant evidence about this case, without saying what the evidence is or what it indicates. In fact, Paula is already aware of that evidence; but, if she were to read Ruth's letter, she would not be justified in accepting as known her conclusion that Quilty is the murderer. She does not, in case two, read the letter, so she is justified in reaching her conclusion; but the fact that the letter is before her keeps her from knowing that Quilty is the murderer. The letter is actually undermining evidence to her conclusion, even though it is not directly evidence against the truth of that conclusion. In accepting the conclusion that Quilty is the murderer, Paula ends inquiry into the truth of that conclusion, implicitly accepting the proposition that there is no obtainable evidence that would require her to stop accepting *h* as known. Such evidence does not have to be directly evidence against the truth of her conclusion; it can, as in this case, be evidence against the truth of the proposition that there is no actually undermining evidence to the truth of her conclusion.

Or consider case three, which is like case one, in which Paula does come to know that Quilty is the murderer, except that, unknown to Paula, it has been widely reported that Sam witnessed the murder and can identify the murderer.

Authorities are now trying to locate Sam to ask him what he saw. In fact, Sam was somewhere else and knows nothing about this crime. Here again, Paula does not know that Quilty is the murderer. She does not know because of evidence possessed by others in a relevant social group to which she belongs, even though this evidence is not directly evidence against the truth of her conclusion. For in accepting her conclusion as known, she accepts it on grounds that she takes to be adequate to end the group's inquiry. But, given the widely held view that Sam witnessed the murder and can testify about it, Paula's grounds are not in fact adequate to end the group's inquiry.

Now, a problem arises when one tries to specify what sort of evidence that is obtainable or possessed by relevant others is to count as actually undermining evidence to h. One could say, truly, "evidence such that if one were to possess it one would not be justified in reaching one's conclusion." But what possible evidence has that property? What will it be evidence against? It does not have to be evidence against the truth of h; it only has to be (as it were) evidence against accepting that conclusion. But how is this to be specified as evidence against the truth of something? Here we seem led to an infinite regress: it can be evidence against the truth of h, or evidence against the truth of the claim that there is no actually undermining evidence against the truth of h, or evidence against the trugh of the claim that there is no actually undermining evidence against the truth of the claim that there is no actually undermining evidence against the truth of h, or etc., *ad infinitum*.

In fact, we can avoid this regress. Evidence that is obtainable or possessed by relevant others is actually undermining evidence to h if and only if it is evidence of sufficient strength against the truth of the following self-referential conjunctive claim: "h and there is no actually undermining evidence to the truth of this whole conjunction." Clearly this covers evidence against the truth of h, evidence against the truth of the claim that there is no actually undermining evidence against the truth of h, and so on.[24]

This seems to indicate that, when one explicitly accepts the conclusion h as known, one implicitly accepts that self-referential claim, "h and there is no actually undermining evidence to the truth of this whole conjunction." The implicit acceptance of this conjunction is part of what is involved in accepting h as known.[25]

2. Digression on Self-Reference

The idea that one's conclusions are implicitly self-referential may seem so bizarre as to indicate that something must have gone wrong. But that would be an over-hasty reaction. On reflection, I believe we can see that this is not such a bizarre result and indeed that there are reasons to suppose that conclusions of reasoning are self-referential in certain other respects anyway.

One source of worry about such self-reference is the thought that it may lead to semantic paradox. Consider the self-referential conclusion consisting in the belief that that very belief is not true. That conclusion is either true or not true; but either assumption appears to lead to a contradiction. Now, it is sometimes thought that the trouble here is due to the fact that the conclusion in question refers to itself. But that is a superficial thought which does not withstand scrutiny. A general prohibition on this sort of self-reference and on other sorts, where one conclusion refers to a second which refers back to the first, is extremely implausible. The real source of the paradox is our prima facie willingness to accept *all* instances of the schema "the belief ·that *h* is true if and only if *h*." The semantic paradoxes show that there are instances of this schema that cannot be accepted.[26]

The suggestion that our conclusions are self-referential may begin to seem less bizarre when one sees that similar suggestions seem plausible in connection with somewhat different issues. For example, H. P. Grice's analysis of speaker's meaning is best presented as he originally presented it, as ascribing a self-referential intention to the speaker: the intention that *A* will react in such and such a way by virtue of *A*'s recognition of this very intention. Out of misplaced fear of the semantic paradoxes, Grice himself reformulated his analysis so as to avoid self-reference; that has led to incredible complication and the real possibility of infinite regress.[27] But the original self-referential formulation remains highly plausible as an account of a speaker's intention.

Similarly, consider the notion of common or mutual knowledge, as explicated by David Lewis and Stephen Schiffer. Lewis and Schiffer avoid self-reference only by allowing an infinite regress: We have mutual or common knowledge if and only if each of us knows *h*, each of us knows each of us knows *h*, each of us knows each of us knows each of us knows *h*, and so on.[28] It is more plausible, I think, to say that what is mutually known is something that refers to itself, e.g., "*h* and we know this" where "this" refers to the whole conjunction and not just to *h*.

To take a different example that I have discussed at length elsewhere, the most common form of intention, which I call a positive intention, is the self-referential intention that, because one has that very intention, one will do a certain thing.[29] So, the suggestion that a certain belief or other attitude might refer to itself arises in a number of areas and not only in connection with our principle (Q).

Furthermore, there are other reasons for supposing that conclusions are self-referential, reasons that are independent of principle (Q). Consider, for example, Alvin Goldman's "Causal Theory of Knowing."[30] Goldman argues plausibly that, in cases of inferential knowledge, one knows only if the proper sort of quasi-causal (I would say "explanatory") connection exists between the fact known and one's corresponding belief and only if one has "reconstructed" this connection in one's inference. This suggests something like the following requirement on justified reasoning:

> (R) One can justifiably reach a given conclusion only if one is justified in accepting the proposition that a certain quasi-causal or explanatory connection holds between the fact one takes to make one's conclusion true and one's acceptance of that conclusion.

The relevant quasi-causal or explanatory connection will vary from case to case. It is therefore not implicitly indicated simply by one's acceptance of the first conclusion but must itself be explicitly indicated in what one accepts. So, here, if we are to avoid an infinite regress we are forced to interpret (R) as telling us that our conclusions are self-referential. In one of the examples Goldman discusses someone might reach the following conclusion: "This volcano erupted long ago, spewing out lava which has remained here until now to be seen by me leading me to believe all this" (where the "all this" refers to the entire proposition quoted).

We might be able to use this application of Goldman's theory to help distinguish theoretical conclusions (beliefs) from practical conclusions (intentions). We are led to suppose that theoretical conclusions have roughly the form: "I accept all this because of something that logically implies or causes or explains the truth of h in such and such a way," for short: "I accept this because of something that settles it that h is true." I have argued elsewhere that practical conclusions have roughly the form "Because I accept this, it is settled that h is true."[31]

More might be said about this application of Goldman's causal theory. For example, it vividly brings out a way in which various explanatory assumptions are essential to a conclusion. But we must recall that our main interest in all this is the independent reason it gives us to suppose that conclusions are self-referential. The fact that our discussion of (Q) leads to the suggestion that accepting a conclusion as known is implicitly to accept a self-referential conjunctive claim does not show that something has gone wrong.

3. The Scope of "Obtainable Evidence"

I now turn to a different issue. Might (Q) be used, with (P1) and (P2), to account for Gettier examples without invoking the theory that explanatory considerations play a crucial role in reasoning, e.g., so that a purely probabilistic account of reasoning might be defended after all? Consider the sort of Gettier example that suggests the relevance of explanatory considerations. Seeing a milk truck in front of Betty's house on Mondays and Thursdays, Albert concludes that milk is delivered in his neighborhood on those days. He is right, but the truck he sees belongs to Betty's brother stopping by for coffee, so Albert does not come to know that milk is delivered in his neighborhood on Mondays and Thursdays. This is supposed to show that an assumption about why the milk truck is parked in front of Betty's is essential to Albert's reasoning, a point which counts against a purely probabilistic theory of reasoning and in favor of the theory that inference seeks to promote explanatory coherence. But can we not defend a purely probabilistic theory of reasoning at this point by invoking principle (Q)? Can we argue not that Albert's lack of knowledge is due to there being obtainable evidence that would undermine Albert's reasoning, namely, the fact that the milk truck he sees belongs to Betty's brother who is merely stopping by for coffee?

This is a hard question to answer because we have not been able to give a rigorous definition of what counts as "obtainable evidence" in (Q). But it is perhaps doubtful whether the fact in question, that the milk truck belongs to Betty's brother who is merely stopping by for coffee, should be allowed to count as available *evi-*

dence. Perhaps the relevant obtainable *evidence* here is that if to take milk into Betty's house, that if Albert peered through the window, he would notice the driver sitting down in the kitchen holding a coffee cup, that if he was hidden in the shrubbery he would hear Betty call out on the truck's arrival, "Oh, brother dear!" and so on. But what if Betty's brother always brings her in some milk? What if Betty and her brother never allude to their relationship in their conversation? What if he has his coffee quickly, standing up? Then the obtainable evidence might have to be such things as that the records of the milk company indicate that that particular truck is driven by someone whose last name is the same as Betty's, that that particular truck never seems to stop at anyone else's house in the neighborhood and so on.

Consider another case. Carol asks David what the score was and David tells her "5 to 1," thinking she has asked for the time. By coincidence the score was 5 to 1. In this case Carol does not know what the score was, but what obtainable evidence undermines her knowledge? Presumably that David thinks she asked what time it is and that he says "5 to 1" because he thinks that the time is 5 to 1. But that does not seem to be the sort of thing that counts as *evidence* in a case like this. Relevant evidence here, it seems, would have to be something the person does that reveals these aspects of his state of mind. The problem is that David's behavior may be unrevealing.

We can bring this out more clearly by modifying the example so that David wrongly thinks the score was 4 to 1, hears Carol's question, and says "5 to 1" in order to mislead her about the score. If David is careful, nothing in his behavior will reveal his state of mind, so what could be the obtainable evidence that undermines Carol's knowledge in this modified example?

Of course we *could* understand "obtainable evidence" so as to count such things as David's belief that the score was 4 to 1 as obtainable evidence. But that would be pointless, for now there are two kinds of obtainable evidence: first, the sorts of things that would normally count as evidence and that count as obtainable evidence in our original theory; second, facts that are incompatible with assumptions that would be essential to one's reasoning if reasoning were not purely probabilistic and involved the sorts of explanatory considerations that figure in reasoning according to our original theory. Furthermore, and crucially, the rationale we have found for (Qa) works only for what is literally "obtainable evidence." For this rationale is that one is justified in ending inquiry only if one is justified in thinking that there is no sufficiently negative evidence that would be uncovered in further undogmatic inquiry, so here "obtainable evidence" must be the sort of thing that could be discovered in further inquiry. A different rationale is therefore needed in order to account for the second sort of fact that would be labeled "obtainable evidence" if we were to extend the interpretation of that phrase in the suggested way, and this second rationale will be exactly the same as whatever the rationale is for the role of explanatory coherence in reasoning. So, extending the interpretation of "obtainable evidence" in this way, so as to include such things as David's belief that the score was 4 to 1, is a purely verbal maneuver which in no way simplifies the substantive theory. It is therefore less misleading to stay with our original version.

4. The Relevance of the Objective Likelihood of Being Wrong

I conclude with some brief remarks concerning a possible further application of our psychologistic strategy. In a recent paper,[32] Alvin Goldman discusses a class of Gettier examples that do not seem to be best accounted for in terms of the principles we have so far considered. We would hope by means of our strategy to use the existence of such examples to learn something more about reasoning.

One example is this: While driving through the countryside, Olive sees what she takes to be a barn. It happens that in this area many farmers have erected barn facades facing the road, which look exactly like barns, but are not. Olive knows nothing of this practice and indeed happens to be looking at an actual barn, not a mere facade. But she does not know she is seeing a barn. Now the explanation Olive accepts concerning the way things look is absolutely right. So that is not the source of her lack of knowledge. Furthermore, in this sort of case her lack of knowledge seems due to the actual existence of all those facades, not simply to obtainable evidence that the facades exist; and the rationale for (Qa) in terms of ending inquiry, etc., does not seem to apply to this case.

The examples Goldman describes are all examples of perceptual knowledge, and it is controversial whether they involve reasoning, but there are also other examples clearly involving reasoning. Max sees the lava here and infers that the lava is here because of a past eruption of the volcano. Max is unaware that often around here people spread out lava so as to make it seem that one or another volcano has been active, although in this case the lava is the result of a volcanic eruption in the way Max supposes. It seems that Max does not know that the lava he sees comes from a past eruption of this volcano.

What happens in cases of this sort might be roughly expressed as follows. In each case there is a significant objective likelihood that the belief in question is false. Some sort of *objective* likelihood of falsehood is relevant here, not just epistemic likelihood.[33] Given Max's evidence, it is epistemically quite unlikely that this lava did not come from an eruption of this volcano, but it is objectively not all that unlikely.

Now our strategy for exploiting Gettier examples has us try to account for them in terms of principle (P2), which says that reasoning that depends essentially on the acceptance of a false proposition does not give one knowledge. The false proposition in each of these cases seems to be that there is no significant objective likelihood that one's conclusion is false. We are therefore led to the suggestion that the acceptance of some such proposition is essential to reasoning. We might begin by proposing the following principle:

(S)   It is essential to one's reasoning for a given conclusion that one accept the proposition that there is no significant objective likelihood that that conclusion is false.

But we must try to be more precise. Objective likelihood is a relational notion; something can be likely in relation to certain facts and unlikely in relation to others. Even though there is a significant objective likelihood that lava surrounding a volcano around here did not actually come from an eruption of that volcano, there may be no significant objective likelihood that lava surrounding this particular volcano did not come from this volcano. There is a significant objective likelihood that this lava is not from this volcano, given that most lava surrounding the volcanos around here has been brought in and spread around by the local villagers. There is no significant likelihood that this lava is not from this volcano, given that none of the lava around this particular volcano has been put there by the local villagers. Can we say then that Max does not know that the lava here came from a past eruption of this volcano as long as there are some facts or other in relation to which there is a significant likelihood that his belief is false? No, because for example Nora, who is accompanying Max, may know about the local practice of lava spreading and also know that none has been spread around this particular mountain. Nora can come to know that this lava came from a past eruption of this volcano even though there is a fact in relation to which there is a significant likelihood that the lava did not, namely, the fact that most lava surrounding the volcanos around here has been brought in and spread around by local villagers.

This suggests making (S) more precise as follows:

(S)   H is essential to one's reasoning for a conclusion h that one accept the proposition that there are no facts F and no proposition P such that
(1)   given F, there is a significant objective likelihood that P is true
(2) P is incompatible with h
(3)   if one knew that, given F, there is a significant objective likelihood that P is true, one would not be justified in reaching the conclusion h.

I am not confident that this is an adequate formulation, but however it should be formulated, (S) is not iterable in the way that (Q) is. When (Q) applies to a conclusion h, it also applies to the implicit conclusion that there is no actually undermining evidence against h. But (S) cannot be iterable in this way. In applying to h, (S) does not apply also the claim that there is no significant objective likelihood that h is false. If one could be justified in reaching a conclusion only if one were justified in accepting the proposition that there is no significant objective likelihood that there is no significant objective likelihood . . . that there is no significant objective likelihood that that conclusion is false, one would presumably have to be justified in accepting the proposition that there was no positive finite chance at all that the conclusion was false. For example, suppose a significant likelihood has to be .10 or more. Then, if there is only a .001 likelihood that h is false, there is a significant .10 likelihood that there is a significant .10 likelihood that there is a significant .10 likelihood that h is false. But, for almost any of the things we think we know, we are aware there is some positive finite objective likelihood that we are wrong. Allowing (S) to be iterable is therefore incompatible with the assumption that we know pretty much what we think we know, given (P1) which says that reasoning is justified if it gives one knowledge.

Indeed, (S) seems to apply only to one's explicit conclusions. It does not apply to what is implicit according to (Q), for example. Given that Norman recently mailed Mary a letter from Italy by way of San Francisco, saying that he is now in California, there is a significant objective likelihood that Mary is wrong in implicitly accepting the proposition that there is no obtainable evidence that would undermine her conclusion. But that does not keep her from knowing he is in Italy if the letter never reaches her because of a mail fire somewhere along the way,[34] although it does keep her from knowing that there is no obtainable evidence that would undermine the conclusion that Norman is in Italy.

This indicates two very important things. First, explicit conclusions are more constrained than implicit conclusions are, since (S) applies to explicit but not implicit conclusions. That may help to explain why (Q) can strike many people as too strict a principle, with skeptical consequences. (Q) says that to be justified in accepting a given conclusion, one must also be justified in accepting a further conclusion about the first conclusion. If you suppose that this means one must be justified in explicitly accepting this further conclusion, you will interpret this as a stronger requirement than it actually is, since it is enough to be justified in implicitly accepting that further conclusion.

A second and related point is that, to know the truth of a given conclusion, it is not necessary to know the truth of everything essential to one's reasoning; it is enough that everything essential should in fact be true. Mary can know that Norman is in Italy without knowing that there is no obtainable evidence that would undermine that conclusion, as long as it is true that there is no such evidence. This, by the way, shows that Mary can know something without knowing that she knows.

Notice that, although (S) does not apply to what is implicit according to (Q), (Q) does seem to apply to what is implicit according to (S). Obtainable evidence or evidence possessed by others indicating a significant objective likelihood of one's conclusion being false can keep one from knowing the truth of that conclusion.

Of course, much more needs to be said about (S). Here, as earlier with (Q), we will want to see whether there is any reason to think there really is a principle of reasoning of this sort and we will want to consider what possible rationale such a principle would have. I suspect that some such principle is plausible as an expression of the idea that in accepting a conclusion as known one accepts it as (at least) highly probable, the point being that it is objective probability that is in question, not subjective or epistemic probability. And I suspect that (S) is also plausible as a way of capturing part of the idea that, in accepting a conclusion as known, one takes oneself to be in a position to know. But I must leave this for future investigation.

Notes

1. I am indebted to Aron Edidin, James Cargile, William Smith, and Paul Benacerraf for their comments on an earlier version of this paper.

2. Edmund Gettier discusses a few examples of this sort in his brief but famous paper "Is Justified True Belief Knowledge?" *Analysis* 23 (1963):121-23. Since then many other examples have been described in what is now a vast literature: see the review article by Robert R. Shope, "Recent Work on the Analysis of Knowledge," forthcoming.

3. Gilbert Harman, "Reasoning and Explanatory Coherence," forthcoming in the *American Philosophical Quarterly.*

4. For this distinction I am indebted to William G. Lycan, "Evidence One Does Not Possess," *Australasian Journal of Philosophy* 55 (1977):114-26. Lycan treats the second way as a special case of the first, but that seems wrong, as I argue below.

5. Judgments vary about this and other cases. Here and elsewhere I report my own judgment. See note 7 below for discussion of this variation in judgment.

6. Lycan, "Evidence One Does Not Possess," p. 117.

7. Lycan gives similar examples in *ibid.,* pp. 118-19. I have for a number of years been systematically testing people's judgments about these and related Gettier examples, and I have found considerable variation. Concerning the cases involving Jane reading about Dr. Kirby's assassination, some people are unwilling to allow that Jane might come to know about the assassination even in case one simply by reading about it in the newspaper. Other people are willing to credit Jane with knowledge of the assassination as long as she is right, even if the newspaper story is a hoax that happens by gruesome coincidence to be right. Suppose we disregard all these people (who may make up as much as 20-25 percent of the total). Then, of the remaining people, 100 percent of course say that Jane knows in case one, where the newspaper story is not denied. Roughly 10 percent say that she knows in case two, where she is unaware of official denials that have been widely reported; 40-50 percent say that she does not know in case two; and 40-50 percent say they are not sure whether she knows in case two. 60-70 percent say that she knows in case three, where the denials are given only to inmates of a certain prison and she is an ordinary citizen; hardly anyone says she does not know in case three; and 30-40 percent are not sure.

Lycan reports somewhat similar results in "Evidence One Does Not Possess," p. 121. He observes that, because of this sort of variation exists, judgments in this area cannot be used by themselves to *prove* the inadequacy of proposed analyses of knowledge or to *establish* principles like (Q), stated in the text below. That is perfectly correct. But judgments in this area can legitimately be used as heuristic aids to *suggest* the existence of principles like (Q). We can then try to see whether there are independent reasons to think there are such principles. If we find independent reasons for (Q), as I go on to argue we do, that will tend to support the original judgments that suggested (Q).

Ultimately, of course, I would like to be able to explain the variations in judgments about cases using principles like (Q) and other principles.

8. Alvin I. Goldman describes a different sort of example in which one fails to know even though one is apparently right in the explanatory claims one accepts. See his "Discrimination and Perceptual Knowledge," *Journal of Philosophy* 73 (1976): 771-91. I discuss these examples below, in the last section of this paper.

9. Cf. Ernest Sosa, "The Analysis of 'Knowledge that P'," *Analysis* 25 (1964)-65):1-8. Sosa states a principle like (Qa) and gives an example that might support (Qb).

10. C. G. Hempel, *Philosophy of Natural Science* (Englewood Cliffs, N.J., 1966), p. 143.

11. Karl Popper, *The Logic of Scientific Discovery* (New York, 1959), p. 251.

12. Richard C. Jeffrey, "Probability and Falsification: Critique of the Popper Program," *Synthese* 30 (1975): 95-117, especially p. 104.

13. I can see no way to give a purely probabilistic explanation of why this dogmatic strategy is irrational. Popper clearly means to be objecting to exactly this sort of strategy, so I think that no purely probabilistic interpretation of his view could be adequate.

14. See John Dewey, *Logic: The Theory of Inquiry* (New York, 1938), especially pp. 7-9. James Cargile points out to me that even after accepting *h* one might continue inquiry into

h in the sense that one might continue to do experiments and look for further evidence in order to convince others or for some other reason, even as an end in itself. I want to say that in such a case one has ended inquiry in the relevant sense, however, since one is not doing the experiments and so forth in order to find out whether *h* is true.

15. Having tentatively accepted something as a working hypothesis, one might go on to accept other things as further working hypotheses within that framework. One will also come fully to accept still other things as known, within that framework. We are, I think, sometimes willing to allow that this last sort of acceptance can give one knowledge even if one's tentative acceptance of the framework does not give one knowledge. For example, one normally accepts the working hypothesis that one is not dreaming. Within this framework one might fully accept the proposition that one is walking down the street. Observe that we are much more willing to credit one with knowledge that one is walking down the street than we are to credit one with knowledge that one is not dreaming.

16. "Dewey took this . . . to show, not that we ever do thus have the right to terminate inquiry, but rather that there is very little, if anything that we ever really know," Roderick Chisholm, *Theory of Knowledge*, 2nd ed. (Englewood Cliffs, N.J., 1977), p. 117. But the passage Chisholm refers to (Dewey, *Logic*) does not support this interpretation. Dewey says, "there is no belief so settled as not to be exposed to further inquiry. . . . In scientific inquiry, the criterion of what is taken to be settled, or to be knowledge, is being *so* settled that it is available as a resource in further inquiry; not being settled in such a way as not to be subject to revision in further inquiry" (pp. 8-9). Presumably Dewey's point here is merely that ending inquiry at one time does not rule out reopening it later if there should be some reason to do so. See Douglas Arner, "On Knowing," *Philosophical Review* 68 (1959): 84-92, especially 87-90.

17. Peter Unger, *Ignorance* (Oxford, 1975).

18. Norman Malcolm, "Knowledge and Belief," in *Knowledge and Certainty* (Ithaca, N.Y., 1963), pp. 67-68.

19. Unger, *Ignorance*, pp. 105-18.

20. See Harman, "Reasoning and Explanatory Coherence."

21. Sometimes this is justified, if, for example, one is about to be hypnotized into thinking there is counterevidence.

22. J. L. Austin, "Other Minds," *Proceedings of the Aristotelian Society*, supplementary vol. 20 (1946); reprinted in J. L. Austin, *Philosophical Papers* (Oxford, 1961), quotation from p. 67.

23. Cf. Austin, pp. 49-51. Notice that, normally, if one believes what one has been told by someone else, one acquires knowledge only if the other person knows (Sosa, "The Analysis of 'Knowledge that P'"). This is the usual case even though there are unusual cases, e.g., in which one knows that the reporter is trying to mislead one although he himself is as it happens confused. Given (P1) and (P2), this suggests that normally in such cases, when one accepts what one is told at face value, one's reasoning depends essentially on acceptance of the proposition that the reporter knows the truth of what he says. Perhaps one concludes that the reporter says what he says because he knows it to be true and would not have said it if he did not know it. (One might have no idea *how* he knows!)

24. There is a probabilistic analogue of this. Recall our earlier discussion of the probabilistic rule (Z), which we can now modify to allow for (Qb) as well as (Qa).

(Z)   One may accept a conclusion *h* if and only if

(1) the probability of *h* is at least .9,

(2) the probability is also at least .9 that there is no *ab*-evidence (i.e., evidence satisfying (a) or (b) of (Q)) in relation to which the conditional probability of *h* is less than .9.

This covers only actually undermining evidence that is directly evidence against the truth of *h*. To cover other cases, an infinite number of additional clauses are needed.

(3) the probability is also at least .9 that there is no *ab*-evidence in relation to which the conditional probability is less than .9 that there is no *ab*-evidence in relation to which the conditional probability of *h* is less than .9.

(4) etc., *ad infinitum*.

To avoid this infinite regress we can replace (Z) with (Z*):

(Z*) One may accept a conclusion *h* if and only if the probability is at least .9 of the following self-referential conjunction: *"h* and there is no *ab*-evidence in relation to which the conditional probability of this whole conjunction is less than .9."

(Here and throughout this section and in the earlier discussion of (Z) I am indebted to William Smith.)

25. This shows that something might be implicitly believed even though it is not an obvious consequence of what one explicitly believes, if it is part of what is involved in believing what one believes. I overlooked this in my discussion of implicit belief in "Is There Mental Representation?" *Perception and Cognition: Issues in the Foundations of Psychology,* vol. IX in Minnesota Studies in the Philosophy of Science, ed. Wade Savage (Minneapolis, 1978), pp. 57-64.

26. For a useful recent discussion of some of the issues here, see Saul A. Kripke, "Outline of a Theory of Truth," *Journal of Philosophy* 72 (1975): 690-716.

27. H. P. Grice, "Meaning," *Philosophical Review* 66 (1957): 377-88; "Utterer's Meaning and Intentions," *Philosophical Review* 78 (1969): 147-77.

28. Stephen Schiffer, *Meaning* (Oxford, 1972), p. 30. David Lewis, "Languages and Language," in *Language, Mind, and Knowledge,* vol. VII in Minnesota Studies in the Philosophy of Science, ed. Keith Gunderson (Minneapolis, 1975), p. 6; or David Lewis, "Languages, Language, and Grammer," in Gilbert Harman, *On Noam Chomsky* (New York, 1974), p. 256. Elsewhere Lewis defines a weak sort of "common knowledge" in such a way that something may be "common knowledge" in a population P even if no one knows it and even if it is not the case; see David Lewis, *Convention* (Cambridge, Mass., 1969), pp. 52-56. More recently, Lewis adopts the term "overt belief" for the weaker notion; see David Lewis, "Truth in Fiction," *American Philosophical Quarterly* 15 (1978) at p. 44, fn. 13. (But Lewis's definition would sometimes seem to count something as overtly believed in a population even though no one believed it.)

29. Gilbert Harman, "Practical Reasoning," *Review of Metaphysics* 29 (1976): 431-63.

30. Alvin I. Goldman, "A Causal Theory of Knowing," *Journal of Philosophy* 64 (1967): 357-72.

31. "Practical Reasoning." (I there say "guaranteed" rather than "settled," but Pat Greenspan has convinced me that "guaranteed" is too strong.) Note, by the way, that this does not fully distinguish intentions from mere beliefs, since, as Derek Parfit has observed, there are neurotic beliefs of the wrong form, e.g., the insomniac's belief that he will stay awake by virtue of having that very belief.

32. Alvin I. Goldman, "Discrimination and Perceptual Knowledge."

33. Marshall Swain appeals to what is "objectively likely" in his discussion of Goldman's examples in "Reasons, Causes, and Knowledge," *The Journal of Philosophy* 75 (1978): 240-41. Goldman suggests that what is at issue is whether the speaker, who says that someone knows something, considers a given alternative possibility to be relevant. But that is oversimplified, since the speaker too may be ignorant of the many nearby barn facades or the local practice of spreading lava around mountains. It is the objective likelihood, in some sense, of the alternative possibilities that makes them relevant. Of course, the speaker's *standards* (of how objectively unlikely an alternative has to be to permit knowledge) may be relevant, but that is a different point.

34. This also shows that obtainable evidence cannot be defined simply as evidence such that there is a significant likelihood that one would obtain it if one undogmatically pursued

one's inquiry. Given that Norman recently mailed his letter, there is a significant likelihood that Mary would obtain undermining evidence if she were undogmatically to pursue her inquiry; but again this does not keep her from knowing Norman's whereabouts if the misleading letter gets burned up along the way. Cf. Lycan, "Evidence One Does Not Possess," p. 119.

Coherence and the Racehorse Paradox[1]

KEITH LEHRER

This paper is concerned with a paradox revealing that a principle of rational acceptance based on probability alone, or any combination of probability and informative content, will lead to unsatisfactory results. The lottery paradox illustrates that a principle directing us to accept what is highly probably will lead to the acceptance of a logically inconsistent set of statements. A number of philosophers, including most notably Levi, Hempel, Hintikka, Pietarinen, Hilpinen, and myself, attempted to avoid such inconsistency by proposing principles of rational acceptance that combined probability and informative content.[2] The paradox presented here shows that some factor other than probability and content must be brought in to yield a satisfactory principle of rational acceptance. The missing ingredient is coherence.

I

There are three conditions of adequacy for principles of rational acceptance which, though not beyond controversy, provide us with familiar desiderata of rationality. They are as follows:

1. Consistency. The set of accepted statements should not be known to be a logically inconsistent set, that is, a set from which one knows a contradiction is logically deducible.

2. Closure. Any statement that is known to be a deductive consequence of accepted statements should also be accepted.

3. Nonarbitrariness. One should not be arbitrary in what one accepts, that is, if one accepts a statement, then one should accept every other statement that is not known to differ from it in any relevant respect.

183

Both the consistency condition and the closure condition have been contro-verted, most notably by Kyburg,[3] and so some justification is appropriate. Note that the consistency requirement only disallows *known* inconsistency. It may be reasonable for a person to accept an inconsistent set of statements because it is reasonable, though erroneous, for him to accept that the set is consistent. Such a person would not know that the set of statements he accepts is inconsistent. It also may seem reasonable for someone who accepts a great deal to accept that at least something he accepts is false. If he accepts this, then not everything he accepts can be true, but, as I have noted elsewhere,[4] following Harman,[5] the set of state-ments he thus accepts need not be logically inconsistent. Moreover, if a person were to note than he accepts S_1, S_2, S_3, and so forth, and then were also to accept that S_1 is false or S_2 is false or S_3 is false, and so forth, so that the set of statements he accepts is logically inconsistent, then he would be unreasonable. It is, of course, highly probable that one or the other of the statements S_1, S_2, S_3, and so forth is false, but he may note that this is highly probable without accepting the statement that it is so. There are advantages of refusing to accept such a statement. Let us assume that one embraces the objective of accepting what is true without accepting what is false. If one accepts the statement in question, this will guarantee that one fails in one's objective of not accepting what is false, for if S_1, S_2, S_3, and so forth are all true, then the statement affirming that one or the other of these statements is false must itself be false. By accepting the latter statement one would convert the high probability of error which we naturally confront into an unwanted neces-sity. Moreover, by maintaining consistency we preserve the integrity and utility of what we accept for the purposes of prediction and explanation. Thus the suggestion that it is reasonable for a person to accept that at least some of things he accepts are false is erroneous. One should remain content with accepting that it is very probable, though not certain, that at least one or the other of things one accepts is false.

Similar remarks are appropriate to the closure condition. It may be reason-able for a person not to accept a deductive consequence of what he accepts because he may reasonably, though erroneously, accept that it is not a deductive conse-quence of what he accepts. But when one knows that something is a deductive consequence of what one accepts, then one should accept it. Harman[6], objecting to closure, has noted that a person who discovers some untoward consequence of what he accepts may reasonably reject something formerly accepted rather than accept the consequence. That observation is compatible with the intended inter-pretation of the closure condition. That condition applies only to what a person accepts at one time. So if one accepts a set of statements at time t_1, deduces a consequence at t_2, and then decides to alter what one accepts at time t_3 so that what one accepts does not have the consequence deduced at t_2, that is perfectly compatible with the closure condition. Moreover, on this closure condition, as contrasted with others, there is no violation of the condition at t_1 when the person does not accept the deductive consequence, because at t_1 the person has not yet deduced the consequence and does not, we suppose, know that it is a consequence.

Other objections to the closure condition rest on rejection of the consistency condition and on attempts to avoid including a contradiction in what one accepts. However, if one is adverse to accepting contradictions, that is because what one thus accepts is certainly erroneous. Such adversity to error implies, however, that one should accept the consistency condition.

The nonarbitrariness condition may seem the least controversial of the three. It is not beyond controversy, however. Consider the lottery paradox. There are a million tickets in a fair lottery numbered in numerical order with one winning ticket. I know this. I hold ticket 124,318. I accept the hypothesis that my ticket will not win. If I conform to the condition of nonarbitrariness, then, for each ticket in the lottery, I should accept that it will not win. For there is no relevant difference between the ticket I hold and any other ticket in the lottery on the basis of the information I possess. But if I accept the hypothesis that each ticket will not win, the set of such hypotheses is inconsistent with what I know, namely, that one of the tickets will win. Thus the nonarbitrariness condition together with the consistency condition yields the result that one may not accept any of the hypotheses affirming that a specific ticket will not win in the lottery.

The lottery examples are two-dimensional because there are only two alternatives for each ticket, either it wins or it does not. We shall now consider some paradoxes that are n dimensional since there are n possible outcomes for each number. The best realization of this is a horserace in which each horse can place first, second, third, and so forth. The paradox is presented in terms of horseraces. The horseraces, like the lotteries we discuss, are somewhat idealized, however. When thinking about the horseraces, all the information about horseraces should be disregarded except that supplied in the example.

II

As a first illustration of such paradoxes, suppose that we use a high probability rule, one saying that any hypothesis that was more probable than 1/2 should be accepted. Consider, then, that one is informed that there is a horserace to be run with horses numbered 1, 2, 3, and that one of the following patterns will prevail, these being outcomes of previous races, and that each is equally probable.

Example A

First	1	2	3
Second	2	3	1
Third	3	1	2

Notice that it is more probable than 1/2 that horse number *1* will beat horse *2*: he does so in two out of three patterns, so you may accept that. It is just as probable that *2* will beat *3*, so we may accept that, and it follows deductively that *1* will beat *3*. But, alas, it is probable that *3* will beat *1*: he does so in two out of three patterns. So one should accept that *3* will beat *1*. Thus one should accept, on the high probability rule, the statement that horse *1* will beat horse *3* and also that horse *3* will beat horse *1*.

To those familiar with the lottery paradox, the foregoing result will not be unexpected, and the proper conclusion to be drawn is that the high probability rule is unsound. However, such horserace examples also generate difficulty for more sophisticated kinds of rules, namely, those that combine considerations of probability and informative content. Indeed, horseraces provide problems that cannot be solved by appeal to considerations of probability and informative content. Suppose that we are informed that the horses in the race are numbered *1, 2, 3, 4, 5*, and that one of the following twenty-five patterns will prevail in the next race, these being the results of previous races, and that each is equally probable.

Example B

First	2 1 1 1 1 1 1 1 1 1 1 1 1 1 1 1 1 1 1 1 1 1 1 1 1
Second	1 2 2 2 2 2 2 3 3 3 3 3 3 4 4 4 4 4 5 5 5 5 5 5
Third	3 3 3 4 4 5 5 2 2 4 4 5 5 2 2 3 3 5 5 2 2 3 3 4 4
Fourth	4 4 5 3 5 3 4 4 5 2 5 2 4 3 5 2 5 2 3 3 4 2 4 2 3
Fifth	5 5 4 5 3 4 3 5 4 5 2 4 2 5 3 5 2 3 2 4 3 4 2 3 2

We should, in this example, accept that the number *1* horse will win the next race, for he virtually always does, but we should not accept anything about how the other horses will place since they place virtually randomly in the patterns supplied. Now let us consider the hypothesis that the number *1* horse will win. That is equivalent on our information to a disjunctive hypothesis saying that one of twenty-four patterns will prevail. That hypothesis is equal in probability to any disjunctive hypothesis saying that one of any twenty-four patterns will prevail. The patterns are equal in informative content: each tells us exactly how the race will come out, and so any disjunction of *n* distinct patterns is equal in content to any other. Each disjunctive hypothesis of twenty-four distinct patterns tells us on the basis of our information that the excluded pattern will not prevail. So if we accept all such twenty-four pattern disjunctive hypotheses, the set of such hypotheses will exclude all the patterns. That is inconsistent with the information that one pattern will prevail. If we are restricted to probability and content as relevant factors, then either we must not accept the disjunctive hypotheses equivalent to the hypothesis that the number *1* horse will win, or, to avoid arbitrariness, we must accept all twenty-four pattern disjunctions and fall into inconsistency. Thus, if we are restricted to content and probability as relevant factors, we shall violate the condition of nonarbitrariness or the condition of consistency if we accept the hypothesis that the number *1* horse will win. We may reinforce the argument by noting that if the fact that the number *1* horse wins in twenty-four of the twenty-five cases is not convincing enough, we could add one more horse and generate 121 patterns in which the number *1* horse wins in 120, or two more, and generate 721 patterns in which the number *1* horse wins in 720, and so forth.

There is a reply to this line of argumentation, derived from Levi[7], which has some plausibility. It is that the measure of content is generated from a question posed and the possible answers to the question. Thus, if the question is — will horse *1* win or not? — then the hypothesis that horse number *1* will win, and the hypothesis that he will not win, are equal in content. The hypothesis that he will win being as probable as it is, it becomes reasonable on the basis of the content and probability to accept that the number *1* horse will win. One reply, which is by itself adequate, is that how the other horses pattern themselves in a horse-race is germane to whether the number *1* horse will win, and, therefore, content should be measured in terms of the patterns cited above. Each pattern is equal in content to each other since each tells us exactly what will happen. Measuring content in that way, the hypothesis that the number *1* horse will win is equivalent to a disjunction of twenty-four patterns, whereas the hypothesis that the number *1* horse will not win is equivalent to the single other pattern. The latter is much more informative, since it tells us exactly how the race will turn out, whereas the hypothesis that the number *1* horse will win is much less informative since it tells us only that one or the other of twenty-four different patterns will prevail. Moreover, it will not do to insist that if what interests us is whether the number *1* horse will win or not, then the information about how the other horses will place is otiose. For we are interested in how *all* the horses will place. It is just that, given our information, we cannot tell how any of the horses will place, except horse *1,* and we can tell that he will win.

Moreover, even if it be allowed that questions generate content measures, so that we may accept that the number *1* horse will win because it is equal in content to its denial, this solution will beget another paradox. For suppose we allow that if horse number *1* wins in all patterns but one, where the number of patterns is sufficiently large, then, if one asks whether number *1* will win or not, it is reasonable to accept that he will. By parity of reasoning, then, we should subscribe to the principle that, if the *n*th horse comes in *n*th in all but one of a sufficiently large number of races, then if one asks whether the number *n* horse will come in *n*th or not, it is reasonable to accept that it will. For, there is no relevant difference between finishing first and finishing *n*th.

Now suppose that we are given the information that there are as many consecutively numbered horses in the race as you care to imagine and that one of the following patterns will prevail:

Example C

First	1	2	3	4	5	. . .
Second	2	1	2	2	2	. . .
Third	3	3	1	3	3	. . .
Fourth	4	4	4	1	4	. . .
Fifth	5	5	5	5	1	. . .

. . .   .

The paradox is immediately obvious. Suppose we allow that if the *n* numbered horse places *n* in four out of five patterns, then if we ask whether the *n*th horse will place nth, it is reasonable to accept that it will. When we ask whether the number 5 horse will come in fifth, it will be reasonable to accept that it will. Similarly, when we ask whether the number 4 horse will come in fourth, the number 3 horse third, the number 2 horse second, it will be reasonable to accept that they will. So for each of the horses 5, 4, 3, and 2, we will accept that it will place according to number. Closure commits us to accepting that the number 1 horse will come in first. But when we ask whether the number 1 horse will come in first, we find that in 4 out of 5 patterns it does not come in first, and so we accept that it will not come in first. Therefore, once again, we violate the consistency condition.

It might be replied that the answer we gave to each question was consistent, and that is all that can be required. We have argued, however, that the consistency condition should be satisfied for the total set of statements one accepts and not just for answers one gives to individual questions. A rational person does not think in logic tight compartments, refusing to consider the answer he gave to one question when answering another.

What should we say about what it is reasonable to accept in the last example? Notice, first of all, that we can add as many horses to the race as we wish by expanding the pattern, and in a thousand horse race, the number n horse, for all n greater than 1, will finish nth in 999 of the patterns and finish otherwise only once. So the frequency can be made as great as the frequency with which the number 1 horse finished first in example B. Nevertheless, if we accept that the number n horse, for all n greater than 1, will finish nth in example C, closure leads us to also accept that the number 1 horse will finish first in example C, which is extremely unlikely and must not be accepted. Therefore, in this example, example C, we should not accept the hypothesis to the effect that the number n horse will finish nth, or we shall be led to paradox. In example B, however, we should accept that the number 1 horse will finish first. The problem is to formulate a principle that allows us to accept that the number 1 horse will win in example B but not allow that we accept that the n horse will finish nth in example C.

As a first step toward formulating a solution of the problem formulated above, I should like to consider a rule I had formulated earlier to deal with the lottery paradox.[8] This principle does not cope with the paradox formulated above, but a modification of the principle does so. The principle is based on the idea here defended that reasonable acceptance is to be explicated in terms of prevailing over competition. The problem is to specify the relations of competition and prevalence. Competition, here referred to as r-competition, is defined as follows. A statement H r-competes with K on E if and only if K is negatively relavant to H on E, that is, the probability of H is greater on E than on the conjunction of K and E. On this notion of competition, H may r-compete with K on E even though they are logically consistent with each other. Moreover, in the lottery example, the hypothesis that the number 1 ticket will not win r-competes with the hypothesis that the number 2 ticket will not win, and in the horserace examples, any disjunction of all patterns except pattern i r-competes with any disjunction of all patterns except j, where $i \neq j$.

Now consider the rule that tells us that we should accept H on E if H is more probable than any K that H r-competes with on E. This rule also fails in example B to allow us to accept that the number 1 horse will win. For the statement that one of the first twenty-four patterns will prevail is an r-competitor of the statement that the number 1 horse will win, and both are equally probable. Moreover, the example may be reinforced by supposing that each of the patterns after the first two is ten or fifty times as probable as the first two, those two being equally probable. Again the statement that the number 1 horse will win is equivalent on our information to the statement that one of the twenty-four patterns after the first will prevail, and the statement that either the first pattern or one of the twenty-three patterns after the second will prevail is equally probable to the former statement. Thus the rule fails to allow us to accept that horse 1 will win when it is even more obvious that it will. The rule avoids unwanted acceptance in example C, but it is too restrictive in example B.

The solution to the problem before us is to recognize the importance of coherence. The hypothesis that the number 1 horse will win in example B race is more reasonable than any other twenty-four pattern because it is more coherent. On the other hand, in example C, the hypothesis that the number 2 horse will come in second is not more reasonable than the hypothesis that the number 3 horse will come in third, and not all hypotheses telling us that the n-numbered horse will come in nth can be accepted. To accept all such hypotheses would lead to incoherence. It is no more coherent to suppose that the number 1 horse will come in first in example C than that he will finish in any other place.

The crux is that it will not do to consider hypotheses about how a certain horse will finish in isolation from hypotheses about how other horses will finish. In deciding whether to accept a hypothesis about how a given horse will finish, one must consider what to accept about how every horse will finish. Of course, one might be able to accept hypotheses about how one horse will finish and not accept any about how others will finish. But, to obtain a coherent account, one must accept the consequences that follow from the statements one accepts about how any specific horse will finish. So if there are five horses and if one accepts that number 5 will finish fifth, number 4 fourth, number 3 third, number 2 second, then to avoid incoherence, one must accept that number 1 will finish first. One must not do that in case C, however. In short, when you consider the strategy of accepting that the number n horse will come in nth, you must consider where a coherent use of that strategy will lead you in the resulting system or set of accepted statements.

If it is granted that it is more reasonable in case B to accept the hypothesis that the number 1 horse will win than to accept any other twenty-four pattern disjunction, and that it is not more reasonable in case C to accept that horse 5 will come in fifth than that horse 4 will finish fourth, then we can formulate a rule articulated in terms of reasonableness that yields the result that it is reasonable to accept the hypothesis that the number 1 horse will win in case B but not to accept any of the hypotheses about how horses will finish in case C.

The rule is as follows:

Accept *H* on *E* if it is more reasonable to accept *H* on *E* than any statement *K* that *H* r-competes with on *E*.

This rule differs from the preceding rule by requiring that the accepted hypothesis be more reasonable rather than just more probable than its competitors. This is crucial. For, as we noted above, the hypothesis that the number *1* horse will win in the *B* case is no more probable than any other twenty-four pattern disjunction with which it competes, nor, for that matter does it have higher content. It gives us a more coherent account of what will happen than do the other disjunctions, since they do not allow us to draw any conclusion about how any horse will finish. This proposal resolves the paradox. It does so in terms of a notion of reasonableness that cannot be explicated in terms of probability and content. The notion of coherence, though unexplicated, is not entirely mysterious. Three of its components are consistency, closure, and nonarbitrariness discussed above. These are objectives of reason, desiderata of epistemic rationality. Their satisfaction increases the coherence of the account we give and, in that way, makes it more reasonable.

The conclusion I propose is that the reasonableness of accepting a hypothesis depends on systemic considerations, on what sort of overall account one can give. Two hypotheses that are equal in content and probability may differ in an important way. One may be such that if we accept it and are not arbitrary and do not violate closure, we shall be led to inconsistency. Examples *A* and *C* illustrate such situations, as does the original lottery paradox. In other examples, such as *B*, we may accept a hypothesis without inconsistency though we observe closure and are not at all arbitrary. I conclude that reason mandates consideration of the system of statements or hypotheses we accept and does not permit us to decide what to accept in terms of the intrinsic features of hypotheses considered in isolation. Rational acceptance is a matter of coherence within a system.

Notes

1. I am greatly indebted to Glenn Ross, Donald Hubin, Lee Carter, and W. V. O. Quine for their remarks and proposals pertaining to this paper.

2. I. Levi, *Gambling with Truth* (New York, 1967); C. G. Hempel, "Deductive-Nomological vs. Statistical Explanation," vol. III in Minnesota Studies in the Philosophy of Science, ed. H. Feigl and G. Maxwell (Minneapolis, 1962), pp. 98-169; J. Hintikka and J. Pietarinen, "Semantic Information and Inductive Logic," in *Aspects of Inductive Logic* (Amsterdam, 1966), pp. 96-112; R. Hilpinen, *Rules of Acceptance and Inductive Logic, Acta Philosophica Fennica,* Fasc. 22 (1968); and K. Lehrer, "Truth, Evidence, and Inference," *American Philosophical Quarterly* (1974): 74-92.

3. H. E. Kyburg, Jr., "Conjunctivitis," in *Induction, Acceptance, and Rational Belief*, ed. M. Swain (Dordrecht, 1970), pp. 55-82.

4. K. Lehrer, "Reason and Consistency," in *Analysis and Metaphysics*, ed. K. Lehrer (Dordrecht, 1975), pp. 57-74.

5. G. Harman made this observation at an A. P. A. meeting in his comments on an early version of the paper cited in note 4. His comments are, unfortunately, unpublished.

6.   G. Harman, "Induction," in Swain, *Induction, Acceptance, and Rational Belief,* pp. 83-99.

7.   Levi, *Gambling with Truth.*

8.   K. Lehrer, *Knowledge* (Oxford, 1974), pp. 192-97.

The Theory of Questions, Epistemic Powers, and the Indexical Theory of Knowledge

HECTOR-NERI CASTAÑEDA

The real danger of oversimplified models is not that they are over-simple, but that we may be satisfied with them, and fail to compare them with regions of experience other than those which suggested them.

> Wilfred Sellars, *The Structure of Knowledge*

A main cause of philosophical illness—one-sided diet: one nourishes one's thinking with only one kind of example.

> Ludwig Wittgenstein, *Philosophical Investigations*

Philosophical method has the anti-Augustinian property. When somebody asks me about philosophical method I know what it is. But when nobody asks me, and I am philosophizing, I often do not know what it is.

> Oscar Thend, *Philosophical Method*

INTRODUCTION

To have knowledge is to have a network of beliefs that stand in a most important isomorphism with some facts in the world. What is the nature of that isomorphism? This is the question of *basic epistemology*. My general purpose here is twofold: protophilosophically, to heighten our understanding of the methodology of the answer to the question; theoretically, to deepen our insights into the nature of epistemic isomorphisms and the contextual structure of justified belief and of knowledge. This is, therefore, a study in philosophical method and a contribution to basic epistemology and to the philosophy of cognitive language.

This essay is dedicated to:
RODERICK CHISHOLM, *the great philosophical analyst*
and
EDMUND GETTIER, *the great philosophical iconoclast*

193

My plan involves several intertwined lines of development. Two general lines deserve foremention. *First*, I propose to look at the phenomenon of knowledge directly, not through the existing theories or definitions.[1,2] By exegizing our cognitive experiences we are bound to gather some insights into the role of knowledge in our normal transactions with the world. Such insights will be a positive gain, whatever the destiny of the theories we build upon them. In any case, they crystalize in criteria of adequacy for any future theory of knowledge. *Second*, I propose to subject those criteria to theoretical criticism so as to distill from them valuable hints for one or more initially plausible theories, even definitions, of knowledge. The more hints for alternative theories we can place in our theoretical cellar, the better able we are to build a most comprehensive and beautiful theory. Unfortunately, we do not have enough space here to consider all the useful theoretical hints. We must hurry our exegesis and criticism of the phenomenon of knowledge to outline a tentative analysis of knowledge. Although this analysis is only a temporary way station, it may not be amiss to provide at this juncture a general idea of its nature.

The exegesis of data reveals that our concept of knowledge is actually that of a *family* of particular species of knowledge determined by rich contexts of epistemic assessment. These epistemic contexts are normally pinpointed by the context of thought and speech. Hence the epistemic words, particularly 'know' and 'knowledge', turn out to be *indexical*: they either denote a generic state or have a semantic incompleteness of denotation analogous to, although somewhat different from, the denotational incompleteness present in the indicator 'here' and the one present in the color words in their perceptual uses. We shall explain these contrasts.

Our analysandum is the indexed 'X knows$_i$ that p' (for a species of knowledge determined by context i). Our analysans differs from all the standard analysantia because of our exegesis of data, it goes deliberately outside the circle of just truth and belief. It adopts the Plato-Powers principle that knowledge involves essentially the non-doxastic component of a power to answer questions. It also includes the non-doxastic component of some mechanisms of inference. In short, our preliminary analysis includes six conditions about: (i) belief; (ii) relevance; (iii) an appropriate epistemic power; (iv) the normality or limited abnormality of the truth circumstances; (v) some appropriate inferential powers, and (vi) evidence.[3] The standard truth condition is implied by these conditions.

There are other non-standard features of our analysis, e.g., it requires no conception of, let alone belief in, probability; it is non-Fichtean since it does not require self-knowledge, indeed it does not even require the knower to have the concepts of self, belief, or of any other mental state. We shall see all of this and other things in detail and in their proper order later on.

I. SOME UNAVOIDABLE CRITERIA OF ADEQUACY FOR ANY THEORY OF KNOWLEDGE

Gettier has taught us that knowledge is not equivalent to, nor is it identical with, justified true belief. What else is needed? What is justified belief? What is truth?

Here we shall not go into the theory of truth. It will suffice to fix this parameter by simply assuming that what one believes is either a truth or a falsehood and that truths correspond to facts. We may even adopt the *fact/truth equational view* and take truths to be identical with facts. Naturally, no analysis of knowledge is fully illuminating until it is placed in the context of a theory of truth and facts.

What other conditions are required for knowledge besides justified true belief? This most important question demands a careful examination of what is involved in our attributions of knowledge. We must scrutinize the ways our concept of knowledge functions in experience in order to glean crucial points about the function and nature of that concept. Then we must posit a concept of knowledge characterized by a pattern that threads those crucial points. Such points are our criteria of adequacy for the posited conceptual pattern. The formulation of criteria through the exegsis of data I call *protophilosophy*, and the positing of theories or patterns *symphilosophy*.[4] Protophilosophy must be pursued systematically.

Undoubtedly, our use of the verb 'know' is vague and imprecise. There is, therefore, no good reason for arguing whether a certain proposed analysis of knowledge captures exactly our ordinary use or meaning of 'know'. The issue should be, rather, whether a certain proposal characterizes the pattern of a fruitful concept that coincides with a large segment of our ordinary use of 'know' and its inflections, thus illuminating our actual cognitive dealings with others and with the world. The criteria of adequacy fix the crucial points of the illumination and hence both demarcate the field of theorization and provide tests for all proposed analysis or theories of knowledge.

Let us proceed to our protophilosophical disquisition.

1. The Criterion of Knower Reliability

The most obvious and general feature of our concept of knowledge is that to attribute to a person, say, Sharon, knowledge that p is to attribute to Sharon a maximal degree of reliability concerning p. This reliability has several dimensions, and it grounds other criteria. If Sharon knows that p, then Sharon not only has a true belief but has beliefs that both guarantee that p and make her an unimpeachable source of information about that p.[5] Let us develop these points in some detail.

2. The Gestalt Character of Knowledge

Both the points made above about the knower's maximal reliability involve a nonatomist structure of knowledge. Each belief, like each piece of knowledge, is indeed associated with a proposition, or a state of affairs (or a fact, if you wish). Each true belief that p and each piece of knowledge that p is, on the equational view of truth mentioned above, a fact. But note our language! Here we have a clue to the nonatomist character of knowledge. We speak naturally of each belief, but we need a fragmentation operation in the case of knowledge, and then we speak of each *piece* of knowledge. This linguistic datum suggests that knowledge, unlike belief, is a nonindividuated massive whole. Indeed, going beyond the linguistic datum, it seems that at a certain surface level of analysis believing is atomistic in that a person could conceivably believe each proposition he believes in isolation of his other beliefs, without taking into account its implications relationships. At that surface level of analysis, on the equational view of truth and fact, the isomorphism between true beliefs and facts is an identity isomorphism of a set of beliefs.

Knowledge is, on the contrary, non-atomistic. For a person to know some truth, she must have evidence for the truth in question, or she must be at least justified in believing that truth because it agrees or coheres with other beliefs she has. A person who knows a truth must believe a whole battery of truths, and even know other truths. To have knowledge is to have beliefs about propositions and about their implication relationships. To know is to have a network of beliefs with a certain *Gestalt*. Thus the belief-fact isomorphism constitutive of knowledge connects networks of beliefs with networks of facts, as wholes, not piecemeal through the association of the individual beliefs with their corresponding facts. On the fact/truth equational view, the knowledge isomorphism may still be an identity isomorphism, but it must be the identity isomorphism of a set of sets of beliefs (or truths).[6]

3. The Knower's Beliefs Must Guarantee Truths

Let us return to the knower's maximal reliability. Patently, the knower cannot be maximally reliable if he is not reliable without the faintest possible correction to his reliability. Since we are dealing with thinking sources of information, the only relevant reliability in basic epistemology is the reliability of what our thinkers believe. In basic epistemology we can assume that if a person attempts to communicate, he or she will, if successful, communicate candidly. We can, that is, assume that the person's utterances will convey the truths, or falsehoods, he or she believes—at least to the extent that language is propositionally transparent.[7] Furthermore, in basic epistemology we do not concern ourselves with the information provided by the circumstances of the speaker, by the speaker's body, movements, or vestment, or by the circumstances of the speaker's speech acts. All of these and other sources of information are valuable and must be studied by later, more sophisticated branches of epistemology. In basic epistemology we deal with fundamental structures to be assumed by those later branches.

In short, the maximal reliability of the knower requires that the knower's beliefs (whether we call them evidence or not) guarantee in a very strong way the truth of what he believes and knows.

4. The Cognitive Irrelevance of Probability

Patently, the criterion that the knower's beliefs guarantee the truth of what he believes leads immediately to the irrelevance of probability in the central structure of knowledge. It is a triviality that to believe that it is very highly probable that *p* is *not* to know that *p*, regardless of how high the probability one believes to obtain may turn out to be, regardless of how correct this belief may be, and regardless of how deeply and thoroughly justified one may be in believing that it is very probable that *p*. To illustrate, consider

The Supercautious Gambler. There are 1000 tickets in a lottery. Ann, our cautious gambler, has bought 999 tickets. The prize will be won by the ticket with a number, between 1 and 1000, which also appears on a wooden disk to be picked out of an urn, completely at random.

Obviously, given the knower's reliability criteria, our supercautious gambler does *not* know that she will win the prize. To be sure, she has a right to believe with confidence that she will win; but neither she nor we know that this will happen, even if in fact she will win.

The Supercautious Gambler is the gambler who does not know that she will win when she will in fact win. This is an unavoidable datum for any theory or analysis of knowledge. Interestingly enough, it rebuts the very sophisticated analysis of knowledge proposed by Keith Lehrer in [42]. Indeed, Lehrer's analysis is rebutted by the weaker datum contained in:

The Minimally Cautious Gambler. Like the Supercautious Gambler, except that this gambler buys only 501 lottery tickets.[8]

The moral of these examples, when they are properly exegized, is that the beliefs of the knower must guarantee the truth of what he knows.[9]

5. The Paradox of Empirical Knowledge

Clearly, the reason the supercautious gambler does not know that she will win is because she is not as supercautious as she may be: she could have been maximally cautious if she had bought all 1000 tickets. Then she would have had, assuming the circumstances to be normal, a full guarantee that one of her tickets would be the winner. Requiring probability 1 for knowledge would guarantee truth. But probability 1, as *The Maximally Cautious Gambler* illustrates, requires logical implication. Lehrer knows this very well, and he mentions [3], [39], and [59] as having shown that a hypothesis h has probability 1 on evidence E only if E logically implies h ([42], p. 145).

This seems to raise a paradox. Our contingent claims about the world, including claims about physical objects in our neighborhood, are not logically implied by our evidence for them. For instance, our sensory experiences do not imply our perceptual claims; our perceptual claims do not logically imply our claims about other persons' mental states; our perceptual claims, including the testimony of other persons, do not logically imply our claims about theoretical entities, and so on. Thus, if we require knowledge to include a guarantee of truth, we seem to be ruling out empirical knowledge altogether, except perhaps for the solipsistic knowledge of our present contents of consciousness. But perhaps not even this. Thus Lehrer claims:

Nevertheless, for any strictly coherent probability function, restricting justification to a probability of one will lead us deeply into the den of skepticism. All of the contingent and non-general statements we naturally assume we know would turn out to be statements we are not completely justified in believing and could not possibly know ([42], p. 151).

Apparently we have a serious dilemma: either we insist on knowledge beliefs guaranteeing truth, or we do not. If we choose the first horn of the dilemma, we are apparently lost irretrievably in some deep skepticism. If we opt for the second horn of the dilemma, we know even, as in *The Minimally Cautious Gambler*, when we believe correctly that the chances of truth are barely more than 50 percent, just in case what we believe happens to be true. On the first horn we know too little; on the second horn we know too much. Lehrer has chosen the second horn.

There should be a way out of the dilemma without having to endorse either horn. Clearly, our efficient and useful concept of knowledge functions in our experience in a way such that neither horn is a viable alternative. Understanding the nature of our experience and the structure of the world we find ourselves in requires that we dissolve the dilemma, rather than choose one of its horns. Since the dilemma rests on the use of probability, perhaps we can do without probability—or perhaps we can require probability 1 for knowledge and yet salvage empirical knowledge.[10] After all, empirical truths do imply other empirical truths.

The presence of the paradox and the need of its dissolution are themselves a most important datum. A satisfactory theory of knowledge, and even perhaps a satisfactory analysis of a fruitful and illuminating concept of knowledge, should shed light on the paradox, its source, and its dissolution.

6. Belief in Probability Not Required for Knowledge

In our world we often encounter beings with the power to think, have beliefs, and even know (in our ordinary use of this word), even though they lack the concept of probability. Small children, not to mention animals or robots, do seem to have knowledge, perceptual knowledge, if nothing else, even though they lack the power to think of some states of affairs, or propositions, as probable. A proposition of the form "Probably p" or "It is (highly) probably that p" is a modal complex proposition. To think a modalized complex proposition Mp, a thinker must have the ability to think p, but the converse is not generally necessary. The more complex the modality M, the larger the gap between the ability to think the arguments p of the modality and the power to think of the modalized proposition Mp. Naturally, given the syncategorematic character of modalities they cannot be thought by themselves —except as abstractions from modalized propositions.

Clearly, a probabilitized concept of knowledge, like the one Lehrer has constructed, lacks the fruitfulness of the ordinary concept of knowledge. First, the fruitful ordinary concept of knowledge is the concept of a maximally reliable source of information, where, as noted, the constructed probabilitized concept of knowledge can be very unreliable. Second, the ordinary concept of knowledge dispenses altogether with probability as the content of some networks of beliefs that constitute knowledge.

7. Knowledge Does Not Require Knowledge, or Belief, that One Knows

Similar to the previous criterion about the concept of probability is another important criterion for elucidating our ordinary concept of knowledge. A person can know without being able to *think* that he (himself) or she (herself) knows: the person may lack the concept of the first-person. This is a crucial point I raised in detail in [7] and assumed as far back as 1960, when I began writing [4].[11]

In [7] I contrasted the consciousness and mind of a thinking being lacking the power of self-reference, being which I called *Externus*, with the consciousness and mind of a being endowed with the power of self-reference who is such that: for him consciousness is self-consciousness, and whenever he believes, knows, imagines, etc., he knows (believes) that he knows, believes, imagines, and so on. This reflexive property I called Fichtean, and I spoke of *Fichtean knowledge*, *Fichtean belief*, and *Fichtean consciousness*—in honor of Fichte who forcefully claimed that "without self-consciousness there is no consciousness"([26], p. 41).

It is an empirical matter whether there exist, or not, examples of Externus-type of mind or of consciousness. David Schwayder has assured me, in correspondence commenting on [7], that, of course, we are surrounded by Externi, namely: animals, especially pets, and very young babies. He may be right about this.

It is also an empirical matter whether there are, or there are no, Fichtean minds in our midst. Hintikka, as is well known, has produced in [36] formal theories for species of Fichtean knowledge and Fichtean belief. It is not clear, however, that he is committed to the view that ordinary human beings have Fichtean knowledge and Fichtean belief. Lehrer has also proposed in [42] an account of Fichtean knowledge.[12] Perhaps he also holds that ordinary human beings are Fichtean in this sense. Chisholm in [19] and [20] does seem to hold the strong Fichtean view that consciousness is self-consciousness.

It seems to me that we, ordinary human beings, do not possess Fichtean minds. When I read in Sartre's [54] about episodes of unreflective consciousness, I find myself experiencing similar things. Many a time I am aware of something, I think of something, without being aware or thinking that I am aware or thinking of it. I have often been surprised to learn that I have known some important truths all along.

We now have the concepts of Fichtean knowledge and Fichtean belief. They are important concepts. They can be of great value in a general theory of knowledge in which they are used to characterize an epistemic or doxastic ideal limiting case. I submit, however, that our ordinary concepts of knowledge and belief are more general, and have the Fichtean cases as possible limit instances. The generality of our ordinary concepts of knowledge and belief infuses them with great flexibility and usefulness. We must, in order to understand *our world*, produce accounts of general knowledge and belief, which need not be Fichtean.

8. The Concept of Belief Is Not Required to Have Knowledge

Just as an ordinary knower need have neither the concept of probability nor the concept of self nor the concept of the first or second person, so a knower need not have any psychological concept at all. An Externus knower may simply know the physical world, having no idea of other minds or of the contrast between object and subject. In [4] I describe briefly the structure of the contents of consciousness and of belief of the Externus stage of a being called Privatus. Privatus thinks out loud, so that the attributions of knowledge to him can be made on the standard basis both of perceptions of his body and circumstances, and of interpretations of his utterances. As in our normal attributions of knowledge, Privatus may be correctly attributed the maximal reliability characteristic of knowledge.

Briefly, an Externus type of consciousness and mind will think and believe, not *cogito* propositions of the form "I see (hear, feel) that such and such," but perceptual *cogitatum* propositions of the form "There is such and such here (there)," which are states of affairs in perceptual fields. Obviously, an Externus knowledge of physical objects cannot be built upon *cogito* propositions. It has to be built, if 'built' is the appropriate word, from *cogitatum* propositions—if these are not already propositons about physical objects. This is a crucial non-Cartesian aspect of knowledge set aside by philosophers who hold that knowledge has a foundation on experience and who then go on to interpret experience as what *cogito* propositions are about.[13]

9. The Basic Epistemic Paradox of Other Persons' Information

We need other persons to furnish us with information. This raises a problem. I do *not* mean the traditional problem of other minds. This problem, about how we know that there are other beings with mental states, certainly has a place in the theory of knowledge. See, e.g., [4]. But here, in basic epistemology, we can set that problem aside. The problem of other persons that belongs here is different. We assume here that we are in fact surrounded by other persons, that we deal with them, and that they have mental states to which we have access somehow. Yet within these assumptions we have a problem. We consider X, say, as a person. Thus X is endowed with both the power to know and the power to act. Because of X's knowledge, X is a source of information and we can rely on him to the extent that we claim that he knows. But X is also an agent, and, as such, we must think of X as capable of choosing freely at least some of his courses of action. To the extent that he is a free agent, X is naturally unreliable. Thus, whenever we find a free agent in a chain of evidence, we have there a point of unreliability, a point of non-knowledge. This is illustrated by:

The First Cheater. Lottery L is composed of 1000 tickets. The Official Drawer OD will pick out a numbered chip from a revolving urn. Our Cheater has bought ticket no. 5. He has paid OD an appropriate fee, in return for OD's promise that he will pick out chip no. 5.

Our cheater clearly does not know that he will win. Yet he has the relevant information both about the Official Drawer's knowledge of the lottery and about OD's character. OD is known to keep his promises. But the more First Cheater thinks of OD as a free agent, who will be free to choose or not to choose the winning chip at the moment of drawing, the less First Cheater is in a position to know that he will win. Regardless of how many promises he has kept in the past, free agent OD will have to act in the light of all the reasons he considers *at the time* he decides what to do then.

By contrast, the more Official Drawer's action is determined and the more it is known how this action is determined, i.e., the more OD is like a *mechanism* rather than a genuine agent, the more one can claim to know that he will do action A.

An expert agent who is both knowledgeable and free to inform, or not to inform, is a perplexing beast. He is reliable to the extent that he knows, yet he is unreliable to the extent that he is free to inform or not to inform.

This internal conflict characteristic of each free informant presents problems that we cannot even start to consider here. All we can do is note that in practical life we solve the problem by adopting an *attitude of trust*. This attitude grounds beliefs, is itself grounded on some beliefs, but it cannot be the logical consequence of the beliefs grounding it. Having knowledge entails more than having beliefs: it also entails having *propensities* to have certain beliefs and make certain inferences.

10. Propositions Are Evidentially Organic Wholes

We need the testimony of others to secure the certainty that comes with the essential intersubjectivity of physical reality. This need of others' testimony includes a paradox of its own. We need others with their true beliefs, but we must have them with their freedom to deceive, mislead, and lie. Thus the potential for false evidence and true counterevidence are essential components of our dependence on others.

Yet our proneness to error lies deeper than our social dimension. Our finitude creates an enormous potential for error. Our need to believe and to act on our beliefs leads us to plunge into errors and into partial views of things. We must build our knowledge on beliefs that may be falsehoods or misleading truths, simply because we do not know enough about their *connections* with other truths. Falsehoods may sometimes be the best vehicles for reaching truths and even knowledge. Counterevidence at a certain level may turn out to be part and parcel of valuable evidence.

Propositions, or states of affairs, are, with respect to evidentiality, *organic wholes*. They form compound propositions that have evidential values which are not merely the sum of the evidential values of the components. Thus some set E of propositions may provide very strong evidence for a proposition p, whereas a superset E' of E may provide counterevidence for p, and a superset E'' of both E and E' may provide again strong evidence for p. Therefore, it may happen that a superset E'' may justify belief in p much better than E, thanks to the fact that the set E'-E provides, by its subsumption into E', negative evidence.

11. False Evidence and Counterevidence May Be Needed for Knowledge

The preceding feature is nearly a commonplace when it is discussed in its naked generality. However, it has not enjoyed the full appreciation it deserves in the mainstream dialectic about the analysis of knowledge. The dominant tendency among the most distinguished practitioners is a form of what has been called the *indefeasibility approach*.[14] This approach is *puritanical*: it requires the evidence or justification of belief that constitutes knowledge to be pure true belief, or belief purified of falsehoods.

The easiest indefeasibility formula is simply to require both (*a*) that there is no counterevidence anywhere, even outside the knower's realm of beliefs, and (*b*) that the knower does not have counterevidence for what he knows.[15] Each of these two conditions is patently too strong. Each runs against the grain of the principle of organic unities for evidence and justification of belief. Thus the most energetic epistemologists have been engaged in a search for methodologies that modify (*a*) and (*b*) in the appropriate way—recognizing the fact that there are no ways of suppressing counterevidence from the world, or even from the knower's mind.

The best work on defeasibility does not attempt pure justification as in (*a*)-(*b*). The best proposals aim, rather, at the purification of evidence and justification in order to secure knowledge. The idea is to purge the knower's evidence of the bad features and insist that knowledge obtains only if the purged evidence retains its justificatory power. This core idea receives different concrete specifications. The most prevailing view is, roughly, that the knower has a *wholly* veridical evidential path (pyramid or tree, says Sosa) that links a sufficient set of pieces of evidence with what he knows. This is, however, too puritanical.

The purification techniques that have been developed, with ever increasing insight into the nature of justification, are of great value. I am, however, not entirely happy with two implicit *assumptions* that typically underlie the development of those techniques:

(A) counterevidence always has to do with falsehood;

(B) falsehoods must be purged: a set E of propositions that justifies belief in *p* does not yield knowledge if the believer does not have evidence that would justify his believing *p* if the falsehoods in E are purged somehow.[16]

Of these, (B) is the more widespread. The mainstream discussions seem to agree that at least (B) is necessary for knowledge. The issue has been whether it is also sufficient.

Undoubtedly, counterevidence sometimes involves falsehoods—as with false testimony; and evidence containing falsehoods is usually incapable of yielding knowledge. Gettier's classic counterexamples illustrate this very well, and so do many others. But not always. *Sometimes the one who fails to know need not have any false belief.*[17]

I want to urge that (B) is *not necessary* for knowledge. It may occasionally happen that the one who knows needs some false belief in order to come to know. Consider, for example,

The Cross-Wired Rememberer. Crispin has an interesting memory mechanism. Whenever he perceives a date *d* written on a book, if he perceives it very clearly, he will remember it as *d* + 10. (This causes him some problems concerning exchanges of information about times, of course.) He has read only one history book about Columbus's preparations for his first voyage to America. In that book there was a misprint: it gave Columbus's date of departure from Palos as August 13, 1482. He repeated the date in order to memorize it. Naturally for him, his memory mechanism corrected his correct perception. Crispin knows, just like anyone of us, that Columbus left Palos on August 3, 1492. Just ask him!

In sections 14–17 below we shall examine the varying contextual assumptions of different species of knowledge. Then we shall better see in what sense both Crispin and we know that Columbus left Palos on August 3, 1492. For the moment let us simply say that Crispin passes the regular tests we pass: mentioning books where we can find the right information, answering the question "When did Columbus depart from Palos (Spain)?" as we do. We may even suppose that Crispin *knows* of his cross-wired memory for dates, so that he knows that he needs false perceptions, or false initial beliefs, of the appropriate kind to know the dates of events and to lead others to know what he knows.

The general point is this: *within a standard correlation between perception, memory, and belief, there can be systematic exceptions that correlate false perceptions with true, fully justified beliefs*, which are fully justified *because they are grounded on those false perceptions*.[18] The connections among the different operations of the mind are capable of combining in more ways than we are used to and still yield knowledge. This matter deserves thorough study, without which a full theory of knowledge will not be attained. For basic epistemology we need note only that we cannot assume an easy correlation between perception, memory, and belief. In fact, even within our ordinary scheme we can have:

> *The Twitching Color Blind.* Norman is color blind, not capable of visually discriminating between green and blue. He has found, fortunately, that often, when he sees pairs of blue-green objects, one member of the pair causes his eyelids to twitch. To make the story short, it happens that Norman learns to discriminate some blue-green objects from other blue-green objects by his twitching, namely, the ones others see as blue when he sees them paired with green objects.

Given that Norman must see a contrasting pair to have his twitching indicative of a blue object, he must, then, have the initial false perceptual judgment that the two objects he sees are of the same color. This judgment grounds his further judgment about the difference in color. The requirement that eliminates false judgment from knowledge-making evidence would deprive Norman of the proper perceptual basis for coming to know that the object he has seen, or is seeing, is blue.

It is easy to conceive of correcting methods for acquiring knowledge that depend crucially on there being some false steps to be corrected. Indeed, I wonder whether this is not more common than purificational epistemologists have thought. In general we can imagine:

> *The False-Believing Knower.* In certain types of situations Louise reacts by acquiring a belief, which turns out to be false. Louise learns the systematic connection between her circumstances and her acquiring a false belief of the requisite type, and then learns to use her own false beliefs as an inductive basis for positing the corresponding truth. She reasons as follows: "In situations of type s I always acquire a false belief of type t; I am now in situations of type s and I have acquired the belief that p, which belief is of type t; hence, it is not the case that p."

Obviously, the knower can more easily, and naturally, use essentially the false beliefs of others to acquire his knowledge.

Nothing in the preceding discussion contravenes the chief intuition of the analytic epistemologists, namely, that the belief constitutive of knowledge be undefeated and that the evidence for it be undefeated. These intuitions are palpably sound. The discussion shows that the puritanical view, which requires for the undefeasibility of the evidence a wholly veridical path (or pyramid, as Sosa says), is too restrictive. The evidence must be undefeated in the sense of beating up the opposition, but there may very well be strong opposition that, so to speak, leaves indelible scars on the victor.

12. The Objective-Subjective Paradox of Epistemic Justification

The requirement of a wholly veridical evidential path seems like the most natural one to complete the classical list of conditions for knowledge. Yet even full evidence without a taint of falsehood may *fail to be sufficient* for knowledge. We shall show this presently through some easy useful examples. But first, let us reflect about it to find our bearings. The situation is perplexing. Nothing seems to be missing from the list: truth; belief; complete justification; wholly veridical justification. What else can be added?

A look at the standard characterizations of complete justification reveals that the completeness of justification in question is a matter of the knower's beliefs overriding all the counterevidence available to him. What we feel is the need to ask for an objective completeness. This is precisely the idea behind the naive condition (a) discussed in section 11 above. There is, however, the crucial fact that a merely objective condition that we cannot take into account is of little value—except as an ideal. (See Tienson [71].) Hence we must require a subjective completeness, which is precisely what Sosa, Lehrer, Harman, Dretske, and the others do. But then we are back to the position where wholly veridical (subjectively) complete justification may fail to yield knowledge. We face here one of the most fundamental problems: *the subjective-objective paradox of epistemic justification.* It is a most pressing one. It is a special case of our egocentric predicament: We encounter it just because we cannot get outside our circle of beliefs.

Perhaps it may not be amiss to see the paradox illustrated in Harman's very fine perception of the problem in [31]. He devises some examples to show that completely justified true belief may fail to constitute knowledge: some missing evidence keeps knowledge away. I am not entirely sure that his examples are all effective. But the point is clear even on general grounds. In any case, there are the examples in *The Cheater Series* in section 13 below. Harman proposes a solution in terms of a subjective requirement for justified inference:

Q. One may infer a conclusion *only if* one also infers that there is no undermining evidence one does not possess ([31], p. 151; my italics).

This principle *cannot* be part of an account of *our* concept of knowledge. According to Harman's Q, the conclusion the prospective knower would infer is of the form

(1) There is no evidence undermining [. . .] that I do not possess.

The indefinite personal pronoun 'one' in the subordinate clause 'there is no under-mining evidence ONE does not possess' in Q is what I call a *quasi-indicator*. (See [6] and [10].) Propositions of this form can be thought only by entities that have: (i) the concept of, or the mechanism of reference in, the first person; (ii) the concept of evidence; (iii) the concept of belief, which is what one possesses as this word is used in (1) and Q. Thus, as explained in section 7, were Harman's Q a universal condition of knowledge, it would at best govern *Fichetean knowledge*. For non-Fichtean, Sartrean creatures like ourselves, Q would impose an unbearable amount of self-consciousness.

Can Harman's Q be a principal characteristic of the knowledge of those thinkers capable of self-reference (not merely capable of referring to themselves but capable of referring to themselves in the first person)? To decide this, we need to know what 'undermining' means. Harman tells us that "the label 'undermining evidence one does not possess' has been explained in terms of knowledge" ([31], p. 151). A perusal of the text preceding this quotation shows the phrase 'undermining knowledge'. Hence the full version of form (1) is:

> (2) There is no evidence undermining my knowledge that *p* that I do not pos-sess.

Clearly, then, adding to our list of conditions for knowledge (truth of that *p*, belief that *p*, complete justification, wholly veridical justification of one's belief that *p*) the fifth condition that the knower infers in accordance with Harman's Q does not accomplish much. Any believer can so infer. Should we require, instead, as the *fifth condition* guaranteeing sufficiency (not necessity, remember) that the knower infers *justifiedly and correctly* in accordance with Q? This new condition would give us a desirable combination of subjectivity (justified inference) and objectivity (cor-rect inference). Is this the end of the post-Gettier search?

The above fifth condition seems to be successful if 'undermining' means falsi-fying. Clearly, if there is no evidence, whether I possess it or not, that falsifies that I know that *p*, then on the assumption of bivalence, I know that *p*. The trouble with this fifth condition is its unhelpfulness. The five conditions cannot provide an anal-ysis of knowledge because of the circularity of the fifth condition. The conjunction of the five conditions is not equivalent to "X knows that *p*"; it implies, but it is not implied by, "X knows that *p*."

To sum up, Harman's Q cannot help us understand the structure of knowledge. He suspects that this is so, for he merely claims that Q "is a principle concerning in-ference." I am sure that some scientific inferences conform to Q; but Q certainly cannot account for most of the valid and justified inferences we make in daily life—not to mention the inferences made by children who have not yet acquired the con-cept of evidence, or of undermining knowledge, let alone the concept of self.

The objective-subjective paradox of epistemic justification is a most serious matter. It has to be solved, we can be sure, only by a requirement that combines the subjective element of some belief with the objective element of the truth of that be-lief.

13. *Wholly Veridical, Completely Justified True Belief Need Not Be Knowledge: The Cheater Series*

Let us know discuss some examples that establish this criterion. Exegizing them should help us find valuable clue's for solving the subjective-objective paradox of epistemic justification. Consider:

> *The Second Cheater.* Lottery L is composed of 1000 tickets. The winning ticket will be the one with a number matching the number on a disk in a revolving urn picked out by the Official Drawer (OD). Ann bought ticket no. 5. She has ensured that OD picks out disk no. 5 in some way, the mechanics of which do not matter. (On one version Ann arranges to have disk no. 5 magnetized and a fine iron filing inserted in OD's right hand, his lottery hand.)

In an example like this, with more obvious details added, Ann knows that she will win the lottery prize. But that is so only because of a major detail that is seldom discussed, yet it is of the greatest importance in Ann's knowledge that she will win the prize. The general silence on this detail, it seems to me, accounts for a good deal of the difficulties normally encountered in discussions on the analysis of knowledge. That detail is this: *the total circumstances surrounding and linking Ann and the lottery are assumed to be normal.* The normality of the circumstances has been the crucial neglected factor. Such normality is implicitly assumed in the many ingenious counterexamples which show the inadequacy of proposed analyses of knowledge by destroying the normality of the circumstances.[19]

How must we deal with normality? This is the nuclear question. To find a guide to the answer we must exegize the epistemic roles of alterations of normality. Consider:

> *The Third Cheater.* The situation is the same as in *The Second Cheater*, except that without anybody having any idea (knowledge, if you wish) of it, there is a pair of mechanisms M_1 and N_1, say, in the Lottery Hall. Mechanism M_1 replaces the number n on a disk picked up by OD with the number $n + h$. Mechanism N_1 maps a number n on a disk (either in the hand of OD or right upon the disk touching the official lottery tray) into the number $n - h$. Thus, when OD picks up disk no. 5, mechanism M_1 causes the number $5 + h$ to be on the disk. Then mechanism N_1 replaces $5 + h$ with 5 again. M_1 and N_1 are causally independent of each other. Thus, when OD has placed the winning disk on the official tray the disk shows ticket no. 5 to be the winner. Ann collects her prize.

Perhaps it is useful to add a word about the mechanisms. Their physical embodiment is immaterial. What is important is that they operate as noted and that N_1 acts after M_1 during the appropriate time and location. M_1 could be embodied in a chemical process acting on a disk in OD's hand because of chemicals he used to cleanse his hands. N_1 could be embodied in an optical process acting through mirrors reflecting light on the official tray. But this is a problem of engineering, not of philosophy.

Does Ann know before OD picks up disk no. 5, or before she is declared the winner, that she will be the winner? This question cannot be answered immediately, one way or the other, just on the description of the situation contained in *The Third Cheater*. But it is of the utmost importance to emphasize one crucial point: *We are not here concerned with falsehoods*, whether in Ann's beliefs or in the relevant reports made by others. We are deliberately limiting ourselves to wholly veridical evidence.

Does Ann, in *The Third Cheater*, know that she will win, if she will in fact win, the lottery prize? *It depends on the context*. By hypothesis Ann has no idea of the balancing mechanisms M_1 and N_1. If these mechanisms are *normal fixtures of the lottery situation*, Ann knows that she will win the prize—in spite of her ignorance about them! Let the mechanisms be standard elements of the normal circumstances. Then they function normally in the total process that both leads causally to the truth of the proposition "Ann [I] will win the prize" and furnishes Ann's evidence for this proposition. That is, those mechanisms function in exactly the same way as other normal causal segments of the standard situation about which nobody has any idea, e.g., the processes inside OD's lottery hand, or inside the disks in the lottery urn, whose chemical constitution has not been studied up to the time of drawing. Yet such processes and those involved in other objects in the situation have an epistemically relevant place in the proceedings leading up to the declaration of the winning ticket.

The fundamental idea is, then, that the *normality* of the circumstances pertaining to the truth of the known proposition plays a crucial role in the knower's knowing that proposition: that normality is part of the *objective requirement* for knowledge to come about. The *subjective requirement* is this: the knower's assuming, taking it for granted, rather than believing it in a more substantial sense, that the circumstances are normal. Here is, I submit, the first stage in the solution of the subjective-objective paradox of epistemic justification.

Suppose now that, alternatively, neither mechanism M_1 nor mechanism N_1 is a normal part of the standard circumstances; they are instantiated for the first time in the history of Lottery L. Then Ann does *not* know that she will win the prize. To be sure, Ann, as described in *The Third Cheater*, still takes it for granted that the circumstances are normal. This is precisely what creates the discrepancy between her beliefs (and evidence) and the external reality. In short:

Crucial Datum I. In *The Normal Third Cheater*, Ann knows, whereas in *The Non-Normal Third Cheater* Ann does not know, that she will win the prize.

The Non-Normal Third Cheater establishes that the typical undefeatedness analyses of knowledge do not provide universally valid sufficient conditions for knowledge. Ann does not know that she will win the prize. Yet she has wholly veridical justification in her belief that she will win the prize, lacks the slightest whit of counterevidence, and in fact she will win the ticket. Furthermore, we may suppose that she has drawn, on her own initiative, the conclusion that no evidence that undermines her knowing that she will win is not known to her.[20] She has inferred that the best hypothesis that explains the facts as she believes (knows, if you wish) them is that she will win. In *The Normal Cheater* she knows in spite of defeasibility.[21]

The Non-Normal Third Cheater brings out a possible ambiguity in Harman's principle Q. Does mechanism M_1 undermine Ann's, or anybody else's, belief that Ann will win the prize? In the context in question *as a whole*, which contains also the reversing mechanism N_1, the answer seems to be an emphatic "NO!" On the other hand, we may consider, not the whole context, but only the context known to Ann, her evidence, and then the extended evidential context that includes M_1 but not N_1. In this *piecemeal* view it is not out of order to hold that there is in reality a piece of evidence that when added to Ann's evidence undermines her knowledge that she will win. I cannot find in Harman's book a text that decides this issue, at least in a way clear to me. But he does include an insightful discussion of how one's evidence may change from time to time. This suggests that *perhaps* Harman at least at some moments adopts the piecemeal view.

If 'undermines one's knowledge that p' is taken in the holistic way, then Ann is correct in inferring that there is no evidence that undermines her knowledge. If the expression is taken in the piecemeal sense, then Ann is mistaken in that inference. But then her being able to make the inference correctly is irrelevant to her knowing that she will win the prize. We can, if we wish, have Ann not engage in irrelevant inferences.

Let us continue our exegesis of the data. Consider *The Modified Non-Normal Third Cheater*. This is like *The Non-Normal Third Cheater*, except that Ann knows somehow, or, more weakly, has strong evidence, about the generally unthought of mechanisms M_1 and N_1; everything else remains the same. Clearly:

> *Crucial Datum II*. In *The Modified Non-Normal Third Cheater* Ann does know that she will win the lottery prize.

Palpably, there are in principle infinitely many pairs of mechanisms, like M_1 and N_1, that can intervene anywhere in the standard causal circuit leading from the setting up of the lottery to the delivery of the prize to the owner of the winning ticket. Furthermore, pairs of mechanisms like M_1 and N_1 can zero in on new members of the expanded causal circuit. For instance, a mechanism $M_{1.1}$ may stop the action of mechanism M_1, or it may operate after M_1, say, mapping $n + b$ onto $n + b/k$, but then another mechanism $N_{1.1}$ reverses the action of $M_{1.1}$.

The requirements are that these mechanisms work in pairs in the appropriate time and order. Naturally, there are also pairs of mechanisms that epistemically cancel each other out, so to speak, even though they do not operate contiguously, converging on one link in the causal chain. There may be all sorts of compensatory pairs of changes.

We shall speak of *The Kth Cheater* to refer to a *Cheater* situation built on *The Second Cheater* by $K - 2$ pairs of compensatory mechanisms. Once again, we distinguish between *Normal* and *Non-Normal Cheaters*. We also distinguish, as before, between *The Non-Normal Kth Cheater* in general and *The Modified Non-Normal Kth Cheater*. *The Fully Modified Non-Normal Kth Cheater* is the variant of *The Kth Cheater* in which there are $K - 2$ pairs of compensatory mechanisms such that: (i) they are exceptions to the normality of the circumstances of *The Second Cheater*;

(ii) they are the only such abnormalities; (iii) Ann knows, or is fully justified in believing, that each mechanism obtains, and knows how it is paired with its mate; otherwise she takes it for granted that the truth circumstances of the proposition "I, Ann, will win the prize" are normal.

14. Crucial Results of the Cheater Series and Their Generalizations about the Assumption about Circumstances

A little reflection on *The Cheater Series* reveals the following *most fundamental epistemological data*:

> GDI. In *The Normal Kth Cheater*, regardless of the value of K (even if it is infinitely large), whether Ann has any idea of the mechanisms involved, or not, she knows that she will win the prize.

> GDII. In any *Kth Non-Normal Not Modified Cheater*, in which there are h pairs of mechanisms, for $0 < h \leqslant K - 2$, Ann does not know that she will win the prize.

> GDIII. In *The Fully Modified Non-Normal Kth Cheater*, Ann knows that she will win the prize. Naturally, given the finitude of human minds, K is a small finite number, or Ann has a general principle thorough which she can think of infinitely many abnormalities by means of universal quantifications.

These data readily suggest the obvious *epistemic generalizations* about what a knower must assume (take for granted) and what he must believe about the normality of the truth circumstances of what he knows. Either he must truly assume that the circumstances are normal, or he must truly and justifiedly believe what each of the abnormalities consists of.

The preceding generalizations are, I submit, at the core of the *solution* to the subjective-objective paradox of epistemic justification. They must be the nucleus of any adequate theory of knowledge, and of any satisfactory analysis of knowledge.

15. The Diversity of Normal Epistemological Contexts and the Contextual Semantics of 'Know'

The normality of a context of belief justification is, we have seen, a crucial pivot on which knowledge hinges. *The Cheater Series* suggests that there may be different normal contexts. It does not make it clear, however, that a person may be involved in different normal contexts of belief justification at one and the same time. Evidently, if one is involved in just one normal context at each time, then there would be a linear, temporal arrangement of contexts of belief justification, and in spite of their diversity we can speak of knowledge *simpliciter*. In such a case it would suffice to note the relativization of knowledge to the normal context applicable at each time under consideration.

On the other hand, if there are different normal contexts of belief justification applicable to a person at one and the same time, then we cannot speak of knowledge *simpliciter* but must distinguish *species of knowledge*: at least one for each context of belief justification. Nothing at this stage of exegesis requires that within each context there be no other parameters to which knowledge is relativized.

One consequence of the diversity of normal contexts impinging upon one and the same person at one and the same place and time is this: for some proposition that *p* the person so impinged may know that *p* in one respect or species, without knowing that *p*, in another respect or species. This is an important result. *First*, it is testable in experience. *Second*, it will furnish some aid in understanding the historical puzzle, merely accentuated in the last decades, of the stubbornness of the disputes about the analysis of knowledge: they continue unabated in spite of the tremendous cleverness of the arguments and the ingenuity of the examples taken as data; the debate has provided penetrating and satisfying insights, yet mastering those disputes produces a deep sense of unfulfillment. The stubbornness of such ingenious disputes suggests that perhaps underlying them all there is often no true joining of issues: that sometimes one species of knowledge may be under consideration and sometimes another species may be examined, even perhaps by the same epistemologist—under the implicit, or explicit, assumption that there is just one species of knowledge.

Let us return to our daily cognitive experiences. Let us investigate whether there are species of knowledge. For this we need cases in which for some person, e.g. Andrea, and some proposition that *p*:

(1) At time *t* Andrea knows that P;

(2) At time *t* Andrea does not know that P;

(3) There is no contradiction in (1) and (2);

(4) The common words in sentences (1) and (2) seem to have, on all fours, the same sense or meaning.

There is unavoidable vagueness in condition (4). The reason is that (1)-(4) are descriptions of data, and the data have certain vaguenesses that represent the junctures at which the puzzles they represent are to be solved by the theories to be developed. Naturally, we may say that

(5) The sentence 'Andrea knows that *p*' does not express in isolation, in (1), the same proposition, or truth, that it expresses in (2).

Hence we may say that the sentence 'Andrea knows that *p*' occurs ambiguously in the pair (1)-(2). But we must *not* conclude from this that the word 'know' is ambiguous. In general, the (propositional) ambiguity of a sentence does not imply that any of its words or constituent expressions is ambiguous. Let us consider examples before we theorize about the semantics of the verb 'know'.

Is there any situation in which for some proposition that *p* (1)-(5) obtain? Yes; there is. Powers in [52] has discussed a beautiful simple example, which shows this.[22] (He, however, exegizes it somewhat differently from the way I do.) He considers the following question:

(Q) Is there (in English) a four-letter word that ends in EE, ENN, and WHY?

The reader may want to investigate the answer to (Q) before reading more of this paper. A reflective pause may not be unsalutary.

I assume that the reader has gone through the dictionary and has found that there is, at least initially, a difficulty in locating an affirmative answer to (Q). I am sure that the reader has also found that an affirmative answer to (Q) is delivered by the word 'deny'. Thus we have for proposition that p in (1)-(4):

> p: There is (in English) a four-letter word ending in EE, ENN, and WHY.

Now, Andrea (like Powers himself, me, and many others, when first confronted with question (Q) has run through the alphabet mentally and has not located the word 'deny'. That occurred at time t. Hence (2) is true. But, obviously, Andrea would have emphatically answered "Yes" to the question:

> (R) Is the word 'deny' a four-letter (English) word ending in EE, ENN, and WHY?

To the extent that Andrea can answer "Yes" to (R) she may correctly be said to know that there is an English four-letter word ending in EE, ENN, and WHY. Hence to this extent (1) is also true.

Powers used his example to conclude that we must distinguish between *propositional knowledge*, which is, *roughly*, the power to answer a question of the form "Is P the case?" from *cognitive knowledge*, which is, roughly again, the power to answer some questions [52], pp. 347 ff). This stipulation formalizes an important distinction. More important, the distinction builds on Powers's Platonic idea of construing knowledge as the power to answer questions. The distinction must not be construed, however, as dealing with two different senses of 'know' and 'knowledge'. *The unity of knowledge must be maintained.* That unity is the one that underlies certain constructions that puzzle Powers:

> The situation [concerning the distinction between propositional and cognitive knowledge] is *obscured* by our tendency in ordinary discourse to use "knowing-that" locutions *even where* no merely propositional knowledge is in question ([52], p. 347; my italics).

This fact of ordinary discourse is another *crucial datum*. One must consider it seriously. It seems to me premature to regard that tendency Powers mentions as obscuring a distinction. At least my *desideratum* is to develop an account of knowledge that accepts Powers's datum and illuminates it by showing the reason why ordinary discourse has it. Clearly, the drift of the desideratum is this: we want an account of knowledge that shows the fundamental unity of knowledge through Powers's constructions.[23]

It seems to me that the word 'know' does not have a different meaning in (1), related to question (R), from the one it has in (2), related to question (Q). It must be carefully observed that the unity of sense of 'knows' in (1) and (2), on which I am insisting, is perfectly compatible with the thesis that in some sense we are dealing in (1) with a different kind of knowledge from the one dealt with in (2). This harks back to the exegetical thesis that the ambiguity of a sentence must not be taken automatically as, i.e., does not imply, the ambiguity of a component of such a sentence.

Assuming a sentence S to be ambiguous creates the problem of disambiguation. If we want to adopt a canonical notation that exhibits the ambiguity in question, we must have in the ambiguous sentence two (or more) readings that exhibit the diversity of interpretations. If there is no ambiguous expression in S, then we must suppose that some implicit sentential element has to be introduced. This additional exegetical principle does not automatically determine a path for disambiguation, only a framework.

In our Powersian example we want to recognize the Platonic-Powersian approach, which equates types of knowledge with powers to answer questions. Thus we can introduce the following canonical expressions for the disambiguation of the sentence 'Andrea knows that there is (in English) a four-letter word ending in EE, ENN, and WHY:

> (1a) At time t Andrea knows$_R$ that there is (in English) a four-letter word ending in EE, ENN, and WHY.

> (2a) At time t Andrea does not know$_Q$ that there is (in English) a four-letter word ending in EE, ENN, and WHY.

Here the subscripts refer to questions (Q) and (R) determining the species of knowledge involved. They denote operators mapping generic knowledge on species of it.

The tentatively proposed analyses (1a) and (2a) of (1) and (2), respectively, maintain the common meaning of 'knows' in (1) and (2). Through the subscripts attached to 'knows' they signal a differentiation of the *one genus* knowledge into *distinct species*. Naturally, there are other alternatives. One can take the needed elements to be, not operators specifying species of the relation *knows* between a person and a proposition or propositional function, but operators on propositional functions. In the latter case we could represent, e.g., (1), as of the form:

> (1b) R (at time t Andrea knows that there is [in English] a four-letter word ending in EE, ENN, and WHY).

Powers's example of questions (Q) and (R) partially confirms that, taking questions as determiners of epistemic contexts, *different normal contexts* may apply to a person at one and the same time. Thus we better acknowledge different determinate species of knowledge.

16. One Dimension of the Semantics of 'Know' and 'Knowledge': The Theory of Questions and Propositional Guises

We must generalize upon Powers's example. Both Plato and Powers start with a *what*-question, like (Q), rather than with a *whether*-question. Undoubtedly, there are many other questions: *Where? When? How? Why? What with? Whenceforth?* and so on. All these questions can be asked with the same resources of the sentence that formulates the correct answer. They are all questions that select a component of the correct answer as the interrogation point, so to speak. But such questions do not exhaust *the interrogation points of a proposition.* For instance, we can ask about the logical connection between two propositions, or propositional functions, when these form a compound proposition or propositional function. Yet ordinary language does not have easy mechanisms that allow one to ask such questions without describing, rather than merely presenting, the question-generating proposition.

Consider the proposition expressed by this sentence:

(2) If all the flights were on time today, John is either in the men's room or in a telephone booth, or he did not come.

Logically, even if not practically, we could ask questions that take the main connective 'if' as the interrogation point, or the disjunction 'or' in the consequent, or the universal quantifier 'all' of the antecedent, or the time denoted by the locution 'on time', and so on. In sentence (2), it seems that each word, locution, and clause determines an interrogation point. This includes grouping questions like "If all the flights were on time today, where is John?" and the overall question "Is it the case that (2)?"

Perhaps we can gather the whole family of questions as follows:

(*a*) There is the hierarchy of logical forms of a proposition, which is the correct answer to each member of a corresponding family of questions, e.g., in (2) we have the forms: p [of a proposition whatever], $p \supset q$ [of any conditional whatever], $p \supset (q \vee r)$ [of any conditional with disjunctive consequent], $(x)(Fx) \supset (q \vee r)$ [of a conditional with a universal antecedent and a disjunctive consequent], and so on. There are the deeper and deeper forms of (2), for instance, which result from analyzing any of its component concepts. If we analyze *flight, men's room, telephone booth, come,* etc., we find a very complex logical form underlying the ostensible form that sentence (2) reveals.[24]

(*b*) We take each component, or part of a proposition considered as having a certain logical form, as an interrogation point, whether the part is a proper part or not. If we analyze any component in (2), e.g., 'flight' or 'telephone', we find more interrogation points.

The result is a hierarchy of the family of questions determined by a given proposition. Each level of questions corresponds to what in [11], part II, I have called a *propositional guise.* A propositional guise is, roughly, a proposition conceived as having a certain logical form. The theory of propositional guises permits a unified account of Moore's paradox of analysis, the discrimination of attention, and the increase of knowledge and belief through the exegesis of propositions.[25] Here I mention it because it has additional unifying power in bringing under the same account the diversity of questions and the diversity of epistemic contexts.

Following the Plato-Powers line, we take a person's powers to answer certain questions as determining species of knowledge. Perhaps some properties, whether qualities or relations, of objects are ultimate, truly unanalyzable. Perhaps some properties can be fully analyzed in terms of primitive properties. Most of the properties we consider in daily life, however, do not seem to be truly analyzable in a finite number of steps into ultimately primitive ones. Thus there seems to be no ultimate analysis of many propositions we know to be true. Hence the hierarchy of logical forms (and guises) of most propositions is not composed of (definitely) a finite number of rungs. Thus the hierarchy of questions determined by most propositions is not a finite system. Hence there is in principle an indefinite, and even infinitely large, number of species of knowledge.

The preceding result seems to explain why we lack in ordinary language a systematic mechanism for denoting, or signaling, the species of knowledge with which we are concerned. Obviously, we are not concerned in practical life with the whole hierarchy of logical forms (and guises) of a proposition, at least not as such. The interrogative locutions we have mark points of interrogation. By placing them in an interrogative sentence, we reveal both the level of logical form (and guise) and within this form the interrogation point in which we are interested. Compare, e.g., in the case above, the questions: "*Is it* the case that (2)?," "If all flights were on time today, *where* is John?," and "If all the flights were on time today, then, since he is neither in the men's room nor in a telephone booth, *where* is he?"

Now the question appears: If in ordinary language we lack a systematic mechanism for specifying which questions and, *a fortiori*, which species of knowledge we are interested in, how do we manage? For we do seem to manage to communicate about what certain persons know or, for that matter, fail to know. The answer seems to be this: *We manage to communicate about species of knowledge in exactly the same way we manage to communicate about the species of other properties, when we need a specification from a genus with indefinitely and perhaps infinitely many species*, namely: the context of communication pinpoints the relevant species.

What I am claiming for 'know' and 'knowledge' is in detail somewhat different from what happens to demonstrative words like 'here' and 'there' and from what happens to color words. Of course, there are fundamental reasons for the differences. The common claim is that in their primary uses all these types of expressions are at bottom indexical. (See [6].)

With 'here' and 'there' the expressions themselves, and the sentences in which they occur, need to be complemented by an association with a place of *possible* (*not actual*) utterance. In perceptul uses color words and the sentences containing them need an association with actual shades of color; but they can be used in a generic way. One reason, I suppose, is that the actual determinate color content of experience is normally not important in communication. Thus, in some uses, especially non-perceptual uses, color words do not denote a determinate shade determined by context, including pointing. They must, then, be understood as either denoting a generic, a determinable quality, or as being implicitly quantified. For instance, 'The book on the table in the chairman's office is red' may be taken as of the form 'There is a shade ϕness of the red family such that the book on the table in the chairman's office is ϕ'.

The epistemic words 'know' and 'knowledge' may perhaps be used in a generic sense, as the color words are. As in the case of these words, the generic use rests on their use in which they denote determinate species contextually pinpointed. With 'know' and 'knowledge' it is not perceptual context, but the *assumed context of inquiry*, that pinpoints the determinate species relevant to episodes of assertion or of thought.

In each context of communication we are concerned with certain questions. Often there is no need to formulate them, because the courses of action we are engaged in, or are planning to engage in, demand certain answers. Thus the implicit set of relevant questions determines by itself the species of knowledge we are interested in. The context of communication, and the context of inquiry, whether the inquiry is carried out by one person or another, determines, therefore, a species operator, like the subscripts 'Q' and 'R' in section 15, which maps the generic knowledge into a relevant species of knowledge.

Aside from inquiry, a person has at a given time the epistemic powers to answer certain questions pertaining to a certain proposition p. Hence, independently of any inquiry, or of any context of communication, a person has *knowledge$_a$* that p for several classes a of questions that include questions pertaining to that p. The linguistic point we are making is that in a given context of speech, even if it is not communicational, a speaker will, in choosing his topic of discourse, select at least one class a of questions, with respect to which he attributes knowledge to persons. Patently, the selection of a is here chiefly the setting in readiness, even if not the actual triggering, of a bundle of dispositions to think of (and formulate) certain questions. Hence the selection of a class a of questions need not be exhibited in a listing of the members of a or in the formulation of a description of a.

17. Another Dimension of the Semantics of 'Know' and of the Theory of Questions: Methodological and Contextual Constraints on Interrogation Ranges

Each proposition, or state of affairs, we claim, determines a hierarchy of questions. This hierarchy is determined simply by the hierarchy of logical forms of the given proposition (or state of affairs). But the total logical hierarchy of questions is often too broad for practical concerns. We are normally interested in a modest segment of the interrogative hierarchy pertaining to a proposition. The segment in question is cut off from the total hierarchy by means of a set of constraints. In a given context of inquiry we are interested in questions that comply with certain conditions embodying the relevant constraints. Such conditions are part of the circumstances determining the truth of the proposition to which the question-*cum*-constraints, as well as the hierarchy of questions containing it, belongs. Obviously, a person may have the power to find a proposition P upon thinking a question $Q^c(P)$ with constraint c belonging to P, and yet that person may lack the power to think of P upon thinking a question $R^d(P)$ with constraint d also belonging to P.

The constraints on the relevant questions for a certain inquiry are part of the context of the inquiry. To the extent that a person may be simultaneously involved in different inquiries, that person may be involved in different sets of *normal circumstances* for the truth of the propositions of the inquires in question. More generally, a person's power to offer a proposition P as the true answer to a question $Q^c(P)$ may not be matched by a power to offer P as the true answer to a different question $R^d(P)$. Yet the set of circumstances involved in the truth of P by constraint c and question Q may be just as normal as the set of circumstances involved in the truth of P by question R and constraint d.

In Powers's example of questions (Q) and (R) in section 15, there are no methodological constraints on the questions; the two normal contexts include simply the capacity of thinking the questions and of English words. In that sense the examples are oversimple.

Let us take a closer look at questions with constraints.

Each point of interrogation in a propositional guise (i.e., a proposition considered as having a certain logical form) determines both *a blank in the proposition*, so to speak, and a range of possible *fillers of that blank*. For example, the proposition (2) of section 16 above, analyzed as far as sentence (2) shows, has the point of articulation represented by the expression 'flights', which yields, among others, the following two questions:

(Q1)   What events are such that if all of *them* were on time today, John is either in the men's room or in a telephone booth, or he did not come?

(Q2)   What commercial events scheduled to take place here are such that if all of *them* were (occurred) on time today, John is either in the men's room or in a telephone booth, or did not come?

Patently, an analysis of the concept *flight* will open up more interrogation points within this concept in the proposition P expressed by sentence (2). Such interrogation points will yield further questions belonging to P with their proper ranges of fillers.

Question (Q1) determines a large number of fillers for the blank represented by the italicized pronoun '*them*'. However, the context of inquiry in which the question is raised may make it clear that certain fillers are not relevant. Question (Q2) cuts down the set of fillers by introducing some important constraints. Yet it may still be too broad as the formulation of the problem of the actual context of inquiry. Further constraints may make the set of relevant fillers a yet smaller subset of the total range of logically viable fillers.

There may also be methodological requirements on the relevant answers. These are external requirements that need not have anything to do with the logical structure of a proposition, or of each of the questions in the hierarchy of questions the proposition determines. The interrogation context may establish that a question is not answered by simply finding the proposition to which the question belongs. It may require that the proposition be found in accordance with certain processes or techniques. In order to know$_\beta$ that p, for some set β of questions with methodological constraints, not only must one have the power to think that p as the answer to mere questions in β: one must have the power to think that p as also conforming to the constraints attached to the questions in β.

The preceding becomes apparent through a simple reflection on: (*a*) what counts as knowing that Columbus discovered America on October 12, 1492, in a television quiz show, with (*b*) what counts as knowing that in a high school student's essay on Columbus's discovery of America, with (*c*) what counts as knowing it when a historian defends the traditional date of the discovery from some ingenious and famous Harvard historian's claim that Columbus discovered America on October 11, 1492.

18. The Hierarchy of Epistemic Powers and the Fundamental Question-Proposition Complexes

The Plato-Powers view, as discussed and endorsed above, makes knowing not just a matter of believing a truth with a certain type of justification but a matter of having the power to find a (true) answer to certain questions. This needs to be clarified in terms of the concept of power or ability used here; the conditions that activate such powers or abilities; the answering relation between question and answer; what it means for a person to believe that a certain proposition is a (true) answer to a question, and so on.

We have already provided the basic theory of questions by developing the conception of a hierarchy of constrained questions, determined first by the logical forms of a proposition, and then reduced both by the stipulation on conditions on the fillers for the blanks at the interrogation points and by methodological constraints. Naturally this theory of questions needs additional development. But what we have presented above suffices for the elementary sections of basic epistemology. We opt here for the simple terminology: *an answer P to a question Q is a true proposition P such that P satisfies the constraints on Q and Q belongs to P in the sense explained above*, namely: Q arises from P by the occurrence of a blank in a propositional guise of P, with the blank determining a subset of all the logically possible fillers for that blank. Thus 'true answer' and 'answer' mean the same thing.

Consider the following:

(1) At time *t* John believed that 'deny' was (is) a four-letter word (in English) ending in EE, ENN, and WHY.

(2) At time *t* John believed that 'deny' was (is) an (incomplete) answer to the question "What is a four-letter word (in English) ending in EE, ENN, and WHY?"

These sentences can be taken *literally* at face value, that is, as having all the expressions of the subordinate clause *internally* (*de dicto* many writers would say, in a terminology I do not like). If so taken, then the John talked about in (1) and (2) is claimed to believe the propositions formulated in the subordinate that-clauses. On that interpretation, (1) and (2) would express true propositions if John can understand the question and think of 'deny' at the same time. Thus in the internal syntactical construal neither sentence (1) nor sentence (2) describes John's ability to offer 'deny' as an example of a word ending in EE, ENN, and WHY when asked to do so.

Perhaps we can express that John has that ability by taking the expression 'deny' in (1) and in (2) as occurring *externally* (or *de re*, again in a terminology I do not like[26]). On this construal, (1) and (2) are not perspicuous, for they represent what is better put as follows:

(1a) At time *t* John believed 'deny' to be a four-letter word (in English) ending in EE, ENN, and WHY.

(2a) At time *t* John believed 'deny' to be an (incomplete) answer to the question "What is a four-letter word (in English) ending in EE, ENN, and WHY?"

These sentences, in their perspicuous use, assign the reference to the verb 'deny' to the speaker of the whole sentence (1a) or (2a). Sentences (1) and (2), on the other hand, in their internal construal represent a cumulation of references both by the speaker and by the John spoken of. Therefore, (1a) and (2a) leave it unspecified how John refers to the verb 'deny'; they leave it unspecified what exactly is the proposition John is said to believe, and thus they are *propositionally opaque* with respect to the subject of the proposition believed by John. Hence sentences (1a) and (2a) may express truths when (1) and (2), construed internally, express truths; but they may also express truths when (1) and (2) do not express truths, because John refers to the verb 'deny' in other ways than by using the expression '(the verb) 'deny''.

Yet neither (1a) nor (2a) describes John's ability to *offer* 'deny' as an example of a word ending in EE, ENN, and WHY when asked to do so.[27] This ability is not identical with, or part of, John's belief that 'deny' is composed of DEE, EE, ENN, and WHY and his ability to *understand* the question "What is a four-letter word (in English) ending in EE, ENN, and WHY?"

Whatever abilities a state of believing that *p* may consist in, it is clear from the discussion of the Powers example above, and from the generalization to all types of constrained questions, that the ability to offer an answer to a question does not consist in, but it does presuppose, both understanding the question and believing the proposition that answers the question. The ability to answer a question has to do with one's ability to *marshall evidence*, and this, in its turn, has to do with the organization of one's beliefs in the unconscious depths of one's mind. Knowledge has to do with structures of evidence. Clearly, a passive account of knowledge, in terms of beliefs and truths *only*, as we have already intimated, cannot be adequate; the analysis of knowledge must connect a person's beliefs with his abilities to marshal evidence.

The Plato-Powers Principle, that knowledge is power, particularly the power to answer questions, is, therefore, an important criterion of adequacy for any analysis of knowledge.

Socrates believed that knowledge is power in a much stronger sense than that enthroned in the Plato-Powers principle about knowledge. For Socrates, knowledge is a power to act, to produce physical movement other than the cerebral and vocal activities required, causally, for thinking and asserting. Socrates may have been right, and a comprehensive theory of knowledge should include the subtheory about the general connections between knowledge and action. These general connections include not only the most fundamental ones, e.g., that every proposition a person believes, *a fortiori*, every proposition a person knows, is a possible premise both for the acquisition of further beliefs and for the determination of what he or she ought to do. The general connections between knowledge and action include causal relationships between the beliefs and the powers composing knowledge, on the one hand, and the production of action, on the other hand. These causal connections include, but do not exhaust, the phenomenon of volition which welds together a person's action with his knowledge of what to do.[28]

Basic epistemology, our concern here, must deal with the most pervasive and fundamental connection between knowledge and action. This is the connection embedded in our powers to think answers to questions. These are the epistemic powers *par excellence*. They depend on the organization of our beliefs; their exercise, in its turn, reorganizes our beliefs. But this organization and reorganization of beliefs, which feeds and results from, respectively, our thinking questions and looking for their answers, is *not* itself a belief, not even the additional belief that the other beliefs stand in a certain hierarchical arrangement. The evidential organization of beliefs, which the engaging in questioning and answering brings about, is a *causal organization* of degrees of readiness one has to think (assertively, for the most part) this or that proposition.

In brief, *our most basic epistemic powers have to do with the causal arrangement of our degrees of readiness to bring forth premises we may need in our reasonings.* Because our reasonings may lead to diverse courses of action, our most basic epistemic powers are at the foundation of the connection between knowledge (and belief) and action.

The basic epistemic powers consist of powers to think questions, to think corresponding answers, and to be caused to think the answers by the very thinking of the questions. One need *not* have the additional linguistic power to use the second-order words 'answer' and 'question'. Consider, for instance, the case of a very young child, Amy. A visitor asks Amy: "Where is your baby doll, Amy, the one Santa brought you?" And Amy, unable to articulate the answer, takes the visitor's hand and leads her to her bedroom upstairs and says, "Here Baby."[29] Undoubtedly, Amy can think propositions and can think questions and can think propositions as answers to questions. These thinking powers have, of course, a foundation in her linguistic powers. But thinking powers, however grounded in linguistic power and control they may be, do run ahead of linguistic development.

Now, aside from the powers of articulation, we must distinguish between first- and second-order thinking. The fundamental thinking ability one needs is simply the ability to think first-order propositions and first-order questions. Thus one must be able to think, say, (*a*) *John is happy*, (*b*) *Is John happy?* and (*c*) *Who is happy?* in order to "see" that (*a*), if true, stands in a special relationship to (*b*) and (*c*). One can, to put it differently, think (A) or (B) below:

(A) Is John happy? . . . [Examination of beliefs and perceptions] Yes, John is happy.

(B) Who is happy? . . . [Examination of beliefs and perceptions] Ah! John is happy.

One can do so *without* being able to think either of the following:

(A+) Question: "Is John happy?" . . . [Examination of beliefs and perceptions]
Answer: "John is happy."

(B+) Question: "Who is happy?" . . . [Examination of beliefs and perceptions]
Answer: "John is happy."

What we need at the foundation of our epistemic powers is merely the power of making an *Operational connection* between answers to questions as in (A) and (B). These illustrate the primary dialectic of thinking. We can, I suppose, speak of this operational connection as the *Ah!-Yes* or, simply, YES connection between a question and a proposition taken to be one of the question's answers. This operational connection must be carefully distinguished from the *predicative relation*, which one can passively contemplate as holding between a question and each of its answers. This relation is the one being thought of in (A+) and (B+). This relation is expressed by the predicative locution *is an answer to* and, naturally, the sentences expressing the second-order propositions involving this relation require nouns to flank 'is an answer to'. For an example consider:

(3) "John is happy" is an answer to "Who is happy?"

Here the quotation marks form nouns. On the other hand, the expression 'YES', which we have just stipulated to be a signal of the operational connection in underlying (3), needs no nouns, but applies directly to sentences, and perhaps forms with them a sentence expressing a compound proposition. Thus we need no quotation marks or any other nominalizing device and may simply write:

(3*) Who is happy? *YES* John is happy

to represent the operational connection underlying the relation *answering* denoted in (3).

In general, I am proposing here to use the word 'YES' as a technical symbol for the most basic connective linking a question and a proposition that may be thought to be an answer to that question. Thus we have *question-proposition complexes* of the form:

(4) Q? *YES p*.

Once again, complexes of form (4) are *not* second-order relational statements like (3); they are first-order complexes. They are not questions. They may be regarded as propositions, since they seemed to be believed by a person who reasons as in (A) and (B) above. The main principles of truth values for such complexes are these:

(Qp.Tg) A question-proposition complex of form "*q YES p*" is true, just in case the question *q* belongs to the hierarchy of questions determined by the proposition that *p*; otherwise it is false.

($Qp.T_i$) A question-proposition complex of the form "q YES_ip," where i denotes, or signals, a set a_i of constraints, is true, just in case the question q belongs to the subhierarchy of questions determined by that p
and is governed by the constraints in a_i; otherwise the complex
"q YES_ip" is false.

We have no room here to develop the fundamental logic of the question-proposition complexes. Obviously, no analysis of knowledge along the Platonic-Powersian
lines followed here can be fully illuminating, until that logic is fully developed, too.

Evidently, a thinking being may be able to think question-proposition complexes, even if it is not able to think the corresponding second-order classificatory
relational propositions about questions and their answers. A small child, for instance,
may be able to think complexes like (3*), but not propositions like (3). Thus there
is a hierarchy of basic *epistemic powers*: at the very bottom, the raw epistemic power
is the power to be caused to think that p by the very thinking of the question q. This
is the power that children, and perhaps sophisticated primates and pets, acquire first.
Then there is the power to think complexes of the form "q YES p" and "q YES_i p"
for constraints that merely demand the normality of the assumed circumstances.
Then comes the power to think complexes of the form "q YES_ip" for abnormal
constraints, and later on the powers to think the most sophisticated constraints.
Somewhere along the development between normality and abnormality there comes
the power to raise to the meta-language: to have thoughts of the relational kind of
the form "The question q has as an answer (the proposition) that p."

This hierarchy of epistemic powers provides room for broad and narrow uses
of the epistemic vocabulary, especially the words 'know' and 'knowledge'. Do house
cats or domestic dogs know, e.g., that their owner is in the house, is angry, is loving?
This all depends on what powers of thinking we attribute to cats and which ones to
dogs. And small children?

19. The Truth-Circumstances of the Known Truth Involved in the Constraints of Questions Need Not Connect the Knower Causally with That Truth

It is widely taken for granted that for a person to know that p there need be neither
a common cause of the person's believing that p and of that p nor a causation path
from that p to the person's believing that p.[30] I believe this to be correct.

We cannot review the arguments in favor, or against, the causal account of
knowledge. To the attentive reader, it will be obvious that some of the examples offered above, especially *The Non-Normal Cheater* subseries, raise problems for most
causal accounts so far proposed. Yet our present interest lies in revealing some general features of epistemic contexts of justification.

The Blind Tiresias. Tiresias, blind seer, has the extraordinary power of seeing
very vivid visions in his imagination. This happens after he has eaten cucumbers
marinated in a mixture of tequila and some very secret concoctions. Tiresias's
visions come, he says, with a date at the bottom. His visions have been found

to correspond point by point to events in the past, or events in the future, or events simultaneous with his visions, in accordance with the dates he sees. Yet there is no way those events can be causally connected with Tiresias's visions. This power came to Tiresias, as his memory goes, on his twenty-fifth birthday. He paid no attention to his visions for about three years. But then some reports on the newspapers described what he had seen, and then be began to believe his dated visions correspond to reality.

Does Tiresias know that his current vision is true? Do we know—we who have tested him thousands of times and have found no single failure? Here again we need the notion of stable, normal circumstances. Tiresias's early beliefs were not grounded at all. His later ones are grounded on the generalization that *caetaris paribus* his visions depict reality, that is, given the assumption of a *normal context of circumstances*, connecting the occurrences of his visions with what they depict. If the generalization, relative to the normal circumstances, only part of which are described in *The Blind Tiresias*, hold, then his belief corresponds to reality and, it seems to me, it constitutes knowledge.

Perhaps Tiresias's normal circumstances include elements we have no idea of. If so, regardless of how bizarre those elements may be, the implicit assumption that the circumstances are normal remains valid. If some bizarre circumstances affect the normality of the context, then Tiresias will fail to know, even if those circumstances come in balancing pairs, just as, the reader may recall, it happens in *The Cheater Series*. Then, if Tiresias knows of (or has reasonable belief about) those circumstances and considers them in his claims about the truth of his visions, Tiresias again knows that his revised generalization is, by hypothesis, true.

There is *no* need for Tiresias to know that his beliefs are causally connected with what he believes. This is more clearly so, the more detailed his visions and beliefs are about the events depicted in his visions. At this juncture serious and profound problems appear regarding how he can think of events he cannot be causally connected with. Undoubtedly, if the contents of consciousness are essentially universals, then Tiresias, like anybody else, thinks of all sorts of particulars in terms of traits or characteristics, and their relations to himself and to the particulars present in his perceptual fields.[31] These issues are difficult, yet they must be dealt with in a comprehensive epistemological theory.

20. Normal Truth Circumstances and World Order

We have returned to the most crucial and deep-seated assumption underlying our cognitive claims, namely: that the truth circumstances of the known propositions are normal or have identifiable abnormalities. We have already formulated in sections 13–17 some of the most fundamental principles governing the epistemic role of normality. Let us say something about what normality consists of. To begin with, the most general and fundamental principle is this:

> MNP*. *The master presupposition about normality.* The changes in our immediate environment have a reliable order, determined by: (1) a hier-

archy of general principles and laws, which we cannot for the most part (at least at the moment) specify, and (2) a set of particular relevant regularities, which we can specify, and both the general order and the particular regularities remain in operation at least during the period with which we are concerned.

The idea that there is an underlying world order that abides but that we cannot specify at a given moment is the permanent assumption that not only unifies each personal life but also unifies all of us as members of one epistemic community. The assumption of a deep-seated world order that sustains our actions, but an order we cannot specify beyond some particularly relevant regularities, is needed to plan actions and count with our being able to carry out our plans. Given our thorough ignorance of the ways of the world, we need the master presupposition MPN*. This is a most economical assumption: we can carry on our tasks without tarrying to formulate the principles that govern the order of the world. It is a vital assumption, since we must live and do our things, regardless of how much knowledge of the order of the world we have and regardless of how much time we have to find out what the structure of that order is.

We cannot know that the world is fully ordered. Some of us, scientists and philosophers, are discovering more and more principles of world order. But we lack the power to answer *all* the questions about the order of the world, especially if we place on our questions some strenuous methodological constraints, like those now applicable to the natural sciences. Thus the fundamental principle MPN* is part of the unspecifiable framework within which we determine that a certain person knows certain truths. On the other hand, the fundamental presupposition and the other structural presuppositions constituting frameworks within which beliefs turned out to be justified, or not, cannot themselves be justified within those frameworks. Whether there are more abstract, or more comprehensive, frameworks within which we can ask whether MPN* is justified, or not, is a most important topic—but it goes beyond basic epistemology. In any case, we have the principle:

NSSJ. Structural assumptions or presuppositions about the world, or a part thereof, which determine epistemic frameworks, are not self-justifiable and are not justifiable in the frameworks they determine.

This principle ties the *Gestalt* character of knowledge, introduced in section 2, and the contextual determination of species of knowledge, discussed in section 15. To know something, a person must have a battery of beliefs of sorts, but these beliefs, which by converging together on other beliefs confer upon these the status of knowledge$_a$, are not themselves known$_a$.

Several pervasive assumptions govern the epistemic role of truth circumstances. They are of different sorts: some stipulate general features of the world order, others stipulate connections between the world order and the mind. The following are just *some* of the most widely discussed:

EP. *Experience principle*. Every proposition that a person is justified in believing must be available to the person through experience.

EBP. *Empirical-basis principle*. The strongest availability through experience of a proposition P for a person S at a time *t* is for P to be fully present in a specious present experience of S at *t*, i.e., for P to be at *t* either the total content of an episode of consciousness of S or the total content of a segment of one such episode.

RP. *Rationalist principle*. Propositions available to a person S need not be exhaustive contents of S's episodes of consciousness (as in EBP), at a time *t*, or during a set of times, but then such propositions must be connected to the experiential contents of S at some time or other and to S's beliefs, through a network of principles that compose in part the order of the world.

LKP. *Leibniz-Kant's principle*. Both the principles of deductive logic and the principles governing structural relationships between concepts (or properties) are principles of world order.

PHOW. *Principle of the Hierarchial Order of the World*. The different categories of entities or states of affairs composing the world are connected to one another by principles of ranking of the categories, escalation from one category to another higher up, descension from one category to another lower down, and commutation across categories not linearly ordered. Principles of these different types link: (a) sensory experiences to physical objects; (b) physical states of affairs to mental states of affairs; (c) perceived objects to unperceived ones; (d) experienceable states of affairs to theoretical ones; (e) particular propositions to generalizations; (f) witnesses' testimony to attested matters; (g) facts to values; (h) values to obligations and rights; and so on.

PIAWO. *Principle of the inferential nature of our attitude toward the world order*. We tend [for economy of thinking and action] to treat the principles of world order we recognize as built-in mechanisms of inference, rather than as formulable beliefs and explicit premises in reasonings. The most abstract and pervasive principles of world order [like the ones on this list] are seldom, if ever, thought of, although they structure most of our reasoning and thinking.[32]

HHP. *Heidegger-Hahn's principle*. We always find ourselves in the midst of a world, which has an assumed general order, and we have a conception of some aspects of that order.

DHP. *Duhem-Hahn's principle*. The world order is not fixed for all times; it may be changed at will, but only piecemeal.

QP. *Quine's principle*. The hierarchy of the world order for a person S at time *t* is a hierarchy of X's degrees of willingness to resist a renunciation of a given proposition.[33]

DA. *Descartes's axiom*. The *cogito* propositions about a person S and a time t to the effect that S is at t having *himself* such and such experiences *then* are maximally resistant to renunciation by S at t [Here '*himself*' and '*then*' are quasi-indicators.[34]]

CP. *Cogitatum principle.* The *cogitatum* propositions pertaining to a person S and a time t to the effect that, within S's total field of consciousness, including S's perceptual fields, such and such occurs, are maximally resistant to renunciation by S at t.

These general principles do not deliver particular regularities that a person can use as premises in building up his knowledge of the world. They, with other similar generalities, merely constitute the broadest schema within which we posit less pervasive, more definite, and more rigorous principles and laws. All such principles and laws, then, constitute the framework within which a person's beliefs are to cohere.

The abnormalities of the truth circumstances of a given proposition about particular matters of fact always deal with specific regularities within the general framework. More general propositions may involve abnormalities revolving around more general regularities. More general laws may be involved in the abnormalities of the truth circumstances in which laws are considered. Finally, the very innocuous-seeming principles listed above and their ilk may yield abnormalities, at least merely thinkable ones, in the truth contexts in which the most general laws of nature, or other fundamental principles, are examined. This hierarchical arrangement of real and merely thinkable abnormalities of the relevant truth circumstances for the justification of belief is simply a consequence of the hierarchical structure of the world order.

We have barely touched the surface of the huge topic of normal relevant truth circumstances. But this must suffice for our present reflections in basic epistemology. We must bring these reflections to an end by tying the several strands of the fabric of knowledge, which we have deployed, in order to take a preliminary look at the weave of knowledge.

II. A PRELIMINARY ANALYSIS OF KNOWLEDGE THAT *P*

1. The Elements of Epistemic Contexts

In our exegesis of data in part I, we saw how species of knowledge that p come about, and how those species are determined by different parameters. We noted how there is a framework of beliefs taken for granted, which scan the surface of an assumed normal context, and beliefs explicitly formulated or formulable, which constitute specific pieces of evidence and justification for other beliefs. These latter beliefs are the ones whose epistemic status is at issue. We noted how a set of questions with constraints, often assumed and left to the context of communication to reveal, determines both a set of epistemic goals and a set of possible epistemic powers. We also noted that our beliefs depend on, and include, the beliefs of others, in spite of the inherent unreliability of the reports of others.

In brief, an epistemic context is an ordered sextuple:

$C_i = \langle F_i, A_i, S_i, R_i, Q_i, P_i \rangle$, where:

1. F_i is the set of presupposed "facts": the relevant beliefs about the issues pertaining to P_i, which the members of A_i have, including beliefs about what other members of A_i believe and say, if the testimony of others is relevant.

2. A_i is the set of agents in the relevant epistemic community involved in deciding the issues pertaining to P_i.

3. S_i is the hierarchical network of structural presuppositions and assumptions, held by at least some members of A_i, which are presumed relevant to the determination of the truth, or falsehood, of the propositions in P_i by the members of F_i and of R_i: these are the presuppositions and assumptions that function in the mental economy of the persons in A_i as mechanisms of inference, rather than as major premises.

R_i is the set of relevant respects of abnormality applicable to S_i.

Q_i is the set of questions, governed, perhaps, by some constraints on the range of the blanks in the questions and by some methodological constraints.

P_i is the set of propositions whose epistemic status is at issue: they are the possible answers to the questions in Q_i.[35]

2. A Tentative Analysis of Knowledge that P

The proposal that ensues is only tentative. I am not even sure that an explicit definition of 'X knows that p' is the accomplishment we should expect in basic epistemology. As I have argued elsewhere, the definitional method of classical analytic philosophy cannot, in spite of the illuminating power it may attain, provide the full philosophical illumination some of us desire. This is so, partly, because definitions are subject to the strict rule of deploying sets of conditions that are necessary and sufficient. Thus we can easily miss the illumination that the discovery of conditions that are necessary, but not sufficient, or vice versa, may deliver.[36]

Naturally, definitions of certain concepts are sometimes feasible. Furthermore, we can offer here a tentative analysis of knowledge that p, which brakes the standard approach at several junctures. *First*, we provide a development of the Plato-Powers principle that cognitive knowledge has to do, not just with beliefs and truths, but also essentially with powers to answer questions. *Second*, we assume the theory of questions sketched out in sections 16–18. *Third*, we take into account the multiplicity of species of knowledge and their indexical specification by epistemic contexts. *Fourth*, we weave into our analysis the crucial feature of the normality of a context and its respects of abnormality. *Fifth*, we are not, besides, providing a Fichtean analysis of knowledge. *Sixth*, we are also not requiring probability computations; but probability may be included in the constraints on the questions in Q_i. Recall, nevertheless, that the analysis schema is only the tip of the iceberg described in part I.

Now the plunge: Recall that '$q\text{YES}_i p$' means, as explained in section 18, the first-order non-classificatory proposition that (question) q has (proposition) p for a (true) answer; also recall the truth-condition for such propositions given in section 18.

The Contextually Indexed Analysis of Knowledge that p is tentatively deployed in the following schema, where the subscript '*i*' is a schematic letter signaling epistemic contexts, its proper substituents are expressions denoting epistemic contexts, each of which expressions, by being subscripted to 'know', represents a contextual operator having generic knowledge as operand and having a (contextually identified) species of knowledge as value. We assume, thus, an epistemic context:

$$C_i = \langle F_i, A_i, S_i, R_i, Q_i, P_i \rangle$$

as characterized above. Then:

CiK. At time t X knows$_i$ that p, if and only if:

   (i) At time t X believes that p;

   (ii) that p is in P_i;

   (iii) There is at least one question q in Q_i such that:

      1) q YES$_i$ p,

      2) if at t X considers q and reflects, searching within his beliefs for an answer to q, X can psychologically think, believingly, at t' that qYES$_i p$, where the interval (t, t') is a retrieval and computation time that conforms with the constraints governing question q, and

      3) at t X believes that qYES$_i p$;

   (iv) There are truth circumstances Z for at least some members of P_i, there is a positive number h, and there are respects of abnormality r_i, . . . , r_h in R_i, such that:

      1) Z is a set of normal circumstances for that p, except for including r_i and . . . and r_h,

      2) Z obtains, and

      3) at t X believes that the truth circumstances for that p are normal except for including respects r_i and . . . r_h;

   (v) There is a subset s_i of S_i such that at t X has the propensity to make inferences in accordance with the members of s_i; [it is not ruled out that there may be unconscious, or subconscious, processes of inference and that some of them may occur in accordance with the members of s_i];

   (vi) There is a conjunction E_i of members of F_i such that:

      1) given Z and s_i, if E_i, then p,

      2) both s_i and E_i are true, and

      3) at t X believes that both E_i and, *ceteris paribus* [that is, given his believing-inferential attitude toward s_i and his believing that the truth circumstances for that p are normal except for r_i, . . . , and r_h], if E_i, then p.

NOTES ON THE SCHEMA

   1. The locutions within square brackets in clauses (v) and (vi) indicate remarks and references by us, or whoever uses schema CiK to attribute knowledge that p to

someone; they do *not* represent references or parts of the thought content of the person X who is said to know.

2. Particular exemplifications of schema C*i*K may have to be carefully formulated because they may require quasi-indicators, so as to attribute to knower X demonstrative references to time (by his using, in English, mainly 'now'), space (by his using 'here'), self (by his using 'I'), and so on. See [6] and [10].

3. Schema C*i*K applies to mathematical knowlege. The stringent standards for mathematical proof prevailing now at the end of the twentieth century are much higher than those prevailing during the seventeenth century, and these were higher than those prevailing two centuries before. All those differences belong to different epistemic contexts, and are generically represented in the constraints built into the questions in Q_j.

4. Schema C*i*K has the following pattern:

(i): the belief condition;
(ii): the relevance condition;
(iii): the epistemic-power condition;
(iv): the normality-abnormality condition;
(v): the inferential-power condition;
(vi): the evidence condition.

3. Skepticism, Scientific Knowledge, and Other Matters

Schema C*i*K conforms, I believe, to *all* the criteria of adequacy encountered in part I. The reader will, undoubtedly, investigate whether this is so or not.

C*i*K has the virtue of indicating where different developments belong. Each of the different parameters of an epistemic context gives rise to a branch of general epistemology. In particular, different problems in the methodology of science concern different sets of constraints to be placed on the questions determining unified sets of epistemic goals.

The issue of skepticism, its types and variants, must be reopened. Obviously, different epistemic contexts give rise to different types of skepticism. The most radical forms of skepticism involve contexts with the slimmest possible parameters. A radical version of skepticism, for instance, works with the following epistemic context:

⟨ϕ, {X}, {deduction rules}, ϕ, {all logically possible questions}, {all propositions}⟩, where ϕ is the null set.

Clearly, some extreme forms of skepticism are indefensible, whereas others, especially local ones about some definite small group of propositions, are wholly defensible. Determining where to draw the line between defensible and indefensible skepticisms requires careful investigation. Things concerning skepticism are, it seems to me, more complex than they are usually taken to be. One thing is certain: however indefensible a form of skepticism may be, this should be shown by the nature of the epistemic context involved in that form of skepticism. All simple appeals to the nonsensicality of skepticism are better shunned. No skeptic need use 'know' in a nonordinary way.

4. Colophon

This essay has naturally culminated in analysis schema C_iK—not so much because it unfolds a new, Platonic-Powersian inferential, and indexical approach in basic epistemology but because it represents a sustained methodological effort at complying with both admonitions, Sellars's and Wittgenstein's, quoted under the title.[37]

Notes

1. The similarity between this sentence and Husserl's slogan about returning to the things themselves is *not* coincidental. What I am calling protophilosophy, i.e., the collection and exegesis of data about certain types of experience is, in general terms, similar to Husserl's phenomenological description. One crucial difference is this: protophilosophy is more outspokenly linguistic than is Husserl's description of essences, because it regards syntactical contrasts in ordinary languages as fundamental philosophical data. For additional discussions of philosophical method see [9] chap. 6, [13], [14], and the complementary references mentioned in them. In the first reference, the contrast between local and comprehensive theories is illustrated and discussed.

2. We will not survey here the huge post-Gettier literature. This literature is impressive not only because of its bulk but also because of the complexity and the ingenuity of a large portion of it. We will only be able to make some contrasting references to a few of the best or most influential pieces. But others not mentioned are, if not better, equally ingenious and intriguing. *One question for the sociology of philosophical knowledge*: the search for a definition of knowledge during the last fifteen years has been typically an American quest—why?

3. This tentative analysis of contextually determined species of knowledge is inspired by the analysis of the justification of actions in terms of what I call the Legitimacy of actions practically considered, or practitions. (See [9], chaps. 5 and 6.) The pivotal analogy is that of 'X knows$_i$ that p' to 'X ought$_i$ to A', the subscript 'i' signaling in the two cases a context of justification: in the case of *ought$_i$* we have the context i of Legitimacy of the action (or practition) X --- *to A*; in the case of knows$_i$, the context i of the justification of the state of affairs *it being the case that p*, rather than that of the psychological state of *believing that p*. See [9], chap. 8 for the justification of norms, or ought-statements, in the sense of the establishment of the truth of a norm. In spite of the analogy between ought$_i$ and knows$_i$, it is worth noting that the "ethics" of belief, to use Chisholm's expression in [15], is not really an ethics or a genuine system of norms. This is so for many reasons. One is this: a person does not have the crucial freedom, characteristic of actions, whether to believe or not to believe. Another reason, grounded on the finitude of the mind is this: whereas one ought$_i$ to do the actions (practitions) implied by what one ought$_i$ to do (see [9], chap. 7 for relevant distinctions), it is just not the case that one knows$_i$, or believes, or ought epistemically to believe, a proposition implied by what one knows$_i$ or believes. One may even be unable to think such a proposition, let alone believe it. There are no obligations, epistemic or otherwise, to believe a proposition. (Of course, it may be *better* to believe than not. But this is something else.) On the other hand, whether one can, or cannot, think of an action implied by what one ought$_i$ to do is immaterial; one still ought$_i$, derivately, of course, to do it.

My original plan was to write a series of essays, or one with a section devoted to the justification of belief, which section could show in detail the connections depicted in the following chart:

		reasons for:	*reasons for:*
Y	$\begin{cases}\text{believing}\\\text{supposing}\end{cases}$	the proposition that X is P	X's being P
Y	$\begin{cases}\text{endorsing}\\\text{wanting}\end{cases}$	the command X to A	X's A'ing
X	$\begin{cases}\text{deciding}\\\text{intending}\end{cases}$	to do A	My (X's) A'ing

A very brief preliminary discussion of this chart appears in my note "There Are Command Sh-Inferences," *Analysis* 32 (1971):13–19. The issue is yet of the utmost importance. It has to do with the fact that reasons for believing that *p* (*a fortiori*, grounds for knowing) are founded on reasons for *it being the case that*, just as reasons for wanting agents to do action A are grounded on reasons for *agents' doing A*. Here *agents' doing A* is not a propositional matrix. (See [9], chaps. 6 and 7.) This connects with the sense in which propositions, rather than states of belief, are warranted. But all this must be left for another study. See note 17 of this paper for another influence of my theory of action on my theory of knowledge.

4. See the essays mentioned in note 1.

5. This crucial and pervasive feature of knowing is, probably, part of what moved J. L. Austin in [2] to claim, outrageously, that one's assertion "I know that *p*" is like one's assertion "I promise to A": one gives one's word that *p*. I say "outrageously" because, for one thing, whenever one asserts something one gives one's word, so that the likeness is too general to be informative. For another thing, the contrast between "I know" and "He knows" does not correspond to the contrast between "I promise" and "He promises": My "He promises" about Karl is parasitic on Karl's "I promise"; my "He knows" is not parasitic on Karl's "I know." Furthermore, to the extent that my "I know" gives my word non-trivially, my "Karl knows" compromises me just as much as it compromises Karl, in a way in which my "He promises" does not compromise Karl or even me.

6. The elementary *Gestalt* character of knowing has been emphatically affirmed by Sellars (see [56]–[58]), Leibniz (see [43]), Kant (in [38]), and others. It appears in the coherentist view of knowledge and in the coherentist view of truth. It is a datum for epistemological coherentism, but not for truth coherentism. In any case, the fundamental *Gestalt* character of knowledge must be carefully distinguished from all coherentisms. Thus it must not be confused with the issue between coherentism and foundationalism in epistemology. On this issue there is a huge literature, but a large amount of ground is covered by [1], [18], [31], [42], [48]–[50], [53], [56]–[58], and [64]–[67], and [74].

7. For a fundamental theory of communication and for a discussion of the propositional transparence of language, some of its limits, and its contrasts with Quine's referential transparence, see [10], [12].

8. The original plan for this essay included the writing of an appendix devoted to an assessment of Lehrer's definition of knowledge in [42]. That definition is the culmination of many years of reflection on the topic, and it is mounted on the most complex and illuminating examination of alternatives and consideration of rich data. But there is no space here for that. It must suffice to note that Lehrer's analysis suffers seriously because it hinges on probability comparisons. (It is also too restrictive to illuminate fully our ordinary cognitive experiences. It is too drastic in its ruling falsehoods out of the path to knowledge, as we note in section 11; that ruling is also not sufficient, falling prey to the data labeled *The Non-Normal Cheater Series* in section 13. It is Fichtean, as noted in section 7.) Lehrer's main clause for belief justification is literally as follows:

>   (iv) *h** is the strongest competitor of *h* for S if and only if *h** competes with *h* for S and, for any *k*, if *k* competes with *h* for S, then $p(h^*)$ is at least as great as $p(h)$. . . .
>   [Here, '$p(h)$' means (as Lehrer explains on p. 201): 'the chance S believes *h* to have of being true within his corrected doxastic system'.]

>   . . . Thus we obtain the following *final result*:
>   (v) S is completely justified in believing that *h* if and only if $p(h)$ is greater than $p(h^*)$. (See [42], p. 207; my italics.)

The hero in *The Minimally Cautious Gambler* believes correctly that *p* (he will win the prize) = .501, and that *p* (the strongest competitor) = *p* (he will not win) = .499. Hence, by Lehrer's (iv) above, our minimally cautious gambler is completely justified in believing that he will win. That belief conforms to Lehrer's other conditions for knowledge: it is true that *p*; S believes that *p*, and "S is completely justified in believing that *p* in some way [in every way, in our case] that does not depend on any false statement" ([42], p. 21). Therefore, the minimally cautious gambler knows in Lehrer's analysans sense of knowledge that he will win the prize. Patently, as far as normal experience goes, he does *not* know that he will win the prize.

Pastin, in [50], has raised some serious difficulties against Lehrer's analysis. A very tough one, also arising from Lehrer's stipulation of a deep, thorough, and essential involvement of knowledge with probability, pertains to our perceptual knowledge. Remembering that one has often experienced illusions, and sometimes hallucinations, decreases the probability one believes one's perceptual judgments to have.

9. This idea that the evidence must suffice for the truth of known propositions has been appreciated by most writers on basic epistemology. A particularly interesting discussion is Tienson's [71] and Tomberlin's [73]. [71] argues that most of our attributions of knowledge are literally false—just as most of our attributions of flatness to the ordinary surfaces we encounter in experiences are literally false. This is an important thesis that needs serious reflection. It accounts very well for our use of the word 'flat', and it illuminates the difficulties encountered by basic epistemologists in their search for an analysis of 'knows'.

Most basic epistemologists simply follow a line like Lehrer's: allow the evidence to remain insufficient for the truth of what is known. But this raises difficulties. Two apparent exceptions are Skyrms in [60] and Dretske in [25]. These writers hold that the reasons for what one knows must be *conclusive*. I said that they are "apparent exceptions" because the conclusiveness of their reasons is not logical, but causal or subjunctive, depending on the circumstances. This is actually a step in the right direction, but it needs to be complemented with a study of normal and abnormal circumstances. (See sections 13 and 20 below, where we provide the beginning of that study.) Thus Skyrms's and Dretske's definitions of knowledge fall prey to the data contained in *The Non-Normal Third Cheater Series*, discussed in section 13. Valuable and ingenious attacks on Dretske's [25] appear in Sosa's [64] and Pappas and Swain's [47].

10. For a sustained and impressive argument for the view that induction does not include, or rest on, the calculus of probability, see Cohen's [24].

11. Other reasons against the rule that knowledge implies one knows appear in Hilpinen [34], Powers [52], and Tomberlin [72]-[73]. The original defense of the rule, which gave rise to much discussion, appears in Hintikka [36], pp. 17-22, 24-28, 104-13, *et al.* Most critics of Hintikka's defense of the rule have not noticed that Hintikka insisted from the very start that he accepted the rule with one qualification, namely: "only if the person referred to by *a* (the subject expression in 'a knows') knows that he is referred to by it" ([36], p. 106). He first formulated that qualification on pp. 158f. Hintikka's qualification conforms to what he characterized as his data, which includes the situation a person is in when he or she is in a position to say "I know" ([36], p. 33). Thus the main issue is whether Hintikka's [36] studies, and illuminates, a concept of knowledge that is widely used in life, *not* whether the rule, which he takes the concept of knowledge he is discussing to obey, holds; it does hold for that concept. A secondary issue is whether Hintikka's formulations of the main rule, and of the additional condition for it, in his system, are satisfactory. This issue is taken up in [7], sections V-VII.

12. This was first pointed out by Pastin in [50] without calling it Fichtean.

13. Given his Fichtean view of the mind, Chisholm is a notable example of a *cogito-foundationalist*. For his building knowledge on *cogito*-propositions and assimilating *cogitatum*-propositions that are not about perceived physical objects to adverbial modalities of the self, see, e.g., [19], chap. 1; and see [14] for a discussion of these views of Chisholm's.

14. See, for instance, the works, mentioned in the bibliography, by Clark, Dretske, Ginet, Harman, Hilpinen, Klein, Lehrer, Paxson, Sosa, Swain, and Thalberg. A nice survey of the main branch of the defeasibility approach appears in Swain [69].

15. Condition (*a*), strengthened with a causal stricture, appears in Swain [68]. Condition (*b*) has been demanded by Clark in [21], Dretske in [25], Ginet in [28], and Thalberg in [70]. For examples of critical responses, sometimes with very ingenious, even brilliant counterexamples, see Coder [22]-[23] (against Thalberg), Pappas [46] (against Dretske), Harman [31], and Lehrer [42]. *The Non-Normal Cheaters* described in section 13 below are useful counterexamples. See note 21 below.

16. Lehrer has formulated several versions of condition (B) in a string of essays that preceded [42]. This book contains a record of those earlier proposals of his as well as of others.

17. This important datum has been appreciated by a good number of epistemologists. Yet it has not been appreciated fully that, as we show in this section and next, with *The Non-Normal Cheater Series*, that datum condemns the puritanical view of the evidence constitutive of knowledge. An excellent protophilosophical paper presenting examples of this datum is Coder [23]. Coder makes clear the role of the normalcy of the truth circumstances of the known proposition by exegizing a three-piece datum. I must confess, however, that I did not appreciate the force of Coder's unified set of examples, nor the depth of his suggestion, until I had reflected on the topic on my own and was surveying the post-Gettier literature. His suggestion is this: "A comparison of the three cases with one another suggests that what is needed for knowledge in addition to justified true belief is *simply* that *one's total picture of events, from first evidence to last belief, be not too skewed*" ([23], p. 116; my italics). He is essenially right: this is simply the condition that has to be added to the classical conditions. On the other hand, it is not a simple matter to spell out this condition. The present essay is, in fact, a preliminary effort at giving an account of what is needed for a person's picture not to be too skewed for him or her to have knowledge.

I diverge from Coder when he requires that the knower's picture cover all the ground from first evidence to last belief, if 'first evidence' is taken in a strong foundationalist sense. I doubt very much, however, that Coder had this sense in mind. I hold very firmly the view that there is an important analogy between knowledge and intentional action. For some foundationalists of intentional action, an action is intentional only if *every* segment of it is intentional, including some basic actions. I believe that this is incorrect. Whether they are just bodily movements or not, basic actions are intersubstitutable. See [13] for five arguments against this view in the sophicated form Alvin Goldman has given it. Similarly, I believe that for John to know that *p* it is not necessary that someone, whether John or not, be able to trace his belief that *p* to evidence going back to basic knowledge, e.g., John's perceptions. *Perceptions are also intersubstitutable.* At any rate, our exegesis of the phenomenon of knowledge in this essay does not reveal any such foundationalist character of knowledge.

18. This principle became very clear to me in 1963, when I was composing [5], which on p. 511 describes the kernel of all those examples in this section 11 illustrating it.

19. Most basic epistemologists have made references to the circumstances of the knower and of what he knows. Yet it has been a troublesome, often unacknowledged factor. For some of the difficulties it has created, see the papers mentioned in note 15. As far as I can detect, the constructive awareness of the normality of the circumstances appears more clearly first in Coder [23] (see note 17 above), and, even more definitely, in Sosa [64]-[65]. In [64] Sosa presents a valuable discussion; he attempts to elucidate the reference to normal circumstances in terms of nomological connections and discusses a series of interesting cases. He distinguishes knowledge from a human context from knowledge from a layman's perspective and from an expert's point of view. His relativized analysis of knowledge that *p* is this: "S knows (from the K point of view) that *p* iff: (a) it is true that *p*; (b) S believes that *p*; and (c) there is a non-defective epistemic pyramid (from the K point of view) for S and the proposition that *p*" ([64], p. 118).

My source for the role of the normality of the circumstances is twofold Leibnizian-Kantian. On the one hand, I have been impressed by the role the parameter of normal circumstances plays in Sellars's theory of perception. (See [56]-[58].) I learned my first Kant from Sellars. On the other hand, the reference to the normality of the circumstances as a whole is precisely the central point of the lawfulness of the phenomena, characteristic of empirical knowledge, as argued in Kant's transcendental deduction of the categories. This idea, I learned later on, is Leibnizian.

20. Of course, putting Harman's inferential principle Q as a defining conditon in a definition of knowledge introduces a devastating circularity—unless some (incomplete) recursive schema is adopted.

21. *The Normal Third Cheater* affects, thus, the analysis of knowledge proposed by Lehrer, Skyrms, Dretske, Ginet, and others. The reader can examine this in the case of the de-

fining passages that have been quoted, e.g., Lehrer's. One more illustration: Ginet defines thus: "S knows that p if and only if: S is confident that p, this confidence is supported by a disinterested justification that S has for it, and *there is no truth r such that*, were S to be justified in believing that r and to retain all his properties that are compatible with his having justification for believing that r, then he would be very far from justified in being confident that p" ([28], p. 80; my italics). Clearly, this is a view of type (*b*) as characterized above in section 11. Evidently, *The Normal Cheater* refutes this; the requisite statement r present in the example is simply: "There is a mechanism M_1 operating as described." Ann knows in spite of such r.

22. Powers's [52] is one of the most insightful studies in basic epistemology. In a field filled with ingenious, penetrating, and even brilliant papers, Powers's [52] stands out for its deep insights. Villoro in [74] connects 'conocer', but not 'saber', with the power to answer questions.

23. We maintain the unity of the propositions about, and the unity of the content of, propositional attitudes. Instead of multiplying senses of 'believe', 'suppose', 'think', 'know', etc., we recognize that these verbs appear in constructions canonically put as follows: "X believes (knows, etc.) of – – – that . . . ," where the dashed blanks are to be occupied by a list of expressions, or a description of a set of entities, and the dotted blank is occupied by a sentence or a clause. We consider as a limiting case, although it is the fundamental case, that in which the dashed blank is occupied by a null list or null description of a set of entities. In that case, the whole sentence occupying the dotted blank expresses a truth or a falsehood. In short, there are no senses of 'know', 'believe', etc., but different constructions, in which the *oratio obliqua* is sometimes a proposition and sometimes a propositional function. See [10] for additional discussion.

24. See [9], chap. 3 for a discussion of the hierarchy of logical forms of a proposition and for some of the basic laws governing such hierarchies. See Appendix.

25. See [11], part II, for a detailed discussion of propositional guises and their application to the analysis of perceptual judgments, sensory fields, and so on.

26. See [10] for some reasons for prefering the terminology 'internal'-'external' over the terminology '*de dicto*'-'*de re*' to refer to occurrences of expressions in *oratio obliqua* constructions, and for a discussion of propositional transparence and propositional opacity.

27. Powers has, it seems, a different view of sentences (1) and (2), if we can construe him as holding for 'believes' what he claims for 'knows', namely: "Again, we use '*x* knows that the answer to the question Q is P' *not* to mean that if *x* were asked 'Is the answer to Q P? he would answer yes, but rather to mean that if *x* were asked Q he would answer P. Thus, what we call 'knowing that the answer to Q is P' is more than merely knowing (correctly accepting) the proposition that the answer to Q is P" ([52], p. 348; his italics).

28. See [9], chap. 10 for an account of volition and chap. 12 for a discussion of several types of intentional action.

29. I owe this example to Miriam M. Castañeda. See also [12] for a double generality of language.

30. See e.g. Skyrms [60], Sosa [63], Paxson [51], Pappas [46], Lehrer [42]. One of the earliest causal accounts of knowledge is the one proposed by Goldman in [29]. Skyrms attacked it with an example that was regarded as conclusive by later writers. Loeb in [44] makes an important clarification to Skyrms's argument and shows that it is not as devastating as it was thought to be. *The Non-Normal Third Cheater Series* shows the insufficiency of Goldman's causal principle.

31. See [12] and [11] for accounts of the nature of our consciousness of particulars.

32. For a fascinating discussion of the different roles of principles of inference, especially their role in the structuring of concepts, see Sellars [55]. An insightful discussion of inference appears in Harman [31].

33. It may seem improper to formulate Quine's axiom in terms of propositions rather than sentences. But we are using the word 'proposition' to mean either a truth or a falsehood, and obviously propositions in this sense are not sentences. In fact, they are not even classes of equivalent sentences, under some equivalence or other, as is shown in [9], pp. 34f. Yet we still leave it open that the truths (and falsehoods) of the world may be reducible to sentences, or, better,

classes of sentences (in order to allow for intra- and inter-language equivalences), together with something else. If the student of Quine is not yet comfortable with the word 'proposition', he may accept the axiom above as a Quinelike axiom, rather than as one of Quine's very own.

34. For the characteristics and crucial referential roles of quasi-indicators, see [6], [10], and [11], section II.9. For an anti-Cartesian interpretation of the *cogito ergo sum*, see [11], section II.4.

35. As is explained in note 2 above, the main inspiration for the account of contexts of epistemic justification developed here is the account of contexts of justification for actions, intentions, and norms proposed in [9], chaps. 5, 6, and 8. I must note an error in the latter account, kindly pointed out by Michael Bratman. This error consists in not having maintained in an actional context the important parameter consisting of a set of *prime actions*, i.e., actions which are for the context in question like atoms of action—even though in other contexts they may be analyzed, into either pure compound actions, whose components are nothing but actions, or mixed actions, having some propositional components. Bratman proved the important theorem that a context that has as prime actions actions that are compounds of prime actions, may lead to contradictions. The counterpart epistemological error is avoided in this essay by having each epistemic context C_i of belief justification contain the crucial parameter P_i. In the epistemic case the rationale for this parameter is, fortunately, even more obvious: P_i is, as noted, the set of answers, whether true or false, to the questions in Q_i. Conversely, given the theory of questions sketched out here, the members of P_i are the propositions that yield hierarchies of questions containing the questions in Q_i. Thus the relevance of P_i to Q_i is obvious and deep.

36. See [13] and [14] for complementary discussions of the role of definitions in philosophy and for a critique of the classical method of philosophical analysis.

37. I am very grateful to Peter French for having put me in the position of having to finish, at last, this essay, even if it is only the first part of a series conceived and planned in 1970 on the model of theory of practical thinking. See note 3 above. The delay was, actually, beneficiary. It allowed me to learn from and to refer to the rich post-Gettier literature. And it also allowed me both to utilize Powers's data and to incorporate his approach. I am grateful to Victoria Haire of the University of Minnesota Press and to Howard Wittstein for having thoroughly overhauled the grammar and style of this paper.

References

[1] Alston, William, "Two Types of Foundationalism," *The Journal of Philosophy* 73 (1976): 165–85.

[2] Austin, John, "Other Minds," *Aristotelian Society Supplementary Volume* 20 (1946):148–87.

[3] Carnap, Rudolf, *Logical Foundations of Probability* (Berkeley, 1949).

[4] Castañeda, Hector-Neri, "Consciousness and Behavior: Their Basic Connections," in *Intentionality, Minds, and Perception*, ed. H.-N. Castañeda (Detroit, 1963).

[5] Castañeda, Hector-Neri, "Knowledge and Certainty," *The Review of Metaphysics* 18 (1965): 508–47.

[6] Castañeda, Hector-Neri, "Indicators and Quasi-Indicators," *American Philosophical Quarterly* 4 (1967):85–100.

[7] Castañeda, Hector-Neri, "On Knowing (or Believing) that One Knows (or Believes)," *Synthese* 21 (1970):187–203.

[8] Castañeda, Hector-Neri, "There Are Command Sh-Inferences," *Analysis* 32 (1971):13–19.

[9] Castañeda, Hector-Neri, *Thinking and Doing: The Philosophical Foundations of Institutions* (Dordrecht, 1975).

[10] Castañeda, Hector-Neri, "On the Philosophical Foundations of the Theory of Communication: Reference," *Midwest Studies in Philosophy* 2 (1977):165–86. Reprinted in *Contemporary Perspectives in the Philosophy of Language*, ed. P. French, T. Uehling, and H. Wettstein (Minneapolis, 1979).

[11] Castañeda, Hector-Neri, "Perception, Belief, and the Structure of Physical Objects and of Consciousness," *Synthese* 35 (1977):285–351.

[12] Castañeda, Hector-Neri, "The Causal and Epistemic Roles of Proper Names in Our Thinking of Particulars," in *Contemporary Perspectives in the Philosophy of Language*, ed. P. French, T. Uehling, and H. Wettstein (Minneapolis, 1979).

[13] Castañeda, Hector-Neri, "Intentionality and Identity in Human Action and Philosophical Method," *Nous* 13 (1979):235–60.

[14] Castañeda, Hector-Neri, "Philosophical Method and Chisholm's Direct Awareness of Self," *Grazer philosophische Studien* (forthcoming).

[15] Chisholm, Roderick M., "Epistemic Statements and the Ethics of Belief," *Philosophy and Phenomenological Research* 16 (1956):281–312.

[16] Chisholm, Roderick M., "Evidence as Justification," *The Journal of Philosophy* 58 (1961): 739–48.

[17] Chisholm, Roderick M., "Contrary-to-Duty Imperatives and Deontic Logic," *Analysis* 14 (1963):33–36.

[18] Chisholm, Roderick M., *Theory of Knowledge* (Englewood Cliffs, N.J., 1966).

[19] Chisholm, Roderick M., *Person and Object: A Metaphysical Study* (Chicago, 1976).

[20] Chisholm, Roderick M., "Castañeda's Thinking and Doing," *Nous* 13 (1979):385-96.

[21] Clark, Michael, "Knowledge and Grounds: A Comment on Mr. Gettier's Paper," *Analysis* 24 (1963):46–48.

[22] Coder, David, "Thalberg's Defense of Justified True Belief," *The Journal of Philosophy* 67 (1970):424–25.

[23] Coder, David, "Naturalizing the Gettier Argument," *Philosophical Studies* 26 (1974):111–18.

[24] Cohen, L. Jonathan, *The Implications of Induction* (London, 1970).

[25] Dretske, Fred, "Conclusive Reasons," *Australasian Journal of Philosophy* 49 (1971):1–22.

[26] Fichte, Johann Gottlieb, *Science of Knowledge*, trans. P. Heath and J. Lachs (New York, 1970).

[27] Gettier, Edmund L., "Is Justified True Belief Knowledge?" *Analysis* 23 (1963):121–23.

[28] Ginet, Carl, *Knowledge, Perception, and Memory* (Dordrecht, 1975).

[29] Goldman, Alvin, "A Causal Theory of Knowing," *The Journal of Philosophy* 64 (1967): 355–72.

[30] Goldman, Alvin., "Discrimination and Perceptual Knowledge," *The Journal of Philosophy* 73 (1976):771–91.

[31] Harman, Gilbert, *Thought* (Princeton, N.J., 1973).

[32] Heidegger, Martin, *El ser y el tiempo*, trans. José Gaos (Mexico, 1951).

[33] Heidelberg, Herbert, "Chisholm's Epistemic Principles," *Nous* 13 (1979):73–82.

[34] Hilpinen, Risto, "Knowing that One Knows and the Classical Definition of Knowledge," *Synthese* 21 (1970):109–32.

[35] Hilpinen, Risto, "Knowledge and Justification," *Ajatus* 33 (1971):7–39.

[36] Hintikka, Jaakko, *Knowledge and Belief* (Ithaca, N.Y., 1962).

[37] Johnsen, Bredo, "Knowledge," *Philosophical Studies* 25 (1974):273–82.

[38] Kant, Immanuel, *Critique of Pure Reason*.

[39] Kemeny, John G., "Fair Bets and Inductive Probabilities," *The Journal of Symbolic Logic* 20 (1955):263–73.

[40] Klein, Peter D., "A Proposed Definition of Propositional Knowledge," *The Journal of Philosophy* 68 (1971):471–82.

[41] Klein, Peter D., "Knowledge, Causality, and Defeasibility," *The Journal of Philosophy* 73 (1976):792–812.

[42] Lehrer, Keith, *Knowledge* (Oxford, 1974). This book supersedes a dozen or so previous essays by Lehrer.

[43] Leibniz, Gottfried Wilhelm, "On the Method of Distinguishing Real from Imaginary Phenomena," in *Gottfried Wilhelm Leibniz: Philosophical Papers and Letters*, ed. L. L. Loemker (Dordrecht, 1969).

[44] Loeb, Louis, "On a Heady Attempt to Befiend Causal Theories of Knowledge," *Philosophical Studies* 29 (1976):331-36.

[45] Lucey, Kenneth, "Scales of Epistemic Appraisal," *Philosophical Studies* 25 (1974):423-28.

[46] Pappas, George, "Knowledge and Reasons," *Philosophical Studies* 25 (1974):423-28.

[47] Pappas, George, and Swain, Marshall, "Some Conclusive Reasons against 'Conclusive Reasons'," *The Australasian Journal of Philosophy* 51 (1973):72-76.

[48] Pastin, Mark, "Foundationalism Reux," *The Journal of Philosophy* 71 (1974):709-10.

[49] Pastin, Mark, "Modest Foundationalism and Self-Warrant," in *Studies in Epistemology*, ed. N. Rescher (Oxford, 1975).

[50] Pastin, Mark, Review of Lehrer's *Knowledge, Nous* 11 (1977):431-37.

[51] Paxson, Thomas D., "Prof. Swain's Account of Knowledge," *Philosophical Studies* 25 (1974):57-61.

[52] Powers, Lawrence, "Knowledge by Deduction," *The Philosophical Review* 87 (1978):337-71.

[53] Rescher, Nicholas, "Foundationalism, Coherentism, and the Idea of Cognitive Systematization," *The Journal of Philosophy* 71 (1974):695-708.

[54] Sartre, Jean-Paul, *Being and Nothingness*, trans. Hazel E. Barnes (New York, 1956).

[55] Sellars, Wilfrid, "Meaning and Inference," *Mind* 62 (1953):313-38.

[56] Sellars, Wilfrid, "Empiricism and the Philosophy of Mind," vol. I in *Minnesota Studies in the Philosophy of Science*, ed. H. Feigl and M. Scriven (Minneapolis, 1956).

[57] Sellars, Wilfrid, "Phenomenalism," in *Intentionality, Minds, and Perception*, ed. H.-N. Castañeda (Detroit, 1967).

[58] Sellars, Wilfrid, "The Structure of Knowledge," in *Action, Knowledge and Reality: Studies in Honor of Wilfrid Sellars*, ed. H.-N. Castañeda (Indianapolis, 1975).

[59] Shimony, Abner, "Coherence and the Axioms of Confirmation," *The Journal of Symbolic Logic* 20 (1955):1-28.

[60] Skyrms, Brian, "The Explication of 'X knows that p'," *The Journal of Philosophy* 64 (1967):333-89.

[61] Sosa, Ernest, "The Analysis of 'Knowledge that p'," *Analysis* 25 (1964):1-8.

[62] Sosa, Ernest, "Propositional Knowledge," *Philosophical Studies* 20 (1969):33-43.

[63] Sosa, Ernest, "Two Conceptions of Knowledge," *The Journal of Philosophy* 67 (1970):59-66.

[64] Sosa, Ernest, "The Concept of Knowledge. How Do You Know?" *American Philosophical Quarterly* 11 (1974):113-22.

[65] Sosa, Ernest, "On Our Knowledge of Matters of Fact," *Mind* 83 (1974):388-405.

[66] Sosa, Ernest, Review of Harman's *Knowledge, Nous* 11 (1977):421-30.

[67] Sosa, Ernest, "The Foundations of Foundationalism," *Nous* (forthcoming).

[68] Swain, Marshall, "Knowledge, Causality, and Justification," *The Journal of Philosophy* 69 (1972):291-300.

[69] Swain, Marshall, "Epistemic Defeasibility," *American Philosophical Quarterly* 11 (1974):15-25.

[70] Thalberg, Irving, "In Defense of Justified True Belief," *The Journal of Philosophy* 66 (1969):795-803.

[71] Tienson, John, "On Analyzing Knowledge," *Philosophical Studies* 25 (1974):289-93.

[72] Tomberlin, James, "Knowing without Knowing that One Knows," *Philosophia* 2 (1972):239-46.

[73] Tomberlin, James, Review of Carl Ginet's *Knowledge, Perception, and Memory, Nous* (forthcoming).

[74] Villoro, Luis, "Conocer y saber," *Critica* 10 (1970):75-91.

[75] Wittgenstein, Ludwig, *Philosophical Investigations* (Oxford, 1952).

APPENDIX

1. After the preceding essay was copy edited, Nuel Belnap showed me that the hierarchy of questions described in section I.16 does *not* include all the questions to which a given proposition is a true answer. For instance, the following question escapes that hierarchy: Can you formulate a proposition that is a member of the set S? In general, the questions that are left out seem to me to be questions that arise from propositions containing P as a component. If this is so, then the hierarchy described in section I.16 is only the *proper* or *characteristic hierarchy* of questions determined by P. I wonder now whether what are called constraints on questions in the essay can, at least in some cases, be considered parts of propositions that have as a component a given proposition in which we are interested.

There is much more to the theory of questions than we have touched upon in our discussion. Given our concern with knowledge and the state of mind constitutive of knowledge, it was crucial, however, that we did not consider a question as a set of propositions, but as a special thought content, which stands in the relations YES$_i$ to its answers. I am not sure that the logic of questions that treats questions as sets of propositions offers us a fully serviceable object of interrogative attitudes. But this is a large issue that we cannot decide here.

In any case, the tentative analysis of part II remains the same, I believe, if the parameter Q_i of questions is understood to include more questions than our discussion in part I concentrated on. See the rich bibliographies in [1] and [2] below.

2. On October 30, 1979 George Nakhnikian gave me the following quotation:

If by 'omniscience' we mean the ability to answer with certainty every conceivable question, including questions concerning the future . . . ([3], p. 121).

Thus, instead of speaking of the Plato-Powers principle as I did above, I should have spoken of the Plato-Popper-Powers principle.

Bibliography for the Appendix

[1]   Belnap, Nuel, and Steel, Thomas B., Jr., *The Logic of Questions and Answers* (New Haven and London, Yale University Press, 1976).
[2]   Hintikka, Jaakko, *The Semantics of Questions and the Questions of Semantics* (Amsterdam: North Holland Publishing Co., 1976).
[3]   Popper, Karl, "Indeterminism in Quantum Physics and in Classical Physics," *The British Journal for the Philosophy of Science* 1 (1950-51).

Believing

J. F. M. HUNTER

1. INTRODUCTION

Both in ordinary life and in philosophy, we can use the word 'believe' altogether competently without having an opinion as to what believing is. Although many of us can construct explanations about why we used the word in this or that situation, we are not, in doing so, saying anything, or anything useful, about what believing is. If I say "I described myself as believing it because while I hold it to be true, I recognize that I might quite well be wrong," then my explanation, although acceptable enough, does not advance our understanding of what believing is, because if there is a problem about that, there is one of the very same kind as to what holding something true, while recognizing one may be wrong, is. If there is something that happens, something that prevails, or something we do, on the occurrence, prevalence, or performance of which we can properly say either that we believe or that we hold true, while recognizing we may be wrong, neither of these expressions tells us anything about *what* it is, given which we are entitled to use them.

It is not very clear what we would be after, in wanting to know what believing is, but it could perhaps be explained in one way on the analogy of the difference between explaining what a car is by giving synonymous terms in English or in other languages and giving a description not employing synonymous expressions, of such a kind as to enable a person to identify a car on sight and distinguish it from a truck, a van, or other such vehicles.

Similarly, when we ask what believing is, we would like to be able to describe, in terms generally intelligible, something, or some family of things, or some set of things, or some set of families of things, that are called believing. We would like to be able to do this in such a way that a person unfamiliar with the word 'believe' or with any of its synonyms or paraphrases in English or other languages could by means of our description identify the phenomenon of believing and distinguish it from knowing, remembering, or imagining.

It is assumed that there is *something* that believing is, not necessarily the same kind of thing in all cases, but something; and it is our job to ascertain *which* something, or if it is different in various cases, which somethings, and to describe it or them in terms sufficient by themselves for their identification.

Do we not all know which something it is? It might be argued that we surely must in some sense know this, otherwise we could not use the word correctly and on appropriate occasions. We may not, the argument might continue, be able to *say* what it is, but it is surely at least an intuitive or an implicit understanding of its nature that guides us in our use of the word 'believe'. Do we not say we believe something when, somehow or other, we recognize that it is true that we do? The problem is to make explicit what it is that we have identified, perhaps instinctively, when we say we believe something—or if not that, the problem is to work out why it is that although we do identify something, we cannot say what it is. (Perhaps it is a distinctive but indescribable experience of such a kind that once we have had it a few times, we will hardly fail to recognize it when it recurs.)

There is not a vast philosophical literature on believing, but it seems to me that in the unhappy history of our struggles with this concept, although there has been well-justified dissatisfaction with particular answers to the question what believing is, there has been almost no skepticism as to whether it is a fair question what it is. If one is untroubled by the question itself, then however much one may doubt that believing is a distinctive experience, a pattern of behavior, or a state of the nervous system, the problem as to what it is will remain and be the more acute. Thinking themselves to be following Wittgenstein, some people may try saying that believing may be quite different in various cases and that the roadblock has been the attempt to find something common to all the cases; but they will have made no advance if they cannot go on, in at least a few cases, to show that *this* is what believing is here, anyway.

My aim in this paper is to mount an attack on the asking of the question what believing is. In section 2 I will illustrate how we flounder when we try to answer this question. In section 3 I will offer a diagnosis of why there is so much floundering, and in section 4 I will sketch an answer to the question how the word 'believe' is used, if not to record, conjecture about, or inquire as to the existence of the phenomenon of belief.

2. FLOUNDERINGS

Let us begin with a marvellous question, the consideration of which will take us round and about through some interesting parts of this boggy territory: can one both know and believe the same thing at the same time?

One kind of answer may be derived from the following short dialogue:

"Did you believe his story?"

"Yes I did. I was with him when it all happened, so I know it is true."

It would not be out of the question to fuss over whether this answer is in order, but if it is, it might solemnly be listed as a case of believing and knowing the same thing at the same time. To say that, however, would in the first instance be only to say that such utterances as "I believe it, in fact I know it" are allowable. It would be a further step to the conclusion that there were two distinct things concurrently true of this person, one that he believed his friend's story, and the other that he knew it to be true. Whether *that* is so is the question that might show us something about the nature of believing.

H. H. Price[1] thought it clearly impossible that two such distinct things should be true of a person at the same time, but his reason for saying this is not very clear. He says that he knows by introspection whether he is puzzled, believes or knows, and that "it follows that it is impossible to know and to believe the same thing at the same time"; but how exactly does that follow?

If knowing and believing were two characteristic and distinct mental events or processes and if we believe or know something only when the characteristic believing or knowing thing is going on, it might be a question of whether these goings-on crowd the mind, so to speak, so that when one of them is on stage, there is just not room for the other.

However (a) believing and knowing do not thus "crowd" the mind. We can believe or know something when in pain or when wondering what to have for supper. (b) The "crowding" theorem would entail that we cannot believe one thing and know something else at the same time and that we can neither believe two different things at the same time nor know two different things at the same time, all of which entailments are false. (c) The proposition that we believe or know something only when a characteristic thing is happening is not true. We can believe or know things day in, day out, without giving them a thought, and without anything else happening to show that we believe or know them.

It might nevertheless be true that we believe or know things, not if something characteristic is occurring at the time we say we believe or know, but if the right kind of thing occurs quite frequently or on appropriate occasions. It is not clear whether this possibility would help Price, since if believing and knowing were experiences, one might quite frequently have the experience of knowing Cock Robin was dead and quite frequently have the experience of believing it; but we need not pursue this, because the supposition requires that there be times when we are believing and times when we are knowing; and that is not true.

We do say "I am not just saying this, I believe it," but we say neither "I am not just saying this, I am believing it," nor "I am not just saying this, there were at least six times this week when I was believing it." There is no time when believing is going on, or knowing either. When we read a report in the morning paper, we generally believe it, but nothing happens which is the believing of it. We do not read it and then have believing occur for a while, until we get interested in another item, whereupon that believing stops and another starts. Nor do we find that we cannot concentrate on the next item, because we are still believing the previous one.

We might, in our deliberations so far, have been making the wrong *kind* of supposition as to what believing and knowing might be. We have been supposing they are something one might introspect; but a different kind of supposition might arise from reflecting on the facts that if we know, we cannot be wrong, and that if we believe, we may be. Knowing and believing might be two sorts of epistemic fettle we can be in, not directly observable but adjudged to prevail on the basis of facts about ourselves that we can observe but which are not themselves the fact that we believe something or know something. Perhaps we could not be in two different fettles at the same time and with respect to the same thing.

It is peculiarly difficult to suggest *what* might show the shape we are in, but whatever we might set down as being the evidence, the connection between that evidence and the conclusion that we were in this or that shape would surely only be probabilistic, and hence in every case there would be room for such expressions as "I suspect that I believe," "The indications are that I know," "It is virtually certain that I believe," and so on. We do say some of these things, but only in special cases, none of which are cases of assessing connections between what we have noticed about ourselves and conclusions as to our epistemic fettle. We say "I think I know the answer" as a way of saying "I think my answer will prove to be right," not as a way of saying "I think I could not be wrong about the answer"; and if we are challenged as to why we said "I think I know," we do not provide evidence as to the shape we are in, but evidence in support of our answer. Or again we say "I think I believe that" as a slightly quaint way of stopping just short of subscribing to it, not as a way of not quite subscribing to the proposition that we believe it. We would go on: "It is surprising that it should be true, but the evidence is certainly impressive," not "All the indications are that I believe it, although I have sometimes found I did not believe something in spite of similar indications."

We do not say "I am too tired [or too feverish or too anything else] for knowing just now. The most I can manage is believing," and we know many things in spite of being tired, feverish, anxious, or distracted, and merely believe many things in spite of being as chipper, agile, and clear in the head as we could wish. We can be in poor shape for playing chess or conducting a seminar, but knowing and believing are not activities and do not benefit from our being in good fettle or suffer from our being in bad.

We choose between the words 'know' and 'believe', not in view of the shape we are in, but in view of such things as the character of our information: we say "I know. I saw it happen," or "I believe that is true. I heard it from Monica, who is usually quite reliable."

It is true there are cases in which the shape we are in may be a reason for saying we believe, for example, in giving memory reports. One might say 'I am tired just now, and cannot be sure I have got this right, but I believe these were his words. . . .''; but we would not say "I am tired just now, so I suspect I only believe this," or "I am tired just now, that is to say I merely believe this."

If we were to marry the fact that if we know, we cannot be wrong, whereas if we believe, we may be, with the idea that we can establish whether we know or believe by some kind of self-examination, we might be onto a marvellous new way of assessing the truth of propositions: if self-examination shows that I know it, then it is true. Moore danced very close to endorsing such a connection between knowledge and truth when he wrote: "Isn't it possible that I merely believe [these common sense propositions]? ....In answer to this question I think I have nothing better to say than that it seems to me I do know them, with certainty."[2] That answer is far from clear, but he *might* have been saying "If I know anything about knowing, and I do, the state I am in with respect to these propositions is certainly one of knowledge. Hence they must be true." So taken, he would be thinking along lines similar to Prichard, who wrote, "We must recognize that when we know something, we either do, or at least can, by reflecting, directly know that we are knowing it. . . ." (Note the continuous present here.)[3]

We flounder in a different way if we think: who, after all, is incapable of being wrong, at least with respect to most things? Ought we not for the most part, if not absolutely always, to cease and desist from saying we know and recognize that we mostly only believe? Here we would be taking "If I know I cannot be wrong" to express the requirement that anyone said to know should be infallible with respect to what he is said to know, and questioning whether that requirement is ever satisfied.

The idea of infallibility makes sense with regard to actions done repeatedly, like predicting the weather or doing calculations, where one may invariably get something right, but it is not clear that it makes sense to speak of a person invariably being right in saying some one thing, such as that Hume was a Scot. No more does it make sense to say that Emil is sometimes wrong in saying Hume was a Scot. Yet there is something right about "If I know, I cannot be wrong, and if I believe, I may be": can we give an alternative account of what it means?

These propositions would come out as the obvious truth they are mostly taken to be, if we read them as statements about the correct use of 'know' and 'believe'. It is permissible to say "This might be false, but I believe it," whereas it is not permissible to say "This might be false, but I know it is true."[4] It is permissible to say "This proposition is false, but he believes it," whereas it is not permissible to say "This proposition is false, but he knows it is true."

These provisions for the use of 'know' and 'believe' do not reflect any extraordinary psychological facts, such as that the knowing state never occurs with respect to anything that is false, or that when something ceases to be true, then all over the world, wherever the knowing state had prevailed with respect to it, that state is automatically reduced to one of believing. If, last week, Mary knew that the old town hall was still standing, but yesterday, unbeknown to her, it was torn down, she no longer knows, but at most believes, that it is still standing, not because the demolition has resulted in any change in her, but just because to say she still knows it is standing would be to say it still is standing.

If there were two identifiable states that we called believing and knowing, it would be quite conceivable, even if it never happened, that a person should know something, although it was not true. She would just have to be unmistakably in the knowing state with regard to it. Similarly it would be quite conceivable that a person should believe it was raining, while seeing it was not. If neither of these things ever happened, it would be an argument for divine providence.

Lest all this sound too farfetched altogether, let us remember that Locke described believing as one of the actings of the mind, perceivable by internal sense;[5] that Hume searched desperately for a mark by which the experience of believing could be distinguished from those of imagining or remembering;[6] that various philosophers (e.g., Braithwaite,[7] Prichard,[8] Moore[9]) were not bashful about using such expressions as "I am believing this," "I am knowing that," "I am having this belief," and so on, as if one's believing or knowing were a recognizable current fact; and that Prichard said, "For obviously a condition of knowing cannot be the result of the use of imperfect faculties."[10]

A second question, which will take us through a rather different wonderland, is whether believing is an action. We may want very much to suppose that it *is* an action, because we like to regard it as being up to us what we believe; and if it is not an action, it will threaten to be an event, which just happens when it happens, and with the occurrences and failures to occur of which we must just learn to live.

The initial prospects for its being an action can be made to look good. We ask people to believe things and urge them not to. This would hardly make sense if believing could not be performed or refrained from at will. We describe things as hard or easy to believe, and it is characteristic of actions that they can be difficult or easy to perform. We explain our reasons for believing, just as we explain our reasons for doing something.

We may be scornful of a request that we believe something, but only in particular cases, and for such reasons as that the proposition to be believed is too implausible. It is not like being scornful of the request that we should not omit to mean it when we say we will cut the lawn. Yet although "Please believe it" makes sense and "Please mean it" does not, there is no action we perform which we call believing. "All right, I will believe it, but not right away" makes no sense, nor does "I said I would believe it, but then never got around to it." We do not plan on believing something this afternoon, and there is no time when we are in the thick of believing it. The question "When did he believe that?" does make a kind of sense, but does not ask for a time at which an act was performed. "In his school days" or "In his Idealist phase" are acceptable answers, but "At five past two" rings strangely. If it is currently true that he believes it, it will of course be true at five past two, but not more then than at any other recent date, and not because anything in particular was happening at five past two.

We do say "I am unwilling to believe" and "I refuse to believe," as if believing were an act we were sometimes reluctant to perform; but while under duress I can reluctantly act as if I believed, no one has the least idea what to do by way of yielding to threats and believing. (The idea of Grace is an offshoot of this crux. "Believe in me and ye shall have everlasting life." "But I cannot just turn on belief." "Right.

Belief is a gift of God, and there is no saying to whom He will grant it, but if you open your heart . . ." Not an action, so it happens when it happens.)

People say "How can you believe that?" but we do not respond by explaining some trick we have learned, given which it is a cinch, nor do we advert to our long experience at believing implausible things. Rather, we try to show that the proposition is not so implausible as it may appear. Doing that is not explaining some facility we have acquired, which might help anyone who learned it to perform such believing tasks.

"It is hard to believe that she is the murderer" does not mean that it takes a skilled believer. We would not, to cope with the problem, prescribe a course in believing ever harder things, until the best students got so that they could believe six impossible things before breakfast, and then have them take on the proposition that she was the murderer. If, instead, we constructed a case against her, showing that her character is not so pure as it might appear, and so on, it might become quite "easy to believe," but we would not add 'even beginners can believe it now'.

We do not say "It is hard to believe this" and go on to say it is impossible late at night or when you have a fever; and that is not because fatigue and fever are in fact not among the things that impede the harder believing tasks. Noise, hunger, and anxiety do not interfere with the task of believing either; nor does anything else, because believing is not a task. We may be unable to think when rock music is playing, and so not come to have any new beliefs, but the activity impeded here is thinking, not believing.

There are things we do such that, had we not done them, we would not have come to believe certain things we do believe. We read newspapers, listen to witnesses in courtrooms, conduct inquiries, and so on. That this is so, incidentally, is all that is necessary to relieve any legitimate anxieties as to whether it is up to us what we believe. It would be absurd to complain that something was so obviously true that one could not stop oneself from believing it, and this would in any case not be a complaint that a state of belief had set in despite one's best efforts to prevent it.

On due consideration we *come to the conclusion* that the defendant is innocent, and thereafter say we believe it, but that is a way of saying what conclusion we reached. Our so concluding did not, right away or soon, have the result that believing set in.

When we listen thoughtfully to testimony, we are not engaged in believing. Our efforts are not directed at getting believed what we finally do believe; nor even at having some belief. When a juror is listening attentively he would hardly say that he is trying to believe something, he does not yet know what, but that he is trying to decide who is at fault.

"People always know when I am lying, so when I want to persuade someone of something false, I always cunningly believe it first." There *are* things that this person might cunningly do. He might tell himself firmly, "Now this is true!" or he might think resolutely of some truth while he uttered the falsehood. None of such things is called believing, nor is anything else. None of us knows what he might cunningly do which is called believing.

Griffiths was talking nonsense when he said, "Whatever else one does with a truth, believing the proposition that expresses it is the first and most fitting thing to do with it."[11]

If we are thus crowded out of supposing that believing is an action, but still never doubt that it is *something,* we may sadly see ourselves as bound to conclude that it just happens: it comes when it comes, and we just have to live with it. As with a cold or a dream, there may be a few things we can do that affect whether it happens, but like these things it has a perverse way of not always responding to our machinations, and it may often occur unbidden. So, when we hear a patter on the roof, luckily the belief that it is raining normally occurs, and normally stops occurring when we see that the rain has stopped; but the belief that it is raining might, even if it never does, persist after we had noticed that the rain has stopped, or annoyingly occur on a fine sunny day.

Do beliefs happen? We do say "I found myself believing it," as if they did; but there is nothing that might set in which on inspection would prove to be the belief that it is raining in Moscow, or which, if it persisted after I listened to a radio report of fine weather in the Russian capital, would require me to say, "The weather in Moscow is fine, but I believe it is raining there."

"It was a strange story he told, but I found myself believing it." We do not "find ourselves believing" an average newspaper report of a strike or a forest fire. The reason we say we find ourselves believing is not that, to our dismay but yet quite palpably, believing starts happening. 'To find oneself believing' is a stock expression that we use (a) as a way of acknowledging that what we believe might well not be believed, and (b) when we are unable to be very specific as to why we believe it.

We assure people that we believe something, but not that the believing of it is going on at this very moment, or has been going on continuously over the last three minutes, or has happened every time we thought of it in the past week.

If believing happened, then when it stopped happening we would stop believing, but for any proposition we believe, if anything happened when we began believing it, it has long since stopped happening, but we have not therefore long since stopped believing it.

If believing is neither an activity nor a passivity, it may seem uncommonly perplexing what other kind of thing it could be. There are other possibilities, however. If there is no action or event that is called believing, believing might yet be a disposition to act or to have various things happen.

The philosophical concept of a disposition is a dark one in many ways. It is not always very clear whether by a disposition is meant the known or unknown cause of a certain kind of tendency, or just a tendency, however caused; and if the latter, it is not always clear what manifestations are to be expected, given the attribution of this or that disposition. With uncontroversially dispositional concepts, as when we say that someone is a nervous or an irascible person, there is no problem as to what will count as a manifestation, or not much of a problem; but here each of the manifestations can be described using the words following 'having a tendency to' that we use in explaining the meaning of the concept. 'Irascible' means having a tendency to become angry quickly, and each display of it, however individually different, is a case of becoming angry quickly. 'Credulous' means tending to be easily deceived, and some people are so deceived repeatedly.

'Believe' is at least not patently a disposition word. 'Irascible', 'credulous', and 'fragile' are adjectives, whereas 'believe' is a verb; and 'believe' is transitive, whereas if there were verb forms of 'irascible' and 'credulous', they would surely be intransitive. Irascibility and credulity are character traits, but believing that P is not. Anyone who knows English knows that 'irascible' means having a tendency to become angry quickly, but English speakers do not know what to say in answer to the question "What tendency are we attributing to a person when we say he believes that P?" They do not even know whether we *are* attributing a tendency.

The possible answers to the question what this tendency is will perhaps divide into sayings and other doings, and sayings will divide into saying "P" and saying "I believe that P."

Certainly if a person believes that P, he will normally say "P" if the occasion arises, but to say "He normally says 'P' if the occasion arises" is to stop short of saying he believes that P. His normally saying "P" might be evidence that he believes it; it is not what it is to believe it.

We can say he believes P even if he never said it, or only said it once, but we can hardly say he is irascible on the basis of one display of temper, still less on the basis of none.

When we read a report of the weather in Yellowknife, we normally believe it, and normally right away forget it, but we cannot forget to be irascible, nor can we be an irascible person for just a few minutes.

These difficulties apply equally if we give as the tendency, his saying that he believes that P, but now a new awkwardness arises: the 'believe' in the analysis will be translatable "has a tendency to . . ."—and we will get ' "He believes' means he has a tendency to say he has a tendency to say . . .", and so on indefinitely.

There may appear to be a remedy for this in saying that the actions to which one is disposed if one believes are not those of saying one believes, or anything substantially equivalent, but such actions as taking an umbrella if one believes it may rain, or stepping gingerly if one believes the ice is thin. There are new difficulties now, however, for example:

(i) The theory does not now conform to the pattern of uncontroversial dispositional concepts, like irascibility, in which every manifestation of the disposition, however much it may vary from chewing the carpet to muttering and cursing, is a case of the same thing, becoming angry quickly. If one believes it may rain, one may stay at home, call off the picnic, patch the roof, and so on. There is no one description of these actions paralleling 'becoming angry quickly'.

(ii) Different people will do different things if they believe it may rain, but "He believes it may rain" does not have different meanings depending on who it is that believes it; and it is not our understanding of the language that enables us to say, if we can say, what Jane, believing it, will do.

(iii) Whereas one can say both "I got angry quickly because I am irascible" and "I called off the picnic because I believed it would rain," there is a different kind of relation between antecedent and consequent in the two cases. It was because I thought it wise that I called off the picnic, but it is not wise, in view of one's irascibility, to get angry quickly.

(iv) One can realize, after many displays of anger, that one is irascible, but can hardly realize, after calling off the picnic and patching the roof, that one believes it may rain.

Flounderings of a somewhat different breed arise from the thought that when we hear or read something and believe it, or when we reflect on various things we have noticed and draw conclusions which we accept, we must be different in some way. Some changes, most likely in the brain, have surely occurred; such changes as have the result that henceforth we routinely treat the stories believed, or the conclusions reached, as true. Why could we not say that the new condition that has set in, whatever exactly it might turn out to be, is what we are supposing to prevail when we say we believe something?

The question is not whether some changes, most likely neurological, occur, but whether we are speaking of them when we say we believe something. The latter seems a very doubtful supposition, for at least the following reasons:

(i) Even if it were possible to specify that state of a human organism that prevailed when someone routinely treated something as true, individuals could use the word 'believe' without knowing anything about those states and certainly without knowing anything about their own specific current states.

(ii) If there were a computer that was designed to evaluate evidence and arguments and always deliver a verdict, but to mark verdicts "beliefs" when the evidence or arguments were inconclusive, then although we, having designed the thing, might know all about what state it was in when it marked a verdict a belief, we would still not take it to be *saying* that it was in that state, but rather that the answer it gave was to be preferred, although there was room for doubt. If it was further designed to explain why it marked anything a belief, it would not advert to the state it was in but, for example, to the fact that such and such evidence was missing or to the other explanations of the facts at its disposal which were just possible. Even if the machine were designed in such a way that on detecting a certain state of itself, it marked a verdict a belief, it would not be talking about itself, but about the verdict, in so marking it.

(iii) It would be the normal thing, if believing were the as-yet-undiscovered cause of our affirming and assuming things, to say "I suspect I believe," "It is as if I believed," "There is impressive evidence that I believe," and so on. Yet if there are cases in which we say such things, they are exceptional and are not connected with theoretical considerations about the nature of belief. One might, for example, adduce evidence for *someone else's* benefit that one believes it will rain, but hardly to satisfy oneself; or evidence might lead one to suspect that one believes that thirteen is an unlucky number, but hardly that one believes Myrtle is living in Vancouver now.

(iv) Believing would surely be a different state from knowing; but it can cease to be true that we know and start to be true that we believe without any change taking place in us, for example, when, unbeknown to us, the building we knew last week to be standing is torn down.

3. DIAGNOSIS

I have been exhibiting ways in which we flounder when we press the question what believing is. The fact that the answers we have considered, which represent at least most of the kinds of answer that have ever been suggested, are all so fragile, may only show how difficult the question is or how sloppy or uninventive philosophers have so far been in their attempts to answer it. It is not clear how any number of failures to find a satisfactory answer would show that there is something wrong with the question we are posing, but the flounderings we have seen do at least make it reasonable to entertain that hypothesis; and once suggested, the hypothesis might be supported by considerations of a different kind. To provide such support will be the aim of this section.

1. We have never satisfied ourselves that "What is believing?" is a fair question; we have just never doubted it. The question is after all so like the questions "What is boxing?" or "What is a stethoscope?" or "What is an offside?" which are routinely asked and effectively answered every day, and so we coast right on to ask what believing is.

2. The differences between these other questions and "What is believing?" turn out to be remarkable, however:

(i) The other questions are language-learners' questions, but we know the language and still have a problem about believing.

(ii) In answering the other questions, there is room for no more than the most rudimentary sorts of investigation. One may look it up in the dictionary or think a bit about how to explain it, but the answers are (quite) ready to hand. Competent speakers, doctors, hockey players know the answers, even if they sometimes botch the job of explaining them, and when they say what an offside or a stethoscope is, they are not giving their *theory* or their *analysis*. By contrast, it turns out to be a matter for searching and sophisticated investigation, what believing is, and speaking English does not entitle us to think that we know the answer.

(iii) When competent speakers cannot say, or cannot say to the satisfaction of philosophers, what a game is, they at least know that old maid and soccer are games, and that skiing and carpentry are not, and they can embark on the project of hammering out a definition by setting before themselves uncontroversial examples of games and nongames and trying to find general things to say about them, given which all and only what we call games come out as games (and perhaps borderline cases come out borderline). By contrast, we do not have the first idea what to set before ourselves as the proper instances of believing—witness the remarkable fact that such entirely different answers as "a way in which the mind acts on its ideas," "contemplating a proposition with a feeling of conviction," "having a disposition to say and do various things," and "a state of the nervous system" have been given. We can list my believing this and her believing that as instances, but however clear it may be that I do believe this, it is still not in the least clear what it is about me that is my believing of it.

3. As was pointed out earlier (p. 239), we can in a sense say right off what believing is. It is holding true while recognizing one may be wrong. Such an answer, while it would steer a language-learner in the right direction, would still leave him with other things to learn, such as that we can say "He believes" although he does not in the least recognize he may be wrong, if, for example, he holds a proposition to be true but is mistaken. Whether we could, by adding fine points in this way, ever say all there is to be said about the use of 'believe', we would still not, in the sense we are after, have said what believing is, because it is no clearer what to hold true while recognizing one may be wrong is, than it is what believing is.

The question what believing is presupposes that it is something, whereas we could now say, it is not anything. That is not to say that no one ever believes or that we have been taken in by the myth that people believe things. If there is a myth here, it pertains to the use of 'believe': that it is used to report the occurrence or prevalence of something or other, though we may not yet know what. We are not making a contribution to philosophical deliberations on What There Is. If we were to say that believing never happens, we would not know what we were excluding from the realm of Being.

We might escape the conclusion that believing is not anything if we could suppose that we are descended from an advanced civilization in which they knew what it was and constructed their uses of 'believe' in the light of this information; and if we supposed further that while those uses had been handed down to us through successive generations, the books in which believing was explained and the instruments for detecting it were all lost in a great cataclysm. However, given what has been said so far, one does need to go to that or similar lengths to sustain the idea that there is some answer to the question what believing is.

Still, it would be best to round out the argument by saying enough about how the word 'believe' *is* used, to answer such questions as how it can be true or false that we believe, how we know when to say we believe, or how it is that we can believe intensely, devoutly, doggedly, or secretly. That will be the aim of the concluding section.

4. FEATURES OF THE USE OF 'BELIEVE'

A full account of the use of 'believe' would touch on many curiosities, among them:

The fact that we say "Why do you believe?" but not "Why do you know?" and "How do you know?" but not "How do you believe?";

The fact that knowing what he said is being able to answer the question "What did he say?" while believing what he said is thinking that what he said is true;

The fact that "Do you know that the price of butter has gone up?" is like "The price of butter has gone up. Is this news to you?" while "Do you believe the price of butter has risen?" is like "What do you say as to whether it has risen?";

The fact that one can know but not believe the price of butter, except in the sense in which we say colloquially "You wouldn't believe the price of butter!";

The fact that one can believe intensely but not vividly, secretly but not privately, wisely but not cunningly, for a long time but not unremittingly, mistakenly but not inadvertently;

The fact that one can illustrate a belief with pictures but not believe pictorially, and can express it in English but not believe it in English; and so on.

For the present purposes it may not be necessary to find a place for all these intriguing facts; it may be enough to delineate a few prominent features.

To begin, we could suggest that 'believe' has two distinct strains of use: (i) in taking a certain kind of stand as to the truth of this or that proposition, and (ii) in saying what stand a person has taken, in expressing confidence in or skepticism as to its genuineness, in trying to secure admissions that such stands were not genuine, in trying to persuade stand-takers to revise their stand, or in conjecturing as to what stand someone would take.

The difference here is aptly expressed by Wittgenstein when he says, ' "I believe that this is the case" is used like the assertion "This is the case"; and yet the *hypothesis* that I believe this is the case is not used like the hypothesis that this is the case."[12]

Much confusion arises from not doubting that 'I believe' and 'He believes' have the same function, because then there can scarcely be any other answer to the question "Namely what function?" than "To say that believing (whatever that may be) prevails in the person spoken of." This is one of the places where the flounderings we have seen begin. Clearly, however, "I believe there will be an election soon," whatever else it does, takes a stand on the prospects of an election, whereas "He believes there will be an election soon" does not. I take no stand on whether I believe (if that makes any sense: can I say "I believe I believe there will be an election"?), whereas he does take a stand on this but takes no stand on the political prospects. I can play my part in this scenario without using the word 'believe' or any synonym (just by saying there will be an election soon), but he cannot manage his part without using some word like 'believes', 'thinks', 'expects', or 'supposes'.

The distinction here is not between first and third person uses. 'I believed' and 'I did not believe' are uses of the second kind.

If we have now sufficiently marked out a difference between these two kinds of use, we can look in more detail at each of them in turn. It is the second which is the chief source of bewilderment about believing, and hence consideration of it will be the longer and more difficult task, but there are important things to be noted about the first.

I said that 'believe' is used in taking "a certain kind of stand" as to the truth of propositions. Here I am ignoring such constructions as 'believe in (him, God, getting lots of exercise)' or 'believe him', details of which could readily be worked out. *What* kind of stand?

In the first place, we go all out and mark a proposition true (or false).

In the second place, we recognize that, in so marking it, we have gone beyond what might in some circles (in a court of law, in a physics laboratory) be required in the way of reasons for accepting or rejecting it, or what we ourselves might ideally prefer.

(This second point will not always apply in cases where it is not the speaker who has introduced the word 'believe' into the conversation. To the questions "Do you believe that P?" or "Does anyone here believe that P?" one may reply affirmatively even if one would otherwise have said one knew it.)

The difference between saying there will be an election soon and saying "I believe there will be an election soon" is that the latter specifically recognizes that there is room for doubt as to whether one's assertion is true.

Although grammatically 'I believe' is self-referential, it appears on the above showing to say nothing about the speaker, but only, for example, about (a) whether there will be an election soon, and (b) how good the reasons are for saying this.

One is not making any biographical revelations, such as that one has an inclination to answer "yes" to the question whether there will be an election soon, and has yielded to the inclination before. This may be the first time I have addressed myself to the question whether there will be an election; but even if I have gone around predicting it, my saying now that I believe there will be an election is not a report of having done that but another case of it.

The recognition that there is room for doubt is easily confused, and is widely confused, with being in doubt, which in turn may be thought of as a biographical fact, perhaps consisting in having feelings of anxiety or uncertainty. One may be in some doubt about whether P if what one believes is that P is probably true; but not about whether P is probably true; and, if one simply believes that P, doubt seems to be excluded. One is not, by using the word 'believe', saying that P is fairly true. There is no such concept; and if one's view is that P is partly true or that something like P is true, that is what one should have said.

If I know of evidence against P, but still say P is true, I must suppose that there is some explanation of this contrary evidence, even if I do not know what it is. Hence while I may recognize the possibility that there is no such explanation, if I am at all inclined to think there is none, I ought not to say that I believe that P.

The central distinction here is difficult to express quite unambiguously, but it is between recognizing that, given the reasons one has for believing a proposition, that proposition could rationally be doubted, and actually being in some doubt oneself. The difference comes out in the fact that one can be certain, and still recognize a possibility of doubting, but could hardly at the same time be certain and be in any doubt. When one is in some doubt, the expressions to be used are, for example, "I am inclined to believe that P" or "I think P is most probably true." If we go further and say we believe, then although we may recognize that the evidence is inconclusive or that the topic is controversial, we are partly saying that we are not therefore in doubt. "I believe it" "goes all out" for its truth.

People who have said they believe may, when pressed, sometimes confess to having some doubts, but it is significant that the word 'confess' is natural here and that the question "Have you no doubts?" can arise out of a profession to believe. 'I believe' implies that the speaker is not in doubt, and we therefore sometimes skeptically ask, "Then have you no doubt?"

Saying I recognize room for doubt is not making a report of the state I am in. If there were introspectible states identifiable as this or that degree of confidence, or if I remembered quavers in my voice or other behavioral indicators of degrees of confidence, from other occasions when I had made the same assertion, it would be because I recognized room for doubt, that these states existed, not because I noticed the states, that I said there was room for doubt.

The foregoing puts us in a position to give one kind of answer to the question how we know whether to say we believe: if the evidence for what we are asserting is inconclusive, or if other people do not find it conclusive, or if the topic is notoriously a "matter of opinion," 'believe' is appropriate. One of the comfortable features of the idea that believing "is something" is that it promises an answer and, we may have thought, the only answer to the question when to say one believes: being aware of the phenomenon of belief prevailing, if we are honest, we report it. It only *promises* an answer, however, since there is no such phenomenon; and the answer it promises but fails to deliver can no longer win by default.

We can now turn to the harder topic of the uses of 'believe' in saying that someone believes, expressing doubts as to whether he does, securing confessions from him that he does not, and so on. What is particularly difficult here is that it seems that it can be true or false that a person believes—and we think: must there not be something that makes it true that he believes, or the absence of which makes it false?

We have by now assembled much reason to be skeptical about this very natural supposition; but if we are not so radical as to deny that it can be true or false that someone believes, we stand in need of some alternative way of understanding this fact.

We might begin with the small point that in the normal case in which a person says such things as that John is in poor health or that Mary is in love, he is routinely describable as believing it, especially if he also says something that recognizes room for doubt, such as "there is every indication of it, anyway," or if the topic is one about which uncertainty is natural or about which people do disagree, or if the speaker anyway has doubts about the truth of what was said. In such cases, in describing someone as believing, we have not come to the conclusion that he does. 'Believe' is simply the word to use when a person has said that P and when, for example, the topic is controversial or one thinks P false oneself. Such facts as that the topic is controversial are not evidence that he believes, but rather make 'believe' an apt choice of word.

In thus routinely describing someone as believing John is in poor health, however, we are not just saying he said that. To describe him as having said it is, if not to raise a doubt as to whether he believes it, at least to stop short of saying he does. Yet if we are not saying that believing is going on, or any of the other strange things we considered in section 2, what are we saying?

We can perhaps take a step toward resolving this difficulty if we reflect that "I believe that P" is like "[As for me,] I say that P" but that there is no clear third person construction for this use of 'say', especially in the past tense. 'He said' stops short of 'he believes', whereas 'he says' is not inconsistent with 'but he does not believe'. We might suggest that 'he believes' and 'he thinks' are third person forms of this special use of 'say'. Whatever we make of "[As for me,] I say. . . .," it at least clearly does not advert to any other cases of saying, still less to anything else that might be going on or be true.

We can take a further step by noting that "I said I believe it and I do believe it" is like "I said I believe it and I say it again." It can be significant that someone should say it again if, in the circumstances in which he now says it, someone is attending particularly to his words and has perhaps raised a question as to whether he might not have meant it. By saying it in such new circumstances, he goes on record more particularly, precluding himself from later backing off, saying he did not mean it or was only joking—except at a price, which will be greater having reiterated it. Similarly, if I have said something in such a way that it is unclear whether I might be conjecturing or reporting someone else's view and if I am asked, "Are you saying you believe that?" my replying affirmatively is not saying that I not only said it, I am in a state of belief with regard to it, but is a direction as to how what I said is to be taken: as an assertion, rather than as a conjecture or a report.

Suppose now that, whether or not the stand we are taking has been hardened in such ways as this, someone is skeptical and suggests we do not believe what we said. What sorts of grounds might he have for this skepticism, and why do they count as grounds? In asking the latter question, we will want to know whether (a) the skeptic has noticed something about me that departs from the dispositional manifestations characteristic of a believer, or (b) the skeptic has noticed something about me that is evidence that the phenomenon of belief does not prevail, or (c) the grounds of this skepticism work in some other, perhaps philosophically unstandard way.

When we are taxing someone with our suspicions as to whether he does believe something, some of the sorts of things we say are that he has said otherwise on other occasions, that he has insufficient reasons for believing this or has reasons for believing otherwise, that he denies something one would not likely deny if he believed this, or that he has not done something it would be sensible to do if one so believed.

Such allegations are not *evidence* that he does not believe. If he yields to the pressure and confesses to not believing, it is not that the weight of evidence has finally satisfied him that he does not after all believe. It was not on the basis of these facts that he initially said he believed, and he is not being shown that he has bungled the evaluation of the evidence as to whether he believes.

In a sense he knew all along whether he believed or not; but still one may be inclined to suppose that the evidence is something distinct from, but connected with, the believing, in a way analogous to that in which the weight of a box or the way it rattles or hums is evidence as to what is inside it, and that whereas other people have only the weight, rattling, or humming to go by, the speaker has seen inside and must admit what the box contains when he can provide no other explanation of what other people observe.

However, if that were the model, it ought to be possible to say "Look, I cannot explain why it rattles and hums this way, but what is inside it is of such and such description, and we all know that is a so and so (the analogue of, e.g., the belief that it will rain)." Yet such a move is no part of these transactions, and that is not because if another person is skeptical, he will hardly believe what we say about the "contents." We would not ourselves know what counts as the belief that it will rain. We cannot say "Look, I have a lively idea associated with a present impression," but neither is there anything else we could say such that, if the other person believed it, that would settle the question. The taxing is conducted entirely in terms of what, on this model, is called the evidence.

It will of course be different if one person is explaining to someone else why he thinks a third person does not believe what he says he believes; but it is plausible enough to regard this person as explaining a way in which anyone might challenge the professing believer.

It might be suggested that what the skeptic is showing is that the pattern of dispositional manifestations is not one of those we call believing. Yet in saying one believes, one is not saying that one of the well-known patterns prevails; and it is not a dispositional fact about a professing believer, that he has reasons for believing otherwise. If he heard John speak contemptuously about Mary, he has reason to believe that John is not in love with her, but his having heard this is not part of any disposition of his.

Moreover, an implication of either the evidential or the dispositional view is that when we have heard what the professing believer has to say for himself, we may often have all we need to know for a decision as to whether he believes; yet however strong our suspicions may be, we do not inform him as to whether he believes. There is, to repeat, something right about saying he knows whether he believes. What is right about it is that it is for him to say. We tell a person that he is irascible but press him to confess that he spoke disingenuously; and without a confession, we do not flatly say to third parties that he did not believe.

When someone doubts if we believe, his allegations are not aimed at convincing us, but at obliging us to confess. Let us look more closely at the ways in which we angle for these confessions. When the skeptic is taxing us with the fact that we have said otherwise on other occasions, have insufficient evidence, and so on, without contesting the alleged facts, we can say certain things that will relieve the pressure. We can admit to having lied on other occasions, or say we have since had a change of mind. We can say that in a case like this, we do not see that we need more evidence ("It's not an important matter. Isn't having overheard it on the bus enough?") We can explain away the evidence against what we believe or give some reason for saying that although we cannot explain it, there must be some explanation. We can claim not to have noticed the connection between what we believe and the other proposition that we deny, or explain how what we believe might be true, whereas what we deny is not; and we can give reasons for not having done what a sensible person might do, believing what we believe.

These moves may often be taken at a price: confessing that one has deceived someone or has not noticed an obvious connection; admitting that one has been overimpressed by certain evidence or has drawn faulty inferences; giving implausible explanations of why one discounted contrary evidence, why one did not draw an obvious inference, or why, believing rain likely, one did not call off the picnic.

Two related features of these goings-on are significant: first, that the pressure exerted is not that of the weight of evidence, but that of embarrassment. The power of the skeptic's allegations to embarrass derives from suggestions that we are muddled, dishonest, careless, or foolish. Failing explanations, it is either muddled or dishonest to say conflicting things on different occasions. If the topic is important, it is irresponsible to hold a belief on slight evidence or in the face of unexplained contrary evidence. It may be stupid, believing p, not to infer that q, and if, to avoid this imputation, we attempt to justify not accepting q, our explanation may be implausible or preposterous, and so on. No one likes to admit that he is dishonest, muddled, stupid, or irresponsible, and it is to avoid or minimize such imputations that we respond this way or that to the skeptical pressure.

The second and clearly related point is that we are, in these matters, holding people to a rough standard of intelligence and honesty, and it is in the hope of coming out looking as good as possible that we wiggle and weave when confronted with the skeptical pressure.

As in some games, we do this by backing up the move we have originally made with further moves, any one of which may, while having its advantages, generate further complications.

There is a hard problem about this, to which we will have to return, but just on the question of what sort of logical force the skeptic's allegations have, the view just sketched not only seems fairly obvious, when you think of it, but also nicely explains a number of features of the business of raising doubts as to whether someone believes. In particular:

(a) Since we all have some ability to recognize the implausible, the devious, the inconsistent, in new cases, or to have an opinion as to how much evidence is too little, or fair enough, we avoid the problem that can otherwise loom large, of why, given a complicated set of facts, we find it unsatisfactory to suppose that Julius believes such and such. It is not that this is not one of the paradigms of believing, but, for example, that Julius surely knows better than to believe this, in these circumstances.

(b) We can explain why considerations having to do with evidence for the proposition believed may be treated as relevant here, when saying one believes is not saying one has reason to believe. If someone says he has no particular reason to believe this, he just feels it in his bones, it does not follow that he does not believe; but we do encourage people to have scruples as to what they believe, and hence it is embarrassing to admit to believing without respectable reasons.

(c) We can explain why, for example, overhearing it in a bus is a good enough reason for a belief as to who won the hockey game, but not for a belief as to whether a vaccine one might take is safe. It is not that people are so constituted that they will not believe the latter on hearsay evidence, but will the former, so that if my evidence about the vaccine was slight, one could infer that I did not believe it was safe, but rather that it makes good sense to be more scrupulous, the more important the topic, and therefore it is embarrassing in one case, and not in the other, if I have to confess that my evidence is slight.

(d) We can explain why we stop short of informing people as to whether they believe, and angle for a confession that they do not. The explanation is that confessing to having said something without believing it is a consequential act, and only those who have performed the act can be held to the consequences.

The importance of this view as to the kind of force the skeptic's points have is largely negative: it shows that whatever he is doing, he is not proving that something called belief does not prevail.

The hard question that was deferred just now is this: however the professing believer is induced to make the moves he makes, may his moves not still be false? May he not find it the least embarrassing course to confess that he did not believe, when in fact he did, or may he not contrive ways of casting it as reputable to believe, and reaffirm his belief, when in fact he did not believe? In the game analogy that was suggested, moves may be strong or weak, ingenious or feckless, but they may not be false. When there is a confession, is there not something, quite apart from the considerations that have induced its author to make it, that is what is confessed?

Here clearly the question what believing is returns to haunt us, and we are in acute danger of having the whole structure of the argument collapse. Yet after all that has been said it ought not to be difficult at least to resist the temptation to write a phenomenology of believing, perhaps in terms of having a thought run through one's head, inconsistent with what one says. True enough, if I speak disingenuously, what I say is not what I think, but here 'think' is another word for 'believe' and does not report a process; and when we think out something false to say and then say it, what we have been thinking is not what we think. We know it is false, but not through having mentioned to ourselves that it is. If I think "This is false, but I'll say it," it is not my having said it is false that shows me that I think it is.

To suppose that someone believed or did not believe what he said is to suppose that he spoke ingenuously or disingenuously. We are massively inclined to look for a phenomenological difference here, whereas there is no phenomenology of ingenuous speech and hence nothing from which disingenuous speech might be a departure. Most of the things we say, we believe, but nothing happens around the time of speaking that shows us that we believe them, nor does anything happen that shows us that 'believe', rather than 'know' or 'suspect', is an apt choice of word. Hundreds of times a day we say such things as that Janet is living in Vancouver, that there was snow yesterday in Havana, or that Tom lost his job. Nothing special happens. We have heard these things and we repeat them on suitable occasions. Sometimes we are a little cautious and specifically say we believe this or that, if, for example, we know it to be controversial; but our knowing it to be controversial is not an event, and it is not necessarily or even generally on reflecting that it is controversial that we insert the word 'believe'. If, in a different case, we use the word 'believe' because our evidence is inconclusive, then although we may at some time in the past have so adjudged the evidence, it will not be the recollection of having done so that leads us now to use the word 'believe'.

We can often, on demand, explain why we believe something, or why we said we believed, rather than that we knew it, but if I say I heard it from David, it is the fact that I did hear it from him, not the recollection of his saying it, that puts me in a position to say this; and if I know David to be somewhat of a muddlehead, but think it unlikely he was mistaken on this point, I may give this as my reason for being so cautious as to have used the word 'believe', without having, at the time of speaking, reflected that he was a muddlehead etc.

What I am suggesting is that all these things reach the lips of comprehending beings as if by magic. Hume was making a similar point when he described the soul as a magical faculty;[13] but there is nothing magical about it. It is perfectly ordinary. It appears marvellous only by contrast with our expectation that the things we say should all be channeled through consciousness. Hume expressed a comparable expectation when he said that "one would think the whole intellectual world of ideas was at once subjected to our view, and that we did nothing but pick out such as were most proper for our purpose."[14]

If I am right in claiming that there is no phenomenology of ingenuous speech, there will be no way of analyzing disingenuous speech into differences between what happens then and what would have happened, had we been speaking candidly. The only difference will be that we would not have said what we did in fact say.

This difference, however, suggests a solution to our problem as to how a confession that we said something we did not believe can, unlike a move in a game, be true or false. It is true if, in making it, we are returning to ingenuous speech. We are not then confessing any such irregularity as that, while p was on our lips, not-p was in our mind, but rather that p was not (according to us) true or was not what (we believed) was true. The parentheses here are intended as a reminder that we are primarily talking about the truth of p and that the function of the words 'according to us' or 'we believed' is to show the epistemological status we assigned to p, namely true, though capable of being doubted. The omittability of 'believe' is perhaps clearest in the case in which we call off the picnic because we believe it will rain. It is because of the rain, not because of the state we are in, that we do this. We do not think: since my thinking (my nervous system, my behavior, my anything else) is thus and so, I will call off the picnic, but since it will rain (I believe), I will do so.[15]

In this section I have concentrated on what seem to me the hardest problems. Among the interesting questions I have not tackled are:

(i) How are we to view the business of raising doubts as to whether a person really believes what he thinks he believes? Here there is no prospect of a confession, since in these cases the professing believer has not been disingenuous; and it may look as if he stands to be convinced by the evidence, in much the way that anyone else might be so convinced. Yet is is peculiarly difficult to say what he would be convinced *of*; and just as it is vital to secure a confession in the ordinary cases of skepticism as to whether someone believes, it is vital here to bring a person to see that he has not believed what he thought he did.

(ii) How is it that we can believe firmly or fervently, if there is nothing called believing that might have these properties?

To encourage the belief that these problems are not intractable, I will just briefly indicate a solution to the second of them. The solution cannot lie either in denying that people do firmly believe or in weakening on the point that when they do, there is still nothing that is firm. It is plausible to say, however, that 'firmly believe' is a figurative expression. Things that are firm are resistant to change, and so we call a belief "firm" as a quaint way of expressing our determination not to be shaken from it. It is not upon finding something to be firm that we conclude that we will not easily be shaken, but we say our belief is firm as a way of declaring that we will not soon abandon it.

Notes

1. H. H. Price, "Some Considerations about Belief," in *Knowledge and Belief*, ed. A. P. Griffiths (Oxford,1967), p. 42.

2. G. E. Moore, "Defense of Common Sense," in *Philosophical Papers* (Reading, Mass., 1959), p. 43.

3. H. A. Prichard, "Knowing and Believing," in *Knowledge and Belief*, p. 61.

4. By "This might be false" here I of course do not mean it is merely a contingent truth, but rather that the speaker's grounds for asserting it are in his opinion such as to leave room for doubt. I think, incidentally that a speaker has not misspoken in saying he knows, as long as *he believes* his grounds leave no room for doubt. He has not misused the word 'know' in such an event, even if his grounds can be shown to be faulty. Given what he believed about his grounds, he used the word 'know' correctly. His mistake is not as to the correct use of 'know', but as to whether his grounds leave room for doubt.

5. John Locke, *Essay Concerning Human Understanding*, book I, chap. I, sec. 4.

6. David Hume, *Treatise of Human Nature*, ed. L. A. Selby-Bigge (Oxford, 1967), pp. 84-85, 94-98.

7. R. Braithwaite, "The Nature of Believing," in *Knowledge and Belief*, p. 36.

8. Prichard, *ibid.*, p. 61.

9. Moore, "Defense of Common Sense," pp. 37, 40, and elsewhere.

10. Prichard, "Knowing and Believing," p. 64.

11. A. P. Griffiths, "On Belief," *ibid.*, p. 140.

12. L. Wittgenstein, *Philosophical Investigations* (New York, 1958), p. 190.

13. Hume, *Treatise of Human Nature*, p. 24.

14. *Ibid.*

15. This is quite like J. O. Urmson's main point in "Parenthetical Verbs," in *Essays in Conceptual Analysis*, ed. A. Flew (London, 1956).

Adverbial Theories of Consciousness[1]

PANAYOT BUTCHVAROV

Recent American philosophy discussions of perception often contain expressions such as 'being aware here-ly', 'is appeared to redly', 'senses redly', 'senses rhomboidally', 'sensation of the of-a-red-triangle kind', 'senses a-pink-cube-ly'. We owe this innovation in philosophical terminology to the so-called adverbial theory.[2] But, the adverbial theory of *what?* The answers usually given are: of appearing, of sensing, of sense-impressions, of sensation. But all these terms are suitable in this context only if understood as technical terms, of unclear sense and uncertain reference, not as they would be understood in common discourse. And the adverbial theory is precisely a theory of that which is supposed to require their introduction as technical terms and an explanation of how they should be understood. Therefore, it is not with a statement of the adverbial theory that we can begin a discussion of the adverbial theory. We must begin at the beginning, with the conceptual roots the theory must have in common discourse if it is to be intelligible.

I

If we speak as we do before our immersion in philosophy, we may say that it is a characteristic feature of perceiving (seeing, tactile feeling, hearing, smelling, tasting), of imagining, of thinking, perhaps of everything that is, or in some manner involves, what may conveniently be called consciousness, that one can perceive, imagine, think of, perhaps in general be conscious of, things that do not exist. That this is so in the case of imagination and thought is unequivocally supported by common discourse. In the case of perception, common discourse is not unequivocal. We may correctly say of the delirious drunk, about whom philosophers often write, that he sees a pink rat and of an ophthalmologist's patient that he sees stripes where there are none. But we may also say that the drunk only thinks he sees a pink rat and that the patient only thinks he sees stripes. Should we conclude from this that 'see' has at least two senses? *Pace* Austin, I believe that we should, though mainly for the sake of terminological convenience. What is important for our purposes here is that we recognize the distinction, not that we regard it as a distinction between *senses*. For it is only in that distinction in common discourse that some of the central terminological proposals of the philosophy of perception can be anchored. Indeed, we may also detect in common discourse a third sense of 'see', in which what one sees must not only exist but also be causally related in an appropriate way to oneself. (Not: to one's seeing, for in this third sense of 'see' the seeing would *include,* perhaps even be identical with, the causal relation.) And, possibly, a fourth sense may be detected: that, in addition to what one of the first three requires, the perceiver have some belief about the thing he sees; but the evidence for the existence of such a sense seems to consist merely in the fact that sincere first-person uses of 'see' presuppose, trivially, that the speaker, who is the perceiver, have such a belief; sincere other-person uses presuppose this, again trivially, regarding the speaker but not at all regarding the perceiver. Corresponding distinctions of senses can be made with respect to all perceptual verbs.

There is no genuine philosophical question, I believe, about which of these senses is the most common or the correct one. To appeal to a distinction Ryle made, but for a purpose of which he would have disapproved, that would be a question about usages, not uses, of perceptual verbs.[3] What ought to be clear, however, is that the first sense, that in which what is perceived need not exist, is the one of primary epistemological interest. For only in that sense can we plausibly say that perception is the source of our knowledge of the existence of material things. In the second and third senses, we can determine that the perceptual verb is used correctly only if we can determine independently that what is said to be perceived exists. And, in the fourth sense, it is not the mere fact of one's belief that one can intelligibly regard as evidence for the existence of what one perceives or thinks one perceives; such a belief is precisely what requires, not what constitutes, evidential support (except in the irrelevant case in which it may serve as indirect, inductive evidence, e.g., if we know that someone usually does not make perceptual mistakes, his having a certain perceptual belief may count as evidence for its truth). But that all this is so is not relevant to our concerns in this paper. What is relevant is that the philosophy of perception begins with a question regarding the first sense of perceptual verbs: How can one perceive something that does not exist? (We may also begin by asking, How can one perceive something as having characteristics it does not have? But if we do, we quickly see that our answer must wait upon the answer we would give to the question about perceiving things that do not exist.)

One answer to this question is that no special explanation is required, that sometimes we just do perceive things that do not exist, that we know that this is possible because it is actual. Of course, this answer faces immediate difficulties concerning the status of nonexistent things and the notion of existence, but they are difficulties we would need to face, because of the facts about imagination and thought, even if we steadfastly refused to speak of perceiving nonexistent things. I believe that these difficulties can be met, but of course will not attempt to do so here.[4] In any case, an important advantage of this answer to our question is that it is the natural one, the *prima facie* correct one, the one that seems phenomenologically obvious.

Another answer is that what is ordinarily described as a case of someone's perceiving something that does not exist is really a case of someone's perceiving (seeing, hearing, etc.) something else that does exist but is such that it is naturally confused with the former. This other thing is usually called a sense-datum and, in the central cases of visual and tactile perception, is described as a mere perceptual expanse that has precisely the sort of qualities we ordinarily say we perceive material things as having, e.g., colors and shapes. This is why, we would be told, it is natural to confuse a sense-datum with the front surface of a material thing, to confuse perceiving a sense-datum with perceiving a material thing.[5] And to reflect the fact that ordinarily we speak of perceiving material things, it may be proposed, *solely for the sake of terminological clarity*, that we use a technical term for our perception of sense-data, namely, the term 'sensing'. But if it is added that in the case of veridical perception the sense-datum, the perceptual expanse, which one senses is identical with the front surface of a material thing, an addition difficult to defend but essential I believe to any plausible sense-datum theory, then in that case one's sensing a sense-datum would be identical with one's perceiving (as directly and immediately as one senses the sense datum) a material thing, and the sense-datum theory would coincide with direct realism. Of course, this answer also faces many difficulties which I cannot consider here.[6]

A third answer is that what is ordinarily described as a case of someone's perceiving something that does not exist is really not a case of perception, or of any other kind of consciousness, of an object at all, whether of the object we ordinarily take it to have (a material thing) or of any other object (e.g., a sense-datum). It is really a case of someone's being in a state of consciousness that has a certain nonrelational (whether sortal or qualitative) characteristic. Since a state of consciousness is expressed most naturally with a psychological verb, its nonrelational characteristics would be expressed most naturally with adverbs modifying that verb. Hence the designation of this third answer as the *adverbial theory*. Because its proponents allow (seldom on the basis of argument) for the use of perceptual verbs only in the case of existentially veridical perception, they too introduce a technical term, indeed, usually, again 'sensing', for the psychological state in question, and would describe the theory as the adverbial theory of sensing. Adverbial theories of thinking, imagining, and believing have also been proposed,[7] for reasons similar to those behind the adverbial theory of sensing. We may therefore speak generally of the adverbial theory (or theories) of consciousness. This would make explicit the fact that what is at stake in a discussion of the adverbial theory of sensing is far more general and deeper than any issues specific to the philosophy of perception. Hence the title of this paper. But I shall be concerned directly only with the adverbial theory of sensing, though in a manner relevant to adverbial theories of other modes of consciousness. My reason for this limitation is that the former alone has been developed in any detail.

The adverbial theory of sensing may be understood in three distinguishable, though not always distinguished, ways. First, as a method of reformulating, or para- phrasing, statements in ordinary language that seem to commit us to philosophical views the adverbial theorist wishes to reject: specifically, the view that sometimes we perceive things that do not exist and the view that sometimes, perhaps always, we perceive ("sense") things that do exist but are not material objects.

Second, the adverbial theory may be understood as a philosophical descrip- tion of the nature of at least some kinds of states of consciousness. Clearly, such a description must be, at least in part, phenomenological; it must be defended, at least in part, with phenomenological considerations. For what else can a *philosophi- cal* description of a certain state of consciousness be? Even if a certain state of con- sciousness is identical with a certain state of a brain, we can know this only if we have an independent conception of the former as well as an independent concep- tion of the latter (to know that the Evening Star is identical with the Morning Star we must first know what we are asserting to be identical with what). And whereas the conception of the latter would be based on anatomical and physiological facts the conception of the former surely can be based only on phenomenological facts. It should be noted that the examination of the ordinary uses of psychological terms need not be an alternative to the phenomenological approach. When practiced at its best, it can be regarded as a methodological variety of that approach.[8]

Third, the adverbial theory may be understood as a postulation of certain entities (certain "states of consciousness") possessing certain characteristics, a pos- tulation intended to provide an explanation of various phenomena, especially of the perceptual reports (both correct and incorrect) we make and of our so-called con- ceptual representations.[9]

I shall first consider the adverbial theory as a method of reformulation. Then I shall consider it as a phenomenological description. I shall not consider its third version, partly because of skepticism about philosophical explanations of phenom- ena, partly because of skepticism about philosophical postulations of entities, but especially because it seems obvious to me that both its rivals, the sense-datum theory and the quasi-Meinongian theory mentioned earlier, would serve the re- quired explanatory role much better than would the adverbial theory.

II

Roderick M. Chisholm recommends that we say of a man who has "spots before his eyes" that "the man senses (is appeared to) 'spottily', or 'in a spotty manner'," rather than that he senses "a spotty appearance" or simply, as ordinarily we would, that he sees spots.[10] Elsewhere Chisholm recommends that in order "to eliminate the reference to the thing that appears," we say, "I am appeared whitely to" or "I sense whitely," instead of "Something appears white to me."[11] And Wilfrid Sel- lars suggests that to have a sensation of a red rectangle is not to stand in a peculiar relation to a red rectangle, but rather to a-red-rectangle-ly sense.[12] But it should be noted that Sellars's version of the adverbial theory is part of a rich metaphysics and philosophy of mind. It is by no means a proposal of a mere reformulation, for the purpose of avoiding puzzlement.[13] And although Chisholm usually speaks as if that is all *his* version is, clearly it is motivated by deep ontological and epistemological considerations.

I shall not comment here on the value of reformulation as a general method for the solution of philosophical problems or on the conception of philosophy that encourages its practice. And I shall postpone until the next section the really important question regarding any proposed reformulation, and therefore regarding those offered by the adverbial theory, namely, whether the reformulation captures the structure of the situation described by the original statement, whether it casts light on it, whether it reflects the crucial similarities and differences between it and other kinds of situation in terms of which we may make it intelligible to ourselves. (Whether the reformulation succeeds in dissolving superficial puzzlement occasioned by the original statement seems to me of little philosophical importance.) Here I shall raise only a question so elementary as to be out of place in most cases of the practice of the method of reformulation, but certainly not in this case, namely, whether the reformulations proposed by the adverbial theory make sense. If we think of the Russellian reformulation of a statement containing a definite description as the paradigm of a philosophical reformulation, then the corresponding question about it would be, not, e.g., one of those which Strawson asks in "On Referring," but one that to my knowledge has never been asked, namely, whether it even makes sense. This question has not been asked about the Russellian reformulations because the answer to it is obvious: they do. Even if "There is one and only one thing that is now King of France, and that thing is bald" is not an adequate reformulation of "The present King of France is bald," there can be no question that it is a perfectly meaningful and clear statement.

Let us take the example "Something appears white to me" and its paraphrase as "I am appeared whitely to." We must keep in mind that we are asked to understand the latter in such a way that it does not entail either that something is appearing to me or that something is white. How should we understand it then? The first obvious observation is that, except in recent philosophical discourse, there is no such word as 'whitely'. But of course we may recognize that in general it is in accord with English grammar to form an adverb from an adjective by adding the suffix 'ly' and that we should understand 'whitely' as we understand the familiar results of that procedure. Thus we may appeal to an analogy with statements like "He runs slowly."[14] But such an appeal is useless. We mean by "He runs slowly" exactly what we mean by "His run(ning) is slow," and if we were told that the former should be so understood that it is not equivalent to the latter, we would avow that then we have no idea of what it means. But we cannot understand "I am appeared whitely to" as meaning the same as "My (present) being appeared to is white," since the latter is either necessarily false or senseless. And if it made sense and also were true, then the curious result would follow, that after all "I am appeared whitely to" does entail that something is white, though not that a material thing or a sense-datum is white, but that a state of consciousness is white! The paradox is even more striking when by a similar reasoning the conclusion is reached that a state of consciousness is rhomboidal.

Indeed, C. J. Ducasse held that " 'blue', 'bitter', 'sweet', etc., are names not of objects of experience, nor of species of objects of experience, but of *species of experience itself.* What this means is perhaps made clearest by saying that to sense blue is then to sense *bluely,* just as to dance the waltz is to dance 'waltzily'. . . ."[15] He claimed that "blue stands to sensing blue . . . as kind stands to occurrence of a case thereof," and explained that what he meant is that the sensing, the awareness, is "of the determinate sort *called 'blue',* and not that it has, like lapis lazuli, the property of being blue." He also explained that "when I assert of lapis lazuli that it is blue, what I mean is that it is such that whenever I turn my eyes upon it in daylight it causes me to experience something called 'blue'."[16] In *Perceiving* Chisholm distinguished three uses of the word 'blue' and claimed that "frequently the word 'blue' is used to designate a kind or species of appearing."[17] And Herbert Heidelberger has suggested, in defense of Ducasse's view, that "being-a-blue-patch, being-a-blue-speck, being-a-blue-line, and being-a-blue-spot are qualities, just as being blue is a quality, and that all are exemplified by acts of sensing."[18] It would seem that Ducasse and Chisholm would be willing to say that an awareness, or a sensing, or an appearing (a state of sensory consciousness) is blue as long as we understand the saying of this as analogous to saying that Jessie is a cow rather than to saying that Jessie is white. (Compare Aristotle's distinction in the *Categories* between being-predicable-of and being-present-in.) And I assume that Heidelberger's suggestion entails, together with the reasonable assumption that there are blue patches, that some acts of sensing are blue patches. But I suggest that it makes no more sense to speak of a state of consciousness as being of the species blue or as being a blue patch than it does to speak of it as having the property of being blue. It should be noted that Sellars's version of the adverbial theory is not open to this objection, since he holds that the attributes of sense impressions are only analogous to those of the (facing sides) of the material things that are their standard causes.[19] But I tend to think that in this manner—through trans-categorial analogies between characteristics of states of things and characteristics of things—absurdity is avoided only at the cost of excessive vagueness and perhaps vacuity.

There is a second difficulty. It is not true that "I am appeared whitely to" does not entail that something appears white to me. (That it does not is essential to the adverbial theory for dealing with the crucial case of existentially illusory perception.) Since 'appear' is not intended to be understood as a technical term, but is the term with which the admittedly technical 'to sense' is explained, this statement, on the surface singular and nonrelational, makes sense only if understood as elliptical for the general and relational statement "I am appeared whitely to by something." An analogy may make this clearer. The fact that the statement "John was shot" contains no reference to the person who shot John merely shows that it is elliptical for a certain general relational statement, namely "John was shot by someone" or "Someone shot John"; it certainly does not show that the statement is genuinely singular and moreover nonrelational, that John could have been shot even if no one shot him. It should be noted that to introduce the verb 'to sense' as a technical synonym of 'to be appeared to' would not help. The ordinary verb 'to sense' is, of course, transitive and therefore requires an object if it is to be used grammatically. On the other hand, it cannot be intransitive if introduced as a technical synonym of 'to be appeared to', since, as we have just seen, one's being appeared to in some way entails that something appears to one in that way.

A third general difficulty arises when we consider adverbial reformulations of more complex statements such as "I see a triangular red after-image to the left of a circular blue after-image." (Some specific difficulties that such statements pose for the adverbial theory are discussed in detail by Frank Jackson[20] and I shall not repeat them here. But I believe that, contrary to what he supposes, they do not directly affect Sellars's version of the theory.)[21] What would be the adverb that a reformulation of this statement would contain? 'Triangularly-redly-to-the-leftly-of-circularly-bluely' or 'Triangular-red-to-the-left-of-circular-blue-ly' can only be described as a syntactical monstrosity. To suggest that the use of such a phrase would save us from philosophical puzzlement and befuddlement would be disingenuous. Chisholm attempts to deal with this objection in *Person and Object:* "And what of the sort of thing the sense-datum philosopher is trying to describe when he says 'I sense a triangular red sense datum located to the left of a circular blue one'? We needn't coin an adverb to describe the situation. We could say merely: 'There is a way of appearing which is such that (i) it is the way one is appeared to under optimum conditions for perceiving that a red triangle is to the left of a blue circle and (ii) I am appeared to in that way.' "[22] But it is not true that we could say merely this. Chisholm's reformulation is a general statement about *ways* of appearing, i.e., exactly about what would be expressed by the adverbs we need not coin. Such a general statement is no more intelligible than its instantiations would be. But an instantiation of this statement would be a conjunction, the second conjunct of which (that corresponding to (ii)) would have the form "I am appeared to . . .", the empty place being filled precisely with the adverb we are told we need not coin. Unless we can construct such an adverb, we cannot construct the conjunction. And unless we can construct the conjunction, we cannot attach sense to Chisholm's general statement about ways of appearing which the conjunction would instantiate.

III

But the adverbial theory can also be taken as a description, sufficiently general to count as philosophical, of certain states of consciousness, i.e., of what it would call states of sensory consciousness, and its puzzling alleged reformulations of the ordinary statements describing such states may be thought of not as reformulations at all but as purely technical though phenomenologically more adequate descriptions of those states. The required adverbs would be coined and with the verb 'to appear', no less than the verb 'to sense', would be assigned explicitly technical senses. How this might be accomplished is not clear to me. But let us ignore this question. Let us ask, instead, is the adverbial theory phenomenologically adequate *in general?* If it is not, then even if it succeeds in providing intelligible technical descriptions of particular states of consciousness, these descriptions would be false or misleading or inadequate in some other way. If it is, then we would have reason to believe that the required technical descriptions can be provided and explained adequately, some day, by someone. It may be objected that it is a mistake to take the adverbial theory as phenomenological, that at least since Ducasse's work no expositions of the theory have contained serious phenomenological descriptions. But to say this is not to defend the theory; it is to point out a glaring methodological defect.

I shall begin by recalling several (by no means all!) phenomenological objections to the theory that may be found in the literature. Then I shall attempt to identify the common and deeper ground on which they rest. But they must not be regarded as formal arguments against, or counterexamples to, the adverbial theory. A phenomenological objection to a theory can only consist in drawing attention to a phenomenon, or to a feature of a phenomenon, that the theory does not fit adequately or plausibly. I do not doubt that the adverbial theorist can respond to each of the objections to follow by providing some sort of adverbialist description of the phenomenon or feature in question. What I do doubt is that his description would be phenomenologically plausible (even if it were grammatical and intelligible).

Regarding Ducasse's view that "when I see the sensible quality 'blue', this quality is related to my seeing of it, in the same way in which, when a cricketer makes a particular stroke at cricket, say a 'cut', the kind of stroke he makes is related to the striking of it...," G. E. Moore observed: "It seems to me evident that I cannot see the *sensible* quality 'blue', without *directly seeing* something which *has* that quality—a blue patch, or a blue speck, or a blue line, or a blue spot, etc., in the sense in which an after-image, seen with closed eyes, may be any of these things."[23] Ducasse responded by suggesting that "if the sensible quality blue qualifies anything, what it qualifies is only some region of sensible space."[24] But Moore observed, "An after-image may gradually grow fainter, while it remains in the same sensible region: but that sensible region does not grow fainter. And an after-image may sensibly move from one region in sensible space to another: but no region in sensible space can move from one place to another in sensible space." Moore also urged that "in order that you may be seeing a resting blue spot, it is necessary that you should not only (1) be seeing the colour, blue, but also (2) seeing a region (or 'place') in sensible space, and also (3) seeing the colour blue *as* occupying that seen place. And even if the colour blue could be related to your seeing as is a stroke at cricket to the hitting of it, I do not at all understand how a place could be related to an act of seeing in the same way, and still less what account can be given of seeing a colour *as* occupying a place."[25] Ducasse's reply was that "when I observe the 'after-image' moving, all I observe is that different but continuous regions of sensible space sensibly become occupied by sensible blue at continuously successive sensible times," that "to say that the after-image gradually grows fainter while it remains in the same sensible region [means] that the sensible blues seen there at continuously successive times are blues of continuously smaller intensities," and that "the seeing of a place is an 'emergent' of two specific acts, each of which is related to a species of sensing as a 'cut' is related to hitting . . . the seeing a specific sensible place . . . is the psychological *emergent* of [sensing kinaesthetically in a specific way] and of possession of superior 'clearness' by some one of the color qualities seen at the time."[26] Later he suggested that we "may or must speak of being aware not only *bluely,* but also *briefly* (or perhaps lengthily), *extensionally* (or perhaps punctually), *here-ly* (or perhaps there-ly), *abundantly* (or perhaps scantily), etc."[27] Readers may judge for themselves the phenomenological adequacy of Ducasse's reply to Moore.

Sellars has argued that Chisholm's 'sensing redly' would not do as an adequate description of any sensory state, that a phrase such as 'a-red-rectangle-ly sensing' is required.[28] But even the latter phrase would sometimes be inadequate, as becomes evident when we note the fact we would ordinarily describe by saying that a person may see two red rectangles, e.g., two red and rectangular after-images, at the same time. (This point is related to Jackson's but is concerned with the phenomenological adequacy of the adverbial theory, not with the adequacy of its reformulations of certain ordinary statements.) The adverbial theory must allow for phrases such as 'this-red-rectangle-ly sensing' and 'that-red-rectangle-ly sensing' if it is to do justice, first, to the phenomenological fact we would ordinarily describe by saying that we see, not mere *kinds* of after-images, which presumably would be abstract entities, but *particular,* individual after-images; and, second, to the logical fact that if we can say, e.g., that a cow is grazing in the field then we must be able, in principle, to say that this cow, or that cow, is grazing in the field, since we do not mean that a certain abstract zoological species is grazing in the field. But, of course, the phrases I have suggested, if they make sense at all, contain reference, in virtue of the inclusion of the pronouns 'this' and 'that', to what in such contexts may only be individual things, not any properties or sets of properties of sensings. As the case of the two red and rectangular *after-images* shows, it is not true that, as Sellars says, "the question Impression of *which* red rectangle? makes sense only as a request to know which red and rectangular object is *causing* the impression, rather than how the impression is to be *described.*"[29]

Reinhardt Grossmann has pointed out that when a painter sees a rectangular object as trapezoidal he may draw what he sees by producing a trapezoidal shape on his canvas. And he may do this by carefully *reproducing* the shape he sees on the canvas. Surely he attends to a certain *shape* he sees, even though it is not the real shape of the object; he does not attend to his inner states of consciousness and their monadic properties. And even if he does the latter, why does he draw a *trapezoidal* shape, since no state of consciousness is trapezoidal?[30] Sellars, of course, would reply that the painter's visual impression of a trapezoidal shape, though not trapezoidal itself, is analogous in certain respects to physical objects that are trapezoidal on the facing side, that the latter are the model of the former. But as Romane Clark has remarked, "the model does not illuminate what is special and interesting about sense impressions as mental phenomenon: the fact that, and the way in which, the havings of sense impressions are *awarenesses of* the sensible qualities of material things, or, more accurately, of the way in which they are impressions of sensibly qualified things."[31]

We can strengthen Grossmann's example by revising it as follows. A novice at drawing wishes to represent the rectangular side of a building as it appears to him, i.e., as trapezoidal. He looks at it through a piece of clear glass and with crayon traces on the glass the shape the side appears to him (through the glass) to have. He produces on the glass a trapezoidal shape. He simply draws the shape segment by segment so that each segment obliterates a segment of the shape the side appears to him to have. He does not look at the side of the building and then attempt to produce on the glass a shape that would appear to him in the same way that the shape of the side of the building appears to him. No doubt some sort of adverbial analysis of what he does can be offered. But what phenomenological plausibility would it have?

Chisholm has drawn attention to a difficulty the adverbial theory faces in the case of the perception of a complex thing as complex. Ordinarily, when we see a thing we also see some of its parts. For example, we may see a hen and also see one of its feathers as well as the tip of that feather. What would be the sensory state corresponding to such a case of seeing? Chisholm suggests that we may say: "The way in which a man senses with respect to a thing includes ways in which he senses with respect to some, but not all, of the parts of the thing, and the way in which he senses with respect to any part of the thing is included in the way in which he senses with respect to the thing."[32] James Cornman complained that "the notion of one way of sensing being included in another is at best unclear and perhaps meaningless."[33] The truth, I suggest, is that this is unclear and perhaps meaningless not because the notion of inclusion just happens to be inapplicable, or not clearly applicable, to ways of sensing, but because the application of any notion, except those in terms of which the notion of a way of sensing has been introduced, to ways of sensing is unclear and indeterminate. And this is so because the notion of a way of sensing has no independent phenomenological grounding. What properties do we find ways of sensing to have? What relations? Are ways of sensing countable? What are the criteria of identity for them? To say, with Sellars, that these questions are to be answered with appeals to analogies hardly suffices.

This becomes especially evident when we enlarge the scope of Chisholm's example and ask for an adverbial phenomenological description of one's total visual experience at a given time, of a whole "visual field." Not only would the number of parts and the complexity of their organization be likely to be greater. Entirely novel phenomena must be taken into account. There is the familiar figure-ground phenomenon. Merleau-Ponty has observed: "Already a 'figure' on a 'background' contains . . . much more than the qualities presented at a given time. It has an 'outline', which does not 'belong' to the background and which 'stands out' from it; it is 'stable' and offers a 'compact' area of colour, the background on the other hand having no bounds, being of indefinite colouring and 'running on' under the figure. The different parts of the whole—for example, the portions of the figure nearest to the background—possess, then, beside a colour and qualities, a particular *significance*."[34] There are the differences between the part of the visual field one attends to, the immediate context of that part, and the rest of the visual field. As Aron Gurwitsch has argued, "... every total field of consciousness consists of three domains, each domain exhibiting a specific type of organization of its own. The first domain is the *theme*, that which engrosses the mind of the experiencing subject, or as it is often expressed, which stands in the 'focus of his attention'. Second is the *thematic field*, defined as the totality of those data, co-present with the theme, which are experienced as materially relevant or pertinent to the theme and form the background or horizon out of which the theme emerges as the center. The third includes data which, though co-present with, have no relevancy to, the theme and comprise in their totality what we propose to call the *margin*."[35]

Indeed, the very distinction between attending to what one perceives (senses) and not attending to it but still perceiving (sensing) it is phenomenologically crucial. I can see an after-image but not attend to it (I may be preoccupied with other things), or I can see it and also attend to *it* but not to its shape or its color or to any other quality it may have, or attend to its color or shape but not to both and even not to the after-image itself. Even if what we would ordinarily call the seeing of the after-image were objectless, surely the attending to the after-image is not. But to attend to it is precisely to attend to *what* one sees. It is certainly to be distinguished from attending to one's *seeing* the after-image; one may attend to the after-image but not to one's seeing (e.g., if one is interested in the kind of after-image it is, or in its peculiar color or shape), or to one's seeing it but not to the after-image (e.g., if one is interested in the fact, perhaps medically significant, that one is seeing an after-image and the circumstances in which it is occurring, but not at all in its specific characteristics). Indeed, O. R. Jones has observed that "one can be said to look at an after-image," that one "can focus one's eyes on an after-image that is directly in front of one's eyes and thereby see it very clearly, or focus one's eyes on something in the far distance that happens to be in one's direct line of vision, thereby taking scant notice of the after-image or perhaps not noticing it at all," that "there is such a thing as having a second look at the same after-image, which also means that we could take a second count of the features of the after-image [e.g., the number of the points of a star-shaped after-image], thereby checking on the first count," that one can make sure that an after-image "is in the direct line of vision as against being to the one side."[36]

Moreover, an adequate phenomenology must take into account not only the internal organization of a visual field but also the fact that a visual field ordinarily includes reference to the preceding visual fields as well as to those that will succeed it, that it is given as continuous with a certain past as well as with a certain future visual field, that in a sense the awareness of it includes awareness of what precedes it and of what will follow it. Husserl observed: "A bird just now flies through the sunlit garden. In the phase which I have just seized, I find the retentional consciousness of the past shadings of the duration likewise in every fresh now. ... The bird changes its place; it flies. In every situation, the echo of earlier appearances clings to it (i.e., to its appearance)."[37] And elsewhere he remarked that also "there belongs to every external perception its reference from the 'genuinely perceived' sides of the object of perception to the sides 'also meant'—not yet perceived, but only anticipated and, at first, with a non-intuitional emptiness (as the sides that are 'coming' now perceptually): a continuous *protention,* which, with each phase of the perception, has a new sense."[38]

The adverbial theory ignores such subtler yet quite unquestionable, indeed essential, features of sensory states. Can it give an account of them in adverbial terms? And, far more important, would such an account be phenomenologically plausible?

IV

I have mentioned a number of phenomenological difficulties the adverbial theory seems to me to face. Do they have a common ground? Is there a single chief phenomenological objection to the theory? I believe that there is. The adverbial theory is incapable of doing justice to the most obvious and indeed essential phenomenological fact about perceptual consciousness (perhaps all consciousness), namely, its intentionality, its object-directedness.

Indeed, insofar as it is applied to existentially illusory, e.g., hallucinatory, perceptual consciousness, the adverbial theory *begins* precisely with the denial of the intentionality of such consciousness and *consists* in an attempt to make sense of that denial. If a hallucination were intentional, if it were necessarily directed toward an object, then there would be hallucinatory objects, whether these be existent sense-data or nonexistent quasi-Meinongian material objects. Many of the objections in the preceding section consisted in drawing attention to respects in which the denial of the intentionality of existentially illusory perceptual consciousness is phenomenologically implausible.

But does the adverbial theory do justice to the intentionality of existentially veridical perceptual consciousness? It should be noted that it is not a theory of (veridical) perception but of certain states of consciousness it calls being appeared to or sensing, which it sharply distinguishes from perception. Nevertheless, it is usually offered as a component of a theory of perception, namely, of a causal theory. (That this is so should not surprise us. The chief motive for rejecting both the sense-datum theory and the view that we sometimes perceive nonexistent material objects is that neither of these seems to agree with philosophical naturalism. But philosophical naturalism also encourages acceptance of the causal theory of perception.) Thus in *Perceiving* Chisholm defined what he called "the simplest of the nonpropositional senses of 'see' " as follows: " 'S *sees* x' means that, as a consequence of x being a proper *visual* stimulus of S, S senses in a way that is functionally dependent upon the stimulus energy produced in S by x."[39] Now a state of sensing is, according to the adverbial theory, not directed toward an object. So if seeing, in the sense defined, is to be understood as directed toward an object, this fact could consist only in the causal relation between the object and the perceiver's sensing in a certain way. This relation is dyadic and therefore there is a sense in which the perceiver's sensing is directed toward an object. But, clearly, neither is the relation *itself* a case of consciousness. Perception, so understood, is a case of consciousness in virtue of the state of sensing it involves, not in virtue of any causal relation in which that state enters. But, by hypothesis, that element of perceiving which alone can be described as a case of consciousness is also the one the adverbial theory requires us to regard as *not* being object-directed. To be sure, the adverbial theorist can admit all this and still insist that seeing is (by definition) a case of consciousness and also object-directed (in virtue of its involving a certain causal relation), and ignore the fact that what makes it object-directed is not what makes it a case of consciousness. But such a reply would conflict with the spirit, if not the letter, of the thesis of the intentionality of perception. The fact that x is causally related to S's sensing in a certain way can no more reasonably be described as S's being conscious of x than the fact that the presence of carbon monoxide in the air is causally related to S's having a headache can be described as S's being conscious of carbon monoxide. The classical causal theories (e.g., Locke's) are also sense-datum theories and thus can legitimately ascribe to one and the same element of perception (namely, to the sensing of the sense-datum) both the characteristic of being a state of consciousness and the characteristic of being object-directed. But they deny that the perceiver is conscious of the material object perceived and for this reason usually hold that it is the sense-datum, not the material object, that is "directly," "immediately" perceived. Hence the familiar epistemological difficulties of causal theories. There is a clear sense in which according to them we can never get at material objects but only at our sensations. Chisholm concludes his book *Perceiving* by saying: "one *can* get at them—in the only relevant sense of this expression—by *perceiving* them."[40] But the only relevant sense is that of our being conscious or aware of them and this is precisely what we cannot do in Chisholm's simplest nonpropositional sense of 'perceiving'.

In *Perceiving* Chisholm proceeds to introduce a more complex sense of 'see', in which S sees x only if S takes x to have some characteristic. It can be argued that this sense does capture the intentionality of perception though, so to speak, indirectly, through the intentionality of the belief ("taking") that is a component of perceiving in this sense. Indeed, this is exactly what Chisholm does argue in his most recent work on the subject, "Thought and Its Reference."[41] The chief thesis of that article, applied to perception as well as to thought, belief, and imagination, is that "we need not appeal to any 'dimension of intentionality' other than what is involved in a propositional attitude," that "given the concept of a propositional attitude—for example, *acceptance, entertainment*, or *endeavor*—we have all that is needed to add a theory of objective reference, or intentionality, to logic and ontology." The application of this view to perception is contained in the following series of definitions. (1) "S perceives *x* = Df. There is a property such that S perceives *x* to have that property." (2) S perceives *x* to have the property *F* = Df. There is a proposition *p* which is such that: S perceives *p*; and *p* implies *x* to have the property *F*." (3) "*p* implies *x* to have the property *F* = Df. There is a property *G* such that (i) only one thing can have G at a time, (ii) p entails the conjunction of G and the property F, and (iii) x has G." (4) "p entails the property of being F = Df. p entails a proposition which is necessarily such that it is true if and only if something has the property F." Chisholm adds: "Now we may say that a proposition p per- tains to—or is about—a particular thing x, provided only that p implies x to have some property."

I believe that the sense of 'about' Chisholm's definitions capture is that which corresponds to the sense in which the statement "There is one and only one baby who will be born first in Mercy hospital next year, and that baby will receive a gift from the Chamber of Commerce" may be said to be, if true, about a certain baby, whoever that baby may happen to be. And the sense of 'intentionality', or of 'ob- jective reference', they capture is that corresponding to the sense in which someone who knows that the above statement is true would have been said by Russell to have knowledge by description of that baby. This would be so regardless of how unusual the property G in definition (3) is supposed to be. But the phrase 'inten- tionality of consciousness', or 'objective reference' ('reference to an object'), has ordinarily been understood by philosophers as having a very different sense and is relevant to the issue before us only if so understood. This is the sense that corre- sponds, even if only roughly, to what Russell meant by 'knowledge by acquain- tance',[42] and in recent philosophy of language to what is meant by 'reference' as contrasted with 'denotation' and by 'referential use of a definite description' as contrasted with 'attributive use of a definite description'. Not only does Chisholm's theory of intentionality fail to capture this standard concept of intentionality, or of objective reference, but it seems to leave no room for it. He defines even ac- quaintance as follows: "s is acquainted with x at t = Df. There is a p such that (i) p is self-presenting for s at t and (ii) there is a property that p implies x to have,"[43] a self-presenting proposition for s at t being one that is true and necessar- ily such that whenever it is true then it is certain for s. And oneself is the only ob- ject of one's acquaintance, even in this peculiar sense of 'acquaintance', since, ac- cording to Chisholm, a self-presenting proposition can imply only oneself to have some property.[44] It is fair to conclude, I believe, that Chisholm's theory, when ap- plied to perception, does not do justice to the intentionality of perception, in the standard sense of 'intentionality'; it does not really allow us to say that we can get at material objects by perceiving them in the usual sense in which saying this would be understood; it allows us to be "aware" of material objects only by description.

Of course, one can still hold, independently of Chisholm's theory of inten- tionality, that the intentionality of perception consists in the intentionality of the beliefs involved in perception, rather than in any intentionality of the "sense experience" that is also involved in perception. But this view, though common, seems to me incredibly muddled. What does the intentionality of my present true belief that this page is white consist in? The answer becomes evident when we consider the statement expressing that belief and ask, In what sense is the state- ment "This page is white" about this page? The usual answer is that the subject- term is used to refer to this page. But what does this successful referential use consist in? In part, though necessarily, in the fact that I pick out (single out, identify) this page. And how do I accomplish this? Obviously, by *perceiving* the page, since the statement is one expressing a perceptual belief. We should now say that the intentionality of the perceptual belief also consists, at least in part, in the fact that it is a belief about something I have picked out by perceiving it. And *this* perceiving is nonpropositional and *its* intentionality is direct, not mediated by any belief that may happen to accompany it.

It is the intentionality of perception so understood that alone explains the crucial phenomenological fact about perception that *prima facie* it provides us with evidence for the existence of material objects, that it appears to us as a sort of contact with the external world. (Whether it *really* provides us with such evidence is of course one of the chief problems of epistemology. Its solution would rest not only on phenomenological considerations but also on a detailed philosophical elucidation and defense of a notion of evidence that could yield such a solution, if this notion is primitive; and if it is defined, then in a detailed philosophical elucidation and defense, dialectical as well as phenomenological, of the *primitive* epistemic notions in terms of which it is defined.) Both of the alternatives to the adverbial theory mentioned in section I do justice to this fact. According to one of them, in every case of perception the perceiver is conscious of a material object, even though this object might not exist. According to the other, in every case of perception the perceiver is conscious of an existent object that has properties the front surface of a material object could have and that perhaps could even be identical with the front surface of a material object. For both, the phenomenological fact that we regard perception as providing us with evidence for the existence of material objects, that it appears to us as providing us with such evidence, is completely understandable. But according to the adverbial theory, a state of sensory consciousness is an objectless state. Its occurrence may in fact constitute evidence for the existence of a material object, but it can hardly appear to one to do so. It is not directed toward such an object, or toward an object that is just like the front surface of a material object; it is not directed toward an object at all. Nor, of course, does it itself have any of the distinctive properties of a material object, even if the properties it does have were analogous to some of those of material objects. Indeed, it may be caused by a material object, but this would be precisely the sort of fact for which we require perceptual evidence, not the sort of fact that constitutes perceptual evidence. The occurrence of such a sensory state would not appear to one as evidence for the existence of the material object that stands to it in the appropriate causal relation, just as the occurrence of a headache caused by the presence of carbon monoxide in the air does not appear to one as evidence for the presence of carbon monoxide in the air.[45]

<h1 style="text-align:center">V</h1>

Of course, as I warned at the outset, the above phenomenological appeals are not conclusive. Each can be rejected by the adverbial theorist as either question-begging or phenomenologically unsound. To some extent their inconclusiveness is due to the very nature of such appeals. But, I suggest, it is also due to the fact that the adverbial theory is proposed as an account of the nature of what philosophers and psychologists have called sensations, sense impressions, sense experience. It has been argued repeatedly and by many that there are no such things at all, unless the terms 'sensation', 'sense impression', and 'sense experience' are understood in ways that make them irrelevant to the adverbial theory. If so, then we should not be surprised that our phenomenological objections to its description of them seem inconclusive. It is not so much that the adverbial theory is mistaken as that it has no subject matter.

That the terms 'sense impression' and 'sense experience' are philosophical creatures, introduced for a variety of reasons and in many, very different ways, should require no argument. The latter term is relatively innocuous, since it can reasonably be understood as a synonym of 'sense perception', i.e., as the general term corresponding to specific terms such as 'seeing', 'hearing', 'smelling', 'tasting', '(tactile) feeling', perhaps also 'feeling' as used in speaking of feeling pains in various parts of our bodies as well as feeling the motions of such parts. But the former term is not innocuous. It clearly suggests the pseudoscientific picture of sense perception as consisting in an elaborate causal chain that begins with the object perceived and terminates in a "mental event." Since the chain itself *is* the perception, this mental event must be something else, and the term 'sense impression' is coined as the name of that postulated last link of the chain. In this picture the zoological ("naturalistic") conception of man and the conception of man's mind as a ghost in a machine form a curious and unholy union.

The term 'sensation' is, of course, not a philosophical creature. But, as Gilbert Ryle repeatedly pointed out,[46] its ordinary uses are not at all those required by philosophers. Sometimes it is a name of our consciousness of such things as pains and tickles, sometimes it is applied to the objects of such consciousness. Thus it is a rough synonym of 'feeling', in one of the latter's uses, and shares its ambiguity. (We do not speak of sensing or feeling painfully, but of sensing or feeling, or having, pain in some part of our body, or of some part of our body hurting.) That there are sensations (and sensings) in this sense is phenomenologically obvious, even if, for metaphysical reasons, we were to identify them with certain states of the brain. But this is not the sense the adverbial theory needs. The sense it needs is that in which we may also speak, for example, of visual sensations. But common discourse is entirely silent on the existence of such things. If someone were to speak of having a sensation when seeing something, he would be understood most probably as meaning that his eyes hurt or tickle, or that he is feeling nauseous or excited, and so on. And we say that the drunk sees pink rats, or at least that he "thinks" he sees them, not that he senses, or has a sensation of, pink rats. How seriously should we take this fact about common discourse? How seriously should we take its failure to reflect the existence of what are alleged to be the most common psychological occurrences? Perhaps not very seriously if introspection revealed such occurrences. But does it? Regarding the notion of a sensation understood as just such an occurrence, Sartre remarks: ". . . it is pure fiction. It does not correspond to anything which I experience in myself or with regard to the Other."[47] Merleau-Ponty optimistically concurs: "It is unnecessary to show, since authors are agreed on it, that this notion corresponds to nothing in our experience."[48] The similar views held by Moore and Ryle, among many other English-speaking philosophers, are too familiar to require more than mention.

Of course, the term 'sensation' could be introduced as a technical substitute for 'perception' in the latter's first sense, distinguished in section I, in which we may be said to perceive both existent and nonexistent things; or, if we accept the sense-datum theory, as a technical term for our perception ("apprehension") of sense-data; or, for the purposes of psychology, as a technical term for our perception of "a simple quality like 'hot', 'cold', 'red', 'noise', 'pain', apprehended irrelatively to other things."[49] These technical uses of 'sensation' would be entirely explicable, as they ought to be, in terms of our ordinary perceptual verbs and would be of no use to the adverbial theory, which requires that sensations be objectless states of consciousness.

I shall conclude this paper by drawing attention to the larger implications of the view that there are objectless states of consciousness. In the previous section I argued that it is incompatible with the thesis of the intentionality of perception. But even if it were not so, it would still be incompatible with the more general and more fundamental thesis of the intentionality of *all* consciousness. Is intentionality, object-directedness, an essential characteristic of consciousness? Can anything be both a state of consciousness and nonintentional? This, I suggest, is the most important question to be raised in regard to the adverbial theory. If the correct answer to it is negative, then the adverbial theory is false, for reasons far deeper than those I have discussed so far. Is the answer negative? We are told that at least being in pain and being depressed (in general, not by anything in particular) are states of consciousness that have no objects. But surely to be in pain is to feel, to be conscious of, pain in some part of one's body (even if only a phantom part), to be conscious of that part's hurting (not of our hurting!), and it is plausible to say that to be depressed in general is to be conscious, perhaps only in imagination, of the world as a whole, or of one's life, or of oneself, as depressing.[50] But the defense of the intentionality of consciousness must rest on firmer foundations than ping-pong games with examples and counterexamples. It must issue from an account of the nature of intentionality and of the nature of consciousness. Sartre has argued (as Moore in effect had also done, in "The Refutation of Idealism") that to take the intentionality of consciousness seriously is to recognize that consciousness is perfectly transparent, that it has no contents, that it exhausts itself in its object, that its being consists in its revelation of its object.[51] If this is so, then of course the adverbial theory must be false, since it consists precisely in the claim that certain states of consciousness ("sensings") have an elaborate structure of monadic characteristics ("ways of sensing"), that they are, as Sartre would say, centers of opacity within consciousness.

But if Sartre's rather Moorean view of consciousness is accepted, together with its inseparable companion, his Humean and perhaps also Moorean view that not only is the self, if understood as the subjective pole of a relation of consciousness, unobservable but the very idea of such a self makes no sense,[52] then we are led to the Sartrean conclusion that consciousness is *nothing* distinct from its object. This conclusion is, so to speak, the mirror image of the adverbial theory. Consciousness indeed cannot be a relation, since it lacks one of the needed relata, but the relatum it lacks is the subject, the self, not the object. So the further, no longer Sartrean, conclusion seems to follow that consciousness can be only a monadic characteristic, though not a characteristic of the subject but a characteristic of the object.[53] But we are now faced with considerations that go far beyond the aims of this paper.[54]

Notes

1. I wish to thank Albert Casullo, Evan Fales, and William S. Robinson for their incisive criticism of an earlier version of this paper.

2. The theory has achieved its prominence chiefly through the efforts of Wilfrid Sellars and Roderick M. Chisholm; indeed, it is an essential part of their philosophical views. But there are important differences between their versions of the theory. Moreover, the most extended exposition and defense of it are to be found in the writings of C. J. Ducasse of several decades ago. For textual references to these philosophers, see below. Still earlier, the main principle of the theory was defended by G. Dawes Hicks in his contribution to a symposium, with G. E. Moore, W. E. Johnson, J. A. Smith, and James Ward, on "Are the Materials of Sense Affections of the Mind?", *Proceedings of the Aristotelian Society* 17 (1917): 418-58.

3. Gilbert Ryle, "Ordinary Language," *The Philosophical Review* 62 (1953): 167-86.

4. I discuss these difficulties in detail in *Being Qua Being: A Theory of Identity, Existence, and Predication* (Bloomington and London, 1979).

5. The classical exposition of the sense-datum theory is H. H. Price's, in *Perception* (London, 1932).

6. I consider them in detail in *The Concept of Knowledge* (Evanston, 1970), part 3.

7. See, for example, Wilfrid Sellars, "Ontology and the Philosophy of Mind in Russell," in George Nakhnikian, ed., *Bertrand Russell's Philosophy* (New York, 1974), pp. 97-98; Roderick M. Chisholm, *Person and Object* (La Salle, 1976), p. 203, note 55, but contrast the doctrine in "Thought and its Reference," *American Philosophical Quarterly* 14 (1977):167-72.

8. Cf. J. L. Austin on "linguistic phenomenology" in "A Plea for Excuses," in *Collected Papers* (Oxford, 1961), p. 130.

9. Cf. Wilfrid Sellars, *Science and Metaphysics* (London, 1968), chap. I. But Sellars does not argue that the explanatory role of the postulated sense impressions requires that they be understood adverbially. His theory of sense impressions must not be confused, of course, with the "theory of sensa" which he imagines science as adopting in the future.

10. Roderick M. Chisholm, *Perceiving: A Philosophical Study* (Ithaca, 1957). p. 122.

11. Roderick M. Chisholm, *Theory of Knowledge,* 2nd ed. (Englewood Cliffs, N.J., 1977), p. 30.

12. Sellars, *Science and Metaphysics,* p. 168.

13. See note 9, also p. 6.

14. Chisholm, *Person and Object,* p. 49.

15. C. J. Ducasse, *Nature, Mind, and Death* (La Salle, 1951), p. 259.

16. *Ibid.,* pp. 264-65.

17. Chisholm, *Perceiving,* p. 127.

18. Herbert Heidelberger, review of C. J. Ducasse, *Truth, Knowledge, and Causation,* in *The Journal of Philosophy* 70 (1973):755-59.

19. See, for example, *Science and Metaphysics,* chap. I; *Science, Perception, and Reality* (London, 1963), pp. 91-95; "The Adverbial Theory of the Objects of Sensation," *Metaphilosophy* 6 (1975):144-60. For an argument against such trans-categorial analogies see Bruce Aune, "Comments," and for a defense of them see Sellars, "Rejoinder," both in Hector-Neri Castañeda, ed., *Intentionality, Minds, and Perception* (Detroit, 1967).

20. Frank Jackson, "On The Adverbial Analysis of Visual Experience," *Metaphilosophy* 6 (1975):127-35; Jackson, "The Existence of Mental Objects," *American Philosophical Quarterly* 13 (1976):33-40; Jackson, *Perception* (Cambridge, 1977).

21. See Sellars's reply to Jackson in "The Adverbial Theory of the Objects of Sensation."

22. Chisholm, *Person and Object,* p. 50.

23. "Reply to My Critics," in Paul Arthur Schilpp, ed., *The Philosophy of G. E. Moore,* 3rd ed. (La Salle, 1968), p. 659. Ducasse's view is defended in his "Moore's Refutation of Idealism," in the same volume. This edition also includes letters that Ducasse and Moore exchanged on the topic.

24. A letter from Ducasse to Moore, in *The Philosophy of G. E. Moore,* p. 687b.

25. A letter from Moore to Ducasse, in *The Philosophy of G. E. Moore,* p. 687h.

26. A letter from Ducasse to Moore, in *The Philosophy of G. E. Moore,* pp. 687k-687m. Ducasse develops this view in "Objectivity, Objective Reference, and Perception," *Philosophy and Phenomenological Research* 2 (1941):43-78. See also *Nature, Mind, and Death,* pp. 282-86, 304-53.

27. Ducasse, *Nature, Mind, and Death,* p. 284.

28. Cf. "The Structure of Knowledge," in Hector-Neri Castañeda, ed., *Action, Knowledge, and Reality* (Indianapolis, 1975). p. 312.

29. Sellars, *Science and Metaphysics,* p. 22.

30. Reinhardt Grossmann, review of James W. Cornman, *Perception, Common Sense, and Science,* in *International Studies in Philosophy* 8 (1976):210-13.

31. Romane Clark, "The Sensuous Content of Perception," in *Action, Knowledge, and Reality,* p. 121.

32. Roderick M. Chisholm, *Theory of Knowledge,* 1st ed. (Englewood Cliffs, N.J., 1966) p. 98. Compare Sellars, *Science and Metaphysics,* pp. 24-27.

33. James Cornman, *Perception, Common Sense, and Science* (New Haven and London, 1975), p. 75. But I find Cornman's own formulation, "In some cases, the sensing in a wing-of-a-hen way is also a sensing in a hen-way," no improvement over Chisholm's. In virtue of *what* is one sensing included in both of certain two classes of sensings while another sensing is included in only one of these classes?

34. Maurice Merleau-Ponty, *Phenomenology of Perception,* trans. Colin Smith (London, 1962), p. 13.

35. Aron Gurwitsch, *The Field of Consciousness* (Pittsburgh, 1964), pp. 4-5.

36. O. R. Jones, "After-Images," *American Philosophical Quarterly* 9 (1972):151-52.

37. Edmund Husserl, *The Phenomenology of Internal Time Consciousness,* trans. James S. Churchill (Bloomington, 1964), p. 149.

38. Edmund Husserl, *Cartesian Meditations,* trans. Dorion Cairns (The Hague, 1960), p. 44.

39. Chisholm, *Perceiving,* p. 149.

40. *Ibid.,* p. 197.

41. Roderick M. Chisholm, "Thought and Its Reference," *American Philosophical Quarterly* 14 (1977):167-72. All quotations from this article are from pp. 167-68. Compare Ducasse, "Objectivity, Objective Reference, and Perception."

42. "I say that I am *acquainted* with an object when I have a direct cognitive relation to that object, i.e., when I am directly aware of the object itself. When I speak of a cognitive relation here, I do not mean the sort of relation which constitutes judgment, but the sort which constitutes presentation." *Mysticism and Logic* (London, 1917), p. 209.

43. Chisholm, *Person and Object*, p. 30.

44. *Ibid.*, pp. 24-30. "Thought and its Reference," p. 169.

45. Compare Sartre: " . . . it is sensation which I give as the basis of my knowledge of the external world. This basis could not be the foundation of a *real* contact with things; it does not allow us to conceive of an intentional structure of the mind." (*Being and Nothingness*, trans. Hazel Barnes [New York, 1956] , p. 314.) James Cornman is sensitive to this difficulty of the adverbial theory: "Somehow . . . we must combine the adverbial sensing theory of sense experience with the perceptual presentation view of compatible common-sense realism." He admits that the statement "Each event of a person immediately perceiving a physical object, *p*, occurs when and only when some event of the person sensing occurs as a result of stimulus from *p* appropriately affecting him" expresses neither logical equivalence nor causal connection, and suggests that it expresses "a criteriological equivalence, and about that I am only able to say that it is like the relationship between right-making characteristics and being right." (*Perception, Common Sense, and Science*, pp. 340-42.) He is also sensitive to the implausibility of supposing that in veridical perception perceiving and sensing are two events, and suggests that they are contingently identical (pp. 342-43).

46. See Gilbert Ryle, *The Concept of Mind* (London, 1949), pp. 200-201, pp. 240-44; Ryle, "Sensation," in *Contemporary British Philosophy, Third Series*, ed. H. D. Lewis (London, 1956). At the end of the latter he acknowledges that we need some term to describe the "affinity" of "having an after-image and seeing a misprint." I suggest that the term needed becomes evident if instead of the idiomatic expression 'having an after-image' we use the no less ordinary expression 'seeing an after-image'. That term is 'sense datum', not 'sensation'.

47. Sartre, *Being and Nothingness*, p. 314.

48. Merleau-Ponty, *Phenomenology of Perception*, p. 3.

49. William James, *Psychology* (New York, 1890), vol. II, p. 1. According to James, sensation differs from perception "only in the extreme simplicity of its object or content" (*Psychology*, p. 2).

50. Compare Sartre's theory of emotional consciousness in *The Emotions: Outline of a Theory*, trans. Bernard Frechtman (New York, 1948).

51. Sartre, *Being and Nothingness*, p. lxi.

52. See *The Transcendence of the Ego*, trans. Forrest Williams and Robert Kirkpatrick (New York, 1957). Compare G. E. Moore's important but neglected article, "The Subject-Matter of Psychology," *Proceedings of the Aristotelian Society* n.s. 10 (1910), especially pp. 51-55.

53. Although I would not describe this conclusion as Sartrean, it is worth noting that in *Being and Nothingness* he says: "If sight is not the sum of visual sensations, can it not be the system of seen objects?" (p. 316).

54. I discuss some of these considerations in Appendix B of *Being Qua Being: A Theory of Identity, Existence, and Predication*.

The Intentionality of
Cognitive States

FRED I. DRETSKE

To know, perceive, or remember is to know, perceive, or remember *something*. Subtleties aside, this something may be either a thing or a fact.[1] We remember a party, see a game, and know a person; but we also remember that the party was a bore, see that the game has started, and know that Hilda is a grouch.

It may be, as some have argued, that we cannot know, remember, or perceive a thing without knowing, remembering, or perceiving some fact about that thing. According to this view, what we know, perceive, and remember is always propositional in character. To describe someone as knowing a person, thing, or event is just to describe the person as knowing some relevant facts about the item in question without disclosing, by one's manner of description, *what facts* it is that are known.

I do not intend to quarrel with this view. I think it mistaken, but I do not have the time to argue the point here. My objectives are more limited. I mean to discuss our *propositional* attitudes and, in particular, those propositional attitudes that involve the possession of knowledge. I mean, that is, to discuss those mental states whose expression calls for a factive nominal, a that-clause, as complement to the verb and, moreover, whose expression implies that the subject of that state *knows* what is expressed by that factive nominal. I am concerned with knowing, seeing, and remembering that your dog is lame, *not* with knowing, seeing and remembering your (lame) dog. I shall call such states *cognitive* states. The *belief* that your dog is lame is not, on this characterization, a cognitive state.

1. INTENTIONAL STATES

If I know that the train is moving and you know that its wheels are turning, it does not follow that I know what you know just because the train never moves without its wheels turning. More generally, if all (and only) Fs are G, one can nonetheless know that something is F without knowing that it is G. Extensionally equivalent predicate expressions, when applied to the same object, do not (necessarily) express the same cognitive content. Furthermore, if Tom is my uncle, one cannot infer (with a possible exception to be mentioned later) that if S knows that Tom is getting married, he thereby knows that my uncle is getting married. The content of a cognitive state, and hence the cognitive state itself, depends (for its identity) on something beyond the extension or reference of the terms we use to express the content. I shall say, therefore, that a description of a cognitive state is non-extensional.

Any state of affairs having a propositional content whose expression is non-extensional I shall call an *intentional* state. On this characterization our cognitive states are all intentional states. The truth of the statement "S knows that *a* if *F*" does not depend, simply, on the extension or reference of the terms '*a*' and '*F*'. This statement therefore describes an intentional state of S. I think that this use of the word 'intentional' is in reasonably close agreement with current philosophical usage—even if it does not capture all the Brentano intended in speaking of intentionality as the mark of the mental.

Intentional states (and, therefore, cognitive states) appear to have something like *meanings* (propositions) as their object (content), as that *on which* the mind is directed. I say things appear this way since virtually any change in meaning (in the terms used to express the content) generates a different content and, thus, a different intentional state.

A materialist confronts the task of explaining, or explaining away, this intentional feature of cognitive states. Some account must be given of how a purely physical system could occupy states having a content of this sort. Or, failing this, some explanation must be given of why we systematically delude ourselves into thinking that *we* occupy states of this sort. What follows is a crude blueprint, an attempt to sketch, along realistic lines, an explanation for how purely physical systems *could* (because even the simplest mechanical systems *do*) occupy intentional states of the appropriate kind. The distinctive character of our cognitive states lies, not in their intentionality (for even the humble thermometer occupies intentional states), but in their *degree* of intentionality.

2. BEHAVIOR AND MEANING

Central state materialists find themselves tugged in two directions: *inward* as the locus of our mental states; and *outward* as the locus for whatever meaning or content these central states might have. The result of this tension is often a curious blend of behaviorism with psychological realism. Our psychological states are genuine *inner* states (to be distinguished from the behavior they help to produce), but everything that makes them psychological (in contrast, say, to gastronomical or *just* neurological) is borrowed, so to speak, from the sort of behavior they help to determine. The flower of mentality has its roots inside, but all the blossoms are outside. It is behaviorism with a displaced reference. Some call it functionalism.

The approach to intentionality is typical. The output, or some of the output, of language-using creatures has a semantic dimension (a meaning) that neatly parallels the kind of content we (as materialists) want to attribute to the system's internal physical states in describing its cognitive processes. Why not let the internal states "borrow" this content?[2] This, of course, would make our attributions of content to the internal states themselves (in our ordinary descriptions of people knowing and remembering things) a bit of a fiction. The internal states would not literally have this content. Nevertheless, this is the best that can be done with the confused ontology of ordinary language. The idea, roughly, is that if S utters the words, "The sun is shining," and if his utterance of these words is causally explicable in terms of a central neural state, then this central state acquires the content: The sun is shining. It, so to speak, shares in the glory of meaning this. By virtue of this borrowed content, the central state acquires the status of a *belief:* the belief that the sun is shining. Harnessing this account of belief with a causal theory of knowledge, one then goes on the say that if this state is brought about (in the right way) by a shining sun, then it constitutes S's *knowledge* that the sun is shining. The verbal output provides the "pattern" for assigning semantic properties (meaning or content) to those internal, neurological states that produced it. The intentional structure of our cognitive states is merely a reflection of the semantic properties of the output they produce.

What about creatures that do not have a language? One option is to simply deny that they (dogs, cats, birds) know or believe anything at all—at least nothing expressible in *our* language. My dog does not know (believe, think) that I am leaving. He just *acts* that way. My preparations to leave may *cause* him to act that way. It may even be true to say that the dog sees me getting ready to leave (and his seeing me getting ready to leave is why he is getting so excited), but he does not *see that* I am getting ready to leave. He has no internal state with this content because he exhibits no output with precisely this meaning (a meaning, it should be noted, that contrasts with "My master is putting on his coat and moving toward the door").[3]

Another option in the case of creatures without language is to appeal to other, non-verbal, behavior as the source of cognitive content. Food is to be eaten. Predators are to be avoided. It is the appropriateness of these responses to one thing rather than another, just as it is (given the ordinary meanings of the words) the appropriateness of the utterance "The sun is shining" to one state of affairs (a shining sun) rather than another, that confers on the internal source of this behavior the derived content "This is food" or "That is a predator (or dangerous)."[4] Roughly speaking, if the dog eats it, he must think it is food. But thinking it is food is an explanatory artifact—nothing more or less than being in a state (whatever neural state this is) that prompts the dog to salivate, chew, swallow, etc. Once again, the intentional character of the internal state, its having a content expressible as "This is food," is only a reflection of the properties of the consequent behavior. The dog knows or believes that there is food in front of him, he occupies a physical state having this content or meaning, *only* because the state prompts the dog to exhibit behavior appropriate to food. If the dog has no response that is appropriate to X (e.g., to daisies *qua* daisies), then he is incapable of believing or knowing that anything is an X.

This behavioristically inspired approach to the analysis of intentional structure has a certain degree of plausibility. Nevertheless, it always stumbles on the circularity inherent in analyzing cognitive content in terms of something (verbal behavior, appropriateness of response) that lacks the relevant properties (meaning, appropriateness) unless the internal source of that behavior is *already*, and *independently* of its producing that output, conceived of as having a determinate content. The appropriateness of what we do depends on what we know and believe (not to mention what we desire and intend). There is nothing inappropriate about my saying, "The sun is shining" at midnight if I sincerely believe the sun is shining. At least there is nothing inappropriate about it in any sense of 'appropriate' that tells us something about what I know or believe. Is it inappropriate for the hen *not* to run from the fox? This depends. It depends, among other things, on whether the hen *recognizes* the fox, on whether she *wants* to protect her chicks, on what her *purposes* are. Independently of these factors, the hen's behavior is neither appropriate nor inappropriate. To describe the hen, for example, as engaging in diversionary tactics (to protect her chicks) is already to describe her behavior in a way that presupposes an intentional structure for the internal source of that behavior. The appropriateness of response, then, insofar as this is relevant to what the organism believes and intends,[5] is a property the response acquires only in virtue of its production by internal states having a content.

This is particularly obvious with verbal behavior. If what I *say* is to have a content of the sort required, then it cannot be understood as merely the *sounds* I make. It must be understood as the meaning, the semantic content, of these sounds. But this, I submit, is circular.[6] Until we have a system, or community of systems, with beliefs and intentions, the output does not have the requisite *semantic* structure (meaning). Internal states cannot acquire their meaning from the output they produce because until the internal states have a content, they cannot produce a relevantly meaningful output. Replacing a door bell by a device (tape recorder, etc.) that announced "Someone is at the door" whenever the door button is pushed brings one no closer to a system with internal states having content. The output of such a device may be said to *mean* that someone is at the door, but this is either Grice's *natural* meaning (in which case the ringing bell means the same thing) or it is a meaning *we* assign it in virtue of the acoustic pattern's significance in *our* system of communication. In the latter case the output may be said to mean something in the relevant *linguistic* sense, but this is a meaning it derives from its occurrence in an appropriate community of fully intentional systems (speakers of the language). Output or behavior has nothing relevant to give except where the gift is not needed.

3. THE INTENTIONAL STRUCTURE OF INFORMATION

The problem of intentionality loses some of its mystery if we think of simple communication systems. If we approach the problem in this way, it soon becomes clear that intentionality, rather than being a "mark of the mental," is a pervasive feature of *all* reality—mental and physical. Even the humble thermometer occupies intentional states. What is distinctive, and hence problematic, about our cognitive states is not the fact that they have a content, not the fact that this content has intentional characteristics (for this is true as well of the thermometer), but the fact that they have a *higher order* intentionality.

To see why this is so, consider a simple information processing device. The fundamental idea of Communication Theory is that the amount of information transmitted between two points is a function of the degree of nomic or lawful dependence between the events occurring in these two locations. The mathematical details are not really important for our purposes. What is important is that the quantity of information arriving at R (the receiver) from S (source) depends on the set of conditional probabilities relating events at R and S. If there is only a chance correlation between what occurs at S and what occurs at R, then no information passes between them. From this extreme we pass through a continuum of possible gradations until we reach a situation in which the flow of information between S and R is optimal: a noiseless (or equivocation free) channel between S and R. For this condition to exist, a certain set of conditional probabilities must obtain. Every conditional probability must be either 0 or 1—strict nomic dependence between the events occurring at S and R.[7]

It is important to emphasize that the conditional probabilities governing the flow of information are *nomic* or *lawful* in character. It is not enough that the type of event at the receiver should correspond, one-to-one, to the type of event occurring at the source. It is essential to the transmission of information that this correspondence have its basis in a lawful dependence, statistical or deterministic, between the events at S and R. For me to communicate, telepathically, with you it is not enough to have thoughts occurring to you that correspond exactly to what I am thinking. For genuine communication to occur, for you to receive information from me, it is essential that there be a lawful dependence between what I am thinking and what you think I am thinking.

If we conceive of information in this way, a thermometer may be said to carry information about its environment to the extent to which its state (e.g., the height of the mercury column) depends, lawfully, on the ambient temperature. And a pressure gauge carries information about, say, altitude.

With only these rudiments of Communication Theory in hand, we are in a position to appreciate an important fact about the transmission, receipt, and processing of information. Information has an intentional structure that it derives from the *nomic* relationships on which it depends. Since a nomic relation between properties (magnitudes) F and G is an intentional relationship, information, understood as the measure of this mutual dependency, inherits this structure. If F is lawfully related to G, and 'G' is extensionally equivalent to 'H', F is not necessarily related in a lawful way to H. If it is a natural law that things having the property F have the property G, it does not follow that there is a law relating the property F to the property H just because, as a matter of fact, everything that is G is also H (and vice versa). To use a well-known example, drunks may have liver problems and these problems may have their basis in a nomic relationship between excessive alcoholic intake and the condition of the liver. But we cannot infer from this fact that there is a nomic connection between sitting on park bench B and liver trouble just because all, and only, drunks sit (have sat, are sitting, and will sit) on park bench B. To reach this conclusion we would first have to be assured that there was some *lawful* regularity between sitting on the bench and being a drunk. This, though, is an assurance not provided by being told, simply, that there is an extensional equivalence between 'is a drunk' and 'sits on park bench B'.

It is obvious that there is a vast network of lawful relationships existing between the properties and magnitudes of our physical universe. Some of these we know. Others we do not. It is this kind of nomic dependence that underlies and supports our assertion of subjunctive conditionals of the form: "The metal would not have expanded unless it was heated"; "If the capacitor had discharged, it would have moved the galvanometer needle"; and "The pressure would not increase unless we were losing altitude." It is also obvious, except perhaps to a few philosophers, that statements describing the lawful relations between properties and magnitudes give expression to something more than an *extensional* relationship between these properties or magnitudes. To assert that it is a *law* that all Fs are G is to assert something stronger than that nothing is (was or will be) F that is not G.

It is not my purpose in this paper to analyze this feature of natural laws. Sufficient unto my purpose is the fact that laws *have* this feature. This, I think, is undeniable. How it is to be explained is another matter.

Since, therefore, the amount of information transmitted from one point to another depends on the system of nomic regularities that prevail between the events at these points, the information reaching the receiver about the events occurring at the source has the very same intentional character as do the underlying regularities. Even when 'F' and 'G' are extensionally equivalent, one can receive the information that something is F without receiving the information that something is G. One can receive information about property F (e.g., x is F) without receiving information about property G (e.g., x is G) even though nothing is F that is not G. This is possible because the signal one receives may have properties that depend, lawfully, on x's being F without depending, lawfully, on x's being G. And in such a case the signal carries information about the one property that it does not carry about the other.

Any physical system, then, whose internal states are lawfully dependent, in some statistically significant way, on the value of an external magnitude (in the way a properly connected measuring instrument is sensitive to the value of the quantity it is designed to measure) qualifies as an intentional system. It occupies states having a content that can be expressed only in non-extensional ways. A device that measures the value of F, and hence occupies a state with the content "F is increasing," does not (necessarily) occupy a state with the content "G is increasing" even though G always increases when F increases.

What this suggests, of course, is that the intentionality of our cognitive states has its source in the intentionality of informational structures. S can know that x is F without knowing that x is G (despite the extensional equivalence of 'F' and 'G') *because* S can receive information to the effect that x is F without receiving information to the effect that x is G. And if we assume, as it seems plausible to assume, that S cannot know that x is G unless he receives *some* quantity of information to the effect that x is G, then we have a tidy explanation for the intentionality of epistemic contexts. One cannot substitute co-referential expressions, *salva veritate,* in the context "S knows that . . ." because knowledge requires information and statements describing the information S has received are themselves non-extensional. And this intentionality derives, in turn, from the non-extensionality of statements describing *nomic* dependencies. Cognitive states exhibit an intentional structure because they are, fundamentally, nomically dependent states.

I have, so far, concentrated on the predicate term in those clauses we use to give expression to what is known. Despite extensional equivalence, S's knowing that x is F is different than S's knowing that x is G, and this difference is to be explained by the difference between receiving information to the effect that x is F and receiving information to the effect that x is G. It may be thought, however, that the parallel between knowledge and information collapses when we examine the subject term, the 'x', in these expressions. Someone can know that the blonde, standing in the corner, is angry without knowing that my sister is angry despite the fact that the blonde is my sister. That is to say, the context "S knows that . . ." is opaque, not only with respect to the embedded predicate expressions, but also with respect to the embedded subject terms. How is this feature of our epistemic descriptions to be explained?

As it turns out, it can be explained quite easily. I would not have raised the point (not, at least, at this time) unless it could be. A signal can carry the information that A is F without carrying the information that it is, in fact, A which is F. S can receive information that a woman (who happens to be my sister) is angry without receiving the information that she (the angry woman) is my sister. A thermometer, immersed in water, can tell us what the temperature of the water is, but it does not thereby tell us *what it is* that has that temperature. When partial information of this kind is received, we can explain why S does not know that my sister is angry even though the person he knows to be angry is my sister. He does not know it because, although he received the information that she (my sister) was angry, he did not (or may not have) received the information that she was my sister.

4. HIGHER LEVELS OF INTENTIONALITY

It seems, then, that the intentionality associated with our cognitive states can be viewed as a manifestation of an underlying network of nomic regularities. If, therefore, the lawful dependence of one magnitude on another is part of the physicist's picture of reality, then intentionality is also part of that picture. Hence, to the extent to which the mentality of our cognitive states resides in their intentional structure, knowledge, perception, and memory are perfectly "natural" phenomena. There is nothing unique about them.

It may seem, however, that I have gone too far. In my efforts to naturalize the mental, have I not succeeded, only, in mentalizing the natural? For if the intentional structure of our cognitive states can be understood in terms of their information-carrying status (where the latter is understood, merely, as their nomic dependence on the condition defining the content of the cognitive state), then not only will living organisms perceive, know, and remember, but such simple devices as galvanometers, television sets, and pressure gauges will also qualify for cognitive attributes. For they also receive, process, and store information of the kind *now* under discussion, and their outputs are variously regulated by this information. Hence, they occupy intentional states of the same kind. Of course, they do not behave in interestingly diverse ways; they do not exhibit what we think of as intelligent behavior; they do not *learn*. But since behavior has already been rejected as the source of intentional structure, their dull, predictable responses to information-bearing stimuli should be irrelevant. According to the present line of argument, simple information-processing devices, mechanical artifacts, should have internal states possessing a content of the same sort that living organisms have when they know or perceive that something is the case.

The danger here is real. If galvanometers occupy intentional states, the conclusion to be drawn is not that galvanometers know things, but that knowledge is not *simply* a matter of occupying an intentional state, a state with a content corresponding to what is known when something is known.

Let me clarify this by contrasting the intentional state of a galvanometer (a device for detecting and measuring electrical current flow) and a genuine cognitive state—the state *we* are in when we know, for example, that there is a current flow between points A and B. Despite the fact that galvanometers receive, process, and display (for the convenience of someone using the instrument) information about affairs external to them, they do not occupy cognitive states. The reason they do not is not because their internal states (the amount of torque, say, on the mobile armature to which a pointer is affixed) fail to have a content, a content to which we can give expression with the sentence "There is a current flow between points A and B." The instrument's internal states certainly *have* this content. If they did not, *we* could never *learn* that there was a current flow between A and B by using the instrument. We get this information *from* the instrument; we depend on it to deliver, transmit, something with this content. This is only to say that such instruments are designed so that their output (hence the internal states responsible for that output) depend, nomically, on the amount of electrical current flowing between points to which their probes are affixed.

No, the reason the galvanometer does not know anything is because those states of the instrument that do carry information, and hence possess a content, carry *too much* information, have *too much* content, to qualify as genuine cognitive states. A galvanometer, and every other simple information-processing device of the sort now in question, is so constituted that it cannot distinguish between pieces of information that, from a cognitive standpoint, are different. If there is, as we know there is, a law that relates current flow to voltage differences (current will flow between points A and B only if there is a voltage difference between points A and B), then the galvanometer is incapable of representing one state of affairs without representing the other. It cannot carry the information (hence have the content) that there is a current flow between A and B without carrying the information (hence having the content) that there is a voltage difference between A and B. This is a consequence of the fact that nomic dependence is a transitive relation: if the position of the instrument's pointer depends on there being a current flow between A and B, and the latter depends on there being a voltage difference between A and B, then the pointer's position depends on there being a voltage difference between A and B. The swing of the pointer carries *both* pieces of information. Both pieces of information qualify as the pointer position's *content*.[8] But there is more. The movement of the pointer also carries information about the intensity of the magnetic field created by the current flow, the amount of increased tension in the instrument's restraining spring, and so on. *All* this information is embodied in the behavior of the pointer. There is, as it were, no way for the galvanometer to "know" that there is a current flow without "knowing" that there is a voltage difference, a magnetic field, an increased tension in the restraining spring, and so forth. All of these are part of the pointer's *informational content*. We, the users of the instrument, may be interested only in one magnitude, but the instrument itself is absolutely undiscriminating with respect to these contents.

This is why the galvanometer cannot know anything—even about those things about which it carries information. Its internal states, although they have a content of sorts, a content whose expression is non-extensional, do not have an exclusive *semantic* content of the sort characterizing genuine cognitive states. What is known when something is known differs, not only from extensionally equivalent pieces of information, but from nomically equivalent pieces of information. Knowledge that there is a current flow between points A and B is *different* than knowledge that there is a voltage difference between A and B despite the nomic inseparability of current flow from voltage differences. This is a distinction the galvanometer cannot make. It is insensitive to such cognitive differences. Hence the intentional states of a galvanometer do not qualify as cognitive states. They are intentional (as this was defined) but they are not *intentional enough*.

The point can perhaps be put more simply in the following way. If there is a natural law to the effect that every F is G, then no information-processing system (man included) can occupy a state having the informational content that something is F without, thereby, occupying a state (the same state) having the informational content that something is G. Every internal state that represents x as being F automatically represents x as being G. This is not a question of unsophisticated filtering techniques. *No* filter can make a structure depend on x's being F without making it depend on x's being G if, as we are assuming, x's being F itself depends on x's being G. Therefore, if a system is to be capable of knowing that x is F without knowing that x is G, and I take this *possibility* to be part of what it means to say that S knows that x is F (where 'F' and 'G', though differing in meaning, specify properties that are nomically dependent), this system must be endowed with the resources for representing nomically related states of affairs in different ways. The system must be given the wherewithal to represent x's being F without representing x's being G even though it cannot carry the one piece of information without carrying the other. For this to occur, the *cognitive* content of the system's internal states must be a function, not only of the information they are designed (or were evolved) to carry, but of *the manner* in which this information is represented or coded.

How is this possible? This is not the place to develop a full account of the matter, but perhaps the following, extremely oversimplified, example will help illustrate a promising avenue of development. Think of an organism that is sensitive to hydrocloric acid (HCl). This is the *only* acid to which it is sensitive. Some kind of receptor system is responsible for picking up and delivering the information that the organism is in the presence of HCl. We put the organism in a solution of HCl and it reacts appropriately (i.e., the way it always reacts in the presence of HCl). Assuming that the organism's response is controlled by some internal nervous state, what can we say about the content of this internal state? If we think merely in terms of the information carried by the organism's internal states, any state having the content "This is HCl" will also have the content "This is an acid." The neural state may be said to carry the information (hence have the content) that HCl is present, but the very same state that carries this information also carries the information (hence has the content) that an acid is present. Such an organism resembles our galvanometer in its inability to distinguish between cognitively different contents. These contents are different (*cognitively* different) because one can know that something is an acid without knowing that it is HCl—perhaps (on some accounts of these matters) even know that something is HCl without knowing it is an acid. The organism we have described does not have internal states that exhibit this kind of difference in content. Hence it does not know that it is in the presence of HCl nor does it know that it is in the presence of an acid. It does not know anything.

Compare the organism just described to one that is sensitive to a variety of different acids—exhibiting the same response to all. Let us suppose, however, that occasionally, in the presence of HCl (but no other acid) it exhibits a unique response. If we assume, once again, that there are different types of neural states responsible for different types of response, then we can begin to see the crude beginning of genuine cognition. For when we place this organism in HCl, there are *two different ways* it can code the information (or represent the fact) that it is in the presence of an acid. If it responds in the way it does to acids in general, then the associated neural state is *one way* it has of representing the acidity of its surroundings. If it responds in the unique way to HCl, then the associated neural state is *another way* it has of representing the acidity of its surroundings. Both internal states carry the information that an acid is present (recall: no state that carries the information that x is HCl can fail to carry the information that x is acid), but the coding of this information is different in the two cases.

Suppose, then, we understand a structure's cognitive content to be determined not solely by the information it carries but by the way it codes or represents this information. We now have a basis for distinguishing internal structures in a way that approximates the way we distinguish cognitive states. We have, in other words, a more satisfactory model of that higher order intentionality characteristic of cognitive content. When placed in HCl, the second organism described can occupy either one of two distinct states: one having the (cognitive) content: This is HCl; and the other having the (cognitive) content: This is an acid. It senses, so to speak, HCl (this information gets in), but this (sensory) information is capable of generating either one of two different cognitive states—either the "belief" that it is HCl or the "belief" that it is an acid. Although no structure can carry the information that x is HCl without carrying the information that x is an acid, a system that is sufficiently rich in the kind of information it can receive can nonetheless *extract* one of these pieces of information without extracting the other. It does so by having different structure types for encoding the incoming information: one structure type "meaning" that x is HCl, the other "meaning" that it is an acid.

On this account of things, the difference between a system that knows that something is F and a system that merely receives, processes, and has its output controlled by the information that x is F is that the former has, while the latter lacks, a representational or coding system that is sufficiently rich to distinguish between something's being F and its being G where nothing can be F without being G. This capacity for differentially encoding the various pieces of information arriving in a given signal is a capacity a system has (or can develop) in virtue of its capacity for receiving information about x's being G without receiving information about x's being F (either because x is not F or because, though it is F, the signal fails to carry this more specific piece of information). If the only way an organism can receive the information that x is an acid is through the information that x is HCl, then it cannot possibly develop a way of coding information about acidity that is different from the way it encodes information about *this specific kind* of acid. It cannot, as it were, acquire the concept *acidity*. Hence its internal states will never reflect the cognitive differences between *this is HCl* and *this is an acid*. This is why our galvanometer can never distinguish between voltage and current flow; it has no way of obtaining information about voltage differences except through information about current flow—hence no way of representing voltage differences in a way that is different from the way it represents current flow.

For a system to know what it is described as knowing, for it to occupy cognitive states with an appropriate content, it must have an informational receiving and coding capacity that is at least as rich in its representational powers as the language we use to express what is known. If it does not, then the language we use to describe what it knows cuts the intentional pie into slices that are too thin for the system to handle. It does not have a representational system rich enough to reflect the kind of distinctions (between various *cognitive* contents) required. Many simple information-processing devices can receive, process, and transmit the information they are required to have in order to know things. In fact, we often rely on them as conduits for the information that *we* require in order to know things. The cognitive inadequacy of these devices lies not in their information-processing capabilities but in their failure to have (and inability to develop) a *singular way* of representing the individual components of information embodied in the signals they do receive. They exhibit intentionality, but they do not exhibit it at the level required for cognitive systems.

5. CONCLUSIONS AND EXCUSES

So much remains to be said that I hesitate to claim much, or anything, for what has been said. What I have tried to do is to indicate how a materialist might go about analyzing cognitive structure in a way that preserved a number of realistic intuitions about the nature of our propositional (more specifically, cognitive) attidues. The resulting picture, assuming it could be fleshed out, yields a view of our cognitive states that (1) makes them internal states; (2) gives them a content exhibiting a significant degree of intentionality; and (3) makes the content of these states independent of the particular way the states themselves happen to be manifested in overt behavior (you do not *have* to eat it just because you believe it is food—even when you happen to be hungry).

Now the excuses. I have not discussed—indeed, I have carefully avoided—the notion of *belief*. I have restricted my attention to states whose contents were *true* (since cognitive states involve knowledge and knowledge implies truth). This was a convenient restriction since it allowed me to characterize a cognitive state's content in terms of the situation (condition, state of affairs) on which it was nomically dependent (about which it carried information). But beliefs can be false; there need be no *facts* corresponding the belief's content in the way there must be for cognitive states. How, then, can we understand a belief's content in informational terms? A belief, or the internal structure that is to qualify as a belief, need not have any *informational* content.

This is a problem, but not, I think, an insuperable problem. A story must be told about the way certain types of structures develop (during learning) as information-bearing structures and, hence, acquire an (information-carrying) role—a role which they sometimes fail to play. This, though, is another story.

I have talked, rather glibly, about levels or grades of intentionality. I have suggested that we can, with simple mechanical models, simulate a system with internal states having a considerable degree of intentionality. But there are still higher levels of intentionality, and our cognitive states exhibit these higher levels. To construct an adequate model of *cognitive* content, we need structures that can distinguish not only between nomically related situations but between *analytically* (or, if you do not like that word, *logically*) related contents. Since knowing that P can be distinguished from knowing that Q even when P entails Q (sometimes at least), the problem is to develop the above analysis of cognitive content in such a way as to reflect this higher grade of intentionality.

There are other problems, but I prefer to dwell on what I have done. What I have done, I think, is to focus the problem of intentionality in a slightly different way—a way that lends itself more readily to reductionistic efforts. The problem is not: how do we build systems that exhibit intentional characteristics? For we already have such systems in the simple mechanical appliances to be found in our kitchens and workshops. Rather, the problem is: how can such physical systems be endowed with a rich enough information-handling capacity so that they can achieve the degree of intentionality characteristic of our cognitive states? This is a problem, I concede, but not a problem of *kind* (building intentional systems out of extensionally describable systems). It is a matter of *degree*. And if I am not mistaken, this is just the kind of difference in degree that work in artificial intelligence is progressively narrowing.

Notes

1. We also use interrogative nominals (know who he is, see where he is going) and infinitive clauses (remember to buy a present) as complements to these verbs. For the purpose of this paper I shall assume that when these constructions are used to describe what someone knows, sees, or remembers, they imply something of the form: S knows *that* . . . For example, if S knows where she is, then S must know that she is, say, in the closet. I shall not be concerned with knowing *how* to do things.

2. Wilfrid Sellars's "Empiricism and the Philosophy of Mind," *The Foundations of Science and the Concepts of Psychology and Psychoanalysis,* vol. I in Minnesota Studies in the Philosophy of Science, ed. Herbert Feigl and Michael Scriven (Minneapolis, 1956), is an early example of this type of approach.

3. I take this to be Donald Davidson's motive for refusing to credit dogs, say, with intentional cognitive states: their output is compatible with a variety of different intentionally characterized inner states and this underdetermination is not merely epistemological. This, at least, is the way I interpreted some of his arguments in a series of lectures delivered in Madison, Wisconsin.

4. This seems to be Daniel Dennett's approach in *Content and Consciousness* (London, 1969).

5. There are, of course, senses of 'appropriate' in which a response can be characterized as appropriate independently of the subject's beliefs and intentions. But these senses of 'appropriate' tell us correspondingly little about what the subject believes or intends and are, therefore, poor candidates for analyzing the content of internal states that produce the response.

6. Dennett puts the point nicely in contrasting the way we treat human snores (mere sounds having a cause but no meaning) and vocal emissions that have a semantic interpretation. "Once one makes the decision to treat these sounds as utterances with a semantic interpretation on the other hand, one is committed to an intentionalistic interpretation of their etiology, for one has decided to view the sounds as the products of communicative intentions, as the expressions of beliefs, or as lies, as requests, questions, commands and so forth." "Two Approaches to Mental Images," in *Brainstorms* (Hanover, N.H., 1978). p. 180.

7. The type of information I am here describing is the type associated with Claude Shannon and Warren Weaver's *The Mathematical Theory of Communication* (Urbana, Ill., 1949). The Mathematical Theory of Communication has had a checkered career in psychology, and most investigators now tend to disparage its usefulness for semantic or cognitive studies. I think this

is a mistake. The present article should help indicate why I think this is so. I exploit this theory—or, better, the principles underlying it—to a much greater extent in *Knowledge and the Flow of Information* (unpublished) from which the present article is derived.

8. This is why one can use a properly constructed galvanometer to measure voltage as well as, or instead of, current flow. Indeed, one can measure *any* magnitude (e.g., pressure, depth, speed) variations which can be converted, by an appropriate transducer, into electrical form. All that is needed is a suitable calibration of the scale along which the pointer moves.

Keeping Matter in Mind

DAVID M. ROSENTHAL

Current discussions of mind-body materialism, intricate and subtle though they often are, frequently leave one with the impression that the central issues have been left untouched. Perhaps the principal cause of the ineffectiveness of such discussions has been the tendency, on both sides of the debate, to neglect the question of how to give a correct characterization of the mental. So, even when materialist arguments succeed in showing that some particular phenomena are physical, they often leave us unpersuaded that the phenomena shown to be physical are, actually, mental phenomena. Antimaterialist arguments, on the other side, frequently appeal to questionable characterizations of the mental, such as being private and not being spatially locatable; such characterizations, though they often derive from familiar theories about the mind, are not part of what reflective people generally have in mind when they talk about the mental. The failure to deal explicitly with the question of the nature of mentality lends false encouragement to materialists and antimaterialists alike. For it persuades antimaterialists that arguments in support of materialism illicitly rely on overly weak conceptions of the mental. And it leads materialists to suppose that the plausibility of immaterialism derives solely from dubious and, perhaps, question-begging characterizations of the mind.

This tendency to avoid the question of how to characterize the mental may result, in part, from a particular complication in theorizing about mental phenomena which has arisen since the seventeenth century. The development of post-Galilean science has seen increasingly impressive success in expressing regularities and laws of nature in mathematical terms. Progress in this direction, however, has led to the problem of what to do about those properties of natural objects which prove particularly recalcitrant to being treated in mathematical terms. Color and sound are two fairly clear cases of this sort of difficulty; however sophisticated the physicist's wave-mechanical descriptions of these phenomena may be, these accounts do not capture the color and sound themselves. The solution usually favored has been to regard such qualities as mere appearances and therefore to relocate those qualities as contents of the mind. Since these mental contents are appearances, it seems intuitively compelling to see ourselves as having unmediated access to them; for our access to them could only be mediated by another layer of appearances, and it is unclear what an appearance of an appearance could be.

But the concept of mind that results from this familiar line of thought is, notoriously, problematic. For, on this conception, the mental is in large part simply a repository for many of the common-sense features of physical things which a mathematically aided science has banished. Since many of the contents of the mind are, in effect, refugees from the nonmental world, considerable difficulties result from trying to develop a clear and coherent account of their nature. And since so many common-sense features of physical objects are relocated in the mental realm, it becomes tempting to think of the difference between the mental and the physical along the lines of the difference between common-sense properties of things and scientifically admissible properties of things. This way of conceiving of the contrast between mental and physical encourages, in turn, such familiar claims as that we cannot compare the mental and the physical without running afoul of category mistakes or that laws linking mental with physical phenomena are impossible or, most starkly, that being mental simply implies being nonphysical. Such views tend to impede efforts to understand the nature of mental phenomena. For they lead us to see the mental as something beyond the reach of scientific understanding and, perhaps, even outside the realm of natural phenomena. And since the view of the mind as a repository of scientifically recalcitrant qualities implies that mental phenomena are a kind of ontological singularity, it is easy to see why a tendency should have arisen to avoid trying to give an adequate characterization of their nature.

Against this background, the eliminative-materialist positions of Richard Rorty and Paul Feyerabend are a natural culmination of the repository view of mind. Once we have come to regard the mind as the repository of properties that are irrelevant to a scientific account of the world, it is but a small step to the conclusion that we can in principle dispose of the repository together with all its contents. Indeed, if the gulf between the mental and the physical is as unbridgeable as the repository picture seems to imply, it may well be that the only scientifically sound position one could take is that the mental is in principle eliminable. But the idea that such a gulf separates the mental from the physical also underlies most antimaterialist arguments, with their appeal to properties of the mental that exclude being physical. So the eliminative materialist, by countenancing the existence of that gulf but urging that the mental is in principle eliminable, combines an antimaterialist view of mental phenomena with an overall materialist outlook.

Despite the great influence the repository picture has had in our thinking about the mental, we need not regard mental phenomena as simply those which a mathematically oriented science cannot accommodate. For the concept of mind did not originate with the repository view's attempt to meet the needs of modern science; rather, the repository view of mind was constructed on the basis of a prior, common-sense conception of mind as the vehicle of our psychological lives. And if we reject the repository picture, it will be open for us to reevaluate the question of whether a dramatic gulf does separate the mental from the physical. In what follows, I argue in favor of an account of the contrast between mental and physical which, unlike the account suggested by the repository view, does not automatically rule out noneliminative materialism. I develop this account against the background of a detailed examination of a recent defense, by Rorty, of an eliminative version of materialism.[1] It is particularly useful to consider Rorty's discussion in this context because it vividly exemplifies the sort of view outlined above. Rorty clearly spells out the way in which his defense of eliminative materialism relies on the account he gives of the nature of the mental. Moreover, he argues for that account on the basis of its being, on his view, the best explanation of the incompatibility of being mental with being physical. Rorty traces his view of the mental to the traditional Cartesian view of mind and not specifically to the repository picture sketched above. Nonetheless, his defense of the imcompatibility of being mental with being physical strongly suggests the influence of some such picture.

In section I, I state, as forcefully as possible, Rorty's arguments for eliminative materialism. In section II, then, I argue that Rorty's characterization of the mental exhibits an unwarranted bias in favor of immaterialism. Moreoover, I argue that Rorty's modification of the traditional Cartesian picture, on which his view of mentality is based, makes his own account too weak to capture our intuitive notion of the mental. In the third and final section, I discuss, in more general terms, the implications for materialism of endorsing different marks of the mental. In particular, I consider the implications of regarding consciousness as being what is essential to mentality. And, having rejected that view, I suggest how a more satisfactory account of the mental might be developed which would be compatible with standard, noneliminative materialism. So, although Rorty's treatment of these issues dominates much of my discussion, my principal concern is to clarify the relationship between materialism and different views about the nature of mental phenomena.

I

Much of the recent literature on mind-body materialism has focused on whether the existence of distinctively mental properties of mental events is compatible with the truth of materialism. Since J. J. C. Smart's classic article, "Sensations and Brain Processes,"[2] the usual materialist strategy for dealing with this problem has been to argue that predicates that attribute such properties can be translated into topic-neutral language, that is, language which is neutral as to whether the properties in question are physical or nonphysical. Much of the attention that materialists and their critics alike have devoted to the mental properties of mental events, as against the events themselves, is probably due to a shared belief that property identity, unlike event identity, is a matter of the synonymy of corresponding predicates.[3] For it may seem that mental properties can only be kinds of physical property if it is analytic that they are. The mere possibility of consistently denying that they are physical will then rule out not only its being analytic that they are physical but also its being true at all.

There is, however, another factor that has led some to focus on the mental properties of mental events. According to most noneliminative materialists, it is possible that we shall discover that mental events are identical with a particular range of physical events, say, certain neural events. But whatever force materialist arguments may have, a pronounced tendency does exist to contrast what is mental with what is physical. Because of this, the idea that mental phenomena are simply kinds of physical phenomena has an air of being irretrievably counterintuitive. So if one accepts, perhaps just for the sake of argument, that mental events may be kinds of neural events, one will be led to look elsewhere for that aspect of the mental by virtue of which it contrasts with the physical. And unless we are willing to return to the dualist hypothesis of a distinct mental substance, it will seem that the only way to retain the contrast between the mental and the physical is by appealing to distinctively mental properties of mental events or to mental predicates that are true of those events. Feyerabend bases a criticism of standard materialism on just such reasoning, writing that the claim that mental events are particular neural events

> backfires. It not only implies, as it is intended to imply, that mental events have physical features; it also seems to imply . . . that some physical events, viz. central processes, have nonphysical features. It thereby replaces a dualism of events by a dualism of features.[4]

Feyerabend is supposing that if the contrast between mental and physical does not obtain at the level of events, then it must be located instead at the level of their properties. But he is assuming also that the mental properties of mental events will have to be nonphysical properties. The reasoning seems to be this: If mental events are particular neural events whose distinctive mental character results from their having mental properties, then the only way to explain the contrast between the mental and the physical will be for those mental properties to be nonphysical as well. In general, if our account of distinctively mental phenomena is to reflect faithfully the mental-physical contrast, and not undermine it instead, something about the mental must be nonphysical.

If this is so, only two strategies remain open to one with materialist sympathies. The first is to accept that, at best, a qualified materialism is defensible and to seek to locate the ineliminably nonphysical aspect of mental phenomena in whatever way minimizes its impact and best serves one's theoretical goals. If, for example, one's view of theoretical reduction required identifying just the events of one theory with those of another, and not the properties as well, then when theoretical reduction were in question it would be useful to try to confine the nonphysical aspect of the mental to the properties of mental events. A second strategy, however, may seem to yield even less ground to the antimaterialist, namely, the eliminative materialism championed by Rorty and Feyerabend. This approach also concedes the irreducibly nonphysical character of the mental, but argues that the very sorts of empirical discoveries that the noneliminative materialist envisages would warrant our dispensing altogether with reference to anything mental. The common-sense contrast between mental and physical is thereby circumvented and its antimaterialist force disarmed. Seen in this way, the objection that mental properties are irreducibly nonphysical is simply a special case of the more general claim that phenomena correctly characterized as mental must, in some respect, be nonphysical. If it is not because they are states of a nonphysical substance or because the events involved are nonphysical, then at least some of the properties of those events must be nonphysical. So the only satisfactory reply to this objection is that of eliminative materialism, that a complete and adequate account of people and their behavior need make reference to nothing mental.

Rorty's recent defense of this position is based on these very considerations. According to him, the contrast between the mental and the physical results from the very meaning of 'mental'; he writes, "it is part of the sense of 'mental' that being mental is incompatible with being physical, and no explication of this sense which denies this incompatibility can be satisfactory" (402). If Rorty is right, then every mental property is automatically nonphysical, and the antimaterialist objection that mental events have irreducibly nonphysical properties is a trivial corollary. Equally, it will be a mistake to grant, as most proponents of that objection do, that mental events might be kinds of neural events; for, according to Rorty, "mentalistic concepts . . . are such that it is wildly paradoxical to say that a mental event might turn out to be a physical event."[5] It follows also, as Rorty points out, that topic-neutral translations cannot be used to defend materialism, because precisely in allowing that what they apply to might be physical, "topic-neutral construals of what it is to be mental lose the mental-physical contrast" (402; see 402-6 and "More on Incorrigibility," p. 195).[6] Nor will this shortcoming be unique to topic-neutral accounts of the mental; Rorty will find no account acceptable unless it implies that the mental is nonphysical. Moreover, it is not simply that, to preserve the mental-physical contrast, at least one aspect of the mental must be nonphysical; on Rorty's view, every distinctively mental aspect must be nonphysical.

Rorty recognizes that, whatever is true about an event's being both mental and physical, there is no inconsistency in an event's being physical and also having some phenomenal quality or intentional character.[7] These properties are not, therefore, "nonphysical properties, any more than the spin of an electron is a nonphysical property" (412). Rorty therefore denies "that the notions of [intentional or phenomenal] states 'about p or 'of-red' give us the notion of something mental, something categorically distinct from everything else" (413). Using the same argument to dismiss a number of other proposed accounts of what it is to be mental, Rorty concludes that what makes an event mental is simply that it can be the subject of incorrigible reports.

Mental events are unlike any other events in that certain knowledge claims about them cannot be overridden. We have no criteria for setting aside as mistaken first-person contemporaneous reports of thoughts and sensations, whereas we do have criteria for setting aside all reports about everything else (413).[8]

And because all that is involved in Rorty's saying "that contemporaneous beliefs about our own mental states are incorrigible, is that there is no assured way to go about correcting them if they should be in error" (417), familiar arguments against the incorrigibility of the mental[9] fail to apply here. An incorrigible belief is not, for Rorty, a "belief that implies its own truth" (417).[10]

Predicates that ascribe phenomenal or intentional properties to particular events or states, therefore, are mental predicates on this view only because they are governed by a "linguistic practice, which dictates that first-person contemporaneous reports of such states are the last word on their existence and features" (414). But we can imagine truly and coherently describing things as having phenomenal qualities or propositional content without there being any such practice. Although phenomenal and intentional properties would still exist, Rorty would not count them as mental, nor would he regard the phenomenal and intentional predicates used to ascribe them nonincorrigibly as mental predicates. What makes these predicates mental predicates is only their being capable of use in incorrigible reports, and not that their meaning involves the attribution of phenomenal quality or propositional content. Rorty therefore endorses, in effect, the specific goal of Smart's and D. M. Armstrong's program of topic-neutral translation, for the aim of that program was simply to show that having phenomenal or intentional properties is, as such, "neutral as between materialist and nonmaterialist theories of the mind."[11] But since Rorty holds that being mental implies being nonphysical, materialism still cannot be vindicated unless suitable empirical discoveries could prompt the decision to abandon the linguistic practice that makes us regard some events as mental and, hence, nonphysical.

Rorty sees two ways in which this could occur. The first involves our regarding the meanings of the predicates 'is a thought' and 'is a sensation', and of specific intentional and phenomenal predicates, as dictating that they can be used incorrigibly. To abandon the linguistic practice of incorrigibility, then, would require abandoning reference to intentional and phenomenal entities. The view that this can happen, say, because of a belief that behavior can be explained "at least as well by reference to brain states as by reference to beliefs, desires, thoughts, and sensations" (421), amounts to that version of eliminative materialism which Rorty espouses in his earlier "Mind-Body Identity, Privacy, and Categories." But Rorty now recommends that we regard the linguistic practice as being due not to the meanings of those predicates but rather to a belief that thoughts and sensations are simply the sorts of things that can be incorrigibly reported. If we follow this recommendation, then abandoning the practice would involve, instead, merely changing our minds about that much of the nature of those events. The same predicates would continue to describe intentional and phenomenal events, but not incorrigibly. Since those very events would therefore no longer count as mental, this possibility too supports an eliminative version of materialism.[12] Although the two cases differ with respect to what shift in linguistic practice occurs and for what reason, in each case empirical discoveries simultaneously induce the abandonment of incorrigibility and of reference to the mental.[13]

Although only Rorty and Feyerabend[14] explicitly adopt an eliminative-materialist strategy for dealing with the mind-body problem, the line separating that strategy from other approaches is a fine one. Daniel C. Dennett, for example,

> recommend[s] giving up incorrigibility with regard to pain altogether, in fact giving up *all* "essential" features of pain, and letting pain states be whatever "natural kind" states the brain scientists find (if they ever do find any) that normally produce all the normal effects . . . . [O]ne of our intuitions about pain is that whether or not one is in pain is a brute fact, not a matter of decision to serve the convenience of the theorist. I recommend against trying to preserve that intuition . . . .[15]

It is not entirely clear, in such passages as this (cf., e.g., Dennett, *Brainstorms,* pp. 187-8), whether Dennett is urging us to replace a problematic view of mental entities with an unproblematic, scientific view or to recognize that what genuinely exists are not the traditional, problematic entities of common sense but only unproblematic entities subject to scientific treatment. Nor is it entirely clear what difference there is between these two proposals.

The 'mental'-'physical' incompatibility that Rorty advocates does not entail the incorrigibility of the mental, any more than the empirical discoveries that both Rorty and noneliminative materialists envisage would necessitate our abandoning the linguistic practice of incorrigibility. What Rorty maintains, rather, is that if all and only mental events are incorrigibly reportable, then the incompatibility of 'mental' and 'physical' can be preserved, and no other extensionally adequate mark of the mental has been proposed which will do that. So the inference to incorrigibility is, in effect, an inference to the best available explanation of the 'mental'-'physical' incompatibility. Rorty does urge that, since "we are never going to identify the property of being the subject of an incorrigible or near-incorrigible report with any neurological property" (422), no theoretical reduction of the mental to the neural is possible. But he does not deploy his linguistic version of incorrigibility to refute standard materialism; the 'mental'-'physical' incompatibility automatically does that, by itself.[16] Rather, the incorrigibility of the mental, by being a matter of changeable linguistic practice, is what opens the way for Rorty's eliminative-materialist strategy.

Rorty's argument requires, however, that particular types of events can be mental at one time and nonmental at another, and he recognizes that this may seem, at best, paradoxical. But he urges that this air of inconsistency will be dispelled once we realize that such a change is no more problematic than what would occur if, owing to new legislation, actions that had been punishable by death were so no longer. Just as one convinced of the rectitude of the death penalty might maintain that, new legislation notwithstanding, some actions were still really capital crimes, so we, habituated to accept the linguistic practice of incorrigibility, can envisage ourselves insisting that some events really are incorrigibly reportable, even in a society in which any report of such an event can be overridden. Similarly, being convinced of the obliquity of the death penalty or the groundlessness of incorrigibility might prompt future generations to regard our beliefs in capital crimes and mental events as simply the results, respectively, of our less advanced social practices and scientific theories. To endorse any of these views amounts to taking the question of whether something is a capital crime, or a mental event, to be straightforwardly a matter of fact.

A more modest stance, however, is usual in the case of capital crimes; we say that they exist just when the law provides for the death penalty. Similarly, one can see incorrigibility, as Rorty urges, as being simply the result of a linguistic practice. These accounts treat the existence of capital crimes and mental events as matters not of fact but of convention. Rorty maintains that, in these cases at least, "nothing much turns on this fact-convention distinction" ("More on Incorrigibility," p. 195); the difference between the alternative accounts is largely a matter of the attitudes being expressed. Since 'mental' is tied to incorrigibility, it resembles 'capital crime' in these respects, and not terms like 'red' and 'square', about which such interchangeable accounts are highly implausible if possible at all. So if Rorty is right about these things, to regard the existence and incorrigibility of mental events as a matter of convention is simply to recognize that different conclusions about these matters can be embedded in convincing ways of talking about things. To regard these questions as matters of fact, then, is to adopt the stance of one such way of thinking, and it will only seem paradoxical that a particular event or type of event can be mental now and not at another time from the point of view of one or another such stance. Rorty's eliminative-materialist purposes, moreover, do not require the endoresement of any particular stance; it is enough that the requisite empirical discoveries would warrant one to conclude that no mental events exist. But Rorty takes the 'mental'-'physical' incompatibility to be common to all possible stances. So the idea that mental events might not be incorrigibly reportable will be, from whatever stance, simply a disguised and paradoxical way of expressing a negative attitude toward the possible practice of permitting all reports of thoughts and sensations to be overridden.[17]

II

Rorty's argument that eliminative materialism can succeed where standard materialism must fail relies, therefore, on two premises: first, that being mental entails being nonphysical and, second, that only the mental is incorrigibly reportable in the way Rorty describes. But neither premise will withstand scrutiny. Rorty maintains that unless 'mental' and 'physical' are incompatible terms, it will not be possible to explain why, and in what way, being mental contrasts with being physical. He thereby construes the mental-physical contrast as equivalent to the contrast between the mental and the nonmental.

But Rorty overlooks that the mental-physical contrast is just one of a number of cases in which we contrast a range of phenomena with what is physical, and so he misinterprets what the mental-physical contrast involves. In the context of chemistry, for example, one isolates properties that are special to chemical compounds and processes as such, counting those properties as chemical in contrast with physical properties. But we also contrast the properties and processes that are special to life forms with physical properties and processes and, in that case, the physical includes the chemical as well. And, as Rorty's own usage illustrates, the biological itself counts as physical when we contrast the physical with the mental.[18] Not only does the range of what is physical vary, but it also encompasses, in each successive case, what was previously contrasted with the physical. In general, contrasting a range of phenomena with the physical does not provide a characterization of those phenomena; rather, it amounts simply to the claim that some distinguishing characterization exists that sets apart those phenomena from all others. Such contrasts, far from being informative about what is set in contrast with the physical, serve instead to fix what counts as physical in particular contexts: the physical is whatever, by being at a lower level of organization, lacks the distinctive features of the phenomena under consideration, whatever those features may be. Physics, proper, studies those phenomena which we cannot contrast in this way with others at an even lower level of complexity. These kinds of contrast, by focusing on an already delineated range of phenomena, suggest the possibility of relatively autonomous theories about them. Unresolved problems may exist about whether chemical, biological, or mental phenomena are really distinctive in the ways they seem to be and about whether they can be theoretically reduced to other phenomena. But the existence of such questions does not presuppose that the phenomena under discussion are nonphysical in any way beyond simply being distinctive; nor does the contrast of particular phenomena with the physical bear on whether they can be theoretically reduced to others. So when Rorty writes that an acceptable mark of the mental must "provide a means for giving the notion of 'physical' a sense by contrasting it with something else" (412), he is entirely correct. But what we must give sense to is only the notion of being physical that figures in the idiomatic contrast between mental and physical, and not any notion of being physical that bears on the issue of mind-body materialism.

It may be thought, however, that the mental-physical contrast is significantly less similar to the contrasts between the biological and physical, and the chemical and physical, than has just been suggested. For whereas we have a relatively clear conception of what would be involved in a reduction of biological or chemical phenomena to phenomena at a level of less complexity, we seem to have no clear idea about what a reduction of mental to physical phenomena would be like. But this disanalogy between the mental-physical contrast and the other two is relatively superficial. For one thing, we are still vastly more ignorant about the nature of mental phenomena than we are about life forms and about chemical interactions and compounds. So it is natural that we should feel we understand far better what would be involved in the reduction of biological and chemical phenomena to simpler terms than we now understand what a reduction of mental to nonmental phenomena would be like. But there is another, somewhat subtler source of our difficulty in envisaging a reduction of mental to physical phenomena. We usually tend to think of such a reduction as if it might go straight from the mental to the phenomena of physics, without first passing through any intermediate reductions at the levels of biology and chemistry. And the leap from the mental all the way to physics does, indeed, seem less than fully intelligible. By contrast, much of the intuitive difficulty we have in thinking of physical systems' having mental states seems to be relieved if we first think of those systems as living things. This suggests that part of our problem in intuitively comprehending how systems of particles, for example, can have mental states is due to a prior difficulty in even getting a clear, intuitive grasp of how such systems can be living things. And this analogy between the two difficulties lends support to the comparison, suggested above, of the mental-physical contrast with the contrast between living things and merely physical objects.

In more speculative contexts, 'physical' follows a similar pattern of usage. We can understand the physical as being, among other things, whatever is extended or natural or subject to causal laws or susceptible of satisfactory explanation.[19] Here, too, what counts as physical is a matter of a contrast with a particular range of phenomena, a contrast with what is unextended, uncaused, supernatural, divine, or unexplained. But in these cases the boundary drawn is of interest because of some belief or theory about things in general, whereas in the previous cases the boundary is of interest because of a concern to understand the particular range of distinctive phenomena set in contrast with the physical. Perhaps because of this, the hierarchical arrangement of the various contexts exhibited in the previous kind of case is absent here. But in both kinds of case what is physical in one context may well not be in another. So although what counts as physical in a particular context is commonly clear enough, it seems unlikely that there is anything that is meant by calling something "physical," as such and independent of one of these specialized contexts. Unlike the mental and the biological, which remain relatively fixed and specific independent of context, what counts as physical and nonphysical does not.

The foregoing considerations, however, may not wholly dispel our inclination to regard the mental-physical contrast as special and revealing in a way that other contrasts with the physical are not. For whatever else may count as physical in some context or other, we do not contrast anything with the physical in a way that leads us to count the mental itself as physical. This is not because we can delineate the mental independently of theory, since nothing beyond common sense is needed to distinguish living from nonliving things, either. Nor is it a result of our special concern with the mental, so exploited by Cartesian epistemology; for emphasis on what is special to life forms can also lead to a degree of reluctance to regard biological phenomena as simply physical, without qualification. Rather, the reason there is no clear and intuitive context in which we count the mental as physical, along with the chemical and biological, is simply that there is no well-entrenched habit of contrasting with the physical some range of phenomena at a yet higher level of complexity than the mental. There is, moreover, no reason to think that the absence of such a contrast tells us anything about the nature of the mental itself. Instead, it is very likely that that absence merely reflects the implicit assumption that no areas of study exist that both are concerned with phenomena at levels of organization higher than the mental and, also, provide us with bodies of knowledge nearly as self-contained and autonomous as are psychology, biology, and chemistry. No counterexample to this seems to be forthcoming from the social sciences, and it is difficult to see where else a counterexample could arise.

Simply to contrast a range of phenomena with the physical, therefore, leaves open for investigation and theory what the nature of those phenomena might be; it does not settle it in advance. And this is so with the mental no less than with the biological and chemical. Independent of such contrasts, a particular form of vitalism might hypothesize that the biological is, in its very nature, nonphysical, just as some theories of the mind have said that about the mental. Perhaps supernaturally inclined theoretical alchemists once so speculated about particular chemical substances. Such theories may have seemed compelling because, in each case, the subject matter under scrutiny is said to contrast with the physical. But for these theories to have content, some particular sense must be assigned to 'physical' and, if it is the sense in which the physical is said to contrast with the subject matter under consideration, the theory will reduce to mere tautology. If, however, some other sense is intended, the resulting theory will not be analytic or inconsistent, but it also will neither be implied nor undermined by the contrast with the physical. To refute standard, noneliminative materialism, however, we need more than a mere contrast between mental phenomena and phenomena that lack the distinctive features of the mental. Rorty has mistaken the use of the mental-physical contrast to focus on what is distinctive about mental phenomna for the idea that what is distinctive about them is that they are not physical.

Rorty maintains "that it is the notion [of the mental] held by Cartesian philosophers that we must explicate if we are to make sense of materialism" (406). And he urges that we are being false to that notion "as long as we give an analysis of the mental that [merely] leaves it open that mental events are taking place in an immaterial stuff" (402). But Rorty's argument for this is unconvincing. For he claims that " 'immaterial' gets its sense from its connection with 'mental' " (402) and that Descartes and Aristotle were driven to the mental to find an example of something immaterial. As a result, he concludes, " '[m]aterial' and 'physical' would be vacuous notions without the contrast with 'mental' " (405). But a variety of other contrasts also give content to the notion of being physical, and the different notion of something's being a material thing gets content from a concern with what things are made of and not from excluding the mental. Moreover, it is hardly true, as Rorty claims, that "the notions of 'ghostly stuff' and 'immaterial substance' would never have become current if Descartes had not been able to use *cogitationes* as an example of what he intended" (402); for, Berkeleian idealism aside, supernatural and divine beings are usually thought of as things that are neither physical nor mental. And although it is difficult to give any nontrivial, informative account of what kind of stuff such beings might consist of, this does not make either notion unintelligible; it is far from obvious that any informative, nontrivial account can be given of what fundamental quantum or wave mechanical entities consist of, either.

What is needed to make sense of materialism and immaterialism alike is, instead, simply an account of what is distinctive about mental phenomena, together with a specific sense to be assigned to 'physical'. But these two matters are independent, and only if one conflates them will it seem plausible that 'mental' and 'physical' are incompatible terms and, therefore, that immaterialism is true *a priori*. The difference between materialism and immaterialism is not, as Rorty suggests, that immaterialism correctly captures the distinctive character of the mental, whereas materialism simply denies or dispenses with it. It is rather than the immaterialist claims that the mental, independently characterized as such, is nonphysical in some particular way, and the materialist denies this. A variety of nontrivial, if controversial, possibilities are available to explain what being nonphysical amounts to, from being a state of an unextended substance to having no causal connections with nonmental, paradigmatically physical things. Or one might simply have in mind the way in which distinctively biological and chemical phenomena are physical without, however, presupposing any particular account of what that way is. All that the colloquial contrast between mental and physical can contribute is the distinctiveness of the mental. Indeed, were Rorty right about the nature of materialism and immaterialism, it would be remarkable that it had gone unnoticed for so long.

Whatever is found to be the underlying nature of mental states and events, whether physical or not, the discovery is almost certain to leave the commonplace contrast between mental and physical wholly unaffected. For the habit of contrasting the two will persist as long as we are able to distinguish mental events as a distinctive kind of event and develop relatively autonomous theories about them. So even if Rorty is mistaken in claiming that the distinctiveness of mental events lies in their being nonphysical, he is entirely correct in insisting that the mental-physical contrast implies that mental events are distinctive in some way or other. But Rorty's argument that being incorrigibly reportable is the best way to capture what is characteristic of the mental rests on the premise that incorrigibility best explains the incompatibility of 'mental' and 'physical', and without that incompatibility Rorty's argument loses all force. So even if Rorty is right about mental events' being incorrigibly reportable, unless being incorrigibly reportable is essential to such events, it may be reasonable to prefer, instead, some other property as a mark of the mental.

The most inviting alternative candidate for such a mark that Rorty considers is that the mental consists of inner episodes with intentional or phenomenal properties, together with dispositions for those episodes to occur.[20] Rorty dismisses this view in part because it does not explain the alleged 'mental'-'physical' incompatibility but also because, although thoughts have intentional properties and sensations phenomenal properties, this account provides no single mark that all mental events and states share (412; see also 409). But unless one's goal is to give an analysis of the meaning of 'mental' which meets fairly particular standards, it is hard to see why a single, uniform mark is required. We do not fault an account of what is distinctive of life forms for proceeding, disjunctively, in terms of the respective distinguishing marks of plant and animal life, though the two differ dramatically. Moreover, it is reasonable to try, in turn, to give an account of an event's having phenomenal or intentional properties by reference to the causal relations the event has to behavior, sensory stimulations, and other phenomenal and intentional events.[21] If this succeeded, the totality of such clusters of causal relations would be extensionally adequate to determine the mental and would very likely point the way to a more illuminating mark. Rorty himself seems to subscribe to the possibility of some such account of phenomenal and intentional properties (411-12). And, in a subsequent article, he allows that being incorrigibly reportable and having particular causal connections with behavior and stimuli are distinct, and potentially competing, criteria for determining whether something has mental states.[22]

Rorty offers the incompatibility of 'mental' and 'physical' as a reason for rejecting standard, noneliminative materialism. Perhaps, however, a different argument is available that does not require such incompatibility but instead relies simply on mental events' being incorrigibly reportable. For whatever empirical discoveries could convince us that thoughts and sensations are, say, neural events would perhaps at the same time also convince us that no reports of them are incorrigible. Yet if everything mental is incorrigibly reportable, as Rorty believes, we would still not have shown that mental events are physical events, but rather that thoughts and sensations are not mental and, indeed, that nothing mental exists.

Rorty's treatment of these matters, however, involves a double standard. Being able to be the subject of incorrigible reports, he claims, can be viewed in two distinct ways, either as the result of a general belief about the nature of thoughts and sensations or as due to the meanings of the terms 'thought' and 'sensation'. If we see a connection of meaning between being a thought or sensation and being incorrigibly reportable, the discovery that nothing is incorrigibly reportable would take the form, as in Rorty's earlier "Mind-Body Identity, Privacy, and Categories," of a discovery that no thoughts or sensations exist. If we see no such connection of meaning, we can envisage discovering simply that thoughts and sensations are not incorrigibly reportable. Rorty regards it as dogmatic to believe that thoughts and sensations are incorrigibly reportable because of what 'thought' and 'sensation' mean (415-16).

But even when Rorty concedes that causal connections with behavior provide a potentially competing criterion of the mental, he still insists that " 'mental' just means "the sort of state people are incorrigible about" " ("Functionalism, Machines, and Incorrigibility," p. 215, fn. 16). This conviction is based on Rorty's belief that incorrigibility best explains the 'mental'-'physical' incompatibility. But without that incompatibility, it is no less dogmatic to see being incorrigibly reportable as part of the meaning of 'mental' than to see it as part of the meanings of 'thought' and 'sensation'.[23] Empirical discoveries might well lead us to believe that all reports of thoughts and sensations can be overridden. But coming to believe this would not force us also to conclude that thoughts and sensations are not mental; rather, it would merely amount to the discovery that our privileged access to our own mental states is not "the last word on their existence and features" (414). And with characterizations of mental events available in terms of phenomenal and intentional properties and causal ties with stimuli and behavior, this discovery would no more undermine the colloquial contrast of mental and physical than would the discovery, considered above, that the mental is, in some specific way, nonphysical. For all that that contrast requires is a set of relatively autonomous descriptions that apply solely to the mental. Rorty may be right that "nothing would count as finding a neurological property that *was* the property of being the subject of incorrigible reports" (422). But this could concern no materialist who did not believe, with Rorty, that 'mental' and 'physical' are incompatible terms and, therefore, that being incorrigibly reportable is part of the meaning of 'mental'.

Moreoever, it is far from obvious that Rorty's permissive attitude about construing statements as reflecting meanings or beliefs is sound. If we accept that no nonarbitrary distinction is possible between matters of meaning and matters of fact (e.g., 415), it will be reasonable to regard all statements as expressing factual beliefs and none as solely matters of meaning. Perhaps one might even maintain that the rejection of a nonarbitrary fact-meaning distinction entitles us to take all assertions as only reflecting meanings, as some of the more extreme claims of the hermeneutical tradition seem to suggest. But it does not follow from the absence of a principled fact-meaning distinction that we are at liberty to construe some statements as matters of meaning and other, related statements as expressions of belief; adopting one construal for some assertions can affect what construal it is reasonable to adopt for others. Indeed, much of the unintuitive character of Rorty's argument seems to stem from his at once taking it to be a factual question whether thoughts and sensations are mental while insisting that it is a matter of meaning that nothing mental is physical.

The discovery that no reports of thoughts and sensations are incorrigible, therefore, would not by itself vindicate eliminative materialism. Nor does something's not being incorrigibly reportable clearly imply that it is physical. Nonetheless, it is probable that whatever could persuade us that something is not incorrigibly reportable would equally persuade us that it is physical, at least in whatever way distinctively chemical and biological phenomena both are. And this, in turn, would support any reasonable version of noneliminative materialism. But Rorty must believe that an even stronger connection holds between being physical and being incorrigibly reportable. For since he regards 'mental' and 'physical' as incompatible terms and believes that 'mental' entails being incorrigibly reportable, he is committed to its being a matter of meaning that nothing physical is incorrigibly reportable. And if the meaning of 'physical' is tied to incorrigible reportability no less than is the meaning of 'mental', then 'physical', too, will have to resemble 'capital crime', and so what is physical now may cease to be later. This feature of that notion of the physical which concerns Rorty, however, shows decisively that that notion is not relevant to the issue between materialism and immaterialism. For, given that notion, it cannot be completely certain that even neural or other somatic states and events will always count as physical. (Carter, "On Incorrigibility and Eliminative Materialism," p. 120, makes a similar point.)

It is commonly recognized that we are able to report our own thoughts and sensations without relying at all on observation or inference, at least in any obvious way. Less often noticed is that there is also a range of nonmental events, such as veins' throbbing and bodily movements, which we also seem able to report independently of observation and inference. Rorty envisages our coming to regard reports of thoughts and sensations as capable of being overridden by observation, inference, or well-confirmed empirical theory, just as we now regard all reports of bodily movements. But we do not now know whether discoveries are possible that would enable this change to take place on a rational basis. If none are, this might well lead us to conclude that mental events are nonphysical in some nontrivial way. But then, at least insofar as incorrigibility is concerned, materialism and immaterialism alike must wait the outcome of future investigation.

Moreover, putting the question of incorrigibility to one side, introspection, itself, need cause no difficulty for materialism. Rorty is right in noting that we count only our direct access to our own thoughts and sensations, and not to physical events such as veins' throbbing, as cases of introspection. But this is not, as he claims, because events like veins' throbbing are physical and thoughts and sensations are not (409);[24] rather, it is because thoughts and sensations are mental and the throbbing of veins is not. Nor is Rorty right that "we cannot explain what introspection is except by reference to an antecedently understood notion of what is mental" (409). For our noninferential access to mental events is nontrivially distinctive in not relying on any of the bodily senses, whereas we learn about bodily movements by way of our proprioceptive sense and about veins' throbbing through our sense of touch. It may also be that our noninferential awareness of these events appears to be nonobservational because there is no perceived spatial separation between the event and the relevant sense organ. And apart from a claim of 'mental'-'physical' incompatibility, there is no reason to maintain, with Rorty, that introspection is definitionally nonphysical (409) or incorrigible ("Dennett on Awareness," p. 155). Introspection is simply our noninferential and nonsensory access to inner events. Indeed, our having such access only to phenomenal and intentional events is very likely responsible for our intuitively classifying both sorts of event as species of a single genus.

Rorty has recently offered an argument for the incorrigibility of the mental which does not rely on a claim of 'mental'-'physical' incompatibility. He considers the case of a person who, though "having normal skills at counting sides of things," nonetheless "*always* sincerely reports an $(n - 2)$-sided after-image after contemplating an n-sided polygon (for n greater than 4)" ("More on Incorrigibility" ["MI"], p. 196). On Rorty's view,

> [i] t seems rational to believe that he gets funny after-images, and that it is up to psychologists to explain why. A psychologist who kept saying "But you can't! Your retinal images are normal, so your after-images must be!" would be fighting the data. What we want is a criterion [of incorrigibility] which captures this privileged reporting — this ability to fend off well-confirmed theory by simple sincere insistence ("MI," p. 196).

Rorty seems to think that this discussion supports his belief "that the reason why we say that after-images are mental and retinal images are not is simply that when all the chips are down we have to take the subject's word about the former but not about the latter" ("MI," p. 196). But although Rorty's specific diagnosis of this case is convincing, his general remarks are not. For in giving the person "normal skills at counting sides of things," Rorty adds a factor that prevents the situation from being an unaided conflict between "well-confirmed theory" and "simple sincere insistence." If these skills are to apply not only to sides of physical objects but also to the sides of phenomenal polygons in afterimages, the possession of these skills by itself gives very substantial reason to accept as veridical the person's surprising reports. If, however, these skills apply clearly only when counting the sides of perceived physical objects, Rorty has given no reason to rule out the possibility of systematic error in the person's judgments about his own afterimages. Although counting sides of physical objects may depend on responding appropriately to phenomenal representations, this would not entitle us to conclude that our judgments about such representations, even in cases such as afterimages, are invariably unproblematic.[25]

If it turned out that no discoveries could lead to our regarding all reports of mental events as capable of being overridden, we would be warranted in concluding that introspective access is the last word about them. But if no discoveries ever enabled us to override introspection with observation, this would almost certainly be because mental events prove recalcitrant to being explained in neural or other somatic terms. And it would be this recalcitrance to theoretical explanation by reference to the physiological which would make us count mental events as nonphysical and would also make introspection the last word about them. If theoretically reductive explanation is possible, however, we would have convincing reasons to regard mental events as somatic and to override introspective reports of them with observation. In either case, the idea that introspective reports are incorrigible would be based not on a linguistic convention about what reports are immune from being overridden but on new knowledge about the nature of mental events. In advance of our knowing whether such explanation is possible, however, whatever incorrigibility may attach to introspective reports can only be a matter of our current relative lack of grounds on which to override them. For as long as we do not know whether observation and theory can override introspection, we have nothing stronger on which to base a practice of taking introspection to be the last word. And since we are largely ignorant of the nature of mental events, save what we learn from introspection and what relatively little we now know of their causal connections with behavior, stimuli, and each other, it is not surprising that some such practice would have arisen. But there is, also, a fact of the matter about whether introspection can justifiably be overridden, and we can hope to discover it by determining whether a theoretical reduction of the mental is possible. If, prior to such a determination, we nonetheless regard mental events as incorrigibly reportable, it is simply because we do not yet know enough about them to know whether they really are.

III

Traditionally, there have been two different ways of delineating the distinctively mental, one cast in terms of the special, immediate access we have to our own mental states, the other based on the phenomenal qualities[26] and propositional content by reference to which we distinguish among types of mental states.[27] Phenomenal qualities are unique to mental states, at least if we do not conflate them with the perceptible properties of physical objects. And except for speech acts that express mental states, only mental states themselves have propositional content. But there is no clear reason to think that there is anything about intentional or phenomenal properties themselves which resists a thoroughgoing naturalist treatment, at least if one does not identify giving a naturalist account of something with reducing it to physics.

By contrast, if we take consciousness of our mental states to be the key to what makes them mental, obstacles to a naturalist treatment arise. One can explain such consciousness as one's awareness of one's own mental states and this, in turn, by reference to one's mental states' regularly causing one to have roughly contemporaneous thoughts that one has them.[28] Such an account is entirely compatible with mind-body materialism. Although it may not seem to us that we have such second-order thoughts about our mental states whenever those states are in our stream of consciousness, this causes no problem for the account. For that is exactly what we should expect, except when we have thoughts, in turn, about those second-order thoughts and are, thereby, aware of them as well. When we just have a thought about a mental state, that state is conscious; when we also have a thought about the second-order thought, we are then self-conscious, in that we are aware of ourselves as being conscious of the original mental state, and can then consciously regard that mental state as introspectible. So introspection, by itself, need cause no difficulty for materialism.

But if, following the Cartesian tradition, one holds that to think something and to know that one thinks it are the same thing and, therefore, that we are at least potentially aware of every mental state we have,[29] the foregoing account will fail. For, then, we shall not be able to explain why we often do not seem to have the second-order thoughts postulated by the above account by appealing to our lack of awareness of them. Consciousness of our mental states will, on the Cartesian view, be an intrinsic property that they have, rather than a matter of their being the subject of a distinct thought, which Descartes sometimes seems to deny is even possible.[30] And, conceived as an intrinsic property of all mental states, consciousness will very likely seem to be an irremediable obstacle to a materialist or naturalist account. Since this difficulty stems from the idea that having a mental state involves knowing that one has it and the related idea that no medium separates mental states from our awareness of them, it is natural to describe the difficulty in terms of the incorrigibility of the mental. But it is actually no more than the idea that all mental states are conscious that creates the problem.

The obvious materialist reply to this line of argument is to maintain that having a mental state does not imply knowing that one has it and, therefore, that not all mental states need be conscious mental states. Instead of consciousness, then, we can take being an inner event with intentional or phenomenal properties to be the mark of what is distinctively mental. This reply is not without support.

It is far clearer what it would be like to have states with phenomenal or intentional properties but lacking consciousness than to have conscious states with neither phenomenal nor intentional properties. The idea that what all mental states have in common is their phenomenal or intentional properties, moreoever, does not need to be qualified. But just as Rorty is forced to concede that such states as beliefs, emotions, and intentions only approximate full incorrigibility (420), so, on the classical Cartesian picture, no particular mental state need be more than potentially conscious.[31] Even if the Cartesian picture is wrong and not all mental states are conscious, this would not undermine the idea that consciousness is an important and striking feature of many mental states, though the incorrigibility that results from the Cartesian picture would, at best, have to be modified. Perhaps no organism that is never conscious can have mental states, but an organism's being conscious does not entail that its mental states are conscious. For an organism's being conscious, if this means more than that it is awake, consists simply in its being aware of something, without its necessarily also being aware that it is. Thomas Nagel may be correct in observing that, while "the mind-body problem would be much less interesting" without consideration of consciousness, "[w]ith consciousness it seems hopeless."[32] But the appearance of insolubility results not from having to take account of consciousness at all, as Nagel suggests, but from regarding the consciousness of mental states as what distinguishes the mental.

It has sometimes been maintained that having a mental state requires being aware of it; perhaps the most compelling case of this idea is the claim that having a pain involves experiencing it consciously as a pain.[33] But even if our psychological terminology contains such a suggestion, that is far from conclusive. There could be little reason to talk about pain, or other somatic sensations, of which we are not immediately aware. But we are more motivated to talk about thoughts, emotions, and perceptual sensations even when we are not immediately aware of them, and in these cases having a mental state seems far less, if at all, to imply being conscious of it. So even with somatic sensations, the appearance of such an implication may be no more than a reflection of our usual interests, rather than a reflection of the meanings of our words or the nature of the mental states themselves. Something's hurting does entail awareness that it hurts, and so perhaps the same is true of being in pain. But even if that is so, the state one is aware of when one is in pain or when something hurts might nonetheless sometimes exist without our being conscious of it.

It also may be possible, moreover, to explain the intuition that mental states must all be conscious not as a matter of the necessary nature of those states, but as the result of how we have fixed the extension of the term 'mental' (see "Naming and Necessity," pp. 274-77 and pp. 315-33, and "Identity and Necessity," pp. 156-61). Since, at the very least, not all mental states are conscious without qualification, it is more reasonable to think of the extension of 'mental' as having been fixed by reference to a range of unproblematically conscious states than to regard consciousness as what distinguishes mental states from everything else. In the case of individual objects, perhaps, what fixes the extension of a term must always refer to whatever object the term itself refers to. But this need not be so with terms used to determine kinds of things; in such cases, the kind can be fixed by means of particular identifying marks, which we then discover are not actually true of all, or even any, of the things of that kind.[34] How we fix a range of phenomena for scrutiny is not always a good indicator of the nature of the phenomena thus determined. So it is plausible, for example, to see the subject matter of biology as having been fixed by reference to the capacity for reproduction, even though investigation and theory have led to more complicated and less unified accounts of the nature of biological phenomena. Similarly, there is no compelling and non-question-begging reason to think that what fixes the extension of 'mental' cannot be distinct from what is essential to a state's being a mental state. Regarding the extension of 'mental' as having been fixed by reference to consciousness, therefore, would not rule out the possibility that the states so determined are not all conscious and that what is distinctive of, or essential to, all such states is rather that they are inner states with phenomenal or intentional properties. If such an account succeeds, then consciousness can be a mark of the mental in this qualified way without, however, this implying that all mental states are conscious or causing any difficulty for materialism.

The foregoing account of consciousness[35] is intended, in part, to help dispel whatever difficulty we may have in forming an intuitively clear idea of how living organisms can have conscious states. In this respect, the account resembles the discussion, in the last section, of the mental-physical contrast. It was suggested there that insisting on an intermediatel level of distinctively biological analysis could help bridge the intuitive gap between the mental and the phenomena of physics. Similarly, the foregoing account of consciousness insists on a distinctive level of analysis between the biological and the conscious, namely, the level of nonconscious mental states. In so doing, the account aims at reducing the intuitive gap between merely living things and beings with conscious mental states. These considerations suggest that Descartes contributed to the appearance of an unbridgeable gulf between the mental and the physical in two ways, not only by counting as mental only what is conscious, but also by eradicating the distinctiveness of the biological in urging that living organisms are automata.[36] Repudiating the idea of a distinctive level of biological analysis is not, however, merely a peculiarity of Descartes's position. For the mathematical model of science, which inspires the repository picture of the mind, is primarily regarded as a model for physics and as applicable to biology and even chemistry only insofar as they prove reducible to physics. So the repository picture, too, by neglecting the distinctively biological, seeks to capitalize on the dramatic distance between the mental and the phenomena studied by physics proper.

Against this background, Rorty's views represent a kind of compromise. In keeping with his claim "that common sense is irredeemably Cartesian" (406, fn. 11), Rorty espouses a mark of the mental inspired by considerations of consciousness and so must reject a defense of materialism based on the adoption of an alternative mark, instead. But he does wish to defend a materialist position, and it seems most unlikely that a materialist account of consciousness is possible unless it treats consciousness as an extrinsic property of mental states, that is, as a relation that each mental state bears to something else. Rorty's treatment of incorrigibility as a linguistic convention governing reports of mental states satisfies just this condition (422). But since the convention expresses the import of the Cartesian view of the mental, Rorty's account can explain how, though "common sense is irredeemably Cartesian," materialism can nonetheless be true.

Rorty strikes this particular compromise, however, because it preserves the 'mental'-'physical' incompatibility, for he believes that without that incompatibility the notions of mentality and consciousness involved in his account would not be of genuinely Cartesian notions. This is vividly reflected in Rorty's conception of the mind-body problem. He writes that without

> the opposition between the mental and the physical, . . . considered as an opposition between two incompatible types of entity, rather than [merely] . . . between two ways of talking about human beings . . . , we would not have had a mind-body problem at all (408).

And so the Cartesian notion of the mental and the attendant 'mental'-'physical' incompatibility is, he claims, required "to make sense of materialism" (406), at least if we are to regard materialism as a response to the mind-body problem. Since this conception of that problem rules out all solutions but immaterialism and eliminative materialism, it is tempting to think that it is, in effect, tailored to yield Rorty's eliminative-materialist solution. But many other contemporary discussions of mind-body materialism seem also to presuppose some form of a priori 'mental'-'physical' incompatibility, though few would follow Rorty in explicitly locating the source of the a priori opposition with the meaning of 'mental'. For example, the widely accepted idea that the existence of irreducibly psychic properties of mental events is incompatible with materialism betrays the tacit assumption that being psychic implies being nonphysical.[37]

Taking immaterialist doctrine to be definitive of the mental may be to beg the question against materialism, but conflating theory with definition in this way is hardly a singular occurrence. For it is not especially uncommon that a theory that succeeds in explaining a particular range of phenomena comes tacitly to be taken as also defining the nature of those phenomena. The effect of so construing scientific theories is normally benign, at least until we are faced with competing theories that purport to deal with the same phenomena. But in the case of the mind-body problem, it is notorious that we already face competing theories. In this case, therefore, the idea that a 'mental'-'physical' incompatibility is constitutive of the mind-body problem is perhaps simply an example of the general doctrine that philosophical problems are conceptual in nature and, therefore, cannot yield to empirical considerations.

There is more than tradition that might prompt one to take Rorty's view of the mind-body problem. For unless that problem is regarded as the result of something given that is in conflict with a thoroughgoing scientific and empiricist picture of things, it may seem difficult or even impossible to explain why the relation between mind and body was ever thought to be problematic, and why it has so persistently continued to seem so. Rorty appeals to this consideration in arguing against a functionalist view of the mental ("Functionalism, Machines, and Incorrigibility," p. 204). And he may be right in saying that unless "people thought that there was a natural kind—indeed an 'irreducible ontological category'—in the area," they would never have "thought there was a mind-body problem" ("More on Incorrigibility," p. 197).

It hardly follows, however, that the mere existence of the mind-body problem entails that the mental really does constitute an "irreducible ontological category." All that is required is that this should seem to be so and seem so in a way that, if not conclusive, is still reasonably compelling. And the pervasive idea that some such thing as consciousness is distinctive of the mental provides exactly what is needed for this; if all mental states are conscious or if the consciousness of mental states is not an extrinsic property of such states, it is far from clear that a materialist account can succeed. So Rorty may be correct when he says that without the notion of immediate awareness as applied to mental states but to nothing else, we would not have had "the mind-body problem which has bothered philosophers from Descartes to Feigl."[38] But just as the relation between mind and body will not seem to constitute a problem without some plausible appearance of opposition between the two, there will also be no problem if, as Rorty believes, it is clear from the outset that this opposition cannot be dissolved or reconciled. A problem will exist only so long as we do not know what to make of the apparent opposition. For the mind-body problem is simply the question of the nature of the mental, specifically with regard to such competing theories as materialism and dualism. Rorty has permitted the mind-body problem to dictate the nature of the mental, rather than allowing the nature of the mental to determine the correct solution to the mind-body problem.

Rorty believes that since the mind-body problem, properly so called, derives from the Cartesian notion that the mental and physical are incompatible, no account of the mental that fails to incorporate this notion will be germane to the problem (406). Any naturalist account of the mental must, therefore, be automatically unresponsive to the problem and so fail. But even if Rorty were right about the nature of the mind-body problem, contesting a central presupposition of a problem can be entirely germane and responsive to the problem. The nature and history of intellectual problems is no more a privileged area of knowledge to which other areas must conform than is the study of the meanings of words, whose claim to special status and "magisterial neutrality" Rorty rightly rejects ("Mind-Body Identity, Privacy, and Categories," p. 25).[39] When properties thought essential to a subject matter have been abandoned, such as entelechies in biology and Aristotelian essences of various sorts, the typical reaction has been to dispense not with the subject matter, as Rorty envisages our doing, but rather with the view that the property in question really is essential to the subject matter. Moreover, the withering away of whatever incorrigibility now belongs to reports of thoughts and sensations could only enhance the prospects of a scientific study of those states. In general, a subject matter is abandoned only if it emerges that a scientific study of it is impossible.

This conservatism with respect to subject matters is not simply an accident of history. For abandoning a subject matter along with a mistaken theory about it makes needlessly difficult the comparison of our current theories with those of the past. Perhaps Feyerabend and others are right in thinking that, strictly speaking, distinct theories are always incommensurate and that no theory-neutral descriptions of subject matters are possible. Even so, the usefulness of regarding our current theories as being about the same subject matters as past theories will generally outweigh whatever advantage there may be in seeing ourselves as having jettisoned the subject matters of theories we have rejected. Perhaps no ahistorical overview is possible from which we could compare the Cartesian idioms of the present with the non-Cartesian idioms Rorty envisages for the future. But even if any attempt to compare the views of different eras must reflect the perspective of the then current era, this does not by itself imply that any such comparison is erroneous. As long as we can validly compare Cartesian theories and idioms with non-Cartesian theories and idioms, there can be little if any reason to take Cartesian theories as definitive of mental subject matter. Rorty's belief that the connection between being mental and being incorrigibly reportable cannot be severed is an example of an unwarranted essentialism with respect to subject matters.

Putting aside the question of a 'mental'-'physical' incompatibility, whatever empirical discoveries could lead us, on Rorty's eliminative account, to dispense with reference to the mental would also vindicate standard, noneliminative materialism. The two views differ principally on the question of that incompatibility and, therefore, about that much of the nature of the mental.[40] But Rorty takes what is mental to be a conventional matter, roughly like what is a capital crime. So his account will fall short of commonly accepted beliefs about mental phenomena no less than do more standard materialist accounts, such as those implicit in Hobbes's *a priori* materialist arguments or in Smart's and Armstrong's rather cavalier topic-neutral construals of mentalistic statements.

If the foregoing arguments are correct, neither considerations pertaining to consciousness nor the nature of the mind-body problem will warrant Rorty's incompatibilist interpretation of the mental-physical contrast. More generally, since a naturalist account of the mental-physical contrast is defensible, we need not adopt the view of that contrast implied by the repository picture of the mind. A naturalist view may require us to repudiate particular theories of mental phenomena, at least insofar as those theories purport to define the nature of those phenomena, and perhaps, in some cases, even insofar as the theories offer explanations of the phenomena. But a naturalist view of the mental-physical contrast and of the mind-body problem itself need not cause us to renounce our traditional, common-sense intuitions about the nature of the mental.

Nor are such maneuvers as Rorty's appeal to an incorrigibility based on linguistic convention necessary to defend materialism while also preserving the distinctive insights of the Cartesian picture. For we need not hope to explain the peculiar importance of consciousness and related notions by claiming that they provide a mark of the mental, even in the qualified way suggested above. It is arguable that these notions are, instead, what enable us to distinguish persons from all other beings. We must take care, here, not to confuse being a person with simply being a member of the human species. But, equally, having mental states is, by itself, clearly not unique to persons, though the notion of a being with mental states has not infrequently been unthinkingly conflated with the notion of a person.[41] If, for example, Rorty is right in holding that being mental is being incorrigibly reportable, then the attribution of mental states to nontalking animals will be problematic at best. Rorty might plausibly maintain that we are all Cartesians at least in denying the existence of any mind-body problem for such animals, though even this can be forcefully disputed (see Nagel, "What Is It Like To Be a Bat?" *passim*). But whatever we may say about that question, we clearly are not Cartesians in holding also that nontalking animals never have any mental states. And even if our conceptual descendants came to think that what such animals have are not mental events, proper, but only thoughts and sensations, it is clear that, at present, we think that they have both. The behavior of nontalking animals may even seem sometimes to indicate the presence of higher-order mental states (see, e.g., Dennett, pp. 274-5), though that inference may seem somewhat unconvincing when one notices that such cases seem never to involve our concluding that the animal has a higher-order mental state that is just about its own mental states and not at least in part about those of another creature. Whatever the case about that matter, what no animals other than persons have is the particular kind of reflective consciousness that involves some fair degree of general rational connectedness or, intuitively, a lack of "mindlessness" in the awareness of its mental states. A compelling case has been made for the related view that what distinguishes persons is their having a particular sort of higher-order mental state, specifically, second-order volitions (see Frankfurt, "Freedom of the Will and the Concept of a Person," *passim*). The temptation to equate being a person with simply having mental states may result in part from our being able to know the mental states of creatures with introspective consciousness, at least in familiar cases, in which introspection is sometimes articulated, in a way we cannot know the mental states of others when such consciousness is absent. But we need no more rely on introspective reports to know the mental states of nonpersons than we must, or typically do, rely on such reports to know the mental states of other persons. Rorty's eliminative-materialist strategy relies on separating the notion of being mental from that of being a thought or sensation, that is, from the notion of being an inner state with intentional or phenomenal properties. But the unintuitive consequences that derive from Rorty's way of combining the Cartesian and materialist pictures can be avoided if, instead, we simply distinguish the notion of having mental states from that of being a person.[42]

Notes

1. Richard Rorty, "Incorrigibility as the Mark of the Mental," *The Journal of Philosophy*, 67, no. 12 (June 25, 1970):399-424 (henceforth "IMM"). References in the text to this article will occur as parenthesized page numbers. Rorty advances related but distinct views in "Mind-Body Identity, Privacy, and Categories," *The Review of Metaphysics*, 19, no. 1 (September

1965):24-54 (henceforth "MBIPC") and in *Philosophy and the Mirror of Nature* (Princeton, N.J., 1979), chap. 2.

2. J. J. C. Smart, "Sensations and Brain Processes," in *The Philosophy of Mind*, ed. V. C. Chappell (Englewood Cliffs, N.J., 1962), pp. 160-72, especially pp. 166-68. This is a slightly revised version of an article of the same title in *The Philosophical Review* 68, no. 2 (April 1959):141-56.

3. Max Deutscher and Hilary Putnam have convincingly challenged this belief. See Deutscher, "Mental and Physical Properties," in *The Identity Theory of Mind*, ed. C. F. Presley (St. Lucia, Queensland, 1967), pp. 73-78, and Putnam, "On Properties," in *Essays in Honor of Carl G. Hempel*, ed. Nicholas Rescher et al. (Dordrecht, 1970), pp. 235-54. This difference between property and event identity will disappear if, as is sometimes proposed (e.g., in Richard Brandt and Jaegwon Kim, "The Logic of the Identity Theory," *The Journal of Philosophy* 64, no. 17 [September 7, 1967] : 516), events are defined in terms of properties.

4. Paul Feyerabend, "Mental Events and the Brain," *The Journal of Philosophy* 60, no. 11 (May 23, 1963):295.

5. Richard Rorty, "More on Incorrigibility," *Canadian Journal of Philosophy* 4, no. 1 (September 1974):195 (henceforth "MI"). See Jerome Shaffer, "Mental Events and the Brain," *The Journal of Philosophy* 60, no. 6 (March 14, 1963): 161, for an excellent statement of that objection. Perhaps because Rorty does not grant that mental events might be neural events, he regards topic-neutral translations as designed not to rebut the charge that mental properties are irreducibly nonphysical but to rebut the claim that applying mental predicates to neural events constitutes a category mistake, and so rules out the identity of mental with neural events ("MBIPC," p. 25-28; see "IMM," p. 399).

6. Rorty's objection to such construals differs, therefore, from the more common complaint that they are too weak to do justice to the phenomenal quality and intentional character of mental events, and he would reject topic-neutral construals even if they succeeded, as David Lewis's very likely do, in capturing intentional and phenomenal properties. See his "An Argument for the Identity Theory," *The Journal of Philosophy* 63, no. 1 (January 6, 1966):17-25, and "Psychophysical and Theoretical Identifications," *The Australasian Journal of Philosophy* 50, no. 3 (December 1972):249-58.

7. Cf. my "Mentality and Neutrality," *The Journal of Philosophy* 73, no. 13 (July 15, 1976): 386-415, sec. i.

8. In response to a criticism by R. I. Sikora, Rorty has modified his claim that there are "no criteria for setting aside as mistaken" such reports, in an attempt to express more successfully the "epistemic favouritism" we accord first-person contemporaneous reports of mental events ("MI," p. 196). See Sikora, "Rorty's Mark of the Mental and His Disappearance Theory," *Canadian Journal of Philosophy* 4, no. 1 (September 1974): 191. Rorty's modification is not, however, germane to the following discussion.

9. E. g., D. M. Armstrong, "Is Introspective Knowledge Incorrigible?" *The Philosophical Review* 72, no. 4 (October 1963): 417-32; Armstrong, *A Materialist Theory of the Mind* (New York, 1968), p. 101; and A. J. Ayer, *The Problem of Knowledge* (Baltimore, 1956), pp. 56-57.

10. For a statement and defense of the traditional view of incorrigibility, which Rorty rejects, see Kurt Baier, "Pains," *The Australasian Journal of Philosophy* 40, no. 1 (May 1962): 1-23, especially pp. 1-7, and "Smart on Sensations," same journal and issue, pp. 57-68, especially pp. 58-61. Baier's notion concerns what we think about our mental states and not simply what we say about them (e.g., "Smart on Sensations," p. 64). For a thoughtful and generally convincing criticism of several incorrigibility theses, see Kathryn Pyne Parsons, "Mistaking Sensations," *The Philosophical Review* 79, no. 2 (April 1970):201-13.

It is far from obvious that even the more cautious "epistemic favouritism" that Rorty attributes to mental events actually obtains. For although reference to behavior, stimuli, and other thoughts and sensations may not provide decisive criteria for the occurrence of particular mental events, criteria are seldom decisive in other cases either. In Rorty's earlier "MBIPC," moreover, he makes a compelling case for his claim that "[o]ur neighbors will not hesitate to ride roughshod over our reports of our sensations unless they are assured that we know our way around among them, and we cannot satisfy them on this point unless, up to a certain point, we tell the same sort of story about them as they do. . . . As in the case of other infallible pronouncements, the price of retaining one's epistemic authority is a decent respect for the opinions of mankind" ("MBIPC," pp. 45-46; see n. 25 below). And his arguments apply at least as well to thoughts as to sensations. Even if some epistemic favoritism is part of "the opinions of mankind," telling "the same sort of story" about our thoughts and sensations as others tell seems to require that we have something along the lines of those criteria which Rorty now maintains we lack. Whatever the case on this matter, there is a marked reluctance to override first-person contemporaneous reports of thoughts and sensations which is not matched in cases of other sorts and seems to exist to roughly the same extent whether or not evidence is present that would justify overriding such reports.

Gerald Doppelt explicitly recognizes the pragmatic character of Rorty's notion of incorrigibility. See "Incorrigibility, the Mental and Materialism," *Philosophy Research Archives* 3, no. 1213 (December 1976): 507-8, and "Incorrigibility and the Mental," *The Australasian Journal of Philosophy* 56, no. 1 (May 1978): 4 (henceforth referred to by year). ([1978] is a shortened and revised version of [1976].) And Doppelt presents a number of convincing arguments against that very notion ([1976] : 512-28 and [1978] :7-19). As he notes (fn. 13 in both articles), his arguments do not hinge on imagining scientific results that may be forthcoming. Similar arguments occur in Parsons, "Mistaking Sensations," pp. 210-13. The present discussion does not, however, rely on evaluating any claims for or against incorrigibility. But see n. 20 below.

11. Smart, "Further Thoughts on the Identity Theory," *The Monist* 56, no. 2 (April 1972): 149. Italics original throughout.

12. It seems likely that Sikora's insistence that a well-confirmed theory could not be used to override repeated sincere avowals of intense pain depends on his tacitly disregarding the force of the discoveries and changes of linguistic usage envisaged by Rorty. See R. I. Sikora, "Rorty's New Mark of the Mental," *Analysis* 35, no. 6 (June 1975):194. Similarly, being wedded to the belief that thoughts and sensations are necessarily or analytically mental may be responsible for arguments against Rorty that are wide of the mark. See, e.g., Doppelt, [1976] :531-32 and 535, and Carol Donovan, "Eliminative Materialism Reconsidered," *Canadian Journal of Philosophy* 8, no. 2 (June 1978): 301-2. The conviction that thoughts and sensations cannot fail to be mental may also result in the conflation of the distinct versions of eliminative materialism Rorty propounds in "MBIPC" and "IMM." William G. Lycan and George S. Pappas argue that "MBIPC" does not claim that it is a straightforwardly empirical matter than no sensations exist. See their "What Is Eliminative Materialism?" *The Australasian Journal of Philosophy* 50, no. 2 (August 1972):154-55. But it is perhaps more plausible to construe "MBIPC" as arguing that, though it is a straightforward empirical truth that no sensations exist, the pragmatic status of the belief that none exist is strikingly and importantly different from the status of other, more ordinary beliefs that something does not exist. This pragmatic status would provide one crucial way in which Rorty's view in that article diverges from the more standard reductive materialism of Smart and others.

13. See Donovan, "Eliminative Materialism Reconsidered," *passim,* for a discussion of what empirical discoveries are necessary, on Rorty's view (though the conditions she quotes [on p. 290] from "IMM" are offered by Rorty in connection not with materialism but with "a certain form of parallelism," which he regards as closely resembling the identity thesis ["IMM," p. 423]). Donovan may be right in urging (on pp. 296-99) that Feyerabend's somewhat looser view of the requisite empirical discoveries is preferable to Rorty's, but suitable adjustments in Rorty's account would leave the central features of his argument intact. Also, David R. Hiley may be correct, in his sympathetic defense of Rorty's position, in claiming that as a general matter Rorty believes it to be impossible to "provide criteria for evaluating the adequacy of alternative vocabularies" ("Is Eliminative Materialism Materialistic?" *Philosophy and Phenomenological Research* 38, no. 3 [March 1978] :336). But the alternative vocabulary Rorty envisages in

"IMM" varies only slightly from our own, and Rorty does state what would warrant the shift ("IMM," p. 421; cf. "MBIPC," p. 27, fn. 6).

14. For Feyerabend's views, see "Mental Events and the Brain"; "Materialism and the Mind-Body Problem," *The Review of Metaphysics* 17, no. 1 (September 1963):49-66; "Reply to Criticism," vol. II in *Boston Studies in the Philosophy of Science*, ed. Robert S. Cohen and Marx W. Wartofsky (New York, 1965), pp. 256-59; "Problems of Empiricism," in *Beyond the Edge of Certainty*, ed. Robert G. Colodny (Englewood Cliffs, N.J., 1965):185-97 and 254-60; and "Science without Experience," *The Journal of Philosophy* 66, no. 22 (November 20, 1969): 791-94.

15. Daniel C. Dennett, *Brainstorms* (Montgomery, Vermont, 1978), p. 228.

16. So it is misleading to suggest, as Pappas does, that Rorty's discussion is an example of the sort of antimaterialist argument that claims materialism is incompatible, by way of the sub-stitutivity of identity, with the incorrigibility of the mental ("Incorrigibility and Central-State Materialism," *Philosophical Studies* 29, no. 6 [June 1976] :456, fn. 5). Recent arguments by M. C. Bradley and Lycan have sought to refute the claims of such writers as Armstrong and Baier that materialism and incorrigibility are indeed incompatible. See Bradley, "Two Arguments Against the Identity Thesis," in *Contemporary Philosophy in Australia*, ed. Robert Brown and C. D. Rollins (London and New York, 1969), pp. 173-80; Lycan, "Materialism and Leibniz' Law," *The Monist* 56, no. 2 (April 1972), pp. 279-82; Baier, "Smart on Sensations," pp. 59-60 and 64-65; and Armstrong, *A Materialist Theory of the Mind*, pp. 100-103, and "Incorrigibility, Materialism and Causation," *Philosophical Studies* 30, no. 2 (August 1976):125-27. But Bradley's and Lycan's refutations bear on the traditional notion of incorrigibility, which implies truth (e.g., Bradley, p. 174, and Lycan, p. 277). So these arguments do not, as Pappas suggests, affect Rorty's position (Pappas, p. 456, fn. 5). But since the incorrigible reportability of mental states is, on Rorty's view, a matter of linguistic practice, such incorrigibility would not be incompatible with the identity of mental with neural events, even if the neural events failed, as such, to be incorrigibly reportable. But cf. n. 24 below.

17. Though Doppelt rightly stresses the pragmatic character of Rorty's views on these matters ([1976] :510 and [1978] :6), he goes on, somewhat surprisingly, to claim that "Rorty needs to distinguish 'almost-incorrigibility' as a *practical* attitude . . . from this concept as an *epistemic* attitude" ([1976] :515 and [1978] :10). Perhaps Doppelt maintains this because he regards "Rorty as a framework-pragmatist but not a case-pragmatist" ([1976] :510 and [1978] :6). This distinction, however, strongly echoes Carnap's between external and internal questions ("Empiricism, Semantics, and Ontology," in *Meaning and Necessity*, enlarged ed. [Chicago, 1956], p. 206), and Rorty's avowed Quinean propensities (e.g., "IMM," p. 415) make it unlikely that he would regard either distinction as being tenable and unlikely, therefore, that Doppelt's use of his distinction accurately captures Rorty's position.

18. P. E. Meehl and Wilfrid Sellars' distinction between 'physical$_1$' and 'physical$_2$' corresponds roughly to the difference between the physical taken to be what contrasts with the mental and the physical construed as what contrasts with the biological, respectively. See their "The Concept of Emergence," vol. I in *Minnesota Studies in the Philosophy of Science*, ed. Herbert Feigl and Michael Scriven (Minneapolis, 1956), p. 252.

19. Cf. Noam Chomsky's suggestion that the notion of a physical explanation gets progres-sively extended to cover any explanations that are scientifically satisfactory, even future ex-planations of the mental. Chomsky notes that this is an "uninteresting terminological" point (*Language and Mind*, enlarged ed., [New York, 1972], p. 98).

20. Such dispositions seem needed to cover such longer-range states as intentions, beliefs, desires, emotions, and the like. Rorty calls these sorts of states "mental features" and contrasts them with mental events, proper ("IMM," pp. 406-8), though he does not construe mental features as dispositions for mental events to occur. Rorty accords mental features only the qualified status of being able to be subjects of near-incorrigible reports (pp. 419-20). Moreoever, he recognizes that momentary mental features "tend to collapse into" mental events (p. 420 [though his words leave it unclear whether what is momentary is the mental states or their

propositional content]). So he casts the event-feature distinction principally in terms of mental events', but not mental features', making "up the content of the stream of consciousness" (p. 407). It seems far from plausible, however, that reports of mental features are even nearly incorrigible. And since it also seems clear (though Rorty appears to deny this; see p. 407) that the occurrence of particular kinds of mental events is closely connected with having particular sorts of mental features, the corrigibility of reports of mental features will undermine the incorrigibility Rorty claims for reports of mental events. (Doppelt has independently made this point. See [1976] :524-26 and [1978] :17-18.)

21.See, e.g., Sellars, *Science, Perception and Reality* (London and New York, 1963), chaps. 2 and 5; Lewis, "Psychophysical and Theoretical Identifications"; and Sydney Shoemaker, "Functionalism and Qualia," *Philosophical Studies* 27, no. 5 (May 1975):291-315. David Coder distinguishes two "different and competing viewpoints on the concept of mind." According to one, what is essential to mental states is what "one gets . . . by abstracting from what one's consciousness reveals," whereas the other maintains that what is essential to such states are "the causal relations that, on the first viewpoint, mental states have [merely] contingently" ("The Fundamental Error of Central State Materialism," *American Philosophical Quarterly* 10, no. 4 [October 1973] :291). It is not clear, however, that one need regard these viewpoints as either competing or conflicting, for what is revealed in consciousness may turn out to be a matter of the causal relations that mental states bear to each other and to particular nonmental states.

22."Functionalism, Machines, and Incorrigibility," *The Journal of Philosophy* 69, no. 8 (April 20, 1972):215.

23.W. R. Carter makes this point in "On Incorrigibility and Eliminative Materialism," *Philosophical Studies* 28, no. 2 (August 1975):119.

24.Also "Dennett on Awareness," *Philosophical Studies* 23, no. 3 (April 1972):155.

25.In "MBIPC," discussing the putative infallibility of first-person reports of pains, Rorty maintains that such reports can be in error. Having argued that no helpful distinction exists between misnaming and misjudging as distinct sources of error in introspective reports of sensations (p. 45), Rorty urges that "the common-sense remark that first-person reports always will be a better source of information about the occurrence of pains than any other source borrows its plausibility from the fact that we normally do not raise questions about a man's ability to use the word 'pain' correctly" (p. 46). Rorty concludes that "if 'always be a better source of information' means 'will never be over-ridden on the sort of grounds on which presumed observational errors are over-ridden elsewhere in science,' then our common-sensical remark is probably false. If 'always be a better source of information' means merely 'can only be over-ridden on the basis of a charge of misnaming, and never on the basis of a charge of misjudging,' then our common-sensical remark turns out to depend on a distinction that is not there" (p. 46). (Cf. the somewhat similar discussion in Parsons, "Mistaking Sensations," p. 207.) But in supposing that skills in counting sides apply to the phenomenal polygons of afterimages, Rorty must be assuming that the words used in reporting such afterimages are being applied correctly and, hence, that error arising from misnaming has been ruled out. It would be useful to know how Rorty would propose to distinguish the two sorts of error in the case under consideration.

26.Phrases like 'how such-and-such feels (looks, sounds)' and 'what it's like to be (see, hear) such-and-such' refer at once to particular phenomenal qualities and to the conscious awareness of them, thereby encouraging the conflation of these two components of experiences. But as long as we can distinguish these components, the distinction suggested here is not threatened.

27.This distinction has been central in the history of discussions of the mental and of the mind-body problem. Gareth B. Matthews has recently maintained, e.g., that the modern notion of consciousness, conceived as "the function of a self-transparent agent (the mind)," as well as "the problems of a Cartesian philosophy of mind . . . [both] arise from a rather deliberate decision by Descartes and his followers to conceive and talk about perception and thinking in a new way . . . " ("Consciousness and Life," *Philosophy* 52, no. 199 [January 1977] :23 and 26). Similarly, Freud, in talking about unconscious mental states, seems to some extent to have regarded himself as having proposed a new way of thinking and talking about the mental.

> Everyone—or almost everyone—was agreed that what is psychical really has a common quality in which its essence is expressed: namely the quality of *being conscious* . . .
> All that is conscious, they said, is psychical, and conversely all that is psychical is conscious: that is self-evident and to contradict it is nonsense. . . . Moreover the equation of what is mental with what is conscious had the unwelcome result of divorcing psychical processes from the general context of events in the universe and of setting them in complete contrast to all others. . . .
> Psycho-analysis escaped such difficulties as these by energetically denying the equation between what is psychical and what is conscious ("Some Elementary Lessons in Psycho-Analysis," vol. XXIII in *The Standard Edition of the Complete Psychological Works of Sigmund Freud*, ed. and trans. James Strachey [London, 1964] p. 283).

Freud did not think this view was original with him, however; see, e.g., p. 286.

28. It is not enough for this roughly contemporaneous thought just to be about one's own mental state; it must also be a thought that one is, oneself, in that mental state. For useful discussions of this sort of reference, see Hector-Neri Castañeda, "On the Logic of Attributions of Self-Knowledge to Others," *The Journal of Philosophy* 65, no. 15 (August 8, 1968):439-56 and works cited therein, and G. E. M. Anscombe, "The First Person," in *Mind and Language,* ed. Samuel Guttenplan (Oxford, 1975), pp. 45-65.

29. For a particularly vivid account of this idea, see Zeno Vendler, *Res Cogitans* (Ithaca and London, 1972), pp. 190-94.

30. Elizabeth S. Haldane and G. R. T. Ross, trans., *The Philosophical Works of Descartes* (Cambridge, 1931), vol. II, p. 64 (henceforth *HR*).

31. John Cottingham, trans., *Descartes' Conversation with Burman* (Oxford, 1976), p. 7; *HR*, II, p. 343.

32. Thomas Nagel, "What Is It Like to Be a Bat?" *The Philosophical Review* 83, no. 4 (October 1974):436 (reprinted, along with several related articles, in *Mortal Questions* [Cambridge, 1979], p. 166); cf. Brandt and Kim, "The Logic of the Identity Theory," p. 519, fn. 6.

33. See, e.g., Saul A. Kripke, "Naming and Necessity," in *Semantics of Natural Language,* ed. Donald Davison and Gilbert Harman (Dordrecht and Boston, 1972), pp. 339 (henceforth "NN"), and "Identity and Necessity," in *Identity and Individuation,* ed. Milton K. Munitz (New York, 1971), p. 163, fn. 18.

34. "NN," pp. 315-25, especially p. 316; cf. Putnam's use of his notion of a stereotype in, e.g., "The Meaning of 'Meaning'," vol. VII in *Minnesota Studies in the Philosophy of Science,* ed. Keith Gunderson (Minneapolis, 1975), pp. 169-173.

35. The foregoing six paragraphs and the last paragraph of this section summarize my argument in "Two Concepts of Consciousness," forthcoming.

36. *HR*, I, pp. 115-16 and II, pp. 103-4. See Matthews, "Consciousness and Life," for a similar view of Descartes.

37. See my "Mentality and Neutrality," sec. ii, for a discussion of this point.

38. "Cartesian Epistemology and Changes in Ontology," in *Contemporary American Philosophy,* Second Series, ed. J. E. Smith (London and New York, 1970), p. 278.

39. Cf. "IMM," pp. 415-16, and "Criteria and Necessity," *Nous* 7, no. 4 (November 1973): 313-29, especially pp. 323 and 327.

40. Cf. Lycan and Pappas, "What Is Eliminative Materialism?" and Eric Bush, "Rorty Revisited," *Philosophical Studies* 28, no. 2 (August 1975):113-21. Both articles, however, are about "MBIPC" and not the somewhat different view put forth in "IMM."

41. See, e.g., Harry G. Frankfurt, "Freedom of the Will and the Concept of a Person," *The Journal of Philosophy* 68, no. 1 (January 14, 1971):5-6.

42. Part of an earlier version of this paper, entitled "Against Eliminative Materialism," was presented at the American Philosophical Association, Eastern Division, December 29, 1975. I am grateful to Margaret Atherton, Richard E. Grandy, and Robert Schwartz for helpful comments on earlier drafts.

Conceptual Schemes

NICHOLAS RESCHER

1. INTRODUCTION

Philosophers have often said things to the effect that those whose experience of the world is substantially different from our own are bound to conceive it in very different terms. Sociologists, anthropologists, and linguists say much the same sort of thing, and philosophers of science have recently also come to talk in this way. According to Thomas Kuhn, for example, scientists who work within different scientific traditions—and thus operate with different descriptive and explanatory "paradigms"—actually "live in different worlds."[1]

Supporting considerations for this position have been advanced from very different points of view. Thus consider a *Gedankenexperiment* suggested by Georg Simmel in the last century—that of approaching the problem of cognitive adequacy from the standpoint of an entirely different sort of cognitive being.[2] Imagine intelligent and actively inquiring creatures (animals, say, or beings from outer space) whose experiential modes are quite different from our own. Their senses are highly responsive to quite different physical parameters—relatively insensitive, say, to heat and light, but substantially sensitized to various electromagnetic phenomena. Such intelligent creatures, Simmel held, could plausibly be supposed to operate within a largely different framework of empirical concepts and categories—the events and objects of the world of their experience might be very different from those of our own—their predicates, for example, might have altogether variant domains. In a similar vein, William James wrote:

> Were we lobsters, or bees, it might be that our organization would have led to our using quite different modes from these [actual ones] of apprehending our experiences. It *might* be too (we cannot dogmatically deny this) that such categories, unimaginable by us to-day, would have proved on the whole as serviceable for handling our experiences mentally as those we actually use.[3]

Different cultures and different intellectual traditions, to say nothing of different sorts of creatures, will, so it has been widely contended, describe and explain their experience—their world as they conceive it—in terms of concepts and categories of understanding substantially different from ours. They may, accordingly, be said to operate with different conceptual schemes: with different conceptual tools used to "make sense" of experience—to characterize, describe, and explain the items that figure in the world as best one can form a view of it in terms of their features, kinds, modes of interrelationship and interaction. The taxonomic and explanatory mechanisms by which their cognitive business is transacted may differ so radically that intellectual contact with them becomes difficult or impossible. Accordingly, we are told such things as, for example, that one cannot secure a grasp on the thought-world of an animistic society if one is unable or unwilling to enter into the conceptual-framework characteristic of such an approach, adopting what the Germans would call their *Denkmittel*—the conceptual tools they employ in thought about the facts (or purported facts) of the world.

Recently, however, some philosophers have begun to question this perspective. If the idea is conceived of in the standard way, as marking a potential contrast between distinct conceptual schemes—ours vs. theirs—then, so they argue, this whole notion of "alternative conceptual schemes" does not make sense, because the appropriate sort of alternativeness contrast cannot be developed.[4]

The present discussion will examine this position and its supporting arguments, and will endeavor to show that the rejection of the notion of conceptual schemes is not warranted. The conception of "alternative conceptual schemes" has its natural home primarily in four disciplinary settings: (1) in descriptive sociology to contrast (e.g.) kinship systems or other such mechanisms for the categorization and explanation of human affairs, (2) in intellectual history to contrast different perspectives of understanding of different *Weltanschauungen*, (3) in the history of the sciences to contrast the diverse explanatory frameworks of (e.g.) Galenic and modern biochemical medicine, and (4) in philosophical epistemology to contrast fundamentally diverse approaches to descriptive or explanatory issues. In brushing aside the idea of "different conceptual schemes," we also give short shrift to what those who invoke them to clarify such differences were getting at, incurring the risk of an impoverishment in our problem-horizons. There is, after all, something a bit eccentric about rejecting the idea of alternative conceptual schemes—something that smacks of the unrealism of one who closes one's mind toward what people are actually saying and doing.

2. THE TRANSLATION ARGUMENT

One influential argument against the conception of alternate conceptual schemes is a line of reasoning, offered by Donald Davidson, that may be characterized as the Translation Argument.[5]

The first step of this argument is the relatively unproblematic association of conceptual schemes with languages. A "concept," after all, is not a shadowy and problematic entity of some obscure sort. It is determined by the meanings of words and stands correlative with the communicative tasks we assign to them in the operations of language. The concept of a certain color or a certain species of flower is given in the complex of rules that govern the use of the pertinent terminology in the language(s) we use to discourse about them. Concepts, in sum, are linked to meanings, and meaning is a functional conception correlative with the rules that govern the communicative employment of language. After all, for effective communication, sender and receiver must not only exchange signals but must decode them the same way. They must "speak a common language" and be in conceptual communion with one another. This indicates a need for *common* concepts to convey information in communication. To speak of "concepts" is to do no more than indicate what is inherent in the meanings of words—the jobs that we assign to them as instruments of communication.

The next step is to supplement this association of conceptual schemes with languages by adopting linguistic intertranslatability as a criterion for the identity of these associated conceptual schemes. To quote Davidson:

> We may accept the doctrine that associates having a language with having a conceptual scheme. The relation may be supposed to be this: if conceptual schemes differ, so do languages. But speakers of different languages may share a conceptual scheme provided there is a way of translating one language into the other. Studying the criteria of translation is therefore a way of focussing on criteria of identity for conceptual schemes. If conceptual schemes aren't associated with languages in this way, the original problem is needlessly doubled. . . .[6]

This leads to the useful and innocuous idea that a difference in language is a necessary, though, to be sure, not sufficient condition for a difference in conceptual scheme.

A further step in the argument is the rather more controversial contention that one is entitled to call something a language only if one is prepared to claim that one can translate its (putative) "assertions" into one's *own* language. It is argued that we can know *that* something is a conceptual scheme only if we can transpose its concepts and categories into those of *our* conceptual scheme. And then, of course, it is not really a radical alternative. Davidson defends this position as follows:

> [To make sense of the idea of alternative conceptual schemes] we wanted to make sense of there being a language we could not translate at all. Or, to put the point differently, we were looking for a criterion of languagehood that did not depend on, or entail, translatability into a familiar idiom. . . . But whatever plurality we take experience to consist in—events like losing a button or stubbing a toe, having a sensation of warmth or hearing an oboe—we will have to individuate according to familiar principles. A language that organizes *such* entites must be a language very like our own.[7]

From here on in, the argumentation is now straightforward: Intertranslatability establishes sameness of conceptual schemes; translatability into *our* lingo is the test criterion for something's being a language, ergo there are no other, genuinely alternative conceptual schemes. The position is that the very idea of *"alternative* conceptual schemes" involves a *contradiction in terms*—to establish that a conceptual scheme is present we must translate into our language, to establish alternativeness the translation must break down. And clearly one cannot have it both ways! The very idea of *"alternative* conceptual schemes" becomes unworkable. And so this whole notion, whose reason for being is, after all, to provide for a certain sort of *contrast*, comes apart at the seams.

Note, moreover, that someone who maintains that *total* intertranslatability between the "languages" associated with "conceptual schemes" is incompatible with alternativeness is not in a position to concede that alternativeness can obtain in the face of *partial* intertranslatability. For a sequence of partial intertranslatabilities along mediating links can coexist with a total absence of intertranslatability between the mediated extremes. This is readily shown by considering a situation of the following sort. We have three languages (A, B, C), each having two sectors. These are such that sector #1 of A is intertranslatable (only) with #1 of B, and #2 of B is intertranslatable only with #2 of C. If alternativeness could be preserved by *partial* intertranslatability, then (given the obvious transitivity of this conception) we would have to regard A and C as alternative *despite* the fact that there is no intertranslatability between them at all. So if a *total* lack of intertranslatability is to be incompatible with alternativeness—as Davidson and others insist—then we are seemingly constrained to admit that alternativeness cannot subsist on a basis of merely *partial* intertranslatability either.

One thus arrives at the anomalous-seeming consequence that languages (or conceptual schemes) merely having pockets that are translation-intractable from one another's standpoint cannot be looked upon as alternatives to one another. The fact that the camel terminology of classical Arabic and the automobile terminology of modern English yield mutually untranslatable contentions must be construed to mean that we are precluded from looking on these linguistic frameworks as reflecting distinct conceptual schemes. This sort of upshot seemingly leaves no room for any useful application of the conception.

3. IS TRANSLATABILITY NECESSARY?

There is good reason, however, to think that the whole focus on actual *translation* is misguided. The key category in this area is surely not *translation* but *interpretation*. What counts for "their having a language" is not (necessarily) that we can literally *translate* what they say into our language but that we be able to *interpret* their sayings —to make some sort of intelligible sense of them through paraphrase, "explanation," or the like. This, of course, is something we must do in our own language, but it certainly does not require the sort of transposition we standardly characterize as "translation"—a far looser sort of reinterpretative reconstruction will serve. And such "interpretation" may well involve a complex process of theory building, rather than being anything as cut-and-dry as what is generally understood by "translation."[8]

How do we know that the sounds or movements or "writings" being made by those creatures represent the use of a *language* at all? The imputation of language-use is not the result of intellectual inspiration or insight; it is an item of theory building. The closer we can push toward translation the better. But translation is a disideratum, not a *sine qua non* necessity. Interpretative reconstruction can serve perfectly well. Language-attribution like all empirical theorizing is a matter of theoretical triangulation from observational data. And such theoretical systematization of the data can render attributions of language-use an eminently reasonable proposition. We knew well from the factual context that cuneiform inscriptions represented writing well before we had decoded them. As any cryptanalyst knows, we can tell *that* a language is being used, and even a good deal about *how* it is being used, short of any ability to translate.

To establish that a purportedly "alternative language" is a genuine language, there is certainly no need to claim intertranslatability with our own language (be it total or partial). This requirement would be much too stringent. We need to be able to report intelligently and informatively about what they are saying—to *interpret* it— but not necessarily to *translate* into the verbal resources of our language. Paraphrase, circumlocution, and all the other makeshifts of linguistic approximation can come into the picture. But *translatability* into our own language is certainly not the touch-stone.[9]

An insistence on translatability into our language as test-criterion of the presence of a conceptual apparatus aborts any prospect of grasping how the differences between conceptual schemes actually work. For such schemes differ precisely where and just to the extent that the resources of paraphrase and circumlocution become necessary. "The congressman appealed to his constituents for understanding regarding his opposition to the economic policies of the administration." Think of translating this into classical Latin! Or of so translating a treatise on quantum electrodynamics. And the same sort of thing holds when the tables are turned.

Consider the reverse process of "translation" of a passage into English in the case of the Melanesian utterance whose nearest English equivalent (so we are told) runs as follows:

We run front-wood ourselves; we paddle in place; we turn, we see behind their sea-arm Pilolu.[10]

It is obvious at a glance that there is no real *translation* going on here, but only a pseudo "translation" that leaves various key terms virtually untouched—a mere start at explanation.

There is and can be no genuine translation where the descriptive, taxonomic, or explanatory mechanisms—the whole empirically laden paraphernalia of empirical reportage—are substantially different. But the lack of such a linkage to "our" language (whatever that may be) does not thereby establish the absence of alternative-ness. For what is crucial here is the prospect of circumlocution and paraphrase, of explication and approximation—in short, of *interpretation*. And, of course, when one makes this shift from *translation* to *interpretation*, the scheme-countervailing

contention "But where *translatability* obtains, there is no difference in the conceptual apparatus at issue" no longer obtains, since *interpretability* is clearly not incompatible with scheme-differentiation.

In fact, the translatability argument against alternative conceptual schemes becomes trapped in a dilemma: If "translation" is construed literally and narrowly,
then it indeed follows that language-intertranslatability is incompatible with scheme-
alternativeness, but it certainly does not then hold that only translation can establish
the claim of another language to qualify as bearer of a conceptual scheme. If, on the
other hand, "translation" is construed broadly (to include any sort of explanation
or interpretation), then a demonstration of scheme-embodiment does indeed require
such translatability, but *this sort* of "translation" no longer suffices to show that one
selfsame conceptual scheme is at issue. (If merely "giving *some* idea of what is being
talked about" is to be called for, then we could indeed "translate" a modern chemistry text into the Ionic of Thales and Anaximander.) Either way, the argument
comes to grief.

4. THE FUNCTIONAL EQUIVALENCY CONSTRUCTION
OF ALTERNATIVE CONCEPTUAL SCHEMES

The use of an analogy may help clarify the issues. The *intertranslation* standard of
"counting as a language" is akin to an *exchange* standard of "counting as money."
On such an approach, it is only natural to take our own money as a fixed basis of
reference. What makes the German mark *money*—one would then hold—is just that
it can be traded against ours at a certain "rate of exchange." If something could not
be so exchanged, then it just would not be money. This seems a plausible line, but it
has serious deficiencies. Consider the Roman denarius. There is just no possibility of
exchange rate across the centuries.[11] As far as exchange rates go, modern dollars and
cents and imperial Roman coinage are simply incommensurable units. But that surely
does not preclude Roman "money" from qualifying as real *money*.

What qualifies the Roman "coin" to count as a *coin*, a genuine unit of money,
is its *functional* role—the way it was used. Various Roman coins are the *functional*
equivalent (given the *modus operandi* of Roman life) of our nickels and dimes, and
it is this which establishes their claims to be real coins that serve as real money.
Coins are what they are because of how they work.

A closely similar story holds for language use in the contexts of "talk" or
"writing" or the like. What makes such processes into uses of a language is their
function in communicative transactions in transmitting information, coordinating
action, eliciting responses, and the like. Not *translatability* as such, but *functional
equivalency* is the determinant of language use: the issue is one as much of sociology
as of semantics.

But consider the following counterargument:

To assess the functional equivalency of their putative use of "language" with
our unproblematic use of our own, we must know about their aims and purposes. To know this requires knowledge of their beliefs. But we now come up

against the purported fact that "knowledge of beliefs comes only with the ability to interpret words."[12]

But this objection does not stand. For it is clear that in suitable circumstances we can ascribe beliefs plausibly on the basis of data regarding *non*-verbal action and behavior—or on the basis of interpretations of linguistic behavior that stops well short of a capacity to achieve *translations*. That someone holds certain sorts of beliefs can be a matter of plausible theorizing well short of any capacity to *translate* his putative communicative endeavors. The ascription of beliefs does not demand a prior decoding of communicative data, however much it may be facilitated thereby.

Other languages accordingly qualify as such not necessarily because what they *say* is invariably something that we can say in our own terms, but because what they *do*—their communicative job or function in conveying information and coordinating behavior—is something we can understand as a linguistic process, something that can be made intelligible to us on sufficiently intimate analogy with our own language-using processes. What is at issue is a matter of different ways of going at a common job. To make a go of the idea of functional equivalence, we must, of course, have some conception of the functions at issue: some insight into the relevant structure of purpose and teleology.

To be sure, the determination of the goals of other sorts of beings is a complex matter. Perhaps some components of it are simple—things having to do with the preservation of the individual and the propagation of the species. But in general, the imputation of purposes calls for a substantial element of theory-building, of explanatory conjecture and of imputation, which is at work when we attribute language use to others. But there is nothing anomalous about that. The same holds for the attribution of any talent, skill, or capacity, and indeed even for descriptive categorization (e.g., the claim that yonder tree is elm).

After all, the teleology of language is nothing mysterious and occult. Language is primarily a purposive instrument whose cardinal aims are the transmission of information for the sake of implementation in action. Language is geared to afford us the mechanisms of information storage and to provide for the exchange of information that facilitates the programmatically coherent pursuit of individual goals and the coordination of effort in the pursuit of common goals.

On this account, then, it is the *functional equivalency* of the operations at issue that affords the needed principle of unification and renders diverse linguistic schemes as distinct instances of a common species. Functional equivalency is the collecting principle that makes them congeners. What, then, renders them *distinct* as instances of this common type?

5. ALTERNATIVE CONCEPTUAL SCHEMES INVOKE VARIANT FACTUAL COMMITMENTS

To become clear regarding what a conceptual scheme *is*, it is helpful to become clear as to what it *does*—how it *works*. A conceptual scheme is inherent in and coordinate with the *modus operandi* of concepts. And concepts are themselves laden with empirical and factual commitments. For at this time of day it seems plausible to adopt the no longer novel idea—argued by all the American Pragmatists against Kant—that all the categories of human thought are empirical and none a priori. Our taxonomic and explanatory mechanisms are themselves the products of inquiry[13]; the fundamental concepts in terms of which we shape our view of nature are a posteriori and not a priori. And schemes differ in just this regard—in undertaking different sorts of factual commitments.

On such a view—and it is surely correct—it transpires that all our concepts are factually committal—i.e., theory-laden—and that language is not an empirically neutral vehicle for making substantive commitments but itself reflects such substantive commitments.[14] A conceptual scheme comes to be correlative with and embedded in a substantive position as to how things work in the world. These factual commitments are crucial for an understanding of the conceptual scheme at issue. And so, as one moves to a non-Kantian (because empirical and a posteriori) conception of categories, one arrives at the familiar and widely agreed point that the concepts we deploy upon factual issues are themselves the products of our empirical inquiries and factual commitments.

We form our conception of the sun in terms of reference very different from those of Aristotle, and that of a heart in terms of reference very different from those of Galen. Consider how many facts about his own sword were unknown to Caesar. He did not know that it contained carbon or that it conducted electricity. The very concept at issue ("carbon, "electricity-conduction") were outside Caesar's cognitive range. Key facts (or presumptive facts) about even the most familiar things—trees and animals, bricks and mortar—were unknown 100 years ago. And this is so not just because of an ignorance of detail (as with a missing word in a crossword puzzle). Rather, the ignorance at issue arises because the very concepts at issue had not been formulated. It is not just that Caesar did not know what the half-life of californium is, but that he could not have understood this fact if someone had told it to him: it lay beyond—or, to put it less prejudicially, outside—his conceptual grasp. Our categorical frameworks (descriptive and explanatory mechanisms) reflect our view of the facts. They are inseparably linked to our picture of the truth (or purported truth) of things and stand correlative to the cognitive "state of the art."

One way of motivating the idea of different conceptual schemes is thus to approach this issue from the angle of conceptual innovation, a process clearly bound up with scheme-differentiation in that the new is (ex hypothesi) something different from the old. Consider what happened in the wake of a shift from (e.g.) the world view of contact-interaction theorists of the early seventeenth century to the electromagnetic conception of matter in the post-Maxwellian era. The issue here is not just that of new phenomena but one of new ways of looking at old phenomena, of different modes of classification, description, explanation. Such innovation makes it possible to say things that could not be said before—and so also to do new things. We have here a broadening—or at any rate a displacement of the conceptual horizons—and deal with things simply not dreamed of in the old conceptual dispensation.

A conceptual scheme for operation in the factual domain is always correlative with a *Weltanschaung*—a view of how things work in the world. And the issue of historical development becomes involved at this juncture, seeing that such a fact-committal scheme is clearly a product of temporal evolution. Our conceptions of things are a moving rather than a *fixed* target for analysis.

Innovation—the availability of assertions in one scheme that are simply unavailable in the other—is one important key to their difference. One conceptual scheme will envisage assertions that have no even remote equivalents in the other framework. They lie beyond the reach of effective transportation exactly because they involve different factual commitments and presuppositions. Given the change, it is not just that one says things differently but that one says altogether different things.[15]

6. SCHEME-DIFFERENTIATION AND THE TRUTH-STATUS OF THESES

Important consequences follow from this general line of approach to the idea of conceptual schemes.

What is involved with diverse schemes is a different way of conceptualizing facts—or rather the *purported* facts—as to how matters stand in the world. Different conceptual schemes embody different theories, and not just different theories about "the same things" (so that divergence inevitably reflects disagreement as to the truth or falsity of propositions), but different theories about different things. To move from one conceptual scheme to another is in some way to change the subject. It is not a quarrel about the same old issues.

If the conceptual scheme C' is to be thought of as an *alternative* to C along the lines we have in view, then one cannot think of C' as involving a different assignment of truth-values to the (key) propositions of C. One must avoid any temptation to view different conceptual schemes as distributing truth-values differently across the same propositions. The fact-ladenness of our concepts precludes this and prevents us from taking the difference of schemes to lie in a disagreement as to the truth-falsity classification of one selfsame body of theses or doctrines.

The difference between conceptual schemes is *not* a matter of treating the *same issues* discordantly (distributing the truth-values T and F differently over otherwise invariant propositions). The key contrast is that between saying something and saying nothing—not that between affirmation and counteraffirmation, but that between affirmation and silence. The difference between schemes does not lie in disagreement and conflict; it turns not on what they *do* say but on what they do not and cannot say at all, on matters that simply *defy* any attempt at actual *translation* from the one scheme into the other and that call for the evasive tactics of paraphrase, circumlocution, and "explanation."

Donald Davidson characterized the conceptual innovation involved in going over from one scheme to another as follows:

> We get a new out of an old scheme when the speakers of a language come to accept as true an important range of sentences they previously took to be false (and, of course, vice versa).[16]

But this does not get the matter quite right. If one is going to insist in this way on describing scheme-change in terms of a truth-value *redistribution*, then one will need a three-valued framework of truth-values, one that adds the neutral truth-value (*I*) of interdeterminacy or indefiniteness to the classical values of truth and falsity (*T* and *F*). For the issue of scheme innovation at bottom turns not on differences in determinate truth-values but on the having of no truth-value at all, because the item in question lies outside the boundaries of the conceptual horizon of a certain scheme.

The crucial point is thus that differentiation of conceptual schemes does not lie in different allocations of the determinate truth-values *T* and *F*. It operates in regard to truth-indeterminacy and turns on the fact that some truth-determinations from the angle of one scheme are simply *indeterminate* from that of the other in that it has *nothing whatsoever* to say on the matter.[17] A change of scheme is not a change of mind but a change of subject. (Shades of Feyerabend and conceptual incommensurability—at any rate at the local level.) And the key schematic changes are those from a definite (classical) truth-status to *I* (i.e., from *T* or *F* to *I*) or those in the reverse direction (i.e., from *I* to *T* or *F*). In the former case, the schematic frame of reference of an old issue is rejected and it ceases to be meaningful; in the latter, a new schematic frame of reference is introduced and gives meaning to a previously inaccessible question. The "disagreement" of schemes does *not* turn on a varying truth-assignment to *overlapping* theses but on differences in conceivability (formulatability) of the theses—the *nonoverlap* of theses.

Galenic and Pasteurian medicine, for example, in *some* respects simply *change the subject* so as no longer "to talk about the same things," but rather to talk differently—each about things of which the other takes no cognizance at all. The difference in "conceptual scheme" of modern and Galenic medicine is not that modern physicians have a different theory of the operation of the four humors from their Galenic counterparts but that modern medicine has *abandoned* the four humors, and not that Galenic physicians say different things about bacteria and viruses but that they have *nothing* to say about them—that they lie entirely beyond their conceptual horizon. (As was already noted, the connectability and mutual relevancy of these enterprises is not at bottom a semantical matter, one that turns on the meaning-content equivalency of their assertion, but a matter of their *functional* equivalency.)

We are told that all talk of "fitting" or "facing" or "accounting for" the facts in our experience in the world "adds nothing intelligible to the simple concept of being true."[18] But when the idea of truth-indeterminacy enters upon the scene, the untenability of this position emerges. For it is clear that even a false thesis can present a greater part of the truth than can an indeterminate one. Thus if the real position is

I	II
AAA	ABBBBB
AAAB	BBBB

It is clear that the falsehood "All the A's there are lie in sector I" gives a far better—a more helpful or informative—statement of "the real truth" of this situation than the blankness of know-nothing silence manages to do.

The most characteristic and significant sort of difference between one conceptual scheme and another thus does *not* lie in the sphere of *disagreements* or *conflicts* of the sort arising when the one theoretical framework holds something to be *true* that the other holds to be *false*. Rather, it arises when the one scheme is committed to something the other does not envisage at all—something that lies outside the conceptual horizons of the other. The typical case is that of the stance of Cicero's thought-world with regard to questions of electricity and magnetism. The Romans of classical antiquity did not hold *different* views on these issues; they held no views at all regarding them. This whole set of relevant considerations simply lay outside their conceptual repertoire. They did not assign the assertions in question a different truth-status from the one we favor; they assigned them no truth-values at all because they lay outside the conceptual reach. It is not just that Caesar did not know what the half-life of californium is; it is that he could have understood it if the Recording Angel had whispered it into his ear.

Certainly the upshot of the present defense of conceptual schemes is not just the truism that there are different languages, nor yet the truism that different cultures and eras have different theories about how things work in the world, important though these truisms are. Rather, the point is that in different cultural/linguistic settings one finds different conceptual mechanisms bound up with different world views in such a way as to make conceptual access difficult, complex, and perhaps even in some measure unattainable.

Different conceptual schemes carry us into literally different spheres of thought. They are not disjoint or incommensurate in the manner of geometric line segments—where, after all, very much the same sort of thing is at issue. Rather, they go their separate ways in very much the same way that different subject matter specialties do—even when (as per the demographer, the designer, and the materials specialist) they address themselves to something that (to a detached bystander) appears to be the same thing.

The different schemes are conceptually disjointed: certain key questions, theses, and issues of one scheme are *unavailable* in the other—where one is eloquent, the other is altogether silent. Certain perfectly ordinary assertions from the perspective of one scheme are altogether *ineffable* from that of the other. The central thesis of our deliberations is that the difference of different conceptual frameworks lies not so much in points of *disagreement* (that #1 says *true* where #2 says *false*) as in points of *mutual incomprehension*, in their lack of mutual contact. For it is not a matter of different schemes assigning a different determinate truth-status (T or F) to scheme-overlapping theses; the key to scheme-differentiation lies in the nonoverlap of theses —the fact that what can be said by one is simply outside the range of the other. The difference between schemes is accordingly a matter of difference in orientation rather than one of disagreement in *doctrine*. It is less like that between the Christian heresies than like that between Christianity and Buddhism. The denizens of different schemes live in—to at least some extent—different "thought worlds," as it were. What is at issue here is something relatively familiar in an era when the phenomena of cultural relativity are well known. (In earlier times, when education in the classics was in vogue, one knew at first hand the contrast between the thought-world of classical antiquity and that of one's own day.)

7. COGNITIVE COPERNICANISM AND THE IMPLICATIONS OF COGNITIVE PROGRESS

Given that different linguistic-conceptual schemes are possible along such lines as have been sketched (with conceptual disjointness superengrafted upon functional equivalency), what can be said regarding the comparative status of our own scheme? Seeing that it provides us with the paradigm standard against which all else is measured —a consideration that establishes its epistemic *priority*—must we not concede to it a position of conceptual *primacy* as well? By no means! The present position does not entail the view that we ourselves constitute the center about which everything moves.

On first thought, it might seem that we have to construe the idea of different conceptual schemes along such lines as the following:

The descriptive practices of Scheme #1 differ from those of Scheme #2 in that Scheme #1 treats such and such an issue A-wise, whereas Scheme #2 treats it B-wise.

Such a view immediately advances our own language/conceptual scheme into a controlling position. For it is going to be necessary to use *our* machinery to do the crucial work of (1) specifying the issue in question and (2) describing the two different manners in which the schemes at issue treat this issue. It becomes a matter of transacting all the relevant comparisons and contrasts within the framework of our own conceptual scheme. Our own language/scheme becomes the pivot point around which all else revolves.

But this just is not how the matter actually stands. Establishing that different things are at issue is not a matter of having to transpose everything into our own terms so as to establish that two schemes treat "the same thing" differently, but simply of noting that there are some issues that one scheme treats and the other does not. The comparison lies immediately between the schemes themselves, without the necessity of obtruding ours between them as a vehicle of mediation. The camel-descriptive terminology of Arabic vs. Chinese or the kinship-pattern taxonomy of Bali and Sardinia need not be contrasted through the mediation of English (i.e., this need not be so done *per se*, though, to be sure, it may have to be so done *by us* if we are sufficiently inept).

Neither on a cultural nor on a temporal basis are we committed to the idea that the framework of our own thinking is inherently superior. Our notion of "a real thing" is inherently such that the possibility of learning more about any thing will always have to be kept in mind as an open prospect. This "inexhaustibility" of the potential knowledge of things is implicit in the very concept of a "real thing" as it figures in our conceptual scheme. And in view of this, we must never lay claim to a cognitive monopoly or cognitive finality. It is a crucial fact about our epistemic stance toward the real world to recognize that every part and parcel of it contains compartments that lie beyond our present cognitive reach—at *any* "present" whatever.

The fact that we ourselves do not occupy the conceptual center of the universe about which all else revolves in the cognitive domain becomes especially clear in the context of historical development. For, in all due realism and humility, we need to adopt an *epistemological Copernicanism*, a view that rejects the egocentric claim that we ourselves occupy a pivotal position in the epistemic dispensation. We must recognize (e.g.) that there is nothing inherently sacrosanct about our own present cognitive posture vis-à-vis that of other historical junctures. There is no reason to think that *our* view of things—be it of individual things (the moon, the great wall of China) or of types thereof (the domestic cat, the common cold)—is any more definitive and final than that taken by our predecessors in the cognitive enterprise. We have little choice but to regard the view that current science captures the truth of things as a fiction that must be presumed to be contrary to fact. The original Copernical revolution made the point that there is nothing *ontologically* privileged about our own position in space. The doctrine now at issue effectively holds that there is nothing *cognitively* privileged about our own position in time. Given a sensible view of how we ourselves stand vis-à-vis the past, one must suppose a position of parity with respect to how we ourselves will stand vis-à-vis the future.

This perspective suggests the humbling view that just as we think our predecessors of 100 years ago had a fundamentally inadequate grasp on the furniture of the world, so our successors of 100 years hence will take the same view of *our* knowledge (or purported knowledge) of things. No primacy—and certainly no finality—can automatically be claimed for our own conceptual posture, be it within the historical course of events or the geographic diversity of cultures.

8. THE MYTH OF A UBIQUITOUS, SCHEME-NEUTRAL INPUT

It will clarify the nature of conceptual schemes to consider some misconceptions regarding them and to set aside some of the errors attributed to the partisans of conceptual schemes that they in fact are not or need not stand committed to.

Objections to the idea of different conceptual schemes are sometimes predicated on the view that recognition of such schemes would commit one to the view that there is one selfsame underlying substratum—one ubiquitously present, uniform, cognitive raw stuff of pure experience, bare sense, elemental stimuli, or whatever—which different conceptual schemes (languages) proceed to process differently. Let us accordingly begin with the following objection:

> To adopt the idea of conceptual schemes is to commit oneself to the notion of a scheme-neutral epistemic basis—an ur-text, as it were, of raw (conceptually "uncooked") experience, sensation, or some such "given"—which different languages transpose into their own conceptual idiom. The concept presupposes the model of *mediation* through language and concepts of a "thought-independent" givenness—an "an sich" world of pre-schematic represented

which we schematize into representations by means of concepts and language. The partisans of conceptual schemes must think of language as a way of depicting or encoding extralinguistic reality—of transforming one determinate structure into another. But (so the objection continues) any reality we can conceive of—any reality we can *say* anything about—is *already* linguistically and conceptually mediated. The idea of a "thought-independent reality" that is *prior* to the mechanisms of conceptualizing thought—a reality that lies "behind the curtain" of schematic conceptualization—is thus a misleading myth. The real is simply "what we can really and truly say or think to be the case" and not an extraconceptual substratum represented in our thought by the mediation of languages and conceptual schemes. The idea of conceptual schemes accordingly stands committed to an incorrect and improper model—that of a linguistic/conceptual processing of preschematic yet determinate experiential inputs.

The model of scheme-operation at issue here is objected to as producing a mistaken form/content dualism in projecting the picture of common, invariant, universal, preschematic input which different conceptual schemes process differently. Conceptual schemes, so it is held, are predicated on the Myth of a Ubiquitous, Scheme-Neutral Input. Donald Davidson, for example, sees the idea of a conceptual scheme as committed to the objectionable picture of an empirical *substratum* which "is in turn explained by reference to the facts, the world, experience, sensation, the totality of sensory stimuli, or something similar."[19] The objection at issue views the conception of a conceptual scheme as predicated on the model of a common, preexistent raw material input which is processed differently by different schemes,[20] subject to the idea of a single, common reality which is represented differently from the different "point of view" of various conceptual schemes[21] that themselves are so many distinct conventionalizations each filtering reality through concepts in its own way, so that each filtering medium imposes its own characteristic inprint upon scheme neutral reality—the way the world *really* is.[22]

It is only too clear that this model of the schematization of a preschematic raw material is indeed objectionable.[23] For it is always problematic to postulate the existence of something whose nature we cannot possibly describe. And there just is no way of specifying whatever "input" our cognitive processes may have apart from the content with which these processes themselves endow it. (As Kant saw, there is no positive descriptive information that can be offered regarding the *Ding an sich* that sensibility is thought to deliver up to the cognitive processing of our understanding.) Even if one were to grant *in abstracto* the existence of a preschematically *given* over and above the schematically graspable, there is nothing one can *do* with this conception—there is no way of implementing this distinction, of applying it to something or other. Our cognition of the real is a matter of a transaction in which the respective contributions of thought and reality just cannot be separated from one another.[24] The decisive shortcoming of the idea of a preschematized "given" as an explanatory instrument of the theory of cognition is simply that *ex hypothesi* no one can possibly say what the given is—that it is inherently and necessarily beyond the reach of conceptualization. No intelligible content can be given to this idea. To invoke it is thus not to explain the obscure by the yet more obscure; it is to explain it by the impenetrable. As Richard Rorty has trenchantly put it, "the suggestion that our concepts shape neutral material no longer makes sense once there is nothing to serve as this material."[25] We must not become entranced by the metaphor of "seeing the same thing from different points of view" in a case where it is only too clear that there just is no earthly way of saying *anything* about "the same thing" that is purportedly at issue. If all "objects of thought" are constituted relative to conceptual schemes (which, after all, represents the role and mission of such schemes), then there cannot—*ex hypothesi*—be a thought-accessible presystematic something for such schemes to schematize.

Let all this be granted, as it should and must be. All the same, the presently envisaged use of these considerations as a *point d'appui* for an objection to conceptual schemes is emphatically improper and inappropriate. For this objection is based on the mistaken idea that the conception of diverse conceptual schemes rests on the presupposition of an incorrect and objectionable processing model according to which there is an invariant identifiable and thus describable raw material that is viewed differently from the perspective of different conceptual schemes. This is quite wrong. The idea of a preexisting "thought-independent" and scheme-invariant reality that is seen differently from different perceptual perspectives *just is not* a presupposition of the idea of different conceptual schemes. The Kantian model of a potentially differential schematic processing of a uniform preschematic epistemic raw material is nowise essential to the idea of different conceptual schemes.

The supporter of the idea of different conceptual schemes certainly need *not* espouse the thesis:

(1) that there is a pre- or sublinguistic cognitive substratum and that different languages afford us different ways of telling about IT (this preexisting substratum).

Rather, he stands committed only to what results when the difficulty-generating words of this proposition are deleted, to yield the contention

(2) that different languages afford us different ways of talking—of saying different sorts of things, rather than saying "the same things" differently or making different claims about "the same thing."

If one holds—as seems only proper—that all individuation, all identification, and all description must proceed from the angle of a conceptual scheme, then it would clearly be inappropriate to say there is an identifiable something (reality, experience, *materia prima*, the matrix of sense-stimuli, or whatever) that is prior to and independent of any and all scheme-based conceptualization. On such an approach, the conception "scheme-independent reality" is not *constitutive*, not a substantive constituent of the world—in contrast with "mere appearance"—but a purely regulative idea whose function is to block the pretentions of any one single scheme to a monopoly on correctness or finality.

Accordingly, the objection at issue does not apply to the present approach to the idea of different conceptual schemes. The erroneous conception of an input of some common identifiable raw material is thus by no means an inherent and inevitable facet of the very idea of a conceptual scheme. As we have seen, in speaking of different conceptual schemes we need not say that different language communities "formulate *the same materials* (experience, sensation, or whatever) differently" but just that they employ different sorts of formulations. We can say that their describing practices differ without saying that they formulate different descriptions for the same thing. Accordingly, different conceptual schemes need not disagree about *the same thing*. To implement the notion that different conceptual schemes are at work, we emphatically do not need to say that Aristotle, Newton, and Einstein "are saying different things about the same thing" (in saying that the world is spherical in the one case and that space-time is a four-dimensional and finite-but-boundless manifold in the other case). It is enough to hold that different schemes say different things "on the same theme" (*functionally* identified) rather than talk differently about the same object (*substantively* identified). The correlation at issue can proceed through *functional* equivalency rather than equivalency of designation. The view that failure of translation affords concurrent evidence against the presence of a language founders on the fact that language use never exists *in vacuo* but always functions in a purposive context in which functional equivalency can fill the vacuum of conceptual inaccessibility.

In sum, given a proper conception of what conceptual schemes are and how they actually work, one can abandon entirely the myth of a uniform, shared, preschematic input without giving up the idea of different conceptual schemes.

9. THE MYTH OF FORM-CONTENT SEPARABILITY

Kant stressed that perception cannot be separated from conception—that in the domain of empirical fact, observation cannot be separated from descriptive characterization. Extending this line of thought, his latter-day Quinean successors stress that conception cannot be separated from judgment, that issues of *meaning* cannot be separated from issues of *fact* or purported fact, that "what we mean by words" in descriptive discourse and "what propositions we accept as true" are issues that are inseparably and inextricably comingled. There is an intimate, nay indissoluble, interlinkage between the meanings of one's terms and the facts (or purported facts) one uses them to state: the meanings of words are shaped in terms of their user's beliefs about the issues. Meanings (concepts) are thus fact-correlative: they are bearers *and also the products* of our factual beliefs. They are not only the tools of inquiry but the products of inquiry.

In consequence of this interlinkage it follows that "one will not be able to draw a clear distinction between the foreigner's using words different in meaning from any words in our language and the foreigner's having many false beliefs." [26] Where concepts are concerned, there is no priority of form over content. One cannot take the view: concepts first, theses later; one cannot adopt the imputation: settle all issues of meaning first, and all issues of truth subsequently. Inquiry into meanings (word use) and into judgments (opinions) must accordingly be handled as one holus-bolus unit within the overall cognitive framework of which they are inseparable components.

This general line of thought envisages paradigm situations of the following type. Consider the case of someone whom we take (at first blush) to say about dogs exactly what we would say about cats (that they meow rather than bark, that they generally chase mice but not mailmen, and so on). As this circumstance emerges more fully, we ourselves would (very rightly) begin to wonder if we have got it right in thinking that they are talking about *dogs* but have very bizarre ideas about them, rather than that we have got it wrong and that they are really talking about *cats* after all (but using a somewhat odd nomenclature).

There is an inevitable tradeoff between the attribution of weird *beliefs* to others and the prospect of *misunderstanding*—of error in our construction of their assertions. For that they really mean to talk about DOGS is in fact a *theory of ours* (re. a certain equivalency in translation or interpretation), and in framing such interpretative theories we are governed by the standard rule: adapt your interpretative hypotheses so as to maximize truth, to make as much as you can come out to be true. Interpretation is, after all, a matter of theory-building, and here the usual inductive principle of inference to the best answer applies, with "best" understood in terms of the overall smoothness of its dovetailings of our systematization.

One thus cannot separate questions of the *meaning of terms* (how our concepts function in their linguistic setting) from questions of *truth* (views on how matters go in the world). It follows that one cannot handle meaning and truth *sequentially*. Meaning and truth (semantics and natural science) are inseparable and symbiotic in the factual domain. To grasp a language requires understanding the conceptual scheme it implements and thus requires knowing (at least in rough outline) what sort of world view its users hold—their picture of the "laws of nature" (or some functional equivalent thereof).

Now there is certainly a questionable and erroneous way of conceiving of a *conceptual* scheme—viz., as separable from and somehow "underlying" the *cognitive* scheme of its exponents (their *Weltanschanung*)—as dealing with the conceptual machinery of their thought quite independently of their material beliefs. Donald Davidson has put the matter as follows:

> [R]etaining the idea of language as embodying a conceptual scheme . . . [means that] in place of the dualism of the analytic-synthetic we get the dualism of conceptual scheme and empirical content. . . . I want to urge that this second dualism of scheme and content, of organizing system and something waiting to be organized, cannot be made intelligible and defensible.[27]

On the view being criticized in this passage, the form-oriented issue of how people think—of the categorial and taxonomic framework of their discourse—is hermetically separated from the content-oriented issue of *what* they think, of the substantive materials of their beliefs.

This criticsim is right-minded; the view it condemns is surely incorrect.

But this incorrectness is nowise built into the idea of a conceptual scheme as such. There is—and this warrants emphasis—no need whatever to subscribe to this view and to construe the conception of a conceptual scheme as involving an irrevocable commitment to this rationalist notion of a neat form-content separability. There is no obstacle to construing conceptual schemes as part and parcel of a comprehensive belief-structure that is committed to the facts (or purported facts) about things over a relatively large domain of issues.

It would seem that the animus of various recent writers against the idea of conceptual schemes is largely due to their construing the notion as committed to the Myth of a Ubiquitous Scheme-Neutral Input (as per the deliverances of Kant's *sensibility*) and the Myth of Form-Content Separability (as per the schematizing labor of Kant's *understanding*). But this perspective unjustly visits upon conceptual schemes a construction geared too closely to the Kantian processing-faculty model, a construction from which this resource can certainly be extricated and from which it is in fact free throughout most of its recent invocations. It is widely stressed nowadays that our conceptual schemes in the empirical domain are built upon *Weltanschauungen*, i.e., views on the facts or purported facts about the world; that empirical concepts are "theory permeated," to use Karl Popper's term; that they involve facts and are inconceivable without them. Our conceptual mechanisms evolve in a historical dialectic of feedback dialectic between cognitive projection on the one hand and experiential interaction with nature upon the other. They are globally *a posteriori* as products of past experience; they are only locally *a priori* in that we bring them to the context of current experience and never encounter situations with a conceptual *tabula rasa*.

The idea that a conceptual scheme is altogether *a priori* and free from substantive commitments is thus clearly mistaken. But the conception of a conceptual scheme as such is patently strong enough to survive the abandonment of such mistaken conceptions. The fact that conceptual schemes can be misconceived is no reason for invalidating the very idea at issue. (Mistaken conceptions can be had of anything!)[28] The notion of a conceptual scheme can survive the abandonment of such misconceptions which are based on an erroneous construction of how conceptual schemes work.

10. THE APPRAISAL OF CONCEPTUAL SCHEMES

In what sense can it be said that distinct conceptual schemes are *alternative* to one another? If it cannot be maintained that they process the same material differently, how can they conflict? If their relationship is one of discontinuity and mutual incomprehension, how can they disagree? The answer is that, strictly speaking, they do not disagree. They do not involve the sort of logical conflict that arises when one body of commitments says one thing and another something else about the same item and the two statements are incompatible.

But if conceptual schemes do not *disagree*, then why not simply conjoin them? Why not simply combine them adjunctively, espousing one alongside the others? Several things must be said (somewhat telegraphically) in reply: (1) We do in fact to some extent do this, superimposing the scheme of science and the scheme of every-day life, for example. Or, again, think of the scholar's ability to move in the thought-worlds of different cultures or civilizations. (2) There are, however, weighty practical reasons why the extent to which we can do this is very limited: It is enormously demanding in learning and effort and attention. Just as very few people can master more than one language well enough to "pass for a native" in it, so only few can achieve a conceptual repertoire that makes them fully at home in significantly diverse conceptual frameworks. And one further consideration might be added: (3) In general, any fairly comprehensive conceptual scheme has an associated value-orientation in point of specifically *cognitive* values. It incorporates its own characteristic sched-ules of what sorts of things are important, interesting, puzzling, worthy of attention, and so on. And this circumstance produces limiting restrictions.

As these considerations suggest, conceptual schemes do not conflict in the man-ner of mutually contradictory bodies of assertions. Rather, they conflict in the man-ner of diverse instrumentalities—the manner in which we cannot make effective con-current use of hammer and saw. It is this sort of *practical* incompatibility that is at issue with diverse conceptual schemes rather than the theoretical incompatibility of mutual contradiction.

But an important consideration remains. For—usually at any rate—the "alter-natives" at issue with "alternative conceptual schemes" are such in the sense of being alternatives *for somebody* rather than in that of being alternatives for us. Given that we ourselves operate in the conceptual domain as we do, we ourselves could not adopt them, short, at any rate, of our undergoing the sort of conversion experience (*intellectual* conversion experience, to be sure) after which one tends to view oneself as no longer quite the same person. Given that we stand where we do, we simply "cannot get there from here."

In closing, it is germane to consider briefly the question of the appraisal and evaluation of the relative merits of alternative conceptual schemes. If the situation were simply that the difference between schemes resided in a different distribution of the determinate truth-values T and F over fundamentally the same range of con-tentions, then the assessment of relative merits would be a relatively simple process: we would simply ask ourselves which is right more of the time. And then, of course, we would have no alternative but to answer this question with reference to the truth-commitments that emanate from *our own* conceptual scheme. Scheme-assessment would have to be a matter of simply determining which scheme has a fuller grasp on the facts as we ourselves see them—of determining which, by our own lights, is right about more things and wrong about fewer. And, of necessity, it lies in the very na-ture of this process that our own scheme will always emerge victorious from such comparisons.

But the actual situation is quite otherwise. Different schemes talk about things differently—and do this not just in terms of disagreement about the same things but also in terms of mooting altogether different sorts of things (different sorts of facts or worlds). Regarding the meaning-content of their assertions, they are—or may be—

simply out of touch with one another and stand in a condition of Feyerabendian incommensurability. Accordingly, comparison cannot be made on the basis of comparative *correctness* (embracing more truths and fewer falsehoods). Nor is comparison feasible on the basis of subject-matter *coverage* (being ampler, richer, fuller, and so on). For *whose standards* of what is a genuine enlargement and what is a pointless proliferation are going to be used here—which scheme can appropriately be used as the arbiter?

Such considerations indicate the inappropriateness of a content comparison approach to the issue of appraisal. They suggest—surely rightly—that comparative appraisal must be detached altogether from the sphere of *semantical* issues—truthfulness, subject-matter coverage, or any other such consideration relating to a comparison of meaning-content. For otherwise we would have little alternative but to advance our own scheme automatically into a position of standard of comparison and so run afoul of the strictures of a cognitive Copernicanism.

But how can linguistic frameworks and their correlative conceptual schemes possibly be compared on a linguistically neutral, meaning-abstractive basis? The answer here lies in recognizing that the appropriate basis of comparison is *pragmatic efficacy*. The traditional pragmatists have put the key point well. C. I. Lewis, for example, has written:

> [T]he point of the pragmatic theory is, I take it, the responsiveness of truth to human bent or need, and the fact that in some sense it is made by mind. From the point of view here presented, this is valid, because the interpretation of experience must always be in terms of categories and concepts which the mind itself determines. There may be alternative conceptual systems, giving rise to alternative descriptions of experience, which are equally objective and equally valid, if there be not some purely logical defect in these categorial conceptions. When this is so, choice will be determined, consciously or unconsciously, on pragmatic grounds. New facts may cause a shifting of such grounds. When historically such change of interpretation takes place we shall genuinely have new truth, whose newness represents the creative power of human thought and the ruling consideration of human purpose. . . . [O]nce the categorial system, in terms of which it is to be interpreted, is fixed, and concepts have been assigned a denotation in terms of sensation and imagery, it is this given experience which determines the truths of nature. It is between these two, in the choice of conceptual system for application and in the assigning of sensuous denotation to the abstract concept, that there is a pragmatic element in truth and knowledge. In this middle ground of trial and error, of expanding experience and the continual shift and modification of conception in our effort to cope with it, the drama of human interpretation and the control of nature is forever being played.[29]

Just as scheme-eligibility (i.e., *counting* as a conceptual scheme) is a teleological matter of *functional equivalency*, so scheme merit (i.e., counting as a *relatively good* conceptual scheme) is a matter of *functional efficacy*.[30] The standard judgment is that of the question: Which scheme underwrites more efficient and effective intervention in the course of events so as to produce those desired results in the area of cognition and communication for whose sake languages and their conceptual schemes are instituted as human resources. (This, after all, is the *raison d'être* of our cognitive instrumentalities, language among them.)

As pragmatists have always stressed (and some of the skeptics before them), languages and conceptual instrumentalities are instituted among people in the interests of effective action within our environing world. Successful praxis thus affords a natural and *semantically neutral* arbiter of our conceptual mechanisms.[31] Schemes may be disjoint or incommensurable on the side of issues of conceptual meaning-content, but they do indeed enter into mutual relevancy on the side of praxis. Their relative superiority or inferiority is not an issue of how much of the somehow scheme-neutral truth they manage to capture (how close they come to grasping the content of God's Mind); it is the practical issue of how effectively they enable us to find our way amid the shoals and narrows of a difficult world. Here once again we have a token of the primacy of practical over theoretical reason.[32] And in this regard the question of the merits of our own scheme is by no means an academic one—its victory in the comparison process is by no means a foregone conclusion.

Nothing prevents us from denying that ours is inherently the best conceptual scheme—a kind of *ne plus ultra*. Such a stance is nowise self-inconsistent. Consider how cognitive progress happens. We can admit THAT the scientists of the future will have a better science, an ampler and more adequate understanding of the natural universe, and thus a better conceptual scheme—but we cannot anticipate HOW. We need not take the stance that our own conceptual scheme is somehow the last word. Nevertheless, our recognition *that* our scheme is imperfect, though correct and appropriate in the interests of realism, is of rather limited utility. For it does not of itself afford us any help in improving it. It is a *regulative* conception that preempts any claim to dogmatic finality, not a *constitutive* one that puts substantively informative data at our disposal. A realization of the *en gros* deficiency of our conceptual machinery unhappily affords no basis for its emendation in matters of detail.[33]

Notes

1. Thomas Kuhn, *The Structure of Scientific Revolutions* (Chicago, 1970).
2. Georg Simmel, "Ueber eine Beziehung der Selektionslehre zur Erkenntnistheorie," *Archiv für systematische Philosophie and Soziologie* 1 (1895):34–45 (see pp. 40–41).
3. William James, *Pragmatism* (New York, 1907), p. 171.
4. See, for example: Barry Stroud, "Conventionalism and the Indeterminacy of Translation," in D. Davison and J. Hintikka, eds., *Words and Objections: Essays on the Work of W. V. Quine* (Dordrecht, 1969); Richard Rorty, "The World Well Lost," *The Journal of Philosophy* 69 (1972): 649–65; and Donald Davidson, "On the Very Idea of a Conceptual Scheme," *Proceedings and Addresses of the American Philosophical Association* 47 (1973–74):5–20.
5. Donald Davidson, "Conceptual Scheme."
6. *Ibid.*, p. 6.
7. *Ibid.*, pp. 14–15.
8. It seems plausible to hold that we are actually in possession of a paradign example of two mutually nonintertranslatable languages—the physicalistic and the mentalistic. It seems possible

that we should be able somehow to *interpret* each in terms of the other, but certainly not that we should *translate* from one to the other.

9. Writers on the theory of rationality often stress that whatever we can validly acknowledge as constituting a reason for "them" is something that would also have to count as a reason for *us*. (See, for example, Martin Hollis, "Limits of Irrationality" in B. R. Wilson, ed., *Rationality* [Evanston and New York, 1970], pp. 214-20.) But this fact that what is sauce for the goose is sauce for the gander where "the reasonable" is concerned can be construed in terms of *functional* equivalency considerations and does not hinge on considerations of linguistic *modus operandi* and translational equivalency. Hollis's indispensable "bridgehead hypothesis" ("first that the native perceive more or less what he [the investigator] perceives and secondly that they say about it more or less what he would say") clearly turns on functional rather than translational considerations (else why that "more or less"?), and in fact is—as he points out—an underlying presupposition essential to the substantiation of any translational hypotheses.

10. B. Malinowski, Supplementary Essay to C. K. Ogden and I. A. Richards, *The Meaning of Meaning*, 4th (revised) ed. (London, 1936), pp. 300-301. As Malinowski justly observes, "Instead of translating, of inserting simply an English word for a native one, we are faced by a long and not altogether simple process of describing wide fields of custom, of social psychology and of tribal organization which correspond to one term or another." (*Ibid.*, pp. 301-2.). Compare the discussion of these issues in John Dewey, *Reconstruction in Philosophy* (New York, 1920).

11. We can of course exchange them for our money by buying them in shops. But *that* cannot be what makes them money. One can buy virtually anything in shops.

12. Davidson, "Conceptual Scheme," pp. 18-19.

13. Thus John Dewey contemptuously complained that "rationalism assumes that the concepts of reason are so self-sufficient and so far above experience that they need and can service no confirmation in experiences." (*Reconstruction in Philosophy*, p. 97.)

14. See chap. VI of the writer's *The Primacy of Practice* (Oxford, 1973).

15. C. I. Lewis, in *Mind and the World Order* (New York, 1929), pp. 268-69, put the point at issue in a way that cannot be improved upon:

> Categories and concepts do not literally change; they are simply given up and replaced by new ones. When disease entities give place to mere adjectival states of the organism induced by changed conditions such as bacteria, the old description of the phenomena of disease does not become false in any sense in which it was not always false. All objects are abstractions of one sort or another; a disease entity is found to be a relatively poor kind of abstraction for the understanding and control of the phenomena in question. But in terms of this abstraction any interpretation of experience which ever was correctly made will still remain true. Any contradiction between the old truth and the new is *verbal only*, because the old word "disease" has a new meaning. The old word is retained but the old concept is discarded as a poor intellectual instrument and replaced by a better one.

16. Donald Davidson, "Conceptual Scheme," pp. 9-10.

17. The crucial point at issue is reminiscent of Leibniz's contention that minds that cannot communicate live in different natural spheres and that "whoever asks whether another world or another space, can exist is asking to this extent whether there are minds that can communicate nothing to us." ("On Existence, Dreams, and Space," in Ivan Jagodinsky, ed., *Leibnitiana elementa philosophiae arcanae de summa rerum* [Kazan, 1913], p. 114.)

18. See Davidson, "Conceptual Schemes," pp. 15-17, for the development of this line of thought.

19. *Ibid.*, p. 21.

20. The fundamental idea here goes back to Kant. For modern variations cf. Lewis, *Mind and the World Order*, and H. H. Price, *Perception* (London, 1933).

21. This latter way of approaching the issue invites the very proper complaint that: "Different points of view make sense, but only if there is a common coordinate system on which to plot them." (Davidson, "Conceptual Scheme," p.6.)

22. Compare Nelson Goodman's critique of this view in "The Way The World Is" in his *Problems and Projects* (Indianapolis and New York, 1972), pp. 24–32.

23. One should perhaps be prepared to make an exception of "the world" or "the universe" or "the true facts" or "things at large" or "reality" or "existence" in this regard. Such *ens et unum* formulas present only a vacuous unifier: an inherently empty container into which we can put anything and everything. This is not a *materia prima*—or indeed any kind of material—but a mere placeholder. For an interesting discussion of relevant issues see Justus Buchler, "On the Concept of 'The World,'" *The Review of Metaphysics* 31 (1978):555–79.

24. See the writer's *Conceptual Idealism* (Oxford, 1973).

25. Richard Rorty, "The World Well Lost," p. 650.

26. *Ibid.*

27. Donald Davidson, "Conceptual Schemes," p. 11.

28. To be sure, someone might ask: Why then bother with this conceptual detour at all? Why not simply operate with the notion of different theoretical stances? What work does the idea of "different schemes" do for you that that of "different theories" does not? The answer here lies in the consideration that it is not the generic fact that theories are at issue, but the special facts as to the *sorts* of theories that are involved, which makes it appropriate and helpful to speak of "conceptual schemes" in this connection.

29. Lewis, *Mind and the World Order*, pp. 271–72.

30. Note that in this teleological connection our own conceptual scheme (or language) must once again enjoy a certain primacy. For when it comes to our understanding of the proper work, role, and function of conceptual schemes it is inevitable that our own scheme should afford us the paradigm by which we judge the issue in general.

31. It is, of course, possible that the appeal to praxis may prove indecisive—that for certain ranges of purpose the one scheme is superior and that for other purposes other schemes are superior. Indeed this seems to be true with respect to the schemes of natural science and of ordinary life, where evolution has equipped us with a highly effective organon for social interaction.

32. These themes are developed more fully in the writer's *The Primacy of Practice* (Oxford, 1973) and *Methodological Pragmatism* (Oxford, 1976).

33. Thanks are due to Jay Garfield and Jean Roberts for helpful comments on a draft of this essay.

Is a Criterion
of Verifiability Possible?

L. JONATHAN COHEN

The purpose of this paper is to try to set the record a little straighter about the idea of a verifiability criterion. In its 1946 form[1] Ayer's proposal was that a (natural-language) statement should be regarded as literally meaningful if it is either analytic or indirectly verifiable. S is directly verifiable if either S is itself an observation-statement, or, like "All crows are black," say, S is such that in conjunction with one or more observation-statements it entails at least one observation-statement that is not deducible from these other premises alone. S is indirectly verifiable if two conditions are satisfied: first, in conjunction with certain other premises, S must entail one or more directly verifiable statements that are not deducible from these other premises alone; second, these other premises must not include any statement that is not either analytic or directly verifiable or capable of being independently established as indirectly verifiable. Ayer's proposal provoked two powerful objections, one from Hempel and the other from Church, and it is widely held[2] that Ayer's verifiability principle cannot be further revised so as to obviate all objections of such a nature. I believe, however, that this is a mistake and that when the principle is appropriately revised we are in a better position to appreciate its merits and demerits as a criterion for a certain kind of meaningfulness.

Hempel's objection[3] was that all consequences that can be deduced from S with the help of permissible subsidiary hypotheses can also be deduced from the conjunction of S and N by means of the same subsidiary hypotheses, where N is any statement you please.

Church's objection[4] was that if there are any three observation-statements and none of them entails any of the others, then it is possible to construct appropriate additional premises to be conjoined with any statement whatsoever, or its denial, so as to guarantee indirect verifiability for that statement, or its denial, respectively. Suppose the three observation-statements are O_1, O_2, and O_3. Church argued that for any S, $(-O_1 \ \& \ O_2) \lor (O_3 \ \& \ -S)$ is directly verifiable according to Ayer's defini-

347

tion, because with O_1 it entails O_3. Then this directly verifiable statement when conjoined with S entails O_2. So S is indirectly verifiable unless it happens that $(-O_1$ & $O_2)$ v $(O_3$ & $-S)$ alone entails O_2, in which case O_3 & $-S$ entails O_2, so that $-S$ is directly verifiable.

Now both these objections exploit the fact that Ayer's version of the verifiability principle allows a statement to be directly or indirectly verifiable even if it has more content than is required for the deduction of observation-statements. So the heart of the problem is: how are we to exclude this superfluous content while the vocabulary available for formulating the principle remains just the terms 'analytic' and 'observation-statement', plus standard logical and metalogical terminology? But at the same time, instead of distinguishing between a definition of direct verifiability and a definition of indirect verifiability, and also referring in the latter to statements capable of being independently established as indirectly verifiable, we might as well aim at making our definition of observational verifiability explicitly recursive. The following seems to do the trick:

> An observation-statement, and its negation, are to be said to be observationally verifiable at level 0.

> A natural-language statement S, and its negation, are to be said to be observationally verifiable at level 1 if and only if the following three conditions are jointly satisfied:

> i. S is not analytically true or analytically false.

> ii. At least one observation-statement E is formal-logically deducible from the conjunction of S with zero or more observation-statements that do not themselves suffice to entail E.

> iii. For any class C of statements, if
> > (a) the conjunction of members of C but of no proper subclass of C is formal-logically equivalent to S, and
> > (b) no non-logical term occurs more often in any one member of C than it occurs in S,

> > then there is no C', such that C' is a proper subclass of C and any observation-statement E, that is formal-logically deducible from the conjunction of S with zero or more observation-statements that do not themselves formal-logically entail E, is deducible from the conjunction of the members of C' with the same observation-statements.

> A natural-language statement S, and its negation, are to be said to be observationally verifiable at level $n + 1$ if and only if the following three conditions are jointly satisfied:

> i. S is not analytically true or analytically false.

> ii. At least one statement E that is observationally verifiable at level n is formal-logically deducible from the conjunction of S with zero or more such statements that do not themselves suffice to imply E.

iii. For any class C of statements, if

   (a) the conjunction of members of C but of no proper subclass of C is formal-logically equivalent to S, and
   (b) no non-logical term occurs more often in any one member of C than it occurs in S,

   then there is no C', such that C' is a proper subclass of C and any statement E, that is observationally verifiable at level n and is formal-logically deducible from the conjunction of S with zero or more such statements that do not themselves formal-logically entail E, is formal-logically deducible from the conjunction of the members of C' with the same statements.

A statement S is to be said to be observationally verifiable *tout court* if and only if there is some level at which it or its analytic equivalent is observationally verifiable.[5]

It will be seen immediately that these definitions are not hit by Hempel's and Church's objections to Ayer's definitions. Hempel's conjunction, S & N, is obviously excluded unless both S and N are observationally verifiable. Church's disjunction $(-O_1 \,\&\, O_2) \vee (O_3 \,\&\, -S)$ is also excluded, unless S is observationally verifiable, because this disjunction is equivalent to the conjunction of $(O_2 \vee O_3)$, $(-O_1 \vee -S)$, and $(O_2 \vee -S)$, and every observationally verifiable statement that is deducible from Church's disjunction, with the assistance of zero or more appropriate additional premises, is also so deducible from $(-O_1 \vee O_3) \,\&\, (O_2 \vee O_3)$. Thus, whereas clauses i and ii of the above definitions ensure that a statement satisfying the definition has *some* observational content, clause iii ensures that it has *only* observational content, because the statement's total content cannot be partitioned into a part that is observational and a part that is not. I am assuming, however, that we do not have to exclude a conjunctive statement from being observationally verifiable merely because one of its conjuncts is a tautology formulated in terms of non-observational predicates, like

All crows are black, and either the Absolute is lazy or the Absolute is not lazy.

It is important not to exclude too much when possible classes C and C' are taken into consideration. The point of clause iii (b) in the above definitions is that without this clause they would exclude any generalization $(x)(Rx \to Sx)$ from observational verifiability because of its formal-logical equivalence to the conjunction

$$((x)(Rx \to Sx) \vee ((\exists y)Ry \to (y)Sy)) \,\&\, ((x)(Rx \to Sx) \vee -((\exists y)Ry \to (y)Sy)).$$

Some further features of the revised definitions are worth noting.

1. A multiply quantified statement, even when existential and universal quantifiers alternate in it, turns out to be observationally verifiable by this criterion, provided that the content of the statement is suitably observational. Thus "For every crow, there is some flea that bites it" is observationally verifiable, whereas "For every river, there is some Nymph that haunts it" is not. But for any statement S,

any term T, and any natural numbers m and n, if T has an occurrence within the scope of n alternating quantifiers in S, and $m < n$, then S is not verifiable at level m. So philosophers who think there is something metaphysical about "all"-and-"some" statements can be interpreted as accepting only level $\leqslant 1$ verifiability and rejecting the thesis of recursiveness. (I am assuming that in this context an observation-statement is conceived to have one or more proper names or demonstrative phrases as referring expressions, to contain just one k-adic predicate ($k \geqslant 1$), and to contain no quantifiers.)

2. The generalization "All emeralds are grue," in Goodman's sense, is a problem for inductive logic, not for the analysis of verifiability. The generalization comes out clearly as observationally verifiable if 'grue' is replaced by the natural-language predicate 'is examined before t and is green or is not examined before t and is blue', provided that both the expressions 'is examined before t and is green' and 'is not examined before t and is blue' are suitable predicates for observation-statements. But the latter expression would presumably not be such a predicate if t was understood to be, say, the End of the World; then the generalization would come out as not being observationally verifiable.

3. It may be tempting to suppose that the above definition of verifiability still embraces certain kinds of hypotheses that incorporate non-observational terminology. For example, let Rx and Sx be two mutually independent forms of observation-statement and Mx a form of metaphysical or otherwise undesirable statement. Then it may seem that

$$(x)((Rx \to Mx) \& (Mx \to Sx))$$

passes the test for observational verifiability, because it obviously satisfies clauses i and ii in the definition of level 1 verifiability. But in fact it fails to satisfy clause iii of that definition because it has an equivalent that is the conjunction of

$$(x)(Rx \to Sx), (x)(Rx \to (Sx \to Mx)), \text{ and } (x)(Mx \to Sx),$$

and just the first of these three statements suffices as a premise for the deduction of all its observational content. Of course, there is no automatic way, in each particular case, of deciding whether clause iii is satisfied, any more than there is for clauses i or ii. Verifiability is no more effectively computable by my criterion than by Ayer's. But, if we always have to put up with the fact that even logical consistency lacks a comprehensive decision procedure, we ought not to feel especially disappointed that verifiability also does. Questions about verifiability are normally raised only where all relevant questions about consistency and inconsistency are assumed to have been already settled.

4. Perhaps, therefore, it will be objected instead that by rejecting statements like

$$(x)((Rx \to Mx) \& (Mx \to Sx))$$

the proposed criterion rejects too much. What if M here were not a metaphysical predicate, for instance, but a respectable theoretical term in natural science, signifying some unobservable attribute? Ayer's criterion apparently allowed such a statement to be indirectly verifiable; and, if the proposed revision of Ayer's criterion disallows this, how can that revision treat scientific theories as verifiable? The answer is that scientific theories remain "verifiable" only on the assumption of a phenomenalist analysis for their theoretical vocabulary. The definition of 'observational verifiability' will still embrace them just so far as their vocabulary is analyzable in terms of that of observation-statements. Without such reductionist analyzability, a theoretical hypothesis cannot be linked to observation-statements in such a way as to guarantee its 'observational verifiability'. Accordingly, on a realist interpretation of the vocabulary of nuclear physics, say, or electromagnetism, much important scientific theory will inevitably remain "unverifiable," if the verifiability criterion is amended as above so as not to admit metaphysical statements. You cannot exclude observationally superfluous content, on the ground that it may be metaphysical, without also excluding any implications about nature that are superfluous to the observational content. Indeed on a realist interpretation the difference between hypothesizing about devils and hypothesizing about electrons should not be expected to be wholly captured by a criterion that operates *a priori*. Instead we need to discover empirical confirmation for the greater predictive accuracy of hypotheses linking electrons with our observations, as compared with hypotheses linking devils with them. For a realist, the domain of scientific verifiability is not a static one that philosophers are professionally competent to determine, with their standard vocabularies of logical or epistemological terms. Rather, this domain enlarges with each acceptance of an experimental procedure that assumes a linkage between observables and hitherto unknown unobservables. For a realist, it is not empiricism that sets permanent limits to science, as the phenomenalist claims, but science that progressively extends the horizons of empiricism. In short, the strategy of adopting a positivist criterion for verifiability is not consistently combinable with a realist interpretation of scientific theories. But it is here that the strategy meets its Waterloo, if it ever does, and not in the logical paradox skirmishings of Hempel and Church.

5. The above definitions have been presented as an account of observational verifiability. But they are obviously transformable into an account of some other kind of verifiability, if the term 'observation-statement' is replaced by one denoting some other appropriate type of statement and the term 'observational' by an analogous one. For example, 'observation-statement' might be replaced by a subordinate term, like 'statement reporting the content of an observation made under appropriately controlled conditions', 'statement reporting an observed incident in the life of a wasp', 'statement reporting the content of an observation made at some time in the Clarendon Physics Laboratory', or 'statement reporting the content of a pre-1977 observation'. Also 'observation-statement' might be replaced by a term that is coordinate with it rather than subordinate, such as 'statement reporting a fact established by such-or-such an experimental apparatus', 'statement in the terminology of such-or-such a theory', 'statement ascribing to a particular person a specified legal right or duty', or 'statement ascribing a particular act or attribute to a particular supernatural entity'. Moreover, it is evident that verifiability, thus construed, is indistinguishable from falsifiability. So any generalization can be assigned to a particular

pure and unmixed category of verifiability or falsifiability in accordance with the particular adjustments (of this kind) that need to be made to the above definitions for the generalization to satisfy those definitions. For example, on a covering-law theory of explanation, the definitions could be used to distinguish laws that explain only phenomena of type-O (as we might call the phenomena described by the basic "observation"-statements) from hybrid laws that also explain phenomena of other types.

6. Despite the vistas that thus open up for a useful generalization of the verifiability principle, as the touchstone of a statement's purity of content within a given framework of subject matter, one must beware of the possibility that, on certain assumptions, shortcuts may be available. In particular, if a phenomenalist analysis of scientific theory is accepted and basic type-O statements are characterized (once their logical structure has been stipulated) by a list of the non-logical terms that may be used in their construction, why should not the whole extension of type-O verifiability be so characterized? After all, that was more or less the way the literature went[6] when positivists despaired of patching up Ayer's criterion. But it all depends on how the basic type-O statements are to be characterized. A linguistic shortcut like this is available only when all that matters in the specification of basic type-O statements is (apart from their logical structure) their non-logical vocabulary. And there might be other things that matter (even for a phenomenalist philosophy of science), such as rules of lexical combination within such statements, or the conditions under which their truth or falsity have been—or may be—observed, and so on. So restriction to a listed vocabulary will not be a sufficient condition of type-O-ness in every case. Also, it will not always even be a necessary condition of this. In some contexts one might not wish to exclude the occasional introduction of new descriptive terms into the vocabulary of basic type-O statements by an appropriate form of ostensive definition.

Notes

1. A. J. Ayer, *Language, Truth, and Logic*, 2nd ed. (New York, 1946) p. 13.

2. An influential judgment here was that of I. Scheffler, "Prospects of a Modest Empiricism," *Review of Metaphysics* 10 (1957): Part I, 383–400; Part II, 602–25.

3. C. G. Hempel, "Problems and Changes in the Empiricist Criterion of Meaning," *Revue internationale de philosophie* 4, no. 11 (1950):50.

4. A. Church, *Journal of Symbolic Logic* 14 (1949):52 f.

5. An earlier redefinition of observational verifiability was given in my "Why Should the Science of Nature be Empirical?" in *Impressions of Empiricism*, ed. G. Vesey (New York, 1976), p. 176. I am much indebted however to Professor D. H. Sanford for pointing out some flaws in this redefinition and in several of my subsequent suggestions for amending it. The present paper owes a lot to the stimulus of correspondence with him on the subject. I am also very grateful to Professor J. Adler for some helpful comments on the issues raised in this correspondence. If there are still some flaws in the definition, I hope at least to have given the problem a new lease of life.

6. Cf. Scheffler, "Prospects of a Modest Empiricism," p. 390-96.

Truth, Realism, and
the Regulation of Theory

SIMON BLACKBURN

I

In this paper I want to approach an area where our metaphysics and our theory of knowledge are apt to become scrambled. Few would deny that a general theory of what it is that marks a statement as true should have implications for the theory of knowledge—of what is necessary, or sufficient, to know such a statement. Equally a view of knowledge might carry with it a picture of the kind of thing that makes true the statements said to be known. My trouble is this: I begin to doubt whether familiar ways of characterizing debates in the theory of truth—realism vs. instrumentalism, and so on—actually succeed in marking out interesting areas of dispute. I doubt too whether, if this is so, the theory of knowledge will provide a solution, so that by looking at conflicting views of what knowledge is we might come to understand genuine metaphysical oppositions. I shall pursue these doubts through the figure of the *quasi-realist*, a person who, starting from a recognizably anti-realist position, finds himself progressively able to mimic the intellectual practices supposedly definitive of realism. In effect, quasi-realism is the program begun by Hume in his treatment of both causal and moral belief. I take it that its success would be a measure of the difficulty of defining a genuine debate between realism and its opponents. There are certainly images and perhaps attitudes to our discourse within a field which seem to be associated with realism, but I shall argue that unless these are given some concrete employment they represent not so much subjects for decision as for nostalgia. This concrete employment would, in effect, be a practice that a quasi-realist cannot imitate.

Some of us think of ourselves as realists about some things, but as more like pragmatists, instrumentalists, idealists or, in a word, anti-realists about others. We are happy that the world contains certain kinds of states of affairs—perhaps physical or phenomenal ones—but no more. We might not be happy with additional realms of conditional or counterfactual or moral or mental or semantic or social or mathematical states of affairs. If this is not where we would draw the line, nevertheless, we might think, there is a line to be drawn; or, even if we prefer not to draw a line, still, we think, we can understand the position of those who do. One possible response is to seek a reduction, so that although there exist no further independent facts corresponding to truths in a certain area, nevertheless there are familiar lesser states of affairs in which their truth consists. Another response is to advocate that we abandon the area of thought in question. It was pessimism about reduction, and about the existence of a distinct area of fact, making truths about what people believe or mean, which led Quine to denigrate psychological and semantic theory.[1] But the interesting issue for quasi-realism arises if we remain anti-reductionist but also are unwilling to abandon the way of thinking in question. There is no real option to abandon conditional, moral, mathematical, etc., thought, even if we become squeamish about the existence of distinct states of affairs corresponding to our beliefs in these matters. We would like to continue behaving as though there were facts, even if we feel the anti-realist pull.

But how are we to tell, from a society or a language or the conduct of an intellectual discipline, or just from our own thought, when we are in the presence of commitment to a realm of fact? One might try saying, with due emphasis and seriousness, that one thinks that there is a fact of the matter whether . . . We are all used to debates, say in the theory of morals, in which one side asserts this and the other denies it, and they appear to themselves and probably to us to have located an issue. But why? Two problems suggest themselves. The first is that from the standpoint of the anti-realist the assertion "there really is a fact of the matter (often: an objective, independent, or genuine, fact of the matter) whether . . ." is itself suspicious. For if his puzzle arises from the thought that no kind of thing *could* possibly play the role of (moral, conditional, etc.) states of affairs, then he ought to translate his doubt into difficulty about what the realist *means to be asserting* when he claims that there are such things. We face the familiar philosophical trouble that in failing to imagine something we also fail to imagine what it would be to imagine it. One may have a picture of what the realist means, but I shall argue below that this is not enough.

The second problem is that it is not so clear that the anti-realist must take issue over any sentence of the kind: "there really is a fact . . ." This is because it may belong to a discipline to think such a thing, and it is no part of the anti-realist's brief to tamper with the internal conduct of a discipline. The point would be obvious enough if we accepted Ramsey's redundancy theory of truth: serious assertion of some statement p transforms into 'it is true that p' and 'it is really a fact that p' without any escalation of ontology or metaphysics. But part of what is at stake in accepting Ramsey's theory is whether there is a genuine issue over realism and anti-realism, and we cannot yet rely on it. Nevertheless, the threat remains that the anti-realist blandly takes over all the things the realist wanted to say, but retaining all the while his conviction that he alone gives an unobjectionable, or ontologically pure, interpretation of them. Both these feelings can arise when reading apologies for objectivity and fact in, say, moral philosophy. Often nothing is conveyed except that their authors are very well brought-up and serious people. In the face of philosophical doubt, one cannot simply ladle out objectivity and facts.

Here is an example to illustrate both these points. I might embrace an anti-realism about conditionals by thinking along these lines. Imagine a thin time slice through the universe, capturing a momentary array of regions of space manifesting properties, like a large three-dimensional photograph. Nothing in it corresponds to a conditional fact. Imagine a succession of these: things change, order appears, yet neither in a single slice nor in a succession of them is there room for a conditional fact. But our universe is just such a succession. So there are no conditional facts. Now, if we are persuaded by this Humean picture (it is no part of my claim that we should be), we lose grip not only of what a conditional fact could be but also of what somebody could *mean to be asserting*, what point he could be making, when he counters that there are indeed such things. The temptation is to rely upon simile: the realist thinks of them as like a fixative or stabilizing glue somehow explaining order. But if pictures and simile fail, as I shall argue they do, and if we cannot use them to make sense of the realist's position, there is still nothing to stop us from using conditionals in the practice of our thought, from asserting them, and for all we have yet shown, from emphasizing our commitment to them with notions of truth and fact. We become quasi-realists in following out the discipline—appearing in as many ways as possible like realists but believing that we have saved our souls in the process.

Clearly, images of what the original realist vs. anti-realist debate is about do come to mind. The realist thinks of it as though the moral order is there to be investigated like a piece of geography, that numbers are like eternal objects spread over space, that the past and the future are laid out, even now, in a state of deep-frozen existence, and so on. But the presence or absence of such images cannot define an interesting issue. It must depend on some other way of directly identifying bad realist (or anti-realist) practice, and without such a way it is irrelevant. The only serious debate arises about the propriety of *using* or *succumbing* to these images. But we do not know *what it is* to use or succumb to them. We have seen the anti-realist fearing that the realist gives an improper *role* to the realm of fact and believing that he alone gives a defensible interpretation of his utterances by seeing them in the spirit of a quasi-realist. But what is the role that is improper, and what are the contrasting interpretations? The similes and images do nothing to answer this question: in themselves, indeed, they are harmless, and until we can define a harm that they do, to lack them is to miss nothing worse than a mildly poetic sort of pleasure.

A direct description of the contentious role that a realist gives to his states of affairs is therefore needed, unless the meta-debate, about whether there was ever a point at issue, is to give the verdict that there was not. Some philosophers have so concluded. Yet it is not easy to believe that such a hardy perennial has such infirm roots. I now turn to some proposals and try to relate them to what we should want to think about knowledge.

II

The debate would be on again if we could see that the quasi-realist can imitate the realist so far but no further, or alternatively that the realist must balk at certain intellectual practices of his anti-realist opponent. If we can identify a practice or thought that we can agree to be available to a realist but that even a quasi-realist must avoid, then we have identified a contentious role for the conception of fact, and in sorting it out we will be joining in what is revealed as a genuine debate. I shall discuss four such thoughts. The first is the thought that a theory to which one is committed could, even if only as a bare possibility, be false. This suggests a conception of facts as "transcending" theory, which the pragmatist or idealist might dislike. Anti-realist schools are often supposed to accept that truth is "theory-relative." The second is the thought that reality must be determinate—that at any point and whatever the infirmities of theory, there is a truth of fact of the matter whether . . . This too can appear to be a thought that a quasi-realist must deny himself. The third, which is closely connected, is that an anti-realist can, or must, make a certain equation, which to the rest of us with our realist propensities, appears invalid. The equation I shall try to identify is made by denying a distinction between a regulative and a constitutive status for principles, in Kant's sense.[2] The Kantian distinction between maxims of procedure in our intellectual inquiries, on the one hand, and truths known about the world, on the other, may appear tenable only if we are real realists about the world. The particular way of taking certain principles (particularly that of bivalence, I shall argue), which is forced upon us if we deny the distinction, seems to be that adopted by Ramsey.[3] Eventually I shall conclude, although tentatively, that a competent quasi-realist can make as much sense of the distinction as the rest of us, so that here there is no distinct intellectual practice separating the quasi-realist from us. The fourth and currently the most discussed view is that realism is the best way of explaining our scientific success, that the existence of facts explains the way in which our knowledge expands and progresses: here an explanatory role seems to carry with it an ontological commitment which, again, is surely problematic to the quasi-realist. All these suggestions are current in the literature. Should we accept any of them? I shall start with the first.

Putnam says:

What does show that one understands the notion of truth realistically is one's acceptance of such statements as:

(A) Venus might not have carbon dioxide in its atmosphere even though it follows from our theory that Venus has carbon dioxide in its atmosphere.

and

(B) A statement can be false even though it follows from our theory (or from our theory plus the set of true observation sentences).[4]

But as he himself remarks, the modal facts (A) and (B) are themselves commonsense facts about the world. They are consequences of our beliefs about the ways in which we gather knowledge or (to beg no questions) form opinion. In other words, when we describe to ourselves what makes us form opinion, we will see that (A) and (B) are true. But we cannot yet rely on anti-realist views about how we gather knowledge (or opinion) being different from anybody else's. It seems possible then that the quasi-realist will intone (A) and (B) but not regard them as denoting a sell-out to the opposition. And if this is permissible, then they fail to provide the necessary litmus test. To come to understand whether it is permissible, let us consider a quasi-realist attempt on ethics and then on statements made with the subjunctive conditional.

I take an emotivist starting point: we see the meaning of moral utterances as essentially exhausted by their role in expressing the speaker's attitude. I have argued elsewhere that a surprising degree of quasi-realism is consistent with that view.[5] For example, it need not be surprising that moral utterances characteristically take an indicative form. Nor need we be worried by, for example, their appearance in the subordinate clauses of hypotheticals. "If it is wrong to allow secondary picketing, then the government has been negligent" need not be regarded as hypothesizing the existence of a state of affairs, and we do not immediately declare ourselves to be realists by using it. An emotivist can perfectly well describe the role of such a conditional: it expresses a conviction that if one attitude is held then so must the other be held; this conviction may itself be moral, but there is nothing to prevent an emotivist from holding attitudes to the inter-relations of attitudes and to the relation of attitude and belief. In fact, he must do so, for to hold this last kind of attitude is what it is to hold a moral standard, and these too gain expression in conditionals with the moral sentence on a subordinate clause: 'if lying causes harm, then it is wrong.' For this reason we should not accept Geach's test for whether we hold an indicative sentence to have a truth-condition, if this is itself a commitment to realism.[6] It fails to give the quasi-realist a proper run. But Putnam's test seems more compelling. What could an emotivist be up to in thinking: "perhaps there is no such thing as a right to strike, even though it follows from my moral theory that there is?" Must he deny himself such thoughts? Is he to say that truth is "theory-relative"?

An analogue of Putnam's theory about how our opinion is gathered would be a view about the genesis of moral attitude. Let us suppose, as seems possible, that prominent in such a story we would find a capacity to sympathize, and an imaginative capacity to put oneself in another person's place, or to see what it is like from his point of view. There would no doubt be other ingredients, but these illustrate my point. Suppose too that one recognizes that these capacities vary, from person to person and time to time. Suppose finally that one admires those in whom they are boldly and finely developed. All these thoughts and attitudes are perfectly accessible to the emotivist. But they seem to give him all that is needed for a concept of an *improvement* or a *deterioration* in his own moral stance. He can go beyond saying "I might change" to saying "I might improve." For he can back up that possibility by drawing the change as one which from his own standpoint he would admire. But now he has the concept of a possible flaw or failure in his present standards. A simple example would be the worry that a certain attitude, or the way in which one holds a certain attitude, is not so much the outcome of a proper use of imagination and sympathy, which one admires, but is the outcome, say, of various traditions or fears which one does not. Hume, of course, has been here before us:

> A man with a fever would not insist on his palate as able to decide concerning flavours; nor would one affected with the jaundice pretend to give a verdict with regard to colours. In each creature there is a sound and a defective state; and the former alone can be supposed to afford us a true standard of taste and sentiment. If, in the sound state of the organ, there be an entire or a considerable uniformity of sentiment among men, we may thence derive an idea of the perfect beauty. . . .[7]

So the quasi-realist can certainly possess the concept of an improved standpoint from which some attitude of his appears inept, and this, I suggest, is all that is needed to explain his adherence to the acceptance of the apparently realist claim: "I might be wrong." I think this view is confirmed if we ask: could one not work oneself into a state of doubting whether the capacities generating moral attitudes are themselves so very admirable? The answer is that one could, but that then the natural thing to say is that morality is all bunk and that there is no pressure toward objectivity for the quasi-realist to explain. For this kind of reason we should be skeptical of John Mackie's claim that we can detect a mistake about objectivity in our ordinary moral thought.[8] For at least as far as the modal test goes we can find ourselves holding fast to emotivism yet perfectly imitating the allegedly realist thought.

Another example comes from the suggestion, again from Mackie, that counterfactual claims are best regarded as condensed arguments. Once more we might advance the Putnam test: surely I ought to recognize that it *may* be false that if Mary had come to the party she would have gotten drunk, even though I know that by far the best arguments, given what we know and the supposition that she came to the party, support the view that she got drunk? Again, the suggestion is that this makes sense only if we have a realistic conception of the truth or falsity of a counterfactual. But again the defense will be that anyone can and should recognize the partial nature of any given evidential basis of argument, including our own present one about Mary; that once we recognize that we can permit ourselves the concept of an improved standpoint from which our present argument takes account of only part of the facts; and that this gives us a sufficient grasp of its fallibility to enable us, quasi-realistically, to say that it might be true that if she had come she would have stayed sober.

When Putnam talks of his modal criterion he admits that it is possible for an anti-realist to oppose truth-within-a-theory against truth as that which would be agreed upon in the limit of investigation. Peirce and Sellars are famous for this conception of truth, and in the remarks I have just made I may appear to be approaching it. But this is not yet certain. It may be that the notion of an improvement is *sufficient* to interpret remarks to the effect that my favorite theory may be wrong, but not itself sufficient to justify a notion of the limit of investigation; if these things are each so, then the notion of a limit cannot be necessary to interpret the fear that my favorite theory is wrong.

There are bad reasons for thinking that we must possess and justify the concept of a limit toward which improved investigation must converge. Perhaps we are misled into thinking that the notion of a limit to which improved opinion must converge is necessary if we are to believe that truth can be found or finally settled, rather than be forever fugitive. But the notion of a limit is not sufficient to remove that worry; it is itself forever fugitive. And it is not necessary. The possibility of an improvement is perfectly compatible with the existence of particular certainties. We can understand the concept of an improvement even if it on occasion remains a bare or notional possibility that such an improvement should result in modification of a particular component of our views—an attitude toward textbook examples of evil or the belief in the shape of the solar system, for instance. Truth can be achieved, and in many places it has been. The second motive to define a limit may be that it alone gives value or point to the search for knowledge. But, again, it is insufficient for that purpose: it would be no particular source of pride to know that my opinion was one on which all judges would converge in the long run unless I had already attached value to the processes that would lead them to do so. For instance, it would be by itself no merit for a house to be one on which all modern architectural design would converge. This is the element that is unattractive in Peirce's definition of truth: unless there is a value in the processes leading to convergence, there is no merit in an opinion's being true in his sense.

We then get two different cases. It may be that the virtue in the processes can only be described as their tendency to act as midwives to the truth; that this is why we appreciate, say, simplicity, elegance, the drive to unified explanation, and so on. Or it may be, as in the moral case, that we can see the virtue in increases of sensitivity, sympathy, freedom from prejudice, and so on regardless of any belief that they are instrumental in advancing a cause of truth. If the latter is true, then we can accept Nietzsche's words:

> Can we remove the idea of a goal from the process and then affirm the process in spite of this?—This would be the case if something were attained at every moment within the processes.[9]

Or, in other words, the mere idea of improvement is after all sufficient to give content to our concepts of self-doubt and of fallibility and error.

But is it sufficient? One might object: it is all very well to say that an attitude M could appear inept to one with an improved use of faculties generating such attitudes (call the improved use F*). But in itself it is consistent with the possibility of a further improved use of those faculties F**, which reinstates M, and so on for evermore. It is only if one is entitled to a concept of convergence toward a limit, in which M is either vindicated or not, that the modal claim makes sense. In short, it is objected that we need more than the concept of *an* improved use of the relevant faculties. Perhaps we need the concept of a perfect or ultimate use of them, and this is something to which the emotivist has established no right. But is this argument cogent?

It is the final conclusion that is at fault. Suppose we are wondering whether a particular view is true. The argument may establish that we need the belief in a possible improvement of opinion to a point at which it is asserted to be true, or to be false, and *beyond* which any admirable change in theory merely serves to confirm that verdict. But this is not a belief that a quasi-realist needs to reject. And it is *not* a belief that demands that we understand the concept of a perfect or ultimate use of the relevant faculties. It is of course true that the quasi-realist may take a pessimistic view over the ease of finding such points, or of our security in believing that we have ever found them. But so may a realist. Or he may optimistically regard a large core of opinion as already in that state, and express this by saying that certainty, or even knowledge, can be had. And like anybody else, he can take into account the empirical question of whether the history of a discipline shows an increasing core of solid fact, rendered more or less immune to successive revolutions of theory, or whether it shows little or no such tendency.

Two issues remain to trouble us. One, which I discuss in section IV, is the possible claim that realism is the best explanation of such convergence in opinion as we do find. The other, which I discuss in section V, is the specter of indeterminacy, or the possibility of equally rational or admirable processes generating inconsistent or incommensurable opinion even in the face of all possible evidence. This is an obvious threat to the realist, who must react either by shrinking the area of fact to a point below that at which the possibility arises or by allowing that truth transcends all possible ways of knowing about it. But it is equally a threat to the anti-realist. For I would summarize the results of this section by saying that they justify the quasi-realist in a conception of truth as a regulative ideal, or a *focus imaginarius* upon which the progress of opinion is sighted. A direct result of the indeterminacy theses would be that we are not entitled to that notion. I try to cope with this threat at the end of the paper.

The net result so far is that apart from raising these two problems there is nothing in the modal claims to distinguish realism. The quasi-realist need not wallow in the unattractive or incoherent idea of truth being "relative to theory," and if we are to find what marks him off, we must turn elsewhere.

III

The second proposal for a distinguishing test for real as opposed to quasi-realism is the thought that there must be a fact of the matter whether p or whether not-p. This takes us into the area defined by Dummett, in which the law of bivalence, that every statement is true or false, is seen as something to which the anti-realist cannot owe any allegiance. The question must be whether in pursuit of a theory we might quite naturally find ourselves needing to be governed by bivalence, regardless of any attitude toward the existence of facts or states of affairs which the statements of our theory describe.

Dummett himself talks as though 'true' and 'false' were in some sense derivative from a fundamental division of utterances into those which it is right to make and those which it is wrong to make; acceptable, unacceptable; correct, incorrect. This alone prompts the thought: why should not such an apparently normative division be made, and rigidly applied to every possible statement, regardless of any theory of what it is, if anything, that makes a statement come down on one side or the other? We are investigating the credentials of realism as such a theory, but the *purposes* of theory may be quite sufficient to drive us to think in terms of the universal application of such a division. To take an example (I shall take more later): the discipline of moralizing may be subject to the regulative constraint that everything is either permissible or impermissible, and this may be reflected as a commitment to bivalence, which an anti-realist would therefore wish. He will happily say "it is either true that you did wrong or false that you did wrong" as a prelude to discussion without in the least regarding himself as subject to any unfortunate lapse.

The lapse would, perhaps, be unfortunate if it involved the suspect notion of completing an essentially uncompletable task. Thus if we need an idea corresponding to God seeing the whole of the natural number series, or seeing a completed totality of argument surrounding a very indeterminate counterfactual, or seeing the whole of physical fact before him, and if without that idea bivalence is groundless, then we might agree that it rests on suspect imagery. And the most forceful examples where we want to query it concern infinities. It is not nearly so tempting, for example, to express anti-realism about other people's sensations in terms of doubts about bivalence applied to them, because it is manifestly true of you that you are in pain or false of you that you are. (Wittgenstein's *Investigations*, section 352 seems to me to be counseling us not to *deny* this but to regard it as simply irrelevant, as not containing within itself the key to some understanding of the meaning of pain ascriptions. Nor, therefore, is it a sensible target for suspicion either.) But as we saw in the last section, it is not generally true that to use a concept of truth, even to describe the result of infinite or indefinite or open-ended investigation requires the paradoxical idea of a completion of such an investigation. It requires only the concept of a point beyond which no improved perspective demands a rejection of a given previous opinion. And it may well be that serious theorizing about an opinion requires faith in the existence of such a point: to agree that the revolutions of theory may endlessly bring in and out of favor a particular opinion is just to agree that the theory is worthless or an insufficient foundation for interest in that opinion. It would be equivalent to abandoning the area of discussion.

I do not intend these remarks as more than a preliminary orientation. They certainly do not remove the necessity to investigate the detailed arguments in the theory of meaning which Dummett uses to support his position. Here I can only record my skepticism about those arguments: they all seem to me to trade upon an insufficiently analysed notion of what it is to manifest understanding of a proposition or, to put it another way, neglect of the intellectual powers of the audience *to whom* one is manifesting that understanding. This systematic neglect enables Dummett, and his followers, to generate the astonishing conclusion that one cannot communicate what one cannot be *observed* to communicate as though one had to manifest understanding to the most wooden or passive of possible interpreters.[10] Nevertheless, I hope my remarks are sufficient to raise a general doubt about the use of bivalence as a litmus-test.

Perhaps its most obvious application comes when we have the conception of a certain realm of discourse as grounded in another, but where the grounding can fail to support either a proposition or its negation. The clearest example arises in fiction, where remarks about, say, Hamlet are true in virtue of what is written in or supported by Shakespeare's texts. There may exist nothing at all in those texts to support the proposition that Hamlet had a baritone voice, nor that he had not. It would then seem wrong to suppose that such a proposition *must* be true or false, even if it might also be wrong ever to be sure that it will not turn out to be, as more subtle readings of the text are made. But bivalence does not seem to be so much use in discriminating the ontological commitment *within* an assertion of truth of falsity. For instance, we may be convinced that in some cases it may be that there is nothing to make a counterfactual either true or false. But we may also think that when a counterfactual *is* true a realist account of what makes it true—a realm of conditional facts, or powers or dispositions, or even nested possible worlds—is in order and makes a genuine opposition to anti-realism. In any case, we do not yet know whether the quasi-realist should not accept commitment to bivalence as something forced upon him by the discipline or practice of theorizing, and see no sell-out to realism in so doing.

Since this strategy is crucial to quasi-realism, I shall follow it through in some detail, first as though a regulative-constitutive distinction can indeed be defended, and then in the light of skepticism about it. Corresponding to that distinction we can define two senses of commitment to bivalence in an area of discourse. Such a commitment may be expressed:

> (P_1) In all cases that arise we should say: either this assertion is true, or it is false.

or as:

> (P_2) We should say: in all cases either an assertion is true, or it is false.

(P_1) is regulative, in a sense in which (P_2) is apparently not, because we might see that it should be adopted as a maxim governing practice, even if we do not accept (P_2). To take a particularly simple but illustrative example, it may be that the practical requirements on a judge demand that he should obey (P_1) where the area that the assertion concerns is within his jurisdiction (say: this contract is valid). He must eventually find for one party and against the other, and the requirement regulates his attitude toward the possibilities. This is perfectly consistent with believing that there are likely to exist incompletenesses in the law, or areas of discretion in which truth would not attach to just one verdict. It will be part of the judge's discipline to think of truth as attaching to just one side, which it is his task to find, but it does not follow that in his reflections on legal reality he must suppose that this assumption has any foundation in the facts. The open-ended nature of the discipline may mean that it is never in practice possible to categorize a case as one in which it was neither true that the contract was valid, nor false that it was, in which case the maxim has an imperative force equivalent to 'keep looking for reasons'; its status is exactly like the drive to complete and unitary explanation which Kant saw as governing science.

Using the distinction between (P_1) and (P_2), we can thus give an account of the pressure that leads Dummett to distinguish between rejecting the law of bivalence, which is something he thinks we should do, and rejecting the principle of *tertium non datur*, which is something he equally thinks we should not do. In other words, he thinks we should reject (P_2), but that we should not hold that there are propositions that are neither true nor false. This way of putting it depends upon an intuitionist view of the quantifiers. But without that view, we can see the attraction of a position that is *not* committed to (P_2) in an area but that *is* committed to practice in any case as though (P_2) were true and that on principle refuses to consider an independent third status for an assertion. This position is just one which thinks that on principle we should not be satisfied with less than one of the polar verdicts and that we cannot ever regard ourselves as in a position to assert that something other than one of those is correct. And that seems compatible with a general doubt about whether there will always exist facts in virtue of which just one side is correct, or about whether there must be the points we have defined, beyond which improvement always confirms one side or confirms the other.

Although it is a digression from my main theme, I should mention that this makes it quite wrong to argue, as Professor Dworkin sometimes seems to do, as though the practice of a bivalent or polar legal system implies confidence in its completeness, in the sense of its being sufficiently grounded to provide a right answer to each question.[11] It is particularly obvious that the constraints on legal decisions make the regulative principle necessary. The fact that their practice is so regulated licenses no inference to a need to use a group's political theory, nor for that matter to use a determinate moral reality, to fill the gaps in their law that may exist after we consider all the other actions they may have taken to create that law.

The quasi-realist seems, then, to be able to accept the regulative principle, (P_1), provided, indeed, that the purposes of making judgment in the area in question can be seen to demand polar verdicts. But at this point the plot suddenly thickens. For given that this is so, given that his thought is to be governed on each occasion by the application of bivalence, what is to prevent the quasi-realist from voicing acceptance of (P_2)? If it is *on principle* to be his practice to think: either this is true, or it is false, what is to stop him from thinking: in all cases truth falls on one side, and falsity on the other? It is quite natural to argue, as we have done, that something more *is* involved in accepting (P_2), but it might appear at this point that it is only a *realist* who should accept the distinction. A principle may after all be constitutive as opposed to regulative only if there is an area of fact whose constitution it purports to describe. We cannot just accept this contrast: it is the very one whose credentials we are querying. Thus we may think there is a distinction between accepting the maxim of inquiring into nature as though every event has a cause, on the one hand, and believing it to be the case that every event has a cause, on the other. But doesn't this very distinction stamp us as realists about cause? Once one has a view of a causal (or legal, conditional, moral, etc.) fact, as a thing with a distinct ontological standing, perhaps one has a notion of it simply failing to exist in a given case; and this possibility would be there even if reason commands us to comport ourselves as though there were a truth of the matter to be found. But what can an anti-realist make of all this? Surely it would be natural for him to take it that the commitment to the maxim is all that can gain expression in the universal generalization ((P_2), every event has a cause, etc.), which can therefore be bought quite cheaply.

It is interesting in this connection that Kant himself, according to Bennett, can be interpreted as sometimes betraying his own distinction.[12] For although his official position is that the antinomies arise only through mistaking a regulative for a constitutive principle, he seems to have no certain view of the distinction, nor of what it means to make this mistake. One view he may have held, again according to Bennett, is that given the sort of general principles that regulative principles are, there is simply no distinction between "accepting the advice which (one of them) embodies, and believing that it is true as a matter of fact." This is to equate acceptance of (P_1) and (P_2). If Kant did hold this, then the diagnosis of the antinomies becomes epistemologoical. We are supposed to be in danger of mistaking what it is that entitles us to accept one of them: it is not an insight into reality but the "speculative interest of reason." However, this is an unsatisfactory contrast for the reasons we have given. There are indeed images associated with the difference between things we take from the world and things we read into it. But we do not know what it is like to employ or misemploy these contrasting images. Kant, it is true, must have thought he could explain this, for only if we think that a principle is constitutive, which on this account means that it represents knowledge of the world, can we find ourselves involved in the antinomies. But commentators tend to agree that the steps in this diagnosis are not very clear, so if we want to find a distinct employment for the different ways of taking a principle, such as bivalence, we could not rely upon Kant as having paved the way.

Ramsey is probably the best known anti-realist to have equated such pairs as (P_1) and (P_2). I think we can also regard Dummett as seeing no significant difference between them. It explains why if we start with doubts about (P_2), as he tends to do, they become doubts about the policy adopted in (P_1), and abandoning that policy prevents us from using bivalence in the course of a logical proof and demands the intuitionist modification of logical practice. The curiosity in that route is, as I have already remarked, that starting by considering (P_2) and finding doubts about its truth seems appropriate to realists, who, thinking they have a distinct conception of the existence of states of affairs corresponding to truth or falsity of a judgment, also fear a point beyond which the facts simply do not exist. But one would expect the anti-realist to take the reverse direction and, as it were, defuse bivalence rather than reject it. This point is supported if we favor the kind of explanations of meaning that Dummett adopts. If we learn what truth is in moral, or legal, or whatever, contexts by observing and understanding the relevant practices and if we are kept on a very tight rein in any attempt to read more into those concepts than appears on the surface, then the concept of truth that emerges is at least governed by the commitment to (P_1). This is why Dummett has always seemed vulnerable (as he himself recognizes) to the counter that classical mathematical practice is part of what does give a real meaning to, in particular, the concept of an unsurveyable infinite totality.

I do not think such a move is met by the reply that it involves a "holism" that threatens to make any logical practice immune to criticism.[13] In areas where the whole question is what our understanding consists in, and whether it is legitimate in any case, classical logical practice may play a part in locating it, even if in others we have a firm enough grasp of the truth conditions of various propositions for a given practice of inference to be vulnerable to criticism. In any case, and even if I am wrong about Dummett, it appears that hesitation about (P_2) is more a mark of the realist than his alleged opponent.

If this is so, the prospects for a litmus test look bright, even if not in the way that might have been anticipated. For the quasi-realist becomes an embarrassingly enthusiastic mimic of traditionally realist sentiments, and in his very zeal we might expect him to differ from a real realist. "In every case of legal (moral, counterfactual, etc.) dispute," we hear him say, "there is a truth of the matter falling on one and only one side." The very fact that for him there is nothing more to accepting (P_2) than there is to accepting (P_1) entitles him to say such a thing; the fact that for us there is some doubt about (P_2) in spite of our defense of (P_1) shows that we are different from him. This seems to be the position if our quasi-realist accepts the regulative-constitutive equation, and as we have seen it is plausible to believe that the only motive for refusing to accept it is the belief in a real status for facts or states of affairs.

Let us keep with the legal example. Perhaps after all it was not fair to lumber the quasi-realist with Ramsey's equation. Clearly the question is whether the *only* motive for assenting to (P_1) yet not to (P_2) is a belief about the status of legal fact which marks a realist. If it is not, then the quasi-realist may be able to imitate whatever hesitancy about their relationship we ourselves feel. In the legal case the hesitancy about (P_2) arises from our theory of grounding: the belief that a group may not have *got up to* a question such as whether a particular kind of contract is valid and that none of its lawmaking activities or beliefs cover the case or determine a verdict. Now there should be nothing in that theory which offends an anti-realist. He can also see judgments of legal fact as answering entirely to questions about what the group has arranged (or to questions about what the group thinks is right). It would seem *strange* then if he cannot hesitate over (P_2) just as much as we do, since he shares the theory of grounding which *we* express by saying that there can be cases in which there is no fact of the matter, but which could be decided either way with equal propriety. Now in spite of the attraction of Ramsey's view, I think the quasi-realist can admit this, *even if* he knows that on principle we must proceed as though a decision one way or the other were always to be found. The escape is to remember the strategy used in the face of Putnam's test. There we removed the apparently metaphysical implications of the modal fact by seeing it as arising from *a natural view* of the nature of our moral capacities. The parallel here is to remove the similar implications of the thought "even if we must all proceed as though bivalence held, it is still not true that on every legal issue there must be a right answer" by seeing it as a natural reaction to the contingent and unproblematic belief that a society is unlikely to have thought of every eventuality. As with Putnam's test, the commitment supposed to identify realism can be seen as a reflection of a piece of knowledge available to anyone, whatever his philosophy. If this is right, then it is the regulative-constitutive equation that was at fault, but the legal quasi-realist can comfortably conform to ordinary thought.

Although I think this suggests the right solution in the legal case, others may be more complex. For often, as with the example of determinism or with moral or counterfactual reasoning, the theory of grounding is not so easy to sketch. I shall follow through the case of practical reasoning. Here there is no relatively straightforward theory of grounding leading one to any particular view on bivalence. Ramsey's equation seems to be more attractive. Given that on principle we must, once we are considering the question, suppose that either there is, for example, a right to strike or there is not, what else could we be doubting if we ask whether on every moral issue truth falls on one side and not the other? Must we not just see this as a natural propositional reflection of our principle of procedure? What difference could there be between obeying the maxim and believing the generalization? The threat is that by seeing no difference the anti-realist purchases commitment to the generalization too cheaply, so that his very complacency serves to distinguish him from someone with a lively conception of moral fact and hence of its possible absence. But again the matter can be, as it were, naturalized. The brief remarks I made about the genesis of moral opinion already suggest that there might exist persons in whom capacities of imagination and sympathy are equally well developed but to whom parts of our morality, or the structure of our practical reasoning, seem as unattractive as theirs might appear to us. The concept of improvement that we isolated gives us then no basis from which to claim that they are wrong and we are right. The concept of truth that did allow the anti-realist to think "perhaps I am wrong" does not allow him, in the face of such a possibility, any confidence that they are wrong. (This is why the suspicion that a foreign culture is an actual example of this naturally and properly leads us to think that we are not entitled to interfere with it. All that is needed is the admirable (moral) opinion that we have a right to interfere only if the people's sensibilities are inferior to ours; lacking this justification, it is appropriate to live and let live, or perhaps live and learn.) This is Hume's case where "there is such diversity in the internal frame or external situation as is entirely blameless on both sides."[14]

The idea, then, is that a reflection of proper awareness of this possibility might be: "on some moral issues, there may be no truth and no falsity of the matter." Then the quasi-realist can permit himself this, even while admitting that we will, in practice, be committed to bivalence, and while admitting that there is never a point at which we can be sure that there is no improved perspective, from which at most one side will appear to be in the right. As I showed above (p. 360), this is consistent with holding that sometimes there is certainty: we are entitled to certainty that no improved perspective or equally admirable perspective could much differ from us in our most fundamental attitudes. It seems then that a quasi-realist can have just the right attitude to the general principle of bivalence, which he can agonize over with the best. His attitude does not betray him in the way Ramsey's test suggested it should.

I shall not pursue the other example where Ramsey's equation or the test of adherence to bivalence, might seem to be promising methods for discriminating real from quasi-realism. There is no case in which they seem to me to work. The devices I have gone through in the examples of law and morals seem to me to be equally successful in other cases, such as those of counterfactuals, conditionals, and cause. The strategy is always to see bivalence as a natural commitment within a discipline, for more or less obvious reasons, and to see the hesitation which it may be natural to feel about indeterminate cases as available to anyone who reflects on either the theory of grounding of the facts in question or facts about the capacities enabling us to form an opinion of them. So far, then, we have no distinctive range of thought or argument that marks off either side in the original debate. We still face the problem that the issue of whether there is a *casus belli* goes against both realists and their opponents.

IV

The final suggestion differs from the other three in a fundamental respect. Each of them seized upon a relatively formal aspect of our intellectual practice—our assent to a modal claim, to a logical principle, to a form in inference. This one seizes upon an attitude we may have toward our own opinion or knowledge. Of course, our problem all along has been to determine whether a distinctive attitude really is associated with realism, and so far we have nothing but images and similes to gesture toward it. And we know that these are not enough. The purpose of the fourth suggestion is to put, in place of these, a distinct explanatory view which, it is suggested, is available only to a real realist.

The explanatory view that may be adopted by the real realist, but not by the quasi-realist, is this:

(RR) it is because opinion is caused, perhaps indirectly, by the fact that p, that it converges upon p.

A quasi-realist will either deny convergence or seek some other explanation for it. Notice that he need not deny or worry over science's propensity to depart as little as possible from immediately preceding theory or to seek to incorporate as much as possible of that theory into new views. Such a propensity is quite naturally explicable in other ways and requires no mention of the states of affairs making a theory true. It does not even imply that those who are in this way conservative themselves believe in convergence.

Using (RR) to define a realist vs. anti-realist debate accords with many intuitions. A quasi-realist can mimic our formal practice with the concept of truth or fact. But surely he cannot give the facts any role in explaining our practice. To do so is to embrace their real distinct existence, or so it might seem. Again, the most famous examples of plausible anti-realism can be seen exactly as attempts to deny (RR) for the areas in question. Hume explains our opinion of the existence of causal connections not by our exposure to the fact of such connections but only by our exposure to regular successions of events. His main point need not be to propound an "analysis" in terms of regular succession, for he can consistently suppose the mind to inject an ingredient into its conception of causation, which is lacking from the mere idea of regular succession. His point is that there is no explanatory role for any fact beyond that of regular succession in accounting for our opinion; exposure to such succession, given natural propensities in the mind, is sufficient. Moral realism is refuted in the same way. Here, indeed it is not just that explanation of our opinion and practice *can* be had simply in terms of natural perceptions, given our desires and needs. It is also that there are obstacles to any other explanation. A distinct explanatory mechanism, starting with a distinct moral fact, would not be reconcilable with the requirement that its output be logically supervenient on other facts, known in other ways. This contrasts with all other explanatory mechanisms; our knowledge of color, for instance, is explained in ways that leave it *logically* possible that everything else should remain as it is, but color change.

In spite of these attractive examples, the test has one flaw, which suggests that although RR *may* be something that a realist must say, it may be possible to say it without being a realist. It would mark a necessary but not sufficient condition of realism. The problem arises if a test is made to determine whether our attitude is one of real realism or not, when the opinion or theory that we are testing *itself* makes causal and explanatory claims. For example, suppose that upon exposure to a given experimental result a physicist comes to hold that it shows the decay of a radioactive atom: he holds that it is the decay that causes the result. To deny that is simply to abandon the physics. But now we have what Putnam calls internal realism as something integral to the theoretical practice, and there is simply no issue of dissent from (RR). There is no option to "speak with the vulgar" by assenting to the theory, but to "think with the learned" by denying its *own* causal and explanatory claims about the genesis of our opinion. If thinking with the learned *is* an option, it is not identified by adherence to (RR), and we are back on the depressing project of finding another way to determine whether there would be such a thing as assenting to (RR) but with that special attitude which marks one's assent as realistic or not.

I do not think (as Putnam seems to) that this makes (RR) metaphysically useless. It maintains its role as a necessary commitment of a realist. What it does suggest is that it has no part to play in detecting a realistic attitude toward the most interesting theories: those such as our view of the external world, or the existence of the past or other minds, where to hold the theory is *ipso facto* to hold a certain explanation of our opinions. Not all theories have this kind of involvement with their own meta-theory—first order morals does not, for instance.

Yet taking (RR) as even a necessary commitment of a realist has one unattractive consequence. This is that states of affairs are only allowed if they play a part in causing opinion. Now it seems at least possible that one would wish to be a realist about mathematics yet deny that mathematical reality is a cause of anything. Or one might wish to have the same attitude toward the reality of the future and the past yet believe that only past states of affairs play a causal role in generating opinion. This is the obverse of the preceding trouble: (RR) is too generous to states of affairs that enter causal theories and too dismissive of the others. But it is, so far, our only prospect for the required hurdle. We might indeed try to do without mention of causation. We could offer the test of whether a theorist agrees that it is the existence of the fact that p which explains convergence of opinion upon p; leaving it unsettled, whether the explanation is causal. May I say that it is the fact that two plus two equals four which explains the convergence of mathematical opinion upon the belief that it does? Or that it is the fact that people do have the right to strike that explains convergence of moral opinion upon the belief that they do? One imagines that the quasi-realist may take license to say such a thing; it will not be clear why he should not, even if many of us believe that he should not. What may be clearer is that a quasi-realist must think that there is in principle a better or more illuminating explanation of this convergence, if he remains true to his anti-realist starting point. A recognizably Humean picture of causation may go so far as to say "it is the fact that A causes B which explains convergence of opinion that it does." Once the mind has "spread itself on the world," it also regards itself as reading things off the world it has projected.[15] But a Humean also holds that there is a more illuminating and economical account of the convergence. The suggestion arises that a realist, as opposed to a quasi-realist, must hold that the best, most illuminating, and economical explanation of our opinion that p, must cite the state of affairs that p. Yet put like this we lose all touch with the original instincts behind the positions. Might I not believe in the real distinct existence of the external world, yet accept that the most illuminating and economical explanation of my believing in it mentions only the coherence of my experience? Or believe in your mental states, yet accept that my opinions are explained merely by exposure to your behavior? The realist may well jib at the very strong thesis about explanation which this suggestion forces upon him.

V

It seems, then, that the best use to make of convergence is not as a phenomenon of which a realist has a superior explanation but rather as one in which he alone has faith. If we use our faculties properly, and reality is determinate, then surely opinion must converge. Equally, if it is decided that even in the long run opinion need not converge, then to many people this is a powerful argument—perhaps *the* powerful argument—for denying that there is a reality which that opinion is purporting to describe. Hence the importance of indeterminacy theses.[16] It is pessimism about convergence even in the long run, even in the face of reasoning admirably from all "actual and possible experience," the pessimism which is expressed in indeterminacy theses, which is the most potent enemy of belief in a determinate world of moral, or psychological, or semantic, or even physical states of affairs. The lemma is that skepticism must be intolerable: truth cannot be transcendental, incapable of being achieved by any extension of reason and experience; to imagine a truth is to have some grasp of what it would be to know it. If this is accepted, then the response to indeterminacy is to deny realism. Yet indeterminacy also threatens the existence of the points that on my suggestion give the anti-realist a decent surrogate for truth.

But the contemporary confidence placed in such indeterminacy theses is quite improper. For such a thesis cannot be an argument against pursuing our moral, psychological, semantic, or physical theory as best we can. And then reason does not beg but commands us to treat a conflict of theories as a sufficient proof that the truth has not yet become known; reason is not free to order a pursuit of one systematic truth and at the same time tell us that many such unities may be equally in conformity with the world; it cannot in such a way "run counter to its own vocation."[17] To theorize, to assert, at all is to disbelieve indeterminacy theses. Nor is reason here at war with itself, telling us to have confidence on the one hand in our correctness, or at least in our progress toward correctness, and on the other hand in the diversity of equally good opinion that could exist. For it is not observation and reason that tells a theorist in a proper discipline that he is unlikely to be effectively pursuing the truth. It is pessimism or loss of faith among philosophers in the value of science or particular sciences; the loss of the will to believe. Indeterminacy theses are a symptom of our disenchantments, not the products of our reasoning powers: here at least it is true that "the owl of Minerva takes wing only with the coming of the night." In saying this, of course, I do not deny that a history composed mainly of worthless and persistent dispute may be a good reason for abandoning a particular discipline or domain of inquiry. But neither physics, nor common-sense psychology or the science of interpretation and translation, nor even perhaps ethics, reveals such a history. And in a case that does, induction from that history rather than the bare possibility declared in an indeterminacy thesis would motivate us to reject the inquiry. The boot is on the other foot: rejection of an inquiry gains expression in indeterminacy theses. It is topsy-turvy to use fear of indeterminacy to motive a modification of an otherwise rational theoretical practice.

At last, then, can we say that the quasi-realist achieves his goal? No talk of knowledge or certainty, reason or truth, no belief in the convergence of opinion, no proper contrasts between theory and reality nor between regulative and constitutive, seem beyond his grasp. The realist never intended to say more than this, nor should the anti-realist have settled for less. It is true that in getting to this point our sympathies were engaged mainly on behalf of the anti-realist: I would be inclined to say that realism, in the disputed cases of morals, conditionals, counterfactuals, mathematics, can only be worth defending in an interpretation that makes it uncontroversial. Could this be retorted upon anti-realism, from a standpoint of differing initial sympathies? If this is so philosophy indeed leaves everything as it is. Yet there may be reason to sympathize more with the anti-realist. He has earned the concepts associated with objectivity; his opponent merely stole them; he has founded our practices on known facts about human capacities; his opponent invents more. Economy matters. And perhaps we feel less guilt about what we have earned—less vulnerable to skepticism. Or could it be that, after all, the old pictures and metaphors are important to the disputes, it mattering to us not just that people talk, behave, and practice intellectually in the same way that we do but also that they are haunted by the same ghosts?

Notes

1. W. Quine, "Reply to Chomsky," in *Words and Objections*, ed. D. Davidson and J. Hintikka (Dordrecht, 1969), p. 303.

2. I. Kant, *The Critique of Pure Reason*, The Appendix to the *Transcendental Dialectic*. The importance of this part of Kant in this connection was pointed out to me by E. J. Craig.

3. F. P. Ramsey, *The Foundations of Mathematics* (London, 1931), especially "Facts and Propositions," p. 153, and "General Propositions and Causality," p. 240 ff.

4. H. Putnam, *Meaning and the Moral Sciences* (London, 1978), p. 34.

5. Simon Blackburn, "Moral Realism," in *Morality and Moral Reasoning*, ed. J. Casey (London, 1971), especially part III.

6. P. Geach, "Assertion," *Philosophical Review* 74 (1965):449–65. Dummett expresses reservations about the test, *Frege* (London, 1973), pp. 348–53.

7. D. Hume, *Collected Essays*, "Of the Standard of Taste."

8. J. Mackie, *Ethics* (London, 1977), chap. 1, sect. 7.

9. F. W. Nietzsche, *The Will to Power*, sec. 55. I owe the reference to Gordon Bearn.

10. M. Dummett, especially in "The Philosophical Basis of Intuitionistic Logic," *Truth and Other Enigmas* (London, 1978), p. 217.

11. R. Dworkin, "No Right Answer," in *Law, Society, and Morality*, ed. P. Hacker and J. Raz (Oxford, 1977).

12. J. Bennett, *Kant's Dialectic* (Cambridge, 1974), especially p. 276.

13. Dummett, *Truth and Other Enigmas*, pp. 218 ff.

14. Hume, *Collected Essays*.

15. This is why any reliance on the mere feeling of objectivity, to confirm realism about, e.g., values or obligations, is pointless.

16. In a volume originating in the Midwest, it is appropriate to record Mark Twain's classic statement of the principle of the underdetermination of theory by data:

> In the space of one hundred and seventy-six years the Lower Mississippi has shortened itself two hundred and forty-two miles. That is an average of a trifle over one mile and a third per year. Therefore, any calm person, who is not blind or idiotic, can see that in the Old Oölitic Silurian Period, just a million years ago next November, the Lower Mississippi River was upwards of one million three hundred thousand miles long, and stuck out over the Gulf of Mexico like a fishing rod. And by the same token any person can see that seven hundred and forty-two years from now the Lower Mississippi will be only a mile and three quarters long, and Cairo and New Orleans will have joined their streets together, and be plodding comfortably along under a single mayor and a mutual board of aldermen. There is something fascinating about science. One gets such wholesale returns of conjecture out of such a trifling investment of fact.
>
> *Life on the Mississippi*

However, I am referring not to underdetermination by data but to the view that there is indeterminacy in the face of proper *reasoning* from data.

17. *Critique*, A 651/B 679.

Cognitive Issues
in the Realist-Idealist Dispute

JOSEPH MARGOLIS

On the textbook view, realism is the historical opponent of nominalism or of idealism, two seemingly unrelated antagonists. But under the pressure of Kantian and Kantian-like thinking, the oppositions themselves significantly change and elements of both quarrels begin to converge and even to adhere rather naturally to one another—as in more recent confrontations said also to concern the prospects of realism. The idea that material objects exist independently of, without any dependence on, mind—in effect, independently of any conditions of cognition—is an intuitively very compelling conviction, which of course the details of astronomy and the early history of our planet are thought (in a nonquestionbegging way) to support. But that conviction is hard to separate from the corollary that a world independent of mind, in particular, a material world, must have a determinate structure of its own. There is, therefore, a very natural connection between the seemingly metaphysical claim originally termed realist and the epistemological concerns of realist-minded investigators. Hence it is hard to separate the original realist thesis from a further commitment: that either (i) the "real world" is ultimately unknowable; or (ii) being knowable, its actual, determinate structure is open to discovery; or (iii) though unknowable "in itself," that is, on the essential condition of mind-independence, we are nevertheless able to formulate a valid description of the world-as-it-impinges-on-us. One may not unfairly claim that contemporary analytic maneuvers with the dialectical possibilities of these three alternatives mark the Kantian-like character of current versions of realism. If so, however, then, since theories closer to (iii) tend now to predominate in the analytic tradition, it becomes problematic both to distinguish the realist and idealist views from one another and to confirm in a new way that the realist thesis is the correct one. Alternatively put, since in a variety of ways most analytic commentators insist that the description of the world is radically dependent on the theories or categories of description favored by human percipients, it is difficult to see how the original realist commitment regarding the world's independence of mind can be reconciled with *any* putatively valid account of the detailed and determinate nature of the world or its parts. Here, then, adjusted versions of realism are required, to meet the more formidable versions of post-Kantian idealism.

Consider, first, the record, that is, several of the more salient views of our day exhibiting the tendencies in question — without, however, defending or attacking particular doctrines or even adequately classifying positions known to be related or opposed to one another. In the Postscript to his influential and much-discussed theory of scientific paradigms, Thomas Kuhn offers the following explicit finding:

> There is, I think, no theory-independent way to reconstruct phrases like 'really there'; the notion of a match between the ontology of a theory and its "real" counterpart in nature now seems to me illusive in principle. Besides, as a historian, I am impressed with the implausibility of the view. I do not doubt, for example, that Newton's mechanics improves on Aristotle's and that Einstein's improves on Newton's as instruments for puzzle-solving. But I can see in their succession no coherent direction of ontological development. On the contrary, in some important respects, though by no means in all, Einstein's general theory of relativity is closer to Aristotle's than either of them is to Newton's. Though the temptation to describe that position as relativistic is understandable, the description seems to me wrong. Conversely, if the position be relativism, I cannot see that the relativist loses anything needed to account for the nature and development of the sciences.[1]

It is difficult to make sense of Kuhn's thesis unless we suppose that, for him, ontological relativity does not constitute sufficient grounds for construing a theory of scientific knowledge as relativistic. The reason is caught up in Kuhn's conception of "puzzle-solving." Roughly, his view is that, in spite of the fact that, for reasons of a historical nature, different scientists belong to different educational and puzzle-oriented communities, make different "group committments" in terms of the "paradigms" they favor in coming to grips with the world, still "the stimuli that impinge upon them are the same. So is their general neural apparatus, however differently programmed. Furthermore, except in a small, if all-important area of experience even their neural programming must be very nearly the same, for they share a history, except the immediate past."[2] The relativism of ontology, perception, paradigms, and the selection of putatively solvable problems are seen by Kuhn, therefore, to rest on an underlying biological uniformity in the human species in virtue of which divergent paradigms of the *success* of scientific work *themselves confirm their non-relativistic import.*

This may seem a farfetched interpretation of Kuhn's thesis,[3] but it proves both plausible and instructive about other influential views that diverge from his own. He says very plainly: "An appropriately programmed perceptual mechanism has survival value. To say that the members of different groups may have different perceptions when confronted with the same stimuli is not to imply that they may have just any perceptions at all."[4] Only "very few ways of seeing . . . that have

withstood the tests of group use are worth transmitting from generation to generation. Equally, it is because they have been selected for their success over historic
time that we must speak of the experience and knowledge of nature embedded in
the stimulus-to-sensation route."[5] So in spite of the fact that men "who perceive
the same situation differently . . . speak . . . from incommensurable viewpoints"
(since what they perceive is mediated by their different theories and paradigms and
since, though their stimuli are the same, only theory can affirm that), they do gain
knowledge *of nature.*[6]

Here we have a very pretty exhibit of the contemporary problem of realism.
For Kuhn wishes to reconcile the thesis (a) that scientific success in puzzle-solving
empirically confirms that the body of knowledge thus produced *is* knowledge of
nature (of the mind-independent world) and (b) that, historically construed, such
knowledge proves to be ontologically relativized but not ontologically convergent.
Now, the problem is this: *if* realism holds, in the original sense of a material world's
existing independently of mind, then how is it possible to construe ontologically
diverging scientific theories as constituting knowledge of the world when such ontologies may be incompatible or the theory-dependent perceptual schemata with
which opposing scientists work may constitute "incommensurable viewpoints"?
In short, Kuhn wishes to hold that our knowledge is (realistically) *of* the (mind-
independent) world but is not knowlege of the world *as* it is mind-independently.
He wishes, therefore, to incorporate within a modified realist position what, in an
earlier era, had been thought to be part of the opposing idealist thesis. It is fair to
say—we shall pursue the matter shortly—that very possibly all the more recent
versions of realism seek to achieve the same sort of reconciliation, however differently they proceed. But for the moment, we may content ourselves with noting two
paradoxes or puzzles of contemporary realism: (A) that, in spite of the fact that
there is no theory-independent way of specifying mind-independent reality, hence
of matching descriptions of reality with reality itself, we can nevertheless validly
claim to have knowledge of the real world; (B) that, in spite of the fact that if there
is a real mind-independent world, such a world must have a determinate structure
of its own, our knowledge of that world can tolerate, diachronically and synchroni-
cally, incompatible ontologies and incommensurable perceptual viewpoints.

Certainly, it is clear that, in Kuhn's account, the "success" of the "very few
ways of seeing" that have withstood the test of "historic time" must be construed
in a way that is *internal* to the favored paradigms of clusters of such "ways of
seeing." Kuhn says that they have "survival value." In effect, then, his realism cannot but rest on a version of pragmatism: baldly put, we know that we must *in some
sense* be in touch with the actual world because we survive; and the relevant sense
in which we survive corresponds to the paradigms of inquiry by which the successes
of science are themselves marked. Kuhn actually says: "In many environments a
group that could not tell wolves from dogs could not endure. Nor would a group of
nuclear physicists today survive as scientists if unable to recognize the tracks of
alpha particles and electrons."[7] But apart from the fact that the race survives re-
markably in spite of everything it does, apart from the fact that one can imagine

having correct knowledge without the capacity to survive (in fact, knowledge that we cannot long survive), apart from the fact that what precisely is meant by "survival value" is most unclear, it is not obvious at all that survival value can serve to support realism as opposed to idealism. *Any* theory of knowledge, any claim to know the world—its parts and features—is bound to try to accommodate, in *some* sense, survival value. The fact remains that (A) and (B) suspiciously resemble positions that idealists have traditionally favored: they seem in fact to be realistically phrased versions of such positions, and they seem in this respect to concede too much to the idealist point of view. In short, they may be fairly construed as elaborations of our alternative (iii) formulated above: apparently, we know only the world-as-it-impinges-on-us, or, we know the world *an sich* only as it impinges on us; and in knowing that, we cannot ensure the convergence of ontological and perceptual schemata in terms of which the known world is analyzed.

Turn now, briefly, to W. V. Quine's views. Speaking of his famous example of the field linguist's disposition to equate the "gavagai" of an observed native's utterance with our term "rabbit," Quine remarks that he takes the linguist's preference to be "sensible"—he "would recommend no other"—but that, nevertheless, the issue to be settled is "objectively indeterminate." He adds at once:

> It is philosophically interesting . . . that what is indeterminate in this artificial example is not just meaning, but extension; reference. My remarks on indeterminacy began as a challenge to likeness of meaning. . . . Of two predicates which are alike in extension, it has never been clear when to say that they are alike in meaning and when not; it is the old matter of featherless bipeds and rational animals, or of equiangular and equilateral triangles. Reference, extension, has been the firm thing; meaning, intension, the infirm. The indeterminacy of translation now confronting us, however, cuts across extension and intension alike. The terms "rabbit," "undetached rabbit part," and "rabbit stage" differ not only in meaning; they are true of different things. Reference itself proves behaviorally inscrutable.[8]

Hence, as Quine puts it, in adopting "a naturalistic view of language and a behavioral view of meaning . . . we give up an assurance of determinacy."[9] Ontology becomes "doubly relative. Specifying the universe of a theory makes sense only relative to some background theory, and only relative to some choice of a manual of translation of the one theory into the other."[10] The identification and reidentification of things must invoke some system of reference among alternative such systems; and the equivalence of what we say of them is relativized to some system of equivalent expressions among alternative such systems. Beyond that, says Quine:

> The obstacle is only that any one intercultural correlation of words and phrases, and hence of theories, will be just one among various empirically admissible correlations, whether it is suggested by historical gradations or by unaided analogy; *there is nothing for such a correlation to be uniquely right or wrong about.* In saying this I philosophize from the vantage point only of our own provincial conceptual scheme and scientific epoch, true; but I know no better.[11]

It is plain from this that Quine is altogether opposed to speaking of science as acquiring knowledge of the determinate structure of the world as it "really is." Apart from the extravagance of the idiom, "there is nothing . . . to be uniquely right or wrong about." In *Word and Object,* Quine had similarly maintained that, regarding our jungle linguist's effort to translate a native speaker's sentences, "the point is not that we cannot be sure whether the analytical hypothesis [on the basis of which we construe the terms and vocabulary of the native as we do] is right, but that there is not even, as there was in the case of 'Gavagai', an objective matter to be right or wrong about."[12] "Rival systems of analytical hypotheses can fit the totality of speech behavior to perfection . . . and dispositions to speech behavior as well, and still specify mutually incompatible translations of countless sentences insusceptible of independent control."[13]

Still, Quine attempts in various ways to anchor the entailed relativities in a realist manner. However, the adjustments remain extremely subtle and signify once again the seeming convergence of realist and idealist pictures of scientific knowledge. In "Epistemology Naturalized" for instance, Quine offers the following:

> It was sad for epistemologists, Hume and others, to have to acquiesce in the impossibility of strictly deriving the science of the external world from sensory evidence. Two cardinal tenets of empiricism remained unassailable, however, and so remain to this day. One is that whatever evidence there is for science *is* sensory evidence. The other . . . is that all inculcation of meanings of words must rest ultimately on sensory evidence. Hence the continuing attractiveness of the idea of a *logischer aufbau* in which the sensory content of discourse would stand forth explicitly.[14]

Here, Quine resists the deducibility, *à la* Carnap, of physical science from original "sensory evidence." He holds, nevertheless, to the realist-motivated thesis that "the stimulation of his sensory receptors is all the evidence anybody has had to go on, ultimately, in arriving at his picture of the world."[15] The trouble is, as we have already noted in Kuhn's account, that only *theory* can affirm that the *stimuli* impinging on different percipients (as distinct from sensations somehow discriminated) are the same. Quine does not make entirely explicit the relationship between his notion of "stimulus meaning"and the cognitive reliance on "sensory evidence." The two, however, cannot be equivalent. The "stimulation of his sensory receptors" cannot be "all the evidence" one has, since fixing such stimulation must itself rest on sensory evidence of a sort *that one can least report.* In *Word and Object,* Quine sometimes speaks as if there might be a relatively stable order of sensory discriminations—an order at least "closer" to "peripheral" contact with the external world than "collateral information" could provide—that our "analytical hypotheses" build on in the alternatively relativized ways already noted. Thus he remarks: "We have been reflecting in a general way on how surface irritations generate, through language, one's knowledge of the world," and, in an apparently sanguine spirit, signifies that he means to consider "how much of language can be made sense of in terms of its stimulus conditions, and what scope this leaves for empirically unconditioned variation in one's conceptual scheme."[16]

The motivation of these remarks is obviously realistic. For either the appeal to "surface irritations" marks (no doubt inconsistently) a range of empirical evidence that is not inscrutable (that is, relativized to theory and conceptual schemata) in the way in which reference and meaning are inscrutable, or else it marks the minimal constraints on which any putative science may be supposed to yield knowledge of the world. That Quine is drawn in both directions is clear enough: how else to understand such pregnant remarks as: "Occasion sentences and stimulus meaning are general coin; terms and reference are local to our conceptual scheme";[17] "Vaguely speaking, what we want of observation sentences is that they be the ones in closest causal proximity to the sensory receptors;[18] "Like all conditioning, or induction, the process [of ostension] will depend ultimately also on one's own inborn propensity to find one stimulation qualitatively more akin to a second stimulation than to a third; otherwise there can never be a selective reinforcement and extension of responses."[19]

Effectively, then, Quine preserves his realism by at least two doctrines that, on inspection, *cannot properly resolve the dispute between realism and idealism:* first, he holds (in effect) that knowledge of the external world rests on sensory evidence; second, he holds that we must be biologically disposed to favor certain sensory elements as more similar than others. But both these doctrines are as congenial to the idealist as they are to the realist. On Quine's own view, there seems to be nothing to appeal to (the indeterminacy issue originally raised) to decide between an epistemologist "who is willing to eke out his austere ontology of sense impressions with . . . set-theoretic auxiliaries" and another "who would rather settle for bodies outright than accept all these sets, which amounts, after all, to the whole abstract ontology of mathematics."[20] It is easy to see also that the (entirely reasonable) theory of a biological asymmetry favoring certain sets of sense impressions as "more akin" than others may be used to support the idealist's picture of our knowledge of a mind-dependent world (outflanking any charge of miracle regarding the world's reliability) as much as the realist's picture of remaining in touch with a mind-independent world (even though, as both Kuhn and Quine suggest in different ways, we cannot expect science to provide a progressively and demonstrably more adequate account of the determinate details of *that* world). In fact, if one takes a very large view of Quine's entire venture, then, on his own conception of ontological relativity, it would seem unlikely (not of course impossible) that an idealist and realist theory of scientific knowledge would not turn out to be "invariant" in the very sense in which, in Quine's justly famous claim, "the infinite totality of sentences of any given speaker's language can be so permuted, or mapped onto itself, that (*a*) the totality of the speaker's dispositions to verbal behavior remains invariant, and yet (*b*) the mapping is no mere correlation of sentences with *equivalent* sentences, in any plausible sense of equivalence however loose."[21] Notice that the required invariance concerns only the totality of speakers' dispositions *and* that the identity of such dispositions remains, on Quine's (best) view, theory-relative, subject to our analytical hypotheses.

We may, therefore, capture the realist theme to which both Kuhn and Quine adhere—in spite of the enormous differences between them—by characterizing them both as *interior realists*. That is, they interpret their respective theories of scientific knowledge realistically, *but the evidence that they adduce is supportive of realism only on the assumption of that interpretation itself.* The term "interior" is deliberately selected to permit a comparison, without prejudice, between Kuhn's and Quine's accounts and Hilary Putnam's—for Putnam terms his own theory an "internal realism." Quine, however, provides us implicitly with an open and radical (negative) admission about the possibility of grounding the defense of realism on empirical evidence; for the final sentence of *Word and Object* reads: "True, no experiment may be expected to settle an ontological issue; but this is only because such issues are connected with surface irritations in such multifarious ways, through such a maze of intervening theory."[22] And in the closing sentence of "Ontological Relativity," reflecting on the parallel between "regress on ontology" and "regress in the semantics of truth and kindred notions—satisfaction, naming" (partly in the context of Tarski's work), Quine concludes—because in both cases the resolution of pertinent questions of "referentiality" (as of quantification or of the satisfaction-condition of the semantics of truth) demands a background theory of ampler resources—that "both truth and ontology may in a suddenly rather clear and even tolerant sense be said to belong to transcendental metaphysics."[23] The question remains whether that constraint can be overtaken empirically. Obviously not for Quine.

Without a doubt, Hilary Putnam's account represents the most sustained effort to date to construe realism as confirmed on empirical grounds. In "Realism and Reason," Putnam specifically contrasts "internal realism" and what he terms "metaphysical realism" (of which more later), identifies the first as his own preference, and explicitly characterizes that view as "an empirical theory":

> One of the facts that this theory explains is the fact that scientific theories tend to 'converge' in the sense that earlier theories are, very often, limiting cases of later theories (which is why it is possible to regard theoretical terms as preserving their reference across most changes of theory). Another of the facts it explains is the more mundane fact that language-using contributes to getting our goals, achieving satisfaction, or what have you.[24]

His thesis here is explicitly indebted to those (largely unpublished) views of Richard Boyd's that seek to recover a form of scientific realism,[25] though Putnam himself believes there is a significant body of knowledge ("practical knowledge"—not altogether unrelated to Polanyi's "tacit knowledge") that is not part of science but is presupposed by it.[26]

The main thrust of Putnam's thesis incorporates the following two principles of Boyd's (as Putnam himself summarizes the matter):

(1)   Terms in a mature science typically *refer.*

(2)   The laws of a theory belonging to a mature science are typically approximately *true.*

Boyd, Putnam says, attempts to show "that scientists act as they do because they *believe* (1) and (2) and that their strategy works because (1) and (2) are *true.*"[27] The empirical payoff, apparently, is just that "my knowledge of the truth of (1) and (2) enables me to restrict the class of candidate-theories I have to consider, and thereby increases my chance of success."[28] Part of the charm and persuasiveness of Putnam's (and Boyd's) position is that, in a certain relatively unrefined sense, what is claimed is clearly true; but in that relatively unrefined sense (*not* equivalent to the construction Boyd or Putnam would put upon (1) and (2)), one supposes that idealists and realists would agree. There is no reason to think idealists are any less "realistic" in the sense of pursuing what seems to work best. The problem arises, how to construe the claim so as to confirm the *empirical* superiority of realism over idealism. For example, on Putnam's view, neither Kuhn nor Paul Feyerabend believes principle (1) *or believes it in the sense in which Putnam intends it*; similarly, Karl Popper certainly does not believe (2) or does not believe it in the sense in which Putnam intends it. Popper explicitly holds that "we must regard *all laws or theories as hypothetical or conjectural*; that is, as guesses."[29] He goes on to explain: "From a rational point of view, we should not 'rely' on any theory, for no theory has been shown to be true, or can be shown to be true . . . But we should *prefer* as basis for action the best-tested theory."[30]

Doubtless, Putnam would counter that one *ought* to subscribe to the realist interpretation of Boyd's argument,[31] but this runs the risk of being questionbegging or irrelevant; for, apart from the internal difficulties of particular views—Feyerabend's, say—and apart from *non*empirical grounds for favoring the realist interpretation over the idealist (recalling Quine's remarks about ontological indeterminacy), it may well be false that scientists (or philosophers) act as they do because they *believe* (1) and (2) to be true. The trouble with (1) and (2), as both Boyd and Putnam understand these principles, is that they are already formulated in realist terms; also, it may, in the relevant respects, make no empirical difference to the success of science whether one subscribes to a realist or an idealist interpretation of (1) and (2) (or an idealist analogue of same). There is no evidence that Putnam is right, and there is a great deal of evidence —witness the rather different views of Kuhn, Feyerabend, [32] Popper, and Michael Dummett [33] (with whom Putnam seriously contends)—that internal realism (the favored realist interpretation of (1) and (2)) is not actually supported by prominent scientists and philosophers of science. Certainly, *if* the issue between realism and idealism were not empirical, then we should have no pertinent reason either to expect the beliefs of scientists and philosophers to favor the realist position or, if they actually did, to judge that their behavior in this regard relevantly bore on the validity of the realist thesis itself.

Further, regarding (1), it is reasonably safe to say that that principle, construed realistically, is not consistent with Quine's conception of ontological indeterminacy. For one thing, Quine holds that we are ontically *committed* by quantificational practice, *not* that we fix the actual entities of the world. Thus he says very plainly, "we have moved . . . to the question of checking not on existence, but on imputations of existence: on what a theory says exists."[34] This obviously suits the idealist as well as the realist—possibly, the idealist more. And for another, on Quine's view (as we have seen), ontological relativity itself precludes the notion that there could be—or need be—any fixity of reference in order to save the body of science. But this again, at least on Putnam's own say-so, suits the idealist better than the realist.

In fact, Putnam concedes, with Quine, that "an absolutely 'unrevisable' truth [is] an idealization . . . an unattainable 'limit'. Any statement can be 'revised'."[35] But in the context in which he subscribes to ontological relativity, Putnam fails to press the point that, respecting principle (1), terms may be consistently *taken* to refer to the same entities through the changing phases of a science rather than actually *known* to refer to such; and that, on the principle of indeterminacy (the correlative of ontological relativity—in Quine's view at least), the body of science may be preserved despite systematic changes in reference within it. It is also clear that the force of principle (1) is largely conditional on the force of principle (2): if a view like Popper's were adopted, then it would be difficult to see why (1) should be *required* at all; the point of (1) is largely captured by the notion that the preservation of "approximately true" laws through the developing history of a science signifies that the laws hold of just the entities intended in (1). This is why (1) and (2) are already realistically interpreted in Putnam's account; there must be some more neutral ("empirical") ground on which to decide the issue if it is to be decided (rather against Quine) on empirical grounds at all.

The matter is actually exacerbated by Putnam's appeal to the principle of charity or the principle of benefit of doubt.[36] That principle applies where putative misdescription affects *apparent* or *intended* reference or even what "ought to have been the intended" reference. Thus Putnam holds that it is not enough that a theory T_2, which is to replace "the received theory" T_1 of some branch of physics, imply "most of the 'observation sentences' implied by T_1"; it is normally "the *hardest* way" (and preferred) to secure that relationship by "making T_2 imply the 'approximate truth' of the *laws* of T_1." Furthermore, we can, by applying the principle of charity, "assign *referents* to the terms of T_1 from the standpoint of T_2" if T_2 satisfies such constraints. For example, Putnam says, "we can assign a referent to 'gravitational field' in Newtonian theory *from the standpoint of* relativity theory (though not to 'ether' or 'phlogiston'); a referent to Mendel's 'gene' from the standpoint of present-day molecular biology; and a referent to Dalton's 'atom' from the standpoint of quantum mechanics."[37] It is clear that Putnam means to subscribe here to some form of Saul Kripke's principle of rigid designators.[38] But if so, the principle of charity must itself already be construed realistically and contrary to ontological relativity; also, there is no reason why a counterpart idealist version of charity could not be formulated, *particularly if (2) were not construed realistically* (or if the theory of rigid designators proved uncompelling or open to an idealist reading or analogue). The *assignment* of referents to T_1 would then count, precisely, as preserving the internal coherence of historically changing theories. There would be no need to fall back to the extreme—and ultimately incoherent—views of Kuhn and Feyerabend regarding reference.[39]

Here, the general strategy of idealism obviously lies with matching the internal realist's construction of alleged empirical advantage in order to achieve a stalemate.

For, although a stalemate cannot secure an idealist victory, it would restore the dispute (borrowing Quine's term) to its "transcendental" status. Thus seen, the boldness and originality of Putnam's and Boyd's contention cannot be denied. On the other hand, we are led to see the relative modesty of the idealist countermove. Essentially, what Putnam claims is "that science taken at 'face value' *implies* realism."[40] The countermove, therefore, seeks to preserve an "empirical" element in whatever is justified in Putnam's and Boyd's claims and to reach for a "transcendental" stalemate regarding whatever they take to *imply* realism. Thus, following Boyd, Putnam places a great deal of emphasis on *"convergence* in scientific knowledge."[41] Now, it is true that Kuhn and Feyerabend deny convergence, *and* it is true that, in doing so, they deny (in somewhat different ways) that the referents of competing theories are or can be the same. It is also true that, developing the latter thesis, they fail to see "that scientific terms are not synonomous with descriptions."[42] But if, as seems reasonable, we can construe the principle of charity in an idealist manner — in fact, it *must* have a form neutral as between realism and idealism — then convergence itself may be construed neutrally as well. For, for one thing, the ("empirical," neutral) facts of convergence themselves presuppose the application of the principle of charity respecting referents marked as *intended* to be the same through changing and replacement theories. And for a second, the interpretation of the facts of convergence (as favoring realism or idealism) logically depends on the interpretation (realist or idealist) of scientific laws. What this shows, in effect, is the tautologous nature of Putnam's dictum' "science taken at 'face value' *implies* realism"; it implies realism simply because, on Putnam's views, to take science at "face value" *is* to construe (1) and (2), the facts of convergence, *and* the principle of charity realistically.

Boyd is especially candid about the problem. He concedes that, in assessing the plausibility of competing theories that "have exactly the same observational consequences when taken together with those currently accepted theories with which they are respectively consistent," we might well hold one theory to be implausible because the force it introduces "is dramatically unlike all those forces about which we now know"; hence we could construe the estimate of its implausibility as reflecting *"experimental* evidence against [it]." So "the experimental evidence for our current theories of force is indirect experimental evidence that no such force [as is postulated] exists — and that [the theory in question] must be false." But the argument, he acknowledges, requires a principle to the effect that the plausibility of new theories "should, *prima facie,* resemble current theories with respect to their accounts of causal relations among theoretical entities." And *that* principle will be construed as empirically or experimentally decisive *"if and only if* we have already adopted a realistic position with respect to the experimental evidence for the currently accepted body of scientific theories."[43] Here Boyd offers a choice only between ("scientific") realism and "conventionalism" (that is, the doctrine that the differences between competing theories arranged as above are "experimentally indistinguishable"). So formulated, there is no doubt that scientific realism must be favored. But idealism represents a much more vigorous antagonist than mere conventionalism. It seeks in effect to provide a relatively complex non-realist account of scientific knowledge: (a) by tolerating non-convergence (of the sort Kuhn reports) where it obtains and by construing the facts of convergence (of the sort Boyd reports) only in terms of cognitive strategies suited to knowledge of the world-as-it-impinges-on-us; and (b) by conceding conventionalism with respect to ontic commitment.

The idea is that all the "empirical" advantages that Boyd very plausibly adduces (that is, advantages reinterpreted neutrally as far as the realist-idealist controversy is concerned) may be retained in order, precisely, to effect the required stalemate. Hence it is *not* decisive to hold that we may assess implausibility (under the conditions sketched) as constituting "experimental evidence," for it is entirely possible to construe such evidence in idealist terms—once one denies knowledge of the world *an sich* as opposed to the world-as-it-impinges-on-us, denies the realist interpretation of scientific laws, denies the realist interpretation of the principle of charity, and admits ontological indeterminacy. In short, Boyd's position must, on this reading, be construed as essentially circular.

In effect, this is to restore—with a difference—Michael Dummett's emphasis on "the underdetermination of theory" (as well as, if needed, its distinction from Quine's doctrine of "the indeterminacy of translation").[44] Dummett's argument against Quine is to the effect that underdetermination is the only basis Quine offers for the indeterminacy thesis and that it is not sufficient: "If two speakers of a language hold formally inconsistent but empirically equivalent theories," the fact may, unnoticed, affect their interpretation of one another's utterances; but there is no entailment, Dummett thinks, from underdetermination to indeterminacy.[45] Indeterminacy, of course, actually strengthens the idealist alternative (as we have seen). But, apart from that, underdetermination may be softened in a manner mediating Boyd's realism and Dummett's (reasonable) hedging between the alternatives originally posed by Duhem and Hertz, that is, the view (Duhem's) "that physical theory is always underdetermined by the available evidence, in that no falsifying experiment or observation could show conclusively that any single constituent proposition of a theory was false, although it could show that the theory was not correct as a whole" and the view (Hertz's) that that condition is "a defect to be remedied, a defect arising out of the use of a multiplicity of theoretical notions exceeding the multiplicity of the observed facts."[46] Boyd's effort was to demonstrate the untenability of "*radical* underdetermination": that is, that experimental evidence provide at least *indirect* evidence for the truth of a theory still underdetermined in the "direct" respect Dummett explores; and Dummett remains a conventionalist (in Boyd's sense), at least with regard to decisions affected by the still unresolved disagreement between Duhem and Hertz. The intermediary position, which now seems increasingly reasonable, simply argues that we should construe the indirect evidence Boyd adduces neither in the realist's nor in the conventionalist's way. This shows, in effect, that Boyd has rather misgauged the force of his argument: it undermines conventionalism all right ("radical underdetermination") but is ineffective (as yet) against an idealism that *admits* the bearing of experimental evidence on the appraisal of competing theories that are empirically underdetermined. The experimental evidence itself, as well as the postulation of theoretical entities and forces, remains as "mind-dependent" as ever in respects decisive to the dispute.

No doubt, the realist thesis with which we began, that material objects exist independently of mind, remains difficult to resist. But why should one resist it? The sophisticated idealist will content himself with restricting his theories to the nature of the world we know: he will leave to the realist—to the "metaphysical realist," in Putnam's phrase—the unknowable world in itself. For Putnam, metaphysical realism is not an empirical theory but, in a sense, a purported model "of the relation of *any* correct theory to all or part of THE WORLD [presumably, the world as it is independent of the knowing mind]." That doctrine, Putnam believes, "is incoherent."[47] But Putnam appears to conclude that the retreat to "internal realism," which is admittedly coherent, plus the defeat of conventionalism *à la* Boyd is tantamount to a defeat of idealism—which is a palpable *non sequitur. If* there is a viable idealist reading of convergence—which certainly seems facilitated by such views (however diverse) as Quine's indeterminacy thesis and Popper's conception of scientific laws—then the mere defeat of *radical* underdetermination (conventionalism) yields no more than an *empirical* stalemate between realism and idealism. Furthermore, in spite of the polarized way in which realism and idealism are pitted against one another, it may well be, once again in the Kantian spirit, that neither position is entirely satisfactory and that only a theory that combines elements of both in a fresh way—conceding convergence and ontic relativity at least—is likely to be compelling. Alternatively put, it may well be that realism rests not with the *indirect* evidence of convergence but (as Boyd almost concedes, admitting the regress of his own argument) with the ontic import of perceptual knowledge. In that case, it may well be decisive to reconsider the tenability of Quine's radical indeterminacy claims and their bearing on the ontic import of sensory information.

Now, the most original aspect of Putnam's defense of realism rests with his use of Kant's innovations. Putnam holds that "Whatever else realists say, they typically say that they believe in a 'correspondence theory of truth'."[48] Before Kant, "almost every philosopher," Putnam holds, subscribed to that theory, viz., that "there is a world out there; and what we say or think is 'true' *when it gets it the way it is* and 'false' when it doesn't correspond to *the way it is.*" All this was changed by Kant because, with him, "a new view emerges: the view that truth is radically mind-dependent. It is not that the thinking mind *makes up* the world on Kant's view; but it doesn't just mirror it either."[49] Here, one might not unfairly claim, Putnam has provided the basis for the validity of both the realist and idealist views—as opposed to those of the conventionalist. Basically, there are two currently favored views of truth: "'realist' views, which interpret truth as some kind of correspondence to what is the case, and 'verificationist' views [in effect, idealist views], which interpret truth as, for example, what would be verified under ideal conditions of inquiry [a mere example, one actually favoring Peirce's version of verificationism]."[50] It is Putnam's intention to subscribe to *both* (in different regards) and, in doing so, to show that a correspondence theory "is needed to understand how language works and how science works"—hence why realism ("internal realism") is unavoidable.[51]

First of all, Putnam seeks to show that Tarski's semantic conception of truth permits us to construe "true," in terms of its formal properties, as "amazingly, a philosophically neutral notion." It is just "a device for 'semantic ascent'—for 'raising' assertions from the 'object language' to the 'meta-language', and the device does not commit one epistemologically or metaphysically."[52] On this view, since Tarski shows us only the formal properties of the correspondence thesis, accepting his account does not yet commit us to realism and, therefore, remains compatible with Kant's constraint. But the "notion of truth" is *not* "philosophically neutral"; Tarski's work "requires supplementation"; in effect, truth as well as reference is "a causal-explanatory notion."[53]

Here, with important *caveats*, Putnam favors Hartry Field's thesis (ultimately failing in another regard, as an objection to Tarski's account) that truth has a causal-explanatory function (Field would insist that language is a natural phenomenon and truth, a physicalistic notion); also, Stephen Leeds's (unpublished) thesis (directed against Field's claim) that the notions of truth and reference are not causal-explanatory notions but serve a certain expressive purpose under the conditions of human existence (hence justify Tarski's Criterion of Adequacy).[54] The point is that, on Putnam's view, what is needed in a theory of truth is an account of speakers' "reliability," that is, that the sentences they utter "have a high probability of being true."[55] Given human interests (which, on Putnam's view, yields, *à la* Leeds, a " 'transcendental argument' for Tarski's procedure"), we are led to construe "reference" (effectively, Tarski's "satisfaction"-relation) in a realist way: satisfaction or reference is then construed as "a relation between words and things" and, as such, exhibits just the sort of explanatory power that Putnam has found in Boyd's original account.[56] Hence, internal realism is vindicated.

But what Putnam has shown so far is no more than the viability and coherence of a realist interpretation of the satisfaction-relation: Tarski's original conception, remember, was conceded to be philosophically neutral.[57] He has not yet shown that an idealist interpretation is untenable. Here we come to the very heart of Putnam's distinctive thesis. Part of its force, however, is somewhat spent, since adopting the extreme dichotomy with which Boyd originally worked leads Putnam (as we have seen) to a *non sequitur*. His summary formulation quite explicitly pits the realist against the conventionalist, but he draws the moral against the idealist:

> the effect of abandoning realism—that is, abandoning the belief in any describable world of unobservable things, and accepting in its place the belief that all the 'unobservable things' (and, possibly, the observable things as well) spoken of in any generation's scientific theories, including our own, are *mere* theoretical conveniences, destined to be replaced and supplanted by quite different and unrelated theoretical constructions in the future—would *not* be a total scrapping of the predicates *true* and *refers* in their *formal* aspects. We could . . . *keep* formal semantics (including 'Tarski-type' truth-definitions);

even keep classical logic; and yet *shift* our notion of 'truth' over to something approximating 'warranted assertibility'. And I believe that this shift is what would in fact happen.[58]

The shift involved eliminates a full-blooded correspondence theory and replaces it with a verificationist theory, a theory of "truth within the theory" or "warranted assertibility" or the like — a position Putnam takes to have been skeptical of realism "from Protagoras to Michael Dummett."[59] But there can be no question that, in attacking conventionalism thus, Putnam means to attack idealism, for it is in precisely the same spirit that he maintains that "the typical realist argument against idealism is that it makes the success of science a *miracle*."[60] Our own effort, here, has been to recover an idealist interpretation of the very evidence that Putnam draws from Boyd. If the effort is reasonable, then Putnam is caught in the same circle as Boyd.

We may now draw the argument to a close that may yet have some surprising aspects. One must remember that Putnam *does* subscribe to a "'verificationist' semantics" — not, to be sure, "a verificationist theory of *meaning*," but a verificationist model of linguistic competence. "Dummett and I *agree*," he observes, "that you can't treat understanding a sentence (in general) as knowing its truth conditions; because it then becomes unintelligible what *that* knowledge *in turn* consists in. We both *agree* that the theory of understanding has to be done in a verificationist way."[61] What Putnam opposes here is the confusion between meaning and reference and the corollary thesis that "conclusive verificationism [entails that] there must be phenomenal truth conditions for every sentence in every intelligible language."[62] He does, by way of a rhetorical question, concede that "verificationism [is] at bottom a form of idealism"; but if so, it is a doctrine realists can consistently adopt provided they do not, in doing so — like Reichenbach or Carnap, for instance — treat it as a theory or account of meaning.[63] The idealist element is in a sense incorporated in a stricter correspondence theory of truth. But now, Putnam argues that a verificationist theory of truth *tout court* (hence idealism) fails to accommodate error in a sense that we require. Thus assume that we require a causal explanation of the reliability of speakers (in the sense provided, above, favoring Boyd's reflections). If so, then, "in the case of seeing what colour a rug is, [say], it is a part of the causal explanation that there is *room for error* — it is *physically* possible that one seems to see a green rug, etc., and the rug *not* be green." "[A] modal statement [is] implied by our theory. But this shows truth *can't* be warranted assertibility!" For any predicate the idealist may substitute for "true" one can find a statement S such that "S might have property P and still not be *true*."[64]

This is an important finding but hardly decisive against the idealist. It does show that truth cannot be or mean the same thing as warranted assertibility (or warranted assertibility under any merely finite or non-ideal circumstances). And it shows at a stroke that a view like Gilbert Harman's for instance that treats knowledge as inference to the best explanation[65] must fail for precisely the reason

Putnam adduces. But the more serious point is simply that the *falsity* of asserting that the rug is green *must itself wait for the exercise of some verificationist procedure:* the modal statement (i) establishes the evidential *relevance* of what proves to be false for what appeared to be true; (ii) confirms that we are committed to the view that our continuing experience with the world may indeed *warrant* that what we once took to be true may be false; and (iii) entails that it is *possible,* given the way the world is or the way we come to gain knowledge of the world, that whatever we verify as true may actually be false. None of these considerations is incompatible with the idealist thesis. In fact, Dummett, in rejecting a realist conception of truth, that is, a correspondence theory that yields a *criterion* of truth, concedes that "we remain realists *au fond,*" in the sense, precisely, that "realism consists in the belief that for any statement there must be something [in the world] in virtue of which either it or its negation is true."[66] Dummett must, therefore, allow revisions of earlier verificationist appraisals on the strength of later ones. (Whether an intuitionist model of verificationism is preferable is quite another matter.[67])

One could say, therefore, that idealists *are* realists who insist on the *use* we make of the concepts of truth and reference, and that realists *are* idealists who insist that, whatever that use, there must be *something* in the world in virtue of which we take truths to be truths. But if conventionalists are idealists, then that breed is defeated, in just the same sense that, if the advocates of correspondence criteria of truth are realists, then that breed is defeated. So it is an extremely thin claim that Putnam reserves for the advantage of the realist, if the idealist is willing to admit that what he takes to be verified at time t he may, for evidential reasons, be willing, at t', to admit to be false.

On Putnam's view, "one does not need to *know* that there is a correspondence between words and extra-linguistic entities to learn one's language. But there is such a correspondence none the less, and it explains the *success* of what one is doing."[68] There is, however, no way to flesh out any putative, determinate correspondence that can be considered in a manner more powerful that the verificationist's: there is no way to say *what* correspondences obtain in the realist's manner except by way of the idealist's devices; and there is no way to say *that* we have verified that the rug is green except by way of the realist's idiom — that *that is* how we find the world to be. But to say that it is *true* that what verification yields corresponds to what is "really there" raises a very subtle conceptual issue. For *if that* correspondence is to be *true,* then either the force of the original mode of verification will itself be verified within the framework of a more inclusive theory, so that (on the preceding argument) it may be false though it appears to be true; or, since the verificationist picture will lead to a vicious regress, we shall have to construe the metaphysical truth of any such correspondence as *"radically nonepistemic,"* that is, that "verified" does not imply "true."[69] The first limb of the dilemma is indecisive; the second is favored by metaphysical realism. Hence, Putnam takes the latter to be incoherent, and he settles for internal realism. Fair enough. But it obliges him to conclude that "in a certain 'contextual' sense, it is an *a priori* truth that 'cow' refers to [or is satisfied by] a determinate class of things (or a more-or-less-determinate class of things . . .).[70] To challenge the claim that 'cow' refers to cows, demanding, that is, how one knows that it refers "to *one* determinate set of things, as opposed to referring to a determinate set of things in *each admissible interpretation?*," is to confuse internal and metaphysical realism. "'cow' refers to cows" is a "logical truth," given what reference or satisfaction means, remains open to revision in the sense that the theory on which it was introduced may be rejected, cannot be challenged in terms of how the theory should be understood without moving to a theory possessing ampler facilities, and does not meaningfully permit the metaphysical realist's attempt to fix a unique referent.[71] Still, as Putnam himself acknowledges, the truth, the logical truth, the truth that is analytic relative to the theory in accordance with which the reference is taken to hold, would hold "even if internal realism were false."[72] Hence the curious *"synthetic a priori"* truths that Putnam introduces are truths in the purely formal sense in which Tarski provides a formal ("philosophically neutral") account of the correspondence theory of truth. It has, therefore, nothing whatever to do with the quarrel between realists and idealists and must be as compatible with the views of the one as of the other. In particular, these logical truths do not bear at all on the verification of principle (i)—which Putnam attributes to Boyd and which concerns reference in a sense that catches up the actual use and *understanding* of a language. And they cannot serve to explain the realist interpretation of ontological relativity —which does not require that we be able to determine the unique referents of our discourse. Hence their admission has the effect, ironically, of returning us to the finding (not, of course, in the metaphysical realist's sense) that the vindication of realism (or of idealism for that matter) is simply not an empirical issue.

Notes

1. Thomas S. Kuhn, *The Structure of Scientific Revolutions,* 2nd ed. enl. (Chicago, 1962, 1970), pp. 206-7.

2. *Ibid.*, p. 201.

3. Cf. Dudley Shapere, "Meaning and Scientific Change," in *Mind and Cosmos: Essays in Contemporary Science and Philosophy*, vol. III in The University of Pittsburgh Series in the Philosophy of Science (Pittsburgh, 1966).

4. Kuhn, *Structure of Scientific Revolution*, p. 195.

5. *Ibid.*, p. 196.

6. *Ibid.*, pp. 195-96.

7. *Ibid.*, pp. 195-96.

8. W. V. Quine, "Ontological Relativity," in *Ontological Relativity and Other Essays* (New York, 1969), pp. 34-35.

9. *Ibid.*, p. 28.

10. *Ibid.*, pp. 54-55.

11. Quine, "Speaking of Objects," in *Ontological Relativity*, p. 25. Italics added.

12. Quine, *Word and Object* (Cambridge, 1960), p. 73.

13. *Ibid.*, p. 72.

14. Quine, "Epistemology Naturalized," in *Ontological Relativity,* p. 75.

15. *Ibid.*, p. 75.

16. Quine, *Word and Object*, p. 26; cf. p. 68.

17. *Ibid.*, p. 53.

18. Quine, "Epistemology Naturalized," p. 85.

19. Quine, "Ontological Relativity," p. 31.

20. Quine, "Epistemology Naturalized," p. 73.

21. Quine, *Word and Object*, p. 27.

22. *Ibid.*, p. 276.

23. Quine, "Ontological Relativity," pp. 67-68.

24. Hilary Putnam, "Realism and Reason" (Presidential Address to the Eastern Division of the American Philosophical Association, Boston, Mass., 29 December 1976), in *Meaning and the Moral Sciences* (London, 1978), p. 123.

25. Boyd's *Realism and Scientific Epistemology* (Cambridge) is apparently forthcoming; cf. Richard N. Boyd, "Realism, Underdetermination, and a Causal Theory of Evidence" *Nous* 8 (1973):1-12.

26. Hilary Putnam, "Meaning and Knowledge" (The John Locke Lectures, 1976), lecture II, in *Meaning and the Moral Sciences*, p. 20. See also, "Literature, Science and Reflection," in *Meaning and the Moral Sciences;* and lecture VI, pp. 72-73.

27. Putnam, "Meaning and Knowledge," lecture II, pp. 20-21.

28. *Ibid.*, p. 21.

29. Karl R. Popper, *Objective Knowledge* (Oxford, 1972), p. 9.

30. *Ibid.*, pp. 21-22.

31. See Putnam, "Meaning and Knowledge," lecture III, pp. 42-43; lecture IV, p. 47.

32. Paul Feyerabend, *Against Method* (London, 1975).

33. Michael Dummett, "Truth," *Proceedings of the Aristotelian Society* 59 (1958-59): 141-62.

34. Quine, "Existence and Quantification," in *Ontological Relativity*, p. 93.

35. Putnam, "Realism and Reason," p. 138.

36. In *Meaning and the Moral Sciences*, Putnam uses the terms interchangeably; but in "Language and Reality," where he first introduced the issue, he favors the second over the first, which he associates with a principle introduced by N. L. Wilson that is incompatible with his own. See "Language and Reality," in *Mind, Language and Reality (Philosophical Papers*, vol. 2 [Cambridge, 1975]). pp. 274-77; also, N. L. Wilson, "Substances without Substrata," *Review of Metaphysics* 12 (1959):521-39.

37. Putnam, "Meaning and Knowledge," lecture II, pp. 21-22.

38. *Ibid.*, pp. 23-24; also, "Language and Reality," p. 276. Cf. Saul A. Kripke, "Naming and Necessity," in Donald Davidson and Gilbert Harman, eds., *Semantics of Natural Language* (Dordrecht, 1971).

39. Putnam, "Meaning and Knowledge," lecture II, pp. 22-25.

40. *Ibid.*, lecture III, p. 37.

41. *Ibid.*, lecture II, p. 20.

42. *Ibid.*, p. 23. Cf. Hilary Putnam, "How not to talk about meaning," in *Mind, Language and Reality;* and Kripke, "Naming and Necessity."

43. Richard N. Boyd, "Realism, Underdetermination and a Causal Theory of Evidence," pp. 5-8.

44. Michael Dummett, "The Significance of Quine's Indeterminacy Thesis," *Synthese* 27 (1974):390.

45. *Ibid.*, p. 383; see also "Reply to Quine," *Synthese* 27 (1974):414.

46. Dummett, "The Significance of Quine's Indeterminacy Thesis," p. 384.

47. Putnam, "Realism and Reason," pp. 123-24.

48. Putnam, "Meaning and Knowledge," lecture II, p. 18.

49. Putnam, "Introduction," *Meaning and the Moral Sciences*, p. 1.

50. Putnam, "Introduction."

51. *Ibid.*, p. 4; cf. p. 5.

52. Putnam, "Meaning and Knowledge," lecture I, p. 10; cf. p. 9.

53. Putnam, "Introduction," p. 4; Putnam, "Meaning and Knowledge," lecture I, p. 17.

54. Putnam, "Meaning and Knowledge," lecture I, pp. 14-17; Hartry Field, "Tarski's 'Theory of Truth'," *Journal of Philosophy* 69 (1972):347-75.

55. Putnam, "Meaning and Knowledge," lecture III, p. 38.

56. *Ibid.*, lecture II, pp. 30-32; lecture I, p. 16.

57. See Nicholas Rescher, *The Coherence Theory of Truth* (Oxford, 1973).

58. Putnam, "Meaning and Knowledge," lecture II, p. 29.

59. *Ibid.*, p. 30; cf. Dummett, "Truth."

60. *Ibid.*, p. 18.

61. Putnam, "Realism and Reason," p. 129.

62. Putnam, "Reference and Understanding," in *Meaning and the Moral Sciences*, p. 112; Putnam, "Realism and Reason," p. 129.

63. Putnam, "Reference and Understanding," pp. 111-14.

64. *Ibid.*, pp. 108-9; cf. Putnam, "Meaning and Knowledge," lecture II.

65. Gilbert Harman, *Thought* (Princeton, N.J., 1973).

66. Dummett, "Truth," p. 157.

67. See Putnam, "Meaning and Knowledge," lecture II.

68. Putnam, "Reference and Understanding," p. 111.

69. Putnam, "Realism and Reason," p. 125.

70. *Ibid.*, p. 137.

71. *Ibid.*, pp. 135-36.

72. *Ibid.*, p. 136.

Spinoza's Vacuum Argument

JONATHAN BENNETT

INTRODUCTION

Spinoza said that the only extended substance is the whole extended world and that finite bodies are not substances, i.e., are not worthy of a thing-like status in a fundamental metaphysics. He had reasons for this doctrine, though they do not occur in his official "demonstration" that there is only one substance (*Ethics* I proposition 14). One reason was the view that an ultimately thing-like status cannot be accorded to something that is divisible. That was certainly Leibniz's view, and there are textual grounds for attributing it to Spinoza also, though the evidence for that is somewhat diffuse. But there is also an argument that occurs in a localized manner, in a passage I shall quote below; and my purpose in this paper is to expound it.

There are two reasons why this is worth doing. One is that the argument is intrinsically enjoyable: once it has been properly reconstructed, it is sharp and elegant and cogent. The other is that the argument points the way to an interpretation of its conclusion — i.e., of the doctrine that bodies are not substances — that helps one understand other things in Spinoza. The interpretation of Spinoza's metaphysics of the extended world emerging from this argument is better than most of what one finds in the secondary literature on Spinoza. And the literature seems not to contain so much as a serious *mention* of the argument that is my present topic.

THE ARGUMENT

The argument occurs inconspicuously in the course of a long explanatory Note appended to proposition 15 of Part I of the *Ethics*. Here it is:

If corporeal substance could be so divided that its parts were really distinct, why, then, could one part not be annihilated, the rest remaining connected with one another as before? And why must they all be so fitted together that there is no vacuum? Truly, of things which are really distinct from one another, one can be, and remain in its condition, without the other. Since therefore there is no vacuum in Nature (this is discussed elsewhere), but all of its parts must so concur that there is no vacuum, it follows that they cannot be really distinguished, i.e. that corporeal substance, insofar as it is substance, cannot be divided. (For my translations throughout this paper, I have relied almost entirely upon a soon-to-be-published translation of Spinoza's works by E. M. Curley [Princeton University Press].)

The interpretation of this which I favor is not the most obvious one. There is a rival that stays much closer to Spinoza's words than mine does. But I reject the rival interpretation because it represents the passage as arguing from a premise that Spinoza did not accept to a conclusion that is hardly intelligible, whereas on my account it argues from a premise that Spinoza did accept to a crystal-clear conclusion that nicely fits the rest of what he says about the extended world. Either he efficiently expressed a dreadful argument or he made a clumsy job of expressing a superb one; and I prefer the latter hypothesis.

THE WRONG INTERPRETATION

The two interpretations differ in ways that flow from their differing understandings of the term 'vacuum', and thus of the statement "There is no vacuum in nature."

The wrong interpretation takes 'vacuum' in a very natural manner: you have a vacuum whenever you have a region of space that does not manifest any mass. (Here and throughout, take 'mass' as a stand-in for whatever empirical property you think marks the crucial difference between empty space and matter.) On this interpretation, the statement "There is no vacuum in nature" means that *everything extended has mass.*

If that is Spinoza's premise, then his argument must go as follows. If you could hold all bodies still while annihilating one of them and leaving the rest intact, that would have to create a vacuum, i.e., something extended and massless. So from the premise that there is no vacuum we can infer that *such a vacuum-producing event cannot happen.* But why can it not happen? It must be because one body could not be annihilated while leaving all the others intact. Why not? Well, because what happens to one body is logically tied to what happens to others. Why? Because bodies are not really distinct parts of the extended world. Q.e.d.

That argument was used in the contrapositive direction by Locke: assuming that the annihilation of one body implies nothing for any other body, Locke used the possibility of such an annihilation as proof of the possibility of "vacuum" in the sense of something extended and massless (*Essay* II.xii.21). That is a good argument. But taken in our present direction, from the denial of vacuum to the denial that bodies are distinct from one another, it is worthless.

For one thing, it requires the premise not merely that there is not but that there could not be a vacuum. Why should anyone think that there *could-not be* massless regions of space? I can think of no reason, and there is no independent evidence of Spinoza's holding any such opinion, or even of his holding merely that there *are not* any massless regions of space.

Also, the conclusion of this argument is confusing and obscure: it says that bodies must fail to be "really distinct from one another," so that the annihilation of one would result in . . . what? The others' closing in to fill the gap? I cannot see what else emerges from the argument. But that conclusion is just silly—as though bodies failed to be "distinct" from one another because they are joined by metaphysical rubber-bands—as well as being quite out of touch with the main lines of Spinoza's thought.

WHAT SPINOZA MEANS BY "VACUUM"

To get the argument right, we have to get "There is no vacuum" right, which involves getting "vacuum" right. The key to this is Spinoza's "this is discussed elsewhere" *(de quo alia)*, which is presumably a reference to the only other place in his writings where vacuum is mentioned—namely a passage in an early work whose short title is *Descartes's Principles*. In that work, Spinoza presents in his own fashion some doctrines that are Descartes's rather than his own; but he agrees with many of them, so that often he is speaking for himself as well as for Descartes. I am sure he writes with conviction about vacuum. Here is the core of what he says about it:

> The nature of body or matter consists in extension alone. . . . Space and body do not really differ [because] body and extension do not really differ, and space and extension do not really differ. . . . It involves a contradiction that there should be a vacuum [i.e.] extension without bodily substance. . . . For a fuller explanation, and to correct the prejudice about vacuum, [Descartes's] *Principles* II.17-18 should be read. The main point there is that bodies between which nothing lies must touch one another, and also that nothing has no properties. (Spinoza, *Descartes's Principles* II.2-3.)

To see what he is getting at, consider the question: If we pump all the air out of a vacuum jar, what is left in it? There cannot be literally *nothing* left, for if there really is nothing between the two sides then they will be in contact with one another, i.e., the jar will have collapsed. We might try to keep them apart, while not allowing that there is something in the jar, by saying that there is *a distance* between its sides. But Descartes has a good reply to this in the part of his *Principles* to which Spinoza refers. Distance, Descartes says, is a mode—a property or quality or measure—and there must be something it is *of*: you can have a mile *of road*, or a yard *of fabric*, but you cannot have just a sheer mile or a naked yard:

> If it is asked what would happen if God removed all the body contained in a vessel without permitting its place to be occupied by another body, we shall

answer that the sides of the vessel will thereby come into direct touch with one another. For two bodies must touch when there is nothing between them, because it is manifestly contradictory for these two bodies to be apart from one another, or that there should be a distance between them, and yet that this distance should be nothing; for distance is a mode of extension, and without extended substance it cannot therefore exist. (Descartes, *Principles* II.18)

The moral is that if one is to speak of vacuum one must speak of it as *something extended:* it may lack mass, solidity, impenetrability, etc., but it must be thought of as something that has size and shape—not as a nothing that has size or shape, a case in which size and shape are not the size and shape of anything.

This is true and good. But Descartes partly spoils it by making two bad terminological decisions, in each of which he is followed by Spinoza. First, he took 'vacuum' to mean something like "extended nothing," i.e., to mean something nonsensical. Second, he used the terms 'body' and 'matter' to mean nothing more than "that which is extended," so that for him the adjective 'bodily' (or 'corporeal') meant merely "extended."

Where it would seem better to say that extended items divide into matter or body (which has mass, solidity, etc.) and vacuum (which lacks mass, solidity, etc.), Descartes allows the terms 'matter' and 'body' to sprawl over the whole realm of that which is extended, and lets 'vacuum' stand only for a non-realm —viz. for the territory of the nonsense-concept of "extended nothing."

Thus, when Descartes wants to say that the pumped-out jar does not contain a *cylindrical nothing,* he expresses this by saying that it does not contain "vacuum"; and that is all he consideredly means by that remark. Similarly, when he says that the pumped-out jar still contains bodily substance, all he means is that it contains *something extended*—the "something" might well be what *we* would call "vacuum," i.e., something extended by lacking mass, solidity, and so on. His whole point—expressed in unfortunate language which makes a philosophical truth sound like a scientific falsehood—is that there cannot be a region of space "in which there is absolute nothing," (*Principles* II.16.)

As one might expect, Descartes sometimes forgot that he was using 'vacuum' and 'matter' in these peculiar ways, and took himself to be committed to holding that wherever there is extension there is mass, from which he then inferred things that do not follow from his considered premise that where there is extension there is something extended. But my present concern is not with those strayings but only with what he did primarily mean by 'matter' and 'vacuum'; for it is those primary meanings which are taken over by Spinoza, consistently and with no muddle or forgetfulness.

When Spinoza says that there cannot be vacuum, then, he does not mean that there cannot be stretches of space that do not manifest solidity, mass, gravitational force, or whatever. He is not predicting what you will find if you ransack the physical universe. His point is a conceptual one: if the two sides of the jar do not touch, it follows logically that there is *something* between them. With that weapon in our hand, let us return to his vacuum argument in the *Ethics.*

THE RIGHT INTERPRETATION OF THE VACUUM ARGUMENT

I shall express the argument in my own way, and leave it to the reader to reread Spinoza's text and decide whether I am right about what he was getting at.

Suppose there are three contiguous cubic bodies — A, B, and C — of which the middle one, B, is annihilated while every other body in the universe, including A and C, is held still. The annihilation of B is to be thought of as B's being driven clean out of existence, in as radical a manner as we can coherently suppose. It does not matter that such annihilation is physically impossible; we are concerned here purely with what is logically possible and logically necessary.

In particular, we are concerned with the following logical fact. If before the annihilation A and C do not touch one another, and if during the annihilation they do not move, then *it follows with logical necessity that at the end of the annihilation they still do not touch one another.* What does their not-touching consist in? What is the positive fact from which flows the negative fact that they are not in contact with one another? Let us look at three answers to this.

First answer: "A and C do not touch because there is sheer distance between them—an extended nothing—a rectangular expanse that is not an expanse of anything. That explains the logical consequence emphasized above: there was a something in there; it was annihilated; and so of course what remains is a nothing." That is the answer Spinoza is rejecting when he says that there is no vacuum: he means that there is no extended-nothing. So we must look for another account of what the apartness of A and C consists in.

Second answer: "Since it is wrong to say that there is nothing between them, it must be right to say that there is something between them. (As Berkeley said: "We Irishmen are apt to imagine that something and nothing are next neighbors.") Since nothing moved during the annihilation of B, what lies between A and C after the annihilation cannot have moved in from elsewhere. So it must have got there without moving, i.e., must have come into existence in that place immediately upon the annihilation of B." Unlike the first answer, this second one makes perfectly good sense; and it is a defect in Spinoza's argument that it does not mention this possibility. Still, we can see what Spinoza could have said to justify rejecting it—namely that it makes a mystery of the emphasized logical consequence. How can it possibly follow with logical necessity that if one thing is driven out of existence a new thing of exactly the same size and shape comes into existence exactly then and there? We are invited to postulate a new "something" to replace the old "something" and thus to see the annihilation as being accompanied by a creation; but one event cannot logically require another event—there is no conceivable explanation of how such a logical consequence could be valid.

The third answer is the one I take Spinoza to be arguing for. It goes like this. "What we are calling the annihilation of B is not, strictly and metaphysically speaking, a going out of existence of a thing. Rather, it is an alteration—a qualitative change in something that remains in existence throughout. Instead of the replacement of a massy thing by an extended nothing, or by a new un-massy thing, what happens is that something—namely a region of space—stays in existence all along and merely alters from being massy to being un-massy. The annihilation of the body B was just a thinning out (so to speak) in that region of space, so that the 'something' lying between A and C after the annihilation of B is the very same 'something' that lay there before B was annihilated."

This third answer, unlike the first, is not nonsense. It describes empty space as something extended but lacking in certain empirical qualities; and there is no incoherence in that. And unlike the second answer, the third shows why the emphasized logical consequence is valid. For it is free to interpret the premise, that during the annihilation A and C do not move, as meaning that any region lying between A and C at the start of the annihilation still lies between them at the end of it; and the "annihilation" is unproblematic, since it is a mere qualitative alteration of that region. The logical consequence was mysterious when the situation was represented as the replacement of something by something else; but now we can put it on a par with replacement of the heat of a cup of coffee by its coolness—there is no mystery about why "annihilating" one entails "creating" the other.

THE RESULTANT PICTURE

The metaphysical moral is that bodies should be understood in terms of—to put it in shorthand—thickenings of regions of space. Spinoza sees the extended world as a *single* item, perhaps called Space, that is qualitatively varied from region to region: some regions at given times qualify as bodies, other as empty space. It is a single thing rather than an assemblage of regions, for several reasons of which I here give just one. (Others will be discussed in a book I am writing, tentatively entitled *Spinoza's Arguments.*) It is that of the infinitely many alternative ways of dividing Space into regions, none is metaphysically privileged; so that if we wanted to make regions metaphysically more basic than Space, we could not know which regions to select.

That is not to say that any division into regions must be purely arbitrary—a mere mathematical *jeu d'esprit*—for we can reasonably mark off certain regions as qualitatively different from their neighbors in ways that interest us. But those qualitative differences belong to empirical science rather than to fundamental metaphysics. Furthermore, they are seldom if ever permanent: what we mainly have reason to mark off as such subjects for special attention are not *regions* but rather *continuous sequences of regions-at-times*—namely the ones we call "bodies."

In deciding exactly which sequences to count as individual bodies, we shall be deciding whether to allow that two bodies can occupy the same place at the same time. This vexed question will thus be made to depend on a matter of conceptual convenience; it will not drive us down to the deep metaphysics of the concepts of body and of occupancy, because at the deepest metaphysical level neither of those concepts has application.

That is one example of the liberating virtues of Spinoza's way of looking at the extended world. It is indeed a bit of metaphysics that is brimming with health and vitality. Another example is its freedom from the assumption that whatever occupies space must be either a body or a construct out of bodies—so that *forces* must be tendencies-toward-movement of bodies, *waves* must be movements of bodies, and so on. Spinoza can reject all such narrowing assumptions, e.g., allowing for the possibility of waves that do not consist in undulations of particles.

SPACE AS A CONTAINER

With the outlines of Spinoza's doctrine of the extended world before us, we can now deal with a certain gap in his vacuum argument. In reply to the question "What is there between A and C after B has been annihilated?" I produced three answers: (1) "Nothing but sheer extension," which Spinoza rightly rejects; (2) "A thing that has just come into existence," which Spinoza could reasonably have rejected; and (3) "The same thing that was there before the so-called 'annihilation,'" which is Spinoza's own answer. There is, however, a fourth possible answer, expressing a view about bodies and space which may have been more widely held than any other. It is that before the annihilation there were two things between A and C— a region of space and the body B—and that after the annihilation of B there remained only the region of space. That seems intelligible, and it does justice to the logical consequence that all the fuss was about: if of two things one is annihilated, of course it follows that there is just one thing left—there is no mystery about that! How, then, can Spinoza justify rejecting this account of the matter in favor of his own?

Well, for a start he can point to all the troubles that arise over the concept of body and of occupancy if they are allowed to appear at the most fundamental level. But there is something more positive than that to be said. I believe that it is part of what Spinoza had in mind; but I base that only on my impression of what he is up to in this part of his work—I have no textual evidence for it.

The basic objection to the view that before the annihilation there were two things between A and C is just that it is ontologically extravagant for no good purpose. On this double-occupancy view, what we at first have between A and C is the body B and also a region of space R which has exactly the same shape and size as B itself. Now, Spinoza has an account of what it means to say that R is occupied by a body at time T—namely that R has certain empirical properties at T and that the place-time R-at-T belongs to a sequence of place-times satisfying certain conditions. The rival view denies that R *has* those properties, saying instead that it *contains a body that has* them. The body is inserted between the space and the properties, like a silk lining between a hand and a leather glove. But this lining makes no difference; it is a purely verbal insertion, and so we should cut it out.

Of course space contains bodies. I am not denying that. My point is just that the concept of body does not belong at the deepest metaphysical level: it is to be defined one level up, in terms of the concepts of "region of space" and "qualitative variety." We could not distinguish regions of space from one another unless they were qualitatively varied, the variations being subject to dependable regularities; but that is not to say that we could not distinguish them unless they contained bodies.

MORE TEXTUAL EVIDENCE

According to Spinoza's account, just one basic extended thing—Space—is qualitatively ("modally") varied from region to region. That this is indeed his picture of things is confirmed a little later in the Note containing the vacuum argument. Here is what he says, in the words of a sound, conservative translation of Spinoza's Latin (here and throughout I am much indebted to E. M. Curley's forthcoming translation of Spinoza's works):

> Matter is everywhere the same, and . . . its parts are distinguished in it only insofar as we conceive matter to be affected in different ways, so that its parts are distinguished only modally, but not really. For example, we conceive that water can be divided and its parts separated from one another— insofar as it is water, but not insofar as it is corporeal substance. For insofar as it is substance it is neither separated nor divided. Again, water, insofar as it is water, is originated and destroyed, but insofar as it is substance it is neither originated nor destroyed.

Here it is again, in words that express Spinoza's thought a little more clearly to modern ears:

> Space is everywhere the same, and . . . its parts are distinguished in it only to the extent that we take it to be qualitatively varied, so that its parts are marked off qualitatively but not really. For example, we think of water as something that can be divided and its parts separated from one another— but this is only considered as *water,* not considered as *what is extended.* For considered as what there basically is, it is neither separated nor divided. Again, water considered as water can be brought into existence and annihilated, but considered as what there basically is, it cannot be brought into existence or annihilated.

If that is a fair rewrite, then this passage expresses the view I have taken Spinoza to be arguing for in his vacuum argument.

One last piece of evidence. Suppose that we ask Spinoza: "What would be involved in a real annihilation of a body, i.e., an annihilation that was strictly and metaphysically a going out of existence of something and not a mere alteration in a region of space?" If I am right about his position, he would have to reply: "That would be the annihilation of a region of space, which does not make sense unless one means it to be the abolition of space as a whole."

With that in mind, read this extraordinary thing that Spinoza says in a letter to a friend:

Men are not created, but only generated, and their bodies existed before, although formed differently. From this you can infer something which I willingly accept, namely that if a single part of matter were annihilated the whole of extension would vanish in that moment. (Letter 4.)

The first sentence, taken on its own, could reflect any of several metaphysical positions—e.g., the view that the material world consists of sempiternal atoms floating in a container-space. But the second sentence points uniquely toward the metaphysical position I have attributed to Spinoza. On the basis of that position, the sentence is perfectly true; I can find no other basis on which it can be other than madly extravagant and unwarranted.

Understanding and Truth Conditions

HERBERT HEIDELBERGER

Over the past fifty years or so, considerable interest has been shown in the relations that obtain between (i) knowing a sentence's truth conditions, i.e., knowing the conditions under which one who utters the sentence says something true; (ii) knowing its meaning; and (iii) understanding it. Some writers have held that prominent among these relations is that of identity. Thus David Wiggins identifies (i) with (ii):

> . . . for any arbitrary sentence S, to know the meaning of S is to know under what conditions the sentence S would count as true . . .,[1]

as does P. F. Strawson:

> It is indeed a generally harmless and salutary thing to say that to know the meaning of a sentence is to know under what conditions one who utters it says something true.[2]

In much the same vein, but without reference to propositional attitudes, Donald Davidson:

> . . . to give truth conditions is a way of giving the meaning of a sentence.[3]

According to one commentator, it is a "maxim" of Frege's philosophy of language that:

> The meanings of sentences can be grasped by recognizing the conditions under which the sentence is true.[4]

It has also been held that (i) and (iii) are identical. Thus in the *Tractatus* Wittgenstein said:

> To understand a proposition means to know what is the case if it is true.[5]

Echoing the same theme, Quine maintains that:

. . . a man understands a sentence in so far as he knows its truth conditions.[6]

The most detailed statement of the identification that I have been able to discover is contained in Carnap's *Introduction to Semantics:*

> Suppose that Pierre says: "Mon crayon est noir" [S]. Then, if we know French, we understand the sentence [S] although we may not know its truth value. Our understanding of [S] consists in our knowledge of its truth-condition; we know that [S] is true if and only if a certain object, Pierre's pencil, has a certain color, black.[7]

I believe it is clear that Carnap's use of the possessive and of French is incidental; his point could as well have been made in terms of "Chicago is large" and is essentially no different from Wittgenstein's and Quine's. Elsewhere Carnap states the point succinctly and unequivocally:

> . . . a knowledge of the truth-conditions of a sentence is identical with an understanding of its meaning.[8]

So we can see that some writers have identified (i) with (ii); some have identified (i) with (iii); and doubtless there are some who would accept both identities.

There is, however, yet another claim pertaining to language and truth that ought to be distinguished from either of the aforementioned. It is the view, generally associated with Davidson, that a theory or definition of truth for a language is a theory of meaning for that language and the sentences of it. But whereas this last claim has come in for extensive discussion and can fairly be called controversial, the earlier ones, according to many of their proponents, should be viewed as uncontroversial and as an agreed basis upon which such more far-reaching claims as Davidson's can be evaluated. As a result, and as the quotation from Strawson indicates, the identification of (i) with (ii) (and of (i) with (iii)) comes to be thought of as "harmless" and perhaps unworthy of serious discussion.

I think both identifications are worth discussing, since by no means are they obviously true, but I shall approach them somewhat obliquely. That is, in order to avoid extraneous problems about knowledge, I shall almost entirely ignore (i) and much of my discussion will bear on the relations between (iii) and (iv): being aware of the conditions under which a sentence is true. I shall proceed as follows. In the first part of the essay, I shall explain what is meant by (iv) and argue that (iv) does not imply (iii); in the second part, I shall attempt some elucidation of (iii); and in the third part, I shall argue that (iii), nearly enough, implies (iv) and draw a moral from this. I believe that the relevance of what I have to say to the relations between (i), (ii), and (iii) will be apparent.

I

To say that a person, we shall call him Hanson, is aware of the conditions under which a sentence, S, is true is to say that he believes, and believes truly, what is expressed by a sentence of the form:

S is true iff p,

where "S" is to be replaced by a name of the sentence whose truth conditions are being specified and "p" is to be replaced by that very sentence. More specifically, to say that Hanson is aware of the conditions under which the sentence "Smith is pusillanimous" is true is to say that Hanson believes truly that "Smith is pusillanimous" is true if, and only if, Smith is pusillanimous. The contention I want to consider then is this:

1. Hanson is aware of the conditions under which "Smith is pusillanimous" is true

is (necessarily) equivalent to:

2. Hanson understands "Smith is pusillanimous."

It may seem that (1) is so weak a claim that it cannot plausibly be taken to imply (2).[9] For it may seem that just about all English speakers believe the proposition expressed by:

3. "Smith is pusillanimous" is true iff Smith is pusillanimous,

whereas it may be assumed that many among them do not understand the word "pusillanimous" and are therefore unlikely to understand the sentence "Smith is pusillanimous." Plainly, if the truth condition account of understanding is to be taken seriously, it is important to show that the proposition expressed by (3) is not trivial and that, at the very least, most people who do not understand "pusillanimous" do not believe what is expressed by (3).

I think the reason it may be thought that almost all English speakers believe what (3) expresses is that almost all English speakers would assent to it, they would regard it as saying something that is true. But from this correct observation it would be a mistake to infer that almost all English speakers believe what (3) expresses; that they believe that "Smith is pusillanimous" is true if, and only if, Smith is pusillanimous. My reason for holding this inference mistaken is that a person may sincerely assent to a sentence but, being unaware of what proposition the sentence expresses, fail to believe what it expresses. A person may be unaware of what proposition a sentence expresses either because he has a misconception about what the sentence says (he assents to "Smith is pusillanimous" because he thinks "Smith is pusillanimous" says that Smith is fat and he believes that Smith is fat) or because he has no opinion about what it says (he assents to it because "it looks right"). Thus sincere assent, in the absence of understanding, is an uncertain guide to belief. Moreover, we have assumed that most English speakers do not understand "pusillanimous," and since (3) makes use of that word, many of them will not understand (3). So let us consider a sentence that most English speakers, and Hanson in particular, do understand:

4. "Smith is pusillanimous" is true iff Smith is cowardly.

(We must be mindful, of course, that a person may understand an expression that names a word without understanding the word named.) We shall assume that Hanson understands the word "cowardly," that he does not understand the word "pusillanimous," and that the two words are synonymous. Will Hanson assent to (4)? It is unlikely that he will if he sees no connection between the two words; thus, on the supposition that Hanson is sincere, we may conclude that he does not believe what (4) expresses. But (4) expresses what (3) expresses. So, despite the fact that he assents to it, Hanson does *not* believe what (3) expresses.

We can, I think, put all this by saying that (3) may be trivial in the sense that almost all English speakers will *assent* to it; this, however, does not imply that what the sentence says—the proposition it expresses—is trivial in the sense that almost all English speakers *believe* it. It is important, in this connection, to distinguish (3) from:

5. ""Smith is pusillanimous" is true iff Smith is pusillanimous" is true.

Failure to understand "pusillanimous" is no impediment to understanding (5). Presumably Hanson will understand (5), and recognizing that "pusillanimous" is an English word, he will sincerely assent to it and so believe what it expresses. Indeed, the fact that Hanson sincerely assents to (3) shows that he believes that (3) is true, which is to say that he believes what (5) expresses. But from Hanson believes what (5) expresses we must not infer that he believes what (3) expresses.

It appears then that (3) says something that is not trivial, and so we must consider again whether a true belief in what it expresses is sufficient for understanding the sentence whose truth conditions it states. I think that circumstances can be described in which Hanson (truly) believes what (3) expresses and yet does not understand "Smith is pusillanimous."

Suppose that Hanson believes that Smith is not pusillanimous. Suppose further that he believes that "Smith is pusillanimous" says that Smith is witty and he believes that Smith is not witty. Hence he believes the negations of the propositions expressed by either side of (3) and so is likely to believe the true proposition expressed by (3) itself. But Hanson does not understand "Smith is pusillanimous".

To meet this example, we could require that Hanson *know* the proposition expressed by (3). One disadvantage of proceeding in this way is that *knowing* the truth conditions, as distinct from merely having a true belief about them, is not, at least in my view, a necessary condition for understanding. But is it even a sufficient condition for understanding?

Suppose now that Hanson knows that Smith *is* pusillanimous. Further, Hanson is told by an entirely reliable person that "Smith is pusillanimous" is true, although he is not told what the sentence means. It is plausible, in the circumstances described, to say that Hanson knows the truth of the propositions expressed by both sides of (3) and knows the truth of the proposition that (3) expresses. Again, however, he does not understand "Smith is pusillanimous."

I suppose, at this point, we could require that the source of Hanson's knowledge should not be testimony. We should then consider the following case.

Suppose this time Hanson knows that "Smith is pusillanimous" either means that Smith is cowardly or means that Smith is dull witted. He has no convictions about which of these "Smith is pusillanimous" means, and therefore he cannot be said to understand the sentence. But he knows that Smith is cowardly and thus knows the truth of the proposition expressed by the right side of (3). He also knows that Smith is dull witted and, if Hanson is not dull witted himself, he should know that the sentence mentioned on the left side of (3), whether it says that Smith is cowardly or says that Smith is dull witted, says something true. He will thus know the truth of the proposition expressed by the left side of (3), as well as the proposition expressed by (3) itself, without understanding "Smith is pusillanimous," and without, in any ordinary way, relying on testimony.

Normally, of course, we come to believe propositions expressed by sentences like (3) through understanding the sentences they are about. We understand "Smith is pusillanimous," realize that it is true if and only if what it says is true, and that what it says is true if and only if Smith is pusillanimous. But one who claims that awareness of truth conditions is sufficient for understanding cannot reasonably require that awareness of truth conditions be got in the way just described. For then one will be claiming that awareness is sufficient for understanding, *if* such awareness is acquired by understanding the sentence whose truth conditions are being given. I do not believe that anyone has ever wanted to assert anything quite so harmless.

II

What does it mean to understand a sentence? This much seems safe: a person understands a sentence if he knows what it says. I suspect, however, that the converse is not true. Suppose I am told what an unfamiliar sentence says, the account I am given is accurate, and I believe it; in these circumstances, it would seem, I can be said to understand the sentence. Because my informant is not entirely reliable or because he is unsure on this occasion, his testimony may not provide sufficient evidence to give me knowledge of what the sentence means. Nevertheless, I suggest, my (true) belief that the sentence says what it does suffices for me to understand it. I propose, then, the following definition of "understands."

> Df (1) "m understands S" means: There is a proposition p, such that S expresses p and m believes that S expresses p.

(This could be put without "expresses" and "proposition": A person understands a sentence just provided he believes that it says what, in fact, it does say.) This account of understanding is plausible, I believe, if (i) we confine ourselves to eternal sentences and ignore the complexities introduced by the presence of token reflexives, (ii) we take the sentence variable to range over unambiguous sentence tokens,[10] and (iii) these tokens are understood to express truths or falsehoods. To keep discussion within manageable bounds, I shall comply with these restrictions.

Let us return briefly to Hanson and "Smith is pusillanimous." It is a consequence of Df (1) that Hanson understands "Smith is pusillanimous," if Hanson truly believes the proposition expressed by:

> 6. "Smith is pusillanimous" expresses the proposition that Smith is pusillanimous.

The sentence (6), or its idiomatic counterpart "'Smith is pusillanimous' says that Smith is pusillanimous," gives the same appearance of expressing a triviality as (3) does. Thus with (6), as with (3), we should distinguish a proposition that says of the sentence that it is true (in this instance, the proposition expressed by "(6) is true"), from a proposition that the sentence expresses (in this instance, the proposition expressed by (6)). Hanson, like most English speakers is likely to believe that (6) (or its idiomatic counterpart) is true (says something true), but he need not believe what (6) expresses and will not believe what it expresses if he does not understand "Smith is pusillanimous". The argument in support of the significance of what (6) says proceeds, *mutatis mutandis,* like the argument for the significance of what (3) says and I shall not go through it. But I think it is worth noticing that (6) says something distinct from what is said by:

> 7. "Smith is pusillanimous" expresses the same proposition as is expressed by "Smith is pusillanimous."

Where (6) tells us *what* "Smith is pusillanimous" expresses, (7), so far as I can discern, says no more nor less than:

> 8. "Smith is pusillanimous" expresses some proposition.

Hanson may (truly) believe what (8), i.e. (7), expresses, without understanding "Smith is pusillanimous"—thus the necessity for distinguishing what (6) expresses from what (7) expresses. Similarly, we should distinguish:

> 9. "Smith is pusillanimous" expresses the proposition that Smith is cowardly

from

> 10. "Smith is pusillanimous" expresses the same proposition as is expressed by "Smith is cowardly."

What (9) says is identical to what (6) says and so a true belief in that proposition is tantamount to understanding "Smith is pusillanimous." However, a person can be aware that two sentences express the same proposition, but, being unaware of *what* they express, understand neither; so that a true belief in what (10) expresses does not ensure an understanding of either of the sentences it mentions.[11] I refer to these distinctions because Df (1) may suggest a "translational view" of understanding—a view that we understand sentences only through their relations to other sentences—but that certainly is not what is intended.

But what is intended is perhaps not as clear as one might like it to be. In this essay I have made extensive use of the word "expresses" and in Df (1) "expresses" is used to define "understands." Some philosophers have found "expresses" to be a puzzling, if not nonsensical, term when it is used, as I have used it, as a predicate of sentences. John Searle, for example, in his book *Speech Acts*, writes:

> . . . I do not say that the sentence expresses a proposition; I do not know how sentences could perform acts of that (or any other) kind. But I shall say that in the utterance of the sentence, the speaker expresses a proposition.[12]

Searle is willing to say that speakers (persons) express propositions but is unwilling to say that sentences express propositions. I propose to define the use of "expresses" that Searle finds objectionable in terms of the use he finds clear.

> Df (2) "S expresses *p*" means: There is an individual m, and a time period t, such that m utters S at t, and that m utters S at t brings it about that he expresses *p* at t. (An alternative formulation of the definiens is: There is an individual m, and a time period t, such that by uttering S at t, m expresses *p* at t.)[13]

Putting Df (1) and Df (2) together we get something like this: A person understands a sentence just provided he is aware of what proposition (thought) is expressed by whoever utters it.

Without attempting to say what it is for a person to express a proposition, the following features of this relation are, I think, worth mentioning.

1. Df (2) is circular if the relation formulated by the occurrence of the word "expresses" in the definiendum is identical with the relation formulated by the occurrence of the same word in the definiens; but I believe that it is a relatively simple matter to show that they are distinct. If a sentence expresses a proposition, then someone's uttering of the sentence brings it about that he expresses the proposition; plainly, however, a person may express a proposition without it being the case that anyone's uttering of *him* brings it about that he expresses a proposition. So we do not have a single relation that sometimes has propositions and sentences as its relata, and sometimes has propositions and persons. Rather, we have two relations, one that propositions bear to sentences and another that propositions bear to persons.

Searle says that persons who express propositions perform acts and that sentences never do. This suggests, what I have tried to show above, that sentences do not have the same property of expressing propositions that persons have. From this, of course, it does not follow that we cannot say sensibly (and truly) of some sentence that it "expresses a proposition."

2. The property that persons have of expressing propositions is distinct from the property they have of asserting propositions. If, in the right circumstances, I say "Either John wins or George wins," I have expressed the proposition that John wins or George wins and have asserted this proposition. I have also expressed the proposition that John wins and the proposition that George wins, although I have asserted neither. I suppose it is clear enough that I have asserted neither proposition, but perhaps an argument is needed in defense of the claim that I have expressed these propositions. I offer the following. The sentence "John wins or

George wins" is true if and only if "John wins" is true or "George wins" is true. Suppose "John wins or George wins" *is* true, then "John wins" is true or "George wins" is true. A sentence is true if and only if it expresses a true proposition, i.e. it says something true. So either "John wins" expresses a proposition or "George wins" expresses a proposition. And I have uttered both sentences. Thus by the bi-conditional arising from Df (2), we may conclude that I have expressed at least one of these propositions, although I have asserted neither. We would therefore be in error were we to replace "expresses" in the definiens of Df (2) by "asserts."

3. We would also be in error, I believe, were we to say that a person expresses a proposition if and only if he utters a sentence that expresses the proposition. Suppose I am asked whether there is life on Mars. I might reply in any of the following ways: by saying "There is life on Mars"; by saying "Yes"; by nodding my head; or, if I am asked to respond affirmatively by raising my hand, by raising my hand. Whichever of these I do (in the right circumstances), I assert, and thus express, the proposition that there is life on Mars. But if I nod or raise my hand and utter no sentence, there is no sentence to express the proposition *I* express by nodding or raising my hand.

III

A person who (a) understands an unambiguous sentence, i.e., understands a sentence that expresses just one proposition, (b) is aware of what, in general, it is for a sentence to be true, and (c) believes the (simple) logical consequences of his beliefs, is a person who is aware of—has a true belief about—the truth conditions of that sentence. This is what I meant when I said in the introduction that understanding a sentence, nearly enough, implies being aware of the conditions under which it is true. Here is my argument.

Hanson, we shall suppose, does understand the sentence "The moon is round." Applying Df (1) to assumption (a), we get:

11. There is just one proposition p, such that Hanson (truly) believes that "The moon is round" expresses p.

At this point the argument will proceed more easily with the aid of a definition.

Df (3) "(A property) F is doxastically essential to x" means: necessarily, for any person m, if there is a property G, such that m believes that x has G, then m believes that x has F.

Otherwise put, a property F is doxastically essential to an object x just provided that necessarily, any person who has any beliefs whatever about x believes that x has F. I suggest that the property of being true if and only if the moon is round is doxastically essential to the proposition that the moon is round. That is to say, if anyone believes anything about the proposition that the moon is round, he believes that it is true if and only if the moon is round. Analogous things, I believe, can be said of all other propositions.

Sentence (11) tells us that Hanson has a belief about the proposition expressed by "The moon is round." Thus (11) should yield:

12. There is just one proposition p, such that Hanson (truly) believes that "The moon is round" expresses p and p is true iff p.

where p is to be replaced by a sentence that expresses the proposition expressed by "The moon is round." Let us suppose that the only proposition expressed by "The moon is round" is the proposition that the moon is round, so that we have.

12'. Hanson (truly) believes that ["The moon is round" expresses the proposition that the moon is round, and the proposition that the moon is round is true iff the moon is round].

Hanson, we are assuming, is aware of what, in general, it is for a sentence to be true (assumption (b)) and this gives us:

13. Hanson (truly) believes that "The moon is round" is true iff there is a proposition p, such that "The moon is round" expresses p, and p is true.

Applying assumption (a), and again supposing that "The moon is round" expresses only the proposition that the moon is round, we have:

13'. Hanson (truly) believes that ["The moon is round" is true iff "the moon is round" expresses the proposition that the moon is round, and the proposition that the moon is round is true].

The sentences contained within brackets in (12') and (13') imply:

14. "The moon is round" is true iff the moon is round.

On the assumption that a person believes the (simple) logical consequences of his beliefs (assumption (c)), we may conclude that Hanson has a true belief with respect to what (14) expresses and so is aware of the conditions under which "The moon is round" is true.

There is, I believe, this moral to be drawn from the conjunction of the preceding argument and the negative results of the first section of this essay. A person who understands a sentence — one who is aware of what the sentence expresses — is a person who is aware of the conditions under which the sentence is true; but a person may be aware of the conditions under which a sentence is true without understanding the sentence, even if, in both cases, we assume (a), (b), and (c). I suppose that we could express this moral more simply — although somewhat cryptically — by saying that understanding a sentence is more basic than being aware of the sentence's truth conditions.[14]

Notes

1. David Wiggins, "On Sentence-sense, Word-sense and Differences of Word Sense. Towards a Philosophical Theory of Dictionaries," in *Semantics*, ed. D. D. Steinberg and L. A. Jakobovits (London, 1971) p. 17.

2. P. F. Strawson, "Meaning and Truth," reprinted in Strawson's *Logico-Linguistic Papers* (London, 1971) pp. 188, 189.

3. Donald Davidson, "Truth and Meaning" in *Philosophical Logic*, ed. J. W. Davis, D. J. Hockney, and W. K. Wilson (Dordrecht, 1969) p. 7.

4. Samuel Guttenplan in his introduction to *Mind and Language* (Oxford, 1975) pp. 5, 6.

5. *Tractatus*, 4.024.

6. W. V. Quine, "Mind and Verbal Dispositions," in Guttenplan, *Mind and Language*, p. 88.

7. Rudolf Carnap, *Introduction to Semantics* (Cambridge, 1942) pp. 22, 23.

8. Rudolf Carnap, *Introduction to Symbolic Logic and Its Applications* (New York, 1958), p. 15.

9. Compare Gilbert Harman, "Meaning and Semantics" in M. K. Munitz and P. Unger, *Semantics and Philosophy* (New York, 1974), especially p. 4.

10. When I refer to the sentence ". . ." in this essay, the reader should imagine that I have referred to some token of that sentence written on a blackboard.

11. Most of these points were made years ago by G. E. Moore. Cf. *The Commonplace Book* (London, 1962), pp. 303-8 and "Russell's 'Theory of Descriptions,'" in Moore's *Philosophical Papers* (London, 1959), especially pp. 172-77; although they are still denied. Cf. Anthony Quinton, *The Nature of Things* (London, 1973), pp. 342-44.

12. John Searle, *Speech Acts*, (London, 1969), p. 29.

13. On the definition proposed, the sentence "John is a male and John is a sibling" expresses the proposition that John is a brother. It also expresses the proposition that John is a male and expresses the proposition that John is a sibling. If we wish to say, as I think we ought to, that "John is a male and John is a sibling" (strictly) expresses only the proposition that John is a brother, we could define "S strictly expresses p" as follows: S expresses p and for any proper part S$'$ of S, if S$'$ expresses p then S and S$'$ express exactly the same propositions. And define "S$'$ is a proper part of S" as: Necessarily, if anyone utters S, then he utters S$'$ and not necessarily if anyone utters S$'$, then he utters S. We could then say "John is a male and John is a sibling" strictly expresses the proposition that John is a brother, but does not strictly express the proposition that John is a male nor strictly express the proposition that John is a sibling. And we could say that neither "John is a brother and John is a male" nor "John is a brother or John is a male" strictly expresses the proposition that John is a male. Henceforth, "expresses" should be taken to abbreviate "strictly expresses."

14. I have benefited from discussions with: David Austin, Roderick Chisholm, Earl Conee, Fred Feldman, Richard Feldman, Edmund Gettier, and M. B. Smith.

The Problem of the Many

PETER UNGER

It is my intention to propose a new philosophical problem which I call *the problem of the many*. This problem concerns the number of entities, if any, that exist in actual ordinary situations and in counterfactual or hypothetical situations. The problem concerns the number even at a given moment of time, and it becomes only yet more baffling when durations of time, and changes, inevitably complicate the issue.

It is a philosophical commonplace to note that, without any further specification, there is no definite finite answer to the question of how many entities a given ordinary situation contains. Considering my own present situation, for example, it might be said to contain a salt shaker, also each of the grains of salt in the shaker, also the atoms that compose the shaker, as well as each of those in the grains, and this is only to begin to enumerate what seems natural. Artificial or contrived entities, so to introduce them, greatly complicate the picture. There is the left half of the shaker, as viewed from right here, and also the right half; there is the scattered concrete entity whose salient parts are that left half of the shaker and the second largest grain of salt inside the shaker; perhaps, there is even relevantly in the situation, the abstract entity that is the set whose sole members are the two concrete items most recently specified; and so on, and so forth.

To illustrate this commonplace is of course nothing new. But it is not even to rehearse any philosophical problem, about numbers of things. For, what is the problem here? On the contrary, it is natural to suppose that once an available category or sort of entities is specified, a definite answer frequently can be given, often in the form of a small positive finite number. Thus, for example, if the question is how many *salt shakers* my present situation contains, the answer is *one*. And, for another example, if the question is how many *human hands* are in that situation, then the answer is *two*. Supposedly without any serious problem, this is what one is given to think. What is new, I believe, is to suggest that even here, with such ordinary kinds purporting to delimit things, no such manageable answers are tenable. And, insofar as there is something to it, this suggestion does mean a problem.

Perhaps "the problem of the many" is a somewhat misleading name for the problem I mean to introduce. Perhaps it might better be called "the problem of the many or the none." For I shall not suggest that various considerations simply lead us to an extraordinarily high accounting, for example, to the idea that in my present situation, in what I take to be my dining area, there are millions of salt shakers. No; what these considerations lead to, I shall suggest, is a difficult *dilemma:* Either there really are no salt shakers at all, or else, in my dining area, there are millions of these things. Insofar as I find the latter of these alternatives rather absurd, I am that far inclined toward the first, to the nihilistic, or Parmenidian, option. But of course most philosophers will wish to avoid both these alternatives. So, insofar as it can be motivated, such a dilemma will be quite a problem for most philosophers.

In addition to informal discussion of it, I mean to motivate this problem in two main ways. First, I shall offer certain *arguments*, whose conclusion is our problematic dilemma, or else a proposition to the same effect, Along this line, I shall suggest that there are no adequate objections to these arguments. I shall try to support this suggestion, in part, by considering what appear the most plausible of objections and by showing that even these miss their mark. In part, also, I shall disarm any objections by examining the implications of my arguments' premises, by trying to understand what underlies them.

These arguments will be presented first in terms of clouds, those putative ordinary things which, so often, seem to be up in the sky. As our problem is one that concerns *vagueness,* beginning with clouds is natural; it should be helpful in promoting some initial understanding, and sympathy, for my argumentation. Later, I shall extend my arguments, in fairly obvious ways, from clouds to many other sorts of ordinary things: stones, tables, hands, and so on.

Although I think arguments are important in philosophy, my arguments here will be only the more assertive way for me to introduce the new problem, not the only way. To complement that reasoning, I shall ask certain *questions.* To avoid our problematic dilemma rationally, these questions must receive an adequate answer. But, it will be my suggestion, there really is no adequate answer to be given here.

Concerning vagueness, as it does, the problem of the many is a problem in *the philosophy of language* as much as in *metaphysics.* Once the problem itself is presented in detail, I shall sketch certain further problems that it implies. While these implied problems also concern the aforesaid two philosophic areas, they do not end there. Rather, they also concern, or give rise to, certain problems in *epistemology.* Accordingly, it is my belief, the problem of the many should prove quite fertile for philosophical investigation.

1. VAGUENESS AND CLOUDS

Our new problem concerns *vagueness.* Typical vague expressions, such as 'tall man', 'table' and 'stone', purport to discriminate their referents from everything else—

THE PROBLEM OF THE MANY 413

the tall men, for example, from the rest of the world. But as is familiar, and as sorites arguments make clear, their vagueness seems to mean a problem for the purported discriminations. Along the dimension of height, for example, where do the tall men stop, so to say, and the other, shorter fellows first come into the picture? With regard to the range of possible heights, at least, "tall man" must have a *boundary*, if we may use this primarily spatial expression, however "vague" or "fuzzy" that stopping place may or may not be. But, it does not seem to have any; or if it does, where the devil can that stopping place occur? So much, for now, for rehearsing familiar problems of vagueness.

For our new problem, the leading idea is to focus on physical, spatial situations where no natural boundaries, no natural stopping places, are to be encountered. Many cases of *clouds* at least appear to provide such situations.[1] Now, when viewed from far away, certain puffy, "pictured-postcard" clouds can give the appearance of rather a sharp clean boundary, a clean end to them, so to say, where the surrounding sky, then, correlatively begins. But many other clouds, even from any point of view, appear gradually to blend into, or fade off into, the surrounding sky. And even the puffy, cleanest items, *upon closer scrutiny*, also do seem to blend into their surrounding atmosphere. For all our clouds, then, this has the makings of a new sort of sorites argument, as to where any one of them could first start, or stop. But we shall not pursue that matter here and now; for our main present concern is to introduce a really new problem, not to discuss any new variation upon an old one.

What we must become concerned with, at all events, is the underlying concrete physical reality, in which any clouds there might be must find their place. Ordinary appearances may be, of course, widely deceptive. Objects that appear to have no natural stopping place may in fact have just that. In contrast, what appears to have such a boundary, e.g., our putative puffy clouds, may in fact have none. We are to consider the reality and not the appearance.

What should reality be like for a cloud to make a clean break with its surroundings? The best possible case or situation is of this sort: The cloud is composed of continuous, relevantly homogeneous matter, or stuff,[2,3] which, relative to each of the "routes into and out of the cloud," just stops at a certain point. Right after any such points, and so external to the cloud, there first begins stuff of another kind, or empty space, or some mixture of the two. The natural boundary, or "break," need not be shaped anything much like it appears, as long as it does have some shape that is suitably definite, or proper. Thus the boundary may appear rather simple and smooth, whereas closer inspection may reveal it to be quite jagged, with bumps on bumps on bumps. But, in relevant regards, a clean natural separation is effected.

In the sort of situation just imagined, which we are confident is wildly hypothetical but which we are supposing to be real, our problem of the many will not readily arise. In such a situation, with the natural boundary remarked, there is just one entity that, in respects relevant to being a cloud, far surpasses anything else present. This is the entity composed, or constituted, of all the stuff within the boundary, and not of anything outside (and which, we might add, has the identity conditions over time appropriate to a cloud). So there is no other stuff around, in our specified situation, that is, then and there, suited for constituting any other, second cloud.

In this supposedly real situation, what other entity could make an attempt at being a cloud, so to say, to give some trouble to the unique preferred status of our cleanly bounded item? An artificial or contrived entity might perhaps be introduced. Think of a certain nine hundred ninety-nine thousand nine hundred ninety-nine millionths of our item, all together, and then, also, the remaining millionth "seamlessly attached to" what you first considered. The greater of these two masses of stuff may be regarded, we shall grant, as constituting an entity, one with a much smaller entity seamlessly attached. But is that (greater) contrived entity a cloud, so that we shall have at least two clouds in our supposed situation? I think not. For if anything is a cloud, it must be a *natural* item, with a real, objective place in nature all its own, so to say. So our contrived object cannot ever fill the bill that cloudhood requires. Even passing over this, and doing so very cautiously indeed, whatever claim it might have to be a cloud is *much* worse than that possessed by our natural, cleanly bounded item. If we allow our common-sense belief, that there is *at most* one cloud right there, to have any weight at all, the contrived item loses out to the natural object. So, with this sort of an underlying reality, we might rest happy with the idea that the only cloud we seem to see is, indeed, the only one right before us. Thinking only of such an underlying reality, then, our would-be problem of the many does not seem to have much chance to get off the ground. (But a good deal later on, in section 9, we shall see how the problem arises even in such a clean, sharp world.)

To get our problem going, let us consider a *very* different sort of reality, one in which, I hope, the problem will most clearly emerge. In relevant regards, then, this sort of situation lies at the opposite pole, along a series of "possible real situations," from where we should place the reality just considered. (Later on, we shall consider some of the intermediate cases.) Before, clouds would be *simple* entities, composed only of stuff and *not* of smaller, simpler constituent *things*. So, this time, clouds, if there really are any present, will be relevantly *complex*. Here a cloud will not be composed of continuous, homogeneous matter. On the contrary, there will be present a large number of dispersed items, each much smaller than a cloud, for example, a large number of dispersed water droplets.[4] (So far as currently relevant considerations go, each water droplet may itself be either simple or else it may be complex; either way our problem of the many will be quick to arise. In fact, of course, water droplets are very complex, composed of molecules, atoms, elementary particles, and who knows what else.) The water droplets are separated from each other by relevantly different matter, which is not itself water, or by space, or by a mixture of the two. It matters not precisely how their separation is effected, so long as they may be regarded as relevantly distinct from each other.

So we have many water droplets before us now, and they are suitably dispersed. But, for our problem to meet the eye, what is a most suitable dispersion, or arrangement, for these tiny would-be constituents? Where a normal observer would take a cloud to be, we shall have our droplets closer together. Quite a ways out from that, where it seems clear we are well out of the cloud, well into the surrounding sky, the population is a good deal less dense, the droplets are, on the whole, much farther apart from each other. Moreover, there is no place at all where suddenly, or dramatically, the "denseness" falls off and the "sparseness" first begins. Rather, when we look at things closely, all that is there to be seen is a *gradual transition* from the more dense to the less so. In this reality, which in all relevant regards is the *actual* reality, i.e., really is reality, there is no natural break, or boundary, or stopping place, for any would-be cloud to have. Thus there is none that might give any candidate cloud its own real place in nature. Without this, how are there to be any clouds here, in this actual reality?

If it is anything, a cloud is a *concrete* entity.[5] Further, it is a concrete entity occupying some space, as well as being spatially located, one existing for some time, if only a moment, and one constituted of some matter or stuff. Well, then, what are the concrete things in our real situation? There are, we may allow, things even smaller than the water droplets—but none of those is a cloud; not really. There are the droplets themselves—but neither is any of them a cloud. We may allow, too, that there are many very contrived entities present, for example, a "scattered concrete individual," consisting of a droplet here and three way over there. But those contrived concrete things are not clouds either. Of course, the only likely candidates will be concrete complexes composed, at least in the main, not merely of some water droplets but of a great many droplets that are "suitably grouped together."If *none* of *these* things is a cloud, then, I am afraid, our situation will, in fact, contain or involve no cloud at all. But, of course, perhaps one or more of these most promising concrete complexes is indeed a cloud. And, if so, then all will not be lost so far as clouds are concerned.

Whether or not all is lost, there is a serious problem here, and that is our problem of the many. For it seems clear that no matter which relevant concrete complex is deemed fit for cloudhood, that is, is deemed a cloud, there will be very many others each of which has, in any relevant respect, a claim that is just as good. To perceive this plethora takes a bit of visual imagination, but I am hopeful that you can do it. Think of any given likely prospect and, then, think of the very many similar complexes each of which "overlaps" it just slightly, sharing constituents with it, except for a peripheral droplet or two, here or there. With any given first choice, there are ever so many such suitable overlappers. And, of course, any of them might have, equally, been chosen first. No matter where we start, the complex first chosen has nothing objectively in its favor to make it a better candidate for cloudhood than so many of its overlappers are. Putting the matter somewhat personally, each one's claim to be a cloud is just as good, no better and no worse, than each of the many others. And, by all odds, each complex has *at least* as good a claim as any still further real entity in the situation. So, either *all* of *them* make it or else *nothing* does; in this real situation, either there are many clouds or else there really are no clouds at all. This dilemma presents our problem of the many.

2. AN ARGUMENT ABOUT CLOUDS
AS CONCRETE COMPLEXES

In a manner that was, intentionally, both informal and imaginative, we have begun our discussion of our new problem. Beginning with a wildly hypothetical world, or kind of reality, we moved to discuss the real, actual world. The contrast, informally presented, was meant to help us see where and how our new problem might readily emerge. I hope it was indeed helpful. If the problem is beginning to make some impression, then it may be well to give our discussion a bit more rigor or form. Interestingly enough, it seems that however this is done, the problem, rather than dissolving, or being exposed as some trifling confusion, manages only to impress itself upon us still further.

I shall proceed to present our problem by means of two rather explicit arguments, each quite different from the other, though they will of course be significantly related. In this section, I shall present one of these, which I call the Argument about Clouds as Concrete Complexes. I present it first, because it most directly flows from the discussion that ended the previous section. In the next section, I shall present the other of these introductory arguments.

We have discussed clouds as complex concrete entities, composed of smaller concrete constituents; in the actual world, if there are any clouds, that is what they will each be. Although this discussion served a purpose, it perhaps proceeded a bit too briskly. For as I spoke in quite general terms, someone with a strong aversion to our problem might challenge me with the suggestion of a weird counterexample, or what he would take to be such an example. From this putative challenge, the inspiration for our first argument can be derived.

In our discussion, I have drawn attention to a myriad of concrete complexes, each overlapping many others, which multitude would generally pass unnoticed. I then said, quite generally, that in (any) such situations, there would not be any one complex that had a relevantly and sufficiently better claim on cloudhood than each of many others. But although this is clearly true in most such situations, even a putative objector will agree, there might be a few marginal situations, even some actually in the real world, where among the many poor complexes present, only one just manages to sneak over the minimum requirements that cloudhood sets for complex entities. Here, it is imagined, none of the complexes is well off so far as the criteria for clouds are concerned, and just one is only a bit better off than any of the others. We are to imagine that one to be just enough better off so that it manages to be a cloud, even though a very marginal case of one, while each of its nearest competitors fails altogether. What are we to make of this suggestion?

In the first place, I think it extremely doubtful that, in actuality, such a situation ever really does occur. But, second, if it ever really does take place, then, surely among our real situations, these problematic ones are quite rare indeed. So, certainly, in situations involving dispersions of water droplets, where, in the real world, clouds have their best prospects for existence, it will be at most only *rarely* that we shall *not* encounter our problem of the many or an instance of that problem. Now, these rare situations will be ones where, while we may suppose that there is just one cloud present, the "successful" item is a *very* marginal case of being a cloud. It is not even a pretty marginal case, let alone a fair to middling cloud. Most certainly, this marginal item will be quite far from being a *paradigm* cloud, a *good example of* a cloud or, as I shall most often put it, a *typical* cloud.

To get farthest away from this challenge, whether or not there ever really is any substance in it, we may present our problem in terms of typical clouds. This moves us to the statement of our first argument. As we want the argument to concern all putative real clouds, and not just the alleged typical cases, it is best to begin it with a premise that will ensure such a general result, by having the one stand, or fall, with the other:

(1) If there are clouds, then there are typical clouds.

Now, this premise, it must be emphasized, is not offered as analytic, or as a necessary truth, or anything of that strong ilk. On the contrary, it is just offered as true, as a true conditional statement (at least supposing there are any true statements about clouds at all). As such, which is all that matters here, it can hardly be denied by one who would avoid our problem of the many. For if there really are clouds around, then a good many of them have been, now are, and will be typical clouds. It is scarcely credible to suppose that, in fact, *all* the clouds in the world are, if not marginal cases, not much better than fair to middling examples.

It is with our next premise that our imaginative powers are called upon for a clear understanding:

(2) If something is a typical cloud, then *any* situation involving it contains, in addition to itself, millions of other complex concrete entities, each of which differs from it, in any respects relevant to being a cloud, at most quite minutely.

This premise makes the claim, or contains the implication, that any real, actual cloud is a concrete complex entity. This may well call for some further discussion (which will be provided later, mainly in section 6). But, realizing that the premise is put forward merely as a true conditional statement, it is, in this implication at least, no less than extremely plausible. Given this, we move to a more demanding aspect of our premise: Our imagination is called upon to perceive, so to say, all the other relevant cloud candidates. In the argument I shall present next, recently promised, I shall provide a "visual aid" toward this end, for now I rely on goodwill and native ability. Given this, we next face the claim of *millions* of such candidates, as opposed to, say, many. This might appear either excessive or too definite, where no such definite numbers can be gotten. Realizing a gap to be filled here, I pass over it now, postponing this matter, too, for a later detailed discussion (which will be provided mainly in section 5, though certain other sections, in particular 6, will also have considerable bearing on the matter). Finally, regarding this second premise, it is implied that each of these millions of candidates is, if not as well off as the "original choice" mentioned in the antecedent, at least quite nearly as well off, in respect of meeting cloud criteria. So the "claims toward cloudhood" of these overlappers will not be much worse than those of the apparently well-placed original candidate. A detailed discussion of why this should be so will certainly be desirable. I plan to proceed with the matter gradually, through our essay's various further sections. But, even now, the proposition itself is eminently credible.

Our argument requires but one further premise:

> (3) If something is a *typical* cloud, then, if there are entities that differ from it, in any respects relevant to being a cloud, at most quite minutely, then each of those entities is a cloud.

This premise, or principle, surely recommends itself to reason. In the first place, it does not even appear to say that any of those latter entities, let alone all of them, will be typical clouds, as is the first. It is content to have them all be only fair to middling cases of clouds, though we ourselves should think a good many of them, at least, to be better placed than that. So, in effect, all this principle is requiring is that the difference between a *typical* cloud and a candidate that fails altogether to instance cloudhood be, in relevant respects, reasonably substantial; at the very least, that it be more than quite minute. Although the credentials of this premise, like its two predecessors, will be furthered by further discussion, the premise, also like them, has every initial appearance of being an entirely acceptable proposition. (We shall find such further discussion in section 8 and, especially, in section 10.)

From these three premises, our problem of the many can be deduced and, thus, introduced. To begin, from (2) and (3), we obtain:

> (A) If something is a typical cloud, then *any* situation involving it contains, in addition to itself, millions of other complex concrete entities each of which is a cloud, that is, it contains millions of clouds.

Although this deduction is not absolutely formal, the divergence from that austere ideal is trivial. In like manner, from (A) and (1), we may in turn deduce:

> (B) If there are clouds, then there are situations involving typical clouds and, in *any* of these, there are millions of clouds.

Logically speaking, though (B) is conditional in form, it adequately presents our problem. Still psychologically speaking, our problem is in large measure one of confronting a dilemma. So, it is well to have our present argument, which introduces the problem, conclude by offering a disjunction of uncomfortable alternatives. From (B), then, we make our final move to:

> (C) Either there are no clouds at all, or else there are situations involving typical clouds and, in *any* of these, there are millions of clouds.[6,7]

With this argument now before us, our new problem has received a somewhat more formal presentation, to complement our initial, more conversational setting for it. At the same time, by focusing on typical cases, the suggestion of certain small logical moves, as to a single present item alone "creeping over the minimum standard," can be seen not to threaten our problem's seriousness or size. For certain readers, however, my talk of overlapping concrete complexes may, perhaps paradoxically, itself "appear all too abstract." So, especially for them, though for the rest of us as well, I shall proceed to offer a second argument, by which our problem may again be given an introduction. Giving "the mind's eye a visual aid," this second argument may help us all get a more vivid idea of our problem of the many.

3. AN ARGUMENT ABOUT CLOUDS AS BOUNDED ENTITIES

My second argument focuses on the fact that any cloud must be a limited or bounded entity: at least relative to certain routes, traveling from inside the cloud outward, there must be a stopping place for the cloud. Just so, once one is beyond such a stopping place, or group of stopping places, or, as I shall most often say, such a *boundary*, one is outside the cloud, that is, at a place where the cloud is not. This idea makes no great claim for any cloud's boundary, again to use that convenient term.[8] Just as the term 'cloud' is vague, we may allow 'boundary' to be vague as well, at least in our current employment, so that a close connection between the two would not be surprising. But, of course, we are using 'boundary' as something of an abbreviation here, as abbreviating something like 'place(s) of the cloud closest to what is outside the cloud', or like 'place(s) between the place(s) where the cloud is and the place(s) where it is not'. So the vagueness we may attribute to 'boundary', or to our usage of it, will have ample roots in common vague terms: in 'place', in 'cloud', and in lengthier expressions with those vague components. Moving from these linguistic considerations to apparently correlative matters in the extralinguistic realm, our argument will be happy to allow, though it does not require, that clouds have "fuzzy" boundaries with "no determinate width," whatever stricter limits the dictates of reason might, or might not, require.

Just as our boundaries may be treated here in the most liberal, fuzzy manner, so our argument is happy to allow cloud boundaries to have all sorts of shapes and a variety of relations to the clouds they bound. With any typical cloud, I suggest, and any actual cloud in our solar system, the boundary will be fully closed, not "punctured" nor "open-ended." But there may be some possible clouds, I should think them atypical of the kind, with what we may call *open* boundaries. Thus, for example, there might be a cloud with an infinitely long, thin tail. Or, for another, there might be one shaped like an infinitely long cylindrical column. Or, at least, our argument will be happy to allow these things and will even be so generous as to allow some such infinite clouds to be typical clouds. But, at all events, with regard to at least some "routes" out of and into the cloud, there must be limits, however fuzzy those may be. This much our argument will require, but so will the dictates of reason. For otherwise there will not be a world with clouds, or even a single cloud, in it, but only a cloudy or foggy world.[9]

With so much disarming generosity displayed, I trust I may begin my Argument about Clouds as Bounded Entities. For similar reasons, it is good to begin here with the very same premise that began our previous argument:

(1) If there are clouds, then there are typical clouds.

For one thing, as it has already been discussed well enough, we may now immediately move on to add further material.

The second premise of our new argument is a conditional which, for all clouds and not just typical ones, we have just recently provided motivation:

(2) If something is a (typical) cloud, then there is something that limits or bounds the cloud, that is, something that is the *boundary* of the cloud.

In line with our motivating discussion, we shall continue to be generous with any who might be leery of this premise. We may allow that it is poorly phrased and that, as best formulated, its implications are quite scanty. As far as phrasing goes, for all I know, the required limiting entity, which the premise refers to as a *boundary*, may perhaps not be so called in ordinary usage. And perhaps the verb "limit" also might be somewhat out of place here. But to object to the premise on any such grounds is to quibble beside the main point. For the important thing, as our discussion has indicated, is that with any cloud there will be such a "limiting" or "bounding" *something*, however well or badly I may label it. It should be emphasized, next, that *this premise itself* really makes no great claims for any such boundary; the thing need be neither natural nor conventional, neither salient no indiscriminable, and so on. Further, the premise does not explicitly exclude the boundary from itself having width and thus being rather on a par with a cloud (though, of course, no such thing is explicitly required either). Nor, then, does the premise thus exclude the mentioned boundary from itself having boundaries, which in turn may have various properties, including the having of further boundaries, and so on.

It is with its *third premise* that our Argument first threatens to run up the numbers where clouds are concerned:

(3) If something is the boundary of a typical cloud, then there are, in a *bounding envelope* centered on the boundary of any typical cloud, millions of other boundaries of clouds each of which limits, or bounds, a cloud that is different from any cloud thus bounded by any of the others.

Passing over our choice of the phrase "bounding envelope" and other such purely verbal trivialities, there are important substantive and conceptual matters to discuss. In the first place, the function of that chosen phrase is to point out a region that is somewhat thicker than any of the relevant boundaries, but (in case they do have thickness) *not very* much thicker. So, in this region, we may find, side by side, or themselves overlapping, a great many potential boundaries for clouds. Given this, we can see the two key ideas advanced by this premise. The first idea is to focus on the myriad of nearby limiters and, by so doing, on *what they limit*, which then cries out for consideration. Before claiming anything about the presence of clouds, we may notice that *many concrete entities* will be suitably limited: First, each boundary will limit a "region of space" different from every other. Further, in at least many of these regions, the stuff contained will differ from that in many other bound regions. To sharpen the picture, we may note that many of these regions, and their contents, will overlap (slightly) with many others, including (that of) the original typical cloud. In many other cases, there will be no overlap with that original but a rather fine "nesting" between the new candidates and our original item. This first idea is the visual aid, for the mind's eye, that I promised you, in the previous section. So much for the first idea, which brings to our attention many concrete entities, each so similar to our alleged typical cloud, which normally would go unconsidered. The second idea is to judge these newly considered entities with regard to whether or not they are clouds. According to our premise, if our alleged typical item is indeed a typical cloud, then many of these candidates, millions at least, do not fail to be clouds altogether but are clouds of some sort or other. Although antecedently surprising, once the candidates are considered, this judgement seems quite fitting. Indeed, we may say that it even has a certain claim to modesty, or understatement. For, first, this judgement nowhere claims that any but the original choice is a typical cloud, allowing, even, that all the other clouds in the situation are marginal cases. (In contrast, I suggest, our intuitive ideas is that if there are any typical clouds at all, our situation will contain not just one but quite a few clouds that are indeed typical.) And, second, our premise also allows that although many of these candidates are clouds, many of them fail to be clouds, perhaps far outnumbering those whose candidacy is, in any way, successful. (In contrast, our intuitive idea is that not only do many succeed, but none of these "very near neighbors" fail to be clouds.)[10]

Now, our premise mentions *millions* of clouds as present in the typical situation (allowing, of course, that there be an infinity of millions and, thus, an infinity of such clouds). And although we might now agree that many clouds must be present, any such numerical reference as that needs further argument. I shall postpone such argument for the while, until section 5. So our third premise needs further consideration. But, even now, when things are somewhat left up in the air (or sky), this crucial, and most interesting, premise appears at least quite plausible.

There remains but one premise to present for our Argument, and that gap shall now be filled:

(4) If there are, in a bounding envelope centered on the boundary of any typical cloud, millions of other boundaries of clouds each of which limits, or bounds, a cloud that is different from any cloud thus bound by any of the others, then there are situations involving typical clouds, and in any of these there are millions of clouds.

In effect, this last premise adds up, by a procedure that is eminently suitable, only the clouds that we have already agreed to be present and relates the sum to any alleged typical cloud. The procedure is to count the clouds by way of the boundaries limiting them. So where two boundaries limit, or bound, different clouds, there must be (at least) two clouds, and where millions, millions. (We might even *allow* here that two boundaries may both bound the same cloud. But even so, the premise's method cannot falsely add to our judgement.)

Although some of our premises may require a good deal of further discussion, we may agree, I believe, that they together adequately yield our problem. Perhaps discounting small points of grammar, by simple logic, our conditional premises yield us, again, this conditional conclusion:

(B) If there are clouds, then there are situations involving typical clouds, and, in any of these, there are millions of clouds.

For many purposes, our conclusion might as well be left in this conditional form. But, as with our previous argument, to heighten the sense of a dilemma, it is well to put matters in the form of a disjunction:

(C) Either there are no clouds at all, or else there are situations involving typical clouds, and, in any of these, there are millions of clouds.

So we have deduced our dilemma now twice over, by our Argument about Clouds as Concrete Complexes and, again just now, by our Argument about Clouds as Bounded Entities. We want to examine these arguments with some care and to investigate the relations between them. For the dilemma they both yield plainly presents a real philosophic problem. Of course, some philosophers, like Parmenides and, in a smaller way, me, too, would be rather happy to accept the first alternative, feeling an absurdity to attend any putatively common particular, such as an alleged ordinary cloud. Perhaps others, maybe certain followers of Leibniz, might be pleased to accept the second. But most will want to avoid both. To do so rationally, they must refute, or properly deny, both our arguments. This, it seems, is not easy to do. Accordingly, there is much for us to discuss here.

4. SOME RELATIONS BETWEEN THESE TWO ARGUMENTS

There are, I think, some rather interesting relations between our two offered arguments. As they are not entirely obvious, it will be worth our while to draw them out explicitly. Let us begin to do so now. The first of our arguments, concerning concrete *complexes*, specifies a certain sort of constitution, or composition, for clouds, namely, as involving certain smaller *constituent entities*. This is done by way of the argument's second premise, a statement which is not matched by any premise in our other argument. Indeed, our second argument makes no specification at all as to the constitution of any cloud. For this reason, I believe, our second argument is more *general* than is our first, applying to all the sorts of underlying realities (or possible worlds) to which the first applies, and then to some others as well. Of course, as concerns our actual situation, this logical disparity makes no difference, for the actual underlying reality, the actual world, is quite as our more specific, first argument requires. But for a comprehensive understanding, the more general matter should be investigated.

In section 1, we considered a possible world where the underlying reality involved no tiny things, no dispersal of water droplets, molecules, or atoms, in the morass of which putative clouds would have to find their place. In such a world, clouds would all be simple entities, rather than complex ones: such a cloud would not be constituted of any other distinct particulars. The cloud would be composed of some matter, or stuff, to be sure, but that matter would be relevantly continuous and homogeneous. Now, in that first section, we made a further assumption too: There would be a clean, natural break between (the matter of) the putative cloud and whatever was allegedly external to the cloud. Providing that there are clouds, this assumption really is distinct from that of supposing clouds to be (not complex but) simple. So, while still supposing for clouds the aforementioned material simplicity, let us drop this further assumption now.

What sort of underlying reality, or possible world, will we now be supposing? It will be like this: The matter where a cloud is thought to be will not make a clean break with matter that surrounds it but will gradually blend into, or fade off into, such surrounding matter, at every relevant place. For a heuristic, represent the matter "suited for clouds" in red and that "suited for the surrounding sky" in blue. Now, a very close look at "where the two are adjacent" will reveal no sudden change from red to blue (or equally from blue to red). Rather, it will reveal a *gradual* transition from the one color to the other, with at "suitable places in between" various shades of maroon, purple, and so on. In such a situation, we can now easily see, if there is a cloud, the *kind of matter* in it, of which it is composed, gradually blends into *another kind of* matter, at every relevant place, and the cloud is *not* composed of that other kind of matter.

As any such cloud will be a simple entity rather than a complex one, the second premise of our first argument will not apply to it; so in such a world our Argument about Clouds as Concrete Complexes will not apply. But our *second* argument, regarding bounded entities, can apply to such simple things as well as to complex ones. It does not care, so to say, whether the blending between presumed cloud and alleged environment is accomplished by, or instantiated by, a dispersion of smaller items or whether by a true continuity, as just colorfully imagined. So long as our underlying reality exhibits *any* baffling blend, our second argument is well satisfied.

This may come as something of a surprise. For our second argument, mainly by way of its third premise, provides a sort of "visual aid," whereas our first seems to leave things more indefinite, perhaps even, more obscure. It is the first argument that leaves more for the reader to make vivid and concrete. Yet it is not the first, but the second, that is the more general. But though a surprise, there is of course no real paradox here. For the greater concreteness of the second argument is of an *epistemological* sort, relating to a more concrete *understanding* of whatever situations are to be considered, whereas the greater generality of the argument, and thus, in a sense, its greater abstractness, concerns the *metaphysical characters* of those situations.

There is a second relationship between our two arguments that is even less obvious than the one just discussed. But it is at least as important to consider. It is pretty plain, of course, that there is no statement in the second argument that is quite the same as the third and final premise of the first one. What, then, is the relation of our second argument to our first one's final premise?

This final statement may be regarded as a *principle* that *underlies* the third premise of our argument about bounded entities, which premise is, I suggest, the very heart of that more general piece of reasoning. Indeed, so important, then, is this underlying proposition that we may give it a name to remember it by, *the principle of minute differences from typical cases*; for brevity, I shall sometimes just call it *the principle of minute differences*. How is it that this principle underlies our second, more general argument?

We may regard our second argument's third premise, where so many boundaries are first introduced, as doing *two* things. *First,* it calls to our attention, by way of these boundaries, ever so many (bound) relevant entities, overlapping and nesting in their spatial relations. In some possible worlds, including the actual one, these entities will all be complex; in others, they will all be relevantly simple. In any of these worlds, there will be no clean breaks around, but only relevant gradualness. Just so, *in order for anything* in any of these situations to be properly accounted a cloud, the sorts of entities that overlap must be considered real things. Further, we are supposing, at least for the sake of argument, that in each such situation a certain thing there is even a typical cloud. So we focus on one overlapping thing that is a typical cloud and also, we must then suppose, on at least those many others which, as regards criteria for clouds, differ minutely from a certain typical item.

But are any of these other overlapping entities, which we have had to admit as genuine things, of some sort or other, so much as *clouds* themselves? Giving an answer to this question is the *second* thing done by our key premise: If the presumed item is a typical cloud, our implicit reasoning tells us, then each of the many other entities, so recently focused upon, will be at least a cloud of some sort or other. What is it that guides this reasoning? It is the third and final premise of our first argument, the principle of minute differences from typical cases. Slightly shortened, as per note 7, it reads as follows:

> If something is a typical cloud, then, if there are entities that differ from it, in any respects relevant to being a cloud, quite minutely, then each of those entities is a cloud.

So underlying the key premise of our second, more general argument is implicit reasoning which consists of two parts. And the second part of it is quite explicit in our first, more limited reasoning.

If this is right, then a lengthy argument may be constructed which incorporates material from both the two arguments I have actually offered. The constructed argument will be like our offered second one, except that the latter's third premise, just considered, will be replaced by statements that make explicit the reasoning underlying it. For this replacement, we require but two propositions, which together entail the premise they replace. The first of these is our principle of minute differences, rehearsed in display above. The other statement to be employed will then be this rather complex related proposition, which relevantly states the "first part" of the reasoning that was previously implicit:

> If something is the boundary of a typical cloud, then there are, in a bounding envelope centered on the boundary of any typical cloud, millions of other boundaries of entities each of which limits, or bounds, an entity different from that thus bounded by each of the others, and each of these bounded

entities differs from the putative typical cloud in question, in any respects relevant to being a cloud, quite minutely.

With this explicit but complicated conditional, we have an argument of five premises, which is itself, thus, quite complicated indeed. Even so, in relevant regards, this "master argument" is not only *vivid* and *general* but also quite *explicit*. For those who can tolerate complications, I offer it now, perhaps in place of my original formulation of my Argument about Clouds as Bounded Entities; after all, it is also about these putative objects' having a stopping place, or boundary. But I shall offer nothing in place of my first argument, the Argument about Clouds as Complex Entities. For I have found that although many people are interested in discussing the baffling boundaries I have mentioned, there are also many who want no part of any such discussion. Any mention of boundaries, or of anything of the like, turns them away right away. Our argument about complex entities, of course, makes no such mention at all. And, as might be expected, I have found that it is eminently discussable by virtually everyone with whom I have, in conversation, broached the problem of the many.

At all events, in what follows, it will often prove a convenience to speak of clouds, as well as of various other things, as bounded and to contemplate their alleged boundaries. Those who want no part of such a convenience may cast things in terms where no such speaking occurs, as is done in my first argument. They may, then, take my talk of boundaries as merely suggesting an aid in the task of noting all that is there in the morass of concrete reality. But however one chooses to frame the introductory arguments themselves, it should by now be clear that our problem is difficult and persistent.[11] Indeed, we have already left dangling various puzzling loose ends, some of which I hope to connect with later. And other facets of our problem, at least equally baffling, have not yet been even so much as glimpsed obscurely.

5. ON NEARBY CLOUDS AND THE MATHEMATICS OF COMBINATIONS

Up in the sky on rather cloudy days, science tells us, there is a dispersion of water droplets. Here, and also over there, the droplets are closer together than in the regions surrounding the here and the there. In those other regions, there are droplets too, but they are less close together. There is a gradual transition from the here, and from the there, to the lesser density in the surrounding regions.

We are given to think that here is one cloud, there is another, and in those other regions there is no cloud. Just so, we think of clouds as consisting of, or largely of, water droplets, with the droplets in some suitable grouping. As one gets away from here, one gets outside a cloud; one passes a *place*, whatever that is, that is, or is part of, the cloud's boundary.

The "messier" our reality, the better for generating our problem of the many. Our actual reality is plenty messy indeed. In addition to water droplets, clouds may contain impurities (clouds in a smoggy area); the droplets themselves are complexes of constituents (molecules, atoms, particles), and each droplet has its own baffling transitions in store for us. To make our reasoning simple, however, and our exposition concise, I shall discount this extra messiness. For us right now, clouds shall be regarded as being composed entirely of droplets of water.

If a cloud's boundary has thickness, and even "fuzzy" edges, there may be certain droplets whose status as constituents of the cloud is objectively less than clear. (I think this suggestion contains incoherencies, but pass over them now. For, as will become clear, our problem is not helped nor hurt by the suggestion.) If x and y differ in the number of their constituents, they cannot be the same thing, much less, the same cloud. Equally, if x and y differ in the number of their objectively clear constituents, then they cannot be the same complex entity, much less, the same cloud. So, for the purposes of our discussion, it will make no difference, except as regards expository clarity and conciseness, whether we talk of *fuzzy* boundaries and *clear* constituents or, alternatively, and at another extreme, of simple "two-dimensional" boundaries, with no thickness at all, and just plain old constituents. In the sequel, I shall generally speak in the latter idiom, simpler and clearer. For those who must have fuzziness almost everywhere, the translations are easy to make; near this section's end, I shall show how.

In the same spirit, I wish to make one further simplifying assumption: As things have proceeded so far, we must still recognize three, and not two, relations between a cloud's boundary and any of the cloud's droplet constituents. To be sure, there are those droplets, millions of them, within the boundary of any cloud. No trouble there, even for exposition. Also, there are those millions outside the boundary, which likewise present no need for a remark. But there is a third group: the droplets, probably many thousands, at least, that will *intersect with* the boundary of any likely cloud prospect. What of each of these droplets; is it a constituent, or not, of the putative cloud in question? Were we talking of clear constituents, and clear non-constituents, these entities would be assigned, it appears, to some sort of midway status. And, then, we could proceed quickly to our reasoning that would concern only droplets in the clear category. Foreswearing such parlance, I think it most natural to consider these intersected droplets *not* to be constituents of the cloud whose boundary cuts through them. At all events, if I must, then by stipulation I shall now assume as much, since nothing of substance can be lost or gained by so doing. With these simplifications, the key matters emerge without distortion or delay: Our definite claim of *millions* of clouds, in even the smallest typical cloud's most carefully circumscribed situation, is readily at hand, if any clouds themselves ever are. Indeed, as we shall soon see, such a claim is something of an understatement.

Each of the droplets included by a cloud's boundary is a constituent of that cloud and, on our simplifying assumptions, nothing else is a constituent of it. Arbitrarily choose an alleged typical cloud and consider precisely those droplets that its boundary encloses. Now, in close proximity to this alleged boundary, there will be at least one other such boundary, of a *very* similar shape and "size." By only as minimal a deviation from the first as is required for the task, this second boundary includes, in addition to all those droplets just considered, exactly one other water droplet. We may imagine that, except for the slight bulge beyond the first required to include the new droplet, the two boundaries are elsewhere wholly coincident. In any event, this second boundary will include a certain complex entity which, on the relevant reckoning, has exactly one more constituent than does our typical cloud. Its droplets bear to it *very* much the same relation, whatever it is, that the already considered droplets, one less in number, bear to the putative typical item. On the relevant reckoning, then, this second complex entity, larger than the first in number of constituents, and also, we might add, in mass and in volume, is a different entity from our typical cloud. But in any respect important to being a cloud, there is scarcely any difference between the two. So in our situation, right there, there is at least one (concrete complex) entity that is, in those very regards, only *minutely* different from a certain *typical* cloud. By this consideration, it is intuitive, this second entity must also be a cloud, if not a typical cloud, at least a cloud of some sort or other. So our typical cloud's situation, arbitrarily chosen, contains at least two clouds, for it contains two different concrete entities each of which is a cloud.

Let us suppose, what seems very cautious, that the foregoing procedure may be applied distinctly at least a thousand times in the case of any typical cloud. Each application will involve a different single droplet that is very close to, but is external to, our typical cloud's boundary, as well as to the boundaries of every new candidate but one, that single droplet then being a constituent of only that one new candidate. As each candidate has a whole droplet as a constituent that is external to each of the others, each candidate really is a different entity from every other. (With a natural choice of their boundaries, each will slightly "overlap" each of the others, and each will "contain" the original allegedly typical specimen.) As each is only very slightly different from a certain typical cloud, in relevant respects, each is a cloud; so each is a different cloud from every other. Thus, in our situation, in addition to our putative typical cloud, there are at least a thousand clouds. But, of course, what we have just done by "reaching outward," we may do as well in reverse, by "reaching inward." Thus, by similar reasoning, there are at least another thousand clouds, each smaller by one droplet than our original typical specimen.

This rather surprising result, of at least two thousand additional clouds, has been arrived at rather cautiously. For with so very many droplets close to our original boundary, both inside and external, when selecting only a thousand in each direction, we could be very choosey in satisfying cloud criteria, whatever those criteria might be. Given our simplifications, it might seem that if we are to run the numbers up much higher this caution must be sacrificed. For, sticking to our simplified procedure, with whole droplets, it might seem that we should have to extend our boundaries considerably, thus reaching regions where careful selection has been abandoned. But his appearance is illusory. For it results from our overlooking the mathematics of combinations, with its notorious power to escalate.

A boundary that, in addition to the original's droplets, encloses any (combination) of our considered nearby external one thousand, but no other droplets, will enclose a cloud. For, although (most) such enclosed candidates will not be *quite* as similar to our typical specimen as was a candidate with only one differentiating droplet, still, in relevant respects, each will also be only *very* slightly different from a putative *typical* cloud. Now, barring sorites arguments, we may grant that there comes a point where such a slight difference is left behind us.[12] But, surely, we have not even come close to such a point with the variations of boundaries so far envisaged. With just these variations, our previously external droplets produce sufficiently good candidates equal to the number of combinations obtained in taking a thousand items each of the times up to and including a thousand. Each candidate is good enough, that is, not to fail to be a cloud, of some sort or other. And when we include internal selections, and combinations of internal and external, we further escalate matters fast, while never straying far from our original bounded paradigm. So if there are any clouds, there are not only millions of them, but, we might say, a problem of *many* millions.[13]

It will soon be my business to extend our arguments from their original exclusive concern with clouds to cover ordinary sorts of things quite generally, including planets and mountains, tables and their legs, human bodies, and so on. Before I do so, I should like briefly to sketch two things: First, as I promised, I would like to show how our discussion can be put in terms that do not imply the fine boundaries we have recently been supposing. And, then, I would like to say a few words about how the entire discussion of this present section relates to our introductory arguments, which were advanced in sections 2 and 3.

First, then, let us suppose that clouds, even typical ones, do not have the "neat and decisive" boundaries we have been discussing but have, instead, "inherently fuzzy" boundaries. Assuming that this idea is coherent, what does it imply? I take it that, according to the idea of fuzzy boundaries, there are things or stuff, whose status with regard to an alleged bounded item, e.g., a certain typical cloud, is *objectively unclear,* or *indefinite,* or *indeterminate.* Despite this rather mysterious complication, however, fuzzy boundaries occasion no great changes in our arguments.

Consider a typical cloud with such a boundary. In addition to droplets with unclear status, there are many further afield that are *clearly not* constituents of the cloud. Third, finally, and perhaps most important, there are other droplets still, closest to hand, so to say, each of which is a *clear constituent* of the cloud. Consider another fuzzy boundary that encloses a space slightly larger than the first. It does that in just such a way that it encloses a complex entity with all the typical cloud's clear droplets as clear constituents for it, too, *plus one more clear one for it,* which had unclear status for the original, typical specimen. What the new fuzzy boundary bounds is a *different entity* from the typical cloud that is fuzzily bounded, for it differs from the latter in *a certain clear component part.* But, all things considered, and in particular as regards any criteria for cloudhood, the difference between these two fuzzily bounded entities is quite minute. As the one is a *typical* cloud, the other, fuzzy boundary and all, is at least a cloud of some sort or other. Thus, with fuzzy boundaries as much as with neat, we must have, if there are ever any clouds at all, at least two clouds in our situation. The reasoning from here to millions, it is plain, will be entirely familiar. What we have just done is quite obvious: we replaced talk of neat boundaries by allusions to fuzzy ones; then we made compensating changes right down the line. As such compensations are always available, it makes no difference to our problem whether we think of a cloud's limiter as neat, even two-dimensional, or as being not only somewhat thick but inherently fuzzy as well.

In this section, we contemplated certain combinations of water droplets. By that means, we saw many millions of clouds where one would normally suppose only one cloud to be. Or better, we saw a dilemma involving such millions. How do these recent perceptions relate to our two offered arguments? The first of those arguments, our Argument about Clouds as Concrete Complexes, mentions millions of relevant entities in its *second* premise. We have now seen why this premise, *apparently the argument's most controversial* one, is actually correct and might even be considered an *understatement*. As concerns our second argument, our Argument about Clouds as Bounded Entities, its *third* premise would, I think, be considered its most controversial one. It is in this premise, after all, where the argument first makes mention of millions of clouds. (In section 4, it will be remembered, this premise is analysed into our principle of minute differences plus a complex statement where millions of bound items are mentioned.) Here, too, our recent perceptions involve us in seeing the correctness of that multitudinous premise. So, by means of the mathematics of combinations, even the "weakest links" in our arguments may be seen as plenty strong enough.

6. EXTENDING OUR ARGUMENTS TO OTHER ORDINARY THINGS

Clouds, we may say, are *ordinary things* of one particular sort. If things of that sort, clouds, really do exist, then through science we gain an understanding of them as *complex concrete entities*, each composed, largely if not entirely, of many tiny constituents. Now, in addition to clouds, there are, of course, many other sorts of ordinary things about which we appear to think and talk: salt shakers, stones, planets and their mountains, human bodies and their arms, hands, and fingers, trees and their trunks and branches, tables and their legs and tops, swizzle sticks, and so on. Although it takes a bit more doing, science reveals all these things, if they do actually exist, also to be complex concrete entities, with their own tiny components. Through this revelation, I suggest, we may readily apply, or extend, our arguments about clouds to cover all these other ordinary things as well.

If it could be managed properly, the most direct way to do this would be to add to our arguments a premise to the effect that these other sorts of things, typical tables, for example, just are clouds; presumably, they would be clouds of molecules, or atoms, or elementary particles. But although such an idea may be common in trying to view ordinary things scientifically, I should be rather suspicious of any such extension of our arguments. Rather, I am inclined to think that such a characterization is only metaphorical. For it seems to me that, despite the similarities thus alluded to, there remain relevant differences between tables and clouds, that block an identification.

The conditions for the identity of a table through time, for one example, appear to be rather different from those for clouds. A typical table may be readily disjoined into five separated large parts, for instance, its top and four legs. These may later be reassembled or, alternatively, not. Even if never reassembled, there are many situations in which the table would be regarded as existing throughout; the parts might be on exhibit together, to show how such a table looks when taken apart. But no similar strength against separation appears available for the continued existence of any cloud. Now, I am not claiming that, as against the idea that tables are clouds, such considerations are absolutely conclusive. But, surely, they are substantial enough for us to be suspicious of the idea and to look elsewhere for a less controversial means of extending our arguments.

We may do better, I think, by noting that, at least in *those respects relevant* to our arguments, there is *no important difference* between clouds and many other ordinary things. Rather, the relation of a cloud to its constituents is *relevantly the same* as that between a table and what constitutes it.[14] Because of this, parallels to our Arguments may be advanced for many other sorts of ordinary things. For example, wherever 'cloud' occurs in our stated premises, we can put 'table' or 'stone', making whatever grammatical adjustments are then required. In that way, we can obtain arguments, just as good as before, for dilemmas with regard to tables and stones.[15]

For specificity, let us focus on our second argument and on how to extend it. What about boundaries, then, for things other than clouds, thus, for typical stones, or tables? Perhaps even more clearly than with clouds, any of these things will have a boundary, which separates it, and its constituents, from whatever is external to it. Centered on such a boundary, there will be our familiar bounding envelope. And in this envelope there will be many other boundaries, each relevantly enclosing a different complex concrete entity.

Regarding small salient constituents, what are the underlying physical facts that ground this plethora of complex candidates? So far as I can gather from reliable sources, the situation here is, in relevant ways, very much like that before with a cloud and its droplets: At any moment, just about anywhere you please along our stone's boundary there will be some atoms, or molecules, whose status, with regard to our typical stone, nature has left unclear; there is no natural break between the atoms of the stone and so very many others that, *ex hypothesi*, are only outside it. But for our argument to be extended properly, we do not even need anything as cloudlike as that which, it appears, nature so generously does provide. Rather, we require only some such extremely cautious proposition as this following one: Even if there are many places along our stone's boundary where a clean break is given by nature, indeed, even if almost all the boundary's places are of this sort, there are at least a thousand atoms (or molecules) of the stone which are not naturally separate from all relevantly similar ones in the stone's environment. The cautious idea here is that with each of at least one thousand different problematic atoms, we may apportion things variously for want of any natural separation.

Where our typical stone's boundary excludes each of these thousand, as may be assumed, a very similar boundary may be described which includes any one or combination of them, as well as all the atoms in the typical specimen, but no other atoms. In this way many millions of boundaries may be described. Cautiously reckoning by atoms, each will enclose an entity that is, in relevant regards, only *minutely* different from a certain *typical* stone. So each will enclose a different stone. Even with such a cautious supposition, and such cautious reckoning, our argument may thus be extended to cover stones as well as clouds: Either there really are no stones at all, or else, in any situation involving a typical stone, there are millions of stones. Dilemmas for other ordinary things, for example, tables, follow in like manner.

Having extended our arguments from clouds to more earthy things, we might ask: Why did we not begin with these latter, "more cohesive" objects in the first place? Logically speaking, we might just as well have done so; indeed, as I shall soon argue, perhaps we might better have done so. But people are not often as logical as they should be. So for psychological reasons, it was best to begin with alleged entities that, *often* in our everyday experience, even seem to present something of a puzzle: Where the devil does one of these things end and where, in contrast, is what merely serves to surround it? This puzzling experience, where reality itself appears to mirror vagueness, opens our minds to "new possibilities." Further, it provides us with motivation to think logically, at length and in complex detail, about what ordinarily passes as being too simple for argument: How many things of such-and-such *ordinary kind are right there now?* Clouds, then, are good food for thought, when one wants to serve up the problem of the many.

Once the introduction has been effected, however, clouds do not seem especially well suited for our problem, after all. For, as I said early on, our problem concerns reality and not, except perhaps indirectly and secondarily, how reality appears to us. Just so, whereas it is at least probably right that a cloud must have a boundary, we may be still more confident that this much is required for a table, or a stone. Why is the latter idea certainly not worse, and perhaps better, founded?

We think of certain things as *concrete* and of others as, perhaps more or less, *abstract.* When a concrete thing is an *ordinary* kind of *spatial* entity, as in the case of a table or stone, it must have a boundary. Consider, in contrast, certain "more abstract" entities, which have their being rooted, so to say, in particular concrete entities. Thus a *swarm of bees* is somewhat abstract, the bees being thought of as concrete. It is somewhat difficult to think of the swarm as really having a boundary: Does the swarm really include as a part a certain (part of the) space that separates the bees? It seems not, but, then again, certain things do point that way. So it is hard to know quite what to think here. No matter: it is not important for us to decide the issue. Rather, my point in mentioning it is this: *Insofar* as we *can* think of clouds as *concrete,* our boundaries for them seem to have a firmer footing.

How, then, *are* we to think of clouds? I think, though I am not very sure of it, that clouds, if they exist, must actually be concrete things. Part of what underlies my thought is that there seems to be the following important contrast between the idea of a cloud and those of such apparently more abstract entities as swarms of bees: A cloud "could be," with no contradiction in terms, composed purely of homogeneous stuff, with no distinct *constituent things* at all.[16] Further, along the same line, it is at least somewhat odd to say of a certain cloud that it is a ? *cloud of water droplets* even if the cloud is in fact constituted of just such droplets.[17] In contrast, it is at least false to say, if not utterly nonsensical, that a swarm (of bees) "could be" composed entirely of homogeneous stuff, with no (bees or other) distinct constituent things serving to compose it.

While I believe I have been right in treating clouds as concrete, I am surer of the point where many other sorts of things are concerned: stones and tables, to mention a familiar couple. It is utterly absurd, I feel sure, to talk of a * *stone of molecules*, no matter how many molecules may serve to constitute a given stone. Along with this, so far as the logic of the word "stone" is concerned, all the stones "could be" composed, each and every one of them, entirely of continuous, homogeneous stuff, with no small constituent things at all. So I feel quite sure that stones, if any such things do exist, must be concrete entities. Equally, and perhaps for that very reason, I feel sure that if there are stones, each one must have a boundary. (It is a further question, we may allow, what sort of boundary might prove acceptable for a stone.) By reason of their more evident concreteness, most other ordinary things cleave more surely to our problem than do clouds. Epistemologically and psychologically, clouds do better than stones at getting any problem before us, in the first place; but stones do better than clouds at keeping it there. (Even so, clouds do not do badly at that second stage, either.) As experience with extending our arguments thus serves to confirm, our new problem is not only a very comprehensive difficulty but a particularly persistent one.[18]

At all events, we have done quite enough with clouds, at least for the while. So let us continue to think some more about such more evidently concrete things as stones, and of what this concreteness might imply for them and their situations. A fairly obvious point, but one still worth mentioning, is this: If you are thinking of a stone, you must be thinking of a concrete object. Suppose that an ordinary person, looking at what we take to be a single stone, operated according to the following function: If there is at least one concrete object there before him which "we would all take to be" a stone, he thinks of a *certain abstract object*; otherwise, he does not think of that object. Could this object, about which he thus thinks, be the only real *stone* in our story, so that this person might conceivably thus avoid our problem of the many? No, it could not. For since that thought of object is abstract, and not concrete, *it* could *not* be *any* stone at all. For any of those things, the stones, must be concrete entities. Goodness knows what that fellow may be thus thinking of; but we can be sure it is *not* a stone.

Relations of *constitution* may obtain between various sorts of things. Perhaps bees, which are concrete, may constitute a swarm of bees, which is at least somewhat abstract and is thus not concrete. The natural numbers, which are quite abstract, may perhaps constitute the infinite sequence of those numbers which, though not itself a natural number, is also abstract. Various molecules, which are very small concrete things, may perhaps constitute real tables and stones, which are also concrete. Certain stuff, like iron, which is also concrete, may serve to constitute such concrete things as well. (It does not happen, as far as I can see, that abstract things can literally constitute concrete ones.) For our problem of the many it is the alleged constituion of certain concrete things by certain other ones that is of importance.

In any case, no matter what is constituting what, that which constitutes cannot be the very same thing as what is thus constituted; that is, nothing can constitute itself. Now some people will think that by noting the concrete character of a stone, and in promoting our problem of the many, I must be identifying a stone with its concrete constituents, that I must be implying that a stone is "nothing more than" certain atoms, for example. But *nothing* could be *further* from the truth, as my preceding remark indicates. *So far* is it from implying such an identification that the statement that a certain stone is constituted of certain atoms *actually* implies quite the *opposite*: The statement *implies that* the stone is something *other than* the atoms. Still, as my earlier remarks imply, *both* the stone *and* the atoms may be concrete entities; indeed, *if they exist*, they *must* be. Our problem of the many is hardly hindered. In any relevantly typical realistic situation, either there is no stone or else there are so many atoms so arranged that each of *millions* of groups of them has as its members things that constitute a stone, a stone different from that constituted by the members of any other group.

The concreteness of stones disarms thoughts that vagueness might actually enter into the nature of each of these entities itself. And these thoughts certainly should be disarmed. For they can easily lead to others that would seem to produce a solution to our problem. But being as confused as it is quickly effected, such a product would be no genuine solution. According to these thoughts, because stones themselves are vague, or are indefinite things, no particular number of constituents, say, of molecules, can properly be said to constitute any one of them. This, even though stones do exist, as do molecules, and the latter do constitute the former. (Similarly, no particular amount of matter can be said to constitute a stone.) But my bounded candidates for stonehood, it will be pointed out, are definite enough to allow such statements; my complex concrete entities have no inherent vagueness. Hence they are so different from stones that no problem about them need involve other more ordinary, inherently vague objects.

It seems to me that such a common objection, though perhaps well meant, cannot itself be well conceived; rather, it is fraught with confusion. For what can it be for a stone to be constituted of molecules but of no number of molecules? And although in any real situation *we* may have only a *vague idea* as to what is the number, in any given stone, what kind of number can it possibly be if not some particular number? No, either the stone, that presumedly real, typical specimen, is composed of a definite number of molecules, whatever the number may happen to be, or *else* it really is *not* composed of molecules at *all*. But if the putative entity does not number some molecules among its constituents, thus, some particular, definite number of them, it is *not* any real typical *stone* that we are discussing.

As I said, this confused idea about numbers rests on a prior confusion of thinking of stones, of such concrete objects, as themselves being vague or indefinite.

The only things that can be vague, of course, are rather more abstract ones: words, statements, shareable ideas, and the like. And although a statement about a stone may be rather indefinite, even, for example, as to the number of molecules in the latter, the stone itself, which is not abstract at all, cannot be in the least bit indefinite. So the vagueness, and any indefiniteness here, will only be a feature of the expressions employed, such as 'stone', the statements made, the thoughts expressed thereby, and the like; it will *not* figure in any *stone* itself. I suggest that, occurring just where it does, the relevant vagueness, far from avoiding or resolving our problem, serves instead actually to generate the problem of the many.

What I have just done, by focusing upon a stone's required concreteness, I am happy to grant, may be regarded as a refutation of the idea that any ordinary thing may have a *fuzzy* boundary. If so, well and good; for I have also argued that such ordinary entities must have boundaries of some sort or other. Thus we may conclude that, if they exist, such things have boundaries that are not fuzzy but that are as neat as you please.[19,20] This conclusion does not, of course, contradict my previously argued claim that even if fuzzy boundaries are allowed, indeed, even if they are required, our problematic dilemma can be generated. On the contrary, either way our problem arises. What we have just argued is this: The more obvious routes to our problem are also, it seems, the only genuine ones. Thus I have just given an argument *a fortiori*.

7. ON INFINITIES OF NEARBY STONES AND CLOUDS

The idea of any infinity of stones, or clouds, being right there, ready for you to take in with one quick look, may seem preposterous. It does to me. But, then, I am a sort of Parmenidian philosopher, so to say, who does not believe in the reality of any stones or clouds at all, who opts for the first disjunct of our dilemma of the many. Those philosophers who, like ordinary folks, do believe in stones must allow, as a real epistemic possibility, a nearby infinity of the blamed things; they are faced, we might say, with a problem of the infinitely many. Let us see why.

It is easiest to see how an infinite version of our problem arises when we have in mind a certain possible world, or possible underlying reality, that is quite different from (what we take to be) the actual one. This is the sort of possible reality I discussed in section 4, vividly represented there by a transition between putative red regions (clouds) and their alleged blue surrounding (the sky around them). In such a world, clouds are composed, if they really exist at all, of one sort of matter which, within the cloud, is relevantly continuous and homogeneous. The surrounding, if there really is such a distinct thing, is composed of a matter of a different sort which is "spread throughout it" in the same relevantly continuous fashion. Around where a cloud's boundary is (supposed to be) there is a gradual transition from matter of the one sort to matter of the other. This idea may be immediately extended from clouds to other, more evidently concrete ordinary things, such as stones and tables.

Now, any stone must have a boundary, a place or group of places where it stops, on the other side of which the stone is not; otherwise, we would just have a stoney universe. So, somewhere around the (red) stone matter there is a boundary that separates the stone, the thing composed of that matter, from its surrounding. Especially because it makes no difference to the argument, for simplicity of exposition we shall, as we did before, think of such a boundary as without thickness, as two-dimensional, if you will, though curved through three-dimensional space. This fine boundary includes or limits a certain amount, and indeed even a certain batch, of (red) stuff or matter; it is that very matter which constitutes our putative typical (red) stone.

Think of a second fine boundary that for the most part lies coincident with the first but that bulges slightly outward from it in a certain relatively small area. The relations between these two boundaries are just the same as those between our first and second considered before with respect to a complex stone's nearby, or peripheral, atom. The only difference is in what the boundaries enclose. This time, there is no extra atom for the bulging boundary above to encompass; so what it encloses is not greater by one salient constituent than what the other bounds. But the bulger does include, in addition to all the matter the one does, a certain extra bit or batch of matter, which is not enclosed by the other. Speaking quaintly, we might say the bulger encloses about an extra "atom's worth of stuff." So the bulging boundary suitably encloses a (simple) concrete entity which is, in regard to matter, and also mass and volume, greater than that enclosed by the boundary imagined just beforehand. Thus each of the boundaries bounds a different (simple concrete) entity.

Supposing there to be stones in this world, the first of these bounded entities is so lucky as to be a typical stone. In any respect relevant to being a stone, though, the second differs from it only minutely. So, as is intuitive and as our principle dictates, the second bounded entity will also be a stone, if not a typical one, at least a stone of some sort or other. Or it will if there are any stones. Putting one and one together, we get two: Either there really are no stones in this world, or else our chosen situation contains at least two of those things.

That much is by now pretty familiar. But how to make the step from at least two to *infinity?* It is easy. We need only realize that "between" the two boundaries considered there are an infinite number of others. Starting with the original boundary, each of these others is coincident with it for the most part but makes something of a bulge where our second did. Each one, so to say, makes a slightly greater bulge than the one before it, the maximum being the bulge of the secondary boundary. So we have an infinite number of very similar boundaries there. Each bounds an entity different from that bounded by every other; indeed, they all differ, though very slightly, in mass, in volume, and even in shape. We have here an infinite number of bounded concrete entities. In all sorts of respects, including any relevant to stonehood, each differs quite minutely from the original putative typical item. By our principle of minute differences, if there are stones, there will be an infinite number of them in this very simple situation.

There is another way to "see an infinity of stones" here, which connects more obviously with the original third premise of my second argument (The Argument about Clouds as Bounded Entities.) Centered on our first alleged boundary, and extending just a bit to either side, we may describe a thin "band," what I called a *bounding envelope*. Even sticking with our typical stone's shape, now, we may "see" in this envelope an infinity of similarly shaped boundaries. Each of these bounds an item differing in mass and volume from that bounded by every other; but this time, of course, the shape of each bounded item is the same. From here on, the reasoning is familiar.

It will be granted, perhaps, that if our world were of the sort just mentioned, our dilemma would reach into the realm of the infinite. But our world is not much like that one. On the contrary, over *there* stones are *simple* concrete things; in *actuality*, they are *complex*, each constituted by at least very many distinct smaller things, in particular, of so many atoms. But no actual stone is composed of an infinite number of such atoms. So, *realistically*, where does infinity get a chance to enter our new problem?

One way to try to reach that high is to dig deeply, so to say, into our small salient constituents, into our atoms themselves. But insofar as what we find is real, we appear to be left, at some elementary point, with small units that, in fact, cannot be further divided. We thus encounter, perhaps, combinations of elementary particles. But, while running the numbers up, all such reckoning will leave us in the realm of the finite. Focusing on the most realistic situations, this "descending" line of approach does not look promising.

To give infinity a better chance, let us shift our focus from our atoms, or a cloud's droplets, to *whatever it is that separates them from one another*. What is it that does this? Some other sort of matter; empty space, perhaps? For what follows, any such answer will do as well as any other. The important thing is that whatever its nature, this *separator*, as I shall call it, blend gradually into whatever is found in the putative surrounding. And, indeed, no natural break is ever in fact encountered. Now, then, given this realistic blending, the important issue is whether or not the separator is continuous. If our separator is physically continuous, that is, if it is in reality infinitely divisible, then we may argue to an infinity of nearby stones, and clouds.

So far as science can tell us, the separator of a typical stone might really be continuous. With this prospect before us, it is necessary to inquire about the status of the separator with respect to the stone whose salient constituents it serves to distinguish. Is this separator itself part of the stone, a much larger but less easily noticed constituent than the atoms, and any other things, separated by it? I shall argue that an affirmative answer is available to us here, one that follows from our concept or idea of a stone, providing it applies to such realistic situations at all. Now, ordinarily, no one has any conscious or explicit thoughts about this matter, one way or the other. So we must probe a bit for anything to point the way.

First, we may begin our probe by asking what we should say of a tiny item, perhaps a miniscule space ship, that appeared to travel into a stone, upon learning that, in fact, the item went well in between the atom's (and particles) of the stone, never so much as even touching any such constituent. I am confident that we should then judge, as we did at first, that the item was, nevertheless, actually inside the stone though, with a suitable item, not a part of the stone. Now, someone might of course raise various objections to taking this literally, but I cannot see any of these to have much substance. And it does seem to follow from a literal judgment here that the tiny item must then be surrounded by space occupied by the stone itself. But the space surrounding this tiny thing is all occupied by our separator, for it never so much as touched any small constituent. Given that, the only plausible way for the stone to be in that space is for the separator to be part of the stone. So our miniscule spaceship will be suitably surrounded by, and inside, the stone itself only if the separator is actually part of the stone.

Second, considerations of volume, in the sense of amount of space, lead to the same conclusion. The volume of a typical stone, we should reckon as so many cubic feet, or inches, though perhaps without putting a fine point on things. But much of this volume is occupied only by the separator, and not by any of the stone's smaller, more salient constituents. If the separator is not part of the stone, then either our volumetric judgments are systematically in error, and by quite a lot, or else we must face the mystery of how a volume equal to the separator's may be properly reckoned toward the total for the stone itself. Let us not monger such mysteries, nor torture our thought beyond recognition. Rather, let us explain these matters simply, by means of what may be simply put: Everything within a stone's boundary, as we have described such an encloser, is part of the stone. (Our previous "tiny item" will not be part of a stone even so. How, so? The stone will have an internal (part of its total) boundary, separating it from the enclosed foreign body.)

In the *third* place, if we do not count the separator as part of the stone, we should have to say that a stone is a "scattered" entity, though one which may cease to exist when the arrangement of its scattered components is no longer maintained, e.g., when they get "too far" apart from one another. But it is intuitive, according to our concept of a stone, that if there are such things, they are not thus scattered, being instead relevantly continuous, or at least a relevantly good approximation thereto.

Fourth, and perhaps most important, if the separator is not part of our stone, what are we to make of the stone's boundary? Our idea of a stone has it that its boundary should be a continuous limiter, or at least something much of that sort, and that whatever is just inside of the boundary be, if not the whole stone, then some part of it. However, if the stone's boundary is even roughly where we have been considering it, and the separator is not part of the stone, then much of what the boundary encloses will not be part of the stone but, instead, only a quite alien thing. That is absurd. But if the separator is not part of the stone, what is the alternative? The alternative is equally repugnant: To include just the stone itself, and so no alien thing as well, the boundary will have to be a scattered-sum-of-boundaries of constituent particles. I doubt that such a sum is coherent at all; in any case, it is not the *boundary* of any *stone*. As both of the alternatives to it are absurd, the separator is part of the stone itself. Thus we may reason, at least four times over, that a stone's separator is a genuine, though often overlooked, part of it.[21]

Given this requirement, what transpires if it happens that the relevant space, or whatever separates atoms, is relevantly continuous? What happens is just this: With any nearby typical stone, an infinity of nearby stones will exist. Let us see why.

Supposing things to be continuous, an infinite number of nearby boundaries will each limit a different separator, each thus apportioning a different separator to the stone it bounds. (To see the infinity of boundaries, we just follow recipes for the imagination already given earlier in this present section.) Each of an infinite number of different boundaries will bound different likely candidates for stonehood. If there really are any stones, then, in our situation (at least) one of these is a typical stone. But, in any respect relevant to stonehood, any of the others differs from such a one only quite minutely; quite minutely, indeed! So if there are stones, each of this infinity is a stone, at least a stone of some sort or other. Thus a continuous domain for would-be separators yields an infinite version of our problem: Either there really are *no* stones at all, *or else* there are situations involving typical stones and, in any of these, there is an *infinite* number of stones involved. The reasoning to infinity is quite parallel, I trust, for our old friends, clouds, for tables, and even for human bodies.

The argument for this dilemma concerning infinity has made a crucial substantive assumption about physical reality: that whatever separates small items, or at least appears to do so, is in fact continuous. Well, what of this supposition; is it true, or not? To get serious about this is to ponder our current epistemological situation regarding the innermost features of physical reality. As a layman, and no scientist, my own position is at a remove. But it seems to me that no one is as yet so very much better off than I am: As of right now, epistemologically speaking, space, or whatever separates, might really be infinitely divisible; so, it might really be that our alternatives are zero or infinity for nearby stones. By the same token, for all anyone can now say, our separators might really not be infinitely physically divisible. For all we can say, it might really be that our alternatives are zero or, not infinity, but a finite number running into the millions. Either way, of course, we have quite a dilemma.

Whether or not our separators are continuous, so whether or not they generate an infinite version of our problem, they will play a part that is quite in addition to everything done by our smaller, more salient constituents. And a realization of the part they play can prove quite instructive regarding the place of ordinary things, like stones, in the concrete complexity of reality. For consider a rather neater world than ours, relevantly possible, in which the arrangement of particles in a typical stone, as well as in other ordinary things, is as neat and regular as you please, both in the interior and even at what we take to be the periphery. And suppose as well that right outside the "most peripheral layer" of atoms, there is a rather spatious vacuum all around, or some undifferentiated field of rarified stuff. Just so, as regards small, salient constituents, there will be no gradual blending here, between those of the stone and those merely in its environment. In a case like this, nature provides a clean break *of a sort*. But is it a break *that will yield exactly one stone* in the described situation? I think not. Confining consideration to small constituents would have things be that way; but we should then miss out on the part played by that which separates them. For even with such a regular arrangement, many different, equally good apportionments of separators are available. One, as good as any, is to take the smoothest outside tangent surface as a boundary; another, just as good, is to take a surface that *barely* encloses each most external particle, then dipping in a certain amount, perhaps the diameter of such a particle, until it is halfway to the next particle, where it then rises, economically to enclose again. And, of course between these two, there are very many (perhaps infinitely many) compromises, each no worse than any other possible boundary for any such stone. Here, then, and *thus also in the actual world*, we shall have *very many stones each having exactly the same atomic constituents as every other*, providing, of course, that, in any world, there ever are any real stones at all.

8. INTERNAL AND EXTERNAL RELATIONS

Philosophers have meant various things by *relations*, and there are various philosophic contrasts concerning relations that have been marked by 'internal' and 'external'. Seldom, if ever, have these contrasts been clear ones. So it is with some trepidation that I approach such metaphysical matters here. Still and all, it seems to me that some brief remarks in this regard can serve to make clearer the severity of our problem of the many.

Focusing on salient constituents, say, atoms, we find that those of a certain table bear certain relations to each other, regarding spatial distribution, bonding forces, and so on. It is at least largely owing to these mutual relations, we may call them the *internal relations* among the table's (salient) constituents, that those atoms serve to constitute that table. Ordinarily, we are inclined to think that this is pretty much all there is to the matter of having a table in a common realistic situation. But, on reflection, it seems that, if there are in fact any tables, there are some rather different factors involved that are also crucial. I think that we may fairly say that these factors concern the *external relations* between those constituents of the table and, on the other hand, various other entities that are, quite literally, external to the table, for example, atoms in the table's immediate surrounding. Fortunately for our new problem and, so, unfortunately for our common sense thinking, these relations are, in reality, gradually manifested. Accordingly, a consideration of the complexities they might impose will do nothing to avoid, or to solve, our problem of the many. On the contrary, an appreciation of these external relations will impress upon us all the more the persistent character of this problem.

Consider a table made of iron, an iron table. Now, the internal relations of the table, the relations among its (internal) constituents, are important for the table's being there. But so are the relations to other things in the world, things outside the table. Should "too many" other iron atoms be right up against those of the considered putative table, and be suitably bound together by appropriate forces, we might well have a large solid iron sphere. Well, some such thing as that will be no table at all, let alone the particular table we first supposed. So it is important for the table's being there that the relations of its atoms to those others are as they "in fact" are, and are *not* as we *next* supposed them to be.

Consider a less extreme situation involving our supposed iron table. This time there *would not be so many* additional atoms bound to the first group, to the table's, so many that we should have no table at all in the situation. Instead, there would be only a few new atoms attached to the first group. What of those *first* atoms *now*, when these other atoms are attached to them; would *they* still constitute a table? (Would they, perhaps, even constitute the very same table that they did in the previously mentioned situation?) If the answer is affirmative, then, even sticking just with combinations of atoms, there would be, in this situation, at least two tables present: one would be composed of just the atoms in the first group; the other, larger table, of those plus the few atoms attached to them.

I believe that our thoughts here are in conflict. One thought, quite common enough, is that the first atoms now do *not* any table make, that the attached atoms logically prevent them from constituting a table. So this thought is, in effect, that, in this case, those first atoms would have the wrong external relations, for table-hood, to the world's other atoms. But, I have found, there is another thought that quite a few people have. This *second* thought is that those first atoms *will* still constitute a table. (Indeed, a strong but common version of this thought continues, they will still constitute the first table here mentioned.)

For people who have this second thought (even if they also have the conflicting first one), our problem of the many will have yet another way of arising. For while the first atoms will "by themselves" still constitute a table (presumably, the first table), those atoms *along with* the "newly attached" atoms will constitute another, slightly larger table. And where two tables are thus encountered, many more cannot be far off. But, as I have implied, many folks will resist this second, troublesome thought, or not even have it at all. Let us now suppose, what may be quite doubtful, that they alone are right here. If so, then we might say this, regarding our currently considered situation: With even those few other atoms attached, the *absence* of *certain external* relations prevents the first atoms from constituting a table, hence, from being a problematic factor. By the same token, the *presence* of *opposite* external relations will prevent this trouble here.

But, of course, we have just pretended to think about things in a manner that hardly conforms to the complexities of reality. Even forgetting considerations of the separator, and the complexities that they present, we must have had in mind a very nice regular atomic arrangement, like that mentioned for stones toward the end of the previous section. There, a stone's atoms, here, a table's, were so nicely arranged that "there would be no question" regarding any of them, whether or not it was a constituent of a most salient stone, or table, in the situation. Now, in such a *special* case, the largest group of considered atoms has, as compared with any other group in the situation, some rather special external relation or relations. Surrounded by a vacuum, as we supposed, its members alone would "stand free"; they alone would be a group of bonded entities with no such further entity bonded to them. All the "interior groups," in contrast, have no such special, clean, "free" status. So, in *such* a case (and still forgetting about separators), there *seems some reason* to suppose that *only one table* is constituted. But even when matters of external relations are in the forefront, any *realistic* situations will yield *no* such happy result.

In realistic situations, there is, not the pretty arrangement of atoms and surrounding vacuum lately considered, but a more gradual falling off of the relevant forces and materials, from the central part where stones, or tables, may allegedly be found, to the peripheral areas. Now, it is of *course* true that any selected group of atoms will have external relations, to the other atoms in the world, that are *somewhat* different from those of any other. So this fact of gradualness cannot mean that any group's external relations will be identical to any other's. But if we consider any *such* relation that might, with any shred of plausibility, be of *importance* to any *ordinary kind of object*, to tablehood, or to stonehood, then our gradualness would appear to mean quite a lot. For it appears, there is no *such* external relation which *exactly one* group of atoms will have, in any such gradual, realistic state of affairs. Rather, in such situations, *any* such *appropriate external relation that one* complex concrete entity, or its components, may enjoy will be possessed as well by *plenty of others*, which overlap or nest with it. For example, if one such entity "approximates to standing free to such-and-such a degree," many others will similarly approximate to such a relational status. External relations, then, present only another facet of the problem of the many; they do not present us with any promising way to avoid, or to resolve, that problem.

9. COUNTERFACTUAL REASONING, JOINED ENTITIES, AND PARTIAL ENTITIES

If I am to trust them—and what rational alternative is there for me in the matter— scientific sources have it that typical concrete complexes, big enough plausibly to be tables or stones, do not come with any neat natural boundary. In relevant regards, they present the gradualness we associate readily with clouds: in any such regard, stones are to their atoms what clouds are to their droplets. But, let us suppose, for the moment, that this is not so. Let us suppose that I have been misled by my sources, or that they have overlooked some recondite physical factor that, in a typical realistic situation, sets off just one group of atoms there as suitable for constituting a table or stone. And let us suppose, further, that considerations of separators cannot generate our problem (supposing, perhaps, that our reasoning in section 7 was, somehow, actually fallacious). Would nature then have given us a solution to the problem of the many?

Right off, it seems quite incredible that this problem should arise for some kinds of ordinary things, clouds, but not for others, stones. Intuitively, and as I remarked near the outset, the problem appears to concern the vagueness of so many of our common terms, of "cloud" and "stone" alike. Now, anything is possible, so to say, but it seems quite unlikely, indeed, that such problems as these terms may engender can be avoided, or solved, by happy external arrangements of matter.

This intuitive suspicion, that everything should be in the same boat here, however nature should selectively operate, is confirmed by appropriate counterfactual reasoning. For such reasoning, it is apparent, will exhibit our problem of the many in any case, only casting it in a counterfactual form, while retaining its full logical substance. (Indeed, even if clouds themselves were to have sharp natural boundaries, this point would still hold good.) Consider a situation, then, presumably, only hypothetical or counterfactual, in which a typical stone had a clean natural boundary. Perhaps this stone would be made of homogeneous, continuous matter, which presented a proper two-dimensional surface to empty space outside or to surrounding matter of a radically different kind. Well and good, we may first suppose, for such a stone, or for a table carved from it. We must still reason, however, on pain of intellectual prejudice, about other, then hypothetical situations, ones in which any stones present would be constituted of separated atoms, just as all of our actual stones do seem to be. In these latter situations, now presumed hypothetical, all the relevant physical factors fade off gradually—from presumed stone to required surrounding.

It is absurd to suppose that there would be no stones, and no tables, in the more gradual world but that there would be such things in the naturally cooperative world. To be sure, the stones, and tables, in one world would be radically different in kind from those in the other; in relevant regards, we are considering *two kinds of* stones, and of tables. But this even *implies* that, if there are such things in either world, there are stones and tables in both these worlds. Taking the cooperative world as actual, consider the counterfactual gradual world. In a situation involving a typical stone of that world, how many stones *would* there be? By reasoning that is now familiar, or a counterfactual version thereof, one should have to conclude with our dilemma: In the *gradual* world, either there *would be no* stones at all, or else, in any situation involving a *typical* stone, there *would be millions* of stones. But, as we agreed, there will be stones in the cooperative world (if and) only if there would be stones in the gradual world. So, both our well-placed reasoner and we must conclude: Either there are *no* stones *even in the naturally cooperative world*, or else, in the gradual world, in any situation involving a *typical* stone, there *would be millions* of stones. While this is counterfactual, it is quite a dilemma just the same.

Even if nature did not conspire so that we should *more easily perceive* our problem, the problem of the many would still arise. It certainly looks, then, to be a problem about the logic of typical vague terms. In this important regard, then, our new problem parallels the old sorites problem, which, as I have argued elsewhere, is a problem about the logic of such expressions and, so, would arise no matter how the course of nature should run.[22] At all events, we may now be pretty confident that even if my scientific sources have put me on the wrong track, about the putative boundaries of tables and of stones, our problem of the many will still be with us.

There are other considerations which show that not very much depends on getting the actual facts right about the realistic situations we have had so much in focus. Beginning with clouds, as we did, we have been thinking, implicitly at least, of those very boundaries of objects, including boundaries of tables and of stones, that are, so to put it, exposed to the open air. Although it is common for a cloud to have its entire boundary so exposed, it is only rarely, as far as everyday experience goes, that a stone's entire boundary confronts the air, as happens when a stone is hurled through the air. Normally, the stone is resting on the earth, or upon something that is thus resting, or so on.[23] Therefore, in actual typical situations with stones and tables, in contrast to the case with clouds, we find a more problematic part of the object's presumed boundary—the part "adjacent to" (part of the boundary of) some other "solid object." Now, even if there were no problem with the more exposed parts of a stone's boundary or surface, these problematic parts would generate the problem of the many quite well enough. For in these areas, at least, there is no natural break of any sort; there is no natural limiting place for an object, where it leaves off and where another object, which it is touching, first begins.

Situations that we describe as those of two objects touching each other, for example, one with an iron table and an iron ball resting upon it, are on a spectrum with those described as involving two objects joined together. It is mainly, we come to suppose about reality, a matter of *how many atoms* or at least, *how much* matter, the two share at the time in question.[24]

Although cases of these objects touching are extremely common, cases of their being joined are somewhat less so. But, of course, very many of these things that are *not in fact* joined, and which *never will be*, are quite *suitable* for certain sorts of joining. Thus almost any two iron objects can be readily joined, by a suitable use of molten iron or of some other metal. Further, a stone, by way of suitable stone material, may be joined to the earth itself, by being joined to a large rock outcrop, which is part of the earth's crust or mantle. Now, we may assume here that the size of the joining stuff is not great: perhaps, even that only a very slender strand joins the putative items. Thus we might best (try to) preserve our idea that there are still at least two objects in the situation, which are joined, and *not* that there is *just one bigger thing*, into which the two objects were so fused that each of them no longer existed.

Where two things are joined, even by a slender strand, part of the boundary of either must "cut through" the joining material. Throughout this material, even if nowhere else, there is, quite surely, no natural break or separation to be found. Not only is the spatial array of atoms in a baffling blend, but any bonding forces are also quite gradually distributed with regard to any candidate boundary. So, regarding either joined object, *if any* boundary is proper, there will be *many* that are. With either object, let us assume that the "exposed parts" of its boundary present a clean natural separation. Because atoms are so very small and numerous, however, there will still be, in our one example, millions of iron balls joined to millions of iron tables, and in our other, millions of stones joined, right there, with millions of planets. (With continuous, homogeneous matter, the point is, if anything, more obvious; indeed, in such a reality, infinities are easily obtained.) Each stone, we may assume, can share part of its boundary, the exposed part, with each of the others in the situation, but the parts within the joining stuff, quite sufficient to generate our problem, will differ from stone to stone.

With these thoughts about joined entities in mind, compelling counterfactual considerations favor our problem. Unlike those counterfactuals recently considered, these do not concern any esoteric hypothetical worlds but only small variants upon actual situations. So we may consider a typical iron ball and a typical iron table that have not, are not, and never will be joined or, even, ever be touching. And we may ask: What would the situation be, if, contrary to fact, they were joined by a slender band? If they exist now, they should exist then. If they existed then, there must be a boundary separating at least one table there from at least one ball. But, if so, there would have to be millions of such boundaries; thus millions of such balls and tables. So either such a table *does not in fact exist,* and so with tables generally, *or else* in that situation, there *would be millions* of tables.

A related dilemma may be generated entirely in terms of the actual situations of our world: If there are any tables, then, I am confident, somewhere in the actual world there is at least one typical table at some time joined to some other object, while each must retain its distinct identity. But, with that putative table, there are millions of tables in its "immediate situation," or else it does not exist at all. But as far as tablehood goes, that joined entity is not significantly worse off than any prospect. Hence either there really are no tables or else, in that table's situation, there are millions.

It is now a good time for us to consider these issues as they relate to alleged entities that, so to say, are most naturally, or typically, in a joined state or status. I call these *partial entities* because, as with a leg of a table or a branch of a tree, in this natural or typical state, they are each part of some other, larger entity, the implied table, or the tree.[25] The branch, for example, if it really exists, is joined to, or relevantly continuous with, or "at one" with, the tree's trunk and, indeed, with the rest of the tree. If there really is a branch it must stop somewhere, so that it will not include the trunk or, indeed, the whole tree. But any place that the branch stops cannot be better than all the other available places for its stopping. Rather, realistically speaking, it is no better than many others. And even if, absurdly, just one such boundary, or partial boundary, is somehow the very best one there, in regard to yielding an instance of branchhood, millions of others will still be at least very good, too, in the same regard. At all events, if any boundary yields us a *typical* branch, as we may suppose often happens, each of millions of others will yield a "nearby" entity that is, at least, a branch of some sort or other.

It may be helpful, at this juncture, to consider the "opposite" of joining: the separating or breaking off, of a typical branch from a tree. (The typical or optimal state for our stone and planet, so to say, was to be separate, so we joined them, for our consideration. The typical state for our branch and tree is for them to be joined, or together; so we shall separate them, also for our consideration. Thus we are considering each situation along with its "opposite," endeavoring to be comprehensive.) A certain brach was on a certain tree; now it is on the ground. Let us suppose, for simplicity, that there were no losses or gains in the situation, with regard to atoms or stuff, other than those required for this separation. So the atoms that now constitute a certain branch on the ground used to constitute a branch (presumably, the same one) on a tree. Suppose, alternatively, that a break had occurred along a plane very near to our first, actual break but not so near that the material severed would be exactly the same. With this second alternative, we also would have a branch on the ground. This time the branch would be composed of somewhat different atoms, and stuff, than in what went on before; perhaps we now have a slightly greater group or batch. Well, *these* atoms would *also* have constituted a branch back on the tree. So we must conclude that before either break, and even in the absence of any break, really, *each* of these *two* groups of atoms constituted a branch on this tree, providing of course that there was ever *any* branch in the situation (or, even, any tree). But, then, if there was any branch there, there must have been at least two of them, for at a given moment, one given branch cannot both be constituted of a certain number of atoms and, at that same time, also be constituted of another number of them. Equally, at a given time, one branch cannot be constituted of a certain batch of stuff and also of a lesser batch. The reasoning from two to many more is now rather obvious. So this gives us a handy way to see, all over again, our new philosophical problem.

Near the beginning of section 1, I asked what sort of possible world, or underlying reality, would make things hardest for generating our problem of the many. My answer was that it would be a world where ordinary things, clouds, stones, and tables, were composed of continuous homogeneous matter, which made a clean break with, perhaps, entirely empty space that surrounded the object all over. In such a case, we might say, nature itself provided a definite real boundary and, so, in a given situation, just one ordinary object with a uniquely preferred status. But, as our recent reasoning shows, even in such a world as this, our problem of the many arises: it arises counterfactually, of course; still better, it arises for cases of joining balls to tables; perhaps best of all, it arises for cases involving partial entities, for example, a tree and its branches. For it is hard to suppose that a typical, paradigm tree, which we take to have quite a few branches, but not many millions, somehow does exist in such a world either without any branches or with so many as all that. As I said near the outset, of both section 1, and of this present section, our problem concerns the logic of our ordinary terms and not, or not so fundamentally, the underlying arrangements of matter, in this possible world or that one.[26]

Near the beginning of section 6, where I began to extend our arguments about clouds to other ordinary things, I mentioned several sorts of partial entities among the things concerned. Thus I mentioned along with planets, the mountains "upon" them; along with trees, their trunks and branches; and along with tables, their tops and legs. Most importantly, for us, along with human bodies, I mentioned their arms and their hands and even their fingers. I should now mention a further partial entity, another part of our bodies, in the properly broad sense of that term: human brains. Now, in that I believe our bodies to be relevantly like clouds, I do think that the problem of the many arises for our bodies just as it does for clouds, along lines that are, by now, perhaps boringly familiar. So the problem of the many looks to cut deep, and close to home, on that account. But even if there is no relevant similarity between clouds and our bodies, the problem of the many will still be of great philosophic moment, and not just due to counterfactual considerations. For, as a matter of fact, there is no natural separation between any *brain* I have and all of the rest of my body. Since my brain is, I suppose, if not quite a typical one, at least a pretty good example of a brain, this means that my body has, among its parts, millions of concrete complexes, each one of which is a brain of mine. Of course, there is one other alternative, as is characteristic of our problem: Perhaps, instead of having millions of brains, neither I nor you really have any brain at all.

I consider the arguments of this section to be rather important in regard to the problem of the many. But it must be emphasized that their importance is not confined to their providing a hedge against uncertainty, in case my scientific informers have led me astray about the gradualness the real world involves. On the contrary, there are at least two other aspects to their importance. First, because I do believe that my informers are reliable and that our world is relevantly gradual, these present arguments are to be employed, I am confident, *in addition to*, and not instead of, the arguments of previous sections. These present ones, then, are arguments *a fortiori*. Second, and more important, I think, these present arguments, more than those of previous sections, indicate that our problem is one regarding the categories of our own thinking, the logic and meaning of our own terms. The problem is not due to unfortunate circumstances surrounding us, to the messy gradualness that, as it happens, does appear so frequently in the world. That gradualness just helps us to see the problem in the first place; it is no more crucial to the problem itself than is our having started with clouds and not with stones.

10. THE PRINCIPLE OF MINUTE DIFFERENCES, EXCLUSION PRINCIPLES, AND SELECTION PRINCIPLES

Our discussion has confirmed the intuitive idea that the problem of the many is a problem with our *words*, and with such *thoughts* as those words serve to express. Further, it seems from the *vagueness* of the words involved, though perhaps from other of their features as well. That we have a serious problem here, and even that it involves at least the factors just mentioned, I believe quite confidently. What I am less confident of, but do also believe, is that I can provide an *analysis* of this problem, even with a modicum of illuminating detail. Any analysis I should provide would *begin* with what I have called *the principle of minute differences from typical cases*. I should say that such a principle governs (the meaning, or the logic, of) our words for ordinary kinds of things, like 'cloud', 'stone', and 'table', as well as (that of) many other common vague expressions. What I should then do is go on to analyze this principle itself and to exhibit its relations to other principles that also govern these expressions of ours. This latter task, though it perhaps cannot be fully completed, is, I think, one well worth pursuing. But, for various reasons, including the obvious one of space, I will not do so here.

Especially because of the role I expect it to play in our problem's analysis, I used (an instance of) this principle as a premise, the third and final one, in my first introductory argument. Also largely for this reason, in section 4, I construed the third premise of my other introductory argument as being motivated by this principle; then I developed a lengthened "master" version of that argument where the principle figured explicitly. Finally, I appealed many times, in my discussion of examples, to relevant instances of the same proposition. But I do not think that our problem, the problem of the many, can be avoided even if this principle were to be rejected. On the contrary, as I shall argue in this section, and also in the next one, this persistent problem would still be with us and still be in want of any adequate solution.

In a rather general form (and not just confined to clouds or to stones), the principle of minute differences may be put as follows:

> With respect to any *kind of ordinary things*, if something is a *typical member* of the kind, then, if there are entities that differ from that thing, in any respects relevant to being a member of the kind, quite *minutely*, then each of those entities is a member of that kind.[27]

The kinds of things governed by this principle include, of course, clouds and stones and tables; we need not be precise in delimiting the range. The reason the principle governs the kinds is that it governs the terms the kinds' members must satisfy: 'cloud' and 'stone' and 'table', and so on. The reason the principle governs the terms is that they are vague and, without going into the matter, have their vagueness involved in such discriminations as the terms purport to make.[28]

In almost any context, I have found it very easy to get firm assent to this principle and even to principles that are more ambitious. Indeed, people seem so sure of it that they consider it quite trivial, perhaps a trivial exhibition of the meaning of 'typical' and of its near synonyms, like 'paradigm'. Only in the context where our new problem is introduced have I found any resistance to the principle.

Because I have used the principle in introductory arguments, one might think that by rejecting the principle, one could easily reject those arguments and, so, that one could avoid the problems the arguments were used to introduce. But such a thought is *not* correct. In the *first* place, we must notice that the principle is nowhere used in the second of my arguments, the one about clouds as bounded entities. So its rejection would leave that argument just as it is, still introducing our problem. To be sure, in section 4, I advanced the principle as (part of) an *analysis*, or *explanation*, of (part of) that argument. But my explanation of the argument might of course be wrong even though the reasoning to be explained is itself philosophically adequate. In the *second* place, in a manner most harmonious with the preceding remarks, the first of my introductory arguments, about clouds as concrete complexes, may be easily revised, so that the principle is not employed there either. Retaining its first premise, we just compress that argument, so that, instead of its previous (2) and (3), the argument's only other premise now reads like this:

> (2′)   If something is a *typical* cloud, then *any* situation involving it contains, in addition to itself, millions of other complex concrete entities, each of which is a cloud.

Regarding our realistic situations, with a plethora of overlapping concrete complexes, what this premise says may be put like this: either nothing there is *so* favored that it is a *typical* cloud *or else* there are *millions* of things there each of which is (well favored *enough* that it is) a cloud, at least of some sort or other. Our principle may be regarded now as an explanation of (part of) the appeal of this very attractive simple premise, (2'). Although I think not, perhaps that explanation is erroneous. Even so, that would scarcely give one much reason to reject (2') itself, which, in any case, would be very hard to deny in any philosophically adequate manner.

So a rejection of our principle, a dubious move in any event, will fail to solve our problem. That this is so should be rather evident; why it is takes a bit more thought to see. The reason begins to emerge when one asks: If we reject that principle, what should we replace it with, for surely at least something much like it does seem to be required? The answer to be given will be, most likely and most plausibly, a longer, hedged version of the original simpler statement. In the longer version, we begin the same way and, then, tack on at the end an appropriate *exception clause*. Thus we might say that each of those (minutely differing) entities is a member of the same kind *except for those that* share "too much" space, or "too much" matter, with the aforementioned putative typical member. As reasoning can make clear enough, it is *very* hard to state an exception clause that stands up to any scrutiny. (When we realize that the relevant principle must govern the thinking of many stupid little children, things look better and better for our original simple version.) But with regard to the problem of the many, that great difficulty is a somewhat peripheral matter, which we can well afford to pass over.

The main matter here is this. Such an exception clause will provide, at best, only an *exclusion principle*. This sort of principle says, in effect, that, in those situations it governs, *at most* one entity has the status it accords, for instance, the status of being a cloud or a stone. Such a principle says that there can be at most one winner, so to say, and that any other competitors will then be excluded from sharing the same status. With regard to our problem, it is surprising how much stock philosophers want to place in some such principles of exclusion. When I propose our new problem quite informally, as I did in section 1, many philosophers think they can solve it, and right away, too, by adducing some exclusion principle. Indeed, this has occurred with some very able philosophers. But, nevertheless, it is only an unfortunate error.

A certain philosopher thinks he sees just one table right there before him. He is rather baffled by my suggestion of overlapping complexes fading off into the surrounding. To relieve this puzzlement, he reaches into his bag of tools, or tricks. What might he employ? For a start, he might resort to this old saw: Two physical objects cannot both occupy the very same space at the very same time.[29] This is an exclusion principle. For what does such a principle say? In general terms it says something like this: If two entities both satisfy a certain description or, in a very general sense of the term, both have a certain property, then they cannot both satisfy a certain second description or possess a certain second property; at least one of the two compared entities will be *excluded* from satisfying the second description.

What about the saw in hand? So if two entities both satisfy 'physical object', they cannot both satisfy 'occupies precisely all of spatial region R at exactly moment of time T'. So, too, if two entities both satisfy the latter description, then at most one of them can satisfy the former, that is, can be a physical object. (Perhaps one of them will be a shadow, or whatever.)

The exclusion principles employed in an attempt to escape our problem will, experience shows, differ in several ways from the very common sort of proposition just considered. First, instead of speaking so generally of "physical objects," our objector will mention a specific ordinary kind of thing, for example, chairs, or stones. Second, the concrete complexes we must consider, as the only likely candidates for being stones, or chairs, do *not*, at a given moment, occupy *exactly the same* space as each other; rather, they overlap, or nest, or whatever. So for an exclusion principle that even *seems* to apply, one needs some other description that is a suitable approximation to, and substitution for, one that specifies such exact sameness. Hence, vague and dubious as it may be, some such principle as the following is likely to be adduced: If two entities both occupy *nearly*, or *virtually*, all of the same space, as each other, at a given moment of time, then they cannot both be chairs, or both be stones. Or, perhaps, some near variant will be employed: If two entities both are constituted of *almost*, or of *virtually*, the exact same matter, or (group of) atoms, at a given moment of time, then they cannot both be chairs, or both be stones.

Let us assume, what might be true, that our thinking about stones, and about chairs, is governed by some such exclusion principles, perhaps even analytically so governed. And let us take this supposition a good deal farther: At least one such principle is (coherently and properly) applicable to the bafflingly gradual situations reality so often involves. Without further argument, this is a pretty strong assumption for us to be making now.[30] But let us do so anyway and thus give our stimulated objector what he seems to want. Will such a principle allow him to avoid, or to solve, our problem?

In point of fact, it cannot even begin to do anything of the kind. For what is needed for our problem's solution, if there is any to be had, is a proposition of an entirely different sort, which I will call a *selection principle*. A selection principle, one that is both applicable and correct, will single out, or *select*, from among the entities in a situation, those that satisfy a certain description or possess a certain property (or, in particular, that are of a certain kind). For our problem, if a principle will help, we need such a *selection* principle. Further, we need one that will select *just one* entity, from a nearby multitude, as being of a certain kind, one that common sense affirms. So we require *not* any exclusion principle but a *selection* principle that will, in realistic situations, *select* just one complex thing, from among all the concrete complexes present, as, say, *the only stone there*.

But of course finding such an adequate selection principle, or even anything that approaches it, seems to be very much harder than formulating exclusion principles or approximations to principles of exclusion. For the former, but not the latter, amounts to nothing less than a solution to our new problem. Just so, as far as all these principles go, we are no better off with our problem that ever we were. The role of exclusion principles, in these matters, is not what some philosophers have expected.

What *is* the logical role, in these matters, of an adequate exclusion principle (if there be any such adequate proposition)? It will say, as we have noted, that in situations where entities compete with each other for a certain description or a certain status, for example, for being a stone, they cannot both achieve it: there can be *at most one* winner. Consider our realistic situation, with all its complex candidates for stonehood. Suppose that an exclusion principle about stones applies, perhaps concerning the sharing of "too much" space or "too many" atoms. What will the principle say, then, about the concrete complexes present? It will say, simply, that *at most* one of those concrete entities is the situation's sole stone. Of course, such an exclusion principle is entirely compatible with any adequate selection principle, but it is *also compatible* with the *absence* of any such principle of selection.

With or without using the principle of minute differences, what our reasoning has *already* yielded is that we have a *dilemma*: In a relevantly typical situation, at any given moment of time, *either* there are many stones there *or else* there are none. Now, our exclusion principle, supposing the most for it, will provide us with this further information, which is entirely compatible with that disjunction: There *are not many* stones there then. So if there is such an adequate exclusion principle, it will, in the absence of a selection principle, "resolve" our dilemma only in a most radical and Parmenidian way. There really are no stones there then, nor any stones at all.

This, after all, is the depressing truth about exclusion principles: They do nothing to escape our problem; rather, given that problem, which has by now been provided from various quarters, they only force us toward the more radical of the two options it poses. Why, then, have philosophers, perhaps in some hurry to escape our problem, assumed that exclusion principles might be of any use? Although it must be somewhat speculative, I think the answer lies along these lines: These philosophers have simply assumed that there really *must* be *at least one* stone in the situation, that this *must* be an *absolute given*, which shall never be questioned, on any account. Now, *given this as an absolute, unmovable dictum*, an exclusion principle *will* yield the result that there is one, and only one, stone present. But, of course, to reach that conclusion in *such* a manner is just to be so deeply in the grip of our ordinary common sense suppositions as to fail, if only temporarily, to consider our problem at all seriously. It is to forget, to ignore, or to misunderstand the problem, rather than to solve it. For if one does think about the problem seriously, one will realize that, in terms of principles, the problem is one of finding an adequate *selection* principle, which is quite a different matter from bringing any exclusion principle to bear. At the very least, we might say, our problem is one of finding, if not the required principle itself, a *philosophically adequate reason* to believe in the existence of some appropriate *selective* proposition, even while no such reason appears anywhere to be found.

Perhaps the most important point of his section is the one just made, a point which, I suggest, is quite important in its own right. This point also has importance, however, for the examination of our principle of minute differences, as I have already suggested. We may see this a bit more clearly now and, partly as a result of that clearer perception, build a case for that principle, in its simple, original version.

As will be remembered, even those who object to our simple principle are wont to agree that something like it governs such typical vague terms as 'cloud' and 'stone' and 'table'. The objectors think, however, that only a more complex (version of our) principle, holds true here, one with a suitable exception clause. Their motivation for that complicating retreat is that they are supposing that such a complicated principle will serve to solve our problem, while retaining what is right in the simple version. As we already saw, that problem can be introduced without employment of *any* such principle, simple or complex; so, for that reason alone, the motivation is undermined. We can now see more clearly that this must indeed be so. Suppose that our vague terms *are* governed by such a complicated minute difference principle, complete with its exception clause. All that such a principle will do, then, is impose on our problem, which is already upon us, a certain exclusion principle, the one stated or implied in that exception clause. Hence, even if it does govern our key terms here, such a principle will only pressure us *from* the many toward the *none*, a most radical result, and will in no wise afford common sense any comfort.

Because I would like my thoughts about our problem's *analysis* to be right, I tend to favor the principle of minute differences in its simple, exceptionless version. But, even apart from this theoretical partiality on my part, I can see no reason to deny this principle, which is as intuitively appealing as it is simple, especially as doing that will be of no use in solving our problem. Nor have I ever seen any reason to accept the more complicated statements, with exception clauses, which are, apparently, as *ad hoc* as they are complex, especially as doing that will, equally, be to no avail here. The point on which I should like to focus now, however, by way of concluding this section, is neither of these two rather evident ideas. Rather, it is a third thought concerning the relation between them, which, while somewhat less evident, is really not a very difficult conception either. It is this: The simple, original principle and a more complex version, with an exception clause, are *logically compatible* with each other. Thus the acceptance of the latter, dubious in any case, *would not in itself rationally require* the rejection of the simple, intuitive principle of minute differences. On the contrary, the two together may hold, both of them governing the vague terms at issue. What would that joint holding imply? It would imply that key vague terms were logically inconsistent expressions, including 'typical cloud' and 'typical stone'.[31] That is, the supposition that anything satisfied these expressions would logically yield a contradiction: certain complex entities that differed minutely from a putative satisfier of 'typical stone' *both would be* stones (by the simple version) and *also* (by the complicated version) *would not* be. For the strongest of reasons, then, there would be no typical clouds or typical stones. As we have already agreed, if no typical clouds, then, in fact, no clouds at all. Hence, with both principles holding, our dilemma would not only be relevantly yielded but, as has happened so many times before, it would be resolved only in movement toward its more radical side.

11. SOME QUESTIONS FOR COMMON SENSE PHILOSOPHY

Our arguments, I believe, pose a formidable dilemma for common sense thinking. In our time, indeed, since Moore's rejection of idealism, this common thinking has been the cornerstone of the most dominant philosophy, which I call *common sense philosophy*. So our arguments challenge this dominant philosophy as well. They seek to reject, in turn, the ideas of Moore and of his very many followers.

However intriguing this may be, few will allow themselves to be convinced, by these or any other arguments. They will assume, instead, that some flaw, no matter how difficult to specify, must always be present. For common sense philosophy is not just another of philosophy's schools. Rather, it does not only rely on, but also advocates and supports, our common sense thinking, which is society's common ground. Consequently, the power of any mere arguments to move us away from this philosophy will be quite limited. Although I should like to pursue our arguments further, I am also anxious for some of this radical movement to occur. So I will now forego further examination of our challenging patterns of reasoning.

I cannot possibly tell what will prove most effective in getting our problem of the many to be seriously considered as a genuine philosophic dilemma. But it is my hope that *if you ask yourself certain questions*, as I have often done, something toward this end may be accomplished. Now, up until this point, we have often just *assumed* what common sense would have be so: That where people judged, or were wont to judge, that a typical cloud or stone was present, there really was *at least one such* cloud or stone. This assumption led to another implicit in it: *Everything required* for the existence of the assumed cloud or stone, such as a suitable boundary, was in fact there, in the situation. Now, these assumptions are very often made in everyday life, at least implicitly. For the sake of argument, in our philosophic reasoning, we have made them, too, though in a rather more tentative, or even hypothetical, fashion. But let us now become, or at least try to become, a bit more doubtful about these common existential suppostions.

In this mildly skeptical frame of mind, let us seriously ask: What is there in these ordinary situations, with so many small constituents so gradually dispersed about, that could be, or could serve as, the boundary for *any* (typical) cloud or for even a single stone? If you ask this question seriously, and try to think of the underlying situations concerned in all their detail, then, I suggest, you will find no available answer to be very convincing. Nevertheless, as there must be some suitable answer here for there to be any clouds or stones, it should not be hard for you to manage to find an answer that will at first seem a bit plausible. For example, you might hit on the idea that what will do is whatever enclosing curved limiter yields a certain average density throughout a certain more or less well-pictured region. But examining any such answer closely, I suggest, will result in a certain amount of depression; for, in the baffling morass of indicated continuents, there seems no reason to think that our idea of a cloud or of a stone really does require any *given particular* average density, complexity of structures, or whatever, and *not* some *other* one that is only *minutely* different from it. So the result your alleged boundary is to yield seems impossibly arbitrary, rather than well enough determined by real features of the situation. This absurd arbitrariness, and the depression about any allegedly adequate answer, is closely connected with sorites arguments. As we have foresaken these arguments for most of our essay, so we shall now again pass over these annoying causes of discontent.

We shall still have plenty enough to worry about in thinking over such answers as initially seem even remotely plausible. For we must now ask ourselves the yet more pointed question: What can there be, in these bafflingly gradual situations, that can be the boundary of, not just *a* genuine cloud, or *a* real stone, but the *only* cloud, or the *single* stone, there? To obviate our argument's dilemma, we must find an answer to these questions that is philosophically adequate. But what actual feature can there be, in the baffling morass of separated items, which can select just one complex as uniquely filling the bill? If we take anything that is even remotely plausible as a requirement for a cloud's boundary, like whatever encloses a "largest" complex of just such a particular average density, then there will be very many items that meet it equally well, as our thoughts of overlapping have so often indicated. If we take something even remotely plausible for a stone itself, for example, a "largest" item there that has such-and-such a complexity of structure, overlapping complexes again prevent any answer from adequately bringing forth a uniquely well-qualified candidate. And, as we have seen, looking to "external relations" for help will fail to narrow things down adequately.

No matter what property we pick, to use an available expression, it seems inconceivable that, in realistic situations, there is precisely one entity that possesses it and, *in virtue of that*, is actually the only cloud or stone there present. After this is thought over to any great extent, the idea that there *must be* some answer begins to look badly founded, at least, perhaps even quite absurd. Now, it is no good to say something like "the property of being *the* cloud in the situation," hoping to specify thereby the appropriate uniquely possessed attribute. That would just beg the question here. For you may *readily question* on what real basis, and so *whether or not* at all, *anything does satisfy* the offered *demanding* description. Indeed, we may put the matter in terms of these descriptions themselves, assuming them to be well formulated. For when we ask ourselves what it could be, in realistic situations, that would give such descriptions semantically proper application, we are apt to bounce between two walls: Either we shall think of something that, realistically, is absent altogether, such as certain of those natural breaks in reality which have been previously remarked, or else it will be something, like those features so recently considered, that is many times exemplified. Now, for all our queries and failures, there just might, I suppose, really be something present that we are always overlooking and which, by fortunate circumstance, in many typical situations, always picks out just one (putative boundary as proper, and so with just one) putative cloud or stone. But, unless we can describe or specify it, at least vaguely and obliquely, we should have our doubts. For, otherwise, we should have to assume a great deal. We shall have to assume that, very often, many stupid little children are somehow made to get things right, as to the small number of nearby real clouds or stones, by the operation of some imperceptible, perhaps ineffable, and certainly quite mysterious factor. Unless it is some truly Almighty Father Who so manages things for us all, we may question whether those blissful toddlers are so well placed as common sense would have them be.

In answer to the present line of questioning, certain lines of reply are predictable. Perhaps the chief among these, which I shall discuss as representative, proceeds from a certain view about ordinary vague expressions. On this view, such terms are incomplete:[32] In addition to some cases for which they are positively defined, and also some for which they are defined so as not to apply, there are still others where the matter of their semantic application is *left open*. Thus it will be *up to us*, in certain circumstances, to decide whether or not such terms shall apply. Now, it has been argued elsewhere that this view is actually incoherent and so cannot properly represent the semantics of any expressions at all.[33] But we shall now pass over any such great difficulties. For whether or not those problems prove fatal for the view even quite generally, certain more specific questions may be raised regarding any attempt to apply such a view to the questions that we have been asking.

It is not clear exactly how the intermediate steps should go, but if this view about vagueness is to help us with our present questions, it will at some point have to incorporate an idea at least much like this one: Our language and thinking, on the one hand, and the objective external facts, on the other, all as determinate as they are at the time, together specify *that there is exactly one* cloud or stone in our typical situation; but they *leave open* the matter as to *which* entity in the situation is the unique present cloud or stone, which *further matter* is thus *left open for us* to decide. Looking to preserve common sense, as it does, and offering us the sort of putative logical distinction that might seem to explain some confused questioning directed against society's common ground, this reply is bound to have an appeal for us that is both marked and quite immediate. But if we examine the matter with care, the offered distinction will do little to settle our questioning attitude. For according to what it delivers, which entity in our situation is a cloud or is a stone will be, at least in many cases, a matter of human thought and decision; whereas the truth of these matters is that, supposing there is to be any real stones or clouds, which entities are these is *not* something relevantly dependent upon what we happen to think or decide.

It is, to be sure, a matter of human convention, and so in a way dependent on our thinking, *which things we call 'stones', which 'clouds',* and which neither, supposing, of course, what we may now allow, that we actually do call some things by these words or names. This is because we have endowed certain sorts of marks and sounds with certain semantic properties, however accomplished, and we may subsequently change these matters by relevantly similar processes. But all of this, as should be obvious enough, is quite irrelevant to the sort of dependency upon our thought required by our considered line of reply. For one thing, with regard to any situation, it is similarly up to us whether we should call *anything at all* a 'stone' or should ever have done so.

In certain situations, it is of course a matter of human action, and its consequences, as to which things present are stones and, in this century, even which are clouds. In the course of events, we can effect the arrangements of matter, so that even which things are plausible candidates for stonehood can be the result of what we do. And since these actions, or many of them, are in turn dependent on our thoughts or decisions, in many cases these matters are correlatively dependent on what we think or decide, or so we may now suppose. But, like the one just previously considered, this is not the dependence required by our reply, for it, too, applies just as much to each branch of the distinction the reply offers. In this sense or respect, it is even dependent on human thought, in various situations, that there is *any* stone present at all.

No, what our reply requires is a good deal more. It requires that even after everything is so specified and determinate, both in our language and in our environment, so that it is *true* that a certain typical situation does contain a *single stone*, it is *still up to us* to decide *which* entity there is the only stone present. And this, I suggest, is to require of a matter that must be relevantly objective, or independent of our thoughts, that it be thus dependent upon our thinking, that it be *only* a quite *subjective* matter *instead*. Now, with various artifacts, for example, chairs, there may be some *shred* of plausibility in claiming that there is no such condition of objectivity. For example, one might suppose that it may be a matter of which of several nearby things certain people right now most prefer to sit upon, or something of the like. And, just perhaps, continuing this line of thinking, this might mean no relevant objectivity for the matter of which of those things is the sole available chair. Now, even here, with such artifacts, the suggestion is *not* very plausible. But with stones and clouds, which entities, if they exist, are entirely *natural* things, the case for any such relevant dependence on our thought appears to have *nothing whatever* to be said for it. So our considered reply, with the distinction it seems to offer, will not answer our baffling questions about clouds and stones. Nor, then, as some *general* answer is presumably required, will it do even for ordinary artifacts.

I have argued that an attempt to reply to our questioning, a rather good representative of such attempts, will fail for an instructive reason. It will overlook, or ignore, a condition governing the terms for the kinds in question, which it must do in order for a distinction it offers to be applicable.[34] In sum, our questions have led to putative replies, and these in turn to arguments that the replies are inadequate. It appears, then, that there really are no adequate, unobjectionable answers to be found.

12. SOME IMPLIED PROBLEMS

The problem of the many poses a formidable challenge, I submit, to our common sense thinking. Were only this by now familiar challenge involved, with no substantial further difficulties as well, our new problem should be of some considerable interest to serious philosophers. But, in fact, the problematic situation is quite the reverse of the isolated conundrum to which I just alluded. On the contrary, the problem of the many implies, for our philosophical consideration, a number of serious further difficulties. In this final section, I shall discuss, very briefly indeed, three (sets) of these. In each case, my discussion will primarily, if not entirely, concern implications of the second, multitudinous disjunct of our dilemma. The reason for this partiality will be apparent: Generally, if the first, Parmenidian situation is presumed to obtain, things will be *so bad* for common sense that there will be little *room left* for any further particular problems to arise. But just as I shall, for this obvious reason, be mainly engaged in disclosing problems in the multitudinous one of our two alternatives, so it will be the other, nihilistic one toward which these implied difficulties will be pointing the way. As will be apparent, in each of these three problem areas, the trouble first arises in what might be deemed a *metaphysical* version; but as soon as one might think to make light of such a problem, an *epistemological* version is right on hand to mystify.

A. The Problem of Having an Object in Mind

We commonly suppose that, regarding various existing ordinary things, several nearby stones, for example, we can think of each of them, or have each in mind. Sometimes, we may think of them all together. But we also presume that often we think of just one of them, individually: Often, if I choose, I can close my eyes and think of just one actual stone. But if there are millions of "overlapping stones" before me, in the manner that our prior reasoning has brought to light, how am I to think of a single one of them, while not then equally thinking of so many others, with each of which "it" might so easily be confused? The presumed *relations* between us, and our minds, and ordinary material complexes look to be in deep trouble.

I look at what I take to be a single stone, right over there. Then I close my eyes and think to myself, "It is quartz." But *what* is *it*? It had better be a stone, at least, or else it is extremely doubtful that, in *this* very common and in *no way untoward* situation, I am thinking of any real object at all. But, then, there are so many stones right there; if any are quartz, they all are. So, being charitable to myself, in any sense or way, will be of no help here. If there is no particular one I have in mind, then what am I doing in conjuring up the sentence subvocally, as I do, "It is quartz." That will not even be grammatically appropriate for expressing any truth that I might be grasping about real objects over there; I should better think, "They are quartz." But, if relevantly more appropriate, that latter thought would be quite disconcerting.

We think it true, and even important, that each of us often does concentrate upon just such a one existing entity, without then and there having to contemplate as well millions of others so very much like it. Indeed, if we *never* do engage in such *individualistic* thinking regarding members of a certain kind of things, e.g., regarding tables or stones, it might well be doubted that we ever think *at all* of any real things of that kind. So this problem is rather serious. But how is it to be resolved? I suggest that up until now, at least, not one of us has ever really thought of any existing stone or table or human hand.[35]

Supposing there are stones, there are millions right there now. How should I individuate in thought any one of them, so that I might contemplate it alone, without the confusion, or intrusion, of so many competitors for my attention? Any mark I could observe would be shared by so many; so would be any description, or property, I should have even the slightest reason to think is exemplified there at least once. I could, of course, *formulate* a demanding description that *calls* for unique satisfaction, e.g., '*the largest* stone over *there*'. But as just indicated, there is no reason whatever to suppose such a description to be satisfied. With all that overlap going on, it is far from clear that there is a single largest stone there, whether in mass, in volume, or whatever. What might be largest in one regard might well not be in another. And who knows how many "regards" there are here? But even if, perhaps by God's design, there were one, clearly and univocally, largest stone right there, it seems incredible that I should have *it alone* in mind just by my thinking of those quoted five *words*. Rather, there should be some real *connection* between me, and even those demanding words of mine, and, at the other end, the single stone there that is the real object of my thought. With so many stones there, however, what connection could, appropriately and uniquely, link me, or my words, to just the single stone I am supposed to be contemplating?[36]

Perhaps there is some special *causal* connection between me, or my thoughts and words, and a single nearby stone that is to be the sole object of a certain salient idea of mine? Putative causal accounts of things are now much in vogue. This is particularly true as regards a person's thoughts about a given existing concrete entity and as regards such language as may be most appropriate to that thought or to its expresion. Finding the notion of causation itself at best obscure and suspecting it to be even semantically inapplicable, I find little illumination from these fashionable accounts.[37] But even discounting any such general suspicion, an allusion to causal processes would seem futile for the particular problem at hand. For consider two very similar, barely overlapping quartz stones over there. Whatever causal relations the one beares to me are *very* closely matched by those the other bears. How, then, is just one of them to be causally connected to me so that I am thinking now only of it, and not of the other, whose causal credentials seem so relevantly similar?

Whether it involves causation or not, *perception* might be thought to provide the link from my thought to its sole relevant object. Normally, of course, we suppose that this is how most individualistic thinking gets started. But then, normally, we suppose that a person can, and often does, *perceptually discriminate* a certain stone from its background and from whatever other stones might be nearby. However, given our prior reasonings, it seems that such perceptual discrimination never does in fact place, and that our common, sanguine idea that it does is but a comfortable illusion. Indeed, rather than solving our problem of individualistic thought, reflections about perception now mean further problems for us there, as well. For if we *do not ever* perceptually discriminate one stone from millions of others, it is *doubtful* that we ever *perceive* stones at all. What, then, *if anything, do* we actually perceive? This is a question I suggest, that we should take quite seriously. Just so, we should not assume, at the outset, that any affirmative answer, especially one congenial to common sense, will prove philosophically impeccable.

Largely owing to work of Kripke and of Donnellan, *ordinary proper names*, of individual people, places, and things, have recently been the focus of much discussion.[38] Accordingly, we might expect some philosophers to think that by an *act of naming* one might bring before one's mind just a single ordinary concrete entity, just one real stone, for example. Frankly, following the tradition of Russell and Quine, I cannot see how having such proper names around, like 'Plymouth Rock' or 'Felix', can yield solutions to *any* fundamental philosophic problems. But even if one doubts the generalization, in regard to the particular case at hand the negative point is plain. Especially with no help in sight from causal or perceptual processes, how am I to name just one stone here 'Plymouth Rock' or 'Oscar' or 'Felix', while leaving its overlappers quite anonymous? There seems no more prospect of bringing this off than of individually thinking of just one nearby instance of stonehood. So, again, rather than solving our problem, the appeal to a familiarly presumed activity calls that activity itself into question. It is doubtful, then, that we have ever named any ordinary thing without at the same time naming so many others much like it (whatever the situation with regard to naming people). But it is also hard to believe that we have, in some happy act, actually named millions of things each 'The Rosetta Stone' or each 'Plymouth Rock'. So we have another problem to take seriously: Have we ever really *named* any *ordinary things* at all?

If I have never thought individually of any stone, or any other common object, then it seems doubtful, to put it mildly, that I have ever thought of any such things collectively either. Accordingly, it may well be that I have never *thought of* any real stones at all, or tables, or even human hands. If that is so, then it would seem that *a fortiori* I do not *know* anything *about these entities*, however commonly I might otherwise suppose. In discussing this (complex of) problem(s), I have been sketching, then, a new route to a view of epistemological skepticism, concerning much, if not all, of our alleged knowledge of the external material world. The alternative of the many, we may say, means many problems for common sense. What of the none, our first, Parmenidian alternative? Well, if there are no real stones or hands, then it is as clear as reason's light that no real hand or stone will be the object of my thought, nor within the scope of any human knowledge.

B. The Problem of Identity through Time

Throughout this essay, our focus has been upon situations at a given moment, or instant, of time. Such a moment may be conceived as without duration altogether or else, for any who are squeamish of such a fine idea, with only such extremely short duration that any changes taking place therein would be negligible with regard to our problem. In reality, however, time goes on, and various significant changes do occur with respect to any of the putative ordinary things that have been our concern. In particular, with any significant lapse of time, these things, stones, for example, lose some of their salient constituents, some molecules or atoms. (They also gain some such constituents; typically, they lose "a lot" while gaining "a few.") It is commonly supposed that an ordinary thing can survive the loss of some such constituents, even without replacement, providing that their number, and their role in its structural arrangement, is not "too great."[39] I think that this is right and, indeed, that some such condition governs the logic of vague terms like 'stone', at least 'typical stone'. But if we consider our new problem's implications, there is a lot of trouble here.

Consider an atom or molecule that leaves its place within the boundary of a typical stone, stone B, and travels outward a very short distance, so that it is now alongside, perhaps even "nosing ahead of," one of those atoms which, just before, was right outside, and very close to, that aforesaid boundary. In reality, if there are stones, this happens with any one of them, during any hundredth of a second (and, generally, a lot more happens, too). Before the movement of this atom, there were at least two stones in our situation, B and a slightly larger stone, C, which, at our outset, contained all B's atoms plus that one, just mentioned, right outside B's initial boundary. Now, what are we to think once the movement has taken place?

To simplify matters, but not in any way that these present difficulties require, we shall think of stones as distinguished by those atoms which compose them. We ignore, for example, possible infinities that separators might impose. (This mirrors our earlier thinking of clouds just at the level of droplets.) Given this, and even with only the one small movement to consider, it seems there is an impossible problem for the continued existence of stone B, thus for the identity through any significant time of any real stone. We may call this problem of identity, which is of course not confined to stones, *the problem of competition for parts.* The propriety of this name will become apparent soon enough, as we consider along with B and C, a third stone, A, smaller than either of them, and as we then notice the struggles between stone B and each of the two others.

Before the traveler's journey, *the atom that it is now alongside*, or just nosing out, *used to be* a constituent (of stone C) *necessary and sufficient to distinguish C*, the larger of our first two stones, *from* B, the smaller. Given this, can B survive the journey of that traveling atom? Common sense, of course, says "yes." But an affirmative answer leads to a dilemma. This is how the dilemma begins: *The traveling atom, itself,* also before its journey, *distinguished B*, the smaller of our two stones, *from A, a smaller stone still.* That smallest stone of these three had *all the atoms of* B, the middle stone, *except for the to-be-traveler.* So for B to remain distinct from such a smaller A, *B must retain the traveler.* Otherwise B will cease to exist (or else B will entirely coalesce with A so that, *from that time ever onward*, the two will become objectively indistinguishable, which is hardly a serious option). This is the first horn of the dilemma. Let us see the second.

If B, the middle stone, is to *retain* the traveler, then its boundary must move outward, so that that atom is still internal to it and not external. Such an adjustment, however, means that the alongside, or nosed-out, atom will also be within B's boundary and so part of B itself. This means, in turn, that the largest stone of the three, stone C, must now cease to exist (or else C entirely coalesces with B, from then ever onward, those two becoming forever indistinguishable, again not a serious alternative). But the relation of the smallest to the middle, of A to B, is relevantly the same as that of the middle to the largest, of B to C, so that there is nothing to choose between the two horns of our dilemma here. First, it is arbitrary, and so not true, to think that, while losing the traveler, B, but not A, continued to exist. And second, it is just as arbitrary, and so just as false, to think that, while retaining the traveler, B, but not C, continued to exist. As those are the only options for B's continued existence, and neither holds, the traveler's little journey means an end to B's existence.

Like our stone B, any typical real stone can be treated as the middle member in a trio of the kind just considered.[40] Just so, with any such stone, the loss of a tiny peripheral part means an end of it. But such losses occur in any hundredth of a second. So a typical stone, if it exists at all, does so for no more than a hundredth of a second. This result does three things. *First*, it makes the second disjunct of our original problematic dilemma yet more unpalatable: (at any time) in any case involving a typical stone, there are millions of stones, and all of these last for no more than a hundredth of a second. *Second*, again assuming that there are stones, it makes it even more doubtful that we ever have a single one in mind. And, if anything, it is more doubtful still that we ever perceive any stone, much less that we should gain knowledge of any. For not only is any putative one so difficult to discriminate from many others, but, if it exists at all, any stone is so soon gone that we never get much of a chance even to try. Nor are we much better off with any other sort of ordinary material thing. So our epistemological problems, having already been bad enough, get even worse.

Third, and finally for now, we should notice that the argument just sketched does *not* contradict the common sense assumption that, at least in realistic situations, any typical stone can survive the loss of a tiny peripheral part. For *that* assumption does not itself imply the existence of any typical stones. Rather, it says:

(cs)   If there are any typical stones, then, in realistic situations, each of them can, and, given science, even will, survive the loss of a tiny peripheral part; that is, such a stone will still exist, whether or not it is still a typical stone.

What we have argued for is a conditional with the same antecent and a consequent to opposite effect. Thus, joining our recent conclusion with the entirely plausible statement (cs) yields, instead of any contradiction, the result that there are no typical stones.[41] And this, in conjunction with the all but indubitable idea that if there are stones, then some (in fact) are typical ones, yields, in turn, the consequence that there really are no stones at all. So, three times over, considerations about time pressure us to our problem's nihilistic, or Parmenidian, side.

C. The Problem of Minds and Bodies

A person's presumed body, just like its supposed salient parts, is susceptible of our problematic dilemma. Even brains, as we saw near the end of section 10, bear the brunt of our problem. And whereas the numbers, in the second disjunct, might not rise quite so high so fast, individual cells, including neurons, would each also present a momentary overlapping multitude. When changes through time are considered, as sooner or later they must, no typical human body, or any such part of it, would seem to last long enough to be of any use. (Or else, what is less plausible, though hardly less troubling, there will be with respect to any such body, or relevant part, very many indistinguishable from it at any time.) If this is our physical situation, what is one to make of one's own nature and, then, of one's relation to any other sentient beings?

Whether or not he is a physical entity, a person, if a real existent at all, must be an utterly concrete individual and in no wise any mere abstraction. But if one is a physical entity, then, it is only plausible, one should be a rather complex one and not some elementary particle, or atom, or whatever. Granting this, a physical nature will imply for oneself, and for people generally, our problem of the many: Either one does not exist, and there are no people, or else in any case of any typical person, or even of any pretty good example, there are, right then and there, millions of people present. And then, of course, further problems will arise: No typical real person will last for even a hundredth of a second, your alleged self included, not long enough to formulate, or to understand, even a rather simple thought or idea. (Or else, and less likely, right where you are now, there are many objectively indistinguishable people: So, who can you be, anyway?)

At first blush, then, our problem would give comfort to dualistic views regarding the mental and the physical: I am a concrete entity that is *only* mental or spiritual in nature and *not* physical or material. So that I might be distinct from other entities, and last long enough to think, I would lack spatial extent altogether. But although such a move might formally avoid those difficulties we have been disclosing, it leaves one, to put it mildly, with a very puzzling epistemological situation. For one assumes that each of us knows about various other people, whom one distinguishes each from the other. But, given our prior reasoning, no such knowledge seems possessed by anyone.

If I ever am successful in distinguishing one person from others, so that I might know something about him, then at least sometimes I do this by distinguishing a particular body from others, which body I take to be *his* body. This involves the thought, on my part, that this particular body is the body of a single person and that this person has no body but this one. But our problem pulls the ground out from such common implicit thinking. For either there are not any human bodies, in which case this presumed way of distinguishing people is without any real substance, or else there are so many bodies there to go on that the associated thought of other persons runs wild. Given the latter option, we should ask: Are there millions of people right across the way from me now, where there "seems to be just one, or two"? And, if so, who's who?

Even in my own case, trouble is very near. Either I have no body at all, even none as a useful shell or appendage, or else there are millions right around where I take mine to be. The former alternative is obviously troubling, but the latter gives one troubles too. With all these bodies about, and so very many brains as well, how many are really mine (even for a moment)? How can I possibly know? Might there not be, instead of just me with millions of bodies and brains, millions of people "right here now," each "with much of my perspective on things" and a slightly different body and brain (momentarily) to employ? How is *anyone to know* what is going on here, *myself included*? Unless they are extremely skeptical, then, metaphysical dualists, regarding mind and body, can take only cold comfort from our problem. In the associated epistemological area, they face a very severe form of skepticism, a very severe version of the problem of other minds.[42]

BRIEF CONCLUDING POLEMIC

Once the problem of the many is appreciated, the choice we face is clear. First, one may try to break the dilemma posed, in a manner that is, of course, philosophically adequate. But as most of our essay has strongly indicated, perhaps especially our asking of questions in section 11, the prospects here are dim indeed. Second, one may accept the alternative of the multitude. But as the discussion of this present section has begun to indicate, this is only a way of compounding and proliferating problems. What we want, of course, is to find a way that is relevantly free of such difficulties. This leaves the third and final alternative, the way of Parmenides, of the other Eleatics, and of the Megarians: There really are not any of those putative ordinary things we think there are. Within this final option, further more specific routes may be sketched. With the ancients, we may think that "thought mirrors reality"—so that we have been discovering the Oneness that is the Only Reality or have been taking steps toward that philosophical ideal. On the other hand, we may, at this late juncture, finally part with our Parmenidian company: Perhaps there is no available thought that is adequate to concrete reality, and what passes for that is really as to nothing. Here the idea is to strive to find something that is relevantly adequate, before making claims "in its terms" as to what obtains in (perhaps the complex of concrete) reality. This, indeed, is the position I favor. According to it, we must set our sights in wholly new directions, that being the true lesson of our failure to find a proper course between the many and the none.[43,44]

Notes

1. For the idea that I use clouds to introduce my problem, I am indebted to Ernest Sosa.

2. According to certain lexicographers, on the most preferred meaning of 'cloud' such homogeneous clouds are logically impossible. Thus my *Webster's Seventh New Collegiate Dictionary* (Springfield, Mass., 1969) lists for the noun: "1(a): a visible mass of particles of water or ice in the form of fog, mist, or haze suspended usu. at a considerable height in the air. (b): a light filmy, puffy, or billowy mass seeming to float in the air." I am confident, however, that no such ambiguity as the above exists for 'cloud' and that (b), though quite deficient, does more toward giving the only (relevant) meaning than does the ridiculously unsemantic (a).

3. The sort of semantic constraints recently urged by Hilary Putnam and by Saul Kripke for certain terms, e.g., 'cat', do not apply to 'cloud' or to other terms I shall similarly employ later. (Although I was once convinced they were right about 'cat', I now think even that term does not have the constraints they urge for it but is much in the same boat as 'cloud'. For now, this latter issue may be safely passed over.) As regards the putative constraints, see Putnam's "Is Semantics Possible?" and "Meaning and Reference," both available in *Naming, Necessity, and Natural Kinds*, ed. S. P. Schwartz (Ithaca, N.Y., 1977), and the third part of Kripke's "Naming

and Necessity," in *Semantics of Natural Language*, ed. D. Davidson and G. Harman (Dordrecht, 1972).

4. As the previous two notes indicate, this realistic situation is *just one possibility* for clouds, in any relevant use of that thorny term.

5. I cannot offer a good definition of 'concrete', in the sense most relevant to philosophy. Its opposite is 'abstract', which I also will not try to define. By 'concrete entity', I mean much the same thing that many philosophers have meant by 'particular' and that many have meant by 'individual'.

6. I offer no definition of 'situation' but use it in much the same way that many philosophers have done. By it, then, I mean much the same thing that many have meant by 'state of affairs'. Situations can encompass more or less space, and so with time. By my stress and placement of 'any', I indicate that even "quite immediate" situations in space (and, of course, in time) will involve so many clouds if any at all. That *some* situations should (even at a moment) involve so many is of course no problem. Consider the present situation of the earth's entire atmosphere. On this matter, I am indebted to Terence Leichti.

7. Following philosophical and logical tradition, I here understand 'there are clouds' to be made true even by the existence of even one cloud. But, of course, this understanding is for me just a convenient pretense, and it is in no wise required for the argument.

For convenience, and *more important to make note of*: Now that this first argument has been presented, in what follows I shall generally omit the qualifying words 'at most' and just speak of entities that differ *quite minutely*. Should they desire to do so, readers may overlook the omission and say to themselves "*at most* quite minutely."

The qualifier 'at most' provides a needed hedge here in at least two (related) ways: *First*, the spotted entities may differ from each other in certain relevant ways by an amount that is *even less* than what should be regarded as quite minute, perhaps one that is only *extremely minute*. But, then, of course, they should still stand or fall, as regards being clods, together with the allegedly typical item. *Second*, there may be certain respects relevant to the kind in which the spotted entities differ *not at all* from the putative typical cloud. Then, too, as far as just being a cloud goes, the typical item cannot thus succeed while the others fail. Once the need for the qualification is noted, it is painfully boring to keep making it.

8. In a recent paper, "Talk About Talk About Surfaces," *Dialectica* 31, no. 3-4 (1977):411-30, Avram Stroll and Robert Foelber argue that the proper application of "surface" is a good deal narrower than one might suppose. I find some of their arguments pretty convincing, and I expect that a similar case could be made for the ordinary word 'boundary'. But I shall use 'boundary' to cover ever so many cases anyway, thus often employing it as a term of art. As the reader can verify, nothing of substance will depend on this eccentricity.

9. On these matters, I have profited from discussion with Jerrold Katz.

10. I think this intuitive idea is grounded in the adequacy of premise (3) of our first introductory argument. This thought of mine will be developed shortly, in section 4, where I shall discuss some relations between the two arguments.

11. A good deal later on, in section 10, I shall show how *versions of both* our introductory arguments may be given which make *no* mention of the principle of minute differences. So, although I *think* this principle underlies our arguments, and our problem, I am *not relying* on that idea to get the problem going, or to keep it around. Indeed, then, I am not even relying on it for my *introductory arguments*, let alone in regard to asking relevant *questions*, perhaps the most important route to the problem, which we encounter in section 11.

12. *Without* barring such sorites, we get, not only our new problem, but, further, the result that there are no clouds. So I am just being generous here.

13. I do not know how to tote up the numbers, precisely and in detail, but I have been assured that the mathematical results here are *extremely* congenial to our arguments.

14. On matters of physical fact, I have relied on Robert Weingard, a philosopher of physics, and, indirectly, on colleagues of his in the Rutgers University Physics Department.

In section 9, I shall argue that not much depends on the physical facts, anyway. Still, it is nice to have nature, so to say, on our problem's side.

15. Our problem is by no means confined to the putative referents of various common nouns for kinds, like 'table' and 'stone'. If anything, it is even more evident that the problem arises for alleged referents of many ordinary expressions lacking such terms, e.g., 'thing with blue and red stripes', 'delightful gift', 'product of the finest Italian craftsmanship', and so on, and so forth. So, I am just focusing, you might say, on some of the *hardest* cases: If things go badly for common sense *here*, with 'stone', as seems to be impending, an awful lot of "easier stuff" will fall as well.

16. Contrary to the offerings of certain lexicographers. See note 2.

17. My Webster's also lists under the noun 'cloud', "3: a great crowd or multitude: SWARM." If there is such a sense of 'cloud', then it is different from the one I have been using throughout. In *that* sense, the referents of 'cloud', if any, would *not* be concrete things.

18. On the matters of these last four paragraphs, I am indebted to correspondence with John Tienson and to discussion with Terence Leichti.

19. I think this is a good place for me to present an independent argument for the proposition that if stones exist, then each of them must have a two-dimensional boundary, with no width or extent, though suitably curved through three-dimensional space. Consider any alleged stone. With no boundary, or limiting places, one can travel from a point within the stone, in any direction, forever and never get to be outside. But, in that case, we will have a stoney universe rather than a universe with stones. On the other side, with no boundary, from any point outside the stone, and there must be some such, one can travel in any direction forever and never encounter the stone. So, again, nowhere in the universe does the stone exist. The stone has a boundary; but must it be without any width? (I do not care what the ordinary sense of boundary may dictate or allow. If required to do so, I use the term here, as a term of art.) The cloud's boundary must either be part of the stone or else not; we rule out the idea that only part of the boundary is part of the stone. Now, if it *is* part of the stone, then the boundary is *internal* to the stone. But if it has extent, then there must be an "outer" limit to it, otherwise we can travel forever, in any way, and always be in the stone, for being in its boundary. So, it cannot have extent; or, what amounts to the same, whatever limits *that* extent is the stone's *real* boundary and is extentless. All right, now suppose the alternative: the boundary is *external* to the stone itself. If such an external boundary has extent, we can travel through it toward the stone. But unless it has a limit, the *real*, extentless boundary, we shall never get to the stone itself; the stone will not exist anywhere. So, in any case, a stone's boundary has no width at all.

Few philosophers have thought seriously about boundary conditions on ordinary (physical) things. An exception is Ernest W. Adams in "The Naive Conception of the Toplogy of the Surface of a Body," in *Space, Time and Geometry*, ed. P. Suppes (Dordrecht, 1973), pp. 402-24, and in "Two Aspects of Physical Identity," *Philosophical Studies* 34 (1978):111-34.

20. Perhaps this is a good place to present or sketch a sorites argument, which I call *the sorites of the boundary*. For, otherwise, you might think that I believe in the extentless boundaries lately argued for *on condition*. I have no such belief, for I deny the condition itself; I do not believe in stones. Here, with this sorites, is one reason why: Our gradual, messy world has the atoms of an alleged stone fade off into those merely in the putative surrounding. Take a point "well within the stone" and one "well outside" such that the line joining them by least distance is a problematic path toward, or from, a boundary. (If there is even one such problematic path, the argument goes through. In fact, there are "ever so many.") Take *very* small steps inward, each equal to every other. Chosen small enough, it is quite clear that no step will take you to or across the stone's boundary; none will take you to the stone. So, you cannot encounter the stone that way. If the stone existed, then, even with such a small choice, you could. Therefore, the stone really does not exist.

Both the sorites just given and the argument in the preceding note need further elaboration and defense, which I cannot properly do here. But I have examined them for quite a while. The closer I looked, the better they looked.

21. Now, it may also be that an adequate argument, or several, can be adduced to opposite effect, to the conclusion that a stone's separator is *not* part of it. But if there is one, what would it show: It would not necessarily show that our previous arguments were in error. On the contrary, it might show that *in addition to* the requirement on stones that, in these situations, their separators be counted as parts, *there was also a requirement to opposite effect*. Thus it could be that our idea of a stone was *inconsistent*. Reflection on attempts to apply the idea properly to these situations would, in such an event, then serve to reveal the inconsistency. And this, of course, would not avoid our problem of the many. On the contrary, it would not only yield our dilemma but would resolve it in the direction of the first, and the more radical, of its two alternatives.

Not to make things easy for our problem now, we shall assume that our concept of a stone is a consistent one. But then, as we have argued, this means that the *only* relevant requirement regarding the separator is that it *is* part of the stone.

22. This is a main theme of my paper "Why There Are No People," in *Midwest Studies in Philosophy*, vol IV, *Studies in Metaphysics*, ed. Peter A. French, Theodore E. Uehling, Jr., and Howard K. Wettstein (Minneapolis, 1979):177-222.

23. There are in outer space, I suppose, many stones with such entirely exposed surfaces. But while worth noting, that has little to do with our everyday experience. And, out there, one will find, if any, very few tables, pine cones, and so on.

24. These considerations generate a sorites argument in which we gradually increase the size of "the joining part." Such an argument might show, I suggest, that there is no coherent distinction between joining and touching, at least no coherent application of it to ordinary things. But if there are such things, if there are stones and tables, then they must be able, in some possible circumstances, to touch. So such a sorites argument seems an interesting way of challenging the existence of these putative entities and thus of yielding the more radical alternative of our problematic dilemma. But as sorites arguments are, in this essay, always to be in the background, we pass over these difficulties, merely noting them now for work on future occasions.

25. For the suggestion that I consider such partial entities, which in turn sparked the thoughts of joining recently discussed, I am much indebted to Samuel Wheeler.

26. If all this is so, and partial entities do everything one might wish for our problem, why did I not just start out with trees and branches, instead of clouds and then stones, and thus wrap everything up quite neatly and quickly? The answer parallels the one I gave for having started with clouds rather than with stones: People are rarely, I am afraid, as logical as they should be; it is hard to get them to ponder our problem unless we start with psychologically gripping cases. I have found, through my own experiences of philosophical conversation, that the order employed in this paper, while logically somewhat roundabout, is psychologicall superior to more direct approaches.

27. I discuss principles like this one in "Why There Are No People," *Midwest Studies in Philosophy*, especially in section 5 of the paper.

28. This is admittedly quick, sketchy, and without sufficient argument. For elaboration and argument, see "Why There Are No People"; the elaboration is mainly given in section 2; the argument runs throughout the paper.

29. For an interesting discussion of such exclusion principles, see David H. Sanford, "Locke, Leibniz and Wiggins on Being in the Same Place at the Same Time," *Philosophical Review* 79 (1970):75-82.

30. A main difficulty here is that a sorites argument can be given to question, or undermine, the coherence of the "almost," "nearly," and "virtually" just suggested for stating an apparently relevant exclusion principle. Indeed, I believe that such arguments completely undermine the coherence of *any* available departure from an exact sameness version, thus any available exclusion principle that would even seem relevant to our topic. But, as with so many sorites arguments, I pass over this difficulty now. As the sequel quickly makes clear, I can well afford to do so.

31. In "Why There Are No People," I argue for the stronger claim that even such simple

expressions as 'cloud' and 'stone' are logically inconsistent. So although I do not see any reason to accept the more complex statement, and thus the route to inconsistancy which its addition means, I am of course very well prepared to do so.

32. I think that in his paper "Wang's Paradox," *Synthese* 30, no. 3-4 (1975):301-24, Michael Dummett presents this view.

33. I argue this in section 3 of "Why There Are No People."

34. A misunderstanding of this error will falsely promise easy answers here. Thus some will suppose, I am afraid, that *in* arguing *for* the condition:

> Clouds and stones (and so on) are things of a sort such that which things are clouds and stones (and so on) is a *purely objective* matter, and so *not* dependent on human thought in any relevant way,

I *must have been arguing* to *deny* the following condition, at the same time:

> Clouds and stones (and so on) are things of a sort such that which things are clouds and stones (and so on) is *not* a purely objective matter, and so *is* dependent on human thought in some relevant way.

And, supposing this, they may think, in addition, that the latter condition may well be correct and, perhaps, even, that arguments based on the considered reply may show it to be so. (I confess that I cannot myself see any strong reason for accepting this latter condition, but we may *suppose* that there is one.) With all this in mind, they may then conclude that my own arguments for the former condition must themselves somehow be unsound, thinking, as they may, that the two putative conditions cannot possibly both hold true together. Although some of this presumed thinking may be quite valid, the first and, particularly, the last of these ideas, each crucial to the conclusion, are surely mistaken. For both the conditions just exhibited can indeed hold true together. What *cannot all be true* is that both of these should hold *and also* that there be clouds and stones (and so on). Should two such conditions as these hold true, as perhaps they might, the relevant expression, say, 'cloud', will be an inconsistent one, logically on a par with, say, 'perfectly square triangle'. (That this should be so would be rather surprising. But, perhaps, it need not be overly so, once we realize that, only with the former expression, and not the latter, will the considerations needed to bring out the inconsistency be quite elaborate and unobvious ones.) At all events, should the latter condition hold true, that will not negate the one for which I argued. Nor will it, then, obviate the dilemma our problem poses for common sense. For if the latter condition holds as well as mine, that dilemma will have been yielded and even, in an unwanted sense, resolved. Indeed, it will have been, still one more time yet again, resolved in favor of the more radical of the dilemma's two alternatives.

35. I have no theory of *thought about objects* or, as some philosophers say, of *de re* thought; nor do I know of any wholly convincing view. For an interesting and well-argued account, however, I can suggest Sephen R. Schiffer's "The Basis of References," *Erkenntnis* 13, no. 1 (July 1978):171-206. On Schiffer's account, our problems emerge quite strikingly.

36. There are *two* related problems here, which we may distinguish. *First* is the problem of finding, or of finding adequate reason to suppose the existence of, a connection that has actually, with some considerable frequency, been there to serve me in the past. Such a connection has, presumably, even been enough to get many stupid little children thinking individually of stones nearby them. This is the problem of accounting for actual individualistic thought; if it cannot be solved, then our common sense thinking is in very bad trouble. A *second* problem is this one: Especially assuming the first problem finds no adequate solution, how can one, by whatever strategy necessary, get oneself to think, at a certain time, of just one real nearby stone? With this second problem, it is obvious, we may employ many more assumptions than a proper solution to the first will allow. I will make things easier for myself, now, and focus on the first of our problems. But my reasoning about it will, I suggest, indicate that even the second problem may well be beyond any adequate solution.

37. First, of course, there are the doubts one feels upon encountering Hume's writings on

the subject. But I am thinking more of certain other problems with *causation* that closely *parallel* those we have been discussing here regarding *ordinary things*. In my paper "The Uniqueness in Causation," I argued that any particular thing (event, or whatever) can be caused by ¯*at most one* entity. But in our messy, gradualistic, complex world, no one candidate entity, be it object, event, or whatever, seems relevantly better suited than ever so many very similar alternatives. Since it is arbitrary and, hence, false, to say of any one that it causes the event in question, there is *nothing* that *causes* the given particular. As I argued, this uniqueness is not a peculiar nuance of 'cause' but holds for any available locution that would seem, at first, suited to describe the relevant "interactions." The present radical extension of those ideas is, of course, very sketchy and needs much further development. But, for now, I mean only to be raising some doubts. The mentioned paper appeared in *American Philosophical Quarterly* 14, no. 3 (July 1977):177-88 and is reprinted in *The Philosopher's Annual*, vol. I — 1978 (Totowa, N.J., 1978), pp. 147-71.

38. See Saul A. Kripke's "Naming and Necessity" in Davidson and Harman, *Semantics of Natural Language*, and his "Identity and Necessity" in Schwartz, *Naming, Necessity, and Natural Kinds*. See Keith Donnellan's "Proper Names and Identifying Descriptions," in the former volume, and his "Speaking of Nothing," in the latter.

39. This is one of the most conspicuous places for sorites arguments to operate against the alleged existence of stones and other presumed ordinary things. I have in mind the *sorites of decomposition by minute removals*, especially as presented in section 1 of my paper "There Are No Ordinary Things," *Synthese* 41, no. 2 (June 1979):117-54. Also relevant are *the sorites of slicing and grinding*, in section 2 of the paper, and *the sorites of cutting and separating*, in section 3. For those of you who think those arguments to be mere fallacies, the present paper's problems may well help you think them over again.

40. With *certain marginal cases* of stones, such trios may be unavailable. But if they do exist, such trivial exceptions scarcely affect the present argument.

41. So, of course, our argument, together with the commonsensical (cs), *does* contradict *another* common sense assumption, namely, that *there are* typical stones. It is easy to conflate these two common sense assumptions, but that is a temptation to be resisted.

42. It is, I believe, interesting to compare what I have been doing in this essay with what was done by my erstwhile tutor, Professor Sir Peter Frederick Strawson, in his very interesting book, *Individuals: An Essay in Descriptive Metaphysics* (London, 1959), especially in chap. 1 and 3. Roughly, beginning with certain epistemological requirements, assumed to be met, the tutor derives our common sense metaphysics. Just as roughly, the pupil, by first questioning certain metaphysical assumptions of common sense, now goes on to question associated epistemological suppositions.

43. The arguments of this paper are meant to complement those offered in several other recent papers of mine. I have already cited "Why There Are No People" and "There Are No Ordinary Things" I should now mention as well: "I Do Not Exist," in *Perception and Identity*, ed. G. F. Macdonald (London, 1979: 235-51), which volume is a festschrift for Professor Sir Alfred Jules Ayer, and "Skepticism and Nihilism," *Nous*, forthcoming.

The epistemological problems raised in this last section, an outcome of considerations from metaphysics and the philosophy of language,should be taken as complementary to the universal skepticism for which I argue in my book, *Ignorance: A Case for Skepticism* (Oxford, 1975). In "Skepticism and Nihilism," I discuss certain other connections between skepticism (in epistemology) and radical views in those other areas of philosophy.

44. In coming to appreciate the many facets of this problem, I have had helpful discussions with many people. In addition to those already cited, all of whom were quite generally helpful, I should gratefully mention: Tamara Horowitz, Sidney Morgenbesser, Thomas Nagel and Stephen Schiffer.

Natural Kinds, Concepts, and Propositional Attitudes

DIANA ACKERMAN

R ecent work on natural kind terms, primarily by Putnam and Kripke, has caused many philosophers to abandon more traditional views. In this paper I argue that, although some of this abandonment is justified, some rests on an overly narrow view of concepts, whose refutation has interesting general implications for metaphysics and the philosophy of mind. I criticize Putnam's and Kripke's views from this standpoint, and I use these criticisms as a starting point for my own view of natural kind terms, which incorporates what I take to be the correct aspects of Putnam's and Kripke's, and which parallels the view of proper names that I have set forth elsewhere.[1] I also discuss aspects and problems of my sort of view that I have not taken up in my earlier discussions of proper names. As Putnam recognizes, a consistent theory of the meanings of natural kind terms cannot be expected to accord with *all* our pre-theoretical beliefs.[2] This paper explores the possibility of developing a view to preserve a different (and, in my opinion, stronger) set of pre-theoretical beliefs from those he favors, although our sets also have many common members.

I

Putnam's arguments for his view focus on a series of cases that he takes to refute the conjunction of the following two assumptions.

    (I) Knowing the meaning of a word is just a matter of being in a certain psychological state (in the sense of 'psychological state' where, first, psychological dispositions and not just occurrant mental states are psychological states and, second, no psychological state presupposes the existence of any entity other than the individual to whom that state is ascribed).

    (II) The meaning of a term determines its extension.

Putnam says that the conjunction of these assumptions has generally been taken for granted in the history of semantics, except for such recognized exceptions as "obviously" indexical words like 'I', 'now', and so on.[3] His contribution is to show that the conjunction is false even for types of words to which it has been assumed to apply, such as natural kind terms and words for artifacts.

Putnam's arguments center around the following sort of case. Suppose there is a planet, Twin Earth, which is almost exactly like Earth except that the liquid called 'water' on Twin Earth, which superficially resembles water on Earth and is found in the same sorts of locations, is composed of XYZ molecules rather than H_2O molecules. Putnam makes the following claims about this case:

a. It is correct to say that on Earth, 'water' means H_2O and on Twin Earth, 'water' means XYZ, and hence that 'water' means different things on Earth and on Twin Earth.

b. It would have been correct to say this about 'water' in the idiolects of average Earthian and Twin Earthian speakers even in 1750, when average Earthian and Twin Earthian speakers knew nothing about the chemical composition of the liquids they called 'water'.

Putnam concludes that a speaker's psychological state does not determine either the extension of a term like 'water' in his idiolect or its meaning "in the intuitive pre-analytic usage of that term."[4] Similarly, he argues that (supposing that aluminum and molybdenum can be distinguished only by experts) if aluminum and molybdenum were "switched" on Twin Earth (so that what was made of aluminum here would be made of molybdenum there and vice versa), and the words 'aluminum' and 'molybdenum' were also switched (so that aluminum was named 'molybdenum' on Twin Earth and vice versa), then ordinary speakers on Earth would mean something different by 'aluminum' from ordinary speakers on Twin Earth, and similarly for 'molybdenum'. Hence again, he holds, we can see that a speaker's psychological state does not determine either the extension of his terms, or their meaning. He further argues for this point by another example. He points out that many people cannot distinguish elm trees from beech trees, but can identify both only as common deciduous trees. He says:

Suppose you are like me and cannot tell an elm from a beech tree. We still say that the extension of 'elm' in my idiolect is the same as the extension of 'elm' in anyone else's, viz., the set of all elm trees, and that the set of all beech trees is the extension of 'beech' in *both* of our idiolects. Thus 'elm' in my idiolect has a different extension from 'beech' in your idiolect (as it should). Is it really credible that this difference in extension is brought about by some difference in our concepts? My *concept* of an elm tree is exactly the same as my concept of a beech tree. . . .(This shows that the identification of meaning. . . with *concept* cannot be correct, by the way.) If someone heroically attempts to maintain that the difference between the extension of 'elm' and the extension of 'beech' in *my* idiolect is explained by a difference in my psychological state, then we can always refute him by constructing a 'Twin Earth' example—just let the words 'elm' and 'beech' be switched on Twin Earth (the way 'aluminim' and 'molybdenum' were in the previous example).[5]

Putnam points out that his cases show that there is a "division of linguistic labor," i.e. that there are terms "whose associated criteria are known only to a subset of speakers who acquire the terms, and whose use by other speakers depends upon a structured co-operation between them and the speakers in the relevant [subset]."[6] He holds that 'water' is indexical, in the sense that what counts as the extension of 'water' in a given linguistic community is a function of the nature of the stuff normally called 'water' by members of that community. He outlines two views one might have about the indexicality of 'water', as follows, letting W_1 and W_2 be two possible worlds such that the extension of 'water' in W_1 is H_2O molecules, the extension of 'water' in W_2 is XYZ molecules, and the relation between English speakers in W_1 and W_2 is the same as the relation between English speakers on Earth and on Twin Earth.

[Alternative (1)] One might hold that 'water' was *world-relative* but *constant* in meaning (i.e. the word has a *constant relative meaning*). In this theory 'water' *means the same* in W_1 and W_2 [but differs in extension].

[Alternative (2)] One might hold that. . . 'water' doesn't have the same meaning in W_1 and W_2.[7]

As the material discussed above would suggest, he thinks that Alternative (2) gives the correct theory.

Putnam's general view of meaning incorporates the extension of a natural kind term as part of what he calls a "normal form description of meaning." He gives such a description of meaning four components: syntactic markers (e.g. *'mass term'*), semantic markers (e.g. *'liquid'*), stereotype (certain associated descriptive characteristics), and extension.[8]

This is a simplified sketch of Putnam's view. Before I try to assess the view, a point of clarification is in order. Elsewhere, I have distinguished between what I call 'meaning' and 'connotation'.[9] Meaning and connotation diverge for such indexical terms as 'I', 'now', and so on. The connotation of a term-token in a sentence-token expressing a particular proposition is what the term-token expresses, which is that term-token's semantic contribution to determining what proposition the sentence token expresses. The meaning of a term, which is what a competent speaker of the language knows as part of his understanding of the language, determines its connotation in a given context. For example, in the idiolects of different English speakers, 'I' has the same meaning but different connotations. Conversely, I can use 'I' and 'this person' with the same connotation to refer to myself, even though they have different meanings. Of course, I am using 'meaning' and 'connotation' partly stipulatively here; they are not always used to reflect this distinction. But I will use them this way in this paper. Putnam's use of 'meaning' seems mostly to accord with mine, rather than to accord with my use of 'connotation'. For example, he remarks that we normally say that 'I' has the same meaning but different extensions in different idiolects.

II

My criticism of Putnam can begin with the following question, which also points the way to the alternative view I will suggest. Why does Putnam pick alternative (2), above, rather than alternative (1)? The answer is largely that he thinks that alternative (1) would require us to say that 'elm' and 'beech' mean the same thing.[10] He has argued that the ordinary speaker's concepts of elm and beech are identical; hence, he believes, on alternative (1) we would have no resources for individuating ordinary speakers' meanings of 'elm' and 'beech' finely enough to let them be different.

Putnam regards this as obvious. But here he is making an assumption that has also been overwhelmingly pervasive in discussions of this subject. This is the view that if one's concepts of elms and beeches do not differ in *descriptive* content, then they do not differ at all, and similarly for other pairs of natural kind terms. Elsewhere, I have criticized the corresponding pervasive assumption about proper names by arguing for and developing a view on which some proper names have what I call "non-descriptive connotations," i.e., the names do not simply stand for their referents but their connotations are not the same as the connotations of any descriptions.[11,12] I will now set forth a related view for natural kind terms. This view incorporates Putnam's alternative (1) and thus can accommodate what I take to be the best and most insightful aspects of his position.

I support the view I am proposing by means of the principle that, loosely stated, hold that if two terms are not interchangeable *salva veritate* when used in propositional attitude contexts, then the terms differ in connotation. I call this principle "the propositional attitude principle." Many writers on reference rely on this sort of principle, which has considerable intuitive force, but other writers repudiate it. Elsewhere I defend it against the objections and alternatives that have been proposed,[13] but here I will simply assume it. My view can be correct even if the principle is false, but the principle can be used to argue for the view. Before I show how, the following point should be made. For simplicity of exposition, I often talk about the connotation of the word 'elm', about elms, or about someone's propositional attitudes toward the proposition that elms are _____ and similarly for other natural kind terms and other propositions. However, of course, it would be more accurate for me to replace such locutions with talk about the connotations of particular uses of 'elm' in someone's idiolect or about someone's propositional attitudes toward the proposition that a particular use of 'elms are _____' expresses in his idiolect, and similarly for related locutions and for other natural kind terms and other propositions. This should be kept in mind while reading this paper, although I will generally avoid this cumbersome sort of locution.

The argument for my view is as follows. Suppose S is an ordinary English speaker who knows only that elms and beeches are common deciduous trees, and cannot tell them apart; i.e., S is a speaker of the sort Putnam describes. Then, as Putnam would agree, there is no description that has the same connotation as 'elm' in S's idiolect. (I am ignoring such vacuous descriptions as 'the things that are elms'; this obviously will not help specify the connotation of 'elm' in S's idiolect.) Now, even this step would raise some objections. For example, some remarks of Schiffer[14] about proper names can be adapted to argue that S at least knows that elms are the entities of the kind conventionally called 'elm' in his society by other people whose uses are causally related to his own use of 'elm', so that this description can give the connotation of 'elm' in his idiolect. But this seems inadequate for several reasons. First, S may not be sure whether he has gotten right the word other people use; perhaps he has misspelled, misheard, or misremembered it. Second, unless S is philosophically sophisticated, he is unlikely to know (or at least, unlikely to know "immediately," "explicitly," or "at his fingertips") that elms fit any such complicated descriptive condition the way he knows (or knows "immediately," "explicitly," or "at his fingertips") that elms are elms. Thus by the propositional attitude principle, there seems to be no description that has the same connotation as 'elm' in S's idiolect.[15] It does not follow, however, as Putnam seems to assume, that the *extensions* of 'elm' and 'beech' must be included in their meanings to enable their meanings to differ. (In fact, as I will emphasize in Section III, Putnam's view violates the propositional attitude principle.) There is another aspect of meaning that is reflected in my view but that Putnam does not recognize.

My view is that 'elm' and 'beech' differ in meaning and conceptual content in a sort of irreducible way that can be explicated only by means of the different analyses the terms have. A simplified generalization (to be somewhat refined later) of what this view of natural kind terms amounts to is as follows. If S is a normal English speaker and K is a natural kind term in his idiolect, then K and some such description as 'entity that is of the same kind as those (or almost all of those) that stand in causal relation R [where R is the appropriate causal relation spelled out as much as possible] to my use of K' have the same relation in his idiolect as 'knowledge and 'justified true belief supported by a chain of reasoning that does not essentially involve a falsehood' have for an ordinary, philosophically unsophisticated speaker of English, assuming for the sake of illustration that the latter expression gives a correct analysis of 'knowledge'. (This account is set up for natural kind terms, like 'elm', that are count nouns, but it can easily be adapted to mass nouns or to abstract substance or species names.) The relevant aspects of the relation in question between analysans and analysandum are as follows. First, K and the description in question differ in connotation, since they do not have the same cognitive value. Second, K and the description are necessarily and a priori knowable to be coextensive in S's idiolect, i.e. they express properties that are necessarily coextensive and that he can know a priori to be coextensive. Third, the *final* test for the coextensiveness of the terms is that the fact that they are coextensive can be learned by generalizing from S's replies to questions about simple described hypothetical situations about when he would call something K, i.e., by use of the standard philosophical example-and-counterexample method, which Kripke and Putnam use to argue for their views about the correct conditions for determining the *extensions* of natural kind terms. Perhaps the relation between the meanings and the connotations of natural kind terms should be specifically indicated here. The analysis of the *connotation* of a particular use of a natural kind term is given by the description-token that mentions the use in question. Something somewhat analogous for the *meaning* of a natural kind term is given by the description type. Natural kind terms have non-descriptive meanings and particular uses of them have non-descriptive connotations as well.

More needs to be said about this notion of analysis, and I am preparing a separate paper on this topic.[16] But the basic notion of analysis used here should be familiar enough, as it is the sort of thing that philosophers aim at in giving analyses of such terms as 'knowledge' that are supported and tested by the hypothetical example-and-counterexample method in the way I have indicated. The parallel with 'knowledge' is important here. To count as understanding 'knowledge', English speakers do not have to know its analysis, but their use of the term must be such that generalizations from their replies to questions about simple described hypothetical cases would support the analysis. The same is true of natural kind terms.

This parallel is also important in rebutting some criticisms. For example, in a recent paper[17] Tyler Burge makes some derogatory remarks about a group of views of names and indexicals in which he includes my view. The remarks are directed specifically against views of names and indexicals, but if they had any force, they would apply to my view of natural kind terms as well. In fact, the arguments are weak and reflect misunderstanding. They have previously been made orally by several other people, but since they have gotten into print, they may be worth taking up here.

First of all, Burge says that "I think that anyone not already bent on preserving a philosophical outlook will find [my sort of account] thin and implausible.[18] As an empirical generalization, this is simply false. My view of names and natural kind terms arises not from insistence on preserving a philosophical outlook but from recognizing both the difficulties of other views and the parallel between the relation between such terms and the descriptions giving the final tests for identifying their referents or extensions, on the one hand, and the relation between such terms as 'knowledge' and the descriptions giving their analyses, on the other. But if Burge intends the quoted remark not as an empirical generalization but as a (peculiarly expressed) philosophical criticism, it does not have enough philosophical content to be discussed—a deficiency it shares with Burge's repeated characterization of my sort of view as "implausible."

Burge's other criticisms are no more adequate. He seems to think that the absence of *actual* back-up people readily at hand will make it impossible for someone to have a concept determining the referent of a name in terms of other people's references (such as 'by Socrates', I mean whomever my sophomore philosophy instructor referred to by that name'). But he overlooks the possibility that a token of name N or natural kind term K has an analysis of the form 'the entity bearing R to this very use of N' or 'entity that is of the same kind as those (or almost all of those) that stand in R to this very use of K', *regardless* of whether the user knows from whom he got the term in question.

Burge's misunderstanding of the sort of view he is trying to criticize is also reflected in his remark that

> [a holder of this view] might say, for example, that the sense or concept expressed by "Aristotle," in a context, is that of being Aristotle. . . . It is not clear what one is being told when [this] is said. . . . The expression "the concept of being Aristotle" does not suffice to convey what is intended, for it is just as context-dependent as the proper name. This insufficiency takes two forms. In the first place, there are lots of Aristotles—which one is intended? We seem to rely on the context to pick out the "right" one. But intuitively we do not—at least not always—relay on some contextually associated complete sense or concept which eternally determines the referent. In the second place, the name "Aristotle" may carry—even for a given Aristotle, a given speaker or thinker, and a given time—different cognitive values. "Aristotle is Aristotle," as used at a given time, may express a surprising discovery rather than a triviality.[19]

As a criticism of my view, these remarks are inadequate in more than one way. First, I explicate the terms in question by means of their analyses, rather than simply saying something like that 'Aristotle' expresses the concept of being Aristotle or that 'elm' expresses the concept of being an elm. Second, the fact that the very use-tokens in question appear in their own analyses in the way I have indicated vitiates Burge's allegations of "insufficiency." (In fact, the analysis of the person's concept will actually have as a constituent his percept-token of the use-token; the concept will not be, as Burge erroneously seems to suppose, completely abstract.)

Finally, Burge characterizes my sort of non-descriptive connotations as "strained, ad hoc and inarticulate."[20] To the extent that these remarks are not mere invective, they can be undercut by the analogy mentioned between the concepts associated with names and natural kind terms, and the connotations of 'knowledge' or any other such term that does not have an analysis that preserves its connotation according to the propositional attitude principle. The connotations of such terms can be explicated by considering their uses and application conditions and by discussing whether they are analyzable and, if so, what their analyses are. Critics who expect a description identical in connotation to keep the non-descriptive connotation of a natural kind term from being "stained" or "inarticulate" are demanding something that is precluded by the very nature of non-descriptive connotations and, without justification, are setting higher standards for the intelligibility of the connotations of natural kind terms than for the connotations of terms like 'knowledge'. My view has the strength of providing a unified account of such sorts of terms by building on the analogies between them. I criticize Burge's positive views elsewhere.[21]

Following my terminology for the non-descriptive connotations of names, I say that natural kind terms are "indefinable" and express "irreducible" properties. The notions of indefinable term and irreducible property could profit from further explication but here I am using them in an intuitive way, as do the people who criticize my view. I will repeat one distinction I made in my discussion of names, however. Philosophers often use interchangeably such terms as 'indefinable', 'irreducible', 'unanalyzable', 'primitive', and so on. But on the propositional attitude principle, correct analyses need not preserve identity of connotation. I say that an indefinable term is one that has no analysis *that preserves its connotation,* and hence indefinably does not entail unanalyzability. Thus my view has general implications for metaphysics and the philosophy of mind, since it holds that there are many irreducible properties that people grasp but that philosophers have failed to take account of.

Some particular aspects of this account deserve note. First, I have included nothing descriptive in the meanings of natural kind terms to correspond to Putnam's stereotype. This is part of why I have called the above account simplified, because I actually want to leave the question open at this point. Perhaps some natural kind words do have descriptive characteristics as part of their meanings. I do not have clear intuitions on the matter. It would be easy to amend my account to include descriptive characteristics if desired, but I will leave this sort of possible addition aside in this paper. There are other oversimplifications in my account as well. Some of them will be discussed later. But basically the point is that the meaning and connotation are non-descriptive, i.e., not *purely* descriptive and not incorporating the extension, and the analysis is the final test for determining the extension, that can be gotten by generalizing from speaker's replies to questions about simple described hypothetical cases, though I am oversimplifying just what the final test might be.[22] Second, the inclusion of the phrase 'of the same kind' in the analysis allows for the fact that standards for determining what constitutes a kind may change, as well as for the fact that ordinary speakers may defer to the judgment of experts about when an entity belongs to a kind that is identified by paradigmatic instances. This is part of the division of linguistic labor that Putnam points out. My view incorporates some related remarks of Putnam as well. Of course I can accept his view that (equating 'gold' with its cognate words in Greek, Latin, etc) " . . . 'gold' has not changed its extension (or changed it significantly) in two thousand years."[23] My view also obviously incorporates Putnam's application of the causal theory of reference to natural kind terms, as well as his views about the importance of paradigmatic instances. I can also accept the aspects of Putnam's views about artifacts that parallel the aspects of his views about natural kind terms that I have accepted, but I will not be concerned with artifacts in this paper.

Putnam's belief that 'elm' and 'beech' would have the same meaning on alternative (1) is not the only reason he gives for favoring alternative (2). As the material I have cited in section I indicates, he also believes that it is part of our pre-analytic notion of meaning that 'water' means different things on Earth and on Twin Earth and that, in the hypothesized case mentioned above involving 'aluminum' and 'molybdenum' on Twin Earth, the meaning of the two terms would be interchanged. This is, of course, basically just an appeal to intuition, so it seems reasonable to reply that it does not appeal to mine. Similarly, I see no force to his view that 'elm' would mean something different in a possible world where its extension was a different kind of tree. My view denies this, since it does not make the extension of a natural kind term part of its meaning. Moreover, Putnam simply assumes that a difference in the natural kind word type involved is not sufficient to change the concept or meaning; he even derides a denial of this as 'heroic'.[24] But he does not argue for this, and I have just presented by view on which it is false. Some of the drawbacks and benefits of this aspect of my view are discussed in the remaining two sections of this paper.

III

I hope that the preceding section has shown that my view is coherent and incorporates many insights of Putnam's. But the following question still remains: should my view be accepted over Putnam's and if so, why? The fact that Putnam has not taken account of the possibility of my sort of non-descriptive meanings does not by itself show that we should accept a theory incorporating them, rather than extensions, into the meanings of natural kind terms. In this section I discuss an advantage of my sort of view.

Putnam recognizes that his view does not accord with the propositional attitude principle, as can be readily seen by an example. Putnam's own example involves a German-English bilingual, but the point is illustrated even more easily within one language. Thus, suppose that 'elm' and 'gleg' are both natural kind terms that meet Putnam's conditions for having the same meaning, i.e., both have the syntactic marker '*noun*', the semantic markers '*natural kind*' and '*tree*', the stereotype '*deciduous*' and the same extension. None of the components of this meaning would fit alternative (1) on Putnam's view, so, combining Putnam's view with my notion of connotation, tokens of both terms would have the same connotation as well. But suppose that S has acquired the terms separately and independently. Then S can believe that a certain tree is an elm without believing that it is a gleg. Putnam says his bilingual case shows that "it is not just that belief is a process involving representations; he believes the proposition (if one wants to introduce propositions at all) under one representation and not under another."[25] These remarks would presumably apply to the elm-gleg example as well on Putnam's view. But this simply describes, rather than solves, the sort of problem that Kripke sets forth as follows for names: "If reference is *all there is* to [connotation] . . . do not 'Cicero was bald' and 'Tully was bald' express the same proposition? How, then, can anyone believe that Cicero was bald and doubt or disbelieve that Tully was bald?"[26] Here, Kripke states the problem in terms of names, but a parallel problem can be raised for Putnam's view of 'elm' and 'gleg'.

Kripke does not suggest that this sort of problem should lead us to repudiate a Millian theory of names. Instead, he argues that it is unclear how we should handle the problem, because it lies in an area where "our normal practices of interpretation and attribution of belief are subject to the greatest possible strain, perhaps to the point of breakdown."[27] But I will argue that this sort of problem can be solved (at a price) by non-descriptive connotations. This is not surprising because non-descriptive connotations are argued for and individuated by means of the propositional attitude principle.

The fundamental strength of my view is its ability to solve this sort of problem, so I will digress here to discuss the problem and Kripke's views about it. Kripke argues that the problem should not make us suppose that coextensive names or natural kind terms do differ in descriptive sense, because the problem can arise even with coextensive pairs of such terms that are associated with the very same descriptions. My elm-gleg case would be an example here; he gives the example of an English speaker who can identify Cicero and Tully each simply as a Roman orator without knowing whether they are the same. I previously made this sort of point elsewhere about names.[28] Kripke says the following about this sort of case for names.

> The premise of the argument we are considering for the classic position of Frege and Russell — that whenever two codesignative names fail to be interchangeable in the expression of a speaker's beliefs, failure of interchangeability arises from a difference in the 'defining' descriptions the speaker associates with these names — is therefore false. . . . So the apparent failure of codesignative names to be everywhere interchangeable in belief contexts is not to be explained by differences in the 'senses' of the names.[29]

Parallel remarks would apply to such pairs of coextensive natural kind terms as 'elm' and 'gleg'. But this passage clearly overlooks the possibility of my sort of non-descriptive connotation, since Kripke moves without argument from the absence of a difference in *descriptive* sense to the absence of a difference in sense. This is particularly important because of the weight Kripke gives to this sort of objection. He says that it is "the clearest objection [to supposing that the problem can be solved by saying that coreferential names can differ in sense], which shows that others should be given their proper weight,"[30] since it shows that "the view under consideration would not account for the phenomena it seeks to explain."[31] But this seems right only as long as non-descriptive connotations are overlooked, for my view holds that 'Tully' and 'Cicero' or 'elm' and 'gleg' can have different non-descriptive connotations in the idiolect of the speaker in question, as they have different analyses. (The details of my non-descriptive view of names are given in the papers cited above.) In Section IV I consider my answer to the obvious question this raises: when do two natural kind terms have the *same* non-descriptive connotation?

Thus my view has the advantage of easily according with the pre-theoretical beliefs about the cognitive side of natural kind terms that are reflected by the propositional attitude principle, and of giving a unified account of proposition individuation that applies both to propositions expressed by sentences with terms that raise Kripke's puzzle and to other types of propositions. Of course, my view pays a price for these advantages. This will be discussed in seciton IV, but it is important in any case that, contrary to what Kripke seems to hold, a solution to the problem is possible in terms of divergent senses of the terms involved.

Moreover, my view highlights the importance of abandoning the overly narrow and restrictive view of the cognitive side of names and natural kind terms that has been held both by the Frege-Russell tradition and by current views. This particular point can and should be retained even if the rest of my framework is abandoned. For example, some current views, such as Kaplan's, separate the objects of thought .from the cognitive significance of the objects of thought.[32] I argue against this sort of move elsewhere.[33] But the important point here is that as it stands, Kaplan's account is unable to solve any problems about names, since he considers the notion of character—the cognitive significance of demonstratives—to be inapplicable to names. He does not talk about natural kind terms. But in principle, I think that if one wanted to separate content and cognitive significance—which I do not want to do—this could be done with names and natural kind terms as well as with demonstratives, but in the former cases, the cognitive significance of names and natural kind terms should include their non-descriptive meanings. I do not have the space to go into this further here and I also expect, although this is beside the point, that Kaplan would not like this sort of extension.

IV

I have already mentioned that Putnam grants that we cannot combine all our pre-analytic views about the meanings of natural kind terms into one consisten theory.[34] In this section, I discuss some consequences of my view that may seem counterintuitive. I think that some of these consequences genuinely *are* unfortunate but that others are likely to seem unattractive (if they do) mainly because they go against currently popular views and assumptions.

First, Putnam and Kripke emphasize that natural kind terms are rigid. On the face of it, it is not immediately clear what it means to say that a natural kind term is "rigid." The notion of rigidity was originally introduced by Kripke for singular terms somewhat as follows: a singular term T is a rigid designator of entity x if and only if it designates x in every possible world in which x exists and designates nothing in possible worlds in which x does not exist. (Of course, this needs to be relativized to particular uses in idiolects.)

How can the notion of rigidity be extended to natural kind terms? An obvious extension would be to say that a natural kind term is rigid iff it has the same extension in any possible world where it has an extension at all. But in this sense, natural kind terms clearly are not rigid, since a natural kind term would have a different extension in a possible world in which so much as a single member of its *actual* extension failed to exist. A more reasonable approximation of this sort of conception would be

R_1 If an entity or portion of matter is part of the extension of a given natural kind term in some possible world, then that entity or portion of matter is part of its extension in any possible world where that entity or portion of matter exists at all.

Thus, for example; all samples of water would necessarily be water and all gold would necessarily be gold.[35]

Another use of 'rigid', one that is explicit with Putnam, is

R_2 "(For every world W) (For every x in W) (x is water = x bears [the relation of being the same liquid] to the [stuff], referred to as ['water'] *in the actual world* W_1) [and similarly for other natural kind terms]."[36]

Kripke and Putnam also talk about the logical necessity of statements expressing theoretical identities involving natural kinds, such as the statement that water is H_2O or that gold is the element with atomic number 79. Thus we have

R_3 Theoretical identity statements involving natural kinds are logically necessary.[37]

A fourth interesting and related set of statements about natural kinds and necessity are those that hold that the theoretical compositions of the entities or portions of matter that fall under a natural kind are essential properties of them, i.e.,

R_4 Each sample of water is necessarily composed of H_2O molecules, and similarly for other natural kinds.

My view can accept R_4 and I find it quite plausible. But my view cannot accept the first three of the above theses, and I do not find Kripke and Putnam's arguments for these theses as compelling as the intuitions behind my own view. In some cases, Putnam just slips in remarks about rigidity along with arguments of other sorts. Thus, in his section on realism, Putnam ends by saying that "we may give an 'operational definition' or a cluster of properties or whatever, but the intention is never to 'make the name synonymous with the description'. Rather, we use the name *rigidly* to refer to whatever things share the *nature* that things satisfying the description normally possess."[38] But the "rigidly" in the second sentence does not follow from the first. Similarly, in criticizing Jerrold Katz, Putnam says that "the reason we *don't* use 'cat' as synonymous with a description is surely that we know enough about cats to know that they do have a hidden structure, and it is good scientific methodology to use the name to refer rigidly to the things that possess that hidden structure and not to whatever happens to satisfy some description."[39] Putnam gives no justification for including 'rigidly' here and this seems unreasonable. My view can allow that hidden structure can determine membership in a kind. This should be adequate for scientific methodology.

Putnam also gives examples designed to appeal to our intuitions about described hypothetical situations. This is also the sort of argument that Kripke relies upon.[40] These cases also do not seem terribly compelling to me, particularly when care is taken to distinguish cases supporting R_4 from cases supporting R_3.

My own view's account of the application-conditions for natural kind terms may look problematic, however. On my account something is gold iff it bears a certain relation to the term 'gold'. Thus it follows on my account that if there were no word 'gold' there would be no gold (and actually, of course, as suggested above, all this should really be stated in terms of particular uses in idiolects). I agree that this is counterintuitive, but the following replies can be made. First, the result seems less odd if we keep in mind that one's concept of gold does seem inherently to involve the word. Of course, this simply follows from my view that the concept has the word in its analysis, but I think it has inherent plausibility. The final test for the application of a natural kind word, which is what gives its analysis, does seem essentially to involve the word, because it involves a causal relation to the use *of that very word* in question. In this respect, natural kind words are unlike such abstract, non-indexical terms as 'happiness', 'justice', and so on. Second, one should be careful about the scope of the modal operator in the proposition under discussion. Thus, for example, we should distinguish the blatantly false proposition that gold is such that it is impossible for it to exist if there is no word 'gold' from the proposition under consideration, which is that if there were no word 'gold' nothing would be gold. My view entails the latter but not the former. I think that some of the apparent objectionability of the latter—but unfortunately not all of it—derives from confusing it with the former. My consequence is genuinely somewhat counterintuitive.

One possible move at this point is to introduce a version of my view that would eliminate this consequence by making natural kind terms rigid. This could be done with Plantinga's notion of a a-transform, where 'a' is a rigid designator of the actual world and a a-transform of the description 'the F' is written as 'the $(F)_a$' and has the same connotation as 'the F in a'.[41] On this view, natural kind term K and the description '(entity that is of the same kind as those (or almost all of those) that stand in causal relation R to my use of $K)_a$' would have the relation that I attributed in section II to K and this description without the a-transform. This view of natural kind terms would parallel the view of names I offered elsewhere.[42] However, I have since argued that the notion of a a-transform faces some problems of its own.[43] As I have already indicated twice, Putnam himself grants that any consistent theory of natural kind terms will have some counterintuitive consequences.[44] Thus, to decide which view to accept, one must compare all the alternatives as wholes in order to be able to pick the one with the greatest proportion of insights to drawbacks. In a paper already cited,[45] I made this comparison for non-descriptive views of proper names with and without a-transforms in the descriptions giving the analyses of the names. Some of what I said there about the relative strengths and weakness of the two positions also applies to the corresponding positions about natural kind terms that are under consideration here. (However, I am now somewhat more inclined to favor a position without a-transforms, because the difficulties with a-transforms now seem more weighty to me. I do not have new reasons; the old problems just seem more compelling.)

As the above remarks suggest, a full defense of my view over Putnam's would require more than just an account of advantages of my view. It would also require detailed comparison of the strengths and weaknesses of each position, including a detailed assessment of how people in the Kripke-Putnam tradition can handle propositional attitude contexts. Space limitations prevent me from doing all this here, so I have divided up the task, presenting my positive view in this and other papers, and relegating most of the critical material to a separate paper, in which I argue that a major point in favor of my view is that none of the alternatives gives a satisfactory account of names and natural kind terms in propositional attitude contexts.[46] However, I do want to say some more here about further consequences, including counterintuitive ones, of my own view.

Putnam and Kripke both inveigh against the view that natural kind terms normally have different senses for ordinary speakers and for scientific experts.[47] My account allows that ordinary and expert speakers *mean* the same thing by a given natural kind term, since the description I have suggested for the analysis will be of the same type for both sorts of speakers. But the following questions remain about identity conditions for the meanings and connotations of natural kind terms. When do two different natural kind term-types have the same meaning? When do two uses of different natural kind terms or of the same natural kind term have the same connotation in the idiolect of the same speaker or in the idiolects of different speakers?

Since my account, in section II, of the analysis of a particular natural kind term uses that term itself in the analysis, it may seem that on my view, *no* natural kind term-tokens of different types ever have the same analysis or the same meaning. But this is another way in which the account in section II was, as I said, over-simplified. Kripke argues that his puzzle about belief will arise whenever we translate names or natural kind words from one language to another. When then, on my view, do two natural kind words have the same meanings?

Answers to this question and to the above questions about connotation show the price I pay for my solution to Kripke's puzzle. When we have two coextensive natural kind words whose connotations the speaker does not associate with each other, we may be able to generate Kripke's puzzle for Putnam's view. Thus I hold that two natural kind term-tokens of different types will not have the same connotation unless one is intended explicitly as a substitute or abbreviation for the other and is thought of that way, and only two such natural kind term-types will have the same meaning. For example, if 'mol' is an abbreviation for 'molybdenum', and is always thought of that way, so that part of what is necessary to count as knowing the meaning of 'mol' is to know that it is an abbreviation for 'molybdenum', then 'mol' and 'molyb-demnum' will have the same meaning. This sort of case requires modification of my account in section II, because in this case the analysis of 'mol' in my idiolect is "stuff that is of the same kind as that (or almost all of that) standing in relation R to my use of *'molybdenum'*." This view does have the counterintuitive consequence Kripke mentions, the consequence that there are generally no exact translations (i.e., translations preserving identity of meaning) for names and natural kind terms between natural languages, since there is no natural language in which a necessary condition of knowing the meanings of some of its words is equating them with words in a *different* language. Of course, Kripke is right that this is counterintuitive, but as I have emphasized, a full assessment of the seriousness of this result for my view would require a detailed comparison of this result with all the counterintuitive consequences of rival views, and of alternative ways of handling proper names and natural kind terms in propositional attitude contexts.

When do two uses of the same natural kind term have the same connotation? Part of the answer seems to yield the following consequence. Non-descriptive connotations are individuated by the propositional attitude principle, and elsewhere I discuss the fact that a result of a thorough and consistent application of the propositional attitude principle is privacy, since the principle will lead to the view that many of the propositions S expresses are private in the sense that it is logically impossible for them to be expressed or entertained by anyone else. I argue that this principle leads to the view that, specifically, proper names and natural kind terms with non-descriptive connotations are private.[48] Thus, although Kripke says that even "differing private senses peculiar to each speaker"[49] would fail to solve his puzzle about belief, this seems true only if we ignore private nondescriptive connotations. (Of course, even two natural kind term-tokens of the same type will not have the same connotations for one person unless he associates them with each other.)

How unattractive are these conclusions? There are those who hold that any alleged concept that would be private is therefore unacceptable. Sometimes, it is simply stated without argument that private notions are implausible or obscure, but other philosophers give arguments. I do not find the anti-privacy arguments at all convincing, but an adequate discussion of the privacy issue would take much more space than I have here.[50]

A few points can be briefly noted, however. First, the sort of privacy my view entails is privacy of connotation and of propositions entertained, not of meaning. My view does not deny that different people can be in mental states that are qualitatively identical when each entertains a private proposition, so there should be nothing mysterious about the qualities of the states involved and nothing incommunicable about the purely qualitative aspects of the connotations. Moreover, note that the sort of privacy involved here has nothing to do with skepticism about other minds or about the nature of others' mental states. This point is worth emphasizing because there are at least two senses of 'private' that are often conflated in discussions of privacy. First, a term can be private in the sense that no one but S can apprehend what it expresses. Second, a term can be private in the sense that no one but S can know that he is entertaining concepts qualitatively identical to those it expresses. The latter sort of privacy is relevant to skeptical questions about the mental states of others, but the consequences of my view are for the former sort, which does not entail skepticism as it is compatible with such alternatives as critical cognitivism. Hence any force that is had by considerations against skepticism about other minds cannot be used against my nondescriptive connotations.

Of course, I do not expect these remarks to show that my view should be accepted over Putnam's. As I have said, my detailed critical treatment of alternatives to my view is given elsewhere.[51] My aim here has been simply to set forth a new view whose possibility has been overlooked by other writers and which has its own distinctive strengths.[52]

Notes

1. For my view of proper names, see Diana Ackerman, "Proper Names, Propositional Attitudes, and Non-Descriptive Connotations," *Philosophical Studies* 35 (1979):55-69 (which includes some views about rigidity that I have since come to doubt), and Diana Ackerman, "Proper Names, Essences, and Intuititve Beliefs," *Theory and Decision* 11 (1979):5-26 (which gives reasons for these doubts).

2. Putnam acknowledges this in Hilary Putnam, "The Meaning of 'Meaning'," in Hilary Putnam, *Mind, Language, and Reality*, vol. 2 of *Philosophical Papers* (New York, 1975), pp. 269-70, and Hilary Putnam, "Comment on Wilfrid Sellars," *Synthese* 27 (1974):447.

3. See Hilary Putnam, "Meaning and Reference," *Journal of Philsophy* 70 (1973): 709-10.

4. *Ibid.*, p. 702.

5. *Ibid.*, p. 704.

6. *Ibid.*, p. 706.

7. *Ibid.*, p. 707.

8. See Putnam, "The Meaning of 'Meaning'," pp. 269-70.

9. See Ackerman, "Proper Names, Propositional Attitudes, and Non-Descriptive Connotations," p. 56.

10. See Putnam, "Comment on Wilfrid Sellars," p. 453, and "The Meaning of 'Meaning'," p. 270.

11. For some of the many examples of how other contemporary philosophers rely on this assumption, see Stephen Schiffer, "The Basis of Reference," *Erkenntnis* 13 (1978): 181, as well as the Kripke material discussed in Section III. In "Is Sematics Possible?" (in *Mind, Language and Reality*), p. 140, Putnam mentions and dismisses such "unanalyzable" properties as just "the property of being gold." Since he describes these properties simply as unanalyzable and does not characterize them any further, they seem both ad hoc (as he says) and fundamentally unlike the analyzable non-descriptive connotations I will shortly describe in detail and argue for.

12. See the material cited in n. 1.

13. I do this in Diana Ackerman, "Recent Work on the Theory of Reference," *American Philosophical Quarterly*, forthcoming.

14. See Schiffer, "The Basis of Reference," p. 198, and "Naming and Knowing," *Midwest Studies in Philosophy* 2 (1977):35.

15. It might be tempting to suppose that each token of 'elm' is selfreferential and has the same connotation as the description 'entity of the kind referred to by this very token 'elm'". One objection to this move parallels the first objection I made in "Proper Names, Propositional Attitudes, and Non-Descriptive Connotations," pp. 65-66, to a similar proposal about proper names.

16. This material will be treated in detail in my book *Methodology of Philosophy*, in preparation, to be forthcoming in the Prentice-Hall Foundations of Philosophy series.

17. Tyler Burge, "Sinning Against Frege," *Philosophical Review* 88 (1979):398-432.

18. *Ibid.*, p. 427.

19. *Ibid.*, pp. 427-28.

20. *Ibid.*, p. 430.

21. Ackerman, "Recent Work on the Theory of Reference."

22. For example, I am not here taking account of Putnam and Kripke's plausible remarks concerning the possibility of discovering that it is false that all or almost all the members of a supposed kind have a common structure. See Putnam, "The Meaning of 'Meaning'," p. 241, and Saul Kripke, "Naming and Necessity," in *Semantics of Natural Languages*, ed. Gilbert Harman and Donald Davidson (Dordrecht, 1972) p. 328. My account can be amended to accommodate such possibilities, but I will not go into this here. My main concern in this paper is with the relation between connotation and the final test for determining the extension, rather than with the details of the final test itself.

23. Putnam, "The Meaning of 'Meaning'," p. 235.

24. See Putnam, "Meaning and Reference," p. 704 (quoted above) and p. 710, n. 2, and Putnam, "Comment on Wilfred Sellars," p. 453.

25. Putnam, "The Meaning of 'Meaning'," p. 270.

26. Saul Kripke, "A Puzzle About Belief," in *Meaning and Use*, ed. A. Margalit (Dordrecht, 1979), p. 248. Note that Kripke is simply *stating* the problem here; his remarks should not be taken as rhetorical questions intended to refute the Millian view of names. He also mentions a case involving 'furze' and 'gorse' that parallels my case of 'elm' and 'gleg', although the cases were developed independently. The following qualification is important to my discussion of his paper. At the time the present paper went to press, I was able to obtain a copy of Kripke's paper only in page proof form and minus footnotes. I am discussing his paper because of its relevance here, but it should be kept in mind that I do not know about any qualifications or additions Kripke may have made in his footnotes or in corrections of the page proofs.

27. *Ibid.*, p. 269.

28. See Ackerman, "Proper Names, Propositional Attitudes, and Non-Descriptive Connotations."

29. Kripke, "A Puzzle About Belief," pp. 246-7.

30. *Ibid.*, p. 246.

31. *Ibid.*

32. David Kaplan, "Demonstratives" (unpublished, 1977).

33. Ackerman, "Recent Work on the Theory of Reference."

34. See Putnam, "The Meaning of 'Meaning'," pp. 269-70, and Putnam, "Comment on Wilfrid Sellars," p. 447.

35. See Kripke, "Naming and Necessity," p. 328.

36. Putnam, "Meaning and Reference," p. 707.

37. Kripke expresses this view in "Naming and Necessity," Lecture 3. See also Putnam, "Meaning and Reference," p. 709.

38. Putnam, "The Meaning of 'Meaning'," p. 238.

39. *Ibid.*, p. 244.

40. See Putnam, "Comment on Wilfrid Sellars," p. 452, and Kripke, "Naming and Necessity," Lecture 3.

41. See Alving Plantinga, *The Nature of Necessity* (Oxford, 1974) for a more detailed account of a a-transforms.

42. See Ackerman, "Proper Names, Propositional Attitudes, and Non-Descriptive Connotations."

43. See Ackerman, "Proper Names, Essences, and Intuitive Beliefs."

44. See Putnam, "The Meaning of 'Meaning'," pp. 269-70, and Putnam, "Comment on Wilfrid Sellars," p. 447.

45. Ackerman, "Proper Names, Essences, and Intuitive Beliefs."

46. As I have indicated, I discuss my positive views of names in Ackerman, "Proper Names, Propositional Attitudes, and Non-Descriptive Connotations," and Ackerman, "Proper Names, Essences, and Intuitive Beliefs," and I discuss most of my criticisms of other views in Ackerman, "Recent Work on the Theory of Reference."

47. See Putnam, "The Meaning of 'Meaning'," pp. 239-40, and Kripke, "Naming and Necessity," Lecture 3.

48. In Ackerman, "Recent Work on the Theory of Reference."

49. Kripke, "A Puzzle About Belief," p. 247.

50. I am preparing another paper specifically on this topic.

51. I discuss this in Ackerman, "Recent Work on the Theory of Reference."

52. I am grateful to Philip Quinn and Ernest Sosa for helpful discussions of some of the material in this paper.

Thinking about an Object

JOHN L. POLLOCK

1. INTRODUCTION

There is a traditional view that may be regarded as being about either the structure of propositions or the structure of thought. According to this view, when one thinks about an object, one must think about it under some description which it uniquely satisfies. Alternatively, a proposition can only be about an object by virtue of containing as a constituent some definite description $\imath a$ where a is a concept uniquely exemplified by the object. On the assumption that to think about an object is to entertain a proposition about the object, these two theses come to the same thing. The objective of this paper is to argue that they are false. A particular non-descriptive way of thinking about an object will be described, and some of the consequences of its existence will be explored.

2. *DE RE* WAYS OF THINKING OF OBJECTS

The orthodox claim that you can only think about an object under a description is the claim that to have a belief about an object is to believe a proposition containing such a description. A necessary condition for thinking about an object under a description is thus given by:

(1) In believing ψ, S is thinking of x under the description $\imath a$ only if, necessarily, in believing ψ, S is thinking about whatever object uniquely exemplifies a.

This provides a useful test for whether one is thinking of an object under a description.

The clearest examples in which you are not thinking of an object under a description seem to me to be cases in which you are thinking about an object about which you know a great deal. In such cases, although you have many descriptions available to you, you are frequently not thinking of the object *under* any of those descriptions. For example, I might be thinking of my wife, Carol. According to the orthodox view, I must be thinking of Carol under some description. What description might that be? It might first be suggested that I am using some description involving the name 'Carol'. That I am not follows, by principle (1), from the fact that I would still be thinking of the same individual even if it were to turn out that I am operating under a posthypnotic suggestion and my wife's name is not 'Carol' after all. Perhaps, then, I am thinking about her under the description 'my wife'. But this cannot be right either. If it turned out that the supposed minister who married us was an imposter, and hence that our marriage is not legal, this would not have the result that I was not thinking about her, despite its having the consequence that Carol is not my wife.[1] Once again, the proposed description fails the test of (1). It seems that similar tales will establish that I am not thinking of my wife under any simple description. This is reminiscent of the circumstances that led Searle to his theory of proper names, and so it might be suggested that the proper description is of the sort discussed by Searle. I have a great many beliefs about my wife. These beliefs provide many descriptions which I associate together in my mind as being descriptions of a common individual. Suppose these descriptions are $a_1, \ldots, a_n$. Then perhaps I am thinking of Carol under the Searle-type description ⌈the thing that satisfies sufficiently many of $a_1, \ldots, a_n$ and more of them than anything else⌉. In support of this suggestion, it can be observed that if no one satsified *any* of a_1, $\ldots, a_n$, it would seem very reasonable to conclude that there was no one about whom I was thinking.

It is not impausible to suppose that the Searle-type description passes the test of principle (1). But it, and any other complicated description, fails another test. I assume that belief is a relation between persons and propositions. Thought involves mental representations of propositions. Occurrently believing φ consists of entertaining a mental item that represents φ and adopting a mental attitude toward that representation which we might call "mental affirmation." Similarly, occurrently disbelieving φ consists of mentally denying a representation of φ, and occurrently withholding on φ consists of entertaining a representation of φ while refraining from affirming it or denying it. Representations of propositions are mental items in the same sense that after-images and pains are mental items. If one were disposed to talk that way, one might say that representations of propositions are "sentence tokens in the language of thought."

I assume that it is impossible to occurrently believe a proposition φ and occurrently withhold on φ at the same time:

(2) $\Diamond$(S occurrently believes φ & S occurrently withholds on ψ) $\supset \varphi \neq \psi$.

It appears to be equally impossible to occurrently believe and occurrently disbelieve φ at the same time, and impossible to occurrently believe φ twice at the same time. This has an important implication about our mental representations of propositions. If two representations of φ could be phenomenologically distinguishable, it would be at least logically possible for a person to mentally affirm one and mentally withhold on another, and perhaps mentally deny a third, and so on. Thus it would be possible to occurrently believe the same proposition twice at the same time, and at the same time to also occurrently disbelieve it and occurrently withhold on it. But these are all impossible combinations. Thus it must be true that any two of a person's representations of a single proposition are phenomenologically indistinguishable from one another. Consequently:

(3) If occurrently believing φ is phenomenologically distinguishable from occurrently believing ψ, then $\varphi \neq \psi$.[2]

Applying principle (3) to my belief that Carol has red hair, it is phenomenologically unrealistic to suppose that the proposition I believe actually contains a Searle-type description as a constituent. I am not mentally surveying all the vast number of descriptions of Carol I could give and collecting them into a single thought. In fact, I could not even enumerate all those descriptions without considerable mental effort. If I have to search description out, it is not part of my actual thought. The belief I have when I occurrently believe Carol to have red hair is phenomenologically distinguishable from the belief I would have if I employed such a complex Searle-type description, and hence the propositions are distinct.

It must be concluded that in a case like this in which I know a great deal about the object of which I am thinking, I do not ordinarily think of it under a description. If I do not think of my wife under a description, how does my belief pick out its object? It is a bit tempting to suppose that when I think about my wife in this way, she herself is a constituent of my thought. I just *think of the woman*, I do not think of her under a description. According to this proposal, some propositions contain objects themselves as constitutents, rather than descriptions that pick out the objects, and then in thinking about an object we entertain these propositions directly.

It would be hard to imagine how the object itself could somehow be a constituent of your belief, but a little reflection indicates that that is an incorrect picture of the situation anyway. Imagine yourself knowing two people well, and then discovering one day that they were really one and the same person who had been fooling you with disguises. Let us suppose that in his two identities, this person went under the names 'Robinson' and 'Thompson'. Before discovering the masquerade, if you occurrently believed that Robinson was tall and you occurrently believed that Thompson was tall, you were certainly having two different thoughts. Your two states of occurrent believing were phenomenologically distinguishable, so you were believing two different propositions, despite the fact that you were believing the same thing about the same object and you were not thinking about the object under a description in either case. This indicates that even though your thoughts about Robinson and Thompson were not mediated by descriptions, they involved some kind of mental representation. If your belief that Robinson is tall was different from your belief that Thompson is tall, then you must have been thinking about Robinson and Thompson in different ways, and hence the man himself was not a literal constituent of your thought.

There is some kind of mental representation involved in beliefs like the foregoing, but it does not consist of thinking of the objects under a description. Cases of the sort we have been discussing involve thinking of objects in special ways. I propose to call these "*de re* ways of thinking of objects," or more briefly, "*de re* representations." Belief wherein one employs *de re* representations will be called "*de re* belief." I will say that a *de re* belief *involves* the corresponding representation and that the *de re* representation *represents* the object about which it is a way of thinking. That object will be called the *representatum* of the representation. If a belief involves a particular representation, then the representatum of that representation is the (or a) subject of the belief.

3. THE SUBJECT OF A *DE RE* BELIEF

Numerous questions arise concerning *de re* belief and *de re* representations, some logical and some psychological. The most important for our purposes seems to be this: Given a *de re* representation, what determines its representatum? It seems initially reasonable to suppose that the representatum must be determined in some way by the *de re* beliefs one has involving that representation. Such an account is more plausible for some cases than for others. There seem to be essentially two ways in which we come to employ *de re* representations: (1) we may begin with the *de dicto* belief that there is a unique object exemplifying some concept a (a may be a long conjunction), and we subsequently come to think of that object in a *de re* way; (2) we may simply perceive the object and immediately come to think of it in a *de re* way. In the latter case, it is unclear whether we must originally have any beliefs at all involving the *de re* representation, and even if we do, they would seem to be irrelevant to determining the representatum. The perception itself determines the representatum. When we acquire a *de re* representation perceptually, then we are thinking about whatever we are perceiving.

Perhaps we should split the account of *de re* representation in two, giving separate accounts of *de re* representations acquired perceptually and *de re* representations derived from antecedent *de dicto* beliefs. It seems initially plausible to suppose, in the latter case, that if we begin with the *de dicto* belief that there is a unique thing exemplifying a, and there is such a unique object x, then if we move from the *de dicto* belief to a *de re* representation, we are automatically thinking about x. This is the *belief satisfaction* account of *de re* representation. However, an example suffices to show that more is required than just belief satisfaction. Suppose my friend Richard tells me a story about a putative ancient Greek named "Dilapides" whose philosophical view was that everything is broken. Richard is just making the story up, but I believe him and so come to believe that there was a unique individual having all the characteristics attributed to Dilapides in the story. Suppose that at this point I do not think of Dilapides in a *de re* way but merely have the *de dicto* belief that there was a unique individual with all those characteristics. Among the characteristics I attribute to Dilapides may be that of being the person about whom Richard was telling me, but we can suppose that after a bit I forget where I heard the story and simply retain the *de dicto* belief that there was a unique individual having all the characteristics enumerated in the story. Suppose that at that point I come to think of the putative Dilapides in a *de re* way. Suppose further that, purely by chance and unknown to Richard, there was a unique individual having all those characteristics. It would follow from the belief-satisfaction theory that in thinking about Dilapides I am thinking about that individual. But that seems false. A necessary condition for my beliefs to be about a specific individual is that in telling me the story, Richard was telling me about that individual. As Richard was not in fact talking about any individual, it follows that when I think of Dilapides in a *de re* way I am not thinking about anyone, regardless of whether there is someone satisfying all my original beliefs about Dilapides.

Consider another example. Suppose I am in charge of a maximum security building that is protected by all sorts of electronic sensors that will indicate the presence of anything moving in its immediate vicinity. The sensors indicate the presence of a small animal on the roof, and upon hearing a "meow" transmitted from the roof I conclude that there is a cat on the roof. I come to think of this putative cat in a *de re* way, draw more conclusions about it on the basis of the information conveyed by the sensors, and so on. Suppose further that there is a cat on the roof, but it has somehow escaped detection by the sensors which are in fact sensing the presence of a misguided squirrel (who meows). Although there is a unique cat on the roof, I am not thinking of *that* cat when I think in a *de re* way about the putative cat on the roof. There is no connection between my thought and the cat that just happens to be there. A necessary condition for me to be thinking about that cat is that it be the cat detected by the sensors. Nor am I thinking about the squirrel. My *de re* belief is derived from the *de dicto* belief that there is a cat on the roof, and as such it must be about a cat if it is about anything. If this is not obvious, suppose instead that what the sensors detected was a branch blowing onto the roof and that the "meow" was the sound of the branch scraping against something. I am clearly not thinking about the branch when I think in a *de re* way about the putative cat.

When I acquire a *de re* representation on the basis of an initial *de dicto* belief, I begin with the *de dicto* belief that there is a unique a (for some concept a). But the preceding examples indicate that when I come to think in a *de re* way I am not automatically thinking about the unique a (even if there is one). I am not thinking about the unique a *whatever* it is; rather, I am thinking about a particular object (the object Richard told me about or the object detected by the sensors) as the unique a. A necessary condition for me to think about the object in this way is that it be the unique a, but that is not a sufficient condition. I suggest that it is also required that I have epistemic contact with the unique a.[3] If that epistemic contact relates me to a particular object (e.g., the object Richard was talking about or the object detected by the sensors), then my *de re* way of thinking can only be a way of thinking about that particular object.

In defense of this suggestion, first note that for one to come to think of the a in a *de re* way, it does seem to be required that one have a good reason for thinking that there is a unique a. For example, suppose the unsupported belief that there is a unique eleven-toed English mathematician named "Charlie" is implanted directly in Louis's brain through neurological manipulation and that this leads Louis to think in a *de re* way about this putative individual. It turns out to everyone's surprise that there really is a unique eleven-toed English mathematician named "Charlie." As there is no connection between this fact and Louis's belief, we would not agree that Louis has all along been thinking of Charlie.

If epistemic contact with the unique *a* is required, in what does that consist? In the Dilapides example, I had a good reason for believing that there was a unique individual possessing all the attributes enumerated in the story, but that reason was defeasible and would be defeated by the discovery that the unique individual possessing all those attributes was not the individual Richard was telling me about. I also had a defeasible reason for believing there to be a unique cat on the roof, and that reason would be defeated by the discovery that the unique cat on the roof was not being detected by the sensors. I suggest in general that a necessary condition for me to come to think of the unique *a* in a *de re* way is that I have a good reason for believing there to be a unique *a* and that that reason would not be defeated by knowledge of the actual facts of the matter. Knowledge of the actual facts might give you a different reason for believing there to be a unique *a*, but if your original reason were not sustained then you would not have been thinking of the unique *a*. If your reason would not be defeated by knowledge of all the relevant facts, let us describe it as *non-defective*. Thus a necessary condition for me to come to think of the unique *a* in a *de re* way is that I have a non-defective good reason for believing there to be a unique *a*.

I might, however, have a non-defective good reason for believing there to be a unique *a* but ignore it and instead believe there to be a unique *a* for a different reason which either is not a good reason or is defective. For example, if in the Dilapides case I had independent evidence for the existence of Dilapides but ignored it and instead believed in the existence of Dilapides simply because Richard told me that he existed, I would not then be thinking in a *de re* way about the real Dilapides. For epistemic contact we must insist, then, not only that one *have* a non-defective good reason for believing there to be a unique *a* but also that one believe it *for* a non-defective good reason.

The notion of a good reason requires elaboration. There is a distinction between a reason being a good reason by itself and its being a good reason given everything else that one believes. If one not only believes the reason but also believes various propositions that are defeaters for the reason, then the reason may be a good reason by itself but not a good reason given one's other beliefs. The claim that one proposition by itself is a good reason for believing another proposition affirms a logical relationship between the two propositions. It is to say that the one is what I have elsewhere[4] called a *logically good reason* for the other. The preceding observation is then the observation that the justification arising from a logically good reason may be destroyed by one's believing various defeaters for the logically good reason.

Defeaters may prevent one's logically good reasons from giving one knowledge in either of two ways. On the one hand, if one *believes* defeaters, this may destroy one's justification and thereby prevent one from having knowledge. On the other hand, there may be defeaters that are true without one believing them. In that case one's reason is defective, in the sense defined above, and although one's justification remains intact, one still does not have knowledge.

Turning to the notion of epistemic contact, we have required that one's reason for believing there to be a unique a be a logically good reason and that it not be defective. We have not, however, said whether epistemic contact requires that one's reason not be defeated by one's other beliefs. In other words, does epistemic contact require merely a logically good reason or a reason that is good in the context of everything else that one believes? One would naturally suppose the latter to be required, but somewhat surprisingly, it seems that only the former is required. For example, suppose that Jones tells me that there is a unique individual of a certain description a, and on that basis I come to believe that there is such an individual and I come to think of that putative individual in a *de re* way. Suppose further that Jones knows that there is such an individual and is telling the truth. However, I have independent overwhelming evidence to the effect that Jones is a liar and not to be trusted in such matters. Despite this evidence, I believe Jones (perhaps he is my father, and various psychological forces are involved in this irrational behavior). Under the circumstances, I am not justified in believing that there is a unique a. I believe that for a logically good reason, viz., Jones told me that there is a unique a and what people tell me tends to be true, but I also believe defeaters for that reason. Given that Jones really was talking knowlingly about a particular individual and I believed him, it seems that I am subsequently thinking about that individual despite the fact that I am not justified in believing him to exist. This illustrates that epistemic contact requires my reason only to be a logically good one, not that it be undefeated by my other beliefs. Summing up then, epistemic contact consists of my believing there to be a unique a for a non-defective logically good reason.

The way in which my epistemic contact with the unique a may relate me to a *specific* object is that there is a relation R such that my reason for believing there to be a unique a would be defeated by the discovery that it is false that the thing standing in the relation R to me is the unique a. In the Dilapides example, R is the relation in which I stand to an object iff it is the object Richard was telling me about; and in the cat-on-the-roof example, R is the relation in which I stand to an object iff it is the object detected by my sensors. When my reason for believing that there is a unique a is defeasible in this way, then a necessary condition for me to come to think of the unique a in a *de re* way (starting from the *de dicto* belief that there is a unique a) is that I stand in the relation R to a unique object, and that object is the unique a. That this is a necessary condition follows from the requirement that my reason be non-defective. This explains the sense in which my epistemic contact may select a specific object for my *de re* representation to represent. Let us call a reason that is defeasible in this manner a *specific reason* for thinking that there is a unique a. It is a reason for thinking that a specific thing is the unique a.

It is also possible to have a non-specific reason for believing that there is a unique a. For example, I have reason to believe that each person has a unique (biological) father, and on that basis I may believe that Jones has a unique father without having any idea who Jones's father is. Despite the fact that I have only a non-specific reason for believing this, I can come to think of Jones's father in a *de re* way. Thus specific reasons are not required for epistemic contact.

I propose then that we adopt the following as our account of *de re* representation for those cases in which the representation is derived from a *de dicto* belief:

(4) If τ is a *de re* representation derived from S's belief that there is a unique a, τ represents x iff: (1) x is the unique a, and (2) at the time of the derivation, S believed there to be a unique a for a non-defective logically good reason.

According to (4), *de re* representations are devices for thinking of objects whose existence we have found out about in particular ways. You have not found out that an object exists if your reasons are defective. The cases in which there is a unique a but you are not thinking about it are cases in which you have not found out that there is a unique a, because either your reason for believing there to be a unique a was not a logically good reason or it was defective.

Superficial consideration of (4) suggests that it makes representation a peculiar admixture of description satisfaction and epistemic contact. However, that is misleading. To find out that a certain object exists, you must be thinking about it in some way. Principle (4) just deals with the case in which, in finding out that the object exists, you are thinking of it under a description. The belief-satisfaction part of (4) is an artifact of this artificial restriction to cases in which we begin by thinking of the object under a description. There are other ways of thinking of objects, i.e., other representations. For example, in thinking about an object we are perceiving, we do not normally think of it under a description. Given a representation ν, it seems that we should be able to begin with the belief that there is a unique thing that is ν, and then derive a *de re* representation from that. When we speak of "the belief that there is a unique thing that is ν," we mean a belief about a certain object or putative object wherein that object is represented in your belief by ν and you believe that there is a unique thing that is the object. It then appears that we can generalize (4) to:

(5) If ν is a representation and τ is a *de re* representation derived from S's belief that there is a unique thing that is ν, τ represents x iff: (1) ν represents x, and (2) at the time of the derivation, S believed there to be a unique thing that is ν for a non-defective logically good reason.

To illustrate (5), consider *de re* representations that are derived from perception. We have a basically simple account of representation in this case:

(6) If τ is a *de re* representation derived from S's perception of x, then τ represents x.

I suggest that (6) can be derived from (5) together with some facts about perception. You perceive an object by being "perceptually acquainted with" a percept, where a percept is a mental item (in the same sense that an afterimage or a pain is a mental item). Philosophers have long pondered the relationship between the percept and the object of which it is a percept, but I propose that we can think of percepts as ways of thinking of objects, i.e., representations. As such, they fall into the same category as *de re* representations and the representations involved in thinking of objects under descriptions. Percepts represent perceived objects in precisely the same sense that other representations represent objects. This might suggest that the *de re* representations that are derived from perception are the percepts themselves. However, once we have perceived an object, we do not continue to think of that object in terms of the percept after the perception, for two reasons. First, we may continue to think of the object while forgetting what it looked like, so clearly we are not thinking of it in terms of the percept. Second, the percept (which is a repeatable thing) must be available for perceiving (and hence thinking about) another object that looks the same way at a later time. Thus the *de re* representation is in some sense derived from the operation of the percept without being identical with the percept. Given that the percept is a representation, it makes sense to talk about one having the belief that there is a unique thing which is "that object," wherein you think of "that object" in terms of the percept. This is presumably a belief you have in any ordinary case of perception in which you do not take yourself to be hallucinating. The suggestion is then that your *de re* representation is derived from this existential belief and that the representation proceeds in accordance with (5). For this to be correct (and assuming (6)), it must be the case that whenever your reason for holding the existential belief is defective, you are not really perceiving anything. Your (defeasible) reason for holding the existential belief is simply that you are presented with that percept.[5] Is it true that whenever the relevant facts of the case are such that knowledge of them would defeat this reason, you are not perceiving anything in terms of that percept? To evaluate this, we must consider what facts can defeat this reason. There seem to be only two kinds of facts that can do this: (1) there not being any object suitably placed for you to be perceiving it with this percept; (2) your perceptual apparatus being abnormal so that even if there is a suitable object to be perceived, your percept is not caused in the normal way by the presence of that object. If either of these is the case, then you do not perceive anything with your percept. If this is correct, then your reason being defective does entail that you are not perceiving anything with the percept. Hence (6) becomes derivable from (5), suggesting once again that (5) is the basic principle governing *de re* representation.

We arrived at our notion of *de re* belief by examining cases in which, despite a person's having a number of descriptions available to him of the object about which he is thinking, he is not thinking about that object *under* any of those descriptions. Our analysis of representation now enables us to see that there can also be cases in which a person thinks about an object without being able to give *any* description that uniquely characterizes it. If a *de re* representation is derived from an initial *de dicto* belief to the effect that there is a unique thing that is a, then initially one can provide the description 'the thing that is a' for the object. But once one has the use of the *de re* representation for thinking about the object, there is no reason one must remember any longer that the object was the thing that was a. If one forgets this, one's *de re* beliefs about the object may no longer contain sufficient descriptive material to uniquely characterize the object. Donnellan gives an example that might be construed as having this form:

> Suppose a child is gotten up from sleep at a party and introduced to someone as 'Tom', who then says a few words to the child. Later the child says to his parents, 'Tom is a nice man.' The only thing he can say about 'Tom' is that Tom was at the party. Moreover, he is unable to recognize anyone as 'Tom' on subsequent occasions. His parents give lots of parties and they have numerous friends named 'Tom'. The case could be built up, I think, so that nothing the child possesses in the way of descriptions, dispositions to recognize, serves to pick out in the standard way anybody uniquely.[6]

In such a case, upon meeting the man at the party, the child might have acquired a *de re* way of thinking of him. Initially, he may have had descriptions that were sufficient to pick the man out (e.g., 'the man I am now looking at'), and by virtue of those descriptions his representation has a well-determined representatum. He no longer recalls those descriptions, but that does not incapacitate his representation.

4. *DE RE* PROPOSITIONS

When one thinks of an object in a *de re* way and believes something about it, what one believes is a proposition. Such propositions might reasonably be called "*de re* propositions." *De re* propositions have a logical characteristic that is importantly at variance with the traditional conception of propositions. This is that they cannot be entertained or believed by two different individuals. Let us define:

(7) φ *is logically idiosyncratic relative to* S iff $\Diamond$(S believes φ) & $\Box(\forall S^*)(S^* \neq S \supset S^*$ does not believe φ).

It is my contention that *de re* propositions are logically idiosyncratic. To defend this contention, let us begin by considering what is required for one and the same person to believe the same *de re* proposition on two different occasions.

Let us describe two *de re* representations as *doxastically equivalent* if they can be employed interchangeably in belief in the same *de re* proposition. We have seen that if occurrently believing φ is phenomenologically distinguishable from occurrently believing ψ, then $\varphi \neq \psi$. Thus, to believe the same *de re* proposition twice, one's belief states must be phenomenologically the same on both occasions, and hence one must be employing the same *de re* representation on both occasions. Thus a necessary condition for a single person to believe the same *de re* proposition twice is that he be employing the same *de re* representations on both occasions. Hence no two *de re* representations of a single person are doxastically equivalent.

It is doubtful that the preceding criterion is even in principle applicable in attempting to determine whether two different people have the same *de re* belief. That criterion proceeds in terms of whether two different mental states are phenomenologically the same, but I doubt that interpersonal comparisons of phenomenological sameness are intelligible. Our ordinary interpersonal comparisons of mental states are in a broad sense "functional" rather than phenomenological. That is, we compare mental states in terms of the roles they play in perception or cognition, and we say that they are the same if they play the same roles. For example, I judge you to be appeared to in the same ways as I am (i.e., redly) if you are appeared to in that way which, in you, stands in the same perceptual relationship to red objects as does the state of being appeared to redly in me. For this sort of judgment it is irrelevant whether our perceptual states are phenomenologically the same. Furthermore, there is no apparent way to tell whether the states of two people are phenomenologically the same. Considerations based upon the external observations of other people give us only functional information about their mental states. To make sense of interpersonal phenomenological sameness, one is reduced to saying something like, "If God could look into the minds of two different people he could tell whether their mental states are really the same," but that makes no real sense as far as I can see. Thus I suspect that the only kinds of interpersonal comparisons of mental states that do make sense are functional comparisons, i.e., comparisions in terms of perceptual and cognitive role.

However, even if it is insisted that interpersonal comparisons of phenomenological sameness do make sense, it can still be argued that they cannot be used as in the intrapersonal case to generate a criterion for when two people have the same *de re* belief. For suppose that such comparisons do make sense in a way that makes them different from functional comparisons. As phenomenological sameness is something separate from functional considerations, there is no reason to suppose that phenomenologically identical states play the same functional roles in different people. For example, the "inverted spectrum" becomes a real possibility. That is, it could happen that the sensation that, in me, constitutes being appeared to redly, in you constitutes being appeared to bluely. That must be at least logically possible. Analogously, the fact that two people are employing phenomenologically identical *de re* representations gives us no reason to suppose that their representations either represent the same objects or are doxastically equivalent. The latter is a functional comparison, not a phenomenological one, and there is no reason at all to think that the phenomenological comparison gives us a basis for the functional comparison. Thus appeal to phenomenological sameness cannot help us here. If it is to be possible for two different people to have the same *de re* belief, then the relation between their *de re* representations must be a functional one rather than one of phenomenological sameness.

Consider a case in which S and S* employ the *de re* representations τ and τ^*, respectively, and for simplicity suppose that each is derived, in accordance with principle (4), from beliefs that there are unique objects exemplifying certain descriptions. Then it seems that the most that could conceivably be required for τ and τ^* to be doxastically equivalent is that they be derived from the same conceptual description a and that S and S* have the same non-defective reason for believing there to be a unique thing exemplifying a. This seems to be the strongest functional condition we could formulate. However, reflection indicates that even this very strong condition is not sufficient. The difficulty is that a single individual can employ two different *de re* representations that are related to one another in this way. Suppose that on some basis S comes to believe that there is a unique object exemplifying *a*, and he comes to think of that object in a *de re* way, employing the *de re* representation τ. He may subsequently acquire many other *de re* beliefs involving τ, and eventually forget his original belief that the representatum of τ uniquely exemplifies *a*. Much later, he may come to believe all over again and on the same basis that there is a unique object exemplifying *a*, without associating that with the *de re* representation τ, and so come to think of that object in terms of a new *de re* representation ν. τ and ν are derived from the same belief (that there is a unique object exemplifying *a*) held for the same non-defective reasons, but τ and ν are different *de re* representations and so, as we have seen, are not doxastically equivalent. S*'s *de re* representation τ* stands in the same relation to both τ and ν. τ* cannot be doxastically equivalent to both τ and ν as they are not doxastically equivalent to one another, and there is nothing to relate τ* more closely to one of τ and ν rather than the other, so we must conclude that τ* is not doxastically equivalent to either τ or ν. Thus the proposed functional criterion is inadequate to ensure that *de re* representations employed by different people are doxastically equivalent. There appears to be no more stringent condition that could be required which would avoid this argument, so I think it must be concluded that there is no reasonable criterion for *de re* representations of different people to be doxastically equivalent. As there is no way to make such a comparison, it must be concluded that the *de re* representations of two different people can never be doxastically equivalent, and hence two different people can never entertain the same *de re* proposition. Consequently, *de re* propositions are logically idiosyncratic.

This is a surprising conclusion. It requires *de re* propositions to be very different from the way propositions have traditionally been supposed to be. For example, propositions have been supposed to be abstract entities having necessary existence, but if a *de re* proposition can only be entertained by a single individual, it is at least plausible to suppose that its existence is contingent upon the existence of that individual. To suppose otherwise smacks of talk of "merely possible objects," which I at least find repugnant. Various responses are possible here. It might, for example, be suggested that unlike *de dicto* belief, *de re* belief does not have propositional objects, i.e., there are no *de re* propositions. However, the case for *de re* propositions seems no different from the case for propositions in general. One might, of course, deny that there are any propositions at all, but that is a whole different matter unrelated to *de re* belief. It is at least apparent that the recognition of *de re* belief and *de re* ways of thinking of objects must force us to rethink a number of matters regarding both the nature of thought and the philosophy of logic.[7]

Notes

1. Notice that we cannot, without a regress, appeal to "doxastic" descriptions like 'the person I believe to be my wife'. That description does pick her out, because she is the unique person I believe to be my wife. But according to the theory under consideration, in order for it to

be true that I believe her to be my wife, I must think of her under some other description, and it is the existence of that other description that is in doubt.

2. This argument was suggested to me by a somewhat similar argument in Steven Schiffer, "The Basis of Reference," *Erkenntnis* 13 (1978):171–206.

3. This is reminiscent of some remarks of Jaegwon Kim in "Perception and Reference without Causality," *Journal of Philosophy* 74:606–20.

4. In *Knowledge and Justification* (Princeton, 1974).

5. I have defended this at length in *Knowledge and Justification*.

6. Keith Donnellan, "Proper Names and Identifying Descriptions," in *Semantics of Natural Language*, ed. Donald Davidson and Gilbert Harman (Reidel, 1972).

7. I am particularly indebted to Diana Ackerman, Richard Feldman, and John Tienson for helpful discussions about earlier versions of this paper.

Thinking about an Object: Comments on Pollock[1]

DIANA ACKERMAN

I have argued elsewhere[2] that there are non-descriptive ways of thinking about objects, so of course I agree with Pollock on this point. Pollock's arguments for this view are also somewhat similar to mine, although mine occurred in conjunction with additional views about the connotations of proper names, which rest partly on positions about the relation between language and thought that are independent of what Pollock discusses in this paper. I have some disagreements with Pollock too, but first a point of clarification about his use of the term '*de re*' seems in order. As Pollock has indicated to me in conversation, he is not using this term in (what I take to be) its usual sense. This usual sense contrasts *de dicto* ascriptions of necessity to propositions and *de dicto* beliefs in propositions with *de re* ascriptions to entities of necessary properties and *de re* beliefs of entities that they have certain properties, where the *de re* locutions permit existential generalization. Pollock, however, is simply using '*de re*' as a convenient label for the sort of representation he wants to discuss, with no real connection with the usual sense. I will follow this use of Pollock's in these comments.

Since Pollock's notion of *de re* representation has nothing to do with existential generalization, the following question arises. Why does Pollock make the standards for non-descriptive *de re* representation higher than those for representation by the descriptions from which they are derived? Epistemic contact clearly is not required for descriptive representation; any attributive definite description in my thoughts represents whatever fits it regardless of whether I have any reason to believe that anything does. So why can there not be a non-descriptive representation that is derived from a definite description in such a way that the non-descriptive representation simply represents whatever the description denotes? This can be a case of non-descriptive representation that meets the left-hand side of the biconditional of Pollock's Principle 5, but not the right-hand side. Here is such a case. A police chief believes that all of a long series of diverse acts have been committed by a single person, but he does not believe this for a non-defective logically good reason. At first, he thinks of that person simply as the person who did each of the acts (with each act described in detail in his thought), but eventually he derives from this a non-descriptive representation τ, with the following characteristics. In having a thought involving τ, the police chief does not have the descriptions of all the acts immediately at his fingertips (any more than Pollock has immediately at his finger-tips all the descriptions of his wife that he could enumerate with considerable mental effort). For the police chief to get all these descriptions would take reflection and, as Pollock points out, if one has to search out a description, it is not part of one's actual thought. So τ is not a mere abbreviation for the complicated description. The relation between τ and the complicated descriptive representation is like the re-lation between the terms 'knowledge' and 'justified true belief supported by a chain of reasons that does not essentially involve a falsehood' (assuming for the sake of il-lustration that the latter gives a correct analysis of the former). The similarity is that the two representations in my example are not doxastically equivalent, but the fact that the description gives an analysis of τ can be learned by investigating the way the police chief uses τ, and especially by generalizing from his replies to questions about whether something would count as its representation in simple described hypothetical cases. This is the standard philosophical example—and counterexample method for arriving at and testing analyses. It enables us to get at the *final* test for determining the application of a notion. In fact, this case will go through just as well if we sup-pose that the police chief merely entertains without believing the proposition that all the acts in question were committed by a single person. Thus Pollock seems wrong in supposing that "There seem to be essentially two ways in which we come to employ *de re* representations,"[3] and that the way that is launched by a descrip-tion always involves a belief that the description is uniquely exemplified.

It might be objected here that τ has the descriptive force of some description such as 'the man who did all these things'. But since the only specification of "all these things" that the police chief has immediately at his fingertips is that they are the things done by the representatum of τ, this account is too circular to count as descriptive in any interesting sense. (If it did count as descriptive, by similar rea-soning, we could call *any* representation descriptive by saying it has the force of the description 'the thing that has these characteristics', where "these" characteristics are immediately identifiable only as the characteristics of its representatum.)

What about Pollock's own examples of *de re* representation? Does his account or one of the sort just sketched or neither apply to these cases? I think that Pollock has not given us enough information to decide. For example, the fact that S derives a *de re* representation from a description S* gives him supposedly as a description of a specific person S* is talking about does not seem to entail that S's *de re* rep-resentation cannot represent someone who fits the description and is not the specific person S* was talking about. This is because S may have derived the *de re* represen-tation to represent whoever, if anyone, has all the characteristics in the story, regard-less of whether S* was talking about this person, and S may reveal this by the condi-tions under which he identifies something as the representatum of his representation.

If the causal theory for determining the referent of a name one has gotten from other people is correct, this sort of non-descriptive representation is unlike a name in this respect. But that is all right; it is just a kind of non-descriptive representation that analyzes into (but is not doxastically equivalent to) the description in question. S's being in this state does not seem precluded simply by the fact that there was supposedly a specific individual that S* intended to talk about; S's own interests may not be that specific. Thus, in Pollock's Dilapides example, Richard's having actually made up the story may preclude anyone's being the referent of the name 'Dilapides', but it does not preclude someone's being the representatum of some non-descriptive representation of S's of the sort I have indicated.

The claim that Pollock's Principle 5 is true seems either to ignore S's own conditions for picking out his representatum or to assume that they must accord with Pollock's conditions. I have just argued against the second disjunct. And the first seems preposterous; why should we suppose Pollock's conditions are correct if they diverge from the conditions S actually uses to identify his representatum? We must look at these latter conditions in each case to determine the correct condition for identifying the representatum. Of course, I do not mean that S must be consciously aware of these conditions or have them at his fingertips; they are just the conditions that can be arrived at by generalizing from his replies to questions of the sort I have indicated. And I am not claiming that S's use of these conditions is an infallible guide; he may get confused and make a mistake, and there are other possible sorts of problems as well. But, *in general*, a generalization on the conditions that S uses as the *final* test for identifying the representatum in simple described hypothetical cases seems like a better way to get at the condition for identifying his representatum than does abstract theorizing that is not grounded in S's own use. As I have mentioned, such generalizations are basically applications of the standard philosophical example-and-counterexample method. I am also not claiming that Pollock's conditions are never the right conditions for identifying the representatum of any non-descriptive representation. They probably sometimes are. My point is that whether they are right in a particular case cannot be determined by looking only at how S acquired a representation; we must also see how he would identify its representatum. The foregoing examples show that this will not always yield Pollock's principle. In fact, τ can be a non-descriptive representation S derives in a situation of a sort Pollock describes even if generalizations on S's replies to the appropriate sorts of questions will yield results that neither are of the police chief case sort nor conform to Pollock's Principle 5.

One possible response at this point is to stipulate away my purported counterexamples by granting that they are cases of non-descriptive representation, but denying that they are *de re* in Pollock's sense of '*de re*', on the grounds that Pollock's sense is *defined* as applying only to the particular sort of non-descriptive representation that meets his principles. Pollock suggested this sort of response in discussion at the symposium where the original versions of both his paper and this reply were read. But such a response does not accord with Pollock's practice in his paper. For example, in discussing the case of the sensors, he says that the representatum of the *de re* representation in question must be a cat since it was derived from a *de dicto* belief about a cat and adds "*If this is not obvious*, suppose instead that what the sensors detected was a branch blowing onto the roof and that the 'meow' was the sound of the branch scraping against something. I am *clearly* not thinking about the branch when I think in a *de re* way about the putative cat."[4] Now, I would say that in this situation someone can be thinking of the branch if his interest is in representing whatever it was on the roof that caused the sensors to register, in the sense that this "interest" is revealed by his replies to questions about simple described hypothetical situations of the appropriate sort. If Pollock would stipulate away this possibility on the grounds that it does not conform to what he means by '*de re*', he would actually be using his examples to help express stipulative definitions of his sense of '*de re*' and it is hard to see how he could be relying on what is supposedly "obvious" or "clear" about these examples in the way suggested by the words italicized in the sentences quoted above. Similar objections apply to his later remark that "*one would naturally suppose* [a reason that is good in the context of everything else someone believes] to be required [for the epistemic contact necessary for *de re* representation] but, *somewhat surprisingly*, it seems that only [a logically good non-defective reason] is required."[5] How can this be "surprising" if Pollock is really defining '*de re*' partly in terms of the type of epistemic contact required? And again, how can it seem "initially plausible to suppose"[6] that the belief satisfaction account of *de re* representation is true (as Pollock says in introducing the Dilapides example) if this account is false *by stipulative definition*? If Pollock is *stipulating* that cases in which his Principle 5 is not satisfied do not count as *de re*, this cannot be a philosophical discovery that is uncovered by his examples and arguments in the way the passages quoted above suggest. Anyway, regardless of what we call my sorts of cases, they do involve non-descriptive representation in the sorts of situations Pollock discusses and hence are worth bringing up here.

I also have objections to some steps in Pollock's argument for the privacy of *de re* propositions. I will discuss the most interesting ones. First of all, Pollock seems wrong in saying that if two representations of φ could be phenomenologically distinguishable, it would be at least logically possible for a person to mentally affirm one and mentally withhold on another, and perhaps mentally deny a third, and so on. Thus it would be possible to occurrently believe the same proposition twice at the same time, and at the same time to also occurrently disbelieve it and occurrently withhold on it. But these are all impossible combinations."[7]

One way to see the objection here is by considering the relation between the following propositions:

(1) The F is red.

(2) The F is colored.

Surely, a representation of (1) is phenomenologically distinguishable from a representation of (2). But it does not seem to follow that it is possible for a person simultaneously to believe (1) occurrently and to disbelieve or withhold on (2) occurently. The view that these are impossible combinations seems as compelling as the impossibility of simultaneously occurrently believing a proposition and occurrently denying or withholding on it, and for the same reason. Of course the fact that proposition q follows logically from proposition p does not entail that occurrently believing p logically precludes occurrently denying or withholding on q. But with (1) and (2), there is a sense in which the logical relations between the propositions are so blatant that it is attractive to say that S's not occurrently withholding on or denying (2) at t is partly constitutive of the state of his occurrently believing (1) at t. It seems at least equally reasonable to say that it is partly constitutive of the state of S's occurrently believing p that he does not simultaneously occurrently deny or withhold on p. In the case involving (1) and (2), these logical constraints cannot entail that all of someone's representations of (1) and (2) are phenomenologically indistinguishable. The constraints are simply logical constraints on the occurrent propositional attitudes one can have simultaneously, even if one's representations of the propositions involved are phenomenologically distinguishable. This sort of account can apply equally well to the cases Pollock discusses, so his argument for the phenomenological indistinguishability of all of S's representations of any given proposition fails. And of course if one denies that it is impossible for one person simultaneously to believe (1) occurrently and occurrently to withhold on or deny (2), it seems no less reasonable to deny the impossibility of the combinations Pollock calls impossible. I think such denials would be implausible, although I will not try to argue for this view here. In fact, as I have suggested elsewhere, I doubt this sort of view can be effectively argued for if it is not accepted on (what I take to be) its inherent plausibility.[8]

Of course, this objection does not show that Pollock is wrong in his *conclusion* that any two of S's representations of a given proposition must be phenomenologically indistinguishable. I will not try to argue for this condition here. But I think it is not unreasonable, given that (as Pollock has informed me in conversation) what he requires for phenomenological indistinguishability of representations is not identity of words or pictures used to express thoughts, but something closer to phenomenological indistinguishability of the experience of "taking" certain words, pictures, or whatever in a certain way. Many philosophers would object to this whole sort of approach to representations, propositions, and experience. I think these objections fail, but I do not have the space to discuss them here.

Another problem with Pollock's privacy argument comes from his views about interpersonal phenomenological sameness and interpersonal belief comparisons. There are actually several difficulties here. First, Pollock's reason for doubting the intelligibility of interpersonal comparisons of phenomenological sameness is unconvincing. Of course, there is a sense in which he is clearly right in saying that "our ordinary interpersonal comparisons of mental states are in a broad sense 'functional' rather than phenomenological."[9] But this sense is only that our *evidence* for interpersonal comparisons of mental states is functional (and circumstantial, etc.) rather than phenomenological. There is a big gap between this reasonable view and the much more extreme position that the notion of interpersonal phenomenological sameness is unintelligible and that mental states of different people are the same iff they play the same functional role. One way to bridge this gap is by a kind of verificationism. Pollock's remarks seem to suggest this, but he does not argue for it and I cannot accept it. A very strong argument would be needed to show that interpersonal phenomenological comparisons are unintelligible, because the intuitive plausibility seems to be on the other side. For example, it at least *seems* compelling to suppose that a sadistic dentist who has also been a dental patient can intelligibly wonder hopefully whether he is inflicting on his patients pain of the same phenomenological sort he himself has felt in the dentist's chair, rather than just wondering about his patients' actual and counterfactual behavior, even if the latter gives him the evidence he can get to answer his question.

Moreover, Pollock gives only a question-begging argument for his further view that even if interpersonal comparisons of phenomenological sameness do make sense, functional comparisons are what we need for generating a criterion for interpersonal identity of *de re* beliefs. He says that if functional and phenomenological sameness are separate matters, then " . . . there is no reason to suppose that phenomenologically identical states play the same functional roles in different people."[10] And he concludes that "analogously, the fact that two people are employing phenomenologically identical *de re* representations gives us no reason to suppose that their representations . . . are doxastically equivalent."[11] But the attempt to justify this latter supposition on the grounds that it is "analogous" to the former begs the question of what follows about interpersonal *de re* belief identity conditions from a divergence of functional and phenomenological similarity of mental states.

Pollock's divergent standards for interpersonal and intrapersonal belief comparisons also raise the following problem. He says that if interpersonal comparisons of phenomenological sameness make sense, then, since phenomenological sameness is something separate from functional considerations, two people's phenomenologically indistinguishable mental states can have different functional roles. It seems equally reasonable to suppose that if the antecedent of this conditional is true, then two people's functionally identical mental states can differ phenomenologically, and that mental states of a single person can be related in this latter way. But now suppose that S's belief state b_1 is functionally but not phenomenologically the same as his belief state b_2 and that both these states are functionally the same as S*'s belief state b_3. By Pollock's phenomenological criterion for intrapersonal belief comparisons, b_1 and b_2 are not states of believing the same proposition, but by the functional interpersonal criterion, b_1 and b_2 are both the same belief state as b_3. In the final step of his privacy argument, Pollock considers a case somewhat like this for *de re* beliefs and concludes that it shows that no functional condition is strong enough to allow interpersonal identity of *de re* beliefs. But a similar result for *all* beliefs would be preposterous, as it would entail that no two persons could share the belief that $318 + 79 = 397$. Pollock also probably would dislike this result, since he emphasizes that the privacy of *de re* propositions puts them at variance with propositions as traditionally conceived. It seems much less reasonable to accept this result than to abandon the divergent standards for interpersonal and intrapersonal belief comparisons.

As the above remarks suggest, I do not think Pollock has considered the strongest possible condition for interpersonal *de re* belief identity. His condition can be strengthened by adding that the representations of S and S* are phenomenologically identical. Moreover, if the correctness of Pollock's Principle 5 is not taken to be part of a stipulative definition of '*de re*', the condition can be further strengthened by adding that S and S* would make the same replies to questions about described hypothetical cases of the sort described above. But of course these objections do not entail the falsity of the conclusion of Pollock's privacy argument. My own views about the privacy of non-descriptive representations are discussed elsewhere.[12,13]

Notes

1. A version of this paper was read as comments on an earlier version of Pollock's paper "Thinking about an Object" (this volume, pp. 487-99) in a symposium on thought at the Pacific Division A.P.A. Meetings, March 1979.

2. Diana Ackerman, "Proper Names, Propositional Attitudes and Non-Descriptive Connotations," *Philosophical Studies*" 35 (1979):55–69. See also Diana Ackerman, "Proper Names, Essences and Intuitive Beliefs," *Theory and Decision* 11 (1979):5–26.

3. Pollock, "Thinking about an Object," p. 490.

4. *Ibid.*, p. 491. Italics added.

5. *Ibid.*, p. 493. Italics added.

6. *Ibid.*, p. 490.

7. *Ibid.*, p. 488.

8. See my Critical Notice on Jonathan Bennett's *Linguistic Behavior, Canadian Journal of Philosophy* 8 (1978);792, where I discuss Bennett's views about whether one can simultaneously believe both a proposition and its negation.

9. Pollock, "Thinking about an Object," p. 496.

10. *Ibid.*, p. 497

11. *Ibid.*, p. 497.

12. My main treatment of this issue is in Diana Ackerman, "Recent Work on the Theory of Reference," *American Philosophical Quarterly*, forthcoming.

13. I am indebted to John Pollock, Philip Quinn, Ernest Sosa, and James Van Cleve for helpful discussions of the material in this paper.

Not Every Act of Thought
Has a Matching Proposition

ROMANE CLARK

The great thing about Ockham's Razor is that you can have it and your on-tology too. Everything depends, not on the truth of the principle—we all grant that—but on the necessities of the particular case. "To each act of thinking, there is a proposition." For all that Ockham's Razor says, that may be true. Even so, the principle is not completely empty. What it does do is establish a presumption. Given the principle, the onus is on those who invoke propositions to show that things are not otherwise equal, that the necessities of this case demand them. Those who invoke them must, given the principle, show not merely that the facts of mental life can be accommodated if we suppose the claim is true. They must show as well that the facts cannot be accommodated if we suppose that the claim is false.

On the opposite side of things, I do not suppose that it is possible to show that there are no propositions at all. I do not suppose that it is even possible to show that all mental acts are, in some ultimate ontological sense, proposition free. But I do think that the claim that to each act of thinking there is a mated proposition is false. I do think that an appeal to propositions in explaining the ontology of mental hap-penings is in general not necessary, often not helpful, and sometimes not possible. If so, given the presumption laid down by Ockham's Principle, we have reasonable grounds to do without propositions. (At least we do if we have something sufficient to put in their place. But if we do not, then perhaps a false but useful theory of ap-proximate validity is better than none at all.)

Accordingly, we have two main tasks. We need to see why it is that the claim above, the claim that there corresponds a proposition to each act of thinking, is not in general necessary and is sometimes not possible. And we need some suggestion at least of how to get along without propositions in characterizing mental life.

Is it really true that there is a proposition to each act of thinking? The claim is a powerful one, laying down a kind of Comprehension Axiom. "Think a thought, get a proposition." It's hard to believe that things can really be so easy.

In what follows, thoughts are taken to be occurrent mental happenings, the natural expressions for which include complete English sentences. This is a purely verbal decision, for ease in subsequent exposition. It is to be noted that thoughts, on this usage, are *not* a species of propositions and are not themselves the objects of our acts of thinking. They are, rather, kinds of acts distinguished by their contents or their texts, by what it is that distinguishes one act of, say, judging, a judging that *P*, from another, a judging that *Q*. Thoughts are the sorts of things we attribute to persons when we say things like: Jones thinks it is time to go home; or, Smith wishes he were home; or, Robinson has decided to go to the Denver meetings. They are the mental acts to which these persons might themselves give expression, saying: It's time to go home; or, If only I were home; or, I'll do it, I'll go to the meetings.

Thinkings, in this generic sense, include, then, acts of decision, and of doubt, desire, and planning, as well as of judgment. All of these are, on the present, stipulated, usage acts of thought. We express such thoughts, and we record the occurrences of such thoughts, with a range of grammatical forms. In English, at least, these are not all simple indicatives or ones embodying "that-clauses." Infinitive and subjunctive verb forms appear; we exploit the various moods of speech in giving voice to our thoughts.

It seems natural, when describing some man on an interesting occasion of his mental life, to distinguish what he does or suffers mentally from the content of his act. His act, perhaps, is a decision, not a judgment. He decides, not judges, to attend those meetings. The content of his act, what makes it the particular decision it is, is his deciding to go to the Denver meetings, not those in San Diego. Thoughts are thus particular mental acts of at least a certain minimal complexity, each with a certain specific content. In the simplest and apparently least problematic cases, they will at least consist of constituting acts of reference and of what we can awkwardly call acts of ascription. This usage is awkward most importantly for the way in which it blurs differences like those between what we judge to be true of what we think of, on one occasion, by contrast with what we set ourselves to do in making a certain resolution on another. But nothing much hangs on the terminology here. The important point is that we have mental doings of a certain constitutive complexity. These are doings with a certain content which constitutes a person's state of mind on the occasion of an occurrent thought. The point is important for it is this content which determines, presumably, how we can identify which proposition corresponds in the required way to a given act of thought. The relevant correspondence, presumably, is determined by our state of mind. Different contents, different thoughts. And different thoughts, then different propositions. Equally, same content, then same state of mind. And same state of mind, then, though not necessarily same thought, still the same corresponding proposition. It is this, presumably, which justifies saying that you can believe what I fear. We are in the same state of mind and so we have the same proposition before our minds when you judge and I fear, for example, that a constitutional convention will be called.

Well, how *are* propositions and states of mind related? In what does the correspondence consist? No doubt different theories will differ in the fine detail they offer in answer to questions like these. But we can extract a few features that seem to be common to certain theories that invoke propositions. On these theories, propositions are, in the first place, a kind of object. They can be thought of in their own right. And they are what is before the mind when one is in a given state of mind. They have implications and truth-values. They are, in the second place, objects of a certain, essential, complexity. They are constituted of objects which map in order one-to-one with the constituent acts of reference and ascription that constitute the mated thought when it occurs. To an act of reference, for instance, there is a constituent of the corresponding proposition which is uniquely determined by the content of that act and not by that act's referent, should it exist. Further, propositions, when true, are *made true* by the facts and are enduringly so. This leaves open the option that facts are themselves just true propositions. This option, as we know, is frequently exercised. Moreover, that the facts make true the propositions that are true leaves open the option that the match of fact and proposition is not necessarily one-to-one. This option, so far as I know, is not frequently exercised.

(Nonetheless, it might be that many facts make a given proposition true, rather as the proposition that someone is here at the Oberlin Colloquium from Indiana is multiply overdetermined by the facts, given the carload that has arrived. It also is possible that some one fact makes a number of propositions true, rather as John's particular, specific behavior makes it true that he ran, that he ran to the store, that he ran swiftly and directly to the store, and so on. Evidently, these apparent options and possibilities may be ruled out or may be reinforced by different, particular theories of propositions. It is regrettable that relatively little has been said concerning the relations among thoughts, facts and propositions, truth and making-true. The one evident and relevant point that emerges, however, no matter how the missing detail might be supplied, is this: There is an intimate and direct relation between acts of thought and the propositions that, on the occasions of the occurrences of such acts, are before the mind. This is essential. But although there may be such an intimate and direct relation between propositions, when true, and the facts that make them true, it is by no means evident that there must be. We will be occupied now with the former relation, suppressing for now, we hope without harm, questions concerning the latter.)

In any case, having collected these few features commonly endorsed by these sorts of theories of propositions, we return to the claim that initiated our discussion. This is the claim that to each thought there corresponds a proposition. We noted that in the simplest cases this involved the specific claim that there corresponds a certain correlated entity to my act of reference when thinking about an object, and a correlated attributive entity to my ascription of some property to what I think of. Whether or not what I think of exists, the "propositional-reference-correlate" of my act is an entity completely determined in its nature by the content of my act. It is an entity that is essentially or internally just as I think it (but, note: *not* just as I think *of it*. I do not, in ordinary acts of thoughts, think about propositional reference correlates).

One may think of these propositional correlates of an act of reference as Meinongian objects, of Fregean senses, or what you will. But the essential fact is that what is before the mind when one is in a certain state of mind is not, as such, the putative object of reference. That after all may not exist, or, existing, it may not be literally, or uniquely, as I think of it. But the propositional correlate is literally and uniquely as my act of reference specifies on each such occasion of reference. It may well be that given the occurrence of a felicitous act of reference, the object I then think of and the propositional correlate of my reference bear some quite direct and intimate relation. But this relation cannot be so intimate as to constitute identity. The girl I think of when I think of the high school class valedictorian cannot literally be the reference correlate of my thought, for that girl is the only redhead on the block and a proposition with a reference correlate like that is not the proposition before my mind. It was, indeed, just such facts about thinking which in part motivated the appeal to propositions in the first place. Further, although this does not quite show that facts cannot be identified with true propositions, it places a certain stress on the doctrine. Whatever else the facts that make true our beliefs may be like, they cannot literally include the actual physical objects we so often think we think about.

What propositional reference correlates actually are, are a kind of descriptional entity. To my thought of the high school class valedictorian, promulgated in just those terms, there may be an actual object, the girl who is also the only redhead on the block. But there is a distinct propositional reference correlate as well, and this last entity, unlike the former, is one whose nature is essentially constituted of the terms of my act of reference and whose existence is guaranteed by that act. It is an entity consisting exactly of the attribute, or of some unique correlate of the attribute, of being the high school valedictorian. So, too, when I think of my father, although he no longer exists, there is a reference correlate consisting of just the terms in which I on the occasion recall him. Similarly, for complete acts of thought as well, whether these be true, false, or neither (including as they do decisions as well as judgments), there are associated propositions. These are propositions constituted in a determinate way of reference- and ascription-correlates of the thoughts no matter what the actual states of affairs may be.

Theories involving features like these may seem excessive, but they are neither unmotivated nor silly. They nicely suffice to explain how our different mental acts can be the same, and to explain the implications of our thinking what we do even when what we think is not true. And they accommodate some of the recalcitrant facts of intentional contexts. If, given your state of mind, what is directly before your mind is a Meinongian objective or Fregean thought, then it is hardly surprising that identities of the objects of reference of your thought do not translate into identities of the related but distinct propositional objects.

However, even though such theories are motivated by real problems and even should they be adequate to resolve them, it is not clear that any such theory is the right theory. There is no indication in the first place that some such theory is necessary to any explanation of the motivating problems. But fundamentally such theories can be rejected for harsher reasons. The Comprehension Axiom underlying such theories is, if unqualified, false. It is not true that there is to each thought a proposition that corresponds to it in the required way. It is not true that to each act of reference there is a propositional reference correlate.[1] Because of this last point, it cannot be true that to each thought there is a proposition. And apart from this, although for similar reasons, we can *independently* arrive at the same conclusion.

We might have had such doubts all along if we had focused more on those thoughts in which we make decisions or in which we set ourselves or plan to do things. It is easy enough to define matching propositions for these sorts of mental acts. But it is not at all obvious that these are what is before our minds on such occasions. However that may be, the basic point is that there are thoughts for which, on pain of consistency, there cannot be corresponding propositions. It is to this point we now turn.

You think some thought. Perhaps you judge something the form of an expression for which is "a is F." There is then, by hypothesis, a proposition, that-(a^* is F^*), matching your judgment. Here a^* is the propositional reference correlate of your act of reference to a, and F^* is an attributive correlate of your act of ascription. (No conditions have been suggested for the nature of F^*, not even the minimal ones sketched for reference correlates. But we note that the reasons for concluding that a^* cannot literally be the object of reference, a, apply quite as well to the attributive correlate. F^* cannot literally be itself the property F which you ascribe to a. It cannot, for the property F may be identical with the property G although it is not true that $F^* = G^*$. The proposition matching your judgment that the couch is blue is not the proposition that the couch is the color of the sky, even though blue is that color.)

Propositions are objects. They are themselves the objects of our thoughts and references on occasion. And they do themselves exemplify various properties. It is true then that there will be propositions of the form: that-(that-a^* is F^*)* is G^*, matching our *thought* that the indicated proposition has the property G; and there will be states of affairs: (that-(a^* is F^*) is H), when the indicated *proposition itself* actually exemplifies the property H.

Given these things, it may happen in particular that when a proposition is itself the object of my thought, the resulting proposition matching my act of thought exemplifies the very property whose attributive correlate it embodies. That is, the property that I ascribe the object of my thought, a certain proposition, may be true of the resulting proposition as a whole. It may be, for instance, that (that-(p^* is F^*) is F), where p^* is the propositional reference correlate of my thought of the proposition that-p. This may happen. Propositions are objects and have properties. And the attributive correlates, Fregean senses or what you will, that occur within them are not, we have seen, to be identified with the property I ascribe.

We may call such propositions "Flashers." They exhibit externally the very property F whose attributive correlate, F^*, of the thought of the property, F, they contain. On the other hand, other propositions are "non-Flashers." They are such just in case it is not true that they are Flashers, i.e., just in case they do not exemplify the property F when they contain the attributive correlate F^*.

You may judge that some proposition, that-p, say, is a non-Flasher. There exists then a proposition, that-(p^* is a non-Flasher*), matching your thought. Let us call this proposition "X." The question arises whether or not X is itself a Flasher. Supposing that X is a Flasher leads to a contradiction, and supposing that X is not a Flasher leads to a contradiction. The conclusion we must draw then is that X does not after all exist.

(We parenthetically note that this is not of course to argue that there are now contradictory propositions. There are for all of this indeed propositions with internal correlates matching our thoughts of the round-square or with attributive correlates matching our inconsistent ascriptions. Our conclusion is not that X is, in a disguised way, itself internally inconsistent. It is rather that X itself does not exist. There is no such proposition. And so there is no proposition matching in the required way your original thought that the proposition that-p was a non-Flasher. And so it is not true that to every thought there is a proposition [of the sort specified by the theories].)

Supposing that X is a flasher leads, as we said, to a contradiction. We can see this, for its being a Flasher implies that X exemplifies the property whose attributive correlate it contains, and this was the property of being a non-Flasher. And X is a non-Flasher, we recall, just in case it is not true that X is a Flasher.[2]

Equally, supposing that X is not a Flasher leads to a contradiction. As just re-marked, a proposition is not a Flasher just in case it is a non-Flasher. But if X is not a Flasher, then X does not exemplify the property whose attributive correlate it contains. That is to say, X is not then a non-Flasher. But this contradicts our assumption, one step removed, that it is.

There are various ways one might respond to all this. One might, I suppose, deny that we really have thoughts of the indicated sort. But we certainly *seem* to. In fact, the whole reasoning turned on apparent reference to these very thoughts. To deny this strikes me as a move of question-begging desperation, but I leave it to the friends of propositions to sort that out. For the fact is that there remain other, very similar, consequences of any theories of propositions which have the minimal features we have noted. And there are yet other consequences, based on kinds of thought that are part of the mental lives of us all, that also suggest there is not in general a certain, mated proposition to each act of thought. These further conse-quences combine, I think, to deflate any merely local interest in the rehabilitation of Flashers.

We have not, in any case, yet exploited the fact that propositions are, on the theories at hand, bearers of truth and falsehood. In particular, we now wish to con-sider those among these theories which not only endorse the claim that propositions have truth-values but claim moreover that facts just *are* true propositions. (It may be, but it need not be, that *every* true proposition is *also* a fact on such a theory.) We have already suggested that this claim, that facts are true propositions, may need to be qualified. If actual physical things, and the way such things are, sometimes constitute facts, then it is hard to believe that true propositions can literally be facts. For we noted that, on pain of intentional puzzles about identity,[3] the constituents of propositions cannot literally be the physical objects and properties of which we (often believe ourselves to) think. But whatever the constituents of propositions may turn out to be, and whatever the elements of facts are, there remains the question of in what, on the theory, does the truth of a proposition consist. The apparent answer is that an atomic proposition that-p—a proposition an expression of which is, relative to some natural language, some atomic sentence of the logical form "$F(a)$"—is true just in case there is a fact, an ordered structure $\langle a,\phi \rangle$, such that a is a "fact-correlate" of a, a is a "fact-correlate" of F, and a is a. We need of course to know what it is for something to be a "fact-correlate" of something. Holding that for a moment, however, we can say that the proposition that-p is true if there is a fact, f, which is its fact-correlate. Saying this does not commit the theory to the requirement that all true propositions are made true by correlated facts; it is open whether some may be true by propositions that are made true in some way or another but that are not themselves facts. And saying this leaves open whether or not the atomic sentences of differing natural languages that express true propositions have in turn correlated facts that make them true. It may be for all this that an atomic truth in one language is a very complex truth in another.

Given the proposition that-a is F, it seems fairly clear what the fact-correlate, a, of a should be if such a correlate exists. It should be an object, *the* object, that uniquely exemplifies the properties that determine the nature of a. Suppose for instance that you judge that a particular object is F and that the proposition that-a is F is the proposition that is, on the theory, before your mind. a, then, is the propositional reference correlate of your act of reference and is constituted of a content specifically determined by the nature of that act of reference. Suppose that your act of reference is in fact felicitous, that there indeed exists an actual object that uniquely is the referent of your thought. Evidently this object will manifest those properties and features the thought of which constituted your reference to the object and whose propositional mappings constitute the propositional reference correlate. The object that in fact exemplifies these properties, thus related to a of the proposition, is a. In general, then, a is a fact-correlate of a only if a exemplifies the properties whose propositional correlates are constitutents of a. That is, a is a fact-correlate of $a \to (F)$ (F^* belongs to $a \to F(a)$).

It is less clear what the fact-correlate, ϕ, of F should be. Perhaps it is an attribute, or the set of actual instances of an attribute, or some determinate way in which the fact-correlate of the propositional reference correlate exists. Let us suppose that what counts as the fact-correlate, ϕ, of F is fixed by the theory in some plausible way. If so, then it is sufficient for the truth of a proposition that-a is F that there obtains a fact containing fact-correlates of a and f.

Suppose then that some proposition that-p is true and that it is made true by some fact. And suppose as the theory does that facts just are themselves true propositions. It may then be that the proposition that-p is the fact that makes that-p true. It may be its own fact-correlate (OFC), or it may not. Consider the proposition that p is not its own fact correlate, that-(that-p is not OFC), and call it X.

This putative proposition, X, does not exist. For if there is such a proposition, then either it too is its own fact-correlate or it is not. Suppose that it is. Then X makes true X. This last, that X is its own fact-correlate, requires then that its subject term, that-p, is the fact-correlate of that-p itself and that, as such, it exemplifies those properties whose propositional correlates are its own constituents. And it requires that its attributive term is also its own fact-correlate. That is, not-OFC is the fact-correlate of not-OFC. And of course it must be the case that-p is not-OFC.

Taking these requirements in turn, suppose that the subject term, that-p, of X is some ordinary proposition. Perhaps it is the proposition that a is F, for some arbitrary a and F. Since p is the fact-correlate of p, given the nature of X and its being OFC, we have that p is itself OFC and that, in turn, so too are its own constitutents. That is, this requires that a is the fact-correlate of a, that F is the fact-correlate of F, and of course that a is F. But if a is OFC, then a must exemplify the very properties or conditions that determine it to be just the propositional reference correlate that it is. This cannot, however, for every a, be the case.

The argument that this cannot, for every such a, be the case is a variant of an argument set out in the paper, referred to earlier, by William Rapaport, "Meinongian Theories and a Russellian Paradox." The present version of the argument is this: let a be the propositional reference correlate matching the thought of the object whose nature it is solely to be not-OFC. It does not matter whether such an object uniquely exists—in fact it cannot. But there is by hypothesis on the theory at least a propositional reference correlate to the putative thought of such a thing and that is a. a itself is OFC or not. If a is OFC, then a is the fact-correlate of a. And if a is the fact-correlate of a, then a must exemplify the property the thought of which determines the propositional correlate constituting a. That is to say, a is thus not-OFC, thereby contradicting our assumption.

On the other hand, if a is not OFC, then a does not exemplify the property, that of being not-OFC, whose propositional correlate constitutes a. And this is to say that it is not true that a is not OFC, again contradicting our assumption.

In general, it is not true that to every thought of an object there is an object of thought. It is not true that even if in some cases what we think of does not exist, there is nonetheless at least in such cases a propositional reference correlate. But since this is not true in general, it is also not true that there are propositions like X. For X required that there be propositional objects of reference whose own subject terms in turn might be their own fact-correlates. But as we have seen, this is not always possible. We think of objects, like a, that not only do not exist but have no being even as mere objects of thought. Accordingly, we also think thoughts for which there is thus no matching proposition, at least none of the sort so simply specified by these theories of propositions.

To complete the argument, we need to consider what it is for an attributive correlate to be its own fact-correlate. It is not rewarding or possible to do that now. For one thing, the scent of Russell's self-applying universals is strong, and we do not have the space to nose out the complexities there. For another thing, we have not collected enough detail about the nature of attributive correlates to develop the interesting implications of their presence here.

Also, to complete the argument, we need to return to X itself and consider the consequences of supposing that X is not its own fact-correlate. But it is clear by now, no doubt, how this would go. Thus, if X is not OFC, then either the subject-term of X, that-p, is not its own fact-correlate or else the attributive term, not-OFC, is not its own fact-correlate, or perhaps both. Suppose that that-p is not OFC and that it is in fact the proposition, say, that a is F. Then either a is not its own fact-correlate, or else . . . And so on. We might chase through these further possibilities, sprinkling self-reflections where we can. But the central point seems already clear. Theories of propositions, even as so minimally characterized here, are overly powerful. It is not true, as these theories lead us to suppose, that to every thought there is a certain matching proposition. It is not true that to every thought of an object there is an object of thought.

We might have doubted these things anyway, and on more substantive but perhaps less conclusive grounds. Two boys, squared off, each say or think "I can beat you up." It is clear enough, it seems, that each says what the other does and that each thinks, in our present usage, the same thought. That is, each act of thinking is the same. Each is the same kind of act, a judgment, with the same text. But it is equally clear that a fact that makes true one boy's belief does not in this case make true the other's. So there cannot be an intermediate entity, the proposition, poised in the direct and intimate way we have earlier supposed between our acts of thinking on the one hand and the facts on the other.

Indeed, what are the propositional reference correlates of each boy's thoughts on this occasion? How exactly do they differ? Surely, the meanings of the words by which they express their thoughts, and their uses of 'I' and 'you' are univocal in these occurrences. How then does the proposition matching the one act of thinking differ from that of the other with which it shares a text? If the proposition correlated with an act of thinking, or expressed in an assertion, is uniquely determined by the text or content of the act, or by the meanings of what is said, then it seems that but one proposition can correspond to the states of mind of the two youngsters. But, again, it seems this cannot be. It cannot if facts are what make propositions true in a unique and determinate way. For not both youngsters have, on this occasion, a true belief.

Or, to switch examples, I nervously glance down at my watch and think, "It's after nine o'clock. I've got to stop." But nonetheless, caught up by the occasion, your presence and all, I carry on. And five minutes later I look at my watch again and think again, "It's after nine o'clock. I've got to stop."[4] It seems as clear to me as anything can get to be in philosophical discussions that I have thought the same thought on these two occasions separated by just five minutes. And if to the text of any act of thought there uniquely corresponds a proposition, then it must be the same proposition that corresponds to each act of thought. Same text, therefore same proposition. But on the other hand, it seems this cannot be. For suppose my watch is three minutes fast, and suppose that the first of these two thoughts occurred in fact at 8:58, my watch then reading after 9:00. In these circumstances my first thought is false but the second is true. If so, how then can but one proposition match each? But if not, how, on the theory of propositions, are we to distinguish the distinct propositions which we now see must go with these acts of thought which seem to be quite the same but which may differ so radically in truth value?

We have, in our ascriptions of thoughts to ourselves and others, accordingly to account for those which, in such familiar ways, employ such types of pronomial reference. We need this on any account of mental life, and not merely on those which appeal to propositions. We need some characterization of the occurrences in our thought or speech of personal pronouns and demonstratives.

Puzzling as these may be, it would be wrong to make such mental ascriptions overly mysterious. On the golf green you attempt a ten-foot putt, which slides from left to right. I do the same thing. I attempt what you do although of course my ball, club, and putt are not yours. So, too, when we say that the one youngster thinks he can beat up the other, but the other thinks the same thing, each youngster uses his own ball and club as it were. Each makes his own reference and ascription. We need, on pain of ambiguity, to make clear *our* references in saying such things about the youngsters. Does the second youngster, in thinking the same way, think that *he* can beat up the first or does he rather agree with the first that he can be beaten up?

What this shows, I think, is what we should have expected anyway. It shows in the first place that when making mental ascriptions, we do not, at least do not often, attempt to reproduce or express precisely what is before the mind of the agent of the act on the given occasion. And it shows in the second place that our ascriptions are radically relativized. We need to keep clear, and to keep track of, the references and concepts of the mental agents to whom we attribute beliefs both from one another but also from our own.

There are various ways to sort out such pronomial ambiguities in communicating the mental ascriptions we make to others. However this may be done, it seems that an adequate account must incorporate at least these essential features. We need some device to make clear the scope of the terms expressing the references and concepts of the mental agents. We need some device making clear the pronomial cross-references to these which may occur in our making these mental ascriptions. Singular terms act thus rather like a kind of quantifier, each occurrence of which has a determinate scope and each of which possibly binds certain pronomial terms lying within its scope.

For instance, a sentence like this is multiply ambiguous: "John thinks that Harry thinks that he can beat him up." We can sort out the references of the pronouns, perhaps restating it in English: John thinks that Harry thinks that he, John, can beat him up; if that is the intended meaning. But we can also distinguish the speaker's from the agent's reference, saying sometimes: John thinks that Harry (whoever he may be) thinks that he, Harry, can beat him up. Or perhaps saying another time: John thinks that Harry thinks that he, John, can beat him up. There are two sorts of ambiguity in the original example, then, which get sorted out in two main ways. The parenthetical '(whoever he may be)' makes clear that 'Harry' is John's reference, not mine. Its occurrence is meant to sort out an ambiguity in the scope of the name. Its scope is internal to the expression of the thought that I ascribe to John. Ambiguities of scope are, of course, distinct from those carried by the occurrences of personal pronouns. These last are sorted out by making explicit the references of the given occurrence of the pronoun. We say in the example, 'he, Harry'.

Pronomial ambiguities are perhaps familiar enough. The former sort, ambiguities of scope, are nicely highlighted by examples like that used by Castañeda:[5] Columbus thought that Castro's Island was China. Evidently 'Castro's Island' was no part of Columbus' thought. But 'China' for all I know might well have been. 'Castro's Island' then has the larger scope. It is external to, and overarches, the expression of the ascription of the thought to Columbus. 'China' by contrast has a scope internal to the expression of that thought.

We require thus a systematic way of making explicit scope and references and cross-references of the various agents to whom we ascribe thoughts as well as those of our own. (We need as well a way of keeping track of the expression for the concepts we and these agents use. But we ignore that here.) If we think of the logic of our ascriptions of mental acts to psychical agents as a modal logic, as many now do, we will think of it as a logic with certain elements supplementing some version of standard logic. It will contain a set of unary modal operators, T, each of degree two. These are modal expressions for acts of thought, each to be qualified by expressions referring to the agents and occasions of the mental acts. Like other modal operators, the result of prefixing one of these to a sentence is a sentence. In addition, to each occurrence of a singular term, s, there is associated a scope indicator, $[s]$, quite in the manner of Russell's treatment of the scope of definite descriptions. (Like Russell, we take scope indicators to be auxiliary devices, ones not given voice in expressing what the sentence that contains them says.) In addition to these things, the logic will contain a pronominalizing operator, $*$. This when superscripted to a singular term yields a singular term. In particular, we think of $s*$ as a pronoun for the name s. ($s**$ we take to be just $s*$ itself. In general iterations of stars collapse.)

With these resources we can return to our multiply ambiguous example, "John thinks that Harry thinks that he can beat him up." In one of its meanings this can be given an approximate, first formal writing:

$$[j]\ T(j,\ now)[h]\ T(h,\ now)B(j*,h*).$$

We then read: John thinks that Harry (as John calls him) thinks that he, John, can beat him up.

So far as the semantics specifying the truth-conditions of sentences like these go, they can be given expression in a first-order version in the spirit of Hintikka. It runs something like this: in all worlds compatible with all I now believe there is someone, John, such that in all worlds compatible with all he, John, believes there is someone, Harry, such that in all worlds compatible with all he, Harry, believes it is true that John can beat up Harry.

This last version is important if only for showing that the first, formal version above is at best approximate but certainly not complete. It is incomplete in at least two very basic respects. Evidently we require, in addition to the elements already added—in addition to scope indicators and pronominalizing operators and special modalities—two special constants. We need, for the complete specification of thoughts to ourselves and others, singular terms fixing the occasion of the occurrence of our own ascription. We need the special constants 'I' and 'now'. The approximate version above is incomplete in another respect as well. It lacks, what its "world-theory" transcription makes evident, the presence of a modal prefix which, although tacit, relativizes each such ascription to its own agent; yours to you and mine to me. There is for each thought of mine, and so for each of my ascriptions of mental acts to others, a pair of scope indicators of widest compass, [I] and [now]. These are prefixed to the whole of the expression of my thought together with a certain modal operator which although tacit is universally present, governing all my thoughts. It is this which places the ascriptions I make in all the worlds compatible with my beliefs. This tacit universal modifier (TUM) of all my thoughts plays a central role in the attempt to characterize those states of mind for which there seems to be no, or at least no evident, matching proposition. The modifier is welcome anyway. Its presence gives logical force to G. E. Moore's intuition that it is not possible to have a belief with the following text: p but I do not believe that p. This can be true, but it is not something I can (rationally) believe. The attempt to express such a putative belief, with its TUM and all made explicit, contradicts a theorem of any logic with resources like ours. It is a theorem that

It is not the case that [I] [now] Bel (I, now) (p & not-Bel (I, now)p).

In any case, with this much apparatus, we can return to various examples and especially to ones involving so-called indexical references. Consider first this: John believes that he is happy. Once again, the sentence can be used to express quite distinct thoughts. For instance, the 'he' might have a demonstrative use in a given occurrence, meaning perhaps something like "that man, the one before him." John believes then of the man before him that he is happy and perhaps even *that* the man before him is happy. Suppressing the TUM for the moment, we then write in formal, quasi-English:

[j] [the man before him] Bel (j, now) (tmbh* is Happy).

Or it may be that the sentence is used to express the fact that John believes that he himself is happy. The thought "before John's mind" he would perhaps put into words as, "I'm happy." We write:

[j] Bel (j, now) [j] (j* is Happy),

with j* occurring as a first-person pronoun of smallest scope, internal to the expression of the thought I ascribe in this way to John. Or it may be that the sentence is used to express the fact that John believes of himself, however he secures that personal reference, that he is happy. We write:

[j] Bel (j, now) (j* is Happy).

This is to be distinguished from John's belief that he himself is happy. It might even be in certain bizarre circumstances that John, as I call him, forms the belief that John is happy without realizing that he, himself, is John. It turns out that neither of our possible versions of the sentence, "John believes that John is happy," implies that he believes that he, himself, is. That is, neither

[j] Bel (j, now) (j is Happy),

the sentence with the name having the larger scope, nor

[j] Bel (j, now) [j] (j is Happy),

the sentence with the name occurring with restricted scope, implies

[j] Bel (j, now) [j] (j* is Happy).

It is to be noted that, by contrast to such occurrences of 'he', the first-person pronoun (and 'now' as well) always lies within a scope indicator of widest extent. Each such occurrence, however deeply embedded in nested ascriptions of thoughts, has an external force and indicates nothing of how the mental agents to whom I refer in turn (are taken by me to) refer to me. The TUM secures the total ascription of my thought to me on the occasion of its occurrence. It is itself no part of the content of my thought or the text of what I believe. If John believes of me that I am happy, if he believes that I am happy, I record this in full, formal expression, writing:

[I] [now] T (I, now) [j] Bel (j, now) (H(I)).

The content of my thought, the *text of my state of mind*, is initiated by the (silent) scope indicator, [j], for the term, 'John'. The *belief I ascribe* to John, in the manner I ascribe it, is expressed in the internal clause, '(H(I))'. And the reference within it to myself is secured by the prefixed TUM with its associated scope indicators of largest extent. TUM is no part of the content of my state of mind, but it reflects the basic fact that there is in the occurrence of any thought at all a reference to the agent of the act. This reference is not in standard cases before the mind. It is rather a kind of demonstration. It is a reference carried by the production of the thought on the occasion of its occurrence. In general, this backward-looking reference from the occurrence of a mental act to its promulgating agent is unnoticed, unstated, and unnecessary. In general, the thought that occurs and the truth-conditions for it make their own way quite independently of this implicit reference indicated by the occurrence of the act and made explicit in our prefixed TUM. What is thought is, typically, independent of the context of the thought. But in important cases it matters. These include cases in which *the texts* of the thoughts that occur *may be the same* but the *thoughts themselves vary* in truth-value. Such cases include occurrences of mental acts with indexical references.

Professor Geach long ago and G. E. M. Anscombe[6] more recently have each considered certain cases of self-ascriptions with a "vanishing I." In soliloquy, Geach maintained, the 'I' is idle; "I'm in an awful muddle" has a content something like "What a muddle." These cases of the "vanishing-I" are, I think, rather like certain minimal perceptions. There are acts of seeing in which I have sensuous experiences but in which, for lack of knowledge, or attention, or given the duration of the event, I do not identify what I indeed detect, something that moves or flashes. These are perceptions the expression of which might be that *that* (I know not what) moved or flashed. These are not perceptions with a cognitive reference. It is not like seeing that that Volkswagen has moved. The demonstrative reference of these minimal perceptions is not part of their content, the sensuous experience of what is before one. Rather, the perceptual occurrence itself, the sheer occurrence of the experience on the given occasion and in the given context of its occurrence, provides the reference to what we see in detecting the movement or flash. The intentionality of experience has, in its very occurrence, this sort of demonstrative reference to the objects of experience. But in a similar way, I believe, the occurrences of mental acts cast a backward glance along the shaft of the intentional arrow to the agents of their production. "What a muddle" in soliloquy characterizes the agent of the thought. The reference to this agent is a function of the *occurrence rather* than the *content* of the thought, and it is secured by the TUM rather than by the ascribed text.

This feature allows us to specify varying truth-conditions for states of mind with common texts. It allows the natural division of beliefs into true and false beliefs, depending upon the author of the thought for each occurrence, or depending upon the occasion or time of each occurrence, no matter if the associated states of mind are indistinguishable. It is in this way we distinguish varying acts of thought with common texts but without mated propositions. If, before and after a five-minute interval that straddles the hour, I judge that it is after nine o'clock, I have on the two occasions performed a mental act my expression for the occurrence of which runs something like this:

[I] [now] T (I, now) (Later than (now, nine o'clock)).

Thus, in all worlds compatible with all I believe at 8:58, it will be true that it is later than nine o'clock. Accordingly, no one of these is the actual world, itself specified by the prefix for which the time of the first thought is 8:58. Quite the opposite, however, is true with respect to my 9:03 thought; the worlds compatible with all I believe then do include the actual world.

The upshot of all this includes, I believe, the following. It is not necessary to assume that there are propositions. We can characterize adequately our ascriptions of mental acts to ourselves and others without them. And sometimes it appears that there is no adequate way to do so even with them. Those who do appeal to propositions ought to establish at least that they are necessary to explain these facts of mental life.

The role of contextual features governing the references, and so the determination of the truth-conditions, of both certain types of *thought in general* as well as certain minimal forms of *perception in particular* is a nice symptom of broader philosophical parallels between the two areas. For propositional theories of mental acts are very much like versions of indirect realism as theories of perception. These last theories introduce special, phenomenal entities to which we stand in a certain direct relation. Such theories suffer of course the attendant problems of specifying how these special entities are related to the external world, and how they are related to the mind, and whether we can be mistaken about them, and all the rest. But so too propositional theories of thought introduce special, intermediate objects to which we stand in a certain direct relation. And they suffer parallel attendant problems. There is a need to specify how these special objects, the propositions, are related to the external world, and how they are related to the mind, and all the rest. Indirect realism, as a theory of perception, fathered phenomenalism and one or another version of skepticism. We already see a new generation of offspring similarly related to theories of propositions. Objects, I have been told, are really systems of the aspects by which I think of them; the facts about the things of which I think are just the true propositions mated to my thoughts of them. Direct realism, where are you now that we need you?[7]

Notes

1. See the excellent and interesting article by William J. Rapaport, "Meinongian Theories and a Russellian Paradox," *Nous* 12 (May 1978):153–80.

2. If one distinguishes internal, or predicate-negation, from external negations of sentences, then a rupture is created in the inference here. This non-classical treatment of negation has a kind of philosophical motivation in the natural attempt to distinguish properties that things have from mere conditions true of them in the sense, say, in which their names satisfy open sentences. H.-N. Castañeda, in characterizing his views on predication, draws such a distinction. See his "Philosophical Method and the Theory of Predication and Identity," *Nous* 12 (May 1978):189–210.

3. For detail on this sort of issue and a special theory for dealing with it, see, e.g., H.-N. Castañeda's "Identity and Sameness," *Philosophia* 5 (1975):121–50, and his "Thinking and the Structure of the World," *Critica* 6 (1972):43–86.

4. This example is adapted from, and due to, discussions of indexicals by Michael Pendlebury in which he considers a range of cases of this sort.

5. Castañeda is the first, so far as I know, to have seen the importance of these questions of scope and indexical reference, and to have predicated in an explicit way basic philosophical theses on them. See, e.g., his papers: "'He': A Study in the Logic of Self-consciousness," *Ratio* 8 (1966):130–57; "On the Logic of Attributions of Self-knowledge to Others," *The Journal of Philosophy* 65 (1968):439–56; "Indicators and Quasi-Indicators," *The American Philosophical Quarterly* 4 (1967):85–100.

6. See Peter Geach, *Mental Acts* (London, 1956), especially pp. 117–21, and G. E. M. Anscombe, "The First Person," in *Mind and Language*, ed. Samuel Guttenplan (Oxford, 1975).

7. This is a slightly modified version of a paper presented at the Oberlin Philosophy Colloquium, Spring, 1979.

Beliefs and Propositions: Comments on Clark

HERBERT HEIDELBERGER

H ere is a piece of intuitive reasoning familiar to all of us. I state that all men are mortal, that some men are wise, and that the wisest man is mortal, you agree and we are both sincere. Therefore, there are three things, three propositions, three true propositions, that you and I believe in common. If we are impressed by that, we ought to be about equally impressed by this. I state that you are wise, that I am mortal, and that the lectern is made of wood, you agree and again we are both sincere. Therefore, there are (perhaps true) propositions, three of them, that we believe in common. But the beliefs we share in the two cases are with respect to propositions of different kinds. I shall endeavor to explain what these kinds are.

Let us think of a proposition in Chisholmian fashion, as something that can be believed, and define what it is for an object to enter into a proposition as follows:

x enters into p: There is a property F such that for anyone m, necessarily m believes p if, and only if, m attributes F to x.

Making use of 'enters into' we can define 'singular proposition'.

p is a singular proposition: Something enters into p.

A proposition that is not singular will be said to be 'general'. If 'singular' and 'general' are properly defined, then, since nothing enters into them, the propositions that all men are mortal, that some men are wise, and that the wisest man is mortal are general and the propositions that you are wise, that I am mortal, and that the lectern is made of wood are singular. Adopting terminology from the recent literature, we can say that belief *de dicto* is belief with respect to a general proposition, and that belief *de re* is belief with respect to a singular proposition, where the object (or objects) the belief is about is the object (are the objects) that entering into the singular proposition believed. Thus, someone believes the singular proposition that you are wise, a proposition into which you enter, if, and only if, he attributes the property of wisdom, the property of being wise, to you. In fact, we can say that the proposition itself attributes wisdom to you, defining this as follows:

> p attributes F to x: For anyone m, necessarily m believes p if, and only if, m attributes F to x.

And in terms of propositional attribution we may define the metaphysical notion of having or exemplifying.

> x has (exemplifies) F: There is a proposition p, p attributes F to x, and p is true.

Although designed to elucidate essentially the same phenomena, singular propositions are notably different from the propositions Professor Clark describes. Where I speak of ordinary things entering into propositions, Clark has his propositional reference correlates; where I speak simply of properties, Clark has his ascriptional propositional correlates. I am uncomfortable with propositional correlates, being in the dark as to what they are, and would prefer to try to get on with ordinary things and the properties we attribute to them.

Clark has an argument for (ascriptional) propositional correlates which goes something like this. If to believe the couch is blue is to attribute the property of being blue to it and if to believe the couch is the color of the sky is to attribute the color of the sky to it and considering that the property of being blue—the color blue—is the color of the sky, then a person should have one of these beliefs only if he has the other. But as this last is not the case (a person may believe the couch is blue without believing it is the color of the sky), to believe a (singular) proposition is not to attribute a property to an object.

It seems to me that in reasoning in this way Clark may have confused two different properties. The first of these is the property of being blue, that is to say the color blue, which is indeed the color of the sky; and the second is the property of being of a color that is the color of the sky. The first of these properties is expressed by the open sentence 'x is blue', the second by the open sentence 'x is of a color that is the color of the sky', and the first, but not the second, is denoted by the descriptive phrase 'the color of the sky'. The first is exemplified in every world by objects that are blue, but the second is exemplified by blue objects only in worlds in which the sky is blue; thus the two properties, though coextensive, are not necessarily coextensive, and hence not identical. I would say that one can believe the couch is blue without believing that it is the color of the sky, because one can attribute the property of being blue to an object without attributing the property of being of a color that is the color of the sky to it. Hence I would say that this example does not require us to invoke Clark's propositional correlates.

There is a point about singular propositions which may distinguish them further from Clark's propositions and which, I think, merits attention independently. The statement: For any proposition p, properties F and G, and objects x and y, if p attributes F to x and F = G, and x = y, then p attributes G to y is a consequence of Leibniz's Law and therefore something we do well to accept. And the statement:

For any propositions p and q, properties F and G, and objects x and y, if p attributes F to x and q attributes G to y, and p = q, and F = G, then x = y, though not a consequence of Leibniz's Law, is something we ought also to accept. But the statement: For any propositions p and q, properties F and G, and objects x and y, if p attributes F to x and q attributes G to y, and p = q, and x = y, then F = G, again not a consequence of Leibniz's Law, is, I take it, false. Adapting an example of Geach's, let p be the proposition that Brutus killed Brutus, q, the proposition that Brutus was killed by Brutus, let F be the property of killing Brutus, and G the property of being killed by Brutus, and let x and y be Brutus himself. Plainly, F ≠ G, i.e., the property of killing Brutus and the property of being killed by Brutus are distinct, but p and q are identical; that is to say, necessarily, one attributes the property of killing Brutus to Brutus if, and only if, one attributes the property of being killed by Brutus to Brutus; or so it appears to me. I am led by the example to believe that it may be a little too simple to think of a singular proposition as an ordered pair whose first member is the object entering into it and whose second member is the property attributed to the entering object. Clark seems to hold that propositions, at least those that interest him, are pairs of propositional correlates and so I doubt that he will agree with me on this matter.

Clark formulates a paradox with respect to propositions "containing" propositional correlates. Can we formulate an analogous paradox for singular propositions? Lamentably, we can. Let us define 'flasher' as follows:

> p is a flasher: There is a property F and an object x such that p attributes F to x and p has (exemplifies) F.

Thus the proposition that the moon is not round is—or apparently is—a flasher, as it attributes non-roundness to the moon and it itself has (exemplifies) non-roundness. Whereas the proposition that the moon is round does not have the property roundness and is therefore not a flasher. For simplicity of exposition, let us call the proposition that the moon is round, "A," and the proposition that the proposition that the moon is round is not a flasher, "B"; B, that is, is the proposition that attributes not being a flasher to A. Then we can ask: Is B itself a flasher?

Assuming that it is we have:

1. B is a flasher.

Evidently, by inspection we can see that

2. B attributes the property of not being a flasher

is true and so by the definition of 'flasher' we get:

3. B has the property of not being a flasher.

But if (3) is true, so is:

4. B is not a flasher.

On the other hand, assuming (4), we can, it seems, infer (3). If, as before, we can see that (2) is true, then, by combining (2) and (3) and appealing to the definition of 'flasher', we get (1). Therefore:

5. It is not the case either that B is a flasher or that B is not a flasher.

which yields:

6. B does not exist.

Now Clark would go on to claim:

7. Some people believe that A is not a flasher.

And from this he concludes:

8. Some people have beliefs that are not beliefs with respect to propositions,

or, as he puts it, "the comprehension axiom" for propositions does not hold.

Clark regards any denial of (7) as "a move of question-begging desperation," and so I feel somewhat embarrassed in having to admit my inclination to such a denial. Why am I inclined to deny (7), to assert that (7) is not true? In part because with Clark I want to deny that

9. Some people believe the (singular) proposition that A is not a flasher, i.e., some people believe B.

is true; and I believe (7) is true if, and only if, (9) is. Again, if the sentence "A is not a flasher" expresses a proposition, then evidently it expresses B. Hence that sentence does not express a proposition; so neither does (7) and therefore it is not true. But I shall try to do a little better than this.

It is worth noticing that to arrive even at (5) required that we make several assumptions, among them: that there is a property of not being a flasher, that B attributes only that property, and that the property of not being a flasher is both a property that B has and a property that B attributes. Why should we not reject one or more of these assumptions? The point may be sharpened by considering a second paradox.

Let us define what it is for a sentence to be a predicator as follows:

S is a predicator: There is a predicate F' such that S contains F' and F' is true of S.

Let A' be the sentence "The moon is round," let B' be the sentence "'The moon is round' is not a predicator," and let us ask ourselves whether B' is a predicator. B' contains the predicate 'is not a predicator' and thus by the definition of 'predicator' the predicate 'is not a predicator' is true of it; so it is not a predicator. Proceeding from the assumption that B' is not a predicator, we are led back to B' is a predicator. To resolve this paradox, we do not want to say that B' doesn't exist—manifestly, it does. My suspicions rather are aroused by the step from "B' is not a predicator" to "The predicate 'is not a predicator' is true of B'." To assume this step acceptable is to presuppose that there is a property of not being a predicator, something we may be disposed to deny. Returning to our first paradox, in parallel fashion we may distrust the easy transition from (4), "B is not a flasher," to (3), "B has the property of not being a flasher," now on the grounds that there is no property of not-being a flasher. Denying existence to the property of not being a flasher comports well with denying existence to B; for B, after all, would attribute not being a flasher to A. We would then reject not only (9) but:

10. Some people attribute the property of not being a flasher to A;

and to reject (10) is, I judge, tantamount to rejecting (7). By denying truth to each of (7), (9), and (10), we may be able to preserve "a comprehension axiom" for propositions. (I am not sure of this, for among other things, I am not sure how Clark would formulate the comprehension axiom he has it in mind to refute. Instances of the schema "(m) m believes that S if, and only if, m believes the proposition that S" can perhaps be regarded as axioms, and the comprehension axiom may tell us that all such instances are true. If it does, then, so far as I can determine, it is true.)

It is plain that the propositionalist's way out that I have sketched is incomplete and may not, in any case, be the best way of coping with Clark's paradox; certainly, it is not the only way, nor the only way open to a propositionalist. But it does seem to have an advantage over the mere affirmation of (6). Merely affirming (6) is a solution that is not readily transferred to the second paradox, whereas the propositionalist's way out is. Moreover, considering that there are paradoxes similar in structure to the one Clark describes that affect entities whose *bona fides* only a few would question—sentences, predicates, properties, beliefs—I think it is reasonable to conclude that they pose no *special* threat to propositions.

There is a further matter pertaining to Clark's paradox that deserves mention. Clark says, in effect, that (7) seems true, that we seem to believe that A is not a flasher, and I would agree. But the relation between seeming and being, almost always an uncertain one, is especially tenuous when paradox is at issue. It seems that the class of round things is a member of the class of things that are not members of themselves, it seems there could be a barber who shaves all and only those who do not shave themselves, much as it seems that B could exist and that we could believe that A is not a flasher. In each of these cases appearance belies reality—or so it seems.

However, the intuition that prompts assent to (7) may not be easily set aside, and if it is not, a compromise can be offered. While remaining adamant in his unwillingness to accept (7), a propositionalist may propose in its place:

7'. Some people believe that the sentence, "A is not a flasher" is true.

Accepting (7') poses no problem, since the proposition that the sentence "A is not a flasher" is true, i.e., the proposition that attributes the property truth—or better, the property of expressing a true proposition—to the sentence "A is not a flasher," seems unaffected by Clark's paradox. Similarly, while rejecting (10) we may accept:

10'. Some people attribute the property of expressing a true proposition to the sentence "A is not a flasher,"

or even,

10″. Some people attribute the property of satisfying 'is not a flasher' to the proposition A.

I doubt we can offer more to the intuition than this, and if it remains unreconciled I would advocate suppression.

Clark says that there are reasons less conclusive, but more substantive, than the presence of paradox which should lead us to deny that every belief is a belief with respect to a proposition. Let us consider these reasons. John and Harry both believe they can beat up the other. As Clark says, they have a belief, a judgment, with a common text. Thus it would seem they believe the same proposition. If, however, John can beat up Harry and Harry cannot beat up John, then John's belief is true and Harry's is false, and how can this be so if they believe the same proposition? Similarly, if Clark thinks that it is after nine a few minutes before nine, and he has the same thought a few minutes after nine, then, if what he thinks on both occasions is a proposition, it is a proposition that is both true and false, and nothing can be like that. How is a propositionalist to deal with these cases?

There are, I believe, several ways, but the simplest would be to deny that John and Harry believe the same thing and to deny that what Clark thought before nine was identical with what he thought after nine. John, we may say, attributes to himself the (referential) property[1] of being able to beat up Harry, and thus the singular proposition he believes is that he can beat up Harry. Since by hypothesis he has the property he attributes to himself, the proposition he believes is true. Harry attributes the property of being able to beat up John to himself, and since by hypothesis he does not have that property his belief—the proposition he believes—is false. So they believe different, and treading lightly on "can," incompatible propositions; that is why if one is true the other is false, and that is why John and Harry disagree. In the other case, Clark attributes the property of being after nine first to one time and then to another; hence he believes different propositions, which is how it can be that Clark was wrong the first time and right the second.

All of this, I suppose, is obvious, though perhaps not obviously true, and I mention it only because I do not know how Clark would respond to it. Clark says that it is as clear to him as anything can be in philosophical discussion that he had the same thought before nine as he had after nine. My intuitions are different. Had I said yesterday, "The Red Sox won today" and uttered the same words today, I would be expressing distinct beliefs, with respect to distinct propositions, which may have distinct truth values, and I would say the same of Clark's example. In Clark's, as in mine, the same property is being attributed to distinct objects and this may go some way to explaining Clark's intuition that the thoughts on the two occasions are the same.

I shall close with three brief remarks.

Clark maintains that the propositionalist must show that "the facts of mental life" cannot be accommodated except by a theory that invokes propositions. Showing that all alternative explanations are false, or otherwise inadequate, is a lot to ask of a theorist. It seems to me that a proposition theory ought to be (i) plausible and (ii) not less plausible than alternative theories. I cannot show that proposition theories satisfy these conditions, but I believe they do.

Clark ends his paper with an apostrophe to direct realism, and elsewhere he expresses skepticism about the existence of "an intermediate entity . . . poised," as he puts it, between an act of thinking and the facts. I sympathize. But whereas Clark finds the offending element in the supposition that there are propositions, I believe that it is a mistaken conception of their nature that is at fault. Writing in 1903, G. E. Moore said, "There is . . . no question of how we are to 'get outside the circle of our own ideas and sensations.' Merely to have a sensation is already to be outside that circle." I would hold, in almost parallel fashion, "There is no question of how we are to get outside the circle of our own ideas and conceptions. Merely to believe a singular proposition is already to be outside that circle."

There is, I regret to say, much in Clark's paper that I have not understood, or properly understood. And in many cases I lack a clear conception of Clark's motivation for asserting what he does. I am confident that had I been clearer on these matters, I would not have said some of the things that I have said in these comments.[2]

Notes

1. A referential property may be thought of as a property into which something enters, where 'x enters into a property F' is defined: For any object y and any proposition p, necessarily, p attributes F to y only if there is a property G and p attributes G to x.

2. I am indebted, as always, to Edmund Gettier.

Belief and Acceptance

JOHN PERRY

W hen asked what I believe, I typically respond with a sentence, or a sentence embedded in a that-clause: That the Giants will lose; that life is short; that philosophy is noble. I would use the same sentences to describe the world to others, and in my own thinking about it. I shall say that I *accept* them.[1]

I think acceptance is not belief, and not analyzable in terms of belief; rather, it is an important component of belief. It is the contribution the subject's mind makes to belief. One has a belief *by* accepting a sentence. Which belief one thereby has also depends on who the believer is and when the believing takes place—factors that need have no representation in the mind. What one thereby believes is not a sentence, nor a sentence meaning, nor one of Frege's thoughts—an abstract object with a sentencelike structure. It is rather, as Russell thought, a complex of objects and properties—objects and properties which are part of the world, not part of the mind (except in rare instances).

In saying that acceptance is the contribution the subject's mind makes to belief, I mean this. When we believe, we do so by being in belief states. These states have typical effects which we use to classify them. In particular, we classify them by the sentences a competent speaker of the language in question would be apt to think or utter in certain circumstances when in that state. To accept a sentence S is to be in a belief state that would lead such a speaker to utter or think S. Thus my conception allows an animal or a pre-verbal child to be meaningfully said to accept a sentence.

How sentences designed to describe a public world can have this secondary role of describing minds is an interesting question, but one I shall not pursue here. In this paper I merely want to argue that acceptance is not belief, and not reducible to it.

I think confusing acceptance with belief has wreaked havoc in the philosophy of belief, in the philosophy of mind, and in metaphysics generally. It requires that we see what is believed, and so what is true and false, on the model of what is accepted;

belief is thus treated as a relation to a sentence or sentencelike entity. When we come across an ineluctably ordinary belief—a belief that some object has some property—we invent a special name for it ("de re belief") and wonder how it is possible. The conflation of acceptance and belief creates the sort of tension in which metaphysics is inevitable. We want *what is believed* to classify belief states for purposes of explaining thought and action—the proper role of what is accepted—while at the same time being objectively true or false, the common objects of belief for different persons at different times. This requires that the subject's mind conceptualize its own perspective on the world, a condition that cannot be satisfied; at this point we stop just short of an inarticulate groan and begin to talk of "intuition."

My focus shall be on context dependent sentences.[2] The acceptance of context dependent sentences is a matter of some importance. That I accept "This paper is due today" explains, together with certain facts about my work habits, my frantic activity. Section I argues that such sentences are not *what is believed*, and I suspect most will agree with that conclusion. But there remains the possibility that acceptance of context dependent sentences will be viewed as a by-product of having beliefs about the world, having beliefs about one's place in it, and understanding words like 'I' and 'now'. One supposes, for example, that I now believe a certain person to be writing a certain time, and believe this person to be myself and that time to be the present time, all of this consisting in my having the relation of belief to context independent sentences, or Fregean thoughts, or similar entities. And then, it is supposed, because I understand how 'I' and 'now' work, I am prepared to express all of this with "I'm writing now"—that is, I accept this sentence.

In sections II through VI I try to show that this picture is topsy-turvy by showing that no analysis of acceptance of context dependent sentences is possible in terms of such "de dicto" beliefs. My goal is negative and limited: acceptance will not be given an iron-clad definition; my positive views will be ill-explained and largely undefended; de dicto belief will not be totally banished. My hope is merely to establish that acceptance is an important phenomenon, involved in the structure of belief, and involved not as a by-product but as a central component.

I

In "The Thought" Frege says, "If someone wants to say the same today as he expressed yesterday using the word 'today', he must replace this with 'yesterday'.[3] I think he is making a correct point about one familiar sense of 'say'. If I uttered to M. B. tomorrow the same sentence I produced today, viz., "This paper is due today," he could legitimately complain: "That's not what you said yesterday. Yesterday you said that it was due then." And if I say to him tomorrow, "This paper was due yesterday," it would be quite appropriate for him to agree: "That's what you said yesterday." In the first sentence, I would have produced the same sentence on successive days yet said different things; in the second instance, I would have produced different sentences but said the same thing. Thus it seems clear that, in this common sense of 'say', what is said is not the sentence produced. I produce a sentence, and my producing the sentence is crucial to my saying something: it is just what I do *in order to* say something. But the sentence itself is not *what* I say.

The problem is not that we are dealing with lifeless sentences instead of their vital meanings. The meanings, like the sentences, were the same in the first instance and different in the second. "This paper is due today" will have the same meaning tomorrow as it has today, and "This paper was due yesterday" will never come to mean the same as "This paper is due today," barring a radical change in the language.

Now if belief involves, at least paradigmatically and for reasonably articulate adults, saying or being disposed to say sentences to oneself and to others, it would not be surprising if the same points carried over. And they do. If tomorrow I am disposed to say to myself and others "This paper is due today," I will believe something different from what I now believe; I will have changed my mind. And if I do not change my mind, I will be disposed to say to myself and others, "This paper was due yesterday." Acceptance of the same sentence today and tomorrow indicates that I believed different things; acceptance of different sentences is required to believe the same thing. So it seems that what is believed is not a sentence (nor the meaning of a sentence).

Now in these last remarks, in speaking of what I say to myself and others, I have been using 'say' in a sense that contrasts with that used in the quote from Frege. In this sense it seems that what is said *is* a sentence. There clearly is a sense in which, had I uttered "This paper is due today" on the successive days, I would have said the same thing. Now one might think that this is a more "strict" or "literal" sense of 'say', from which the sense discussed before has developed as a strictly unnecessary but practically useful way of grouping sentences which are, for certain purposes, only irrelevantly different. And one might further suppose that any of the verbs denoting activities in which the production of sentences or the disposition to produce sentences is a crucial part would admit of a similar strict or literal sense.

But this would be a mistake. For a particularly clear case, consider promising. My brother first drew my attention to these issues by making a promise to me with these words: "I'll give you a dollar tomorrow." The next day when I asked for my dollar he laughed and said, "I promised to give you a dollar tomorrow, and I will." This kept up for several days until I got what I thought was the point: that tomorrow never comes. I am now sure that the point my brother was after was the difference between the sentence used in promising and what is promised. For of course when he said "I promised to give you a dollar tomorrow," he was not right, as he well knew. To make that promise he would have had to say, originally, "I'll give you a dollar the day after tomorrow." So what is promised, like what is said, cannot be identified with the sentence used in promising. The point is that unlike 'say', 'promise' has no sense in which what is promised is a sentence. Certainly a writer might promise to write a sentence, or rewrite one, but then writing or rewriting the sentence is promised, not the sentence itself.

In this particular, believing is like promising and not like saying. I can discover no sense in which what is believed is a sentence. We can believe a sentence to be true, but that does not make the sentence *what is believed*, any more than the fact that we can believe an automobile to be rusty means that automobiles are sometimes *what is believed*.

In constructing reports of beliefs, we use that-clauses containing sentences. When people report their current beliefs, they will put in the that-clause just the sentences they accept. Thus I now report that I believe that this paper is due today using the very sentence I accept: "This paper is due today." This fact suggests the view that this sentence, or something intimately connected to it, perhaps its meaning, is what is believed. If, in thinking about belief, we concentrate on the beliefs we have now, this suggestion will seem compelling.

But the facts of first person, present tense reports of beliefs are quite special. In reporting beliefs of others, or our own past beliefs, we will not generally be able to produce a singular term denoting what is or was believed by prefacing the sentence accepted with 'that'. You now accept, let us suppose, "I did not write this article." If I report "You believe that I did not write this article," I get it wrong. By accepting "I did not write this article," you believe that you did not write this article, not that I did not. Yesterday I accepted "Nothing is due today." I cannot now report the belief I had by saying "I believed that nothing is due today." It is not my purpose in this paper to say much of anything about the nature of what is believed. But I hope a convincing case has been made for the negative claim that what is believed is not in general the sentence accepted.

II

These arguments show that acceptance and belief must be distinguished where context dependent sentences are involved. One might still try to dismiss acceptance as an important notion in the philosophy of belief by maintaining (i) that for context independent sentences, acceptance may be identified with belief; (ii) that acceptance of context dependent sentences may be analyzed in terms of belief in context independent sentences and certain other notions, such as *understanding* and *meaning*.

I shall not argue against (i) here, though I think it is wrong; I concentrate on (ii).

Now a natural suggestion for carrying out the analysis called for in (ii) is that acceptance of a context dependent sentence is no more than the belief that the sentence is true by one who understands what the sentence means. If I accept a sentence, and have the concepts of a sentence and of truth, it is natural to suppose that I believe it to be true. Nevertheless, accepting a sentence and believing it to be true are quite different things.

Acceptance is a relation a person has to a sentence at a time. The person is the person who accepts, the time is the time that he does the accepting. Believing to be true is a more complex relation. Someone has to do the believing, and he must do it at some time. But that is not enough. A person and a time have to come in again. For most sentences are not simply true or false, but true or false *as uttered by some person at some time*.

Consider "I am the President." The sentence as such has no truth value, and no one understands it would suppose that it does. It would be true if said by Carter now, false if said by him ten years ago, or by Jerry Brown now. To believe it *simpliciter* makes no sense. Thus acceptance is a three place relation, while believing-true is a five place relation.

This shows that acceptance and believing-true are different things, but not that they are very different. There might be an analysis of acceptance in terms of believing-true in which the extra argument places are absorbed by appropriate terms.

The simplest possible move would be this:

(A) At t, X accepts "S" iff For some τ and some a, at t X believes that "S" is true for a at τ.[4]

This is, of course, not plausible. I believe that "I am President" is true for Carter on July 4, 1979, but I do not accept "I am the President."

The problem, it seems, is that "Carter" and "July 4, 1979" do not designate the right person and time. Suppose we add, then, that a must designate X and τ must designate t:

(B) At t, X accepts "S" iff There are a and τ such that: (i) At t, X believes that "S" is true for a at τ; (ii) a designates X and τ designates t.

The idea is that acceptance of a sentence—that is, being ready to use it to describe the world and to characterize one's own beliefs—is just the state one is in whenever one believes that sentence to be true for oneself at that moment. One might, of course, believe this of certain sentences that one does not understand and so is hardly prepared to use. So I shall assume that the believer understands the meaning of S.

However, (B) does not work. Let S be "My meeting starts now." If I know on July 4, 1979, that my meeting is scheduled for noon, July 4, 1979, then I may well believe right at noon on that day:

"My meeting starts now" is true for J. P. at noon July 4, 1979.

And yet I might not accept "my meeting begins now" right at that moment, having lost track of time (or, less probably, having lost track of who I am).

III

The problem is clearly that for any context independent a and τ, my thinking that "my meeting begins now" is true for a at τ does not guarantee that I think the sentence true for *me now*—as I would have put it at the time. It is natural, then, to try to work the 'me' and the 'now' into the right side of the biconditional:

(C) At t, X accepts "S" iff There are a at τ such that: (i) At t, X believes that "'S' is true for me, now" is true for a at τ; (ii) a designates X and τ designates t.

But this condition fails, for the same reason as (B). From the fact that I believe at noon July 4, 1979, that the sentence

"My meeting starts now' is true for me, now"

is true for J. P. at noon on July 4, 1979, it simply does not follow that I then accept "My meeting starts now."

IV

Rather than engage in further futile semantic ascent, we might try an epistemic condition.

> (D) At t, X accepts "S" iff There are a and τ such that: (i) At t, X believes that "S" is true for a and τ; (ii) a designates X and τ designates t; (iii) At t, X believes that *he* is a and it is *then* τ.

I think, on an ordinary reading of (D), it is true—at least if values for X are restricted to those who understand the locution 'true for . . . at . . . .' (D) is true because we ordinarily would take the emphasized 'he' and 'then' in (iii) to be what Hector-Neri Castañeda calls quasi-indicators.[5] Used as a quasi-indicator, "he" performs two functions. First, like a pronoun, it picks up the reference to X. But it also tells us how the believer thinks of X. He tells us X thinks of X as *himself*. He thinks of himself in the way that we think of ourselves when we use the word 'I'. Similarly, 'then' tells us that at t, X thought of t as 'now'.

(D) does not succeed in analyzing acceptance in terms of believing-true, however, for the belief predicate in (iii) is not 'believes-true'. "Smith believes that *he* is Smith" does not mean that Smith believes that "he is Smith" is true, or believes that it is true for Smith, as reapplications of the arguments and examples used above will show.

I think that when we use quasi-indicators we combine a remark about what Smith believes with a remark, or a hint, about *how* he believes it. In the case of 'he', the second bit of information is roughly that he believes what he believes *in virtue of* accepting a sentence with 'I' in it. That is, "Smith believes that *he* is a" tells us that Smith believes Smith to be a in virtue of accepting "I am a." More precisely, it tells us that he accepts it in virtue of being in a certain belief state, which in English-speaking adults typically results in the utterance, in appropriate circumstances, of "I am a."

If this is correct, (D) does not succeed as an analysis of acceptance in terms of belief, for the biconditional is true only because of an implicit remark about acceptance on the right-hand side. But another type of account of quasi-indication is possible and must be considered.

V

The second possible explanation of the quasi-indicators 'he' and 'then' supposes that they go proxy for context independent terms. "Smith believes that *he* is Smith" tells us that Smith believes that a is Smith, where a is a term that plays a very special role in Smith's thinking, though not in anyone else's. a plays the same role in Smith's thinking that 'I' plays in the thinking of English-speakers, so that if Smith believes that a is so-and-so, and speaks English, he will accept "I am so-and-so." On this conception, 'I' can play this role in the thinking of each of us *because* it is linked in our thinking to *some* such context independent term.

Similarly, "At t, Smith believed it was then time to leave" tells us that at t, Smith believed that it was time to leave at τ, where τ is a term that at t, but not at other times, played a very special role in Smith's thinking. τ played the very same role in Smith's thinking, at t, that 'now' plays in the thinking of English speakers at all times. And it is supposed that 'now' plays this role, at any given time, by being linked in our thinking to some such context independent term.

It is clear that a will have to designate Smith, unless he is wrong about who he is, and so each of us will have to have our own special term. This, in the view being considered, explains the usefulness of the quasi-indicator. Often it will be clear to us that a person is thinking of himself with his "special term," though we do not know what term it is.

It seems clear that for many of us, our own proper name will come close to being such a special term for ourselves. Actually, most of us are aware, through hearing of namesakes or through studying Tyler Burge's theory of proper names, that few of us have names that are unique to us. But each of us probably went through a period of time when we were not aware of this. During that time, our proper name played the same role that a is supposed to play for Smith. Indeed, although I have met namesakes *and* studied Burge, this biconditional is probably almost true:

I accept "I am so-and-so" iff I believe that John Perry is so-and-so.

Of course, the special role that 'John Perry' and 'I' play in my thinking goes far beyond their interchangeability. When I accept "I am to be slugged," I feel terror, for example.[6]

The relation between 'I' and my proper name appears to me to be this. 'I' has this peculiar role in the thinking of everyone who understands it. Its having this role is tied to its meaning—not the special meaning it has for each of us, but the common meaning it has for all of us. 'John Perry', on the other hand, does not have this special role in my thinking in virtue of what it means. It means the same for all of us as it does for me, but plays the special role in question only in my thinking. It has this special role in my thinking because I was taught when young to come when I heard the words (roughly) "John Perry better get over here," to say "John Perry is hungry" when hungry, and so forth. *In a sense* 'John Perry' has this special role in my thinking because it stands for me, for if it did not stand for me my parents would not have trained me in this way. But it is the training that is crucial. They could have trained me, perhaps as a patriotic joke, to respond and use 'Dwight David Eisenhower' in this way, and then that name would have played this special role in my thinking. Yet this would not have made 'Dwight David Eisenhower' stand for me, even when I used it. (To see this, imagine my parents had taught me that the state we lived in was California. 'California' would then have played a special role in my thought and action; I would have worried about earthquakes more than I did when I heard that California had many of them. This would not mean that 'California' stood for Nebraska but that I was wrong about where I was.)

I suspect that my own name acquired a special role in my thinking before I learned that 'I' always stood for the person using it, and accepted "I am John Perry." Now, on the other hand, I, like most adults, use 'I' rather than my own name to think about myself. It is conveniently short, and we have learned to use it when speaking to others. And at least for philosophers, 'I' has a certain epistemic advantage over their own name, since it is easier to imagine one's parents playing a cruel joke about one's name than to imagine being systematically misled by one's whole community about the meaning of 'I'.

The importance of 'I', then, is simply that, thanks to its context dependence, we can all be trained so that it plays the same role in our thinking, while being right about who we are. We could probably get along without 'I', or some other context dependent way of referring to ourselves. On the other hand, our proper names seem dispensable in favor of 'I', too.

Now let us return to the account of quasi-indication under consideration. When I say "Smith believes that *he* is so-and-so," it is supposed that I am saying that there is some context independent term a that plays a special role in his thinking, and that he believes a is so-and-so. Although there may be such context independent terms for some people some of the time, there is no reason to suppose that there must be such terms for all of us all of the time. Even if I forget my name, or have such a fit of skepticism that I am not sure I have a name, I can still believe things of myself by using the word 'I' in my thinking.

But I have admitted that there is nothing inevitable about the word 'I'. There could be a person who only thought of himself with his name. Is not the account put forward in the last section disproved by this possibility?

I think it is not. The importance of the word 'I' is not that everyone who has beliefs about himself must use it, or an indexical like it, to think of himself. Rather, it is that because its role in thinking is tied to its meaning, it can be used to *characterize* that cognitive role in a general way. To *accept* "I am so-and-so," a person need not understand the word 'I', but only be in a state that, were he to understand 'I', would lead him to use "I am so-and-so."

Suppose a one and a half year old, with no mastery of 'I', says "Joey wants Post-Toasties." We say, "he says *he* wants Post-Toasties," where the 'he' is a quasi-indicator. We mean he is in a state which would lead him, if he had mastery of 'I', to say "I want Post-Toasties."

As far as I can see, it is unnecessary, for such quasi-indexical attribution, that the child have any term for himself at all. I explain a visually disoriented child's ducking when objects are tossed well to one side of him saying, "He sees them as coming toward him." The 'him' is a quasi-indicator. He would, if he were an adult, say "They are coming at me." But he is not thinking of himself with a name or under a description or with an indexical. He is simply perceiving things in a certain way that leads naturally to the ducking behavior. We can use the first person "pronoun" to help describe such ways of perceiving and thinking, not because it is universally present but because, in virtue of its context dependence, it is universally suitable.

The account of quasi-indication under consideration in this section seems even less plausible when extended to 'then', for there do not seem to be the special terms available to make it work. There is not enough *time* to train people to use context independent terms for times in a special way in their thinking, for they would need a new term for each time. Perhaps I could teach my child to say "Joey wants to eat on September 20 at 5 P.M." if at 5 P.M. on September 20 he wants to eat. But I shall have to teach him something else to use an hour or a day later. What a lot of effort! Much simpler to give him a formula he can produce whenever he is hungry: "I want to eat now!" The meaning of 'now' ensures he will have said exactly what he wanted to say. When we want verbal behavior to replace natural behavior, context independence is our only hope.

VI

I have argued against three proposals for analyzing acceptance of a context dependent sentence in terms of belief, understanding, and meaning. Let me now give a general argument.

Suppose there were a context independent sentence S such that (i) I now accept "I am hungry now" if and only if I believe that S and (ii) this is so simply in virtue of my understanding of S. It seems that S will have to consist of context independent terms that designate me and the present time, and some two place predicate—e.g., '____ is hungry at . . .' or "I am hungry now' is true for ____ at . . .'. Let a and τ be the terms and H be the predicate, so S is $H(a,\tau)$.

The problem is that if my belief that S leads me to accept "I am hungry now" at t, simply in virtue of understanding its meaning, why should it not also lead me to accept it later, at t + 10 minutes? None of the meanings would have changed; S would still be true, since it is context independent, even if I had had a ham sandwich at t + 5 minutes. And you might well believe that S too, since it is as true for you as for me, being context independent. But if my belief that S and my understanding of S suffice to explain my acceptance, then if you understand it and believe that S, you should also accept "I am hungry now," even though you are stuffed. My acceptance of "I am hungry now" cannot be completely explained by my belief that S and my understanding of the meanings of 'I', 'now', a, and τ, for otherwise these other acceptances, which did not occur, would have.

The additional facts needed in the explanation, the facts that separate me at t from me at t + 10 minutes, and me from you, are these: I accepted "it is now τ" at t, but not later, and I accept "I am a," and you do not. Acceptance plays an irreducible role in belief.[7]

Notes

1. A handy word to use for our attitude toward sentences, 'accepts' has been given various technical meanings by various authors. I apologize for appropriating it but ask that the reader

avoid reading more into it than I have put, except insofar as is required by ordinary standards of sympathetic understanding.

2. I would define context dependent sentences as those that when accepted by different people or at different times result in different beliefs. Thus if you and I both accept "I wrote this paper," we believe different things. This definition prejudges the issue in section I, however. So until section II we may rely on the definition that context dependent sentences are those that may be true as uttered by one person at one time, but false as uttered at another time or by another person. A context dependent term is one that stands for different things as used by different people or at different times.

3. Gottlob Frege, "The Thought: A Logical Inquiry," trans. A. M. and Marcelle Quinton; reprinted from *Mind* 65 (1956) in *Philosophical Logic*, ed. P. F. Strawson (Oxford, 1967), p. 24.

4. The letter S is a schematic letter in such displayed formulas, while used in the main text as a meta-linguistic variable. τ and a are variables ranging over *terms*, which may be thought of either as expressions or as concepts or senses, depending on what sort of thing is taken to be *what is believed*. They are supposed to function appropriately after 'believes that'. Thus, if we suppose Fregean thoughts are believed, "X believes that "S' is true for a at τ' means that X believes the thought composed of the sense of "S' is true for', a, the sense of 'at', and τ. 'Designates' will be used later for the relation between terms and what they stand for, and so will share the ambiguity of 'term'.

5. See Hector-Neri Castañeda, "Indicators and Quasi-indicators," *American Philosophical Quarterly* 4 (1967):85–100.

6. See my "The Problem of the Essential Indexical," *Nous* 13 (1979):3–21.

7. Jon Barwise, Michael Bratman, and John Etchemendy gave me detailed and helpful comments on (several) penultimate drafts of this essay.

A Version of Foundationalism

RODERICK M. CHISHOLM

I shall here set forth a version of "foundationalism" in the theory of knowledge. I believe that if we have such a theory before us, rather than a mere program for a theory, then the philosophical issues that foundationalism involves can be more adequately understood. It is my hope that non-foundationalists may thus be encouraged to formulate actual versions of the alternatives to foundationalism.

As a result of criticisms by several philosophers, I have been able to correct and otherwise improve upon my earlier attempts to state such a theory.[1]

I shall accommodate my formulation to a general theory about what is expressed by first-person sentences: these sentences do not express first-person propositions (for there are no first-person propositions); they express, rather, the direct attribution of properties to oneself.

I begin, then, by summarizing my general conception of the primary *object* of intentional attitudes—attitudes like knowing, believing, and desiring.

THE PRIMARY OBJECT OF INTENTIONAL ATTITUDES

It is only within the last decade that philosophers have come to appreciate the difficulties involved in what might be called "the 'he, himself' locution"—the locution 'There exists an x such that x believes *himself* to be wise', as contrasted with "There exists an x such that x believes x to be wise." The difficulties are due to the fact that the first locution implies the second and not conversely, thus leaving us with the question "What does the first tell us that the second does not?"

The second locution could be true and the first false in the following situation. I look in the mirror, or look at my hand, and believe with respect to the person that I see that he is wise: I am then an x such that x believes x to be wise. But it may yet be at the same time that I do not believe *myself* to be wise, for I may have a very poor opinion of myself and not realize that *I* am the person I am looking at.

To understand the difference between the two locutions, we have to rethink the nature of believing and of other so-called propositional attitudes. Instead of thinking of these attitudes as involving, in the first instance, a relation between a person and a *proposition*, we think of them as involving a relation between a person and a *property*—a property that the person attributes to himself. If I believe myself to be wise, then I directly attribute the property of wisdom to myself. If I believe *you* to be wise, then there is a certain *other* property which is such that, in directly attributing *that* property to myself, I *indirectly* attribute to you the property of being wise. Suppose, for example, that you are the only person I am talking with. And suppose I (directly) attribute to myself the following property—that of talking with exactly one person and with a person who is a philosopher. Then I indirectly attribute to you the property of being a philosopher. The property I attribute to myself singles you out as the thing to which I bear a certain relation; by directly attributing the one property to me, I indirectly attribute the other property to you.

Thus we begin with the undefined locution 'x directly attributes to y the property of being F'. And we assume that direct attribution is necessarily such that, for every x and y, if x directly attributes a certain property to y, then x is identical with y. Given this undefined locution, we may now define the locution 'x *indirectly attributes* to y the property of being F' as follows: "There is a property H and a relation R of the following sort: (i) x directly attributes H to x; (ii) x bears R to y and only to y; (iii) H is necessarily such that whatever has it bears R to just one thing and to a thing that is F; and (iv) if R logically implies the property of being F, then R is necessarily such that whoever conceives it conceives the property of being F."

So-called *de dicto* believing—the acceptance of propositions—may be viewed as one type of indirect attribution. If I accept a certain proposition, then I indirectly attribute to it the property of being true. (In so doing, I will single it out as the sole thing I am conceiving in a certain way. The proposition, say, that all men are mortal may be the sole thing pertaining to mortality that I am now conceiving.) But we shall assume that whenever I do attribute a property to myself, then I *also* accept a certain proposition. Thus if I attribute wisdom to myself, I will also accept the proposition that someone is wise.[2]

The version of epistemology that follows, then, presupposes this general theory of believing. But everything that I shall say is readily adaptable to the view that the basic form of believing is propositional. Indeed, if that view were true, the following could be considerably simplified.

PRESUPPOSITIONS OF THE THEORY OF EVIDENCE

The problems of the theory of evidence, like all other genuinely philosophical problems, arise when we consider the consequences of certain presuppositions. Each of the presuppositions seems to be inescapable, and yet, when we combine them, they give rise to philosophical perplexity. The perplexity is philosophical in that, it would seem, we cannot resolve it by appeal to the particular sciences. We must rely instead upon our own deliberation and reflection.

What, then, are the presuppositions of "the theory of evidence"? I shall list six such suppositions. In formulating them, I shall use the first person, but I am quite confident, however, that I am speaking for all of us.

(1) There are certain things I know and certain things I do not know. I can give examples of each. Like Moore, I know that this is a hand and that the earth has existed for hundreds of years past. But I do not know whether it will rain here a year from today and I do not know how many people there are now in East Jaffrey. This first presupposition can be put more generally: there are certain things I am justified in believing and certain other things I am not justified in believing.

(2) The distinction between the things I am justified in believing and the things I am not justifed in believing need not coincide with the distinction between those of my beliefs that are true and those of my beliefs that are false. In other words, it is quite possible that some of the things I am justified in believing are false and that some of the things I am *not* justified in believing are true. Possibly my senses are deceiving me, but even if they are, I am now justified in believing they are not. And obviously, many of the things I am not justified in believing are true. I cannot *now* say, of course, which of my justified beliefs are false. Perhaps there was a time when people were justified in believing the false proposition that all swans are white. This means that they were not justified in believing the true proposition that some swans are not white.

We may say, of the relation between epistemic justification and truth, what John Maynard Keynes said about the relation between probability and truth: ". . . there is no direct relation between the truth of a proposition and its probability. Probability begins and ends with probability. That a scientific investigation pursued on account of its probability will generally lead to truth, rather than falsehood, is at best only probable."[3]

(3) Yet there *is* a positive relation between the epistemically justified and the true. For one thing, I am justified in believing a given proposition if and only if I am justified in believing that that proposition is *true*. There is still another point about the relation between epistemic justification and truth, but this point is somewhat more difficult to formulate. For the present, we may put it by saying that, if I want to believe what is true and not to believe what is false, then the most reasonable thing for me to do is to believe what is justified and not to believe what is not justified.

(4) Epistemic justification, unlike truth, is capable of degrees. Of the things that we are justified in believing, some are more justified than others. We may say, more generally, that certain attitudes are *more reasonable* on certain occasions than are other attitudes on those occasions. (As we shall see, the concepts of the theory of evidence may be explicated in terms of the undefined epistemic locution. '_____ is more reasonable for S at t than _____'.)

(5) Some of the things I know, or am justified in believing, are justified by certain *other* things that I know, or am justified in believing. For example, I know—and am therefore justified in believing—that there were people in this building earlier today. What justifies me in believing this may include the fact that certain people have

told me so and that I am justified in believing what they said. And presumably my justification also includes certain general information I have about buildings like this and the communities in which they exist.

(6) Some of the things I am justified in believing are such that by reflection I can *know* that I am justified in believing them; and I can find out just *what*, if anything, justifies me in believing them. Thus Russell once observed: "The degree of credibility attaching to a proposition is itself sometimes a datum. I think we should also hold that the degree of credibility to be attached to a *datum* is sometimes a datum."[4] This will hold for so-called empirical or *a posteriori* beliefs as well as for beliefs that are *a priori*. Hence, the present concept of the justified differs from the concept of the true in another respect. For in the case of what is empirical or *a posteriori*, deliberation or reflection is *not* sufficient to enable us to find out whether it is true. It is important to distinguish this final point from the first. According to the first, there are some things I am justified in believing and some things I am not justified in believing. And according to the present point, some of the things I am justified in believing are such that I can find out by reflection that they *are* things I am justified in believing; and similarly for some of the things I am not justified in believing.[5]

It may be noted that these presuppositions of the theory of evidence are analogous, in fundamental respects, to the presuppositions of ethics.

SOME EPISTEMIC CONCEPTS

Traditionally, knowledge may be identified with justified true belief. If, as we have asumed, the basic sense of believing is direct attribution, then there is a kind of knowledge that may be associated with justified true direct attribution. We now consider this knowledge.

The simplest way of setting forth the vocabulary of the theory of evidence, or epistemology, is to take as undefined the locution, '____ is more reasonable than ____ for S at t' (or, alternatively, '____ is epistemically preferable to ____ for S at t'). Epistemically reasonability could be understood in terms of the general requirement to try to have the largest possible set of logically independent beliefs which is such that the true beliefs outnumber the false beliefs. The principles of epistemic preferability are the principles one should follow if one is to fulfill this requirement. (It should be noted that the requirement is so formulated that the requirement to have true beliefs receives greater emphasis than the requirement not to have false beliefs.)

The epistemic locution we have taken as undefined is obviously applicable to propositional acceptance, or *de dicto* belief, where we can say that accepting one proposition is more or less reasonable than accepting another. But its application can readily be extended to direct attribution.

In order to characterize the relevant epistemic concepts in their application to such attribution, we shall introduce the concept of *withholding* the attribution of a property. Consider a person and a property such that (a) the person does *not* directly attribute that property to himself and (b) he does not directly attribute the *negation* of that property to himself: such a person may be said to *withhold* the direct attribution of that property.

Among the general principles of epistemic preferability is the fact that such preferability is transitive and asymmetric. If one attribution, or withholding, is more reasonable for a given subject at a given time than a second, and if the second is more reasonable than a third, then the first is more reasonable than the third. And if one is more reasonable than another, then the other is not more reasonable than the one.

We may also affirm the following principle: If, for a certain subject at a certain time, withholding the direct attribution of a given property is *not* more reasonable than the direct attribution of that property, then the direct attribution of that property *is* more reasonable than the direct attribution of the negation of that property. This principle has its analogue in the following *de dicto* epistemic principle: if withholding a proposition is *not* more reasonable than accepting it, then accepting it is more reasonable than accepting its negation. "If agnosticism is not more reasonable than theism, then theism is more reasonable than atheism."[6]

Given these principles and others, we may formulate definitions of a variety of fundamental epistemic concepts. We could say, for example, that the direct attribution of a given property is epistemically *unacceptable* for a given subject at a given time, provided only that withholding that property is more reasonable for that subject at that time than directly attributing it. In saying that the attitude is "unacceptable," I do not mean that the believer *finds* it unacceptable. I mean something more objective—something that could also be put by saying that the attitude ought not to be taken, or that it is an attitude that it would be unreasonable to take. We could say that an attribution is *counterbalanced* if and only if the direct attribution of that property is no more nor less reasonable than is the direct attribution of the negation of that property.

We may also distinguish several different epistemic levels that the direct attribution of a property may occupy for a given subject at a given time. Thus we have:

having some presumption in its favor;

acceptability;

being beyond reasonable doubt;

being evident;

being certain.

Each of these concepts may be said to provide a sense for the expression 'epistemically justified'—"certainty" constituting the highest degree of epistemic justification and "having some presumption in its favor" the lowest.

A direct attribution of a property could be said to *have some presumption in its favor* provided only that the direct attribution of that property is more reasonable than the direct attribution of its negation. A direct attribution of a property is *acceptable* if it is not unacceptable. A direct attribution of a property could be said to be *beyond reasonable doubt* provided only that the direct attribution of that property is more reasonable than withholding that property.

Ascending to still higher epistemic levels, we may now consider *the evident*—where the evident is thought of as that which distinguishes knowledge from true belief that is not knowledge. We may say that the direct attribution of a property is *evident* if the attribution is beyond reasonable doubt and if it is even *more* reasonable than withholding what is counterbalanced. (We have said that the attribution of a property is counterbalanced provided that the attribution of that property is no more nor less reasonable than is the attribution of its negation.) A counterbalanced attribution would provide a paradigm case of that which it is reasonable to withhold. But we are saying that an evident attribution is even *more* reasonable than is any such withholding. (In thus countenancing the category of the evident, we give sense to the remark that the principles of epistemic preferability give "believing the true" a greater emphasis than "not believing the false." Indeed, one of the principles of epistemic preferability could be put by saying this: It is possible that there are properties P and Q such that P is counterbalanced and attributing Q is more reasonable than withholding the attribution of P.)

Finally there is the concept of objective certainty. The direct attribution of a property may be said to be objectively *certain* for a person provided these conditions hold: the direct attribution of that property is beyond reasonable doubt for that person; and it is at least as reasonable for him as is the direct attribution of any other property. If the attribution of the property of being F is thus certain for a subject, then he may be said to be certain that *he* is F.[7]

These epistemic expressions may be read in another way. For example, if we may say, of the property of being F, that the direct attribution of that property is beyond reasonable doubt for a certain subject x, then we may also say: "It is beyond reasonable doubt for x that *he* is F." And analogously for the other epistemic concepts just defined.

We must take care not to be misled by syntax at this point. The propositional locution 'It is beyond reasonable doubt for x that *he* is F' may tempt one to suppose that there is a certain proposition corresponding to the expression 'he is F' and that this proposition is one which is beyond reasonable doubt for the subject x. But 'It is beyond reasonable for x that he is F' does not imply that there is a proposition corresponding to the expression 'he is F'. In this respect it may be compared with the locution 'He believes himself to be F'. The latter tells us only that he has directly attributed the property of being F to himself; and the former tells us only that, for him, directly attributing that property is more reasonable than withholding it.

The epistemic concepts which thus apply to direct attributions have their analogues which may be applied to propositions.

THE SELF-PRESENTING

Let us introduce the concept of a *self-presenting property*. There are certain properties—many, if not all, of them psychological or "Cartesian"—that may be said to "present themselves" to the subject who has them. One example is feeling sad: another is thinking about a golden mountain; another is believing oneself to be wise; and still another may be suggested by the awkward locution 'is appeared redly to'.

In saying that such properties are "self-presenting," I mean this: (i) they are necessarily such that if a person has them and if he considers the question whether he has them (i.e., if he considers his having them), then *ipso facto* he will directly attribute them to himself; and (ii) they are properties such that we *can* consider our having them *while* we have them. (Without the second clause, we would have to say that such properties as being unconscious are self-presenting.)[8] Feeling sad, for example, is necessarily such that if you do feel sad and if you consider the question *whether* you feel sad, then you will believe yourself to feel sad. Similarly for believing and for other intentional attitudes.

These attitudes include the property of *considering* I have just mentioned. Thus considering the question whether one is sad—considering one's being sad—is itself a property that is self-presenting.

And there are *ways of being appeared to* such that being appeared to in those ways is self-presenting. Thus there is a way of being appeared redly to which is such that if you are appeared redly to in that way, and if you consider your being appeared redly to in that way, then you will attribute to yourself the property of being appeared redly to in that way. We shall return to such ways of being appeared to below.

We may leave open the question whether certain logically necessary properties —for example, being either red or nonred—are self-presenting. If they are *not* self-presenting, then we may say that *all* self-presenting properties are psychological or "Cartesian."

We have said that the direct attribution of a property is objectively *certain* for a person provided these conditions hold: the direct attribution of that property is beyond reasonable doubt for that person; and it is at least as reasonable for him as is the direct attribution of any other property. Let us now consider the relation of such certainty to that which is self-presenting.

It will be noted that I have not *defined* self-presenting properties by reference to certainty. But if we think of certainty as constituting the highest degree of epistemic justification, then we may say that a person's self-presenting properties *are* objects of certainty for that person.

Indeed we may affirm the following "material epistemic principle" pertaining to such certainty:

P1 If the property of being F is self-presenting, then for every x, if (i) x has the property of being F, and if (ii) x considers his being F, then it is certain for x that he then has the property of being F.

If, as I have said, being sad is a self-presenting property, then if you are sad and if you consider the question whether you are sad, it will be certain for you that you are sad. And if considering is also self-presenting and if you consider your considering whether you are sad, then it will be evident to you that you are considering whether you are sad.

Every self-presenting property provides us with an instance of P1. Thus we could say:

For every x, if (i) x has the property of being sad, and if (ii) x considers his being sad, then it is certain for x that he then has the property of being sad.

Our principle illustrates what Alston and Sosa have called the "supervenient" character of epistemic justification; for it tells us how positive epistemic status "is supervenient on a set of non-epistemic facts."[9] Other material epistemic principles that I shall formulate also illustrate such supervenience. (We could say that a normative property G "supervenes upon" a non-normative property H provided only: H is necessarily such that whatever has it has G, but not necessarily such that whoever attributes it attributes G. A "normative" property—for present purposes—could be said to be any property definable in terms of preferability.) Thus the instance of P1 cited above tells us that being certain that one is sad supervenes upon the property of being both sad and such that one considers one's being sad.

Principle P1 pertains to what we might call "nonpropositional certainty." But we may affirm as a corollary the following principle about propositional certainty: For every x, if it is certain for x that he has the property of being F, then the *proposition* that something is F is one that is empirically certain for x.

To understand principle P1, we should distinguish two closely related concepts —the concept of the *directly evident* and the concept of an *evidence-base*.

The empirical certainty that may thus be yielded by those of our properties that are self-presenting could be said to constitute that which is *directly evident*. When we have such properties, then our direct attributions of them are directly evident. So, too, for the attribution of those properties which are *entailed* by the self-presenting. (One property may be said to "entail" another if it is necessarily such that whoever attributes it attributes the other.) And the propositions that may be said to be entailed by such attributions may also be said to be directly evident.

It will also be convenient to introduce the technical concept of an *evidence-base*: a person's evidence-base at any time will be the set of those properties which are self-presenting to that person at that time or which are entailed by what is thus self-presenting.

Hence a property may be in one's evidence-base without it being directly evident to one that one has that property. For one may *have* that property and yet not *consider* one's having that property.

If, as I believe, there are no first-person propositions, then one's evidence-base cannot be identified with a set of propositions (even though, as I have said, there *are* directly evident propositions). Yet it will be convenient to speak as we would if one's evidence-base *were* a set of propositions. Thus we shall speak of the logical consequences of one's evidence-base: we shall speak of what is consistent with it, of what follows from it, and of the probability relations that it may be bear to hypotheses that refer beyond it. But this way of talking does not commit us to the hypothesis that one's evidence-base is, after all, a set of first-person propositions, for we can avoid it by using obvious circumlocutions.

Thus we may make statements like "My evidence-base *entails* that I have the property of being so-and-so." This means that the set of properties constituting my evidence-base is necessarily such that (i) whoever has them has the property of being so-and-so and (ii) whoever attributes them to himself also attributes to himself the property of being so-and-so. And if my evidence-base thus "entails that I have the property of being so-and-so," then it may also be said to "*contradict* my *not* having the property of being so-and-so."

THE UNITY OF CONSCIOUSNESS AND CERTAINTY

Kant held that the subject is "in a position" to "unite all his representations into a single consciousness."[10] What does it mean to say that the subject is "*in a position* so to unite them*"? Perhaps the answer is this: "In order to see that the representations are united, the subject has only to ask himself *whether* they are united." And what is it for the representations to *be* thus united?

I suggest we may formulate the *principle of the unity of consciousness* as another material epistemic principle:

> P2 For every x, if (i) it is certain for x that he is F and certain for x that he is G, and if (ii) x considers his being both F and G, then it is certain for x that he is both F and G.

Given what we have said about propositional certainty, we may add that if it is certain for a subject that he is both F and G, then the *proposition* that there is something that is both F and G is one that is certain for him.

The unity of consciousness gives us a means by which we can identify without recourse to a middle term and without appeal to a set of common properties. If there is a property G that is self-presenting to me and if there is a property H that is also self-presenting to me, then, *ipso facto*, I can be certain that I have both G and H. And if I can be certain that I have both G and H, then I can also be certain of the proposition there *is* something having both G and H.

The person's self-presenting properties, then, are such that he can be absolutely certain that they are all had by one and the same thing—namely, himself.

THE UNCONTRADICTED

In the formulation of our first epistemic principle above, we appealed to a certain "justification-making" property—that of being self-presenting—and we defined that property without making use of epistemic terms. Then we were able to say what epistemic status is supervenient upon that property (more exactly, upon that property and the fact that one considers one's *having* that property). I shall now attempt to formulate another such principle.

Let us first try to single out certain things that may be said to have *some presumption in their favor* for our subject at any given time. We have said that the direct attribution of a property has some presumption in its favor for a given subject at a given time provided that the direct attribution of that property is then more reasonable for him than is the direct attribution of its negation.

I suggest now an extremely latitudinarian principle. This is the principle that *anything* we find ourselves believing may be said to have *some* presumption in its favor—*provided* it is not explicitly contradicted by the set of other things that we believe. Hence we may say, more exactly:

> P3 For every x, if (i) x directly attributes to himself the property of being F, and if (ii) x being F is not explicitly contradicted by the set of properties that x directly attributes to x, then his being F has some presumption in its favor for x.

The principle may be extended to propositional belief: for every x, if x accepts a proposition that is not explicitly contradicted by any set of propositions accepted by x, then that proposition has some presumption in its favor for x.

One proposition *explicitly* contradicts another provided only that it *entails* the negation of the other. That is to say, the one proposition is necessarily such that (a) if it is true then the negation of the other is true and (b) whoever accepts it accepts the negation of the other. Analogously, two properties may be so related that the one explicitly contradicts the other. Here, too, one may say that the one property entails the negation of the other: the one property is necessarily such that (a) if it is exemplified then the negation of the other is exemplified and (b) whoever attributes it to a thing attributes the negation of the other property to that thing.

I would take the principle just formulated to constitute one of the fundamental principles of the theory of knowledge. Here we follow Carneades who assigned a positive epistemic status to "the uncontradicted."[11] Such a principle may seem over-permissive, epistemically. But any such over-permissiveness can be corrected by reference to a certain subset of these "uncontradicted" attributions; this subset constitutes our next category.

THE EPISTEMICALLY UNSUSPECT

From among those propositions that thus have some presumption in their favor for our subject, we may single out those that are "epistemically unsuspect" or "epistemically in the clear." An attribution may be said to be *epistemically unsuspect*, or *epistemically in the clear*, for any subject, provided only that it is *not disconfirmed* by any set of properties that have some presumption in their favor for him.[12]

We must say something, then, about the relevant concept of confirmation. Confirmation is normally thought of as being a relation between propositions; but it may also be construed as a relation between properties. One property may be such that it *confirms the attribution* of another property; or, to put the matter somewhat differently, one property may be such that it *confirms that whatever has it* has the other property. The relevant relation between properties is analogous to that which holds when one proposition confirms another. Thus the property of being F could be said to *confirm* the property of being G (alternatively, to confirm that whatever has it has the property G), provided only that these conditions hold: For every x, if it is evident for x that he is F, and if everything that is evident for x is entailed by his being F, then it is epistemically acceptable for x that he is G. And analogously for disconfirmation.

For example, my belief that I am in a building with other people is epistemically in the clear for me. This means that those things having some presumption in their favor for me do *not* confirm the attribution of the property of not being in a building with other people.

According to our second material epistemic principle: anything we believe has some presumption in its favor provided it is not contradicted by anything we believe. We may now add a third material principle:

P4 For every x, whatever is epistemically in the clear for x is also epistemically acceptable for x.

Additional epistemic principles may be formulated by reference to these categories.

THE EVIDENTIAL STATUS OF BEING APPEARED TO

There are ways of being appeared to which are such that being appeared to in those ways tends to make evident the nature of what it is that appears to one in those ways. In other words, there are certain ways of appearing and certain properties which are so related that being appeared to in one of those ways tends to make it evident that one is appeared to by something having one of those properties.

The requisite sense of 'appear' is both causal and psychological: the object of perception, as a stimulus object acting upon a person's sense organs, causes the person to have certain sensations—or, as I prefer to put it, the object of perception causes the person to sense, or *to be appeared to*, in a certain way. One should note the distinction between the two locutions 'x *appears to* y in a certain way' and 'y is *appeared to* in a certain way'. The first implies the second but not conversely. The first, unlike the second, implies something about an external stimulus object and what it causes. In cases of phantasy and hallucination the second could be true and the first false.

Here we will cite a further principle:

P5 For every x, being appeared to in a way that is self-presenting tends to make it evident for x that there is something that is appearing in that way to him.

We have put our principle briefly by making use of the concept expressed by 'tends to make evident'. We may say that the property being F *tends to make evident* the attribution of the property being G provided that these conditions hold: being F is necessarily such that, for every x, if x is F and if his being G is epistemically in the clear for x, then it is evident for x that he is G. If being F does thus tend to make evident the attribution of being G and if in fact his being G *is* epistemically in the clear for x, then we may say, more simply, that being F *makes evident* for x that he is G.

An instance of our principle would be:

Being appeared redly to tends to make it evident that something is appearing red.

The expression 'being appeared redly to', in our example, has what I have called its *noncomparative* sense in this use.[13] 'Being appeared redly to', in this use, refers to a property that is self-presenting in the sense that we have defined.

Let us now consider an important point about principle P5; this pertains to our distinction above between that which may be said to be in one's *evidence-base* and that which may be said to be *directly evident* to one. We noted that a property could be in a person's evidence-base without it being directly evident to that person that he has that property; this might be the case if the person did not *consider* his having that property. Principle P5 pertains *not* to the directly evident but to what is in one's evidence-base. Hence P1 could be fulfilled even if the subject does not consider the ways he is being appeared to. Thus Thomas Reid said that the appearance is likely to "hide itself" behind the shadow of the object perceived and to "pass through the mind unobserved."[14]

PERCEPTUAL EVIDENCE

What I would call the primary sense of perception may be expressed by saying "The property of being F is such that x *perceives* y to have it." This sense of perception may be defined as follows: "y is F; y appears to x in a manner that tends to make it evident that one is appeared to in that way by something that is F; and x directly attributes to himself the property of being appeared to in that way by something that is F." When 'perceive' is taken in this way, the expressions that may replace the letter "F" are restricted to expressions for certain sensible characteristics.

If I perceive a thing to be red, then the way the thing appears to me makes evident to me that the thing that appears to me in that way is a thing that is red. In other words, the way of appearing is necessarily such that if a thing appears to a person in that way, and if his being appeared to by something that is red is epistemically in the clear for him, then such attribution is also evident for him.

Perception, however, is not normally restricted to the attribution of such sensible characteristics. Hence we may introduce a secondary sense of perception, which could be expressed by saying "The property of being F is such that x *perceptually takes* there to be something that has it." This concept may be defined by saying: "x is appeared to in a way such that he directly attributes to himself the property of perceiving the thing that is appearing to him in that way to have the property of being F."[15]

We may now form further principles of evidence by referring to this concept of perceptual taking.

A simple form of such a principle would be illustrated by the following: If a person perceptually takes there to be a sheep in the field before him, then it is *evident* to him that there is a sheep in the field before him. Thus Meinong held, in effect, that the fact that we *think* we perceive confers "presumptive evidence (*Vermutungsevidenz*)" upon the proposition or state of affairs that is the object of our ostensible perception.[16] And H. H. Price has said that the fact that we "perceptually accept" a certain proposition is sufficient to confer some positive epistemic status on that proposition. Price put this point as follows: "We want to be able to say: the fact that a material thing is perceptually presented to the mind is *prima facie evidence* of the thing's existence and of its really having that sort of surface which it ostensibly has: or, again, that there is *some presumption in favor of* this, not merely in the sense that we do as a matter of fact presume it (which of course we do) but in the sense that we are entitled to do so."[17] But such principles, as they stand, are somewhat over-permissive, epistemically.

Using the concept of the "epistemically unsuspect," or of that which is "epistemically in the clear," we might say that certain perceptual propositions are evident—*provided* they are epistemically unsuspect. In this way we could formulate a principle that is less permissive. Thus we might say:

> P6 For every subject x, if (i) x perceptually takes there to be something that is F, and if (ii) his perceiving something that is F is epistemically in the clear for x, then it is evident for x that he perceives something that is F.

Let us note that the first part of the antecedent ('x perceptually takes there to be something that is F'.) pertains to what is self-presenting and that the second part of the antecedent ('his perceiving something that is F is epistemically in the clear') pertains to the epistemically unsuspect. And it should be noted further that the final clause reads: 'it is evident for x that he *perceives something that is F*'. (One can perceive something that is F without thereby perceiving the thing *to be* F—without thereby perceiving *that* the thing is F. Thus if the person that I see is a thief, then I perceive something that is a thief. But even if I know that he is a thief, it is not likely that I *perceive* him to be a thief.)

The emphasis that we have placed in principle P6 upon that which is epistemically unsuspect, or in the clear, has applications for the so-called KK principle— the principle according to which, if one knows, then one knows that one knows. For our ordinary perceptual beliefs will not be instances of *knowing* unless they are epistemically unsuspect. But normally, whether or not such beliefs *are* epistemically unsuspect, they will not be known to be such.

It should be noted that our principle P6 states certain conditions under which we may say of a person that it is evident to him that he perceives something that is F. It does not enable us to say, *de re*, of that person and a certain external object y, that it is evident to the person that he perceives that particular thing y to be F. It may be self-presenting for x that he is *being appeared to* in a certain way (that he *senses* in a certain way). But it cannot be self-presenting to him that there is something that *is appearing* to him in that way (i.e., it cannot be self-presenting to him that an external stimulus object *causes* him to sense in that way). By means of what principle, then, can the person pass from a way of appearing to a particular physical thing that "transcends" that way of appearing? We want, then, a principle that says of two different things, x and y, that it is evident to x that y is F.

The following is a possibility:

> P7 For every x and y, if (i) perceives y to be F, and if (ii) it is evident for x that he perceives something that is F, then y is such that it is evident to x that it is F.

This perceptual principle introduces the *de re* epistemic locution: "y is such that it is evident to x that it is F." Therefore, the principle is, in a certain respect, less pure than the preceding principle, P6. For, in theory at least, one can ascertain merely by reflection whether or not the antecedent condition of P6 obtains. But the present principle, P7, is not applicable unless there is an external physical thing that is causing the subject to sense in the way that he does. And this fact cannot be ascertained merely by reflection. It cannot be self-presenting to the subject that there *is* a certain thing that he perceives to be F; it can be self-presenting only that perceptually takes there to be something that is F. Hence we might call P7 a "quasi-epistemic principle."

OTHER EPISTEMIC PRINCIPLES

The perceptual principles I have tried to formulate have their analogues for memory and also, I believe, for "the problem of other minds," but I shall not attempt to formulate these additional principles here. I shall cite only one additional principle. This is a *coherence* principle, or *concurrence* principle, telling us how the members of a concurrent set of beliefs can lend each other support.

Let us say that a *concurrent* set of properties is a set of properties of the following sort: it is a set of two or more properties each of which is such that the conjunction of all the others tends to confirm it and is logically independent of it.

Our coherence principle is this:

> P8 Any concurrent set of properties, each of which is acceptable for S, is such that each of its members is beyond reasonable doubt for S.

This principle has its obvious analogue for propositions.

IS THIS FOUNDATIONALISM?

In order to see the sense in which the present view may be said to be a version of "foundationalism," let us now list the eight epistemic principles we have formulated:

> P1 If the property of being F is self-presenting, then for every x, if (i) x has the property of being F, and if (ii) x considers his being F, then it is certain for x that he has the property of being F.

P2 For every x, if (i) it is certain for x that he is F and certain for x that he is G, and if (ii) x considers his being both F and G, then it is certain for x that he is both F and G.

P3 For every x, if (i) x directly attributes to himself the property of being F, and if (ii) x being F is not explicitly contradicted by the set of properties that x directly attributes to x, then his being F has some presumption in its favor for x.

P4 For every x, whatever is epistemically in the clear for x is also acceptable for x.

P5 For every x, being appeared to in a way that is self-presenting tends to make it evident for x that there is something that is appearing in that way to him.

P6 For every x, if (i) x perceptually takes there to be something that is F, and if (ii) his perceiving something that is F is epistemically in the clear for x, then it is evident for x that he perceives something that is F.

P7 For every x and y, if (i) x perceives y to be F, and if (ii) it is evident for x that he perceives something that is F, then y is such that it is evident to x that it is F.

P8 Any concurrent set of properties, each of which is acceptable for S, is such that each of its members is beyond reasonable doubt for S.

We may now consider certain philosophical questions.

(1) Are there *self-justifiers*—attributions or propositions that may be said to constitute their own justification?

The self-presenting would seem to be the closest we can come to that which constitutes its own justification. The fact that one has a self-presenting property does not itself make it evident that one has that property. But the fact that one has it and also *considers* one's having it does make it evident that one has it. Self-presenting properties, moreover, are distinctive in the following respect: it can be evident to one that one has the property even though one has no non-deductive—no merely inductive—grounds for attributing that property to oneself. In other words, a self-presenting property is a property such that it can be *evident* that one has it even though the only things that *make* it evident that one has it are things that entail it.

If we look now to our principles, we will see that in our formulations of P1, P3, P5, and P6, antecedent (i) pertains to what is self-presenting. (But this is not true of P2 or P7.) And in our formulations of P1 and P2, antecedent (ii) pertains to what is self-presenting.

(2) Is there a sense in which the self-presenting may be said to justify that which is not directly evident? Principles P5 and P6 state conditions under which the self-presenting may make evident certain attributions that are not directly evident. For in the case of each of these principles, antecedent (i) refers to what is self-presenting and the consequent refers to something that is not directly evident. But application

of the principles does not require that it be *evident* to the subject that he has the self-presenting properties in question—for they do not require that he *consider* his having them. It is the self-presenting, then, and not the directly evident, that may be said to justify that which is not directly evident.

(3) Is everything that is epistemically justified justified *by* that which is self-presenting? Or is there a sense in which something other than that which is self-presenting can be said to serve as a ground or foundation of our knowledge?

Examination of our principles makes it clear that, according to them, our knowledge is not a function *merely* of what is self-presenting. Principle P3 refers to what I have called "the uncontradicted"; this involves the logical relations that one attribution may bear to others. If these relations obtain, the fact that they obtain will not be self-presenting. But, I would say, one can always ascertain by reflection whether or not they obtain. Similar observations hold of "the epistemically unsuspect" (that which is "epistemically in the clear"), referred to in principles P4, P5, and P6, and of the type of "concurrence" referred to in P8.

But the *de re* principle, P7, is an exception. For antecedent (i)—'if x perceives y to be F'—is not something that can be ascertained merely by reflection. The requisite sense of 'perceives', as we have defined it, involves a causal relation between the object of perception and the perceiver. And one cannot determine by reflection whether or not such a relation obtains. Hence I suggested that P7 might be called a "quasi-epistemic principle."

I wrote in the second edition of *Theory of Knowledge*:

> What, then, of our justification for those propositions that are indirectly evident? We might say that they are justified in three different ways. (1) They may be justified by certain relations that they bear to what is *directly* evident. (2) They may be justified by certain relations that they bear to *each other*. And (3) they may be justified *by their own nature*, so to speak, and quite independently of the relations that they bear to anything else.[18]

I would now replace 'the directly evident' above by 'the self-presenting'; otherwise, I would say, the passage describes the present version of foundationalism.

(4) Can we say that, according to our principles, the self-presenting constitutes the *foundation* or *grounds* we have for the other things we know?

We must decide, of course, how the technical term 'foundation', or 'grounds', is to be understood. We could say that a self-presenting property constitutes the *basis* for an attribution provided that the subject has that property and provided that, if he has it and if the attribution is epistemically in the clear, then the attribution is evident. But this concept of a basis is a very broad one. If a self-presenting property is thus a basis for an attribution, then any wider self-presenting property which entailed that property would also be a basis for that attribution. For example, anything that is a basis for attributing the property expressed by "being standing and such that the President is in Washington" would be, in this sense, a basis for attributing the property of standing. But it would not constitute the *ground* or *foundation* for that attribution. A ground, then, would be a special type of basis.

Let us define "The property of being G constitutes S's *grounds* for the attribution of being H" by saying: The property of being G is a basis of the attribution of being H for x, and it is entailed by everything that is a basis of the attribution of being H for x. If we take 'grounds' in this way, then we may say that, according to our principles, the self-presenting does constitute the subject's grounds for what he knows. And, moreover, the principles do not specify any type of grounds other than that which is self-presenting.

These considerations also apply to *a priori* knowledge. Thus we might define an *axiom* as a proposition that is necessarily such that (i) it is true and (ii) whoever conceives it accepts it. Then we could affirm a principle analogous to P1: "If the proposition that p is an axiom, then, for every x, if x conceives the proposition that p, it is certain for x that p." (Here 'p' is schematic, replaceable by any English sentence.) Then we could say that that self-presenting state, which is the subject conceiving the proposition that p, is the ground for his knowledge that p.

"You are saying that logic and mathematics are grounded in certain *subjective* states. That is psychologism of the worst sort!" We are saying only that even our knowledge of logic and mathematics begins with experience. We are not saying that logic and mathematics are about that which is subjective. The objection confuses the *ratio essendi* with the *ratio cognoscendi*. "But how could a proposition be an axiom if it is grounded on some other proposition?" Saying that a proposition is an axiom for a given person does not imply that that person does not ground the proposition on something else; it implies only that he does not ground it upon any other *necessary* proposition.[19]

(5) Are there any *unjustified justifiers*—justifiers that are not themselves justified?

To the extent that the self-presenting serves as a foundation or ground for other knowledge, it could be said to *justify* what is thus known. But these self-presenting properties may serve as justifiers even when one does not *consider* one's having these properties. Hence they may serve as justifiers even when it is not evident to one that one has them. And so in this sense, the self-presenting may be a justifier that is not itself justified.[20]

OTHER SENSES OF JUSTIFICATION

The issues in theory of knowledge between "foundationalists" and "non-foundationalists," so far as I have been able to ascertain, are mostly the result of misunderstanding. Foundationalism, I believe it is agreed, is a theory about the justification of belief, but apparently those who accept it take 'justify' in one way and those who reject it take 'justify' in another way.[21]

The foundationalists take 'justify' in the *epistemic* sense. This interpretation of justification is illustrated, at least, by the concepts of epistemic preferability I have tried to explicate. And the non-foundationalists take 'justify' in one or another of several non-epistemic senses—some of which seem to presuppose some *further* sense of 'justify' and some of which do not. From the fact that foundationalism is false, if 'justify' is taken in one of its non-epistemic senses, it does not follow, of course, that it is false if 'justify' is taken in its epistemic sense.

If you present one account of justification and I present another, is the difference between us merely verbal? Not if our respective accounts are intended to be adequate to the same pre-analytic data. And there is a set of data to which most versions of foundationalism and non-foundationalism are intended to be adequate. Such data are involved in the fact that there is a valid distinction between knowledge and true belief that is not knowledge.

The term 'justification', in its pre-analytic sense, may be thought of as being the name for that which distinguishes knowledge from true belief that is not knowledge. The terms 'warrant' and 'grounds' are other possibilities, as are variants of 'evidence' and 'evident'. Other possibilities are certain broader concepts in terms of which our ordinary evidential concepts can be defined, such as "credible" or "reasonable." Thus I would prefer to make use of terms that can be defined by reference to the comparative concept, "more reasonable than." But for the present let us use 'justification'. (In considering these questions, we will do well to keep in mind that such words as 'perceive' and 'remember' are generally used in a way that implies knowing and therefore that there may be the danger of circularity if we attempt to explicate knowing in terms of perceiving and remembering.)

We presuppose, then, that there *is* a valid distinction between knowledge and true belief that is not knowledge. In other words, we presuppose that it is possible to have true belief with respect to a certain topic without having knowledge with respect to that topic. Let us cite certain examples of this distinction. For then we will be able to ask whether various proposed analyses of the distinction are adequate to the examples. I shall describe three different cases.

(a) We contrast the astronomer who believes that there are at least nine planets with the man who arrived at that belief solely on the basis of an examination of what he took the tea leaves to say.

(b) Consider a case of the sort discussed by Brentano. I happen to have a headache and you believe, solely on the basis of an exaggerated pessimism, that someone in the room has a headache; then you have mere true belief with respect to a topic concerning which I have knowledge.

(c) The possible cases need not be restricted to empirical knowledge. Suppose I believe, solely on hearsay, that a certain mathematical or logical theorem is true. And suppose the theorem is one that certain mathematicians or logicians have *proved* to be true. Then I will have true belief with respect to the theorem and they will have knowledge.

Let us, then, consider other possible theories about the *nature* of the justification in question, about the nature of that which is essential to the distinction between knowledge and true belief that is not knowledge.

Let us consider, then, some of those *other* concepts that are thought to be adequate to our pre-analytic data about justification.

(1) Sometimes it is said: "A belief is justified if and only if it is arrived at by a

reliable method." The word 'reliable' may then be characterized either by reference to truth alone or by reference to some other sense of justification. If we take it the first way, then we could form a simple version of the "reliable method" theory by saying: "A belief is justified if and only if the method by means of which it was arrived at is, more often than not, a method that leads to beliefs that are true and not to beliefs that are false."

Given such a simple interpretation of 'reliable method', it is very difficult to distinguish this sense of 'justify' from that which might be put by saying that a belief is justified if and only if it is true. (Such a theory, of course, would not be adequate to our three examples.) If I *have* arrived at a true belief, however accidentally, then I have followed a method which, on this occasion, *has* led to a true belief. Consider, once again, our three examples above of true belief that is not knowledge. It does not take much ingenuity to formulate, for each case, a general procedure that has been followed in that case and which is such that, whenever it is followed, it leads to true belief. We need mention only our first case: the man who decided that there were nine planets as a result of reading the tea leaves in a certain way. If this reading took place, say, on a Friday afternoon at 2:17 and if, previously and subsequently, the man never consulted the tea leaves about the number of planets at that hour on a Friday afternoon, then he followed a procedure that always leads to truth—one he could describe by saying, "Whenever I want to find out anything about the number of planets, I should consult the tea leaves at 2:17 on a Friday afternoon."

The simple version of the "reliability theory," then, does not enable us to distinguish knowledge from true belief that is not knowledge. Hence one must place certain restrictions upon the simple formula I have proposed. It remains to be seen whether this can be done without importing some other sense of justification.[22]

(2) 'Justify' might be taken to refer to the procedures of decision theory, or game theory. In applying such procedures one may reach conclusions of the following sort: "A course of action is justified (or reasonable) for a particular individual at a particular time if and only if, in relation to the goals of that individual at that time and in relation to the evidence he has, it is more reasonable for him to pursue that course of action than not to pursue it." How would we apply such procedures to the acquisition of belief? One might say: "A belief is justified for a particular individual at a certain time if and only if, in relation to the goals of that individual at that time and to the *evidence* he then has, it is more reasonable for him to have that belief than not to have it." Here, once again, we have a sense of 'justify' that presupposes the epistemic sense, for it refers to the *evidence* that the individual has.

"But might not this evidence in turn be characterized by reference to the procedures of decision theory?" The answer is that the kind of regress that would then be involved will not begin in the right place. ("If there are recordings of musical performances, then there must have been at least one actual performance at some time or other." "No; for all our recordings were made from *other* recordings of musical performances.")

"It is not necessary that we characterize decision procedure epistemically. We can say that the subject should base his beliefs not on the *evidence* that he has but merely on the *other beliefs* that he has." We can, of course, formulate decision theory in such a way. But how would reference to such procedures help us to analyze our three examples?[23]

(3) Sometimes justification is characterized by reference to "science" as in: "A belief is justified if and only if it has as its object one of the statements of science." This says both too much and too little, for it is inadequate both to our first example as well as to our second example. Consider first the case involving the planets. The man who followed the tea leaves *did* accept one of the statements of science—namely, that there are nine planets. Consider next the second example who knew that he had a headache and therefore that there is someone in the room who has a headache. In what sense was the object of his belief one of the "statements of science"?

If, now, we say, "A belief is justified for a given person if and only if he arrives at it by means of a scientific procedure," then we are faced once again with the difficulties we encountered with "the reliable method" theory.

(4) Sometimes, it would seem, justification is characterized in terms of *coherence*: a belief or a statement is said to be justified in this sense provided it coheres in a certain way with certain other beliefs or statements. One may ask "In what ways?" and, more important, "With *what* other beliefs or statements?" The answer, once again, would seem to presuppose some further sense of justification. Thus I have formulated a coherence principle in P8 above, but that principle presupposes applications of our basic epistemic concept. What would be an alternative to such a principle? Here, too, programs have been formulated, but not with such detail that we can apply any of them to our present problem.[24]

(5) In recent years, it has also been contended that a belief or a statement is justified provided only it has a certain *explanatory* power.[25] But it would seem to be impossible to characterize the requisite sense of *explanation* without presupposing some other sense of justification. Normally, a hypothesis is not said to be an explanation for a particular formula unless the hypothesis has *some* positive epistemic status—unless, say, it has some presumption in its favor: ". . . the acceptability of an explanation must be assessed on the basis of the degree to which the explanans as a whole is supported by factual evidence."[26] Moreover, if the suggestion is to be applied to our three examples, then, presumably, we will need an explication, not merely of the logical locution 'E explains O', but of the relativized locution 'E explains O for S'.[27] How, then, are we to characterize the relativized locution? We will be back where we started if we say merely "S has an explanation for O." Suppose E explains O, in the logical sense of 'explains'. And suppose S has true belief, but not knowledge, about E and O. Will he then "have an explanation" for O? In *one* sense of 'have an explanation', the tea leaf man who believes that there are nine planets "has an explanation" for many astronomical phenomena. But this sense of 'have an explanation' has no relevance to the distinction between knowledge and true belief that is not knowledge.

It would seem, once again, that we are considering a theory that needs to be worked out.

(6) 'Justify' may be taken in a strictly ethical sense, as when one says "I have a right to believe whatever I want, provided no one else is affected by my beliefs." This ethical sense of 'justify' does not seem to be relevant to the issues that separate foundationalists and non-foundationalists.[28] Certainly this concept does not help us in any obvious way with our three examples of the distinction between knowledge and true belief that is not knowledge. But I shall leave open the possibility that the epistemic sense of justification can be explicated in purely ethical terms.

Notes

1. These critics include William P. Alston, Bruce Aune, Fred Dretske, Herbert Heidelberger, Ernest Sosa, and Timm Triplet.

2. I assume, however, that there are no "first-person propositions"—e.g., that although the first-person sentence "I am wise" expresses my direct attribution of wisdom to myself, it does not express a proposition. My reasons for holding this are set forth in detail in: "The Self and the World," *Proceedings of the Second International Wittgenstein Symposium* (Vienna, 1978), pp. 407-10; "Objects and Persons," *Grazer philosophische Studien* 5 (1979); "The Indirect Reflexive," in *Intention and Intentionality*, ed. C. Diamond and J. Teichman (Sussex, 1979), pp. 39-53; and "The Logic of Believing," *Pacific Philosophical Quarterly* 1 (1980).

3. John Maynard Keynes, *A Treatise on Probability* (London, 1952), p. 322.

4. Bertrand Russell, *Human Knowledge: Its Scope and Limits* (New York, 1948), pp. 381-82.

5. Compare C. I. Lewis, *The Ground and Nature of the Right* (New York, 1955), chap. 2; and James Van Cleve, "Foundationalism, Epistemic Principles, and the Cartesian Circle," *The Philosophical Review* 88 (1979):55-91, especially pp. 84-91.

6. Other principles are set forth in the second edition of my book *Theory of Knowledge* (Englewood Cliffs, N.J., 1976), pp. 138-39. The principles are there restricted to *de dicto* form; but their analogues for direct attribution are obvious.

7. To do justice to the Gettier problem, we should introduce the concept of the "non-defectively evident"—a category falling between the evident and the certain. The expression "It is non-defectively evident for x that he is F" may be spelled out as: "Either (a) it is certain for x that he is F, or (b) the property of being F is entailed by a conjunction of properties each having for x a basis that is not a basis of any false attribution for x." The relevant concept of "a basis" is defined below.

8. Shall we also say that these properties are necessarily such that a person attributes them to himself only if he has them?

9. Compare William P. Alston, "Two Types of Foundationalism," *Journal of Philosophy* 73 (1976):165-85, especially p. 170; and Ernest Sosa, "The Foundations of Foundationalism," forthcoming in *Nous*.

10. See the *Critique of Pure Reason*, A98-130, A345-49, B131-38.

11. Compare *Sextus Empiricus*, vol. II, Loeb Classical Library (London, 1933), p. 95; "Against the Logicians," vol. I, pp. 176-77.

12. Compare the following definition proposed by John Pollock: "'p is prima facie justified for S' means: 'It is necessarily true that if S believes (or were to believe) that P, and S has no reason for thinking that it is false that P, then S is (or would be) justified in believing that P.'" John Pollock, *Knowledge and Justification* (Princeton, N.J., 1972), p. 30.

13. See the chapter "Three Uses of Appear Words," in my book *Perceiving: A Philosophical Study* (Ithaca, N.Y., 1957), pp. 43-53; the distinction is further defended in "Comments and Replies," *Philosophia* 7 (1978):599-602.

14. Thomas Reid, *An Inquiry into the Human Mind*, chap. V, sections 2 and 8.

15. Suppose a person thus assumes he is being appeared to by something that is a philosopher; and suppose further the assumption is correct. Then he believes himself to be perceiving something to be a philosopher—where 'perceive' must now be understood in its primary sense. Since the primary sense of "perceive" is restricted to the apprehension of sensible characteristics, shall we say that, strictly speaking, the person's "perceptual taking" is false? I think that we should.

16. See A. Meinong, *Gesamtausgabe*, vol. V (Graz, 1973), pp. 398-404.

17. H. H. Price, *Perception* (New York, 1935), p. 185.

18. Chisholm, *Theory of Knowledge*, 2nd ed., p. 63.

19. Compare Franz Brentano, *Die Lehre vom richtigen Urteil* (Hamburg, 1979), p. 168.

20. Hence the classification of types of foundationalism proposed by Pastin ("modest, "radical") should be expanded. See Mark Pastin. "Modest Foundationalism and Self-Warrant," in *Essays on Knowledge and Justification*, ed. G. Pappas and M. Swain (Ithaca, N.Y., 1978), pp. 279-88.

21. This point is recognized by Frederick L. Will in *Induction and Justification* (Ithaca, N.Y., 1974), part II; compare Michael Williams in *Groundless Belief* (Oxford, 1977), p. 115.

22. See Alvin Goldman, "Discrimination and Perceptual Knowledge," in *Essays on Knowledge and Justification*, pp. 120-45. Goldman attempts to develop the "reliability" theory for perceptual knowledge; hence what he says is not strictly applicable to our three examples above. And I think he would concede, moreover, that he has set forth a program rather than a finished theory, for he makes use of the undefined expression 'S's propensity to form an F-belief as a result of percept P has an *appropriate* genesis' (p. 142, my italics). Compare Fred Dretske, *Seeing and Knowing* (London, 1969), chap. 2, and "Conclusive Reasons," in *Australasian Journal of Philosophy* 48 (1971):1-22. Compare James van Cleve's criticism of "naturalistic" theories of epistemic justification in "Foundationalism, Epistemic Principles, and the Cartesian Circle," section X.

23. One could, of course, make use of a principle such as our P3 and then compensate for its over-permissiveness by making certain further *epistemic* stipulations. Compare Keith Lehrer, *Knowledge* (Oxford, 1974), chap. 6. I believe that Lehrer does not intend his theory to be adequate to the type of example I have cited; but if this is so, then the theory should not be thought of as an alternative to the present theory.

24. Compare Lehrer, *Knowledge*, chap. 8, and Nicholas Rescher, *The Coherence Theory of Truth* (Oxford, 1973), chap. 13. The theories proposed by these authors are not readily applicable to our three cases.

25. Compare James Cornman, "Foundational versus Nonfoundational Theories of Empirical Justification," in *Essays on Knowledge and Justification*, pp. 229-52.

26. The quotation is from Jaegwon Kim's article "Explanation in Science," in *Encyclopedia of Philosophy*, ed. Paul Edwards (New York, 1967), vol. III, pp. 159-63; the quotation is from p. 161. Kim also cites additional "epistemic conditions" which must be fulfilled if a theory or hypothesis is to serve as an explanation; one of these is "the requirement of total evidence" (p. 161). Compare Lehrer, *Knowledge*, chap. 5.

27. Thus Cornman, in the article referred to in note 25, makes use of the undefined expression 'x explains y', but he does not introduce 'x explains y for S'.

28. For a definitive study of the relations between the epistemic and ethical senses of "justify," or "warrant," see Roderick Firth, "Are Epistemic Concepts Reducible to Ethical Concepts?" in *Values and Morals*, ed. A. Goldman and J. Kim (Dordrecht, 1978), pp. 215-29.

Notes on Contributors

Diana Ackerman is Associate Professor of Philosophy at Brown University. She has published several papers dealing with problems in the philosophy of language and related issues in epistemology, metaphysics, and the philosophy of mind.

William P. Alston is Professor of Philosophy at the University of Illinois at Urbana-Champaign. He is a past president of the American Philosophical Association (Western Division) and of the Society for Philosophy and Psychology, and is currently President of the Society of Christian Philosophers. He is the author of *Philosophy of Language* and has published numerous articles on philosophy of language, philosophy of religion, philosophy of mind, philosophy of psychology, and epistemology.

Robert Audi is Professor of Philosophy at the University of Nebraska, Lincoln. He has published articles in epistemology, philosophy of action, philosophy of the social sciences, and moral philosophy.

Jonathan Bennett has taught philosophy in New Zealand, England, and Canada. He is now a Professor of Philosophy at Syracuse University. His paper in this volume comes from a draft of a book, tentatively titled *Spinoza's Arguments*.

Simon Blackburn is Fellow and Tutor in Philosophy at Pembroke College, Oxford, and has held visiting appointments at Melbourne and the University of British Columbia. He edited a collection of essays entitled *Meaning, Reference, and Necessity*, and is the author of *Reason and Prediction*, and a number of papers on themes connected with meaning and realism. He is currently engaged in writing a book provisionally entitled *Understanding Understanding*.

Laurence BonJour is Associate Professor of Philosophy at the University of Washington. He has published a number of articles in journals and collections on epistemological and related topics, including most recently "Can Empirical Knowledge Have A Foundation?" *American Philosophical Quarterly.*

Panayot Butchvarov is Professor of Philosophy at the University of Iowa. He is the author of *Resemblance and Identity: An Examination of the Problem of Universals; The Concept of Knowledge; Being Qua Being: A Theory of Identity, Existence, and Predication*; and a number of articles and reviews in philosophical journals.

Hector-Neri Castañeda, the founding Editor of *NOUS*, is the Mahlon Powell Professor of Philosophy of Indiana University and, since 1978, the first Dean of Latino Affairs. He is the author of *La Dialectica de la Concientia de si Mismo; Thinking and Doing: The Philosophical Foundations of Institutions; The Structure of Morality; La Teoria de Platon sobre las Formas, las Relaciones en el Dedon.* He has contributed over 100 essays to different journals and anthologies.

Roderick Chisholm is Andrew W. Mellon Professor of Humanities at Brown University. His publications include *Perceiving: A Philosophical Study; Realism and the Background of Phenomenology*; and *Theory of Knowledge.* He is editor of works by Brentano and Meinong, and has authored many journal articles. He is past president of the American Philosophical Association and the Metaphysical Association of America.

Romane Clark is Professor of Philosophy at Indiana University. He has published journal articles primarily in the areas of philosophical logic, perception, and metaphysics.

L. Jonathan Cohen is Fellow and Praelector in Philosophy at The Queen's College, Oxford. He is the author of *The Principles of World Citizenship; The Diversity of Meaning; The Implications of Induction;* and *The Probable and the Provable.*

Fred Dretske is Professor of Philosophy at the University of Wisconsin, Madison. His chief interests are epistemology, philosophy of mind, and philosophy of science. He has published a book and numerous articles in these fields and is presently preparing for publication a book on knowledge and information.

Carl Ginet is Professor of Philosophy at Cornell University. He is the author of *Knowledge, Perception, and Memory.*

Alvin Goldman will shortly be joining the Department of Philosophy at the University of Illinois at Chicago Circle. He is the author of *A Theory of Human Action* and has written on social power. His papers in epistemology have covered such topics as knowlege, perception, justified belief, and the relation between epistemology and cognitive science.

Gilbert Harman is Professor of Philosophy at Princeton University. He is the author of *Thought* and of *The Nature of Morality*, and is at work on a book about reasoning.

Herbert Heidelberger teaches philosophy at the University of Massachusetts, Amherst.

J. F. M. Hunter is Professor of Philosophy at the University of Toronto. As well as articles on Wittgenstein, philosophical psychology, ethics, and political philosophy, he has written a book, *Essays after Wittgenstein*, and a monograph, *Intending*.

Oliver Johnson is an Easterner by education but a Westerner by birth and inclination. A charter member of the faculty of the University of California, Riverside, he has taught there for twenty-seven years. He is the author of *Rightness and Goodness; Moral Knowledge; The Moral Life; The Problem of Knowledge; Skepticism and Cognitivism*; and a number of journal articles.

Keith Lehrer is Professor of Philosophy and former Head of the Department of Philosophy at the University of Arizona. He is the author of *Knowledge; Philosophical Problems and Arguments* (with James Cornman); editor of *Freedom and Determinism; Analysis and Metaphysics; Reid's Inquiry and Essays*; and *Philosophical Studies* with John Pollock among others.

Joseph Margolis is Professor of Philosophy at Temple University. His most recent books include: *Persons and Minds* and *Art and Philosophy*. He is presently completing a book on the philosophy of psychology.

George S. Pappas is Associate Professor of Philosophy at Ohio State University. He has edited, with Marshall Swain, *Essays on Knowledge and Justification*, and has edited *Justification and Knowledge: New Studies in Epistemology*.

Mark Pastin is Associate Professor of Philosophy and Faculty Fellow of the Poynter Center for the Study of American Institutions at Indiana University. He has published articles on topics in epistemology, value theory, and metaphysics, and is currently completing *Normative Reasoning: The Conceptual Foundations of Normative Thinking*.

John Perry is Professor of Philosophy at Stanford University. He is the author of *A Dialogue on Personal Identity and Immortality* and journal articles.

John Pollock is Professor of Philosophy at the University of Arizona and the editor of *Philosophical Studies*. His major publications are *Knowledge and Justification* and *Subjunctive Reasoning*.

Nicholas Rescher is University Professor of Philosophy at the University of Pittsburgh. Born in Germany in 1928, he is the author of over thirty works on a wide variety of philosophical topics. An honorary L. H. D. was awarded to Mr. Rescher by Loyola University of Chicago in 1970 "in recognition of his contribution to philosophy and the science of values."

David M. Rosenthal is Associate Professor of Philosophy at the City University of New York (Lehman College and Graduate School). He is editor of *Materialism and the Mind-Body Problem* and author of articles in the philosophy of mind and the philosophy of language.

Ernest Sosa is Professor of Philosophy at Brown University. He has published extensively in the major philosophical journals.

Peter Unger is Professor of Philosophy at New York University. His primary interests are in the areas of epistemology, metaphysics, philosophy of language, and philosophy of mind. He is the author of *Ignorance: A Case for Scepticism* and of numerous articles in these areas.